SAP® NetWeaver Portal Technology: The Complete Reference

SAP® NetWeaver Portal Technology: The Complete Reference

Rabi Jay

New York Chicago San Francisco
Lisbon London Madrid Mexico City
Milan New Delhi San Juan
Seoul Singapore Sydney Toronto

The McGraw-Hill Companies

Library of Congress Cataloging-in-Publication Data

Jay, Rabi.
SAP NetWeaver portal technology : the complete reference/Rabi Jay.
p. cm.
Includes bibliographical references and index.
ISBN 978-0-07-154853-3 (alk. paper)
1. Web site development. 2. Web portals—Computer programs. 3. SAP NetWeaver. 4. Business enterprises—Computer networks. I. Title.
TK5105.8885.S24J39 2008
025.04—dc22

2008018951

SAP® NetWeaver Portal Technology: The Complete Reference

1234567890 DOC DOC 0198

ISBN 978-0-07-154853-3
MHID 0-07-154853-X

Sponsoring Editor
Wendy Rinaldi

Editorial Supervisor
Patty Mon

Project Manager
Aparna Shukla, International Typesetting and Composition

Acquisitions Coordinator
Mandy Canales

Copy Editor
Lisa Theobald

Proofreader
Elise Oranges

Indexer
Robert Swanson

Production Supervisor
Jean Bodeaux

Composition
International Typesetting and Composition

Illustration
International Typesetting and Composition

Art Director, Cover
Jeff Weeks

This book would not have been possible without the encouragement and support of a number of people who have crossed my life during the years of my schooling as well as work. I am very grateful to each and every one of them. Following is a small list of persons I would like to acknowledge for their tacit as well as vocal support while writing this book.

To my beautiful wife, Suji, for her love and support while writing this book. She is the inspiration behind all my endeavors.

To my dear one-year-old son, Rohan, who was not unduly upset when his father was steeped into a computer screen.

To my dad, who has been a source of inspiration to me and has instilled in me a sense of optimism and a "can do it" attitude.

To my mom, whose sense of love and sacrifice has been a model for me to live by.

To my other family member, who have always stood by me, helped me, and prayed for me throughout, and for their unmatched love.

To my nephews and nieces, who I pray will achieve great achievements and come up with flying colors in their respective vocations.

To my parents-in-law, who supported me while writing this book.

To my friends and colleagues at work, who helped me learn these new technologies, solve problems, and shared their knowledge and experience.

To Renchy Thomas, who provided a number of useful suggestions that have been incorporated throughout this book.

To Ashok Baskaradu and Surendra, for helping me with the chapter on installation.

To the contributors in the SDN community, too numerous to mention, whose documents have been listed in Appendix B and cited while writing this book.

To my editor, Wendy, and acquisitions coordinator, Mandy, for their support and encouragement when writing this book.

To the project manager, Aparna Shukla, who was kind enough to accommodate my last minute changes and the copy editors, Lisa Theobold and Patty Mon, for doing an excellent job on this book.

To my well wishers Alag Arasan, Govi Rao, Jay Stanell, Jess Aiden, Ramesh Rajagopal, and Sanjay Bodduluri.

Also thanks to Adebowale David Adesokan, Karun Reddy, Raja Jalandaradoss, Sandeep Kumar Jha, Srivatsa Kadambi, and Swapna for their inputs.

To the other members of the McGraw-Hill team who contributed towards bringing out a great book.

And last, but not the least, I want to thank God for giving me the vision to write this book, the commitment to complete the book, and the opportunity to publish the book with one of the prestigious publishers in McGraw-Hill.

Contents at a Glance

Contents

Part II Portal Infrastructure Design

Part VII Portal Security

Preface

While working on a portal implementation project, I found myself searching for useful information at various stages of the implementation. While a lot of information is available in various forms from different sources, the simple act of tracking resources and identifying the most useful and relevant ones became a huge task. It was this need that really motivated me to write this book. If this book serves as a single point of information for anything related to the portal installation, configuration, administration, and maintenance, then it has served its purpose.

Another influence in writing this book is the very positive feedback that I received from students I have been privileged to coach. My students were so impressed with my style of teaching and the quality of content that they encouraged me to put it in the form of a book. I thought this was a great idea because this would help me reach a wider audience than would be otherwise possible.

Another reason for writing this book is the passion that I have for this portal technology and the valuable knowledge and skills I have gained over a period of more than 10 years in JAVA, SAP Portal, SAP ERP, and CRM solutions. I felt obligated to share this exciting technology especially with those new to SAP who are looking to make an entry into SAP Portal.

And last but not least is the lack of a single book on portals that provided a comprehensive treatment of SAP Portal technology, especially with a hands-on approach.

Each and every chapter starts with a brief introduction and then gradually takes you into a tour of the most intricate details of that given topic. The important highlights of these chapters are the hands-on approach and the detailed treatment of every topic. The chapters have been arranged in a logical sequence of how a typical portal implementation project would proceed. After reading this book, the reader should be able to handle a portal implementation in a relatively more confident and successful manner.

While writing this book, I have relied on my own knowledge and skills gained during the various portal implementations of which I have been a part. I have referred to a large number of resources. I have extensively referred to the wealth of information available in the SDN while writing this book, and these documents have been listed in Appendix B of this book. I have also added references to specific documents at the end of some chapters. I encourage you to continue your study by reading these articles as well as the extensive documentation available at http://help.sap.com. SDN is a great website and I recommend that every reader should subscribe to it if they have not done so already. SDN was my default resource for any issues that I faced during my project, such as, for example, when challenged with implementing SSO solutions. This book deals with almost every aspect of the portal implementation, using a very hands-on approach. The chapters in the book and a brief discussion of the contents follow.

Part I of this book deals with the topics related to portal implementation planning and includes six chapters. **Chapter 1** provides an introduction to the concept of Enterprise Portal and discusses why we need portals and how it is it different from an ordinary website. **Chapter 2** deals with the building blocks of portals from a software architecture standpoint and discusses such topics as portal platform, PCD, UME, KM, and Content Management. **Chapter 3** takes a look at the different NetWeaver components from IT scenario, process, and system standpoints. This helps identify the different portal components to be installed during implementation. **Chapter 4** deals with the PAM, release planning and maintenance strategy, and support package strategy. This helps ensure that products have enough support from SAP after implementation. **Chapter 5** takes a look at the Scenario and Process Component list tools that help to identify the various IT scenarios and the corresponding NetWeaver Portal components and support packages to be installed. **Chapter 6** deals with the various components in the SAP J2EE engine architecture.

Part II of the book deals with the portal infrastructure design and contains Chapters 7 to 9. **Chapter 7** deals with the SPOF in the portal system and the measures that can be taken to avoid them to ensure high availability. **Chapter 8** deals with implementing a highly scalable technical infrastructure and explains how to use Quick Sizer to size your hardware system. **Chapter 9** addresses the specific requirements for a web infrastructure and ensures that the conflicting requirements for session stickiness, high availability, and load balancing are met.

Part III of the book covers aspects related to a portal installation and consists of Chapters 10 to 12. **Chapter 10** describes how to go about planning for a portal implementation and coming up with checklists, pointers to documentation and other resources, OSS Notes, and so on. **Chapter 11** walks the user through the various steps involved in the portal installation and helps identify potential trouble spots during the installation. **Chapter 12** explains how to go about troubleshooting when faced with issues during installation and addresses some of the post-installation steps involved when implementing the portal.

Part IV of the book discusses content administration on the portal and consists of Chapters 13 to 20. **Chapter 13** deals with the initial steps involved in content administration and takes a look at the PCD objects. **Chapter 14** reviews the details of iViews and pages and explains how to use the editors to create these objects. **Chapter 15** discusses the details of roles and worksets and explains how to use the editors to create these objects and assign them to users on the portal. It illustrates the use of roles for personalization and navigation on the portal. **Chapter 16** explains the advantages of business packages, the types of business packages, and how to implement them. **Chapter 17** explains how to change the look and feel of the portal and discusses themes, portal desktops, and display rules. **Chapter 18** describes how to configure connectivity with SAP and JDBC databases using JCO connectors, gateway connector service, user mapping, and so on. **Chapter 19** explains the concept of federated portals and describes the steps involved in configuring them in a global scenario. **Chapter 20** covers the concept of external facing portals and describes the steps involved in configuring it in a global scenario.

Part V of the book deals with aspects related to system administration on the portal and consists of Chapters 21 to 25. **Chapter 21** describes the backup and recovery strategy, the procedures involved, and the post-verification process. **Chapter 22** explains how to configure the portal transport mechanism and how to transport portal content, personalization content, permissions, and languages. **Chapter 23** covers the concept of federated portals and the steps involved in configuring it in a global scenario. **Chapter 24** deals with how to implement delegated content and system administration in very large-scale implementations. **Chapter 25** shows you how to implement delegated user administration across regions distributed geographically.

Part VI of the book deals with portal troubleshooting and consists of Chapters 26 to 33. **Chapter 26** explains how to use the various logging tools available, including how to use them for debugging and troubleshooting. **Chapter 27** deals with devising a performance analysis strategy and using performance analysis tools and monitors to assess the current performance. **Chapter 28** discusses how to conduct workload analysis on the portal and assess component, request, and thread analysis. **Chapter 29** explains how to conduct JVM GC analysis. **Chapter 30** describes how to conduct and analyze thread dumps. **Chapter 31** explains how to conduct client-side analysis using HTTP trace. **Chapter 32** covers CCMS monitoring and GRMG availability monitoring, including how to configure and use them. **Chapter 33** discusses aspects related to tuning the portal server, the J2EE engine, and other components of the portal, including development components.

Part VII of the book deals with portal security and includes Chapters 34 to 42. **Chapter 34** discusses the various authorization models available in the portal, such as security zones, UME actions, and permission models. **Chapter 35** discusses the elements of UME architecture and discusses UME objects, user replication, central user administration, and so on. **Chapter 36** describes how to use the UME tool to manage UME objects. It helps to configure e-mail notifications, security settings for SAP ABAP, and portal databases as UME repositories. **Chapter 37** explains how to configure the LDAP as the UME data source, discusses user data partitioning and attribute base partitioning, and explains how to modify data source config files. **Chapter 38** covers the mechanisms involved in implementing authentication, such as basic form-based authentication, Windows-based authentication, Kerberos, X.509, header-based authentication, SAML, JAAS login modules, and so on. **Chapter 39** explains how to implement role transfer between SAP and the portal. **Chapter 40** deals with different forms and SSO and how to implement it for SAP and non-SAP applications. **Chapter 41** describes the various steps involved in implementing SSL on the J2EE engine. **Chapter 42** explains how to implement portal security, including network and application security.

Part VIII of the book deals with NetWeaver system landscape components and consists of Chapters 43 and 44. **Chapter 43** explains the terminologies in SLD and how to administer it and how to import the software catalog from the SAP marketplace. **Chapter 44** describes how to use NWA for system administration and monitoring, and also how to configure with SLD and remote systems.

The chapters have been written carefully, offering the reader basic yet thorough explanations of portal implementation. While it is not possible to address each and every aspect of the portal technology in one single book, I hope that the reader will be well-equipped to take up a real job and perform it successfully after finishing this book.

The book is a complete reference guide for those dealing with portal implementation and a must-read for SAP BASIS administrators and ABAP and Java developers who want to work with the portal technology. This information can serve the occasional needs of project managers, IT managers, and others involved in portal implementation. It is of particular interest to portal administrators, architects, and developers. It deals with the complete life cycle of a portal implementation—including planning, designing and installing, configuring and administering, monitoring, performance tuning, maintaining content, application and network security, and user administration. The book takes a hands-on approach and is intended to serve as an on-the-job reference guide both during and after a portal implementation.

To administer the portal, you need knowledge of both ABAP and Java systems. There is a gap in such skill sets in the market. This book will serve as a hands-on manual for those who know ABAP and BASIS and want to work in Java-based portal technology as well as for those who know only Java (and are new to SAP) and want to get initiated to SAP Portal.

If you have been looking for a book that can aid as a single point of resource for everything related to portal technology, this is the book for you. Knowing the information presented in this book can give you that extra edge you have been looking for in your portal job and could even help beginners to land a lucrative job working with the SAP Portal.

If you have any suggestions or feedback, please feel free to e-mail me at rabijay1@yahoo.com. I also recommend that you visit the book's companion website at http://www.sapportalguide.com. I wish you all the best!

I

PART

Portal Implementation Planning

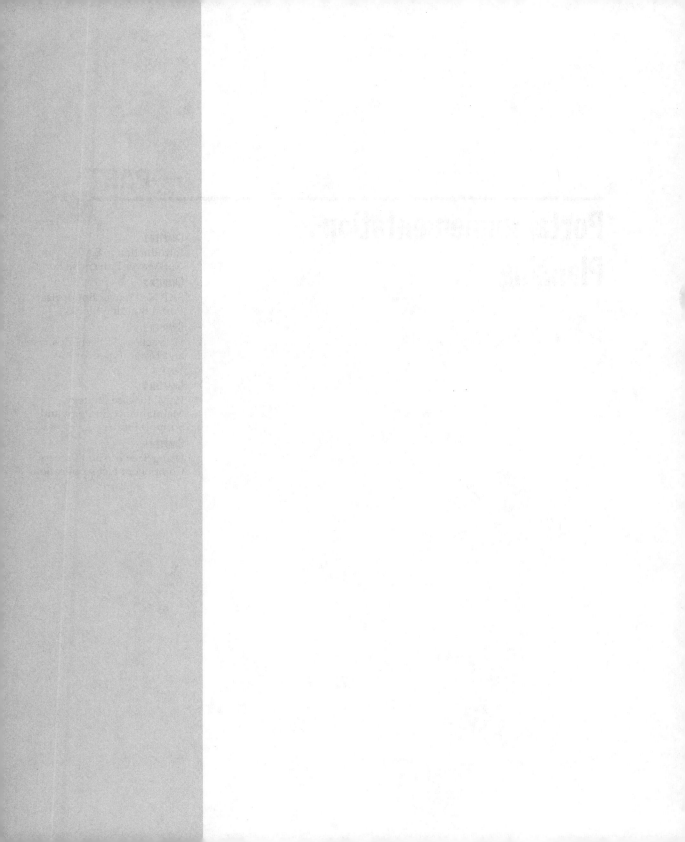

CHAPTER 1

Introduction to SAP NetWeaver Enterprise Portal

In this chapter, we address what an enterprise portal is and how it differs from an ordinary website. We then discuss the business benefits involved in implementing an enterprise portal. In the next chapter, as part of the introduction, we deal with the SAP NetWeaver Portal in particular and analyze the various components that constitute the portal.

We also look at the SAP NetWeaver technology stack and analyze the role of the SAP NetWeaver Portal in the stack. We then address some of the benefits of using the portal, such as navigating intuitively, drag and relate functionality, branding and personalization, integration using iViews, role-based personalization, securing the portal, single sign-on, and ready-made implementation of content using business packages.

Another important component of the SAP NetWeaver Portal is the Knowledge Management (KM) component that is used for integrating unstructured content. This is accomplished using two major components—namely, Content Management and TREX. Knowledge Management provides functionality such as discussion forums, content workflow, and classification. Sitting on top of KM is the collaboration functionality of the portal, which provides functionality such as the collaboration room, the Collaboration Launch Pad, real-time collaboration, and third-party integration.

Why SAP NetWeaver Portal?

One of the first few questions that needs to be answered during a portal implementation is how do we stand to benefit by implementing a portal? Is it really important to use a portal, or is it something that can be avoided? A portal provides a means by which we can improve the business efficiency of a process. For example, by implementing a portal, a company can provide the right information to the right person at the right time. Based on this information, the person can make a decision that is not only correct, but also quick.

NOTE *By implementing an enterprise portal, you can provide the right information in the right format to the right person at the right time.*

The portal provides the required information in one place. Not only does the portal increase the productivity of an employee, it also reduces the turnaround time of a given business process. By implementing a portal, a customer service representative can quickly attend to customer complaints, or a sales representative can place an order at a customer site and answer customer inquiries regarding pricing.

What Is an Enterprise Portal?

While some argue that the portal is merely a website, others argue that it is more than that. An enterprise portal can be viewed as a means by which an organization tries to web-enable its applications, services, and information to its internal employees as well as its external partners. So, to that extent, enterprise portal software should be able to solve some of the complex challenges that arise out of web-enabling systems. To mention just a few examples, the problems could be associated to that of integrating the applications; providing a single sign-on to the end users so that they do not have to remember passwords for different backend applications; providing only the right information to the right user using authentication and authorization methods; ensuring application and network security; increasing usability by using techniques such as role-based personalization; providing content management features; and using KM functionality to integrate unstructured content such as file systems, database systems, and websites.

INFO *Good enterprise portal software should solve the challenges arising out of web-enabling systems and applications.*

As you can see, a portal is a website, no doubt, but it is much more than just that. It is the complexity that surrounds the portal that makes it so much more interesting and worth studying. SAP NetWeaver Portal is one such technology, an amazing one that aims to solve complex issues and tries to bring together the different SAP Business Suite solutions. In a way, it was born out of a need to provide a common user interface for various SAP products and to simplify access to end users using single sign-on. The next few chapters will unravel the potential of the SAP NetWeaver Portal to provide you with a greater understanding of what an enterprise portal is and what it can do for your organization.

Portals come in different flavors, such as horizontal and vertical portals, employee portals, and manager portals. Portals can be classified into different categories based on the functionalities they provide and the user populations they serve.

Why Do We Need SAP NetWeaver Portal?

Let us now discuss some of the differentiating features of an enterprise portal and why is it so important for an organization to implement it.

Increased Productivity

The SAP NetWeaver Portal tries to resolve some of the complex issues that an IT organization faces while trying to integrate its existing applications and information sources. From a purely business standpoint, the SAP NetWeaver Portal is able to provide tremendous business value by providing the right information to the right user at the right time.

By providing role-based content and by using iView techniques, the SAP NetWeaver Portal ensures that the end user sees only the information that he or she is supposed to see and ensures that the information is in the appropriate format. For example, the portal makes it possible for a sales manager to look at the sales performance of her sales reps or the sales performance for her sales territories. Or a marketing manager can look at how well his different campaigns have performed and identify potential sales opportunities or leads. In the same way, customer representatives can quickly address customer complaints because all the information is located in one place.

INFO *SAP NetWeaver Portal increases the productivity of employees and helps improve the efficiency of the different business processes like processing sales orders, responding to customer complaints, and so on.*

Business Packages: A Jumpstart to Implementation

One of the distinguishing features of SAP NetWeaver Portal as compared to other portals is the concept of *business packages*. Business packages are collections of iViews, which are grouped together into worksets. The worksets are based on tasks that are likely to be executed by a user in his or her day-to-day job. The business packages are based on best practices and address three groups of users: *users*, *managers*, and *specialists*.

TIP *Business packages come with readymade content and hence provide a jumpstart for implementing applications on the portal.*

The business package for users consists of iViews that provide internal and external news, travel information, information on people, and other self services. The business package for managers consists of worksets that deal with people management and budget management. This is mainly addressed toward team leads, project leads, and department heads. Using the people management functionality, team leads can assess the performance of their teams. Using the budget management functionality, managers can make sure that the costs are managed properly. Some examples of people management worksets are team overview, compensation planning, recruiting, and so on. Examples for budget management are cost center monitors, budget alerts, and queries for training and travel budgets. Business packages also provide alert functionality, where the user can receive notifications on the portal whenever a customer's payments are overdue or when inventory levels go below a certain level.

Portal Technology: Open Industry Standards

The technological platform on which the portal is built is based on open industry web service standards such as eXtensible Markup Language (XML), Simple Object Access Protocol (SOAP), Web Services Description Language (WSDL), Universal Description Discovery and Integration protocol (UDDI), Java Connector Architecture, and Java Authentication and Authorization Service (JAAS). It is a platform-independent solution that can work on most of the database/operating system combinations.

The fact that the portal is installed on the Java stack of the web application server helps you tap into all the potential benefits of Java. With every new version of the enterprise portal, it has also become so much easier to install due to the tighter integration of the portal software components as well as the increased sophistication and usability of the SAPinst software used to install SAP solutions.

Integration with Applications

One of the other major reasons why companies implement the SAP NetWeaver Portal is because it is very effective in integrating existing legacy and other backend systems.

INFO *Using SAP's iView technology, you can literally extract data from any backend system.*

Usually, over a number of years, companies implement IT solutions using various technologies, which, after some time, become a Herculean task to integrate. When dealing with IT solutions, complex issues arise due to multiple vendors, numerous point-to-point integration systems, communication protocols, and proprietary industry standards. Using SAP's NetWeaver portal, solutions implemented using .Net and IBM WebSphere can be integrated into the SAP NetWeaver portal landscape. SAP NetWeaver Portal also provides drag and relate functionality that helps users take a piece of information from one application and drag and drop it into another iView to retrieve information from another application. For example, users can drag the customer number from a sales order iView and drop it into another iView that fetches customer information. The sales order iView could be fetching data from an SAP R/3 system, while the customer data could potentially come from an SQL database iView or a Business Information Warehouse (BW)–based iView.

The ability to integrate with multiple technologies and application components from multiple vendors often becomes a major factor when a company decides to implement a global portal system to enable end-to-end collaborative business processes.

TIP *SAP NetWeaver Portal results in lower total cost of ownership because you can leverage the existing skill sets as well as the IT infrastructure that supports those solutions.*

SAP's NetWeaver Technology Stack

SAP NetWeaver is the building block for almost all SAP applications and is composed of four layers:

- People integration layer
- Information integration layer
- Process integration layer
- Application platform

The portal, along with other building blocks such as multi-channel access and collaboration, form the people integration layer. The scope of the people integration layer is to bring together all the information and the functions that an employee needs to perform his or her work very efficiently. The collaboration management piece of the portal provides collaboration rooms and real-time tools such as shared e-mail, discussion threads, team calendars, and document stores that enable teams to work together.

The information integration layer is about providing access to both structured and unstructured information in the company. The Business Information Warehouse, KM, and Master Data Management (MDM) are major building blocks of this layer.

In the process integration layer, the SAP Exchange Infrastructure (XI) plays a major role in enabling business processes to run across system boundaries in heterogeneous landscapes. The application platform has both Advanced Business Application Programming (ABAP) and Java runtimes and is actually an extension of the BASIS (SAP System Administration) layer with greater focus on web-enabling applications and services. It consists of the SAP NetWeaver Application Server (AS) that comprises a Java 2 Platform, Enterprise Edition (J2EE) engine and a database. It provides support for standards such as Hypertext Transfer Protocol (HTTP), HTTP over SSL (HTTPS), Simple Mail Transfer Protocol (SMTP), Simple Object Access Protocol (SOAP), Secure Sockets Layer (SSL), single sign-on (SSO), World Wide Web Distributed Authoring and Versioning (WebDAV), X.509, HyperText Markup Language (HTML), XML, Unicode, Wireless Markup Language (WML), and so on. The SAP NetWeaver Portal, by virtue of being installed on top of the NetWeaver AS, enjoys all the benefits that an SAP NetWeaver AS provides.

SAP's NetWeaver Product Strategy

The SAP NetWeaver Portal is one of the building blocks in making an integrated enterprise a reality. It helps to bring together all the different applications such as SAP applications, customer relationship management (CRM), supply chain management (SCM), product lifecycle management (PLM), and so on; various data sources; and even different business organizations. It is a central part of SAP's NetWeaver product strategy.

Single Point of Access

Today's world of e-business requires an increasing need to provide a single point of access to various business partners such as customers, suppliers, partners, and employees. It acts as an interface not only to your own company's applications, but also to your business partners' applications and third-party Internet services.

Portal Platform: Runtime Environment

The portal platform is the main component that allows you to create a role-based portal. The portal platform is based upon the portal runtime, which is made up of portal components and services. The portal components and services together form the development and runtime environment for the portal.

Tip *A role-based portal helps to bring together data from various applications and services for various user groups using the iView technology.*

Collaboration Platform: Enabling Teamwork

Sitting on top of KM, the collaboration functionality of the portal enables users to communicate with each other using functionalities such as team rooms, interactive online meetings, instant messaging, shared e-mail, discussion threads, polls, and application sharing. For the collaboration functionality to work effectively, it is important that KM is implemented in the portal.

Knowledge Management: Unifying Unstructured Content

The KM platform is part of the information integration layer of the NetWeaver stack along with the Business Intelligence (BI) and Master Data Management (MDM) components. Knowledge Management deals with unstructured content and provides content management functionalities such as document authoring and publishing, version management, search and navigation, and classification.

The role of KM functionality in the portal is to manage the unstructured content that exists in various repositories such as file systems, websites, content management systems, e-mail systems, and so on. The portal can also be used to manage structured content such as data that are stored in transactional systems, data warehouse systems, and other legacy systems. The functionality that enables analysis of structured data is known as *Business Intelligence*.

The KM functionality is composed of two major components: Content Management and TREX. TREX is the search component of the KM functionality that enables searching documents and classifying documents using taxonomies. The Content Management portion of KM provides support for approval-based publishing, distributing and locating information based on indexing and classification of documents. It is possible to create subscriptions to documents so as to get notified of changes as well as to provide feedback on documents and discussions.

Business Information Warehouse: Unifying Structured Content

The Business Information Warehouse (BW) is the other major pillar in the portal that brings together structured, but extracted and/or processed, information. An example of such information is the company's top three best-selling products. The BW architecture consists of datasource and extraction systems, data storage and staging systems, as well as data analysis and presentation systems.

Portal Security

Let us now take a look at the various security implementations possible in the portal from an application and network standpoint. The portal allows for integrated user management by enabling the User Management Engine (UME) to store data across various repositories such as the Lightweight Directory Access Protocol (LDAP) and SAP R/3 systems as well as databases such as the SQL Server and MaxDB. It supports a number of authentication mechanisms such as client certificates, user ID/PW (identification and password), SAP logon tickets, basic authentication, Windows-based NTLM authentication, and header variables, as well as third-party authentication. It enables SSO for SAP as well as non-SAP applications, thus providing end users the ability to get data from backend systems without the need to log on every time a new backend system is accessed.

TIP *SSO can be used in the portal to integrate both SAP and non-SAP applications.*

The portal has a permission-based authorization model as well as concepts such as UME actions and security zones to implement application security. This will allow only certain users to administer data and allows data to be displayed to end users. Delegated user administration provides only certain administrators the ability to maintain user administration for a specific group of users based upon the company to which they belong.

TIP *Delegated user administration is useful for managing very large portal implementations.*

The portal architecture allows setting up a network architecture that takes into consideration all the security requirements for the Internet scenario as well as the data integrity requirements when dealing with enterprise class applications such as SAP. Using Secure Network Communication (SNC), you can encrypt the sensitive information that flows between the web server, the portal server, and the backend systems.

Portal User Interface: Branding and Role-Based Personalization

From the user interface point of view, the portal provides a role-based user interface with content displayed according to the user's role. The role of a user is associated with worksets that are bundles of pages and iViews. The worksets address the daily tasks that the user will be required to carry out to complete his or her job.

The role ensures that the user does not view content that he or she is not supposed to view. The role also decides the navigation structure of the portal interface. *Navigation structure* defines how the top-level menu and the tree-like detailed navigation links on the left of the portal user interface are organized. The navigation layout enables easier navigation for the user and allows accommodating virtually all possible design scenarios for the user interface. The Navigation panel iViews help the user to identify where he is in the portal and where he can navigate to. The portal layout can be designed outside the portal using Java Server Pages (JSPs) and then imported into the portal.

The other interesting aspect of the user interface design is the ability for the administrators to change the look and feel of the portal by changing the company logo, colors of the foreground and background, fonts, thickness of the frames, the top-level menus, and other parts of the UI. The portal administrator can create new portal themes and import them into the portal. It is also possible to change the portal framework page to meet the company's specific branding requirements.

TIP *Implementing a role-based portal, and changing the look and feel using themes, can all be done without any significant development effort.*

Using the iView/page personalization functionality, the end user can decide what iViews she wants to see and where the iViews should be placed on the page. Thus users have the ability to customize what content they want to see and on which page.

Portal Development Environment

The portal provides portal developers with the portal development kit that helps them to create custom portal applications using technologies such as portal components, portal services, HTMLBusiness for Java (HTMLB), JSP DynPage, web services, JSP, and so on. Portal administrators and developers can create iViews, pages, layouts, roles, worksets, and other features using the portal content developer studio, and thus the PCD serves as the development environment for the portal.

Conclusion

You can see that portals enable an organization to focus on streamlining processes by bringing together applications and the information required to complete a task. This results in increased productivity, better customer service, and process efficiency.

CHAPTER 2

SAP NetWeaver Enterprise Portal Building Blocks

Before we look at the portal architecture from a hardware standpoint, we'll address it from a software components point of view. As discussed in the first chapter, a portal consists of a basic *portal platform*, a *Knowledge Management component*, and a *Collaboration platform*. While a basic portal platform is mandatory in any portal implementation, whether the Knowledge Management and Collaboration components are installed would depend upon the business requirements in the project.

In this chapter, we take a deeper look at the software architecture of Enterprise Portals. The Enterprise Portal platform is deployed on the SAP Web Application Server (AS) Java and serves as the front end of the SAP NetWeaver platform. The other components, such as Knowledge Management, Collaboration, and Guided Procedures, are nothing but applications deployed within the portal platform.

Portal Platform

The portal platform consists of the following components (as shown in Figure 2-1):

- Portal runtime
- Portal applications
    - Portal components
    - Portal services

A portal platform is basically a portal runtime that is composed of Java libraries. The two primary functions of the portal platform framework are to provide the necessary runtime environment so as to run iViews and to administer iViews.

Portal Runtime

The *portal runtime* is a virtual environment that provides the runtime and development environment in which the portal applications run. We can compare it with the Java runtime, which provides the runtime environment for Java applications. The portal runtime is made

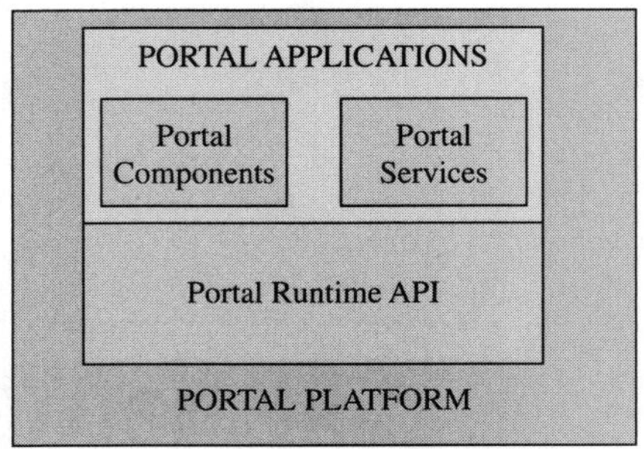

FIGURE 2-1 Building blocks of a portal platform

up of a Java API known as the *portal runtime API,* which is a collection of portal components and services. The portal components and services provide the basic core functionality to help the portal run efficiently. Portal components and services can be either provided by SAP or custom-built.

INFO *A set of predefined portal components and services are loaded by the portal runtime at portal startup.*

Portal Components

Portal components are Java Server Pages (JSPs) or Java classes that produce HTML output, which is displayed on the client browser when a page is rendered. These core portal components include the page builder and administration tools. The portal components are responsible for creating the necessary content for display in the iViews.

TIP *More than one portal component may be involved in generating the page, filling the iView with content, or defining the page layout.*

A portal component can do the following:

- Call other portal components, if needed
- Respond to other events
- Detect another component's profile and properties

A good example of a portal component is a *portal builder component,* which is responsible for the following:

- Receives HTTP requests from the client
- Forwards the incoming HTTP request to the relevant portal components and services
- Receives the response back from the portal server
- Builds the portal page
- Sends the page response back to the client

FIGURE 2-2 List of portal applications, components, and services

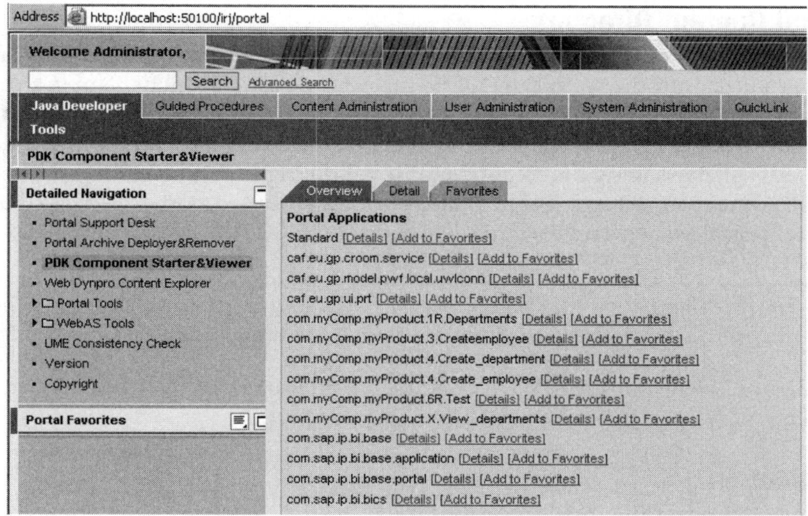

Copyright by SAP AG

Figure 2-2 displays the list of portal applications, components, and services deployed on the portal. This iView is available only if you have the Java Developer role.

Portal Services

Portal services are Java classes that provide functionality that can be accessed by other portal components and services. By functionality, we mean *data, procedures,* and *other resources*. A portal service is often called from the portal component to carry out some basic tasks such as searching for user-related information in the User Management Engine (UME) database.

TIP *Portal runtime (PRT) services are deployed on each server node and are loaded before other applications because they are necessary for the proper functioning of the portal.*

A portal service differs from a portal component in the following respects:

- While portal components have views, portal services do not have views.
- A portal service cannot be directly called by the client.
- Unlike a portal component, a portal service is not tied to a request.

Portal services can be classified as PRT services and external services. Examples of PRT services are caching services, notification services, iView services, application repository services, system landscape services, and services for portal content objects such as roles, pages, and worksets. External services extend the functionality of the PRT. Examples of external services are client eventing, the logger, the URL generator, HTMLBusiness for Java (HTMLB), and the Java Connector (JCO) client service.

Portal Content Directory

We will take a more detailed look at the *Portal Content Directory* (PCD) in a later chapter, but here is a little introduction. The PCD is the central storage mechanism in the portal used for storing content objects such as roles, worksets, pages, folders, and system landscapes. The top-level node is called *portal_content*. The PCD can interact with the UME, access control lists (ACLs), messaging notifications for invalidating caches, and transport mechanisms. The PCD can connect to a single database in a distributed portal scenario that involves several portal servers running on several machines.

TIP *The nice thing about the PCD is that the portal content objects are stored in the form of a tree structure, which enables easy browsing when developing or administering content.*

Figure 2-3 displays the PCD structure, which illustrates the tree structure of the content objects.

Unification

The portal unification feature is based upon the *drag and relate* iView functionality. The unification feature facilitates *object-based navigation* between objects in the backend systems such as Customer Relationship Management (CRM), Business Information Warehouse (BW), and SAP R/3 as well as database systems such as Oracle, SQL, and so on. To implement the drag and relate functionality of the portal, you need to implement *unifiers*. The choice of the unifier will depend on the type of databases and SAP R/3 systems that are used for providing the functionality.

FIGURE 2-3 Portal Content Directory tree structure

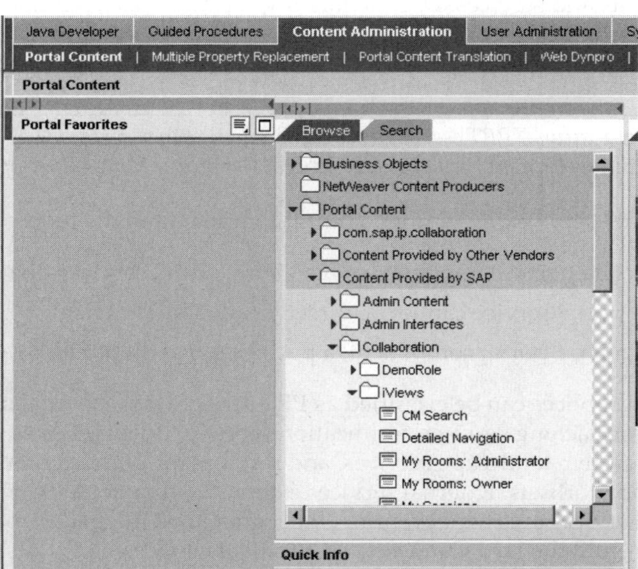

Connector Framework

The *Connector framework* of the portal resides on the Web Application Server (WAS) J2EE engine and provides a set of adapters called *connectors.* The connectors enable the portal to be connected to the backend *Enterprise Information Systems* (EIS). The Connector framework is based on the J2EE Connector architecture (JCA). Because the connectors have been created in line with the JCA specifications, any backend system-related issues such as the connectivity parameters and the protocol to be used are taken care of by the connector. The JCA specification is a framework provided by Sun for third-party vendors to follow when creating their adapters. As per JCA terminology, the connectors are referred to as *resource adapters* and the backend systems as *Enterprise Information Systems.* The various components of a connector framework are displayed in the following illustration.

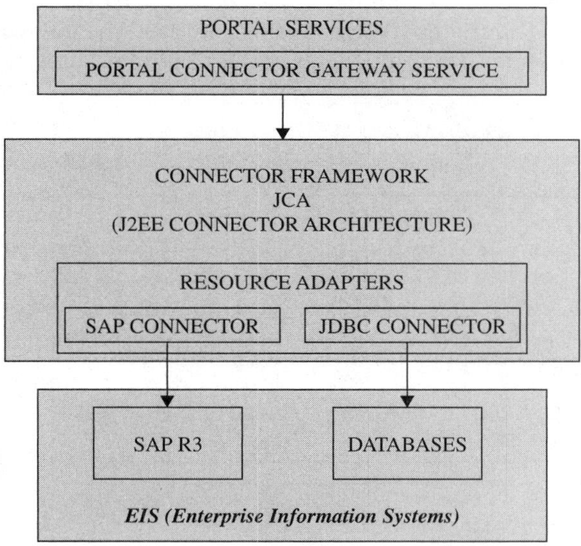

The JCA API is available in the com.sapportals.connector.* package. For the connector functionality to work properly in the portal, the following JAR files are required:

- GenericConnector.jar (comes with Portal)
- Extended Connector.jar (part of the J2EE engine that contains additional functionality for GenericConnector.jar)
- Connector.jar (contains the JCA 1.0 API)
- JTA.jar
- JAAS.jar

Assuming that the *system object* (which represents the backend system) has been defined in the portal system landscape, we can use the *Portal Connector Gateway Service* to call the JCA-compliant connectors for connecting to the backend system. The SAP NetWeaver Portal comes with standard connectors for connecting to a JDBC system, an SAP system, and a web service.

TIP *The standard connectors are automatically included by default in the portal during the initial installation.*

You will learn more about how to create system objects and connect to a backend system using the connectors in Chapter 18. iViews can be created that use these connectors to connect to a backend system using a wizard. The *SAP connector* can be used to connect to the SAP backend systems and the *JDBC connector* can be used to connect to JDBC databases.

Portal Runtime Storage Resources

So far you have seen the *portal runtime resources*, namely, the portal platform, the J2EE engine, the Knowledge Management (KM), and the Collaboration components. The portal runtime resources use the data that are stored in the *runtime storage resources* for rendering the portal framework, the pages, and the iViews during runtime. The following illustration displays the various portal runtime components and the portal runtime storage resources.

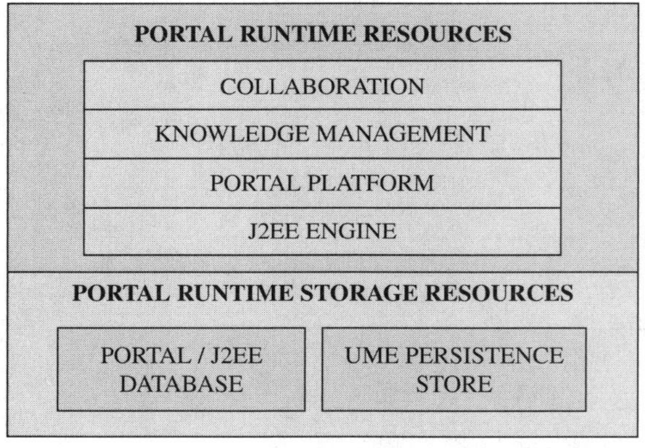

The runtime storage resources are the *Portal/J2EE database* and the *UME persistence store.* The portal database stores the portal data such as the portal objects (iViews, roles, pages, worksets) and portal applications. The user persistence data store refers to the user-related data such as roles, users, and groups that could be stored in one or more repositories such as a database, an SAP system, or an LDAP system.

UME Architecture

UME stands for the *User Management Engine*, which, as the name implies, is responsible for managing objects such as users, user accounts, roles, and groups. The portal provides a UME service that can be used to call the appropriate UME API for executing the necessary activity such as create, change, or delete user management objects.

TIP *The advantage of the UME is that all of the different portal applications can share the same user management objects, thus reducing the maintenance effort.*

UME Components

The components of the UME can be classified into the following broad categories:

- **UME tools** Consists of the user interface for creating, changing, or deleting user objects.
- **UME service** Responsible for calling the correct API when executing user administration–related activities.
- **UME API** Actual source code that is responsible for creating the user objects. The UME API calls the persistence manager.
- **Adapter** Also known as connector, which is used for connecting to the backend system.
- **Replication manager** Comes into play when we configure the J2EE engine to use the replication adapter for creating users in an external system such as SAP R/3 every time a user is created on the portal.
- **Persistence manager** Responsible for coordinating with the different UME repositories that are available for storing the UME data. Also responsible for taking care of all the connection details involved when connecting to a repository, thus absolving the programmer from having to know those details.
- **UME repository** Used for storing the user management objects. Can be an LDAP, an SAP R/3 system, or a database.

The following illustration displays the various components of the UME. For more information on UME, refer to Chapter 35.

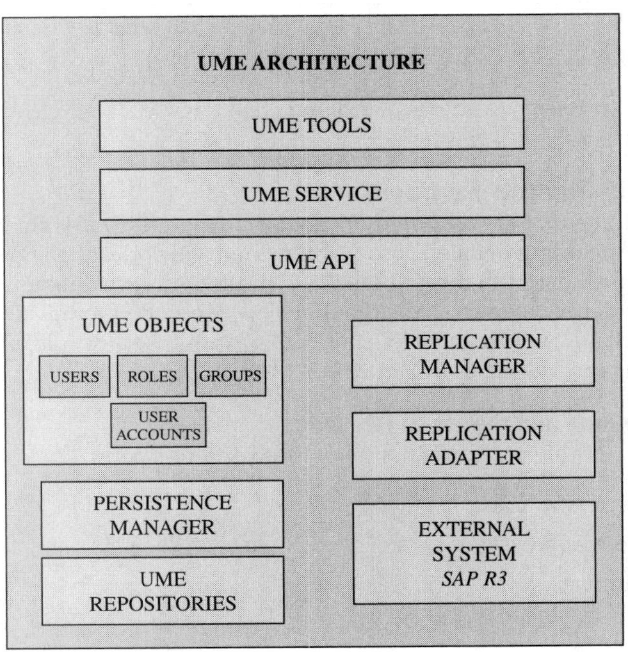

FIGURE 2-4 Portal logon screen

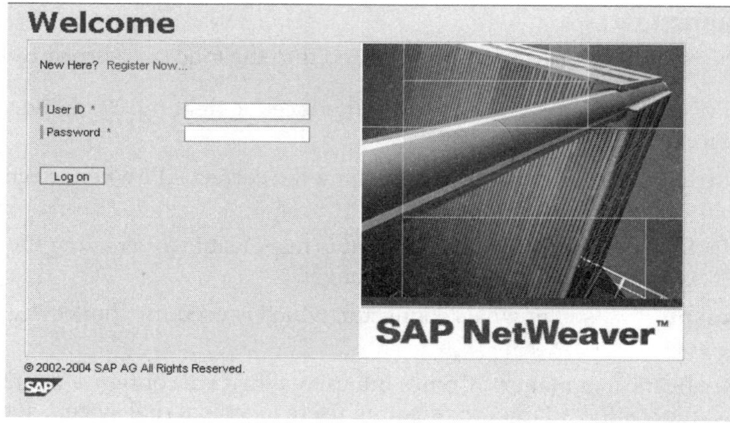

Copyright by SAP AG

Portal User Interface

The *portal user interface* is composed of a number of parts, each of which has a specific purpose.

Logon Screen

Figure 2-4 displays a portal logon screen that appears when the portal is installed out of the box. Depending on the portal version that was implemented, the Register Now link may or may not exist. If the version of the portal that was implemented is 7.0, the Register Now link may be missing.

TIP *To activate the Register Now link, certain configuration steps must be taken in the J2EE engine. This is addressed in Chapter 25.*

After you enter the user ID and password and click Log On, the Welcome screen, shown in Figure 2-5, appears.

Top-Level and Detailed Navigational Menus

Depending on the roles that are assigned to the user, different first-level menus and second-level menus including detailed navigation menus will appear, as shown in Figure 2-6. The top-level menu includes both the first-level and the second-level menus. What appears on the top-level menus depends on the roles that have been assigned to this user, which in this case happens to be the Java Developer role, the Super Administrator role, and the Content Management role, as shown earlier in Figure 2-5.

Super Administrator Role and the Top-Level Menus

The *Super Administrator* role is a combination of three different roles:

- Content Administration
- User Administration
- System Administration

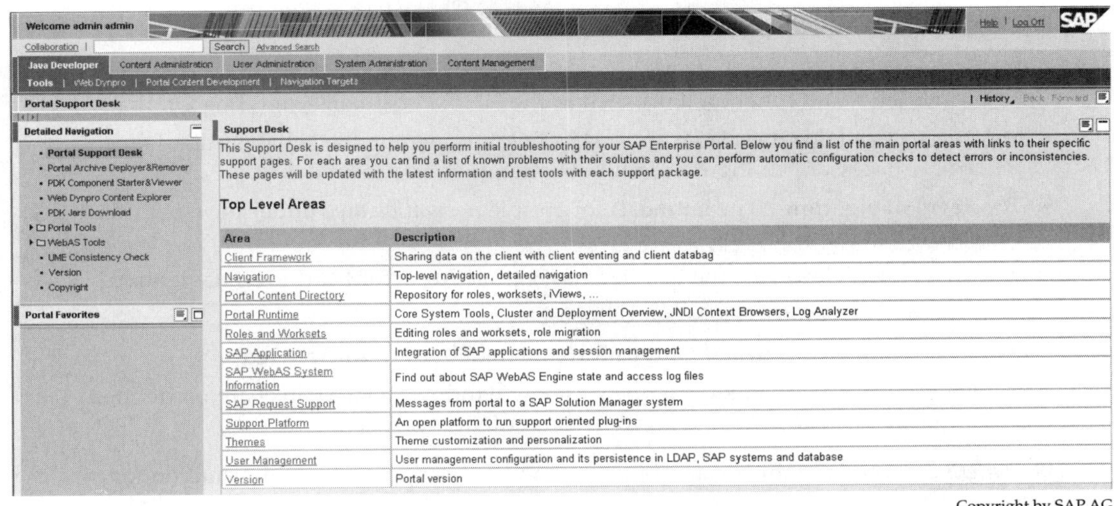

FIGURE 2-5 Welcome screen after successful logon

As a result of the Super Administrator role, three top-level menus appear, one each for the roles that make up the Super Administrator role.

Second-Level Menus

By assigning content to the roles, we can build the *navigational structure* of the portal. For example, by assigning content to the Java Developer role, the corresponding *second-level menus* and *detailed navigational menus* will be created.

In general, the portal user interface can be broadly divided into the following three areas: header area, navigation area, and content area.

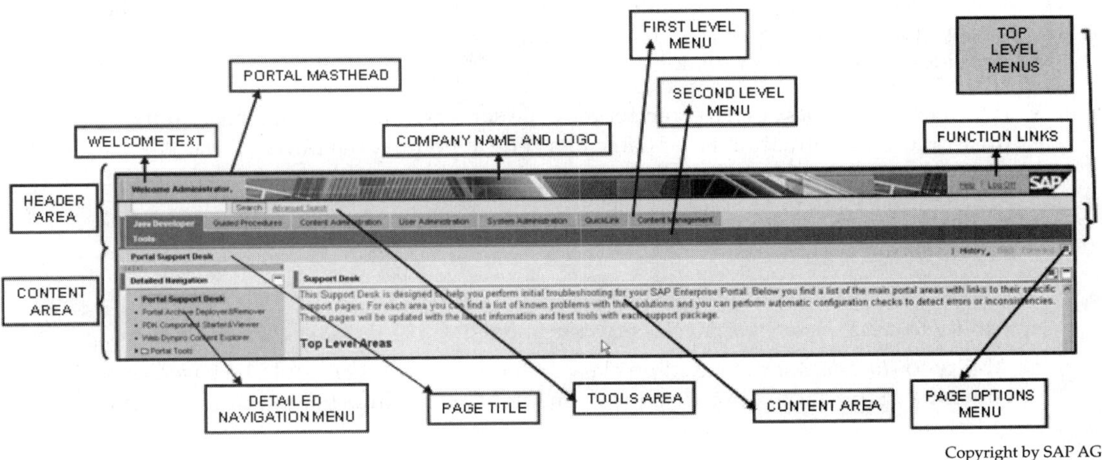

FIGURE 2-6 Parts of a portal desktop

The *header area* consists of the following:

- **Portal masthead** Contains welcome text for the user who has logged in; company name and logo; and function links such as the Help, Personalize, and Log Off links.
- **Tool area** Contains the search area and a link for opening the collaboration launch pad (if the necessary configuration for collaboration was carried out).
- **Top-level navigation** The leftmost, collapsible *navigation area* under the page title bar consists of the following:
  - Navigation iViews like the detailed navigation iView for third-level navigation
  - Dynamic navigation iViews for database access
  - Drag and relate iViews (if Unification functionality is implemented)
  - iViews with related links that open on new window (related links are predefined for the iView and page displayed in the content area)

The *content area* on the right consists of pages and iViews that provide information for the user. The *title bar* contains the title for the page that is being displayed. A History link, Back and Forward links, and a Page Options menu is available on the title bar. The Page Options menu provides links for opening the page in a new window, refreshing the page, personalizing the page, and adding the page to favorites.

Knowledge Management Architecture

Knowledge Management is very useful for organizations that store vast amounts of data among various types of media. It provides for controlled management of a document's life cycle and fosters collaboration between groups and communities.

Knowledge Management deals with making *unstructured information* available to the right audience. Unstructured information is content that is stored across various datasources such as text, web servers, file servers, intranet, mail servers, and database systems. It allows an end user to search and find information or knowledge very quickly, irrespective of where it is physically stored.

KM provides the following functions:

- *Integrates repositories* such as web servers, file servers, and notes database so that unstructured information is available at a central point in the portal.
- Ability to *navigate the folders* across all integrated repositories.
- Ability to access the documents in these repositories based on available *user permissions.*
- Ability to *search documents* in all integrated repositories.
- Ability to *create taxonomies* to classify documents.
- Ability to *store documents* based on classification. *Classification* could be based on content, organization, or other criteria; ensures that the information can be found efficiently.

- Ability to *create documents* based on user permissions.
- Ability to *publish documents* based on an *approval workflow.*
- *Provides Knowledge Management services* that allow internal support activities like the following:
  - Creating direct *feedback* on a document.
  - Creating *subscriptions* for notifying about any changes made to a resource.
  - Creating *reviews, ratings,* and *notes.*

Knowledge Management Components

The Knowledge Management component consists of *content management and search functionality.* The Knowledge Management functionality is provided by the following components (see Figure 2-7) through the portal:

- **KM applications** Such as Navigation and Search applications
- **KM global services** Such as index management and audit service
- **KM repository services** Such as subscription and publishing services
- **KM Repository framework** Such as repository managers for file system, HTTP, and WebDAV
- **TREX** The search engine

KM Application

The KM application consists of *end user* and *administrator iViews* for carrying activities such as navigating through folders and documents, searching for documents, and carrying out file operations such as copying, deleting, and so on.

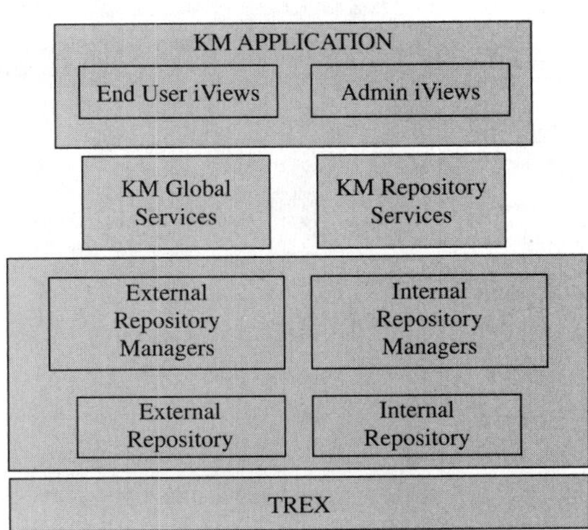

FIGURE 2-7 Knowledge Management components

The following iViews are available for end users:

- KM Classification
- KM Content Exchange subscriber
- KM Documents
- KM Navigation
- KM Quick poll
- KM Search
- KM Subscriptions

The following administrator iViews are available:

- KM Configuration
- KM Index administration
- KM TREX monitor

NOTE *To access the KM functionality for conducting activities such as changing/configuring data sources and KM services, choose System Administration | System Configuration | Knowledge Management | Content Management.*

Figure 2-8 displays the portal screen used for configuring Content Management.

KM Global Services

KM services can be classified as *global* and *repository* services. To manage the KM global services, choose System Administration | System Configuration | Knowledge Management |

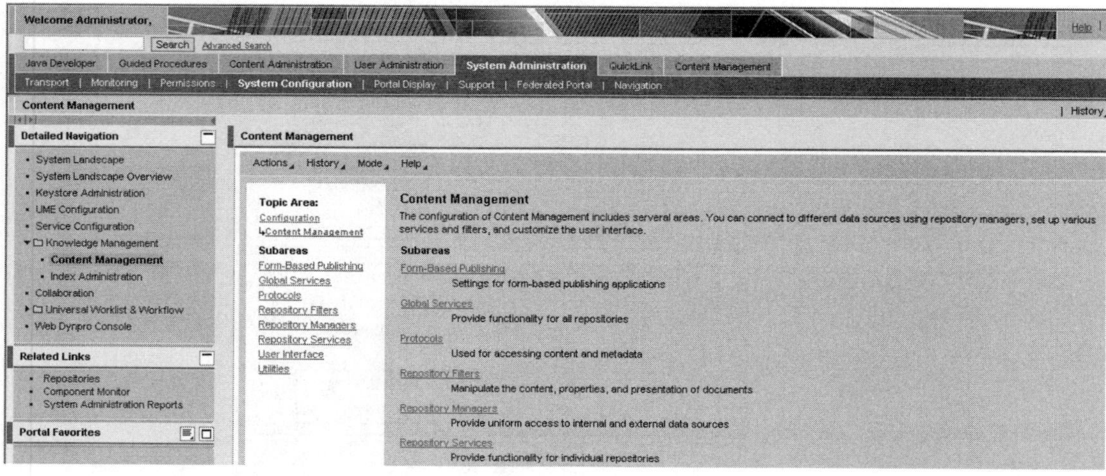

FIGURE 2-8 Portal screen for configuring Content Management

Content Management | Global Services. KM global services are available to all repository types in Content Management. Following are examples of KM global services:

- **Audit logs service** Used for auditing changes to documents and folders.
- **Cache service** Used for managing caches.
- **Index management service** Used for indexing and classification of documents and folders in KM repositories so that they are available during search.
- **MIME handler service** Used for identifying MIME types of documents so that the relevant icons are displayed against the document in the folder view.
- **Notificator service** Used for sending notifications to users when changes are made to subscribed resources and documents.
- **Virus scan service** Used for scanning documents for viruses.

TIP *The KM services require the TREX to function effectively.*

KM Repository Services

The next layer in the KM architecture is the KM services that are used by the various KM repositories. Unlike the global services, the repository services are tied to individual repositories and hence should be registered with the repositories. This is done by maintaining the *Repository Services* parameter in the repository definition. To change/configure the repository services, choose System Administration | System Configuration | Knowledge Management | Content Management | Repository Services.

Examples of repository services follow:

- **Application property service** Used by services or applications to store application properties, which is especially useful for classifying documents.
- **Subscription service** Used for sending notifications to users when changes are made to documents, folders, discussions, and so on.
- **Time dependent publishing service** Used to determine how long the document will be visible to the users.
- **Collaboration services** Enables functions such as feedback, notes, discussions, comments, ratings, and attachments.
- **Status management service** Used for managing documents based on their status in approval workflows.

KM Repository Framework

The Repository framework consists of

- Repositories for storing documents
- Repository managers for managing those repositories

The KM repository framework provides the functionality for storing documents in a physical storage location. It helps to perform some basic functions such as deleting, copying, and reading files. Documents and folders can be stored in the form of a virtual hierarchy and namespace, in both the internal and external repositories.

KM Repositories

When the repositories are used purely for KM purposes, they are known as *internal repositories,* and if they are used by other components such as BW or other Content Management solutions, they are known as *external repositories*. The repositories could be Windows-based file systems, HTTP servers, WebDAV systems, and so on. To create/configure a repository manager, choose System Administration | System Configuration | Knowledge Management | Content Management | Repository Managers.

Figure 2-9 displays the folder and documents for a KM repository. Here we can carry out basic activities like:

- Creating new documents, folders, and links
- Searching for documents

KM External Repository Managers

External repositories are included so as to manage information that is stored external to Content Management. Those included in the standard delivery of the portal follow:

- **File System repository manager** Provides read and write access to the contents in a folder hierarchy in a file system
- **Lotus Notes repository manager** For read access to Lotus Notes database

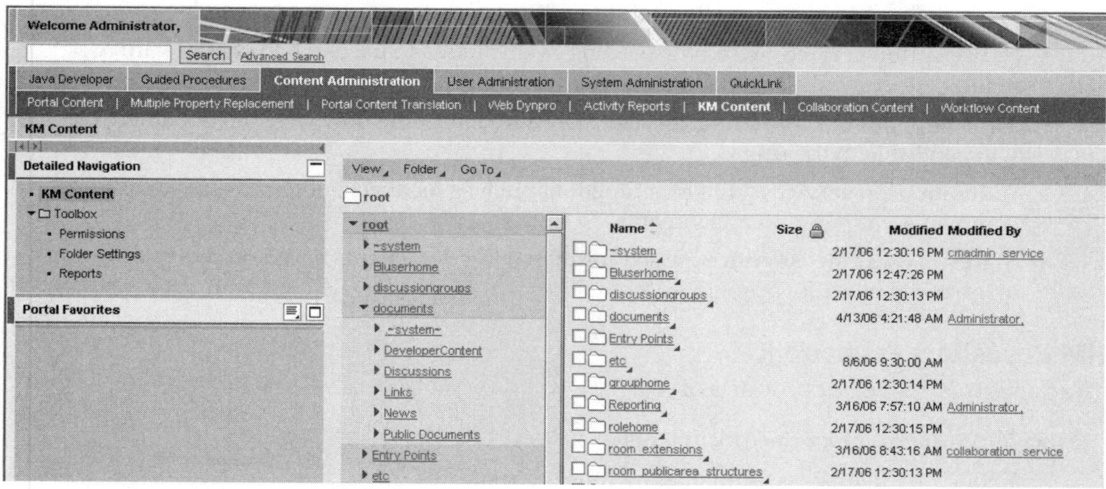

FIGURE 2-9 Folders and documents in KM Repository

- **WebDAV repository manager** For read/write access to information stored in IIS Services
- **Web repository manager** For read access to the contents of a website

KM Internal Repository Managers

Following are some types of internal repository managers:

- **CM repository manager** Manages repositories that are used by CM to store documents and folders. Examples of CM repositories are
  - **/documents** for managing text documents
  - **/collaboration** for managing collaboration content
  - **/discussion groups** for managing discussion groups
- **User Management repository manager** Makes available user information to CM. An example of UM repository is /um.
- **PCD repository manager** For searching portal objects like roles and iViews in the Portal Content Directory (PCD) in KM. The repository is */pcd* in the standard delivery.

Note that this repository managers list contains just a few of the many repository managers that exist on the portal.

Collaboration Architecture

As the name implies, collaboration in the portal is all about bringing together individuals, teams, or groups to work together closely. This is achieved by using a common set of collaboration tools and services under the portal platform. Although a number of standalone collaboration tools, such as e-mail, project management tools, and application-sharing tools, are available in the market, bringing them all together under a common platform is a huge undertaking.

Figure 2-10 displays a sample screen for administering collaboration functionality.

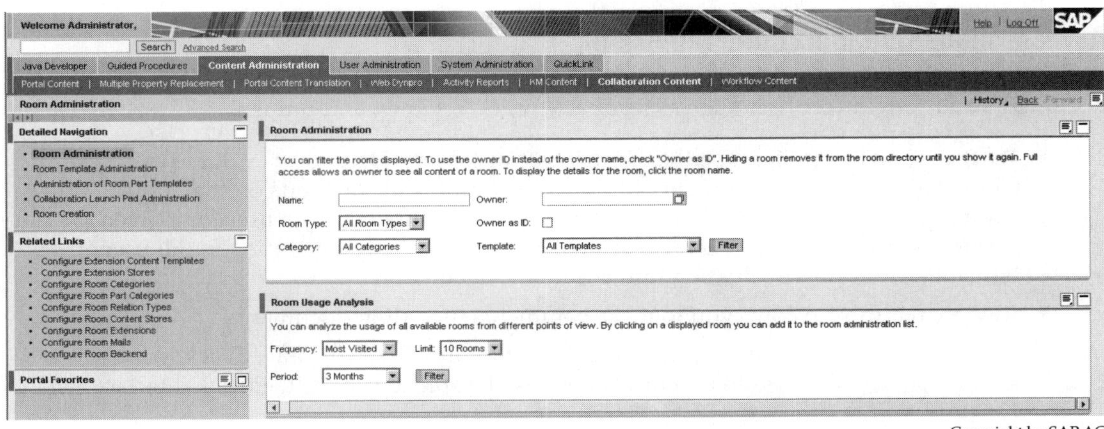

Figure 2-10 Portal screen for administering collaboration functionality

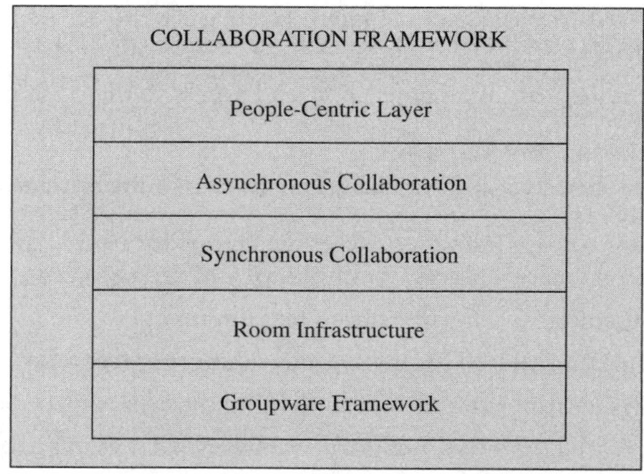

FIGURE 2-11 Collaboration framework components

The *collaboration framework* consists of the following components (refer to Figure 2-11):

- **People centric layer** Consists of iViews for selecting people and displaying information regarding people.
- **Room infrastructure component** Allows you to create, delete, and change *collaboration rooms* (used by project teams to share data and information).
- **Asynchronous tools and components** Allows asynchronous collaboration between users using functionalities such as *discussion groups, feedback, rating*, and so on.
- **Synchronous collaboration framework** Used for real-time collaboration functionalities such as *application sharing* and *instant messaging*.
- **Groupware framework** Allows integration of *e-mail systems* such as Lotus Notes and Microsoft Exchange; helps synchronize the task lists and the calendar between the two groupware systems.

Asynchronous Collaboration Framework

Asynchronous collaboration tools and *components* can be used for online discussions, tasks, and documents and provide services such as feedback, notes, reviews, and ratings.

- **Rating** Can be applied to either documents or folders. Helps you evaluate the content available in a document or folder. The rating scale depends on the company's configuration. Multiple ratings can be maintained by a user for a given document. In such cases when the system calculates the average rating for all users, it includes the latest evaluation rating only for calculation.
- **Review feature** Allows you to make comments regarding documents.
- **Feedback** Can be created on documents and folders. To create a feedback, you should have read access to that object and also be able to use the feedback interface.

TIP *You cannot maintain ratings for your own documents.*

Synchronous Collaboration Framework

The *Synchronous collaboration framework* allows real-time collaboration through

- **Application sharing** Used for product demos, presentations, and customer support
- **Chat** Used for multiple users to communicate with each other in real time
- **Instant messaging** Used for one-to-one communication

Room Infrastructure

The *room infrastructure component* allows you to manage the life cycle of team rooms. *Collaboration rooms* are virtual workspaces with all the necessary tools, services, and information available in one place. They can be integrated with real-time collaboration services and other third-party groupware as well. The room templates allow you to define the structure, content, and access controls for the room.

Collaboration Launch Pad

The *Collaboration Launch Pad* is a central point of access to contacts, e-mails, documents, discussions, appointments, rooms, tasks, application sharing, and instant messaging.

Third-Party Services

Third-party services such as WebEx can also be integrated into the portal. This allows portal users to communicate with non-portal users.

J2EE Architecture

The next system to be addressed is the *J2EE architecture,* because the portal is nothing but a software application that is deployed on an *SAP Web application server*. What it really boils down to is that, from an architectural standpoint, when we speak of the portal architecture, we are really referring to the J2EE architecture. Thus, concepts such as load balancing, high availability, and security ultimately depend upon the J2EE engine. This topic is addressed in detail in Chapter 6.

Summary

This chapter discussed the building blocks of the portal platform from a software architecture standpoint. You learned at a high level the various components of the portal platform, the Knowledge Management component, and the Collaboration platform. A good understanding and knowledge of these topics will help you when you're designing the technical infrastructure as well as gathering the business requirements during the portal implementation planning process.

CHAPTER 3

IT Practices, IT Scenarios, and Usage Types for NW Portal

This and the subsequent chapters address the various steps and tools SAP has provided that could be used when planning for the portal implementation. These tools include the *ASAP methodology for portal implementation, solution maps, Scenario and Process Component List tool,* and the *product availability matrix (PAM).* Combining these tools with the information and guidance available in SAP documentation such as the installation guides, release strategy, maintenance strategy, support package strategy will help you ensure a successful portal implementation. The next chapter deals with topics such as PAM, release strategy, maintenance strategy, support strategy and so on.

Initial Requirements Gathering

When planning to implement the portal, you must gather the initial business and technical requirements, because this will determine the success of the portal implementation after it goes live. In addition, the portal implementation project will move smoothly because most of the potential surprises can be avoided by planning properly.

Gather the Business and Technical Requirements

During the planning phase, the focus should be on gathering the basic business requirements during the business blueprint workshops. These requirements can then be used to identify the various software and hardware components that need to be installed for the Enterprise Portal using various portal planning tools discussed in this and subsequent chapters.

Identify User Population: Size, Nature, and Usage Intensity

You should identify the user population that will be affected by this project and gather information regarding the following:

- The *nature of users* in terms of how intensively they will be using the portal
- The *roles* to which they belong in the organization

The users could be classified into low, medium, or high intensity users based on the *think times*. This information will help you in the later stages of the project to calculate the potential load on the portal and to size the hardware systems accordingly.

INFO *The think time is the time elapsed between two successive clicks by an end user when using the portal.*

The other information that needs to be gathered is the functional positions and jobs of these users. This will not only help you choose the worksets (with iViews and pages) that need to be created, but it also helps you design the portal roles that need to be created.

Identify the Portal Types

Depending on the type of users, the portal could be implemented either for *internal users, external business partners* such as customers and vendors, or even *one time casual visitors*. Examples of portals are intranet portals that usually replace home-grown applications, supplier portals that provide vendor access to company information, customer portals such as the business-to-business (B2B) or business-to-consumer (B2C) scenarios, Business Intelligence (BI)–based portals that provide analytical information, and performance metrics dashboards. This information is important because it will have potential architectural design implications in terms of designing the security topology, required network bandwidth, content development issues, etc.

DO *Identifying the basic portal type at this stage will help you during the technical infrastructure design and content development phase.*

Identify the Applications to Be Integrated

You must take an *inventory of the applications*, both SAP and non-SAP, including the database and operating platforms on which they are deployed. You should confirm whether these applications should be integrated into the portal, and, if so, within what timeframe.

You should make an assessment of the *existing systems* in the company's infrastructure that is proposed to be integrated within the portal framework. You should assess the *type and amount of content* such as documents and transactions that need to be brought into the portal. You should also identify whether any *company specific processes and guidelines* such as branding guidelines and web content guidelines need to be followed. You should analyze whether these applications are already *web-enabled*, and, if they are not already web-based, you should assess the cost of web-enabling them before integrating them into the portal.

Following are examples of applications that can be integrated into the portal:

- Enterprise Resource Planning (ERP) applications such as SAP R/3, JD Edwards, Oracle, Peoplesoft, and so on.
- Customer Relationship Management (CRM) applications such as mySAP Customer Relationship, Siebel, and so on.
- Supply Chain Management (SCM) applications such as mySAP Supply Chain Management, mySAP APO, i2, and so on.
- SAP applications based on Web Application Server, BSP (Business Server Pages), ITS (Internet Transaction Server), and IACs (Internet Application Components).

- Data warehouse solutions such as SAP Business Information Warehouse (BW), Business Objects, and so on.
- Legacy systems and other databases.
- Collaborative groupware applications such as WebEx, Outlook, and Lotus Notes.
- Web content management solutions such as Interwoven, EMC Documentum, and so on.

Do *After identifying the content that needs to be integrated into the portal, you should determine the timeframe for including such content into the portal.*

Identify the Content: Business Packages vs. Custom

Based on the business requirements, you must determine whether additional business packages are required for deploying content or whether custom content needs to be developed.

If you choose to install business packages, you should determine whether the required *technical and functional prerequisites* have been met. For example, you should check the following from a technical standpoint:

- What SAP backend systems are required
- How much of R/3, BW, or mySAP components have been configured already
- Which functional modules will be impacted by the business package
- Whether the R/3 backend systems will be upgraded, which could potentially impact the implementation
- Whether the existing backend system version is compatible with the business package version

From a functional standpoint, you should check the following:

- Identify the roles that will be supported by the business package
- Determine the number of users who are likely to use the business package
- Decide which aspects of the business functionality the users will need
- Determine the nature and intensity of business analytic functions that the users are currently using
- Identify any external non-SAP applications that need to be integrated
- Identify the iViews in the business package that are not needed for the implementation

---

Tip *All technical and functional requirements are laid out in the documentation provided with the business package, and this topic is addressed in detail in Chapter 16.*

Following are some typical examples of business packages: Business Package (BP) for Manager Self Service, Employee Self Service, BP for Projects, Collaboration by WebEx, BP for CRM, BP for mySAP FI, BP for Oracle connectivity, Siebel Connectivity, Peoplesoft connectivity, and BP for FedEx tracking.

Develop the Technical Infrastructure Design

Another aspect of the planning phase is designing the technical infrastructure aspects of the portal installation. The goal of the technical infrastructure design is to provide a robust portal that not only meets the functional requirements but also provides good performance and high availability of the system. Adequate attention should be focused on how the different components of the portal are distributed as well as to aspects such as performance, scalability, and availability. This should be an outcome of the initial planning phase and should be continuously refined as more information becomes available that makes more accurate design possible.

INFO *Refer to Chapters 7 and 8 for more information on designing a robust technical infrastructure.*

Include SAP NetWeaver Landscape Strategy

When planning for the technical infrastructure, you should also plan for implementing the whole scale landscape for SAP NetWeaver using central, shared components such as System Landscape Directory (SLD), NetWeaver Administrator (NWA), and Solution Manager (SM).

Decide the IT Scenarios, Processes, and Systems

Once most of the major business requirements have been gathered, you must identify the various IT scenarios and processes that need to be implemented. Subsequently, you must identify the various systems that should be installed for those IT scenarios and processes.

INFO *This is dealt with in detail later, in the section "Identify Installable Software Units: Systems, Standalone Engines, and Clients" of this chapter.*

Identify the Installable Software Units

Once the IT scenario has been identified based on the initial requirements, you should identify the technical requirements such as the hardware and software components for that IT scenario.

DO *As a part of this process, you should identify the sequence with which the components should be installed.*

For example, if during the business requirements gathering workshops, it was decided that the knowledge management functionality of the portal such as maintaining and publishing documents is required, then you have to plan for installing the knowledge management software components of the portal and design the hardware requirements based on the proposed user population and other workload requirements.

SAP Documentation: A Must Read

In the context of identifying the different software components that need to be installed, it is mandatory to read the *Master Guide* document provided by SAP. This document is available in the SAP Service Marketplace, which can be accessed at the hyperlink http://service.sap.com/instguides. Choose the appropriate version of the document based on the release of NetWeaver that you plan to install. To access the SAP Service Marketplace website, you must request a user ID and password from your company security administrator.

A number of resources are available on SAP's website that can come in handy when choosing the components required for installation. These are the product availability matrix, the release strategy and maintenance strategy information, the scenario and component list information, and the Solution Manager. Before installing, you should always refer to the master guide and installation guides.

TIP *The master and installation guides can provide very useful information while you're planning for the portal implementation.*

Preparing the Checklist

As a part of the planning for the portal implementation, you should come up with a checklist that consists of all the requirements and tasks to be carried out. The checklist should consist of the following information:

- The list of *software components* to be installed
- The *sequence* of the installation of the software components
- The *patch levels and support package levels* to which the software components should be upgraded
- The list of *hardware components* based on the sizing of the systems
- The choice between a *distributed* and a *central installation* based on the requirements of system availability and cost-benefit analysis
- The choice between NetWeaver *AS Java* and NetWeaver *AS ABAP + and AS Java*
- *Sizing* requirements such as the need for additional dialog instances based on an initial analysis of potential user population and the application characteristics
- The list of *supported platforms* such as browser, operating systems, and databases based on the product availability matrix
- The list of additional software and hardware components to meet the *security* requirements of your organization
- Identifying and selecting a list of *installation media DVDs* for installing the database, NetWeaver application server, the Enterprise Portal, Knowledge Management and Collaboration components, and TREX
- Operating system requirements, JDK requirements, NTFS file system, and OS service pack levels
- The list of *business packages* to be installed
- Details of *technical and functional prerequisites* for the business packages
- Information on central NetWeaver landscape system components to be installed

---

NOTE *Please note that the above list is by no means complete.*

Identify IT Practices, IT Scenarios, and Usage Types

It is important for you to address some of the terminology such as *IT practices, IT scenarios,* and *usage types* that needs to be understood to help with the portal implementation.

IT Practices: A Process-Centric Approach

SAP now addresses its NetWeaver products from the angle of *IT practices, IT scenarios,* and *usage types. IT practices* is a process-centric approach rather than a technological component–centric approach to implement NetWeaver-based solutions. Note that SAP NetWeaver 2004s was considered as a major release in and of itself, and also considered to be a minor special release of SAP NetWeaver 04s. SAP NetWeaver 2004s has come to be known as SAP NetWeaver 7.0, which is now the latest version.

Benefits of Process-Centric Approach

The idea behind having a process-centric approach in SAP NetWeaver 7.0 that it is a step toward the objective of implementing a service-oriented enterprise system. The process-centric approach enables a business-centric cross-component view of SAP products and hence makes it possible to bring about a better understanding, communication, and synergy between the IT and the lines of business. So now, instead of speaking of Business Intelligence (BI), Enterprise portal, Exchange Infrastructure (XI), and so on, we speak of IT scenarios and IT practices that are more closely aligned with the business scenarios and practices. SAP is fully backing up this shift, and this new approach is now reflected in the SAP Solution Manager, help documentation, implementation guidelines, and Implementation Guide (IMG) configuration activities.

The *SAP Technology Map,* which provides information and help on choosing the SAP NetWeaver technology components such as Portal, BI, and XI, also reflects this trend. The fact that there has been increasing integration between the NetWeaver technology components such as Portal, BI, and XI and also tighter integration between the SAP applications and technology components strengthens this shift toward a process-centric approach. Instead of different release cycles for SAP NetWeaver products, a synchronized release cycle is used for one integrated NetWeaver platform.

INFO *Because of the increased integration and synchronization across components, it is becoming increasingly easier to identify NetWeaver components requirements and to install them.*

IT Scenarios: Step Toward an Incremental Service-Based Architecture

The IT practices, in turn, consist of a number of predefined *IT scenarios*. The IT practices, in conjunction with the IT scenarios, help to provide the customers with a tangible roadmap that they can follow when implementing NetWeaver solutions on an incremental basis. By combining one or more of the IT scenarios with custom developed solutions, you will be able to leverage the benefits of NetWeaver landscape components as well as the investments that have already been made in the existing IT landscape.

TIP *This phased implementation approach combined with the flexibility to include custom components makes it easier to implement a service-based architecture in an incremental manner and helps to reduce the Total Cost of Ownership (TCO).*

A few examples of the IT scenarios are

- Running an Enterprise Portal
- Enabling User Collaboration
- Business Task Management
- Enterprise Knowledge Management
- Enterprise Search
- Software Lifecycle Management
- Developing, Configuring, and Adapting Applications
- SAP NetWeaver Operations
- Authentication and Single Sign-On
- Integrated Data Access and User Management

IT Scenario Variants: Address a Specific Business Need

For the purpose of this chapter, let's take a look at one of the scenarios, namely, *Running an Enterprise Portal*. This scenario is one of the many scenarios that fall under the IT Practice, namely, *User Productivity Enablement*. Every IT scenario comes with a number of *scenario variants*. The IT scenario variants are designed to meet the business requirements of a specific business scenario such as implementing a global portal, a public website, or a simple intranet website.

For example, the IT scenario variants for Running an Enterprise Portal include the following:

- Implementing an External Facing Portal
- Providing Uniform Content Access
- Implementing a Federated Portal Network

The scenario variant *Implementing a Federated Portal Network* is useful to implement a network of portals (both SAP and non-SAP), some of which could be *producers of content* and some *consumers of content*. Having such a federated network of portals enables the sharing of content between the portals. This concept of federated portals helps to leverage the content available in portals already existing in the organization, irrespective of whether they are SAP- or non-SAP–based systems.

The other scenario variant, *Implementing an External Facing Portal*, can be used to implement a public web portal that can be used by anonymous and registered users on even low-bandwidth networks. This portal can be used by external users such as customers, suppliers, and business partners. This scenario variant has some additional functionality such as enabling caching on the server, using short URLs, using light portal desktops, and so on.

INFO *Refer to Chapters 19 and 20 for more information.*

The scenario variant *Providing Uniform Content Access* is the most basic implementation of the portal functionality and is a prerequisite for installing the *Implement a Federated Portal Network* scenario variant.

INFO *The scenario variants are specific applications of a given IT scenario in order to meet a specific business need.*

Usage Types

Once you have identified the required IT practice, the IT scenario, and the IT scenario variant, the next step is to identify the various software components required for the IT scenario variant. This is done using the *usage types,* which are nothing but various software components. For example, to implement the scenario variant *Providing Uniform Content Access,* you will need the following usage types or software units:

- Application Server Java
- Enterprise Portal
- Developer infrastructure, which is optional and required only if you are developing custom applications for the portal

IT Processes

The next step is to get more specific in terms of what needs to be done to make the IT scenario variant a reality. In other words, you must identify the *processes* required to implement the IT scenario variant. Following are the IT processes required to realize the *Providing Uniform Content Access* scenario variant:

- Configuring the portal
- Creating portal content
- Maintaining the portal
- Using the portal

As you can see, the IT processes are mainly concerned with getting the portal up and running by implementing activities such as

- Configuring the portal
- Developing content for access
- Ensuring the portal runs smoothly by administering user roles
- Monitoring the system operations

The same approach can be used to realize any of the other IT scenarios. Thus, some of the steps involved during an initial implementation would be to identify the required IT scenarios, identify the possible variants of those scenarios; choose the required and optional usage types; and, finally, configure, administer, and use the portal to meet the user requirements.

For further information regarding the different scenario variants and their corresponding usage types, please refer to the *master guide* specific to the version of SAP NetWeaver that you are planning to install. Again, which version of SAP NetWeaver that you would be implementing will depend upon the platform support, which is laid out in the Platform Availability Matrix, the release strategy, support strategy, and so on.

INFO *For more information, please refer to Chapter 4.*

Identify Installable Software Units: Systems, Standalone Engines, and Clients

Now that you understand the various IT scenarios and the processes, let's take a closer look at some of the software units that may need to be installed to implement the scenarios. The installable software units can be broadly classified into *systems, standalone engines,* and *clients.* Using these installable software units, you can install parts or all of SAP NetWeaver.

The usage types help to bridge the gap between identifying a required IT scenario that meets a particular business requirement and then translating it into implementation specifics in terms of what systems and software components should be installed.

Systems

Examples of usage types for *SAP systems* are Application Server ABAP, Application Server Java, Enterprise Portal, Business Intelligence, Business Intelligence Java components, Development Infrastructure, Mobile Infrastructure, and Process Integration. Process Integration is the new name for Exchange Infrastructure.

For a simple IT scenario such as *Running an Enterprise Portal,* Application Server Java and Enterprise Portal systems should be sufficient. As already mentioned, NetWeaver systems that are required for the implementation would depend upon a particular IT scenario that is implemented. Thus, during the planning phase, it is important that you identify the scenario and the corresponding systems (usage types) that are required to be implemented.

Systems are the basic building blocks of SAP NetWeaver that have been built for a specific purpose. An SAP system can have either one software component that belongs to a particular usage type or several software components that belong to multiple usage types. Examples of usage types are Application Server Java and Enterprise Portal. When usage types run separately on different systems, they should be able to work just as they would run locally on one system.

INFO *The usage types are the largest installable units that can be used to implement IT scenario variants.*

Considering that we are more concerned about the NetWeaver AS Java and the EP systems, let's take a quick look at them.

Application Server Java Usage Type

Application Server Java provides the basic Java functionality for SAP NetWeaver and consists of various software components such as a J2EE-compliant Application Server, Web DynPro for Java, Adobe Document Services, and the SAP Composite Application Framework core (CAF).

The *J2EE-compliant Application Server* provides the basic runtime capabilities for running enterprise class applications. *Web DynPro* is the technology advocated by SAP for user interfaces and is the preferred user interface for professional business applications that use either mobile clients or desktop clients. *Adobe Document Service* provides the required runtime services for working with Adobe documents. *Adobe Document Service* is an example of how SAP works with third-party vendors to improve the portal functionality. *SAP Composite Application Framework* provides the ability to create a service-oriented architecture by using services such as entity services for the domain model, application services for business logic, and external services using RFC calls or web services.

Enterprise Portal Usage Type

The *Enterprise Portal* provides the basic web front-end capability for SAP NetWeaver and consists of software components such as Portal, Knowledge Management, Collaboration, guided procedures, Visual Composer, Adobe Flex Server, and an application sharing server. *Guided procedures* are tools that provides the framework for modeling and managing business processes that span across multiple backend systems. *Visual Composer* is a development tool for creating applications based on the model-view controller (MVC) model without manually writing code. *Adobe Flex Server* is used to compile applications that have been developed in Visual Composer into Flash .swf files. An *application sharing server* is used to enable collaboration functionalities that need data streaming services for application sharing features. Enterprise Portal requires Web Application Server Java to run.

TIP *For details regarding other SAP NetWeaver systems with different usage types, please refer to the* master guide *related to the version of SAP NetWeaver that you are planning to implement.*

Change in Terminology

With the advent of this shift from a component perspective to a process-centric perspective, the names of some of the NetWeaver technology components have changed as well. SAP Web AS is now known as *SAP NetWeaver Application Server*, SAP BW (Business Information Warehouse) is now known as *SAP NetWeaver Business Intelligence*, SAP XI is now known as *SAP NetWeaver Exchange Infrastructure*, SAP EP is now known as *SAP NetWeaver Portal*, and SAP MI is now known as *SAP NetWeaver Mobile*.

NOTE *In this book, the above terms will be used interchangeably.*

Standalone Engines

The *standalone engines* and the *clients* are the other pieces of the puzzle that help to fulfill the installation software requirements. The standalone engines are additional software components that can be installed on the server along with the SAP systems such as Web AS Java and EP, as mentioned above, to provide additional functionality.

INFO *These standalone components can run on their own and do not need either Application Server Java or ABAP.*

Examples of standalone engines are Content Server gateway, SAP center jobs scheduling by Redwood, liveCache, search and classification, and Web Dispatcher.

Of particular importance to the portal scenario is the search and classification engine using *TREX* and the *Web Dispatcher*. TREX can be used for implementing the search functionality in Knowledge Management and the SAP Web Dispatcher can be used to implement load balancing across multiple server nodes in the SAP NetWeaver Application Server.

Clients

The third type of installable software component is the clients, examples of which are Adobe Life Cycle Designer, Business Explorer, J2SE Adapter Engine, Mobile Infrastructure Client, SAP GUI, SAP NetWeaver Developer Studio, and SAP NetWeaver Developer Workplace.

SAP NetWeaver Developer Workplace

SAP NetWeaver Developer Workplace consists of both SAP NetWeaver Developer Studio and SAP NetWeaver system consisting of both Enterprise Portal and the NetWeaver Application Server Java. The SAP NetWeaver Developer Workplace can be used for developing applications and testing them before deploying on the portal. It is available only for the Microsoft Windows operating system and for databases such as mySQL, Microsoft SQL Server, or MaxDB.

INFO SAP NetWeaver Developer Studio *is used for developing applications by portal developers.*

SAP GUI Clients

SAP offers three different types of SAP GUI clients for accessing ABAP applications: *SAP GUI for the Windows, SAP GUI for Java,* and *SAP GUI for HTML*. SAP GUI for Windows is the most versatile of all the three and is available only for the Microsoft Windows operating system. SAP GUI for HTML is based on SAP ITS. SAP GUI for Java is the most generic of all the three clients and is available for a variety of platforms. When using SAP GUI for Windows, the iView has the same look and feel as that of the back end system. SAP GUI for Windows can be painful to use because the SAP GUI needs to be installed on all clients. SAP GUI for Java also requires an installation of the SAP GUI on the client, but this happens only for the first time during runtime. SAP GUI for HTML is a little slower than SAP GUI for Windows, because browser rendering time is involved. Also SAP GUI for HTML does not support all SAP transactions because certain screen elements and controls are not supported in the browsers. Compared to both SAP GUI for Windows and SAP GUI for Java, the look and feel is more aligned to that of the portal when using SAP GUI for HTML.

Design NetWeaver System Landscape: Central Systems

As a part of designing the system landscape, care should be given to implementing shared services such as Solution Manager, Solution Manager Diagnostics, SAP NetWeaver Administrator, Alert Monitor, System Landscape Directory, Software Lifecycle Manager, and Adapting Computing Controller, as illustrated in Figure 3-1.

Solution Manager

Starting from SAP NetWeaver SR1, you need to generate the Solution Manager key to install or upgrade the system. At least one productive *Solution Manager* should be present in the system landscape. Solution Manager helps to monitor ABAP-based SAP solutions, thus ensuring that business processes run smoothly.

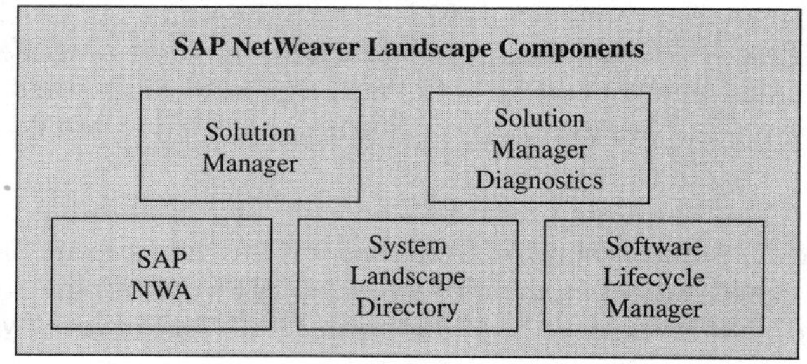

FIGURE 3-1 SAP NetWeaver Landscape Components

Solution Manager Diagnostics

The same concept is extended to the Java world by implementing the Solution Manager Diagnostics. *Solution Manager Diagnostics* contains two third-party solutions: *Wily Introscope,* which is used for performance troubleshooting and problem analysis, and *Mercury Loadrunner,* which is used for load testing.

SAP NWA

SAP NWA is used as a tool for administering local systems for NetWeaver Application Server Java solutions and can be used as a central administration tool for systems containing NetWeaver Application Server Java, NetWeaver Application Server ABAP, and Enterprise Portal. It can be used for starting and stopping Java applications, viewing logs, and providing monitoring and administration functionalities using Web DynPro iViews.

INFO *SAP NWA helps to carry out all monitoring and administration activities centrally.*

System Landscape Directory

System Landscape Directory is used to store all information regarding the current landscape as well as the systems that can be installed in the future. It includes both ABAP and third-party systems. It comes by default in the Application Server Java installation. If you are using just ABAP systems, then SLD is not required because Solution Manager can maintain the same information. You can either maintain a single SLD or multiple SLDs, depending upon your specific geographical and availability requirements.

INFO *Please refer to Chapters 43 and 44 for more information as SLD and NWA respectively.*

Software Lifecycle Manager

Software Lifecycle Manager (SLM) is a new tool provided by SAP that is intended to facilitate easier management of software lifecycle tasks such as installation, upgrade, and patch installation. It provides a graphical overview of the existing and planned system landscapes. It is integrated with the SLD and helps to view third-party solutions and business scenarios stored in SLD. For more information, refer to the master guide document for SAP NetWeaver 7.0 (2004s).

Introduction to ASAP Methodology

AcceleratedSAP (ASAP) roadmaps are methodologies provided by SAP to implement SAP solutions. SAP provides *ASAP Implementation roadmaps for the Enterprise Portal,* which is a subset of the full ASAP Implementation roadmap. It is a useful tool that can be used by project managers, implementation team members, portal consultants and architects, and anyone who is involved in a portal implementation. With particular reference to the portal installation, provision is made for aspects such as how content is organized for various user groups, look and feel design, role-based personalization, user adoptability, and integration with existing systems.

The ASAP methodology broadly classifies the portal implementation phases into the following:

- Project preparation
- Business blueprint
- Realization
- Final preparation
- Go live and support

TIP *The ASAP methodology for portal implementation provides a number of useful tools and documentation templates that can be used throughout the course of the portal implementation.*

Templates are available for project plan, business scenario templates, global delivery templates, performance test plans, scoping statements, iView documentation templates, installation documentation templates, work package templates, and so on.

INFO *The ASAP roadmaps can be accessed from http://service.sap.com/asap. For accessing the roadmap for portal, please click the link* ASAP Implementation Roadmap for SAP Enterprise Portal. *Click the link for downloading the roadmap and follow the instructions provided in the help document* "How-to install HTML version of ASAP Roadmap" *to install the roadmap.*

Project Preparation

In this phase, all the activities that are required to ensure a successful project are carried out. Most of the activities are project management–related activities such as defining the project goals, aligning them with the company objectives, defining the implementation standards, and assigning resources. Some of the technical activities are technical infrastructure planning activities such as designing the technical system landscape and initial sizing, and defining the integration plan and transport strategy.

Business Blueprint

During this phase the focus is on gathering the detailed business requirements for the portal implementation. Details regarding the organizational structure, business scenarios, required master data, development requirements, and design are gathered. Technical infrastructure design is further elaborated with focus on proposed transport strategy, server infrastructure design, network topology design, security planning, rollout strategy, and high availability strategy. By now, the portal development environment is installed and is ready for intensive development.

Realization Phase

This phase is the actual phase where all the major implementation activities are carried out. Part of this phase is the intensive development activities such as content development, integration development, quality testing, and cutover planning. Once the system is ready and tested, you should get ready for production live operation per a go-live plan. By now all the enterprise-wide user roles and authorizations are implemented. Performance tests and the SAP GoingLive check are also conducted.

Final Preparation Phase

During this phase, all the systems are tested, any pending issues are resolved, end user training is conducted, and all the cutover activities are finalized. Adequate procedures are implemented for post go-live technical and functional support activities.

Go Live and Support

This is the final sign off phase where the project has really come to an end and sign off has been obtained for final customer acceptance. The SAP GoingLive check and SAP EarlyWatch check are also conducted.

Using Solution Maps: A Quick Peek

Other useful resources are the *SAP Solution Maps* and *SAP Business Scenario Maps*. An example of a solution map is the SAP NetWeaver Solution Map, which is an infrastructure and services map. To access the solution maps, go to http://service.sap.com/solutionmaps.

The solution map provides process information at two different levels. At the first level, the solution map provides an overview of the processes in the form of process categories and main processes within an organization for a particular industry, cross-industry, or infrastructure and services area. In Figure 3-2, User Productivity Enablement is a process category and the main processes within that process category are Running an Enterprise Portal, Enabling User Collaboration, and so on.

At the second level, the solution map provides information on the functionality required to implement a given process. For example, to implement the main process Running an Enterprise Portal, three possible configuration scenarios are possible, as shown in Figure 3-3. The configuration scenarios represent the possible end-to-end processes that can be implemented in an organization while implementing an IT solution. For the main process Running an Enterprise Portal, the corresponding configuration scenarios are as follows:

- Implementing an external facing portal
- Providing uniform content access
- Implementing a federated portal network

Each of these IT configuration scenarios can be technically realized by implementing the processes. For example, to implement the Implementing an External Facing Portal scenario, you have to implement the four processes shown in Figure 3-4.

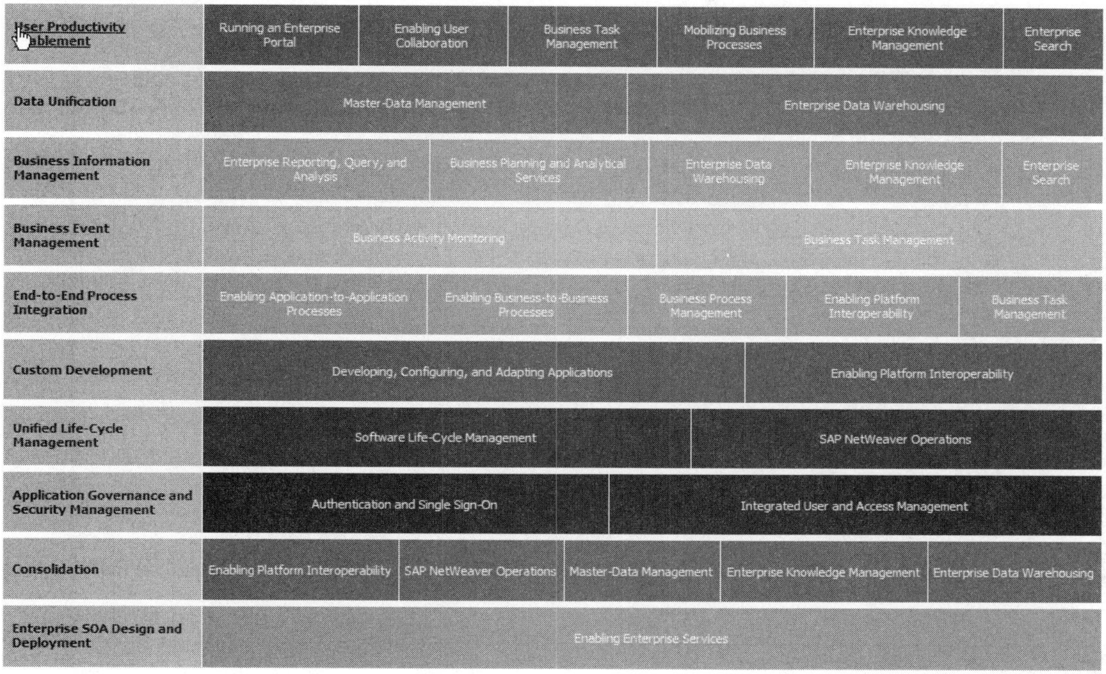

User Productivity Enablement	Running an Enterprise Portal	Enabling User Collaboration	Business Task Management	Mobilizing Business Processes	Enterprise Knowledge Management	Enterprise Search
Data Unification	Master-Data Management	Enterprise Data Warehousing				
Business Information Management	Enterprise Reporting, Query, and Analysis	Business Planning and Analytical Services	Enterprise Data Warehousing	Enterprise Knowledge Management	Enterprise Search	
Business Event Management	Business Activity Monitoring	Business Task Management				
End-to-End Process Integration	Enabling Application-to-Application Processes	Enabling Business-to-Business Processes	Business Process Management	Enabling Platform Interoperability	Business Task Management	
Custom Development	Developing, Configuring, and Adapting Applications	Enabling Platform Interoperability				
Unified Life-Cycle Management	Software Life-Cycle Management	SAP NetWeaver Operations				
Application Governance and Security Management	Authentication and Single Sign-On	Integrated User and Access Management				
Consolidation	Enabling Platform Interoperability	SAP NetWeaver Operations	Master-Data Management	Enterprise Knowledge Management	Enterprise Data Warehousing	
Enterprise SOA Design and Deployment	Enabling Enterprise Services					

FIGURE 3-2 SAP solution map for infrastructure and services

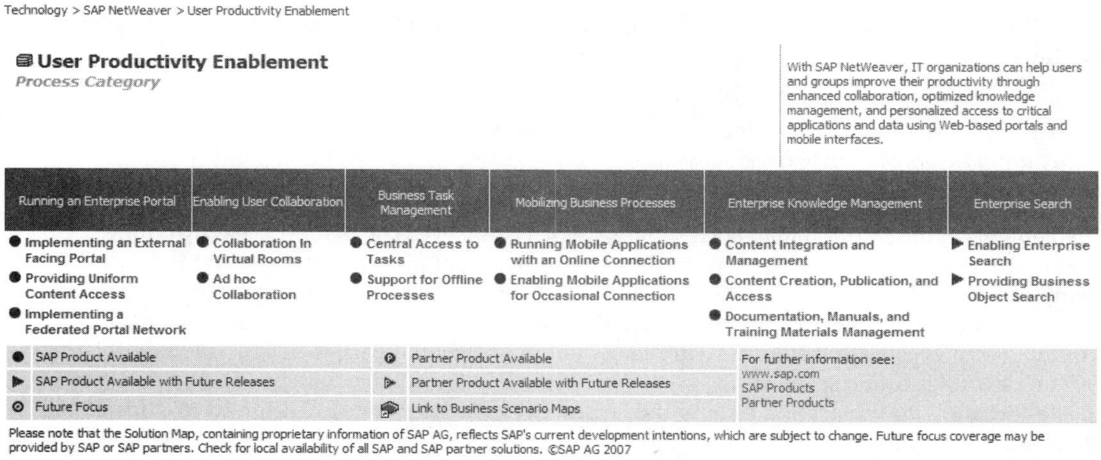

Technology > SAP NetWeaver > User Productivity Enablement

User Productivity Enablement
Process Category

With SAP NetWeaver, IT organizations can help users and groups improve their productivity through enhanced collaboration, optimized knowledge management, and personalized access to critical applications and data using Web-based portals and mobile interfaces.

Running an Enterprise Portal	Enabling User Collaboration	Business Task Management	Mobilizing Business Processes	Enterprise Knowledge Management	Enterprise Search
● Implementing an External Facing Portal ● Providing Uniform Content Access ● Implementing a Federated Portal Network	● Collaboration In Virtual Rooms ● Ad hoc Collaboration	● Central Access to Tasks ● Support for Offline Processes	● Running Mobile Applications with an Online Connection ● Enabling Mobile Applications for Occasional Connection	● Content Integration and Management ● Content Creation, Publication, and Access ● Documentation, Manuals, and Training Materials Management	▶ Enabling Enterprise Search ▶ Providing Business Object Search

● SAP Product Available	Partner Product Available	For further information see:
▶ SAP Product Available with Future Releases	Partner Product Available with Future Releases	www.sap.com SAP Products
Future Focus	Link to Business Scenario Maps	Partner Products

Please note that the Solution Map, containing proprietary information of SAP AG, reflects SAP's current development intentions, which are subject to change. Future focus coverage may be provided by SAP or SAP partners. Check for local availability of all SAP and SAP partner solutions. ©SAP AG 2007

FIGURE 3-3 Details under User Productivity Enablement process category in solution maps

Processes

Process	Process tasks	Configuration Variants
Configuring the External Facing Portal●	Define user profiles for named anonymous, external crawlers and B2B users Configure named anonymous user access Configure navigation cache Create/modify navigation iViews Customize the out of the box light framework page Customize styles (optional) Assign light framework page to users/groups/alias To fully utilize this functionality, the following products should be evaluated SAP NetWeaver	**Configuration Variants** Configuring The External Facing Portal
Creating External Facing Portal Content●	Create light content Define content for EFP usage To fully utilize this functionality, the following products should be evaluated SAP NetWeaver	**Configuration Variants** Creating External Facing Portal Content
Maintaining the External Facing Portal●	Define application quick links Handle B2B user requests Monitor performance Track activities To fully utilize this functionality, the following products should be evaluated SAP NetWeaver	**Configuration Variants** Maintaining The External Facing Portal ɔrtal Content
Using the External Facing Portal●	Request B2B account Register as named anonymous user Work with the portal To fully utilize this functionality, the following products should be evaluated SAP NetWeaver	**Configuration Variants** Using The External Facing ɜcing Portal

●SAP Product Available | Partner Product Available | SAP Product Available with Future Releases | Partner Product Available with Future Releases | Future Focus

Please note that the Solution Map, containing proprietary information of SAP AG, reflects SAP's current development intentions, which are subject to change. Future focus coverage may be provided by SAP or SAP partners. Check for local availability of all SAP and SAP partner solutions. ©SAP AG 2007

FIGURE 3-4 Processes under Implementing an External Facing Portal scenario

Thus the relationship flows from the process category to the processes as shown here:

Solution >> Process Category >> Main Process >>
Configuration Scenarios >> Processes >> Process tasks

Following is an example of a *User Productivity Enablement* category in the SAP NetWeaver solution:

SAP NetWeaver >> User Productivity Enablement >> Running an Enterprise Portal >> Implementing an External Facing Portal >> Configuring the External Facing Portal >> Assign light framework page to users/groups/alias

At the time of this writing, in the master guide, the process category (User Productivity Enablement) in the solution map corresponds to the IT practice. The main process (Running an Enterprise Portal) is referred to as the IT scenario. The configuration scenario in the solution map is the equivalent of the IT scenario variant. Finally, both the configuration scenario in the solution map and the IT scenario variant in the master guide are composed of a number of processes that should be implemented to realize that particular IT scenario variant or configuration scenario.

Following is an illustration of how the IT practices and scenarios are referred to during the process of implementation:

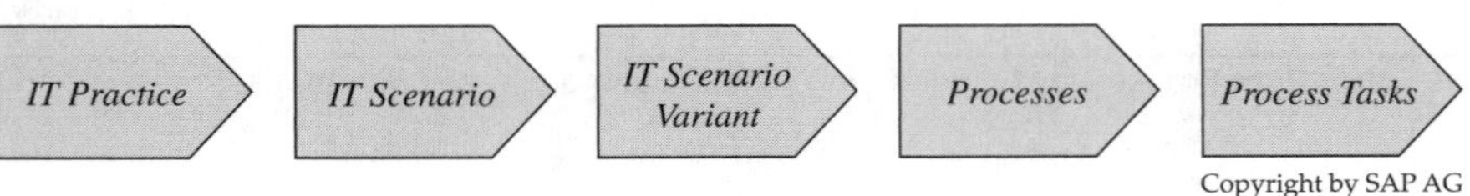

For example, User Productivity Enablement >> Running an Enterprise Portal >> Providing Uniform Content Access >> Configuring the Portal >> Initial Role Assignment to Administrators.

This process flow is referred to in the Solution Map as shown next:

Process Category >> Main Process >> Configuration Scenarios >> Processes >> Process tasks

Benefits of Using SAP Solution Map

The point to be noted here is that the SAP solution map and the process view adopted by SAP provide a high-level, common blueprint of the possible IT practices in an organization. Using the process-centric approach of the SAP solution map, you can implement these IT practices in such a way that they are aligned with the business strategy. This approach enables you to identify the business requirements as well as the IT requirements, and map them to each other using these business maps though at a high level. It enables the business teams and the IT teams to link business concepts with IT solutions and thus provide business benefits as a result of such implementations.

TIP *The SAP solution map helps the IT and business teams design and plan a solution using common language.*

Once the business requirements and the IT practices have been mapped, it is then relatively easy to identify the required software units based on the usage types, standalone engines, and clients enunciated in the master guide for a particular SAP NetWeaver version.

Summary

This chapter discussed the basic tasks that are required during the requirements gathering phase and in compiling a checklist for the portal installation. It then discussed how to identify the required IT practices and scenarios based on the business requirements and then how to identify the required software installation units based on those IT scenarios. The chapter wrapped up by taking a quick peek at ASAP implementation methodology for portal and the SAP Solution Manager, which are both good tools that can be adopted by the project managers and the portal architects during the portal implementation.

4
CHAPTER

PAM, Release Strategy, Maintenance Strategy, and Support Strategy

In this chapter, we shall take a look at the various tools available to check the availability of SAP NetWeaver versions and the releases. While so doing, we will be able to learn more about the release planning, maintenance strategy, support package strategy and support strategy from SAP. This information is helpful when designing the system landscape and choosing the systems required for installing the SAP NetWeaver Enterprise Portal.

Why Is PAM Important

During the project preparation phase, when you are conducting a high-level assessment of the existing system environment, it becomes important to analyze the integration feasibility of the SAP NetWeaver platform components such as Enterprise Portal and NetWeaver Application Server with the existing IT landscape. To do this, you will have to look at the release planning, required upgrades for applications such as SAP R/3, Customer Relationship Management (CRM), and license information. The product availability matrix provided by SAP comes in very handy for undertaking such an analysis.

The *product availability matrix* (PAM) provides information on various SAP components and instances. The PAM provides both *technical release information* as well as *release planning information* for SAP components. The technical release information provides information on the compatibility of these SAP components with respect to different operating systems, database systems, and JSE (Java Standard Edition) platforms.

To access the product availability matrix, go to http://service.sap.com/pam. The easiest way to go to the PAM for the relevant version is to select the versions under the Most Viewed list.

SAP Products or Applications

A number of different categories of SAP products are available, and sometimes the terminology used to identify SAP products can get quite confusing. Let's take a look at the types of SAP products. SAP components can be classified into various types shown in Figure 4-1.

- **SAP application components (cross-industry components)** Examples are SAP Customer Relationship Management (CRM), SAP R/3, SAP Supplier Relationship Management (SRM), and SAP Supply Chain Management (SCM). SAP application components are part of the SAP Business Suite and are responsible for providing the basic business process functionalities such as CRM, SCM, and Advanced Planner and Optimizer (APO).
- **SAP industry-specific components** Examples are SAP Insurance, SAP Pharmaceuticals, SAP Consumer Goods, and SAP Media. These components provide additional functionality that is not available in the more generic application components mentioned above. These components are specific to particular industries.
- **SAP NetWeaver components** These components form the underlying technology foundation platform for SAP NetWeaver. The technology platform is composed of various usage types, standalone engines, and clients. Examples are Web Application Server ABAP, Web Application Server Java, Enterprise Portal, and Mobile Infrastructure. It also consists of standalone engines such as TREX, light cache, and SAP content server. Examples of clients are SAP GUI, SAP NetWeaver Developer Studio, and mobile infrastructure client.
- **Technology components** These are the supplementary software and middleware components that work along with the other mySAP Business Suite components to provide basic business functionality. Examples are SAP Solution Manager, SAP Content Server, and SAP Partner Connectivity Kit.

FIGURE 4-1 SAP product components

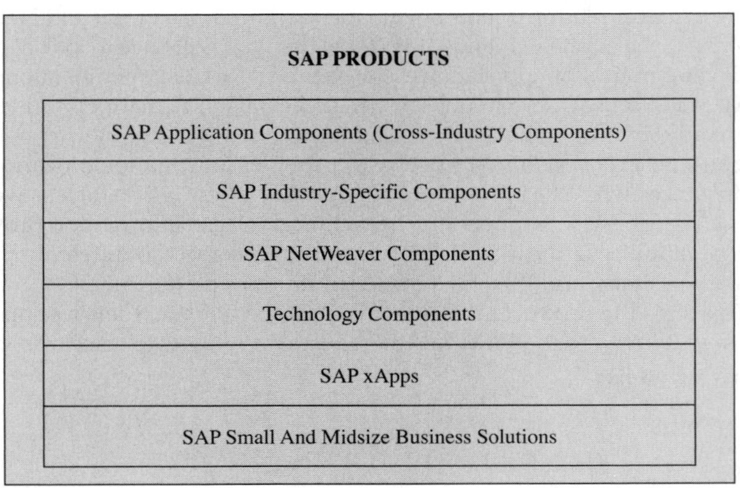

- **SAP xApps** xApps are applications that are based on service-oriented architecture and are built upon the NetWeaver technology components. They provide an additional layer of complexity for portal solutions based on SAP components. Examples are SAP xRPM, SAP xAPP Analytics, and SAP xMII.
- **SAP small and midsize business solutions** These are solutions that are addressed to the smaller and midsize business segments that range from ten to hundreds of users. Examples of these solutions are SAP Business One and SAP BI Integration for SAP NetWeaver.

Application Component Releases, Instances, and Software Component Versions

To interpret the PAM, you need to know some SAP product terminology such as the SAP components, instances, and software component versions. The *SAP component releases* (also known as product versions) are structured into *instances*. The *instances*, in turn, are simply bundles of *software component versions* that are dependent on each other and can be installed in one logical system as one set.

Figure 4-2 shows an example of an SAP component release, namely, SAP R/3 4.6C, which in turn consists of instances such as an R/3 server and front-end GUIs. The R/3 server in turn is a bundle of software component versions such as SAP APPL 4.6C, SAP HR 4.6C, and SAP Basis 4.6C.

Technical Release and Release Planning Information

The *technical release information* of these SAP component releases or product versions (SAP R/3 4.6C) is provided on a per-instance (R/3 Server, SAP GUI) basis. The *release planning information* consists of the availability of these component releases. These component releases are referred to as *product versions* in the release planning information, which contains information on the general availability of the products, maintenance end dates, and upgrade paths.

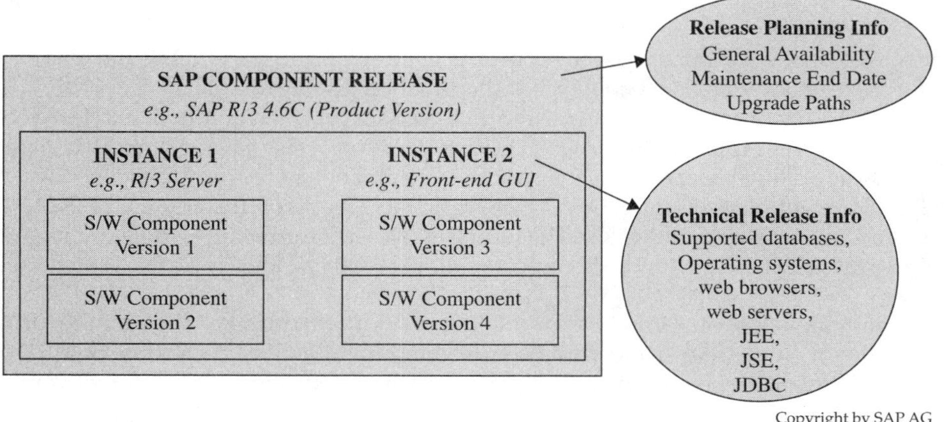

FIGURE 4-2 SAP component release, instance, and component version

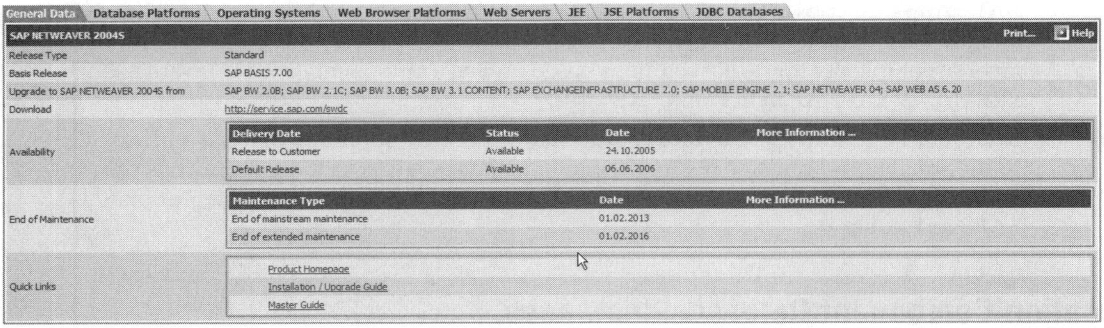

General Data | Database Platforms | Operating Systems | Web Browser Platforms | Web Servers | JEE | JSE Platforms | JDBC Databases

SAP NETWEAVER 2004S	Print... Help
Release Type	Standard
Basis Release	SAP BASIS 7.00
Upgrade to SAP NETWEAVER 2004S from	SAP BW 2.0B; SAP BW 2.1C; SAP BW 3.0B; SAP BW 3.1 CONTENT; SAP EXCHANGEINFRASTRUCTURE 2.0; SAP MOBILE ENGINE 2.1; SAP NETWEAVER 04; SAP WEB AS 6.20
Download	http://service.sap.com/swdc

Availability

Delivery Date	Status	Date	More Information ...
Release to Customer	Available	24.10.2005	
Default Release	Available	06.06.2006	

End of Maintenance

Maintenance Type	Date	More Information ...
End of mainstream maintenance	01.02.2013	
End of extended maintenance	01.02.2016	

Quick Links

- Product Homepage
- Installation / Upgrade Guide
- Master Guide

FIGURE 4-3 PAM for SAP NetWeaver 2004s

In Figure 4-3, SAP NetWeaver 2004s is the component release or product version for which you see the product availability matrix. The release type is standard and is based on the basis release of SAP Basis 7.00.

In the upgrade to SAP NetWeaver 2004s, you can see the *potential upgrade paths* to SAP NetWeaver 2004s. Based on this information, it is known that you can upgrade from SAP XI 2.0, SAP NetWeaver 04 and SAP Web AS 6.0 to SAP NetWeaver 2004s. In the Availability section, you can see that the product was released to the customer on *24.10.2005* and the default release date is 06.06.2006. From the End of maintenance section, you can note that the mainstream maintenance ends on 01.02.2013 and extended maintenance ends on 01.02.2016.

INFO *Mainstream maintenance and extended maintenance are discussed later in this chapter.*

Technical Release Information

On the top menu bar in Figure 4-3, you can see that the technical release information for this component release or product version has been provided for database platforms, operating systems, web browser platforms, web servers, JEE, JSE platforms, and JDBC databases. Now let's see what happens when we click the Database Platforms tab.

In Figure 4-4, you can see that under the SAP NetWeaver 2004s component release are a number of *instances*: Application Server ABAP, Application Server Java, Adobe Document Services, Business Intelligence, BI Java, Enterprise Portal, Content Server, Mobile Infrastructure (MI), Development Infrastructure, Developer Workplace, Process Integration, J2EE Adapter Engine, and Partner Connectivity Kit. The technical release information is therefore provided for each of these instances with details on compatibility with various operating systems and databases.

Now let's look at the information for the Enterprise Portal instance shown in Figure 4-5.

Scroll down on the screen and you'll see the entry for SQL Server; click the SQL Server link and you'll see the screen shown in Figure 4-6. This screen shows the different versions of SQL Server that are supported for Enterprise Portal in NetWeaver 2004s.

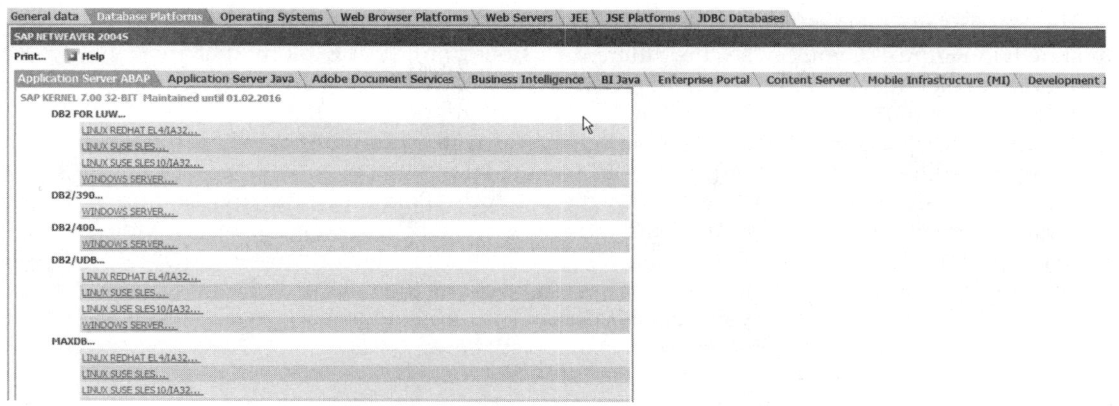

Figure 4-4 Technical release information for SAP NetWeaver 2004s Application Server ABAP

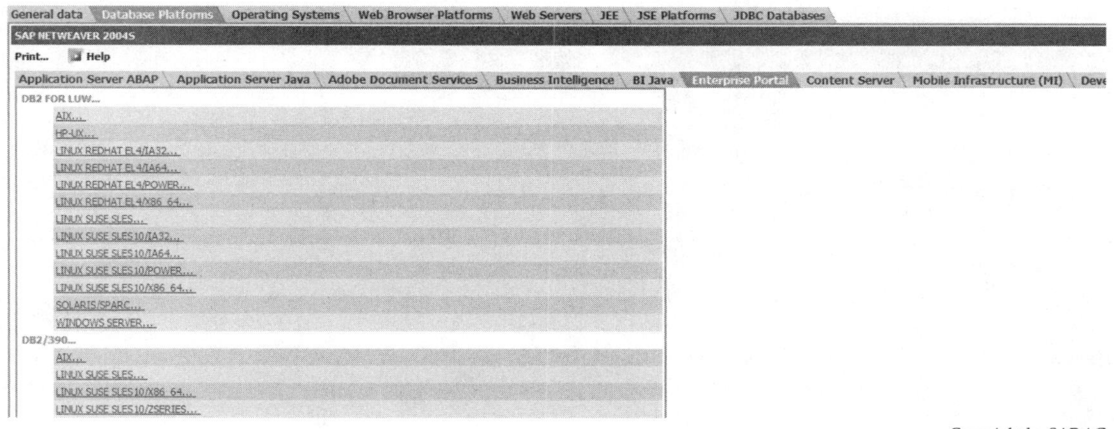

Figure 4-5 Technical release information for SAP NetWeaver 2004s Enterprise Portal

> Releases Enterprise Portal Database Platforms MS SQL SERVER...

Released Database Version	Operating System Version	Date	Status	System Status	Comments
MS SQL SERVER 2000	WINDOWS SERVER 2003/IA32 32BIT	24.10.2005	Released		
MS SQL SERVER 2000 IA64	WINDOWS SERVER 2003/IA64 64BIT	31.01.2006	Released		
MS SQL SERVER 2005	WINDOWS SERVER 2003/IA32 32BIT	28.04.2006	Released		
MS SQL SERVER 2005 IA64	WINDOWS SERVER 2003/IA64 64BIT	28.04.2006	Released		
MS SQL SERVER 2005/X86_64	WINDOWS SERVER 2003/X64 64BIT	28.04.2006	Released		

Close

Figure 4-6 Supported SQL Server versions for SAP NetWeaver 2004s Enterprise Portal

In the same way, when you look at the Web Browser Platform tab for Enterprise Portal, as shown in Figure 4-7, you can see the different versions of Internet Explorer that are supported in NetWeaver 2004s. When this book was being written, the Enterprise Portal in SAP NetWeaver 2004s supported only IE 6.0 and did not support IE 7.0.

Figure 4-8 displays the SAP J2EE engine versions as well as the dates on which they were supported for Enterprise Portal in NetWeaver 2004s.

Note that starting from NetWeaver 2004s, the Enterprise Portal has been divided into two main components: *Enterprise Portal* and the *EP Core.* The EP Core (Figure 4-9) provides the basic portal platform functionality that was previously provided under the *Enterprise Portal* category. The add-on products are now grouped under the Enterprise Portal.

Figure 4-10 shows the latest versions of JSE from various vendors such as HP, IBM, and Sun that are supported for the Enterprise Portal in NetWeaver 2004s.

General data | Database Platforms | Operating Systems | Web Browser Platforms | Web Servers | JEE | JSE Platforms | JDBC Databases

SAP NETWEAVER 2004S

Print... Help

BI Java | Enterprise Portal

PORTAL 7.00 Maintained until 01.02.2016

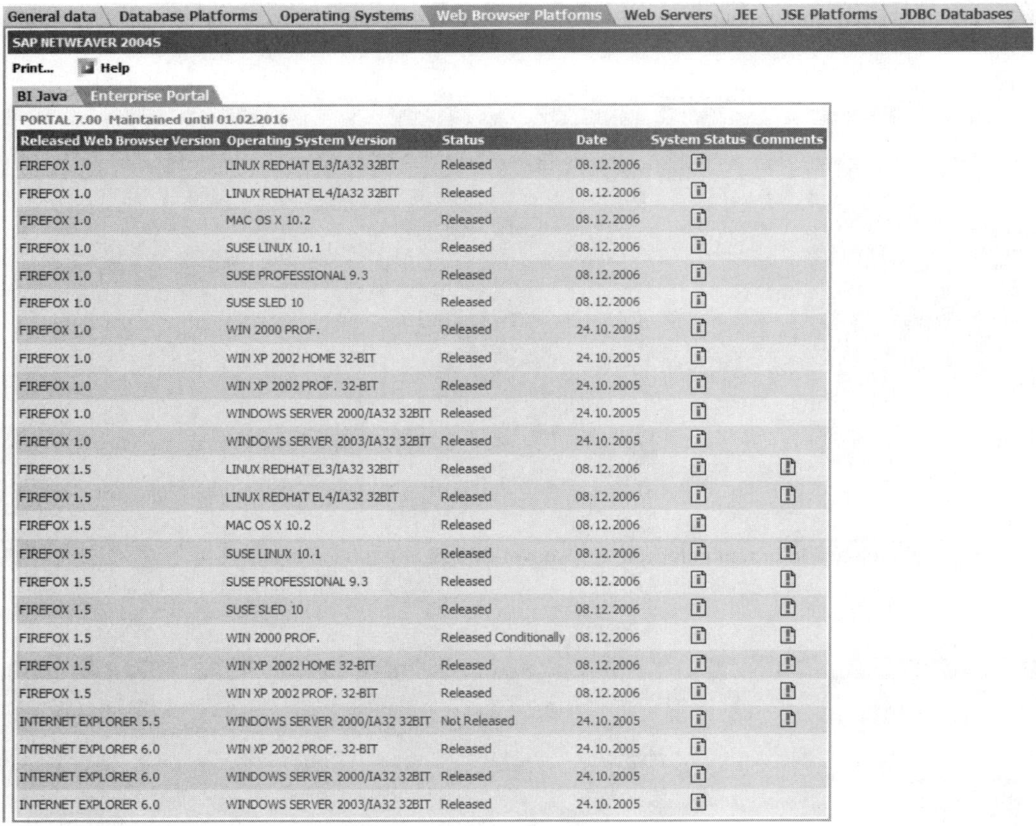

Released Web Browser Version	Operating System Version	Status	Date	System Status	Comments
FIREFOX 1.0	LINUX REDHAT EL3/IA32 32BIT	Released	08.12.2006		
FIREFOX 1.0	LINUX REDHAT EL4/IA32 32BIT	Released	08.12.2006		
FIREFOX 1.0	MAC OS X 10.2	Released	08.12.2006		
FIREFOX 1.0	SUSE LINUX 10.1	Released	08.12.2006		
FIREFOX 1.0	SUSE PROFESSIONAL 9.3	Released	08.12.2006		
FIREFOX 1.0	SUSE SLED 10	Released	08.12.2006		
FIREFOX 1.0	WIN 2000 PROF.	Released	24.10.2005		
FIREFOX 1.0	WIN XP 2002 HOME 32-BIT	Released	24.10.2005		
FIREFOX 1.0	WIN XP 2002 PROF. 32-BIT	Released	24.10.2005		
FIREFOX 1.0	WINDOWS SERVER 2000/IA32 32BIT	Released	24.10.2005		
FIREFOX 1.0	WINDOWS SERVER 2003/IA32 32BIT	Released	24.10.2005		
FIREFOX 1.5	LINUX REDHAT EL3/IA32 32BIT	Released	08.12.2006		
FIREFOX 1.5	LINUX REDHAT EL4/IA32 32BIT	Released	08.12.2006		
FIREFOX 1.5	MAC OS X 10.2	Released	08.12.2006		
FIREFOX 1.5	SUSE LINUX 10.1	Released	08.12.2006		
FIREFOX 1.5	SUSE PROFESSIONAL 9.3	Released	08.12.2006		
FIREFOX 1.5	SUSE SLED 10	Released	08.12.2006		
FIREFOX 1.5	WIN 2000 PROF.	Released Conditionally	08.12.2006		
FIREFOX 1.5	WIN XP 2002 HOME 32-BIT	Released	08.12.2006		
FIREFOX 1.5	WIN XP 2002 PROF. 32-BIT	Released	08.12.2006		
INTERNET EXPLORER 5.5	WINDOWS SERVER 2000/IA32 32BIT	Not Released	24.10.2005		
INTERNET EXPLORER 6.0	WIN XP 2002 PROF. 32-BIT	Released	24.10.2005		
INTERNET EXPLORER 6.0	WINDOWS SERVER 2000/IA32 32BIT	Released	24.10.2005		
INTERNET EXPLORER 6.0	WINDOWS SERVER 2003/IA32 32BIT	Released	24.10.2005		

FIGURE 4-7 Web browser support for SAP NetWeaver 2004s Enterprise Portal

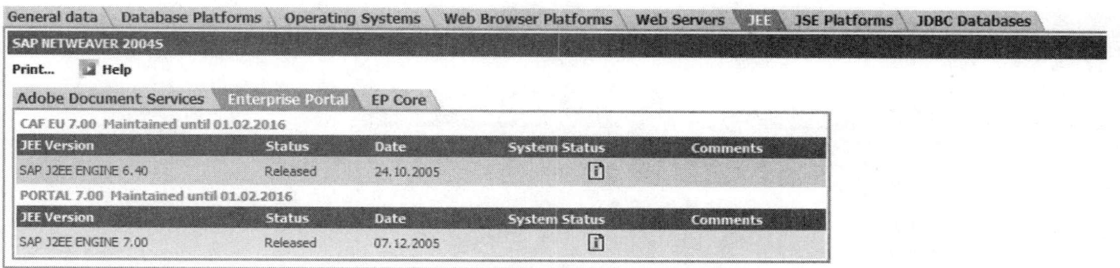

General data | Database Platforms | Operating Systems | Web Browser Platforms | Web Servers | JEE | JSE Platforms | JDBC Databases

SAP NETWEAVER 2004S

Print... Help

Adobe Document Services | Enterprise Portal | EP Core

CAF EU 7.00 Maintained until 01.02.2016

JEE Version	Status	Date	System Status	Comments
SAP J2EE ENGINE 6.40	Released	24.10.2005		

PORTAL 7.00 Maintained until 01.02.2016

JEE Version	Status	Date	System Status	Comments
SAP J2EE ENGINE 7.00	Released	07.12.2005		

Copyright by SAP AG

FIGURE 4-8 SAP J2EE engine version support for SAP NetWeaver 2004s Enterprise Portal

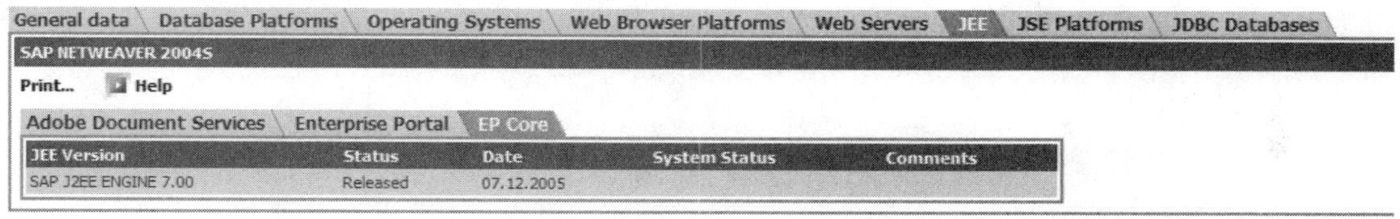

General data | Database Platforms | Operating Systems | Web Browser Platforms | Web Servers | JEE | JSE Platforms | JDBC Databases

SAP NETWEAVER 2004S

Print... Help

Adobe Document Services | Enterprise Portal | EP Core

JEE Version	Status	Date	System Status	Comments
SAP J2EE ENGINE 7.00	Released	07.12.2005		

Copyright by SAP AG

FIGURE 4-9 SAP J2EE engine version support for SAP NetWeaver 2004s EP Core

General data | Database Platforms | Operating Systems | Web Browser Platforms | Web Servers | JEE | JSE Platforms | JDBC Databases

SAP NETWEAVER 2004S

Print... Help

Application Server Java | Adobe Document Services | BI Java | Enterprise Portal | Development Infrastructure | Process Integration (PI/XI)

Released JSE Version	Operating System Version	Status	Date	System Status	Comments
HP JSE 1.4.2 64BIT	HP-UX 11.11/PA-RISC	Released	24.10.2005		
HP JSE 1.4.2 64BIT	HP-UX 11.23/IA64 64BIT	Released	24.10.2005		
HP JSE 1.4.2 64BIT	HP-UX 11.23/PA-RISC	Released	24.10.2005		
IBM JSE 1.4.2 64BIT	AIX 5.2	Released	24.10.2005		
IBM JSE 1.4.2 64BIT	AIX 5.3	Released	24.10.2005		
IBM JSE 1.4.2 64BIT	LINUX REDHAT EL4/POWER 64BIT	Released	24.10.2005		
IBM JSE 1.4.2 64BIT	LINUX REDHAT EL4/X86_64 64BIT	Released	24.10.2005		
IBM JSE 1.4.2 64BIT	LINUX SUSE SLES 9/POWER 64BIT	Released	24.10.2005		
IBM JSE 1.4.2 64BIT	LINUX SUSE SLES 9/X86_64 64BIT	Released	24.10.2005		
IBM JSE 1.4.2 64BIT	LINUX SUSE SLES10/POWER 64BIT	Released	28.12.2006		
IBM JSE 1.4.2 64BIT	LINUX SUSE SLES10/ZSERIES 64BI	Released	31.05.2006		
IBM JSE 1.4.2 64BIT	OS/400 V5R3	Released	15.12.2005		
IBM JSE 1.4.2 64BIT	OS/400 V5R4	Released	14.02.2006		
SUN JSE 1.4.2 32BIT	LINUX REDHAT EL4/IA32 32BIT	Released	24.10.2005		
SUN JSE 1.4.2 32BIT	LINUX SUSE SLES 9/IA32 32BIT	Released	24.10.2005		
SUN JSE 1.4.2 32BIT	WINDOWS SERVER 2003/IA32 32BIT	Released	24.10.2005		
SUN JSE 1.4.2 64BIT	LINUX REDHAT EL4/IA64 64BIT	Released	01.12.2005		
SUN JSE 1.4.2 64BIT	LINUX SUSE SLES 9/IA64 64BIT	Released	01.12.2005		
SUN JSE 1.4.2 64BIT	SOLARIS/SPARC 10	Released	24.10.2005		
SUN JSE 1.4.2 64BIT	SOLARIS/SPARC 9	Released	24.10.2005		
SUN JSE 1.4.2 64BIT	WINDOWS SERVER 2003/IA64 64BIT	Released	24.10.2005		
SUN JSE 1.4.2 64BIT	WINDOWS SERVER 2003/X64 64BIT	Released	26.05.2006		

Copyright by SAP AG

FIGURE 4-10 JSE support for SAP NetWeaver 2004s Enterprise Portal

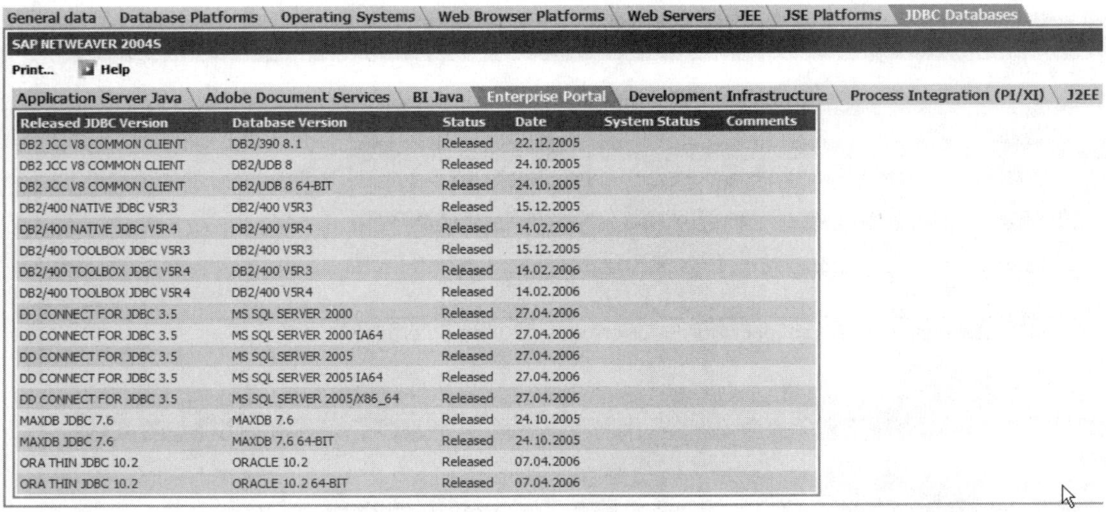

General data | Database Platforms | Operating Systems | Web Browser Platforms | Web Servers | JEE | JSE Platforms | JDBC Databases

SAP NETWEAVER 2004S

Print... Help

Application Server Java | Adobe Document Services | BI Java | Enterprise Portal | Development Infrastructure | Process Integration (PI/XI) | J2EE

Released JDBC Version	Database Version	Status	Date	System Status	Comments
DB2 JCC V8 COMMON CLIENT	DB2/390 8.1	Released	22.12.2005		
DB2 JCC V8 COMMON CLIENT	DB2/UDB 8	Released	24.10.2005		
DB2 JCC V8 COMMON CLIENT	DB2/UDB 8 64-BIT	Released	24.10.2005		
DB2/400 NATIVE JDBC V5R3	DB2/400 V5R3	Released	15.12.2005		
DB2/400 NATIVE JDBC V5R4	DB2/400 V5R4	Released	14.02.2006		
DB2/400 TOOLBOX JDBC V5R3	DB2/400 V5R3	Released	15.12.2005		
DB2/400 TOOLBOX JDBC V5R4	DB2/400 V5R3	Released	14.02.2006		
DB2/400 TOOLBOX JDBC V5R4	DB2/400 V5R4	Released	14.02.2006		
DD CONNECT FOR JDBC 3.5	MS SQL SERVER 2000	Released	27.04.2006		
DD CONNECT FOR JDBC 3.5	MS SQL SERVER 2000 IA64	Released	27.04.2006		
DD CONNECT FOR JDBC 3.5	MS SQL SERVER 2005	Released	27.04.2006		
DD CONNECT FOR JDBC 3.5	MS SQL SERVER 2005 IA64	Released	27.04.2006		
DD CONNECT FOR JDBC 3.5	MS SQL SERVER 2005/X86_64	Released	27.04.2006		
MAXDB JDBC 7.6	MAXDB 7.6	Released	24.10.2005		
MAXDB JDBC 7.6	MAXDB 7.6 64-BIT	Released	24.10.2005		
ORA THIN JDBC 10.2	ORACLE 10.2	Released	07.04.2006		
ORA THIN JDBC 10.2	ORACLE 10.2 64-BIT	Released	07.04.2006		

FIGURE 4-11 JDBC support for SAP NetWeaver 2004s Enterprise Portal

Figure 4-11 provides information on the support for JDBC databases from various vendors such as IBM, SAP, and Oracle for the Enterprise Portal in SAP NetWeaver 2004s.

NOTE *The information provided in these screens is very dynamic and is likely to change. You should go to the* SAP service marketplace *to get the latest information on the support provided by SAP for various combinations of available releases and various instances of SAP NetWeaver.*

It should be obvious by now that the information available on the product availability matrix is useful to help you arrive at the possible combinations of Enterprise Portal and the support for databases, web servers, web browsers, SAP J2EE engines, JSE platforms, and so on, for a particular product version (which in this case is SAP NetWeaver 2004s) that you plan to implement. A prior knowledge of this information will come in handy during initial implementation because it provides information on what is supported and what is not for a product version.

TIP *By using PAM, you can avoid any potential surprises and be able to manage users' expectations as to what can and cannot be implemented based on what is supported.*

Release Planning Information

Armed with knowledge about the platforms that are supported for the Enterprise Portal for a NetWeaver component release, your next logical question is about the releases that are likely to be available in the future as well as the nature of maintenance support that will be provided by SAP. This information is good to have because it will help you plan for future maintenance support and also avoid potential surprises. This information can have some cost implications for future maintenance as well.

The release information and maintenance information are also available in the PAM, but then it is important to know the various terminology associated with such information. SAP release strategy, in particular, helps you to know the availability of new releases in the future, as well as the nature and length of maintenance support for those releases.

TIP *Release strategy information is important because it helps you select the right combinations of SAP business applications and the corresponding SAP NetWeaver platform based on product availability and the future maintenance support information.*

Release and Maintenance Strategy

SAP's release strategy varies depending on whether the product was released before or after 2005. SAP NetWeaver, mySAP Business Suite of applications, as well as industry solutions follow a 5-1-2 maintenance strategy.

INFO *This is all true as of this writing, but this information can change and hence you are recommended to refer to the* service marketplace *for the latest information at http://service.sap.com/releasestrategy.*

The *5-1-2 maintenance strategy* stands for five years of *mainstream maintenance* at the standard maintenance fee followed by one year of *extended maintenance* at an additional percent fee, followed by two years of extended maintenance at an increased additional percent fee per year. After this period, the release enters a customer-specific maintenance program.

INFO *The 5-1-2 maintenance strategy is a new strategy introduced by SAP in 2004 and applies only to NW 2004 and later.*

In general, you can opt for either the complete set of mySAP Business Suite of applications, individual SAP applications, or the SAP NetWeaver platform. SAP, by default, provides access to the latest release when you order a product and also provides procedures to update to the latest release.

INFO *SAP often provides procedures to upgrade to the latest releases provided the existing releases in the organization are either in mainstream or extended maintenance mode.*

SAP often delivers a new release for SAP NetWeaver first, shortly followed by new releases for the SAP application components, which in turn are followed by new releases of business content for those applications. Usually, when a new release is delivered for a given SAP application, such as CRM it is compatible with a defined set of applications. When a new release is delivered for that SAP application, it continues to be compatible with the same predefined set of applications as before. However, if you need to implement any new functionality, it may become mandatory to upgrade one or more of the previous sets of applications.

The combination of the various releases of the applications is usually available in the Master Guide in the service marketplace. The other place to look for is the *Scenario and Process Component List* application, which is discussed in Chapter 5.

Release Shipment Phases

Now let's take a look at the various *shipment phases* for a new release, as shown in the following illustration. This information is important to know as it can have an impact on the availability of products as well as the nature of support that can be expected from SAP.

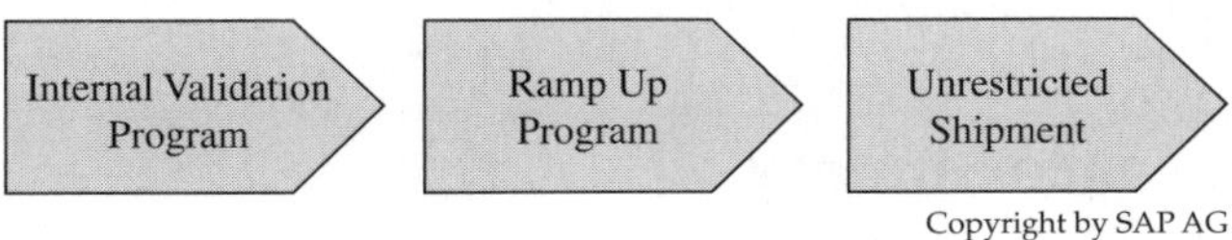

Copyright by SAP AG

Internal Validation Program

Before a release is ready for use in production, SAP subjects the release to an *internal validation program* as shown in the illustration above. During this phase, the release is tested for any errors and for integration into the existing system landscape.

Ramp Up Program

Once the release is ready for use in production, the release enters the *restricted shipment* and the *ramp up phases*. The restricted shipment phase begins with the *release to customer date* and is guided by a *ramp up program*, which signifies a controlled increase in the number of customers. During this phase, SAP provides coaching support and development support and provides corrections in the form of support packages, support package stacks, SAP notes, and any legal changes, if necessary.

NOTE *Legal changes are all changes needed to comply with the legal and regulatory requirements of the government.*

Unrestricted Shipment

Once the ramp up program is over, the *unrestricted shipment* begins. The unrestricted shipment coincides with the *default release date*, which is usually several months after the *release to customer* date. During the unrestricted shipment phase, the release is available to all customers and the most recent release of the application is considered the *current default release*. Shortly afterward, a *support release* consisting of all the previous support packages may be released.

Maintenance Strategy

The mainstream maintenance begins as soon as the restricted shipment begins and continues into the unrestricted shipment phase. SAP support in the form of support packages, notes, and legal changes may continue until the extended maintenance phase.

Release Planning and Maintenance Strategy for General-Purpose Applications

mySAP Business Suite

Please click here for more information on mySAP™ Business Suite.
Please click here for more information on enterprise services.

Application Release	Based On	Availability (Release to Customer, RTC)	End of Mainstream Maintenance	End of Extended Maintenance
mySAP™ ERP 2005 mySAP Customer Relationship Management 2005 mySAP Product Lifecycle Management 2005 mySAP Supplier Relationship Management 2005	SAP NetWeaver® 2004s	October 2005	March 2011	March 2014
mySAP Supply Chain Management 2005	SAP NetWeaver® 2004s	December 2005	March 2011	March 2014
SAP Supplier Relationship Management 6.0	SAP NetWeaver® 2004s	December 2006	March 2012	March 2015

FIGURE 4-12 Release planning for mySAP Business Suite

***INFO** The nature of support during the extended maintenance phase is the same as that in the mainstream maintenance phase.*

After the extended maintenance phase, the customer specific maintenance phase starts. Once the customer maintenance phase starts, there may be no more support in the form of support packages or legal changes. SAP offers support to upgrades for releases that are in the mainstream maintenance mode, but it does not offer support to upgrades that are in the extended maintenance mode.

Based on the release planning and maintenance strategy for both the SAP applications as well as SAP NetWeaver shown in Figures 4-12 and 4-13, you can see that the *release to customer* date, the *end of mainstream* maintenance dates, and the *end of extended maintenance* dates coincide with each other for both SAP applications and SAP NetWeaver platform, which is a good thing. If this were different, you would have to make a choice of a given version based on the relative dates for the SAP NetWeaver components and the NetWeaver applications.

Figure 4-14 shows the availability date, end of mainstream date, and extended maintenance dates for SAP Solution Manager 4.0.

Figure 4-15 displays the release and maintenance strategies for the SAP Enterprise Portal for various SAP NetWeaver product versions.

Release Planning and Maintenance Strategy for SAP NetWeaver

SAP NetWeaver

Please click here for more information on SAP NetWeaver.
Please click here for more information on SAP NetWeaver Master Data Management.

Platform Release	Availability (Release to Customer, RTC)	End of Mainstream Maintenance	End of Extended Maintenance
SAP NetWeaver® 2004 SAP NetWeaver 2004s	March 2004 October 2005	March 2010 March 2011	March 2013 March 2014
SAP NetWeaver Master Data Management 5.5	March 2005	March 2010	March 2013

FIGURE 4-13 Release planning for SAP NetWeaver

SAP Solution Manager

Please click here for more information on SAP Solution Manager.

Release	Based On	Availability (Release to Customer, RTC)	End of Mainstream Maintenance	End of Extended Maintenance
SAP® Solution Manager 4.0	SAP NetWeaver 2004s	December 2005	March 2011	n/a

FIGURE 4-14 Release planning for SAP Solution Manager

Support Packages, Support Package Stacks, and Support Release

You should also be aware of the differences between support packages, support package stacks, and support releases. A *support package* is a bundle of corrections that are available in the form of an ABAP or a Java support package.

INFO *Support packages are released to resolve a particular bug or correction to SAP source code.*

A *support package stack*, on the other hand, is a combination of support packages and patches for a given release at a given point in time. A *support release* is often released shortly after the unrestricted shipment phase begins and consists of all the previously released support packages. *Support packages* can be downloaded from http://service.sap.com/patches or can be ordered from SAP Software Shop at http://service.sap.com/softwarecat.

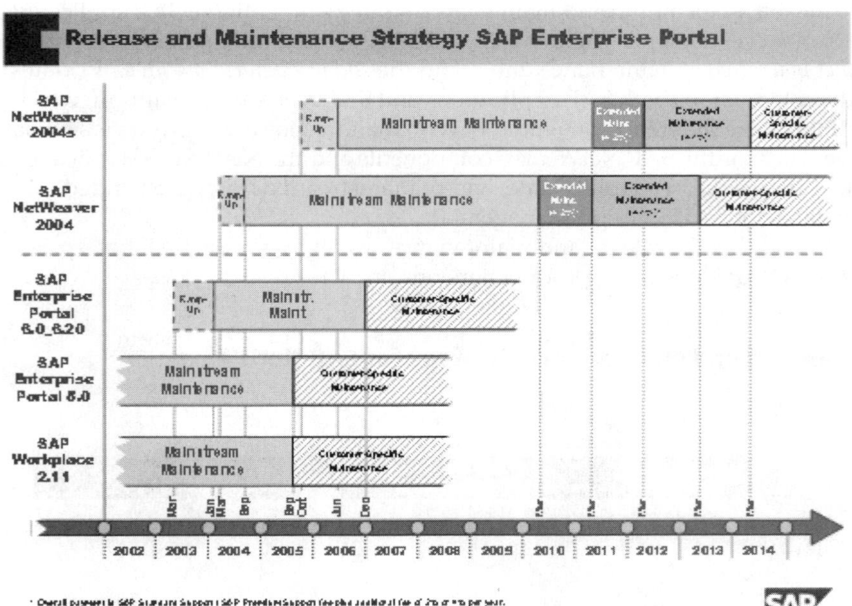

FIGURE 4-15 Release and maintenance strategy for SAP Enterprise Portal

Support Package Strategy

As part of implementation planning, you should define a strategy for implementing support packages (formally known as *hot packs*) and support package stacks both during and after the portal implementation project. Implementing the support packages on a timely basis helps you keep the system current per the latest release as well as guarantees optimal performance and stability by avoiding system bugs.

Do *Handle the implementation of support packages well right from the beginning to avoid running into some costly surprises that can delay the successful and timely completion of a portal project.*

Part of defining the strategy is to decide the frequency with which the support packages are deployed. Usually the support packages can be applied every month before you go live until the integration testing stage is reached.

Don't *Starting from the first integration testing cycle to the Go-Live, it is recommended that you not apply any support packages as they could lead to unforeseen risks to the implementation.*

After Go-Live, you can implement support packages on a quarterly basis. Instead of implementing a large number of Online Support Services (OSS) notes, you may find it better to implement a support package upgrade. While implementing a support package upgrade can involve a lot of business process testing, implementing a large number of OSS notes could be very resource intensive for Basis and may result in more errors.

Do *Because the development and quality assurance systems will be working on a different support package as compared to the production system at some point, it is important that the entire deployment process does not take more than one week.*

The testing strategy should be well defined and should include testing of business processes and interfaces in the quality system using test scripts. Part of the testing plan is to include testing by a business owner.

SAP Support Strategy

Now let's take a closer look at the support strategy of SAP and how it interplays with the maintenance strategy. During the mainstream maintenance mode, the customer can choose between the *Standard support or SAP Premium support*. SAP provides three levels of support, namely, *Standard, Premium,* and *MaxAttention.*

SAP Standard support provides support in the areas of continuous improvement, quality management, knowledge transfer, and problem resolution. Continuous improvement deals with providing new releases, upgrading tools, ensuring compatibility with databases and operating systems, providing support packages, and providing patches for legal changes. Quality management deals with providing support through Solution Manager for monitoring, testing, and providing implementation tools and remote services such as SAP GoingLive Check and SAP EarlyWatch Alert. SAP also provides a 24 × 7 global service for resolving problems that cannot be resolved by the customer.

INFO *More details on Premium and MaxAttention support can be obtained at http://service.sap.com/maxattention.*

SAP support services should be made an integral part of the deployment plan during portal project implementation. The deployment plan should include periodic reviews by SAP during the entire project life cycle. Some of the SAP organizations that can provide invaluable help are the SAP Consulting Organization, the SAP Active Global Support Organization, and the SAP Education Organization.

SAP also provides a *review program*, the details of which can be obtained at http://service.sap.com/reviewprogram. The various types of review program are project reviews (project management), solution reviews (application design), technical reviews (operations), and modification (development) reviews.

Another service provided by SAP is the *safeguarding service* for implementation and upgrade projects. More information can be obtained at http://service.sap.com/safeguarding. If SAP GoingLive Check is not sufficient for your project because of the complexity, you could opt for the SAP Safeguarding for Implementation or Upgrade. During Safeguarding for Implementation, a technical quality manager checks the technical and functional feasibility of the solution, supports integration tests to ensure performance and stability, supports volume tests, supports cutover activities, supports software change control, and supports handover to operations. In a similar way, during the SAP Safeguarding for Upgrade, the technical quality manager identifies upgrade paths, assesses upgrade impacts, checks technical and functional feasibility, and performs other tasks as appropriate.

INFO *For more information on SAP support services, please visit http://www.sap.com/services/index.epx.*

List of URLs Referenced in This Chapter

http://service.sap.com/pam
http://service.sap.com/releasestrategy
http://service.sap.com/patches
http://service.sap.com/softwarecat
http://service.sap.com/maxattention
http://service.sap.com/reviewprogram
http://service.sap.com/safeguarding
http://www.sap.com/services/index.epx

Summary

In this chapter, you learned about the various SAP software components available, and learned how to use PAM to identify OS and DB compatibility for a given version of SAP NetWeaver and Enterprise Portal in particular. We then discussed release planning information, maintenance strategy, and their influence on the choice of product and software component versions. We discussed the importance of a good support package strategy and the various support options available from SAP that can be accessed throughout the course of the portal project.

5

CHAPTER

Using Scenario and Process Component List Application

In this chapter, you will learn about the *Scenario and Process Component List* application tool available from SAP and how it can be used for identifying the software units that you need to install to realize a particular IT scenario. The Scenario and Process Component List application is a useful application for mapping the business scenarios and processes into the appropriate application components and software components, and vice versa. Identifying the software units that need to be installed for a given business scenario is an important step during the installation planning process, and this tool may come in handy along with other tools discussed throughout this book. This tool can be a good starting point to identify various possible scenarios and software units that may be relevant for your portal implementation. However, please note that your final decision should be driven by the information provided in the master guides, SP stack guides and SAP notes as they are more current and reliable.

To access this application, go to http://service.SAP.com/scl. This application helps you identify the different possible scenarios or processes in which a particular selected component or components can be used. It also helps you identify the components required to implement a particular scenario or business process.

This tool also helps you determine whether all the existing business scenarios will continue to be supported after an upgrade. You can find out what additional business scenarios can be supported after the upgrade or by adding new components. You can also identify up to two additional components that are missing or that can be potentially added based on an analysis of the existing components. This information can be used to identify any additional opportunities that may exist to implement new business scenarios.

You can check what other components are included in a particular component as well as the components that are based upon this component. You can also download the components, the support packages, and the support package stacks directly from this application, provided you have the adequate licenses.

Under the Additional Information tab on the Show Realization Alternative page, you can check for the required support packages, support package stacks, and SAP notes.

Application Building Blocks

Before you take a look at the tool itself, you need to understand the terminology associated with the Scenario and Process Component List application

Application/Product, Application Component, Software Component, and Cluster

Copyright by SAP AG

Examples of *applications* or *products* are SAP R/3, SAP Customer Relationship Management (CRM), and SAP Business Information Warehouse (BW). These are essentially software units that are required to implement a collection of business processes that are geared toward meeting the customer's business needs.

INFO *Every application has a* version *associated with it—for example, SAP R/3 4.6C, SAP CRM 5.0, and so on.*

The next building block of an application is the *application component*, which contains the software component version. For example, the application version SAP CRM 5.0 contains another application component such as the CRM mobile client. The CRM mobile client application component, in turn, contains the software component version, such as SAP Internet Pricing and Configurator (IPC) Java 7.00.

The *software component version* is the smallest possible unit that can be delivered, maintained, or deployed. When speaking of components, it is important to differentiate between application and software components. An application consists of application components, which in turn consists of software components. When more than one application component or software component version needs to be installed together as a bundle on one physical server, they are referred to as *clusters*.

Application Capabilities, Processes, and Scenarios

Now let's discuss what is meant by a *key capability*, a *business scenario*, and the *business process*.

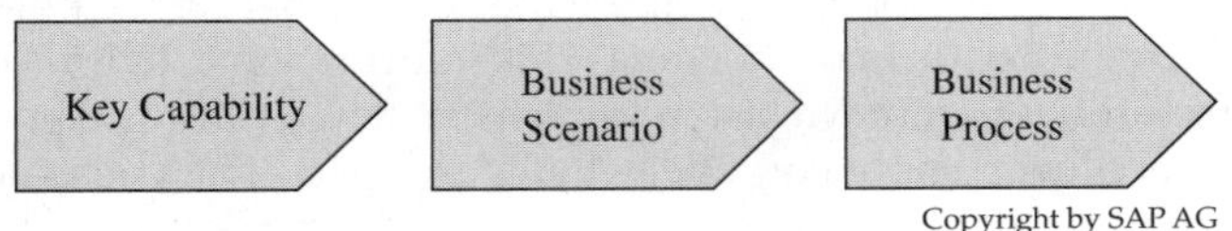

Copyright by SAP AG

A group of related tasks or activities that can be conducted to achieve a certain business outcome is known as a *business process*. A collection of business processes that make up an end-to-end task in a much more comprehensive and a self-contained manner is known as a *business scenario*. While an example of a business process could be creating customer complaints, an example of a business scenario would be customer troubleshooting management, which is much more comprehensive in dealing with customer issues. Examples of business scenarios are *Administering SAP NetWeaver and Implementing an External-Facing Portal.*

When groups of related scenarios are joined together, they form what is known as a *key capability.* One example of a key capability is SAP NetWeaver Operations.

INFO *In the portal scenario, the key capability would be* Running an Enterprise Portal *and the business scenario would be* Implementing an External-Facing Portal.

Realization Alternatives and Scenario Templates

Now let's clarify the terms *realization alternatives, scenario templates, scenarios,* and *solution.*

A *realization alternative* is a collection of application components and software component versions that are required to implement a particular business scenario or process. To realize a particular business scenario such as Implementing an External-Facing Portal More than one valid possible combination of application components and software components may be available. Any given valid software configuration that is required to implement a particular business scenario is known as the *scenario template.*

A *scenario* in turn can contain one or more valid software configurations—in other words, scenario templates. The scenario template is basically a valid combination of application versions, application component versions, software component versions, support packages, support package stacks, relevant Online Support Services (OSS) notes, patch level regulations, and any restrictions.

Finally, the term *solution* can refer either to an industry solution such as SAP Media or a cross-industry solution such as SAP NetWeaver.

Using the Tool

Let's take a look at the application itself. Click Start Application to see the Home page shown in Figure 5-1.

To view a list of components required for a given business scenario, click the SAP Scenarios and Realization Alternatives tab.

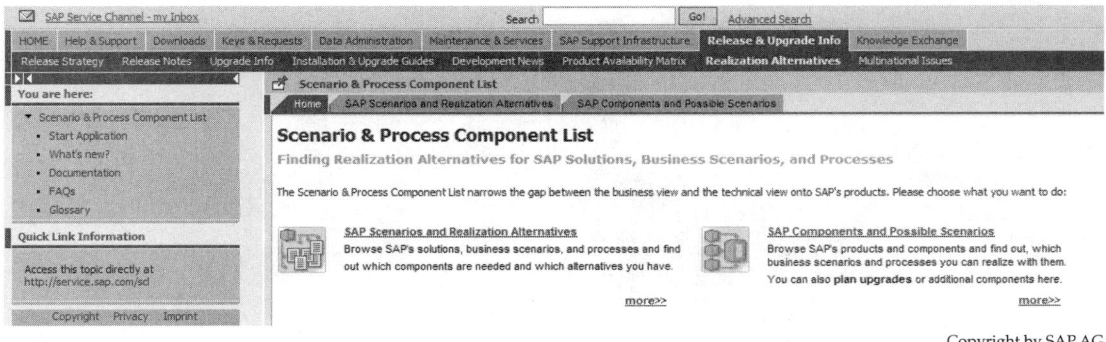

FIGURE 5-1 Home page of the Scenario and Process Component List application

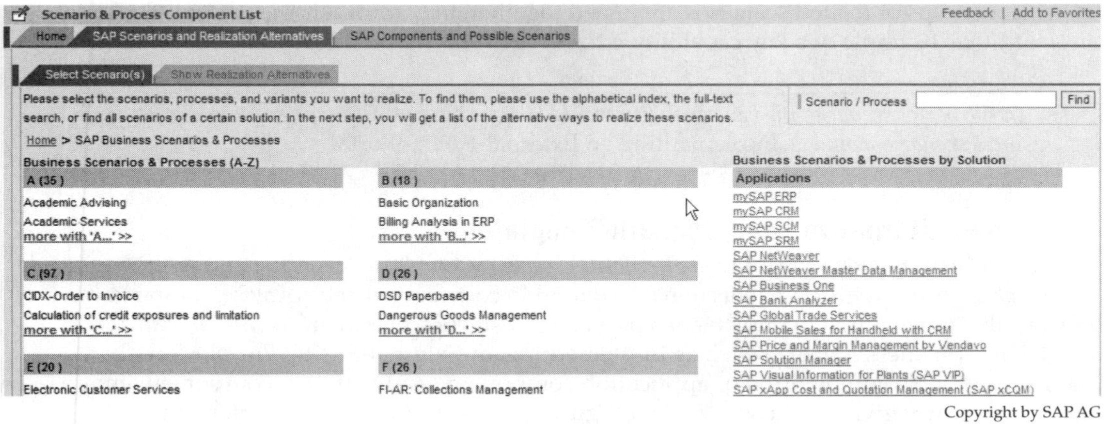

FIGURE 5-2 Selection screen for selecting Business Scenarios

Choosing a Scenario

In the Select Scenarios screen shown in Figure 5-2, you can select the appropriate scenario by clicking the scenario from the alphabetized list, by searching using keywords in the Scenario process field, or by drilling down from the solution. To drill down, click SAP NetWeaver under Business Scenarios and Processes by Solution as the right. The screen shown in Figure 5-3 will appear after you select the SAP NetWeaver solution.

Displaying the Realization Alternatives

Now select the scenario Administering SAP NetWeaver on the left side of Figure 5-3. You can see that Administering SAP NetWeaver is a scenario that belongs to the solution SAP NetWeaver and is a part of the key capability SAP NetWeaver Operations. Click Add and then click Show Realization Alternatives to see the screen shown in Figure 5-4.

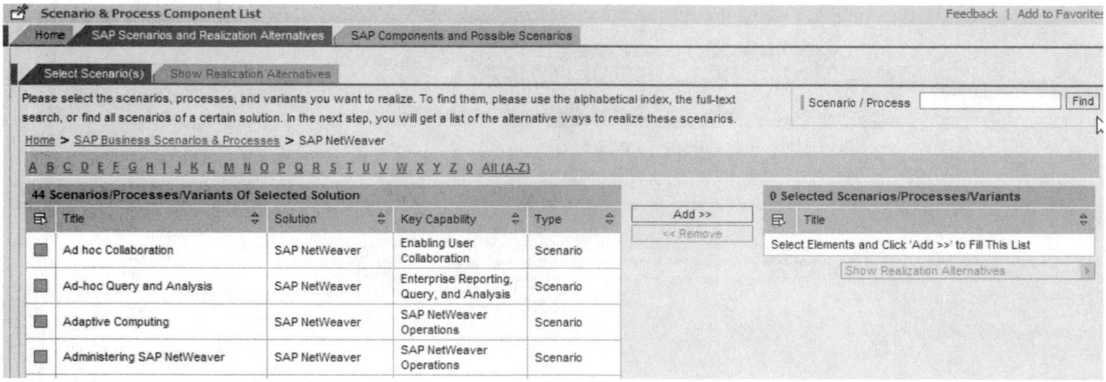

FIGURE 5-3 Scenarios available for SAP NetWeaver solution

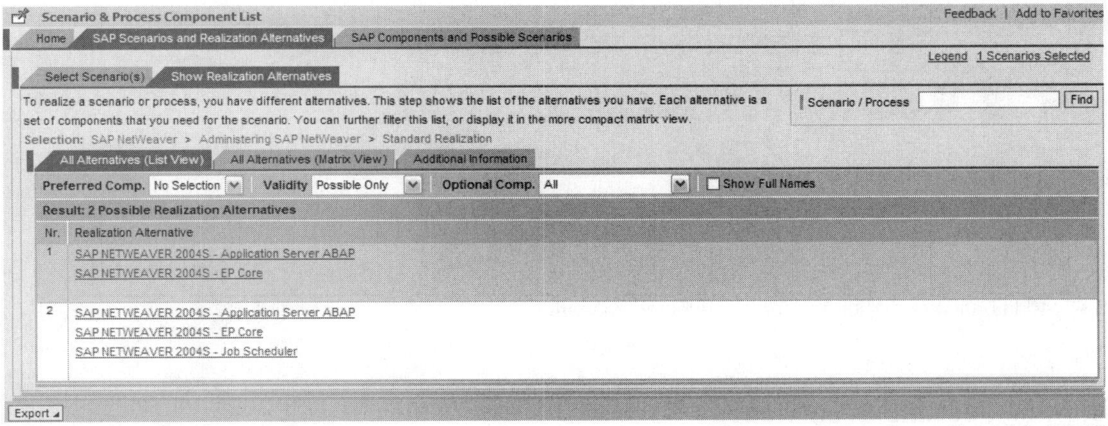

Copyright by SAP AG

FIGURE 5-4 Realization alternatives for administering SAP NetWeaver scenario, including optional components

In Figure 5-4, you can see that to realize the Administering SAP NetWeaver scenario, you need at least two application components: Application Server ABAP and EP Core. Under the Optional Component drop-down, select Without Optional Components. The screen shown in Figure 5-5 appears.

Viewing Additional Information

Click the Additional Information tab to see more information on documentation. Figure 5-6 shows the link for documentation related to installing SAP NetWeaver.

This demonstrates how you can identify the components required for a given IT scenario. Starting from a given business scenario, you can display the various realization alternatives, from which you can select the most desired alternative consisting of the various installable software units.

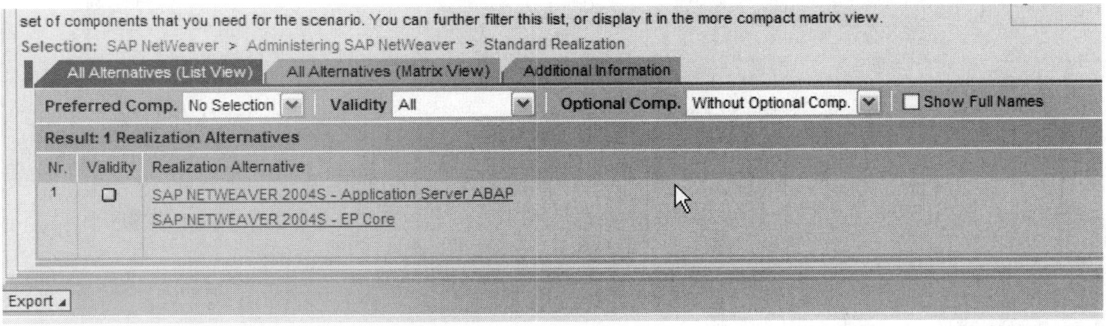

Copyright by SAP AG

FIGURE 5-5 Realization alternative for Administering SAP NetWeaver scenario without optional components

Legend 1 Scenarios Selected
Select Scenario(s) Show Realization Alternatives
To realize a scenario or process, you have different alternatives. This step shows the list of the alternatives you have. Each alternative is a set of components that you need for the scenario. You can further filter this list, or display it in the more compact matrix view.
Scenario / Process Find
Selection: SAP NetWeaver > Administering SAP NetWeaver > Standard Realization
All Alternatives (List View) All Alternatives (Matrix View) Additional Information
Currently Reduced to Your Preferred Components. Reset Selection.
Other Related Links
Also check the following related sites:

- /instguidesnw2004s

FIGURE 5-6 Additional Information tab for the selected scenario

Viewing Possible Scenarios

Now let's proceed by selecting one or more components and then identifying the different possible scenarios that can be realized. Click the SAP Components and Possible Scenarios tab to view the Select Components screen, as shown in Figure 5-7.

Select NetWeaver 2004S in the SAP Products Versions section. Then click the Details link for SAP NetWeaver 2004S–Enterprise Portal, shown in Figure 5-8. Figure 5-9 displays the details for the SAP NetWeaver 2004S–Enterprise Portal application component.

The details consist of information such as the release to customer date, the default release date, the extended and mainstream maintenance dates, the potential upgrade paths, the database and operating system platforms that are supported, and the software component versions that are included in the application component, namely, SAP NetWeaver 2004S Enterprise Portal.

You can also download the component, support packages, and support package stacks provided you have the necessary licenses by clicking the relevant link under the Downloads section (shown in Figure 5-9).

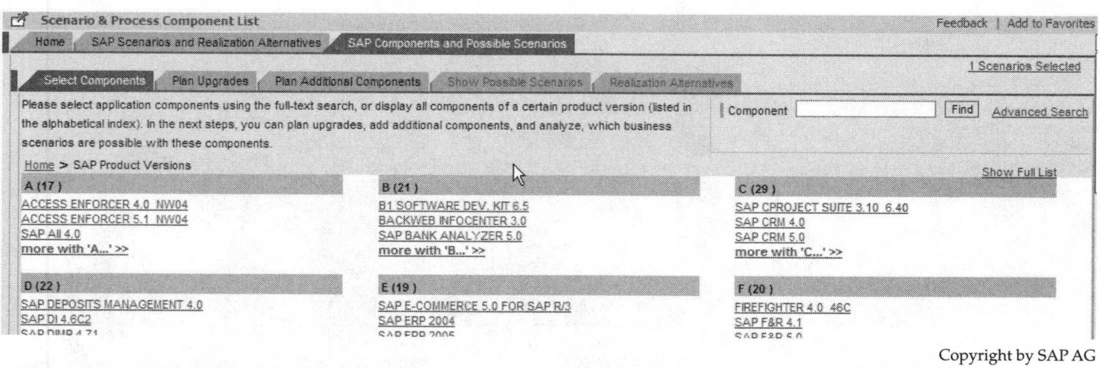

FIGURE 5-7 Select Components screen

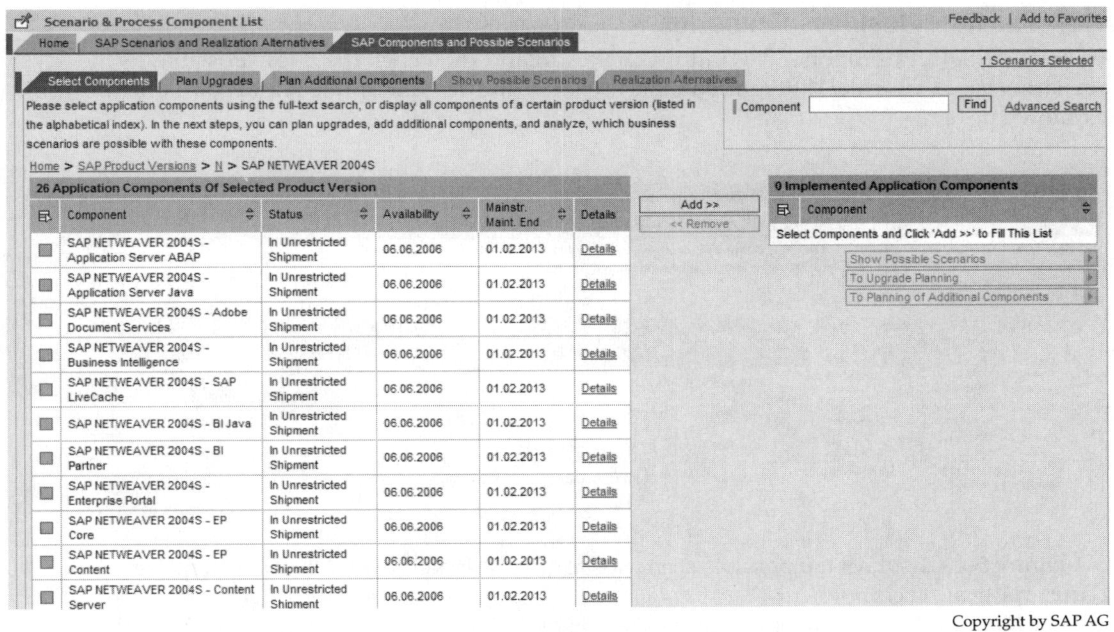

FIGURE 5-8 Application components for selected product version

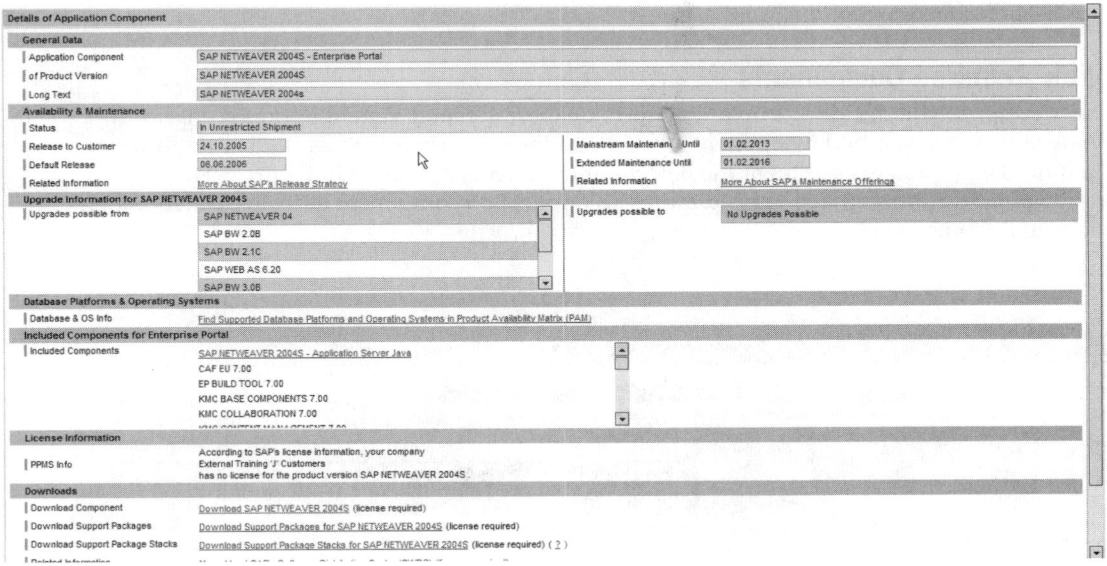

Details of Application Component

General Data

Application Component	SAP NETWEAVER 2004S - Enterprise Portal
of Product Version	SAP NETWEAVER 2004S
Long Text	SAP NETWEAVER 2004s

Availability & Maintenance

Status	In Unrestricted Shipment		
Release to Customer	24.10.2005	Mainstream Maintenance Until	01.02.2013
Default Release	06.06.2006	Extended Maintenance Until	01.02.2016
Related Information	More About SAP's Release Strategy	Related Information	More About SAP's Maintenance Offerings

Upgrade Information for SAP NETWEAVER 2004S

Upgrades possible from	SAP NETWEAVER 04 SAP BW 2.0B SAP BW 2.1C SAP WEB AS 6.20 SAP BW 3.0B	Upgrades possible to	No Upgrades Possible

Database Platforms & Operating Systems

Database & OS Info	Find Supported Database Platforms and Operating Systems in Product Availability Matrix (PAM)

Included Components for Enterprise Portal

Included Components	SAP NETWEAVER 2004S - Application Server Java CAF EU 7.00 EP BUILD TOOL 7.00 KMC BASE COMPONENTS 7.00 KMC COLLABORATION 7.00

License Information

PPMS Info	According to SAP's license information, your company External Training 'J' Customers has no license for the product version SAP NETWEAVER 2004S.

Downloads

Download Component	Download SAP NETWEAVER 2004S (license required)
Download Support Packages	Download Support Packages for SAP NETWEAVER 2004S (license required)
Download Support Package Stacks	Download Support Package Stacks for SAP NETWEAVER 2004S (license required) (?)

FIGURE 5-9 Details for SAP NetWeaver 2004S–Enterprise Portal application component

View Possible Business Scenarios

Back in the Select Components window, click Add and then click the Show Possible Scenarios tab to view the different possible scenarios for this Enterprise Portal component, as shown next.

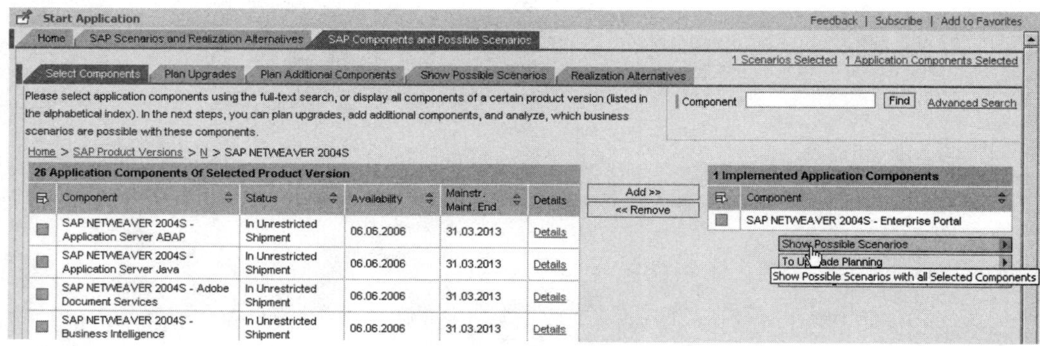

Figure 5-10 displays the possible scenarios for the SAP NetWeaver 2004S Enterprise Portal application component.

Clicking the Additional Opportunities tab displays the screen shown in Figure 5-11. This shows the additional scenarios that can be implemented by adding a maximum of 2 additional application components. The screen shows that you can implement 11 possible scenarios for the SAP NetWeaver 2004S Enterprise Portal component by including 2 more additional application components.

View Required Components

Now suppose you decide to implement the Collaboration and Virtual Rooms scenario. To view additional required components, you select the scenario on the left and click Show Required Components button at the bottom of the screen, as shown in Figure 5-11.

Figure 5-12 shows that you need the TREX application component to realize collaboration in virtual rooms.

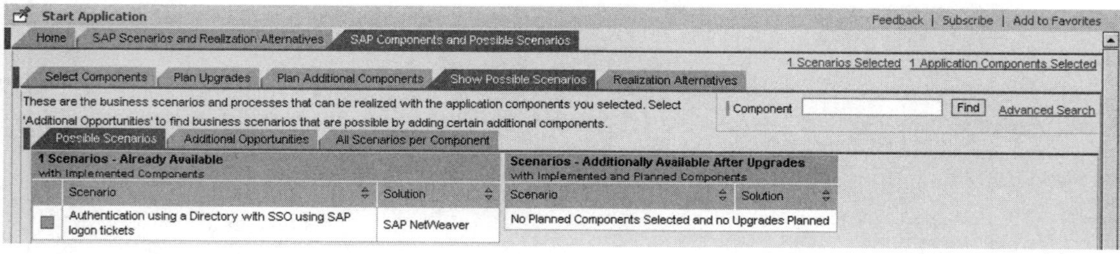

FIGURE 5-10 Possible scenarios for SAP NW 2004S Enterprise Portal application component

Select Components | Plan Upgrades | Plan Additional Components | Show Possible Scenarios | Realization Alternatives

1 Scenarios Selected 1 Application Compo

These are the business scenarios and processes that can be realized with the application components you selected. Select 'Additional Opportunities' to find business scenarios that are possible by adding certain additional components.

Component [Find] Ad

Possible Scenarios | Additional Opportunities | All Scenarios per Component

11 Scenarios - with max. 2 Additional Components and with Implemented and Planned Components after Upgrades

Scenario	Solution
Ad hoc Collaboration	SAP NetWeaver
Asset Maintenance and Oil Field Services	SAP for Oil & Gas
Client and Project Acquisition	SAP for Professional Services
Collaboration in Virtual Rooms	SAP NetWeaver
Content Creation, Publication, and Access	SAP NetWeaver
Content Integration and Management	SAP NetWeaver
Contract Management for Pharmaceuticals	SAP for Life Sciences
Creating Applications using SAP NetWeaver Visual Composer	SAP NetWeaver
Creating Portal Applications using PDK for .NET	SAP NetWeaver
Process Automation	SAP NetWeaver
Project Resource Management	SAP for Professional Services

Show Required Components

FIGURE 5-11 Additional scenarios possible for SAP NW 2004s Enterprise Portal application component

View Potential Upgrade Paths

You can then click the Plan Upgrades tab to see what potential upgrade paths are available from the current selection component, namely, Enterprise Portal 2004S.

Since the SAP NetWeaver 2004S portal was the latest application component version release at the time of writing, no upgrade paths are available, as shown in Figure 5-13.

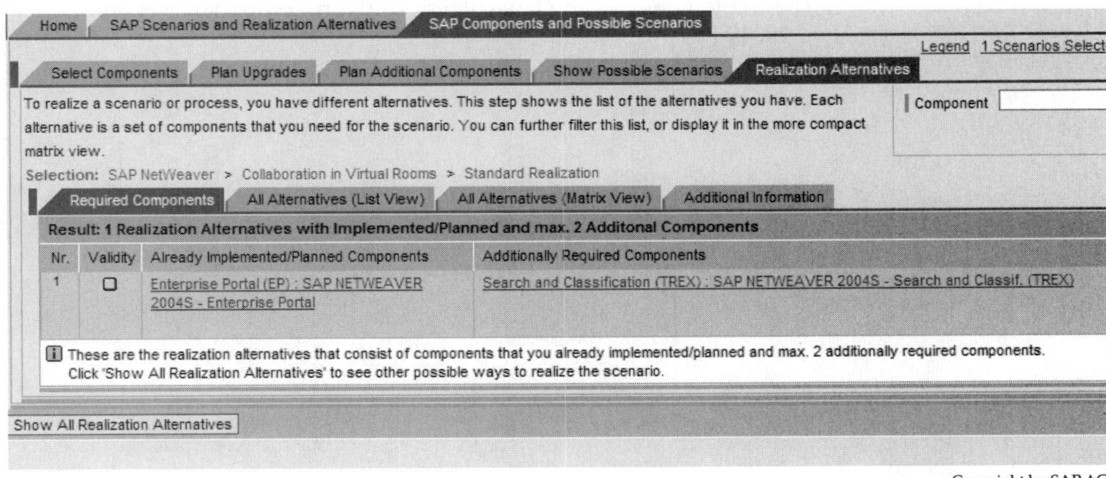

FIGURE 5-12 Additional components necessary to realize collaboration in virtual rooms

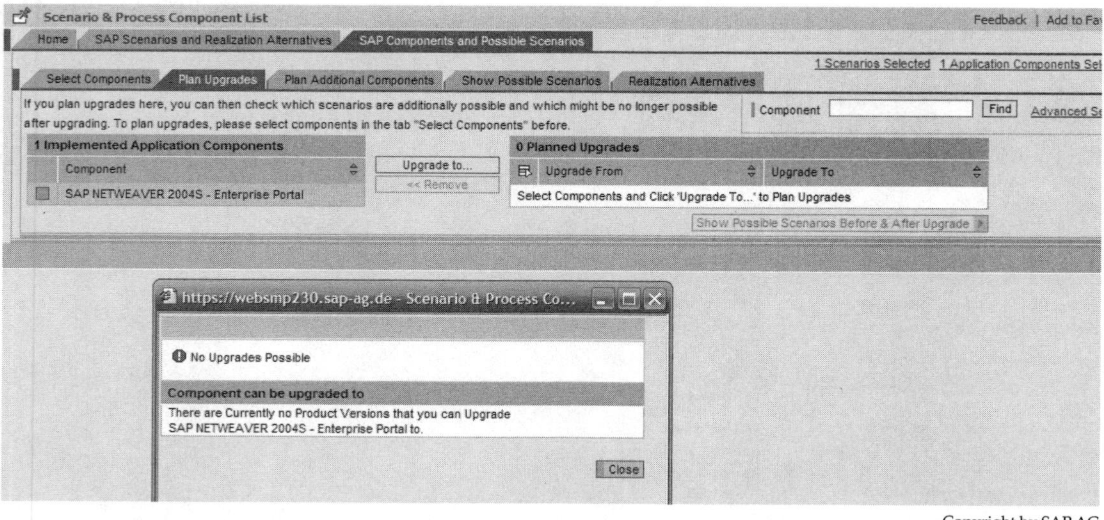

Figure 5-13 Potential upgrade paths for selected component

Summary

Thus the Scenario and Process Component List application is a useful application for mapping the business scenarios and processes into the appropriate application components and software components, and vice versa. For example, you can identify the required and optional components (also known as Realization Alternatives) that are required for implementing a given business scenario, such as Implementing an External Facing Portal, under the key capability Running an Enterprise Portal. At the same time, you can identify the various business scenarios that can be implemented using a particular software component version such as the SAP NetWeaver 2004S Portal.

PART II

Portal Infrastructure Design

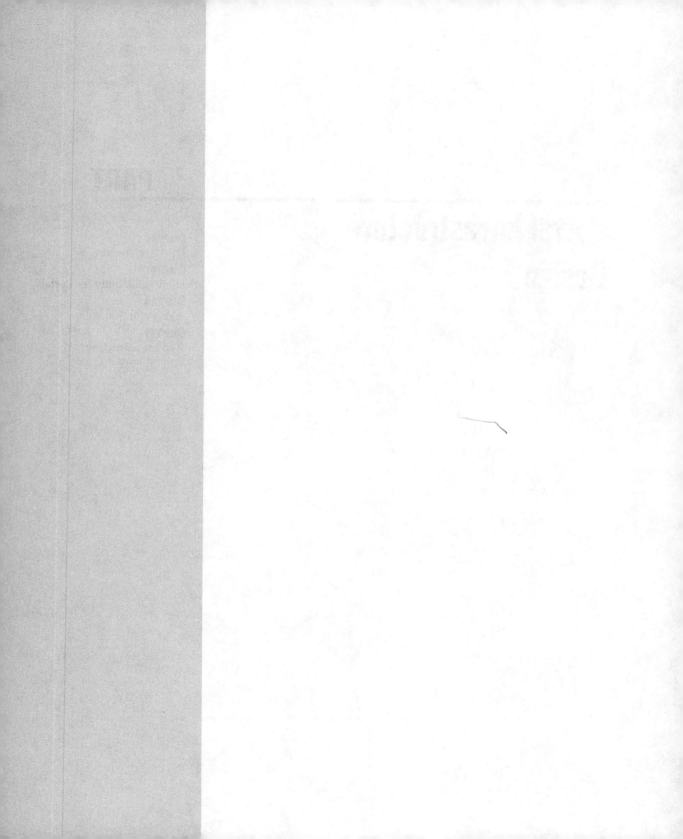

CHAPTER 6

J2EE Architecture

In this chapter, we discuss the important components of portal technical infrastructure, SAP Web Application Server (WAS) Java and Advanced Business Application Programming (ABAP), and finally TREX architecture. We also take a quick look at the minimal Web AS Java and a large Java cluster installation that uses a load balancer. In this chapter, you will learn about the Java versus Add-in installations of NetWeaver as installation such as central instance, central services instance, dialog instance, message service, enqueque service, Java dispatcher process, Java server process and Java startup and control framework. Once you get a basic understanding of the J2EE architecture in this chapter, Chapters 7, 8, and 9 will help you design the portal infrastructure giving due considerations to high availability, scalability, performance, security, and so on.

Components of a Portal Infrastructure

Technical infrastructure in general consists of various components such as hardware systems, operating systems, network systems, firewalls, high availability solutions, load-balancing devices, and storage devices. In addition, any discussion of the technical infrastructure for portals must address the web application infrastructure and the web infrastructure itself. Figure 6-1 displays the *portal technical infrastructure,* which consists of the following major components:

- Web clients
    - Internet browsers
    - PDAs
    - Mobile solutions
- Web infrastructure
    - Load balancer
    - Web servers
    - Web dispatchers
    - Proxy servers

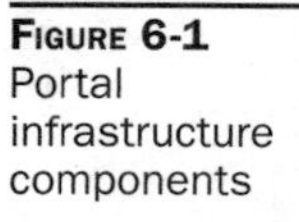

Figure 6-1 Portal infrastructure components

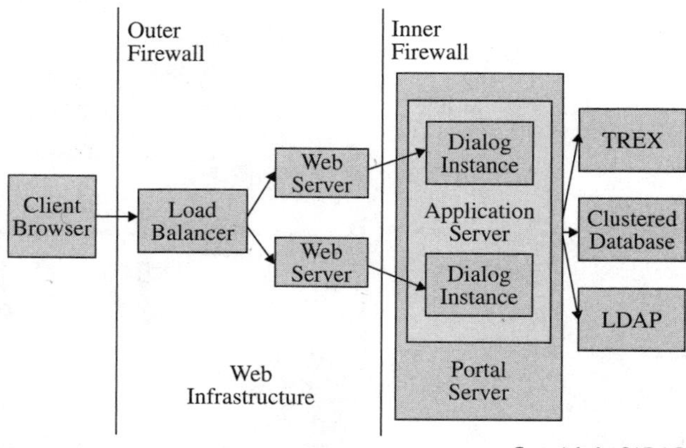

- Portal server
    - Portal platform
    - Knowledge management
    - Content management
    - Collaboration platform
- J2EE engine
- Web AS database
- User Management Engine (UME)
- TREX components
    - Web server
    - Retrieval and Classification Engine
    - Retrieval and Classification Index

The portal server architecture and the UME components were covered in Chapter 2. The web infrastructure components will be discussed in Chapter 9. In this chapter, we discuss the J2EE architecture and the TREX components. As you have already seen, the J2EE engine is just one of the many components in the portal technical infrastructure.

Web AS Java Architecture

Figure 6-2 displays the components in a Web AS Java installation. A typical installation has a central instance, a central services instance, a Java instance, and a database. The central instance contains a dispatcher, a server, and a Software Delivery Manager (SDM). The Java instance differs from the central instance in that it does not contain an SDM. The Java instance can contain a dispatcher and one or more J2EE server processes. The Web AS Java stores all its data in the Java schema.

Note that the central instance, the central services instance, and the Java instance can all be installed on separate physical machines. Such a distributed setup increases system availability and scalability. Chapters 7 and 8 deal with high availability and scalability, respectively.

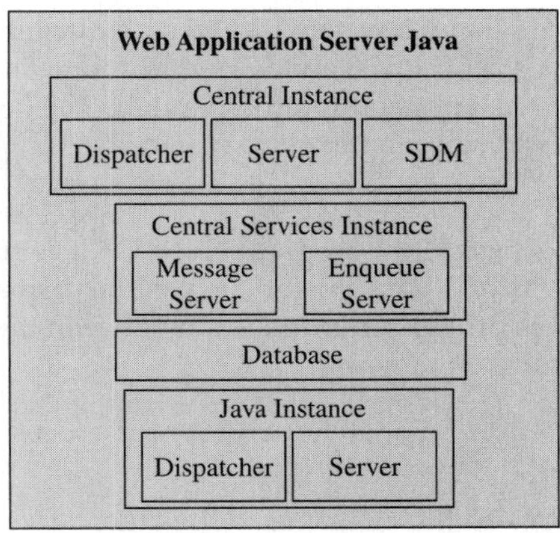

FIGURE 6-2 Web AS Java architecture components

The central services instance contains both the message service and the enqueue service installed together on one machine.

INFO *The machine on which the central services instance is installed can be a high availability machine.*

In a Java cluster, only one central services instance can exist, even though we can have more than one Java instance and more than one database.

TIP *When we have more than one Java instance, we need a load balancer such as the SAP Web Dispatcher to distribute the load across the dispatchers of the Java instances.*

Java Instance

A Java instance contains one dispatcher and one or more server processes. The number of server processes that can be installed in a host would depend upon the available RAM in the host machine. This is discussed in greater detail in Chapter 8, which deals with sizing and scalability. The *Java dispatcher* is a kind of internal load balancer that receives the client request and forwards it to the server process. The Java dispatcher communicates with the message service to identify the server process to which the client request should be routed. The server processes are responsible for processing the request, and they store the user session as well.

NOTE *Since the Java instance contains only the Java stack installed, the Web AS can serve only Java requests.*

A Java instance can run only on one machine, even though more than one Java instance can run on that machine. These Java instances can be implemented on one host or distributed across multiple hosts. This results in what is known as the *central or distributed installation.* The Java instance that contains the SDM is known as the *central instance.* An individual Java instance can be identified by a system ID and a unique instance number. The instance number is a two-digit number between 00 and 97 and is unique for that machine. The Java instance can be started, stopped, and monitored separately. The Java Startup and Control Framework is used for starting and stopping the Java instance.

Message Service

The *message service* is basically a program in the OS layer that can be used for communicating between the elements of a Java cluster such as the dispatcher and server processes. The *message server* ensures proper communication between the various J2EE engine components and is responsible for the following:

- Maintains a list of dispatcher and server process nodes that are running in the J2EE engine.
- Helps to forward the messages to the other server nodes whenever a message needs to be broadcasted to the other nodes.
- Provides the SAP Web Dispatcher with the information on the status of the server nodes, which the dispatcher uses for load balancing between the servers based on the existing load.
- Keeps track of all the active Java instances, and whenever a server node in the cluster fails or is shut down, or when an instance is started or stopped, it notifies the other services of the event.
- Provides support for message server failover and guaranteed transmission of messages, and helps to exchange cache information in the cluster.

Enqueue Server

The *enqueue server* is responsible for maintaining the locks for all objects requested by various portal applications, components, and services. Every time an object needs to be accessed by an application, the server node makes a request to the enqueue service. The enqueue service then processes these requests and either sets or releases the lock. The enqueue service helps to keep track of the locks obtained by the server nodes for the object that is being accessed. It maintains the lock table in the main memory and maps the logical locks to the database.

In addition to maintaining the locks, the enqueue service in the Java stack also synchronizes data in the Java cluster. On the other hand, the enqueue service in the ABAP stack only maintains the locks for data objects.

NOTE *The enqueue server is also known as the* lock server *because it manages the lock table.*

Minimal Java Installation

Figure 6-3 displays the minimal install scenario of the Web AS Java System. This is a simplistic scenario when compared to the Web AS Java installation shown in Figure 6-2. No Java instance is installed and only one database is installed on one machine.

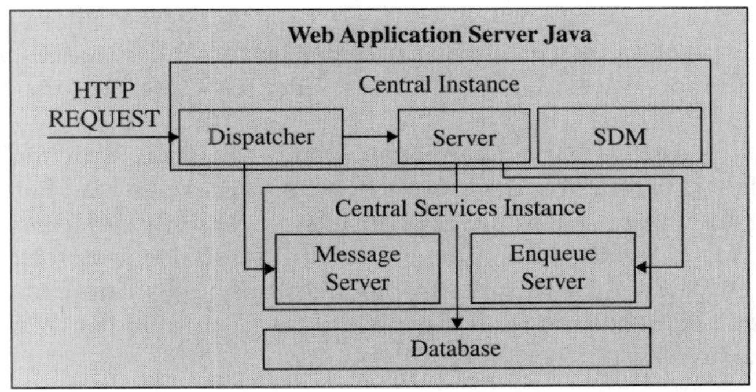

FIGURE 6-3 Minimal Web AS Java installation

Larger Java Cluster Installation with Load Balancer

Figure 6-4 displays a large Java cluster installation that uses a load balancer to distribute requests across the Java instances. This installation provides higher system availability and scalability due to the additional Java instances.

Java Cluster

The *Java cluster* can consist of one or more Java instances and one or more databases and can be installed on one or more physical host machines. Of course, a Java cluster consists of only one central services instance and hence only one message server and an enqueue server exist for the whole J2EE engine.

Load Balancing by SAP Web Dispatcher and Java Dispatcher

With more than one Java instance, it is important for the J2EE engine to be able to distribute the client requests to the different dispatchers based on the availability of the servers as well as the load on them. SAP offers a component called the *SAP Web Dispatcher* that

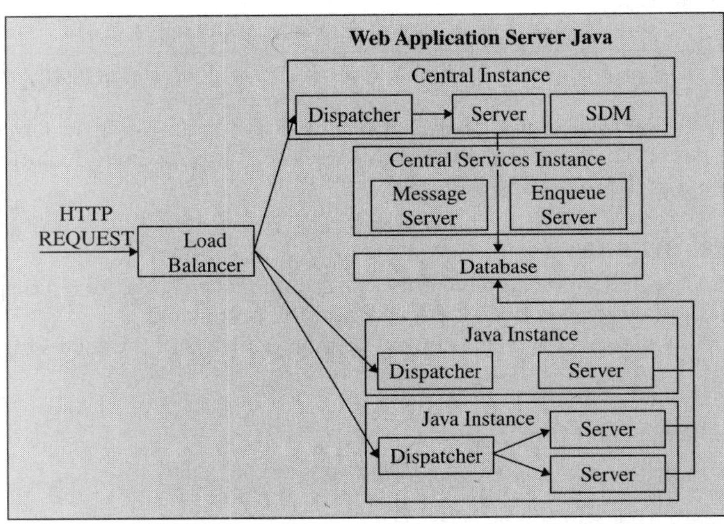

FIGURE 6-4 Large Web AS Java installation with load balancer

does the job of a load balancer. SAP Web Dispatcher gets the hosts and port information of the Java dispatchers as well as the capacities of the J2EE instances from the message server. This information is stored in a profile file. Chapter 9 discusses the SAP Web Dispatcher in greater detail.

It is also possible that a given Java instance has one dispatcher but more than one server process. In such scenarios, the Java Dispatcher serves as a load balancer by distributing the incoming client requests to the appropriate server node based on the availability and the load. The Java Dispatcher obtains the server node information from the message server. The Java Dispatcher uses a round-robin algorithm to distribute the requests. Thus you can notice that load balancing is taking place at two levels, first at the SAP Web Dispatcher and then at the Java Dispatcher.

NOTE *While SAP Web Dispatcher load balances across multiple Java dispatchers, the Java Dispatcher load balances across multiple server processes.*

NetWeaver AS Java vs. Add-In Installation

One of the first important decisions to make regarding the technical infrastructure is whether to install a NetWeaver AS Java only system installation or a NetWeaver AS Add-In system installation. A NetWeaver AS Add-In installation is a dual installation that consists of both Java and an ABAP stack. A NetWeaver AS Add-In is required when you are implementing SAP XI (Exchange Infrastructure). The SAP Enterprise Portal requires only the Java stack to function properly. It is generally not recommended to implement the dual installation for a portal installation because this will expose the ABAP layer to the public Internet. The ABAP stack is often used to host SAP ERP ECC (Enterprise Central Component), SAP CRM, SAP SCM, and so on. Since the information hosted on the ABAP stack is more sensitive in nature, you are recommended to install the portal on the NetWeaver AS Java server. By doing this, you will also be able to fully utilize all the system resources for the portal and ensure better performance.

TIP *In most cases, a Java only installation is sufficient for installing enterprise portals.*

For the sake of completeness, let's discuss the Java Add-In system's installation components. The Java Add-In system (AS-ABAP and AS-Java) includes the components discussed in the following sections.

Central Instance

Each SAP installation can have only one *central instance*. Figure 6-5 displays a Java Add-In installation, which has both the ABAP and the Java stacks.

The Java stack or the Java central instance consists of the following:

- Java dispatcher
- Java Server processes
- Software Delivery Manager (SDM)
- Internet Graphics Service (IGS)

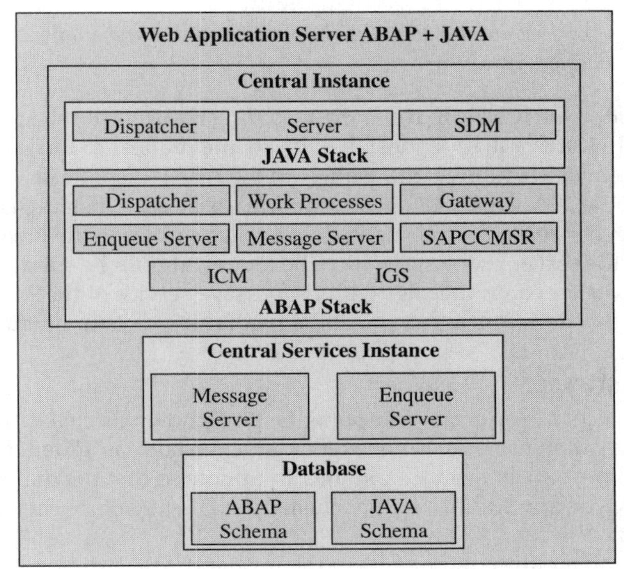

Copyright by SAP AG

FIGURE 6-5 Web AS Java and ABAP components

PART II

The ABAP stack or the ABAP central instance consists of the following:

- ABAP dispatcher
- Work processes
- Gateway
- Enqueue server
- Message server
- CCMS agent SAPCCMSR
- Internet Communication Manager (ICM)
- IGS

The SAP system communicates with the external world using HTTP, HTTPS, and SMTP protocols with the help of the Internet Communication Manager (ICM). The ICM is a thread-based process and handles the incoming requests as URLs with server/port combinations for which it has been configured to listen to.

Central Services Instance

As already mentioned before, the *Java Central Services instance* consists of components that are responsible for the communication as well as synchronization in the Java cluster across server and dispatcher nodes:

- Enqueue server
- Message server

NOTE *The ABAP stack also contains the message server and enqueue server, similar to the Java Central Services instance.*

The role of the ICM is to route the incoming requests to the appropriate dispatcher based on the URL. If it is a Java request, it submits the request to the Java Dispatcher, and if it is an ABAP request, it submits the request to the ABAP dispatcher.

If multiple NW AS ABAP + Java instances exist, each instance should have an ICM. The Java Dispatcher communicates with the message service in the Java central services instance to identify the server process to which the request should be submitted. In the same way, the ABAP dispatcher communicates with its message service of the ABAP central service instance to identify the work process to which the request is to be submitted.

Dialog Instances

Dialog instances are optional components, also known as *application servers*, and are usually installed on different hosts. Whenever a dialog instance is added, it belongs to the software cluster and the central instance initiates an update so that the dialog instance can have access to the deployed applications in that cluster. A dialog instance can refer to either a Java or an ABAP instance.

Following are the components in the Java and ABAP dialog instances:

- Java stack or the Java dialog instance
  - Java dispatcher
  - Java Server processes
  - IGS
- ABAP stack or the ABAP dialog instance
  - ABAP dispatcher
  - Work processes (dialog, batch, spool, or update)
  - Gateway
  - IGS
  - ICM

NOTE *In the ABAP stack, the work processes are the equivalent of the Java server processes.*

Java Dispatcher Components

Figure 6-6 provides a closer look at the Java Dispatcher that has the following components: connection request handler, connection manager, load balancer, session level services, request queue, and communication handler.

The *connection request handler* receives the incoming HTTP request and initializes the *connection object*. The *connection manager* then analyzes the incoming request and submits the

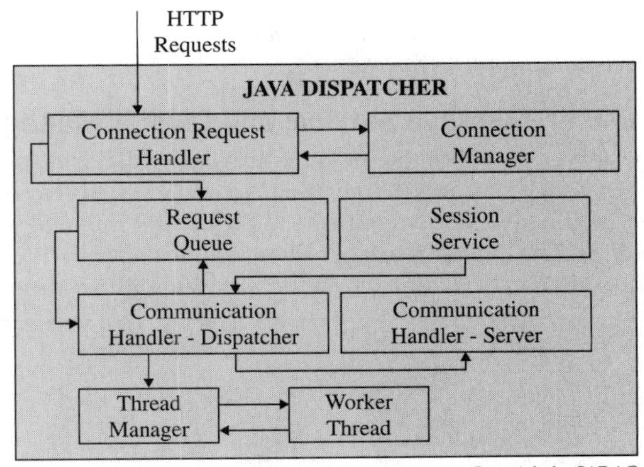

FIGURE 6-6 Java Dispatcher components

PART II

request to the appropriate *session service* such as HTTP, Remote Method Invocation (RMI), and so on. If there are more requests than the dispatcher can handle, the requests are placed in a *request queue.* The *communication handler* in the dispatcher then forwards the request to the communication handler in the server.

NOTE *The Java Dispatcher communicates with the message server to determine which server is active.*

Java Server Process

Figure 6-7 shows the Java server process components. In the case of a Java server process, the *communication handler* of the server process receives the incoming dispatcher requests. If no threads are available to process, the requests are put in a *queue.* The communication handler identifies the required session level service such as RMI or HTTP and sends it to the session service. The *session service* then sends it to the *application level service* for actual processing by the Java application. A good understanding of the components of the Java Dispatcher and the server will help you fine tune the Web AS Java (SAP J2EE engine) performance.

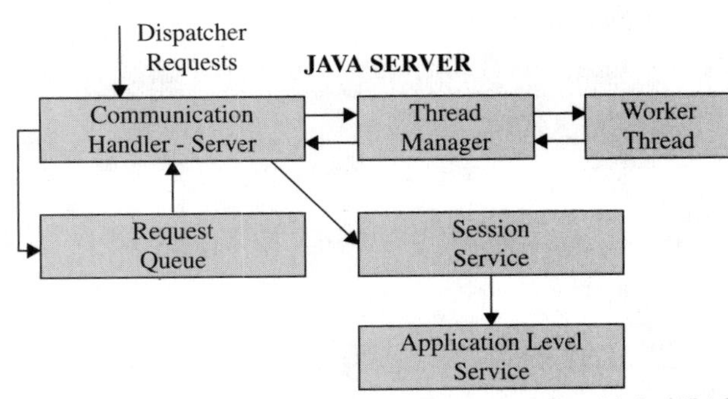

FIGURE 6-7 Java server process components

TIP *You can configure the number of server and dispatcher threads, the request queue's initial size, and maximum size for better performance.*

Message Server, Message Service, and Cluster Manager

The message server provides the message service, which is responsible for monitoring the status of the message server. Whenever a Java server needs to communicate with the message server, the Java server connects to the cluster manager of the Java instance to which it belongs. The cluster manager then communicates with the message service in the central services instance as depicted in the following illustration.

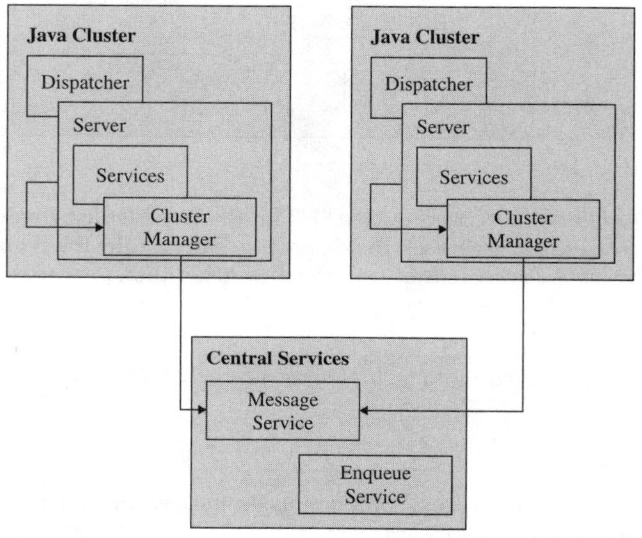

Copyright by SAP AG

SAP Management Console

The Web AS has an SAP management console in Windows as shown in the illustration below. The SAP management console helps you monitor the server and services that are running from one single access point. The SAP management console is installed as part of the portal installation. In the case of UNIX, you have *startsap/stopsap* scripts for starting and stopping the SAP system.

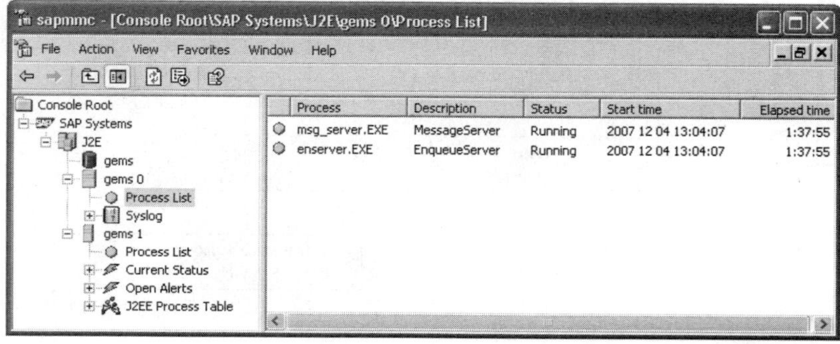

Copyright by SAP AG

In the preceding illustration, J2E stands for the system ID of the SAP J2EE engine. The cylindrical shaped blue icon with the name "gems" is the portal database. gems is the host name of the computer on which the portal has been installed. Below this icon, you can see the rectangular shaped icon with name "gems 0", which represents the central services instance. When you click on the process list under the gems 0 icon, you will see the message service and the enqueue service on the right.

The second rectangular icon with name "gems 1" represents the central instance. When you click on the plus sign before gems 1 and double click J2EE Process Table, you will see the screen as shown in the illustration below.

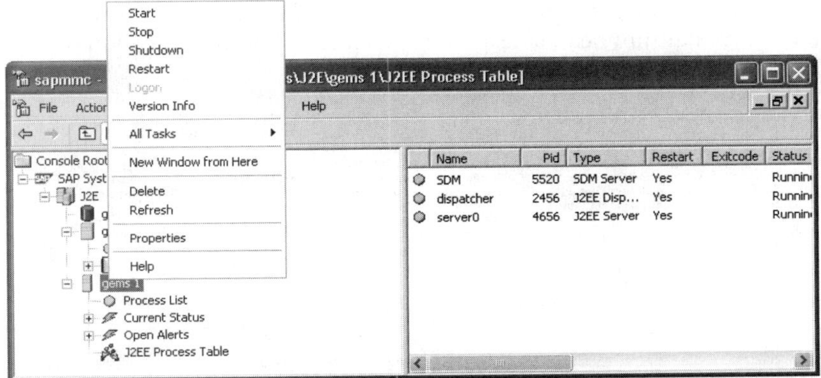

Copyright by SAP AG

On the right, you can view the J2EE server, dispatcher, and the SDM processes. When you right click on any of the processes, you will see a context menu that provides you the ability to start, stop, dump stack trace, and so on. A similar context menu appears when you right click on the central instance, central service instance, the database, or the whole J2E SAP system. Note that this is a minimal installation with only a central instance and no additional Java instances. If there was an additional Java instance, you would see an additional rectangular icon. That will include a dispatcher and server process, but no SDM process.

Java Startup and Control Framework

The next important feature of the SAP NetWeaver Application Server is the *Java Startup and Control framework.* The Java Startup and Control framework contains the JControl and JLaunch programs. When a service stops, the JControl process restarts the service again. This takes care of situations in which someone knowingly or unknowingly stops a service. The Java Startup and Control framework loads the Java Virtual Machine (JVM) and restarts processes that may have crashed/failed.

NOTE *The restart feature of the Java Startup and Control framework helps to increase the high availability of the system.*

The startup framework lies between the OS and the JVM. Some OS-level scripts start the OS collector first. Then, if the database resides on the same machine, the database is started. After that, the enqueue and the message services are started, and then the JControl process is started.

The JControl is the actual watchdog that ensures that all the server nodes are running by monitoring the JLaunch processes. The JControl first checks the instance.properties file and the profile properties for the instance. Then it creates a shared memory segment for holding administrative data for the instance. The instance.properties file is available under <sap_j2ee_engine_install_folder>\usr\sap\J2E\JC01\j2ee\cluster folder and part of the content is reproduced in the illustration below for a better understanding. The illustration contains entries in the instance.properties file relevant to the dispatcher. It contains JVM parameters such as maximum heap size, garbage collection settings, location of the JDK, and so on.

```
ID19021300.ClassPath=./bin/boot/boot.jar:./bin/system/bytecode.jar:.
ID19021300.Debuggable=no
ID19021300.JLaunchParameters=
ID19021300.JavaParameters=-Djava.security.policy=./java.policy -Djava.security.egd=file:/dev/urandom
-Dorg.omg.CORBA.ORBClass=com.sap.engine.system.ORBProxy -Dorg.omg.CORBA.ORBSingletonClass=com.sap.engine.system.ORBSingletonProxy
-Djavax.rmi.CORBA.PortableRemoteObjectClass=com.sap.engine.system.PortableRemoteObjectProxy -Xms15M  -XX:NewSize=5M  -XX:MaxNewSize=5M  -XX:PermSize=10M
 -XX:MaxPermSize=20M  -verbose:gc  -XX:+DisableExplicitGC -verbose:gc -XX:+UseConcMarkSweepGC
ID19021300.JavaPath=C:/j2sdk1.4.2_09
ID19021300.LogName=dispatcher
ID19021300.MainClass=com.sap.engine.boot.Start
ID19021300.MaxHeapSize=170
ID19021300.Name=dispatcher
ID19021300.Parameters=
ID19021300.RootPath=C:/usr/sap/J2E/JC01/j2ee/cluster/dispatcher
ID19021300.Type=dispatcher
```


For each instance consisting of the dispatcher, the server process, and the SDM, the JControl starts/stops the JLaunch process. The JLaunch hosts the JVM process that reads the instance-specific properties. The Java server, dispatcher, and the SDM processes have a JLaunch process associated to each one of them. When you open the task manager in the Windows operating system of the application server host, you will be able to view these individual JLaunch processes as shown in the illustration below. The illustration shown below displays three JLaunch processes, each corresponding to the dispatcher, server, and SDM processes. You can also view processes running for the message server (msg_server .exe), enqueue server (enserver.exe), and JControl (jcontrol.exe). This information is helpful when troubleshooting the portal and this topic is dealt with in detail in Chapter 27.

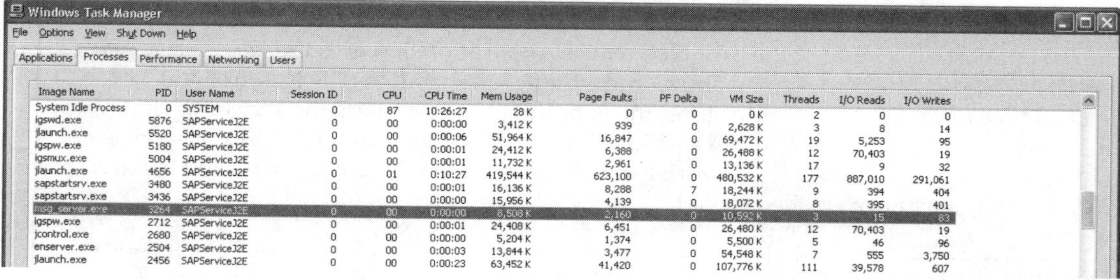

Image Name	PID	User Name	Session ID	CPU	CPU Time	Mem Usage	Page Faults	PF Delta	VM Size	Threads	I/O Reads	I/O Writes
System Idle Process	0	SYSTEM	0	87	10:26:27	28 K	0	0	0 K	2	0	0
igswd.exe	5876	SAPServiceJ2E	0	00	0:00:00	3,412 K	939	0	2,628 K	3	8	14
jlaunch.exe	5520	SAPServiceJ2E	0	00	0:00:06	51,964 K	16,847	0	69,472 K	19	5,253	95
igspw.exe	5180	SAPServiceJ2E	0	00	0:00:01	24,412 K	6,388	0	26,488 K	12	70,403	19
igsmux.exe	5004	SAPServiceJ2E	0	00	0:00:01	11,732 K	2,961	0	13,136 K	17	9	32
jlaunch.exe	4656	SAPServiceJ2E	0	01	0:10:27	419,544 K	623,100	0	480,532 K	177	887,010	291,061
sapstartsrv.exe	3480	SAPServiceJ2E	0	00	0:00:01	16,136 K	8,288	7	18,244 K	9	394	404
sapstartsrv.exe	3436	SAPServiceJ2E	0	00	0:00:00	15,956 K	4,139	0	18,072 K	8	395	401
msg_server.exe	3264	SAPServiceJ2E	0	00	0:00:00	8,508 K	2,160	0	10,592 K	3	15	83
igspw.exe	2712	SAPServiceJ2E	0	00	0:00:01	24,408 K	6,451	0	26,480 K	12	70,403	19
jcontrol.exe	2680	SAPServiceJ2E	0	00	0:00:00	5,204 K	1,374	0	5,500 K	5	46	96
enserver.exe	2504	SAPServiceJ2E	0	00	0:00:03	13,844 K	3,477	0	54,548 K	7	555	3,750
jlaunch.exe	2456	SAPServiceJ2E	0	00	0:00:23	63,452 K	41,420	0	107,776 K	111	39,578	607

The other important point about the Java startup process is the *bootstrapping* mechanism, which is triggered by the JControl process during startup. During this initialization phase, all the startup parameters are read from the J2EE database by the J2EE instance bootstrap process and then passed on to the JControl process. The JControl process then reads the J2EE instance description (containing the details of parameters related to the dispatcher, server processes, and SDM that need to be started) and then starts the J2EE node-specific bootstrap processes.

The node-specific bootstrap processes then ensure that for each server process, the binary information stored in the local file copy has the latest information corresponding to the database; if not, then the file copy is synchronized with the database. Once the files are synchronized, the JControl starts the J2EE instance processes by launching the corresponding JLaunch processes.

The bootstrap functionality, including the watchdog functionality, ensures that all server processes are started correctly and without fail. Whenever a change is made to the J2EE engine configuration, let us say, by using the Visual Administrator, the change is stored in the J2EE engine database. By synchronizing the files in the J2EE operating system with those in the J2EE engine database, it is ensured that the latest configuration changes are incorporated during startup. One example of a configuration change could be changing the JVM heap size of the server. The other notable feature about the Java startup framework is that the Java processes have been integrated into the concept of an SAP instance. The Java startup framework can also be monitored by the JCMon command-line tool, which provides an overview of the instance and the state of the processes.

RDBMS Database

The RDBMS database is a mandatory component for the installation and consists of the following schemas, preferably stored in the same database. The AS-Java schema is named as SAP<SID>DB and contains all the objects needed by the application server as well as the deployed application objects. The ABAP schema is named as SAP<SID>. <SID> is the SAP system ID and the default value is J2E, which can be chosen during installation. So, for a default installation, the AS Java schema would be SAPJ2EDB and the ABAP schema would be SAPJ2E.

The *portal database* can be located on the same host machine, or it can be distributed on a separate physical host. But if it is installed on the same host as the other J2EE components, it is known as a *central installation*. It is known as a *distributed installation* when the database is installed on a separate host machine. At the time of portal installation, you will be prompted to choose between a central and a distributed installation. Depending upon your specific business and technical requirements, you will have to decide your preferred option during the technical infrastructure design phase. Chapters 7 and 8 discuss portal infrastructure design in greater detail.

Monitoring Processes

The *SAPOsCol* is a service that runs on the host machines and is essential for the CCMS functions. The *SAPCCMSR* agent is responsible for collecting all the monitored data and sending them to the CEN (Central Monitoring System). Chapter 32 discusses the role of the SAPOsCol service and the SAPCCMSR agent for setting up CCMS and GRMG monitoring in greater detail.

TREX: Technical Infrastructure

The TREX works independently of the portal. TREX services can be used for the following:

- Searching and retrieving large document collections
- Text mining
- Automatically classifying documents
- Searching information from SAP applications

TREX is based on a client/server setup and can be set up in a high availability mode without using any third-party switchover solutions. Figure 6-8 displays the TREX architectural components.

NOTE *TREX is a separate component and is not part of the Web AS architecture.*

TREX Client

The TREX client is used in content management when we use the search functionality on the portal. Note that TREX is also used in other applications such as CRM and MDM to implement the search functionality. Content management exists as a service in the web application server and it uses the TREX Java client to send the search request through HTTP to the web server in TREX for processing. The TREX Java client (as well as the ABAP client) is nothing but application programming interfaces that can access the TREX functions such as creating indexes and searches, indexing and searching, as well as querying the internal status of the TREX. The web server in TREX has a TREX extension that helps the Java client to communicate with the TREX servers such as Queue server, Index server, and Name server. The TREX extension formats the incoming XML requests into TREX-specific formats that the TREX servers can process. The TREX extension exists either as an ISAPI filter for the Microsoft IIS or as a shared library for the Apache web server in UNIX.

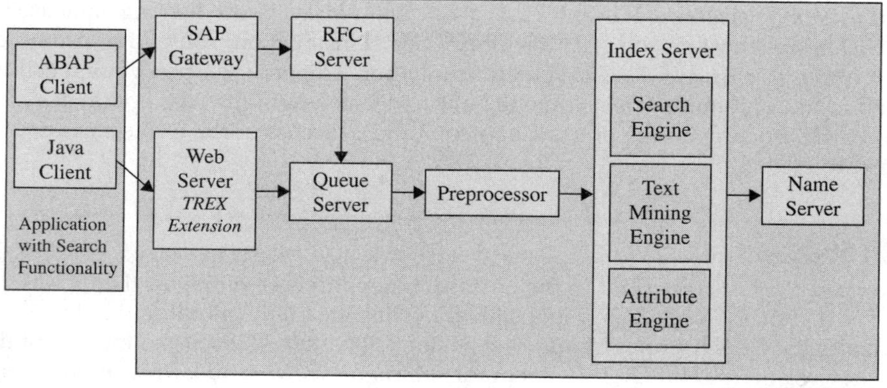

FIGURE 6-8 TREX architectural components

For an SAP ABAP system to communicate with the TREX servers, the RFC server component of the TREX is used. The SAP system sends the request to the RFC server using an SAP gateway. Similar to the web server with a TREX extension, the RFC server converts the incoming requests to TREX-specific formats and routes them to the TREX servers. Note that the RFC server is not required for the Java client to communicate with the TREX servers.

Queue Server

The *queue server* has a number of queues, one each for each index. The queue server is responsible for the following:

- Storing all the search requests in a queue for processing
- Gathering the documents required for creating indexes
- Triggering the preprocessing as well as subsequent processing by the index server asynchronously. This way, the load on the system can be managed by scheduling the indexing during times when the search queries are lower.

Preprocessor

The *preprocessor* is responsible for the following:

- Fetching the documents from the repository based on the incoming URIs
- Extracting the keywords in textual form from a document such as Word, PowerPoint, and so on, and converting them into UTF-8 Unicode format, as well as removing any formatting data
- Performing *linguistic analysis* using a lexicon that exists in different languages and splitting text into words and forms stems (base forms)

Once the linguistic analysis is completed by the preprocessor, the queue server submits the documents to the index server.

Index Server

The *index server* consists of the following engines:

- **Search engine** To carry out searches
- **Text mining engine** To classify documents and to search for similar documents
- **Attribute engine** To search for documents based on attributes such as author, creation, and changed date

The index server builds the indexes, classifies the documents, and retrieves the results. It passes the requests to the core TREX engines, which provide core functionalities such as the search engine, the text mining engine, and the attribute engine. The TREX Java client sends the requests to the name server to find out to which index server the requests should be forwarded.

Name Server

The *name server* is responsible for the following:

- Maintaining the data for the whole TREX system such as the information on TREX servers, indexes, and queues
- Ensuring high availability of TREX servers by launching a watchdog functionality to monitor them
- Conducting load balancing by distributing the indexes and search queries only to the available servers

All these components can be either stored in one machine or distributed in many machines. The actual distribution of the TREX components should be decided during the technical infrastructure design phase.

NOTE *For more details, refer to 'Technical Infrastructures of SAP Enterprise Portal 6.0' and other resources listed in Appendix B.*

Summary

We discussed two major components of the portal architecture, namely, the J2EE engine and the TREX engine. When discussing the J2EE engine, you learned about the Java versus Add-In installations of the Web NetWeaver Application Server and minimal installation versus cluster installation that uses load-balancing functionality. You learned about the various components of an SAP NetWeaver Application Server installation such as central instance, central services instance, dialog instance, message service, enqueue service, Java Dispatcher process, and the Java server process. You learned about the difference between a central instance, central services instance, and a Java instance. You also learned about the importance of Java Startup and Control framework. A good understanding of these topics will be very helpful as you proceed with technical infrastructure design as well as when implementing and supporting the portal after Go-Live.

7

CHAPTER

High Availability for Portals

Part of the planning phase in a portal implementation is to come up with a technical infrastructure design for the portal that delivers a robust architecture with optimized performance, scalability, high availability, security, and reduced total cost of ownership. The technical infrastructure design for the portal is an outcome of the technical infrastructure planning and is often conducted during the project preparatory phase.

In this chapter, you will learn about the following:

- Salient features to consider when designing a portal infrastructure
- Factors affecting high availability on the portal
- Key success factors for implementing high availability
- Creating a high availability requirements checklist for portal
- Aspects to consider when choosing a high availability solution
- Identifying the single points of failure in a portal system
- Securing the single points of failure
- Possible technical infrastructure designs for use in systems demanding high availability.

Designing a robust system giving due considerations to high availability during the initial project implementation will result in reduced unplanned downtimes, reduced unplanned maintenance effort, and ultimately increased customer satisfaction. In the next chapter on scalability, we address how we can scale the system for use in a production environment, giving due consideration to performance and sizing.

Portal Infrastructure Design

When designing the technical infrastructure for the portal, you should focus on the following:

- Designing the solution landscape with focus on high availability
- Sizing the systems that compose the portal system landscape
- Designing the system landscape, which is composed of sandbox, development, quality, and production systems
- Setting up a working environment for the portal project team, such as NetWeaver Development Infrastructure

Tip *Once the technical infrastructure design is ready, it serves as a basis for procuring the physical hardware for building those systems.*

When designing a technical infrastructure for the portal, you should rely on the following:

- Project, technical, and functional scopes
- Business requirements
- Current landscape system
- Company security policy

Essentials of Good Portal Infrastructure Design

Following are the salient features to ensure that the portal infrastructure is well designed (shown in the illustration):

- It should not only be able to serve its customers with the correct functionality, but also have reasonable response times.
- It should be scalable with increases in the user population as well as increases in the functionality of the application.
- Proper sizing of the machines is important so as to ensure satisfactory portal performance and should be considered in the early stages of the project.
- The system should be highly available and meet the service level agreements that exist, especially in the case of mission critical portal applications such as the external customer facing applications—for example, B2B Internet sales.
- The security of the portal should not be compromised, and the security policy of the organization should be followed.
- The new technical infrastructure that comes with the portal should be integrated with the existing network architecture as well.
- The need for reducing the total cost of ownership of the applications should be balanced with the need for a high-end, highly available portal application.

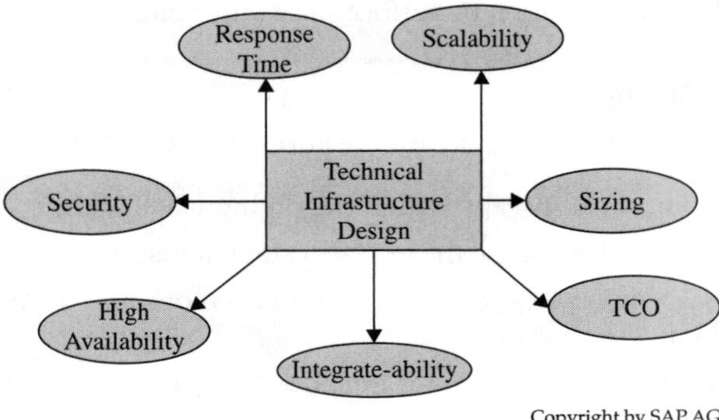

Portal System Landscape Design

In an organization, the portal system landscape is usually composed of sandbox, development, quality, and production systems. For each system landscape, you should design the technical infrastructure.

Copyright by SAP AG

For each system, you should decide upon the number of host machines, which can be calculated based on the *number of installable software units* such as the usage types, standalone engines, and client systems. The specific requirements that those installable software units impose will help you to decide the server requirements. For information on choosing the installable software units, refer to Chapters 3, 4, and 5 as well as the relevant version of the SAP NetWeaver Master Guide. You must decide which software unit will be installed on which host server. Based on that assessment, the load on the host machine should be analyzed. Finally, based on the load requirements, the sizings of the machines in terms of number of processors, gigabytes of RAM, disk size, and other design considerations such as load balancing, reverse proxy, and authentication mechanisms should be considered during deployment.

TIP *In the case of production, aspects such as high availability and sizing based on load will have a major impact on the outcome of the final design.*

High Availability for Portal

The term *high availability* is a relative term, and the definition of high availability is in a way tied to the criticality of the business solution under consideration. High availability for the portal could mean a lot of things, including the following:

- Minimizing planned downtimes for backup, patching, updates, and other maintenance.
- Determining a disaster recovery plan for the portal landscape when unforeseen events such as fire occur in a data center or in a locale.

Importance of High Availability

The topic of high availability for the NetWeaver systems and the portal, in particular, is gaining more importance with the advent of end-to-end business processes that span multiple systems and company boundaries. It is not only important to maintain high availability for single components, but also to maintain *end-to-end high availability* for entire scenarios.

In this chapter, we focus on how to minimize unplanned downtimes, which involves identifying the single points of failure (SPOF) in the portal system landscape and coming up with action items to avoid the SPOF. This basically results in *improved service levels.*

PART II

TIP *Non-availability of a portal system can cost the business its customers, revenue, and reputation, and may result in decreased productivity due to disruption in normal business operations.*

Cost of Implementing a High Availability Portal Solution

The need for high availability of the portal system should be weighed against the cost of producing a solution. The cost of downtime to the business often increases exponentially when the duration of downtime increases. At the same time, the cost of producing a high availability portal solution increases exponentially when the requirements of high availability increase. The cost for implementing high availability is often high due to increased investments on redundant high availability components, disaster recovery planning, monitoring tools, and IT personnel.

Impact of Downtimes

When planning for high availability for the portal, you need to understand the causes of unplanned and planned downtimes.

Unplanned downtimes occur due to hardware, software, or human errors. Hardware failures could be due to hardware, operating system, and environment failures. These failures can be avoided by installing redundant hardware systems so as to eliminate SPOF. The other cause is *human error,* which can be avoided using training in proper change and problem management procedures. Finally, unplanned downtime can also result from application (both SAP and custom) related errors.

Planned downtime can result due to system maintenance requirements such as the following:

- Installation of patches and support packages periodically as part of regular maintenance
- Portal upgrades
- Database reorganization / backup
- J2EE engine configuration changes for performance tuning, troubleshooting, and so on
- Portal transports due to new / changed functionality

NOTE *SAP is constantly striving to reduce downtime by enabling rolling maintenance, improved upgrade processes, and a robust correction and transport system.*

Key Success Factors for High Availability

Following are some of the key success factors for implementing high availability for the portal.

System-Wide Strategy

Implementing high availability for the portal system should be a *system-wide strategy*. Unplanned downtime can be due to issues that lie within any of the layers that form the hardware and software environments. Layers of the hardware and software systems that can fail and hence affect portal availability include the following:

- User interface (also known as front-end services) components such as a web browser, SAP GUI, and so on
- Web infrastructure components (also known as middleware services) such as web servers, firewalls, routers, load balancers, and so on
- SAP business components, such as mySAP CRM, mySAP SCM, and so on, to which the portal is connected
- SAP NetWeaver Technology Components, such as SAP Business Intelligence (BI) integrated with the portal
- Infrastructure components on which the portal depends for proper functioning, such as database services, network services, and operating system services
- Hardware components such as servers, NICs, UPS, hard disks, memory storage, and so on

To implement a robust high availability portal solution, you must focus on all these components that span across the user interface layer, web layer, business functionality layer, infrastructure layer, and the hardware layer so that end-to-end availability can be ensured.

TIP *Even if one component fails in a portal system landscape, the complete end-to-end availability can suffer.*

You should also be responsible for the following:

- Assessing the costs/benefits of providing such high availability portal solutions
- Establishing the goals for high availability of the portal in tangible terms so that performance can be measured against these goals
- Establishing SLAs between departments for high availability of the portal
- Defining proper escalation procedures in the event of unplanned downtimes to ensure quick response to failures
- Establishing proper controls and procedures for managing systems during change management, portal upgrade, system failures, portal monitoring, database administration and failures, disaster recovery, and network administration
- Setting up a proper test portal system that mimics the production environment for simulating failures

High Availability Requirements Checklist

When trying to achieve high availability for the portal, you should maintain a checklist of requirements:

- How much portal uptime is needed? Is the uptime sufficient to take database backups and conduct portal maintenance and portal upgrades?

- How much portal downtime is tolerated?
- Are the portal database backup frequency, restore, and recovery procedures and durations adequate?
- What is the database volume and the transaction load in the portal?
- Do you need redundant hardware components such as switchover software, UPS, and the latest disk technologies such as mirrored disks, RAID, or LVM?
- Do you need redundant network components such as cables and active components such as routers, switches, hubs, and NICs?
- Do you need hot standby systems for enqueue and message services and database services?
- What external factors, such as power failures or floods, might affect the system?
- What internal factors, such as availability and training of personnel, and cost for implementing high availability solutions, affect your needs?

Once you have created a checklist similar to the one mentioned above, you can then use it as an input when choosing between different possible high availability designs identified for the portal.

Highly Available SAP NetWeaver Platform

A key factor that contributes to high availability is the SAP NetWeaver platform, which leverages all the high availability capability available in the industry and works with solutions offered from third-party vendors and partners for various OS and database platforms. Another factor that contributes to high availability is the support provided by third-party vendors. Third-party vendors provide state-of-the-art high availability solutions for various hardware, operating system, database, storage, and network systems. The partners also provide help on actually installing the high availability solutions using their expertise in these areas.

TIP *It may be a good idea to bring in external consultants to help implement high availability solutions using third-party solutions.*

A number of third-party high availability solutions, both hardware and software based, are available on the market; these can work with SAP software. Note that SAP may not take responsibility for the proper functioning of such solutions. Before choosing a high availability solution, ensure that it works well with SAP systems. Some of the available solutions are Microsoft Cluster Service, Sun Cluster, HP Service Guard, HP Service Insight Manager, IBM HACMP, Veritas Cluster Server, Oracle Failsafe, and Oracle Real-Time Application Server.

When choosing a high availability solution, you should give due consideration to aspects such as the following:

- Will all the SPOF be removed after installing the high availability solution?
- Will the high availability solution introduce additional points of failure?
- How many servers are required to implement high availability?
- What software is used for detecting switchovers?
- How much time does it take to failover from one system to the other?

- How much time does it take to implement the high availability solution?
- What is the cost of implementation?
- Will the high availability solution be compatible with future SAP solutions?

Single Points of Failure

When planning to implement high availability, you must undertake two essential activities:

- Identify the SPOF in the portal system.
- Eliminate the SPOF identified above.

Identifying SPOFs

The first logical step when implementing high availability is to identify each and every component in the portal architecture and analyze whether it is an SPOF. Some of the potential SPOF for a typical portal system include the following:

- SAP Web AS Java
- J2EE database
- User persistence store like LDAP or the SAP R/3 system
- TREX engine
- Load balancer, if used

Let us now take a deeper look at the SAP Web AS Java system, which, in turn, can have the following SPOFs:

- SAP Application Server (also known as the dialog instance)
- Message Service
- J2EE Database (either the connectivity between the application and the database is lost or the database data itself is lost)

Other SPOF that should be taken into account are the following:

- Network service issues due to failure of cabling and active components such as hubs, switches, routers, NICs, and routers.
- Disk failure due to SPOF in a power supply, fan and cooling system, internal/external cabling, and so on. This could result in loss of user data, system data, log files, and config data.

Figure 7-1 shows the following SPOFs:

- Central services instances for both Java (SCS) and ABAP (ASCS) stacks. SCS stands for Server Central Services and ASCS stands for ABAP Server Central Services
- The database
- The SAP central file system share

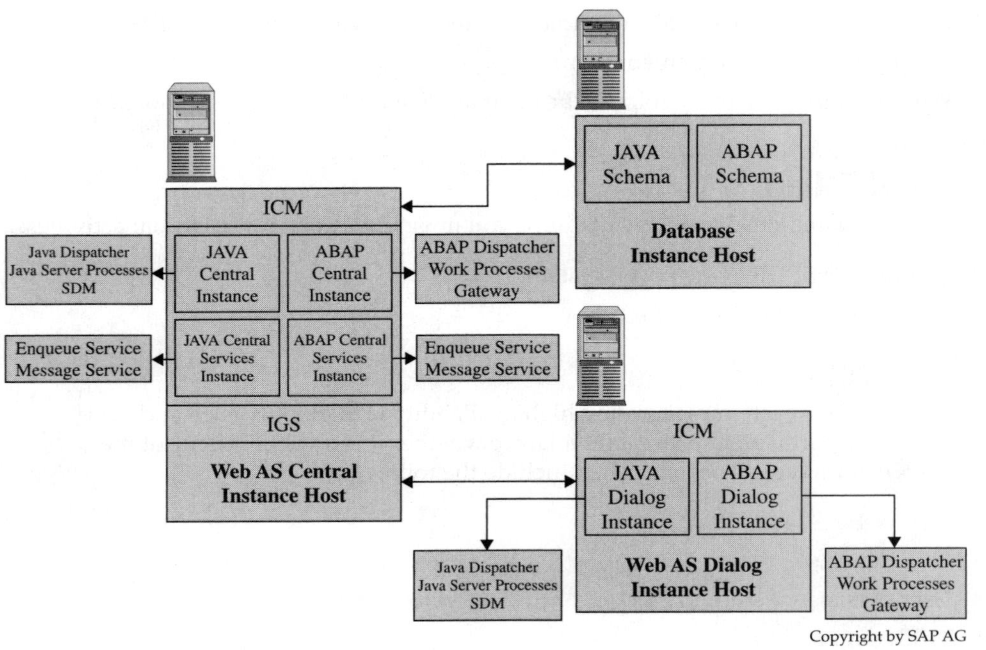

FIGURE 7-1 SPOFs in a Web AS Java + ABAP system

Dispatcher, Java Instance, and Enqueue Service

The dispatcher, the Java instance, and the enqueue service are also single points of failure and hence affect high availability. If the dispatcher is installed on the central instance, the whole system goes down. If the dispatcher is installed on a Java instance, then the users logged on to that instance will be logged out. To recover the dispatcher, either a manual restart of the dispatcher is required or you should have a switchover mechanism to failover to another instance. If the dispatcher fails, usually you cannot detect it, except when it is configured as an NT service.

If the Java instance fails, all the user sessions on that instance will be lost. When the Java instance fails, the dispatcher will detect it and the system will try to restart the Java instance automatically.

When the enqueue service fails, it will be temporarily impossible for the transactions to access the enqueue locks, unless you have a replication enqueue server installed. The dispatcher will detect the failure of the enqueue service and the system will try to restart it automatically.

Securing the SPOF

In a typical portal architecture setup, the *load balancer* is a potential SPOF. So it is important to set up the load balancer in a high availability manner using either hardware or software options. Another option is to avoid the *portal server* as an SPOF by operating the portal clusters in an active-active mode, so that when one of the servers fails, the other server will take the entire load as the requests are now redirected to the server.

It is possible to operate the *clustered database* in a switchover fashion so that when one database server fails, the other one takes over as the database. You can also use load-balanced *LDAP servers* that are synchronized with each other so that both have the same structure and data. Finally, the TREX can be installed in high availability mode (this is discussed in a subsequent section of this chapter).

High Availability Solutions

In this section, we discuss the various options available to implement high availability such as switchover solutions, active versus passive clustering techniques, database clusters, and replication enqueue servers. High availability solutions are identified for components such as SAP Web AS Java, SAP Web AS ABAP, enqueue servers, Java instances, central services instance, databases, config folders, ICM, web server networks, network infrastructure components, and TREX.

Switchover Solutions

To implement high availability solutions, you can implement *switchover solutions* for the various critical SPOF components such as the Central Services instance, the database, and the SAP central file system. No matter how well you have designed the architecture by distributing the components and adding dialog instances, a true high availability solution requires at least one switchover solution.

Switchover solutions are helpful during both unplanned failures and planned maintenance downtimes. When a failure occurs, the switchover takes place from the components in one switchover group to another. Switchover solutions can also increase availability during planned downtimes because a particular node can be deliberately shut down for maintenance.

Components Involved in a Switchover Cluster

A switchover cluster typically consists of the following components:

- Two or more hosts for hosting the replicated software component
- Software for switching over to the other node when the failure occurs
- A mechanism that allows the system to work with the switched node by virtual identity or addressing

---

TIP *While designing a switchover solution, the clustered software components should be hosted preferably on the same operating system.*

Figure 7-2 shows how you can introduce redundant components to eliminate SPOF.

Active Clustering

In an *active clustering* setup, all the machines are running, and when one machine fails, the other machine takes over all the server processes from the failed machine for processing. The load balancer ensures that the requests are no longer forwarded to the failed machine. This setup provides you with the ability to increase the workload capabilities by adding additional servers. Some of the key features of this set up are *keep-alive implementation, load-distribution policies*, and *session-stickiness implementation.*

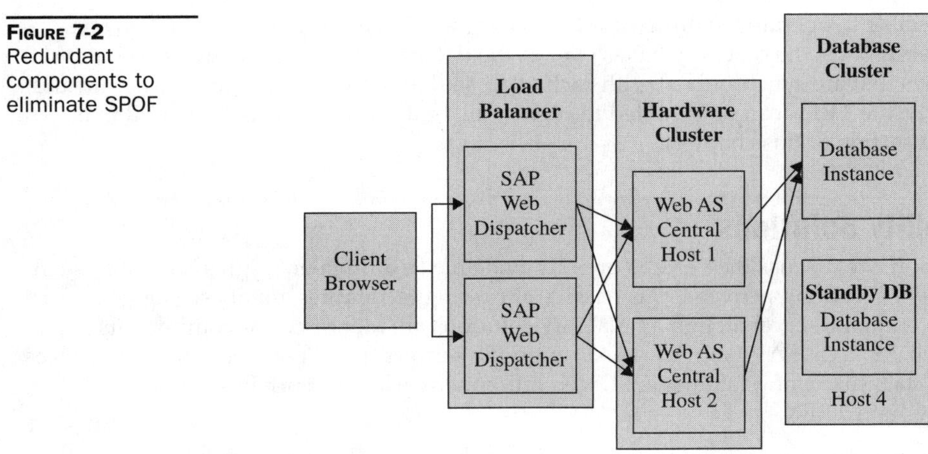

FIGURE 7-2 Redundant components to eliminate SPOF

NOTE *Active clustering is not only a high availability solution, but it's also a load-balancing setup.*

You need either a *software-based or a hardware-based load balancer* to distribute the client requests across the different servers in the cluster formation based on a load-distribution policy such as round-robin.

Also, because a portal is a *stateful application*, it is important that you have *session management* implemented with stickiness so that the subsequent client requests are always redirected to the same server or cluster node. This ensures that the client session information is not lost. Moreover, if one of the cluster nodes fails for whatever reason, the load balancer should be able to redirect the requests to the functioning server.

Passive Clustering

In the case of *passive clustering*, one machine is not running, and when the live machine fails, the passive machine takes over. For this to work, *switchover solutions* must be able to detect the failure and initiate the failover to the other passive machine. Some of the key features of this setup are *error detection/failover initiation, failover duration,* and *fallback initiation.* The issue with this setup, however, is that some delay occurs in the startup of the machine and all the server process information on the first machine is lost.

When a failure occurs in the active cluster node, the cluster software solution detects the error and then initiates the failover. During this process, all the processes that are running in the failed node are now transferred to the standby node. In this setup, the storage is shared between the nodes. So during the failover process, the ownership of the storage is transferred to the standby node. This kind of setup is often used for implementing high availability for databases.

NOTE *Passive clustering is a purely high availability solution, unlike the active clustering mode.*

Switchover Solution for SAP Web AS ABAP and Java

Refer to Figure 7-3, and note that under normal operating conditions, Node A has the central instance and the central services instance running and Node B has the database running.

When a failure occurs in Node B, the failover happens from Node B to Node A, so that both the server and the database both run on the same host—that is, Node A. A similar thing happens when Node A fails: the failover takes place from Node A to Node B, so that both the server and the database run on the same host.

For this configuration to work properly, you must configure *virtual IP addresses* and host names so that both the nodes appear as a single system. When one of the nodes fails, then the functioning node will be reconfigured with the virtual address of the cluster.

When the database fails on one node and it is restarted on the other machine, the application servers will then connect to the database automatically using the *database reconnect* feature.

The database reconnect feature could result in reduced performance; however, the main advantage with this setup is that you do not have to monitor the system manually and the failover occurs automatically, thus saving downtimes.

Another advantage with this cluster setup is that it helps to mask any OS- or hardware-related issues on any one machine. This is because if any of the hardware components fail in one of the cluster nodes, the failover is initiated to the other node. The failover, however, consumes a sufficient amount of time because the running applications have to be stopped and restarted.

PART II

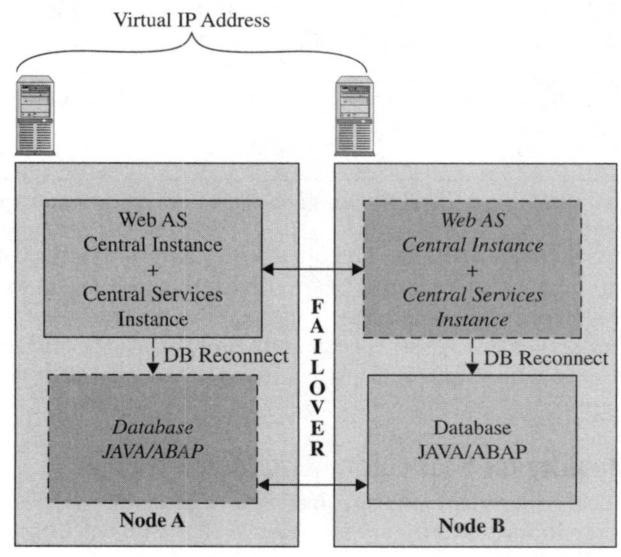

FIGURE 7-3 Microsoft Cluster server system for Windows

It is not recommended that you implement high availability for application servers using a switchover process, because a lot of resources are consumed. In such cases, distributing the dialog instances on multiple servers is used to achieve high availability. However, in such a design, when one application server fails, the client session will be lost and hence special measures must be taken to enable session failover.

The standard switchover solution available for SAP systems to set up this configuration is the Microsoft Cluster Server (MSCS) system for Windows platform. The failover mechanism is enabled by a cluster-aware version of the database management system and the MSCS software.

TIP *Please refer to OSS note* ***106275 from http://service.sap.com/notes*** *for more information.*

ON THE JOB *For SAP Web AS Java, it is recommended that the database and Server Central Services (SCS) instance be located in their own separate switchover groups. It is not recommended that the central instance, SAP Central Services instance, and database be in one switchover group. It is recommended that you separate the SCS instance from the central instance for better performance reasons.*

High Availability and Load Balancing Using Software Cluster

You can implement a highly available system by configuring a *software cluster* consisting of multiple Java instances, with each additional Java instance being installed on a separate host. If any of the Java instances fail, then the load-balancing solution dispatches the client request to another available instance. If any of the J2EE engine processes such as the server or the dispatcher fail, then the Java Startup and Control Framework restarts the process.

Figure 7-4 shows two Java instances, one of which is a central services instance with a message and enqueue service.

NOTE *A Java instance contains one Java Dispatcher but can contain more than one Java Server.*

Switchover software solutions can be used for components such as DBMS and central service components such as message services and enqueue services that are system-wide SPOF. However, for other components that are not system-wide SPOF, such as Java dialog instances and server processes, you can improve scalability and reduce unplanned downtimes simply by implementing a software cluster by adding multiple components (dialog instances and server processes).

High Availability for Standalone Enqueue Server

Another critical component that can affect SAP transactions is the *enqueue server*. When it fails, all the database locks held by it are lost. Hence all the transactions that did not commit must be aborted and rolled back before the enqueue server is restarted, and then the transactions should be re-executed after the restart. If not, database inconsistencies may occur.

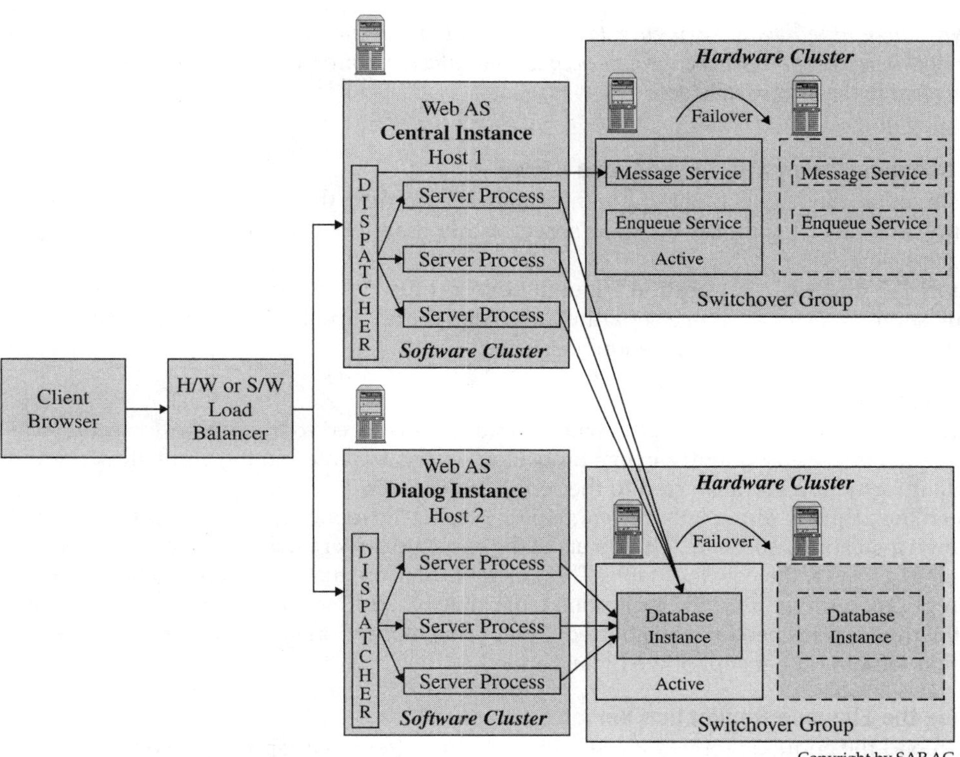

FIGURE 7-4 Switchover Software Solutions for DBMS and central service instance

Managing Infrastructure Locks

The enqueue server contains system-wide information regarding *infrastructure locks* pertaining to the instances. Starting from NetWeaver04 SP15 and NetWeaver 2004S SR1, the application lock service will detect whether these locks were lost, and this will result in a restart of the J2EE instances by the JControl process. This could result in loss of time affecting high availability. This issue is resolved by installing an optional enqueue replication server.

Separate Central Services Instance

Because the enqueue server is an SPOF in the system, and since the enqueue server is a part of the central services instance, the central services instance also becomes an SPOF in the system, unless some form of a high availability solution is implemented. Instead of having the entire central services instance with the enqueue and message server installed along with the central instance, you can have a slim central services instance that consists only of the enqueue and the message service. This way, it becomes possible to implement high availability solutions for the central services instance using the replication enqueue server, for example.

You can also implement high availability for the enqueue service using a switchover solution; however, a standalone replication enqueue server is preferred because the transactions open at the time of failure do not have to be rolled back.

Do *When designing the infrastructure, take care to ensure that the database and the SCS instances are kept in separate switchover groups because the database switchover is more intensive when compared to the SCS switchover.*

Direct Communication with the Enqueue Server

With this setup, the clients that require information regarding the enqueue locks will now communicate directly with the enqueue server rather than through the dispatcher and the message server.

Figure 7-5 displays a replication enqueue server setup. When you use a replication enqueue server, it is located on a separate host. All the individual application servers communicate separately with the enqueue server.

State Transfer Concept

Using the concept of *state transfer*, the whole table is transferred to the replication table from the enqueue table. Subsequently, every time a lock entry is created in the enqueue server, the delta information is transferred to the replication server.

When the enqueue server fails, the enqueue server on the replication server host is restarted by the high availability software. The restart of the enqueue server on the replication server enables it to generate the new lock table. The lock table data are transferred to the enqueue table on the replication server from the replication table; this way, the lock information is not lost and hence the transactions need not be aborted. Finally, the replication table is deleted and the replication server is either shut down or suspended.

Installing the Enqueue Replication Server

To download the enqueue replication server, go to http://service.sap.com/swdc and then choose Download | Support Packages and Patches | Entry by Application Group | Additional Components | SAP Kernel | SAP Kernel 32 BIT | SAP KERNEL 6.40 32 BIT | Windows Server on IA32 32bit | #Database Independent | INSENREP_2-20000182.SAR.

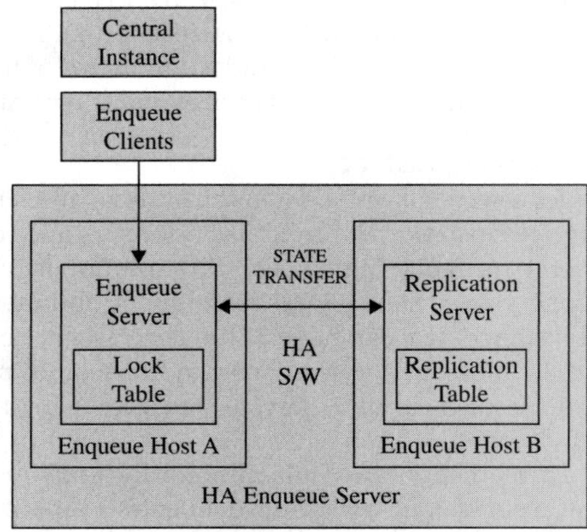

Figure 7-5 Replication enqueue server

TIP *The enqueue replication server can be installed directly from the SAPINST for NetWeaver 7.0 (2004s). Refer to OSS notes 729945, 768727, 804078, and 803018 from http://service.sap.com/notes to learn more about the automatic restart feature of the SAP startup framework for the MSG and the ENQ server.*

High Availability for Databases

Two options are available for protecting databases for high availability. In the first option, shown in Figure 7-6, a single database can run in a *cluster mode*, so that when one node goes down, the other node should start running. The problem with this setup is that if some transactions are running in the first node, these are lost in the second node in the cluster. To avoid the loss of such transactions, you may have to run the redo logs (queue of transactions) to recover the transactions. The user may have to re-execute the transactions manually. The second database system is a copy of the production database. You could use a standard switchover solution to set up such a high availability cluster.

Microsoft Cluster Server solution can be implemented for SQL Server in Windows to implement high availability. In this case, one database runs in a hardware cluster. The portal servers have only one access point to the database even though two cluster nodes exist. A shared storage system is placed between the two cluster nodes that is set up on RAID disks.

The advantage with MSCS is that the failover is rapid and automatic. This solution is supported by SAP and is the standard switchover solution for all SAP systems that run on Windows.

PART II

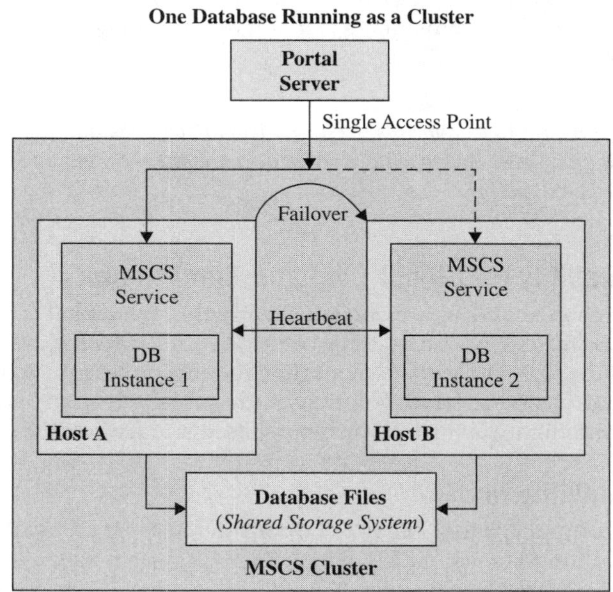

FIGURE 7-6 One database running as a cluster

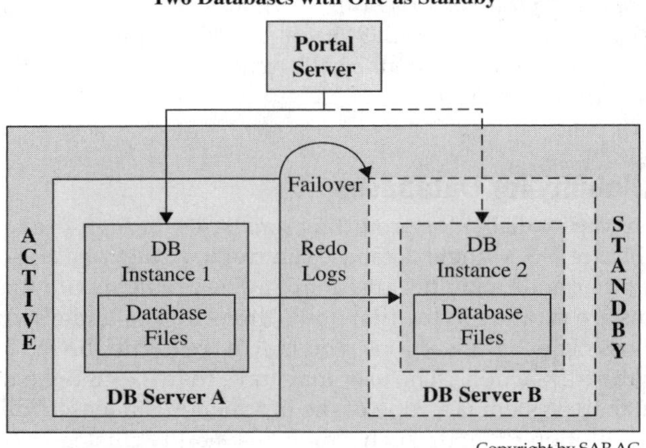

FIGURE 7-7 Two databases with one running as standby

In the second option, shown in Figure 7-7, two databases are used, so that when a failure occurs, data can be replicated from one database to the second database. In this case, all the transactions in the first database are also replicated into the second database. This option is known as the *standby option*. A copy of the production database is created on a standby host.

The standby database server is kept up to date by periodically shipping the backed-up redo logs from the primary to the standby database. When a failure occurs on the primary database, the standby database is brought online after running the appropriate transaction logs from the time of failure. This solution is more suited for avoiding data loss due to failure; however, the disadvantage is that it requires manual intervention after failure and the recovery is slow.

TIP *Another aspect to be remembered for high availability is that the portal licenses should be installed on at least two machines so that even if one machine fails, the license on the other machine is still active.*

High Availability for Global Configuration Directory

Another high availability feature is to ensure that the global configuration directory (/usr/sap/<*sid*>/global), which contains the config data for the Portal Content Directory (PCD) and the Content Management functionality, is set up for high availability. You can use third-party vendor–based solutions such as NFS file share, switchover-based cluster file solutions, and highly available hardware-based storage solutions.

High Availability for ICM

The other component that needs to be considered for high availability is the Internet Communication Manager (ICM), which the SAP system uses to communicate via HTTP, HTTPS, and SMTP. Usually, if the ICM fails, it is not an issue because it does not store any session information and hence only the active requests will be affected. Moreover, the ABAP dispatcher tries to restart the ICM.

High Availability for Server, Access, and Web Server Networks

To implement high availability for networks, you can use some hardware options such as redundant network providers, redundant routers, redundant hardware load balancers, hot standby firewalls, redundant switches, and redundant network access for servers by using redundant network cards. High availability solutions should also be considered for other network devices such as Domain Name System (DNS), mail systems, directory service, domain controllers, and so on.

Depending upon the criticality of the applications, high availability measures should be taken for the server and the access network. As shown in the following illustration, the server network is located between the application servers and the database servers. The access network, also known as the company network, lies between the clients and the application servers. You should have redundant adapters on the database and the application server hosts so that the physical network can still be used when one adapter fails. Critical servers should be connected to multiple physical subnetworks. A separate LAN should be available for the server network. To prevent the server from unplanned downtimes, you can implement options such as redundant power supply, redundant coolers, redundant bus, and additional pluggable components.

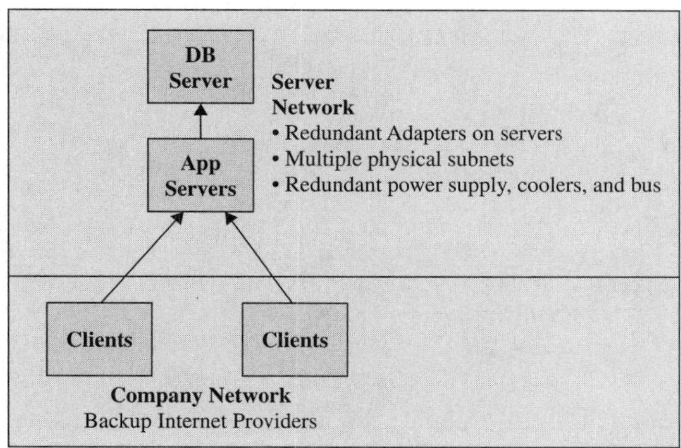

Copyright by SAP AG

The third type of network is the web server network, which consists of the web servers and load balancers such as web switches, SAP web dispatcher, and firewalls. High availability can be established for web servers and DMZs by introducing horizontal scalability. Horizontal scalability involves introducing additional components of the same design. When you add multiple web servers, you can implement load-balancing techniques using web switches, load-balancing servers, redirection, and round-robin DNS.

TIP *For load balancing across SAP Web AS, you can use SAP Web Dispatcher.*

High Availability at the Physical Level

High availability measures should be taken at both the physical and the network and transport layers for the networks. The physical layer includes the *network infrastructure,* consisting of the cabling and the active components such as hubs, switches, and routers; and *network interface cards* on the server and the clients through which all the network traffic passes.

To enable high availability on the NIC, you can either switchover to another backup machine when the NIC fails or switchover to a second NIC on the same machine. You can also use proprietary solutions that allow multiple NICs to be addressed using the same IP address, thus exploiting higher network capacity and reduced downtimes. At the level of the network layer, you can use special routing protocols for exchanging information about potential routes between various network nodes.

High Availability for TREX

Figure 7-8 displays a smaller version of the high availability setup of the TREX system. Here the indexes are replicated from the master to the slave system. So, even if the index server or the preprocessor fails, the slave machine takes over and offers increased workload capabilities.

Figure 7-9 displays a high-end solution in which even if one index server fails, the other one takes over. The TREX system has its own high availability features built in, so there is no need for any third-party solution.

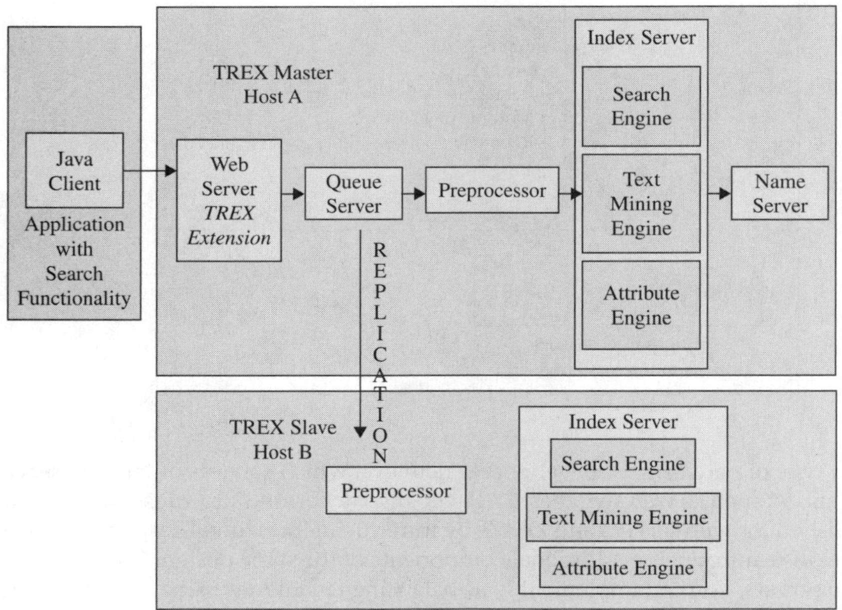

FIGURE 7-8 Highly available TREX system

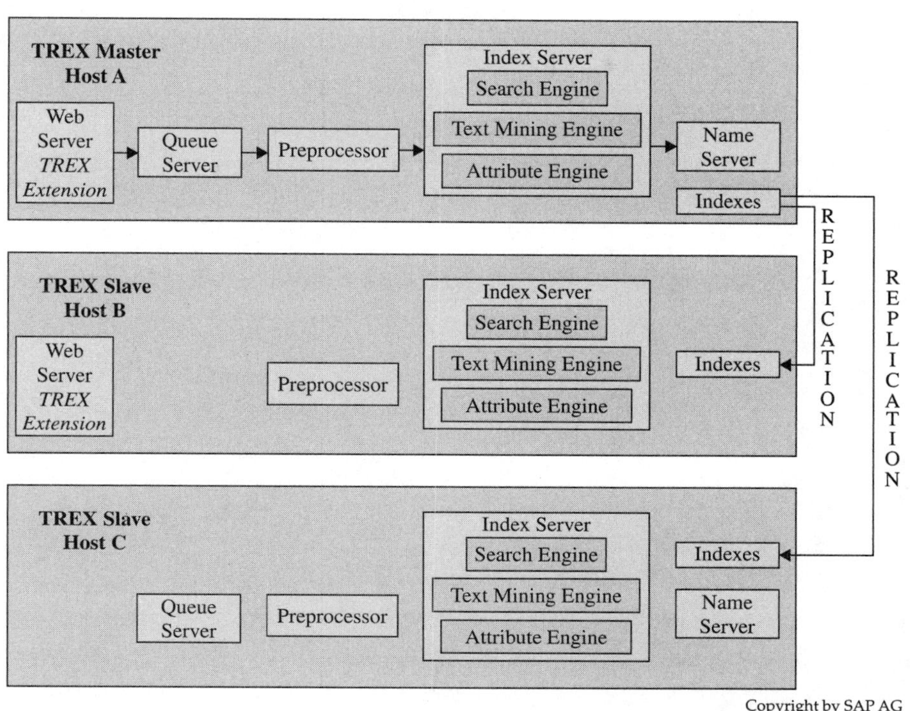

FIGURE 7-9 High-end high availability TREX system

NOTE *For more details, refer to the 'Technical Infrastructures of SAP Enterprise Portal 6.0' and other infrastructure related resources listed in Appendix B.*

Summary

This chapter covered the basic ingredients of a good technical infrastructure design for the portal and discussed in detail the high availability aspects of the infrastructure. You learned the importance of high availability for the portal, the causes of downtimes, and some of the key success factors for high availability. You also learned about some of the typical single points of failure in the portal architecture and the available options to implement high availability for those components. High-availability options such as implementing switchover solutions, active versus passive clustering techniques, database clusters, and replication enqueue servers were covered. The next chapter covers the scalability and sizing aspects of technical infrastructure design for the portal.

Summary

CHAPTER 8

Sizing and Scalability

Chapter 7 discussed the essential objectives required in planning and designing a good technical portal infrastructure and addressed some of the mechanisms available to implement high availability solutions for the portal from a system-wide perspective. This chapter addresses aspects related to scalability, and how to implement scalability by adopting techniques such as sizing and distribution of software and hardware components.

What Is Scalability?

A portal requires *scalability* to ensure that its performance is not affected by factors such as an increase in user population, the geographical distance of the users from the portal, an increase in the portal functionality, the number of objects in the portal content directory, or the size of data used in the KM application.

Scalability is important because by conducting appropriate load tests, you can determine aspects such as how many incoming HTTP requests can be processed in an hour, how many concurrent users can use the portal without significant performance degradation, and how many transactions can be executed in SAP R/3 from the portal.

One of the tasks that can be undertaken to ensure that a portal is scalable is adding new hardware, such as servers, RAM, and hard disks, to maintain the portal's performance at satisfactory levels for the end user with increasing loads. Implementing scalability also involves distributing the portal components to different physical machines so that enough resources are available.

Sizing for Performance and Scalability

An important part of portal infrastructure design is sizing the various components so that the requirements of performance and scalability are met under heavy load conditions. Sizing determines the hard disk, memory, CPU, I/O, and network load requirements so that the end user response time is satisfactory, with consideration for the cost to be incurred to procure those systems. The scope of sizing is to obtain results that provide management with the required information on the cost, time, and effort required to implement the portal functionality. The portal functionality could be implemented in phases over a certain period, say 2 to 5 years.

If the system has been sized adequately, then performance will not suffer when system load increases due to increased users, increased workload activity, and other factors. Considering that performance is such an important factor that decides the ultimate success or failure of a portal project, it is important that sizing of portal systems is done as early as possible during the project. This will allow you sufficient time to procure hardware for the project. Due to the dynamic nature of the factors that affect sizing, sizing should be treated as a continuous, iterative activity throughout the lifetime of the portal implementation project and beyond.

Do *Proper sizing ensures that the portal performance does not suffer due to increased load.*

The factors that influence sizing are portal software versions, database versions, operating system versions, and customer-related factors. Examples of customer-related factors are the number of users, the nature of users in terms of the intensity of use of applications, geographical distribution of users, the workload on the system, and the amount of customizing involved.

From a portal standpoint, factors that can affect sizing include the following:

- Number of top-level menus in top-level navigation (TLN)
- Number of nodes in the detailed navigation iView
- Number of images used when designing the pages
- Layout of the portal desktop and the portal framework page
- Number of iViews in the content area of the portal desktop
- Different types of iViews on the same page
- Number of Java iViews that use Java Connector Remote Function Call (JCO RFC)
- Number of iViews that fetch data from SAP and non-SAP backend systems
- Knowledge Management & Collaboration (KMC) platform iViews
- Custom navigation iViews and the programming model used to create those iViews
- Portal server-side caching and client-side caching, which results in a reduced number of round-trips and the consequent reduction in load
- Number of roles and groups created in the UME database
- Authentication method used to log on to the portal
- Number of concurrent users using the portal
- Think time between two successive clicks
- Distance between the portal server and the backend systems

It is important that you gather as much information as possible during the initial requirements gathering phase regarding the above sizing-related factors. A good understanding of these aspects will help you to choose the appropriate load tests to be conducted on the portal and ensure satisfactory performance after Go-Live.

Sizing at Different Project Stages

During the project preparation phase, *initial sizing* places emphasis on the technical feasibility aspects of the portal implementation. Considering that you do not have much information or a point of reference to measure portal performance, you cannot aim for accurate estimation of sizing during this stage.

During the initial project preparation phase, it is a good idea to install a prototype version of the portal on either a laptop or a desktop with 2 to 4GB RAM, greater than a 30GB hard disk, Windows 2000/2003 operating system with NTFS partition, and either MaxDB or Microsoft SQL Server 2000/2005. For the SQL server, you can use a Microsoft SQL Server 2000 or 2005, both of which are available for download for evaluation purposes on Microsoft's web site. You can even use the evaluation version of the NW portal that is available for download at https://www.sdn.sap.com/irj/sdn/downloads. Download the Java Trial Version, which is a complete package that contains the Application Server Java, SAP NetWeaver Portal, Content Management and Collaboration, TREX, and so on. Once you have installed the evaluation version, the portal database will be based on MaxDB, which is essentially a MySQL database. You can then install the business packages that meet your required functionality and conduct some basic performance testing. This prototype can also be used as a tool to get the end users acquainted with the out-of-the-box functionality and the look and feel of the portal. Once the realization phase of the portal implementation project commences, the portal development systems are in place, and this makes it possible to measure portal performance and benchmark it. So you can now conduct more expert sizing. *Expert sizing* can be carried out by having a single user carry out tasks on a test portal system so that the CPU, memory, and disk consumption can be captured.

Finally, the expert sizing results can be verified just before portal Go-Live and resizing can be undertaken if required. At the time of Go-Live, new users, roles, and content would have been added, and if additional components such as Knowledge Management (KM) and Business Intelligence (BI) have been implemented, resizing will indeed become necessary to get more accurate sizing. This is also true if business packages or custom content have been deployed on the portal. You can conduct load tests at a fraction (5 to 10 percent) of the planned load.

Sizing Techniques

Some of the following techniques can be employed for portal sizing:

- Questionnaires
- Benchmarks
- Expert sizing techniques such as Quick Sizer
- Portal performance tests

Do *When conducting sizing tests, you must decide ahead of time whether to size the systems based on* average load or peak load *on the portal.*

When sizing using the Quick Sizer, you can have three approaches: user-based sizing, throughput-based sizing, and customer performance–based sizing. For more information on the Quick Sizer tool, visit http://service.sap.com/quicksizer.

User-based sizing is usually done for initial sizing and is often less accurate than the other methods because there is limited information available regarding the project. It is also resorted to when there are not too many concurrent users using the system. User-based sizing can test the basic technical feasibility of the portal for initial budget planning.

User-based sizing considers the number of portal users and different types of users based on the *think times* (time elapsed between two successive user interaction steps). The different types of users, based on activity, are *high (power users), medium (knowledge workers),* and *low (information workers) activity users*. The think times between screen changes are around 10 seconds, 30 seconds, and 6 minutes, respectively, for high, medium, and low activity users. The think times, in your project, can vary and you should choose the correct values for the think times for your Quick Sizer analysis. This is an important step because this can distort your Quick Sizer sizing results, if not done properly. Examples of high activity users are customer service representatives who use the portal for customer interaction activities on a constant basis like creating sales orders, answering customer complaints, and so on. Medium activity users could be those working in the back-office such as sales representatives, who use the portal for regular activities like checking sales orders, purchase orders, and so on. Low activity users are larger in number and they log onto the portal maybe once a week or once a month.

When taking the number of users into account, you should only consider the users who are actively using the system during a predefined period of time. This is not the same as the number of named users in the portal, which can be a much larger number.

Throughput-based sizing is based on the workload on the portal and considers factors such as the number of incoming user requests during the day, the number of transactions to be processed, and so on. This method can be employed during the later stages of the portal when there is more information available regarding the applications that have been deployed and the usage levels on the portal.

Customer performance–based sizing is based on customer data and is useful when all the necessary customization and configuration have been completed in the portal. It is done during the final stages of the project before Go-Live. It provides more accurate results, but is expensive and considerably time-consuming.

Standard Application Benchmarks

To verify the portal performance and scalability, you can use the benchmark provided by SAP—*SAP Standard Application Benchmark (SAPS)* is used to identify a suitable hardware configuration for the portal solution based on the benchmarks that have been created by SAP. These benchmarks can be used to test the scalability and performance of the portal application, hardware components, and database.

The SAPS is available for various applications such as Enterprise Resource Planning (ERP), Supply Chain Management (SCM), Customer Relationship Management (CRM), Enterprise Portal (EP), and Product Lifecycle Management (PLM). SAPS is a hardware-independent measurement unit that can be used to derive equivalent sizing requirements by comparing the system loads and hardware configurations.

INFO 100 SAPS *is defined as the ability to process 2000 fully processed order line items per hour.*

SAP NetWeaver Portal Benchmarks

For SAP NetWeaver Portal, the performance benchmarks are available for the Employee Self-Services (ESS) and CRM scenarios. Using these benchmarks, you can compare the performances of various platforms, with the information obtained from testing for sizing the SAP system.

The SAP NetWeaver Portal benchmarks have been created purely for assessing the performance of the portal server. It focuses mainly on assessing the number of concurrent users that can be supported by the portal server when performing activities such as top-level navigation or calling backend applications.

The EP-ESS portal benchmark uses an employee role for testing scenarios such as recording working time, processing leave request, and displaying leave request overview, personal data, and addresses.

The EP-PCC (people-centric CRM) portal benchmark uses a sales representative role for testing scenarios such as displaying activities, account management, and acquisition.

A typical SAPS conducted for a portal will contain information on the following:

- Whether it is an EP-ESS or EP-PCC benchmark
- Who cond… nd when
- Numb… users
- Av… me
- … on steps per hour

… n information such as the operating system, … se, NetWeaver platform release, number of

… sizing. Click on Start the Quick … ick Sizer. Enter a name in the … t appears as shown in the … tform and Communication, … alue of 220 appears in the … CPU and disk size

I…

Copyright by SAP AG

You can see that on the left navigational menu, the Quick Sizer provides a number of business scenarios, such as CRM and SCM, for which you can calculate the sizing requirements. On the left navigational menu, navigate to Tree of Elements | SAP Business Solutions | SAP NetWeaver | SAP NetWeaver | Portal. You will see a screen as shown in the illustration below, where you can select the different portal scenarios and usage patterns for each scenario. The different portal scenarios that are available are given below:

- **NW-EP-URL** NetWeaver Portal for launching back-end transactions using URL iViews
- **NW-EP-INT** NetWeaver Portal for Intranet scenarios
- **NW-EP-PCC** NetWeaver Portal for People-centric CRM (PCC) scenario
- **NW-EP-PRT** NetWeaver Portal for custom scenario

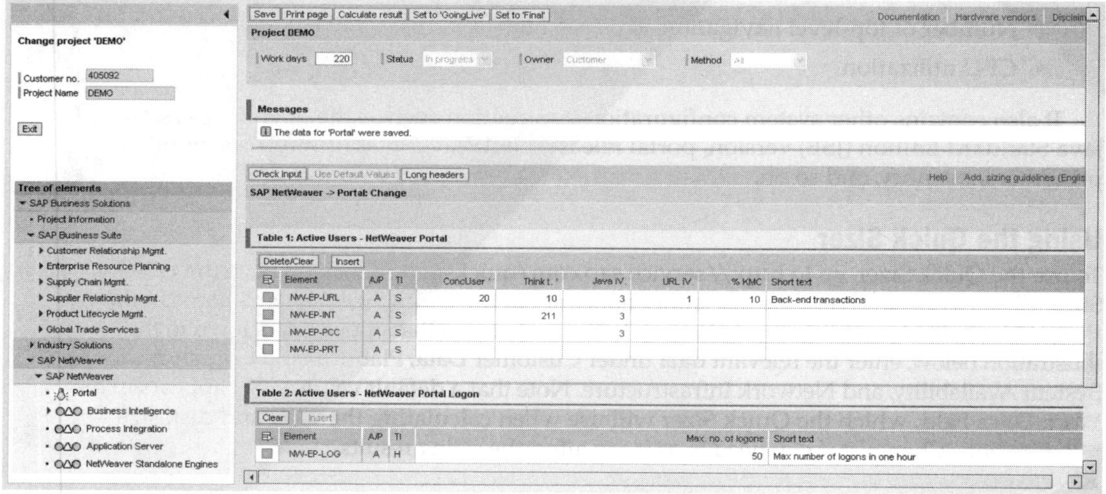

Choose the relevant portal scenario and in the ConcUser field, enter the number of concurrently active users. In the Think t field, enter the average think time in seconds. In the Java iV field, enter the number of Java iViews on an average portal page. In the URL iV field, enter the number of URL iViews on an average portal page. In the %KMC field, enter the value for number of requests for KMC in percentage.

In the Max. No. of Logons under the Table 2: Active Users - NetWeaver Portal Logon section, enter the value for the highest number of users who log on per hour. After entering all the relevant details, click Save and then click Calculate Result. The Quick Sizer results will appear as shown in the illustrations below.

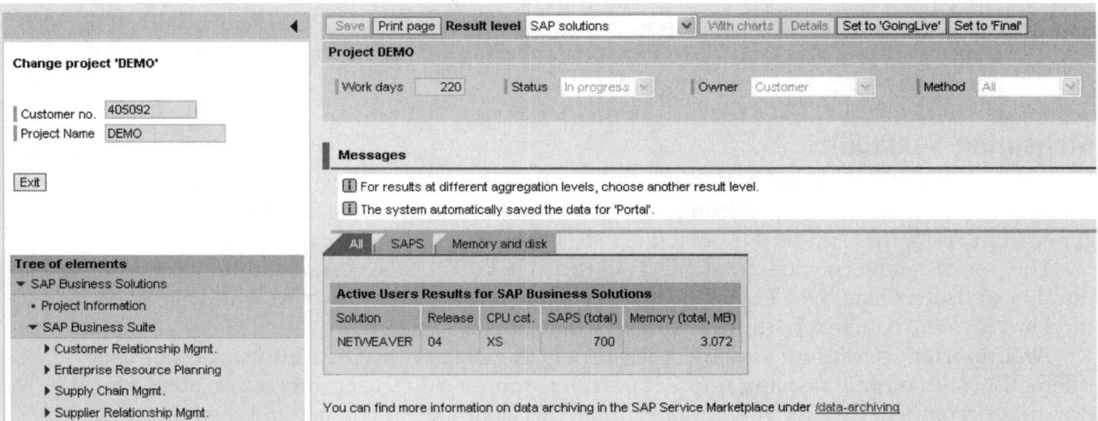

Note that the Quick Sizer results are 700 SAPS for CPU power, and 3GB RAM for memory. At the top, you can view the results at different levels such as the following:

- Project
- SAP Solutions
- Software Components
- Key Capabilities
- Sizing Elements
- Line Results + Inputs
- Results, Statistics, Inputs

Let us choose the option Results, Statistics, Inputs in the Result level dropdown. The results will appear as shown in this illustration.

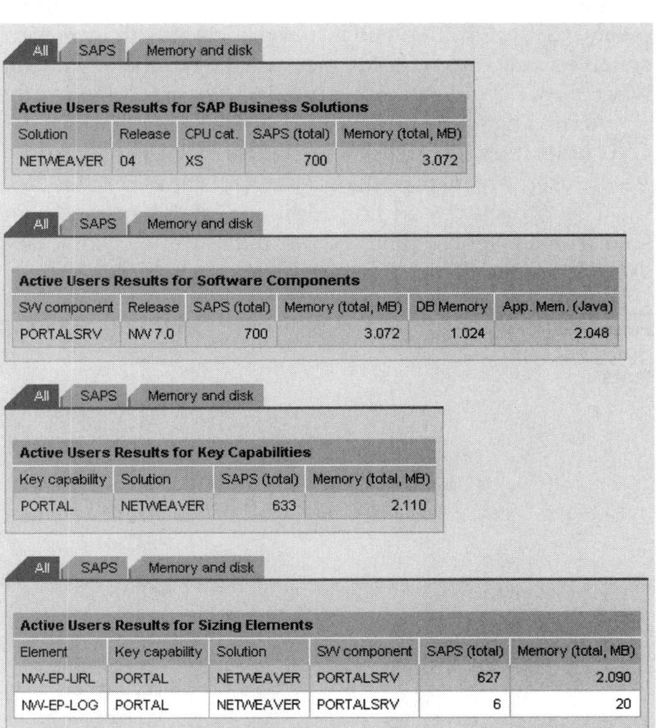

Solution	Release	CPU cat.	SAPS (total)	Memory (total, MB)
NETWEAVER	04	XS	700	3.072

Active Users Results for Software Components

SW component	Release	SAPS (total)	Memory (total, MB)	DB Memory	App. Mem. (Java)
PORTALSRV	NW 7.0	700	3.072	1.024	2.048

Active Users Results for Key Capabilities

Key capability	Solution	SAPS (total)	Memory (total, MB)
PORTAL	NETWEAVER	633	2.110

Active Users Results for Sizing Elements

Element	Key capability	Solution	SW component	SAPS (total)	Memory (total, MB)
NW-EP-URL	PORTAL	NETWEAVER	PORTALSRV	627	2.090
NW-EP-LOG	PORTAL	NETWEAVER	PORTALSRV	6	20

Do *Once the Quick Sizer calculations have been completed, you can provide the project and customer numbers to the hardware vendor to identify the optimum hardware configuration.*

Note that the Quick Sizer results will help you to get an initial idea of the required system hardware, but you should then consult with the hardware vendor to get a more accurate estimate of your required system hardware. In general, a 2 CPU machine with 4GB RAM can support around 500 users, but the actual performance will vary depending upon factors specific to your portal implementation.

Measuring Scalability

You can test the stability and scalability of the portal by adding new hosts that contain additional J2EE instances. By adding additional hosts, you can measure the number of concurrent users that can be supported on the portal.

The portal can be considered stable as long as the CPU usage is constant for a certain number of users. Once the CPU usage reaches a maximum value, you can add hosts and then increase the concurrent number of users that can be supported.

An important part of measuring scalability is to measure the CPU utilization per user interaction step with increasing number of concurrent users. A user interaction step, for example, occurs when a user initiates navigation by clicking the menu bar and then displaying an iView. The value of the CPU utilization per user interaction step should remain a constant even with increasing concurrent users. While the CPU utilization step remains constant, the overall CPU utilization will increase linearly with increasing concurrent users. To arrive at a suitable sizing data, you can measure the number of concurrent users that can be supported when the CPU utilization is around 65 percent, provided the response time is also linear.

According to the measurements shown in the chart in Figure 8-1, you can see that the CPU utilization increases almost linearly with an increase in the number of concurrent users. As the users are increased, once the CPU limit reaches around 65 percent, you can increase the CPU capacity by adding additional dialog instances and continue testing. You can also see that the response time is linear initially and becomes exponential once the CPU utilization exceeds around 65 percent.

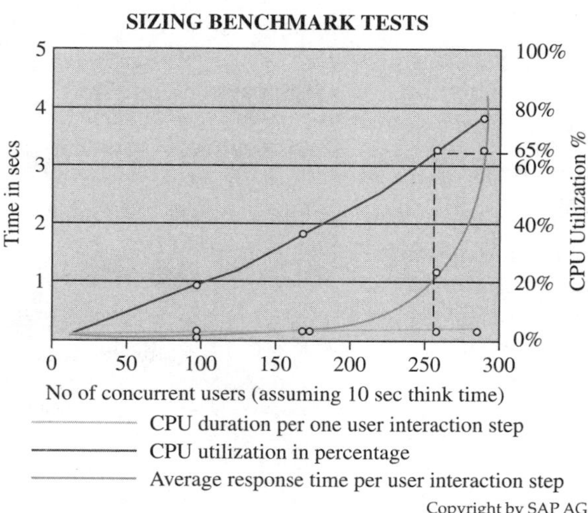

FIGURE 8-1 Sizing benchmark tests

TIP *When determining the scalability, you should consider only the linear section of the response time curve.*

The *response time* is measured for every user interaction step, which could be a portal navigation step such as clicking the navigation menu followed by displaying iViews. The *think time* is the time elapsed between two successive user interaction steps. It is interesting to note that the CPU utilization per user interaction step remains a constant with increase in concurrent users, which is an indication of stability and scalability.

In Figure 8-1, for 65 percent utilization per user interaction step, the number of users is around 260. Hence you can say that the portal is sized for 260 concurrent users.

Implementing Scalability

You can implement scalability using vertical scaling, horizontal scaling, or both.

Vertical Scaling

Vertical scaling, also known as *scale-in*, involves installing multiple dialog instances on the same physical machine, as shown in Figure 8-2. The number of additional dialog instances that can be installed in a host will depend upon the hardware capacity of the host.

The entire central instance, the central services instance, and the dialog instances are installed in one big machine. This is possible if enough processors are available and memory is adequate, as in the case of UNIX machine. The problem with this configuration is that you cannot use the same ports for all the dispatchers, because a port can be used only once for a given machine. Moreover, you need to have a load balancer in front of the machine because you have more than one Java dispatcher and the load needs to be balanced between them. Each Java dispatcher is usually attached to one server process only.

NOTE *Vertical scaling is easier to implement when compared to horizontal scaling.*

FIGURE 8-2 Vertical scaling with multiple dialog instances on the same host

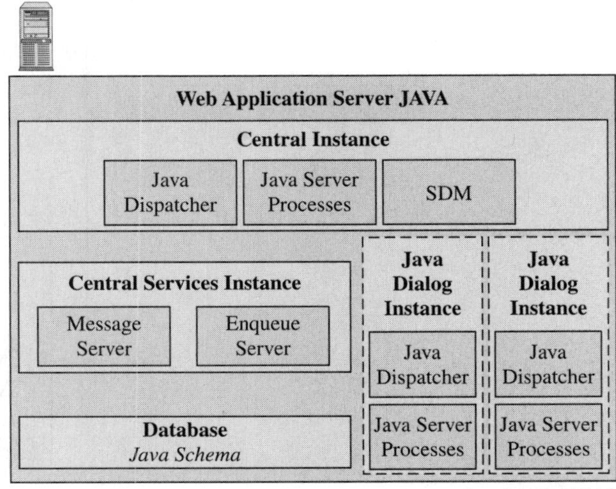

Horizontal Scaling

Horizontal scaling, also known as *scale-out,* involves installing additional dialog instances on separate physical machines. This obviously involves more effort and cost, but it is possible to implement high availability for the application server processes, in addition to implementing scalability.

Combining Vertical and Horizontal Scalings

Even if scale-in techniques are employed, the central services instance, the dispatcher, and the host itself are still single points of failure. To resolve this, you can employ a combination of scale-in and scale-out techniques. Adding new server processes within a host is a scale-in technique, while adding new dialog instances on a separate host is a scale-out technique. Figure 8-3 displays an example showing both scale-in and scale-out techniques. In the figure, the scale-out technique has been adopted by having multiple Java instances on two separate hosts and the scale-in technique is implemented by having multiple server processes for each Java instance in each host.

In Figure 8-3, you would still need a load balancer to distribute the client requests between the two dispatchers. This load balancer now remains a single point of failure. So the load balancer needs to be set up in a high availability mode using clusters if this needs to be a high availability system.

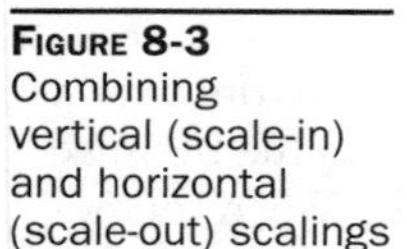

FIGURE 8-3 Combining vertical (scale-in) and horizontal (scale-out) scalings

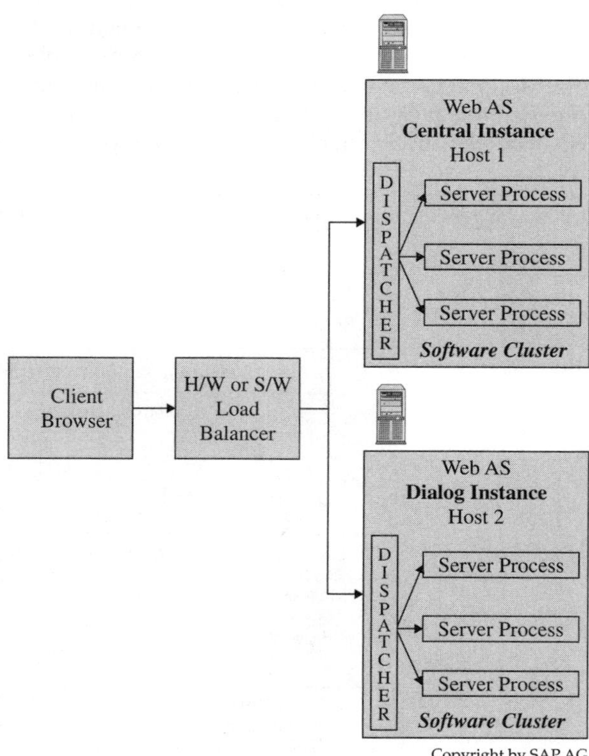

Minimal Portal Installation: Central Installation

Now let's discuss how you can design the system using scale-in and scale-out techniques. The minimal portal installation is the *central installation*, in which all the components such as the *portal platform* and the *TREX components* are installed in one host. This is shown in Figure 8-4.

The portal platform consists of the portal database, the SAP NetWeaver Application Server Java server, the central instance, the central services instance, the portal server, and content management components. Each of these components can be installed in a separate host if necessary.

The TREX is composed of the web server, index server, preprocessor, queue server, and the name server. In this case also, the individual components can be installed on a separate host. However, for a central installation, all the TREX components are installed on the same host.

This is not suitable for a productive system, because all the components are competing for the system resources. As a result of this, performance is likely to suffer. Moreover, implementing firewall security and high availability is also difficult in such a configuration.

NOTE Scaling-in *means adding another dialog instance on the same machine and* scaling-out *means adding another dialog instance on a different machine.*

Scale-In Options

Several options are available when implementing scale-in techniques.

Maximum Number of Nodes

The maximum number of nodes that can be installed in a cluster is 32, which includes the dispatcher and the server nodes. A maximum of 20 to 24 application server nodes can be used in the cluster. It would be reasonable to expect the system to be scalable in a linear fashion with additional cluster nodes.

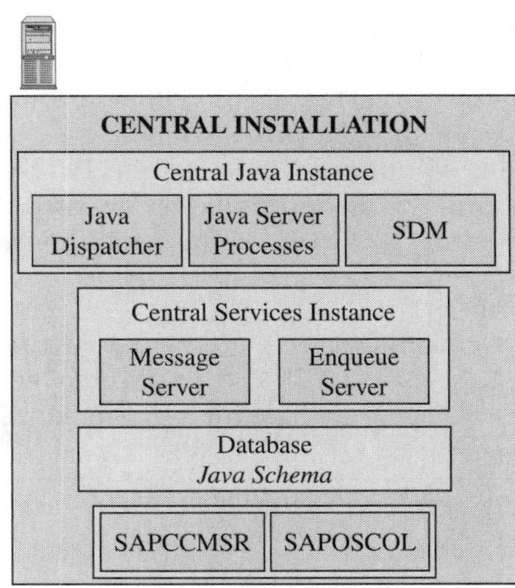

FIGURE 8-4 Minimal portal installation: central installation

Adding Server Processes vs. Dialog Instances

The NetWeaver Application Server Java system can handle 40 threads, by default, when processing requests. If all the threads are active most of the time, it may be helpful to add server processes. If the server processes are active all the time and if the host machine cannot hold additional server processes (usually 2GB for one server process), you would have to add dialog processes on a separate machine.

It should be noted that the system is not necessarily scalable with more CPUs. The application node scales well for up to two CPUs, but doubling that to four CPUs does not necessarily double the capacity of the portal servers. Instead, an additional server node can be created, provided of course enough RAM is available.

Distribution of Dispatchers, Server Nodes, and Central Service Instances

Various distributions of dispatchers, server nodes, and central services instances are possible based on the fact that you can have a maximum of 32 nodes in the Java cluster.

If you have 2 CPU machines, you can have 1 dispatcher and 1server on each host. So you can go up to 15 hosts, considering that you can have a maximum of 32 nodes. One host may contain an additional central services instance and another may contain a backup central services instance. In this scenario, you will have a total of 15 dispatchers and 15 server nodes. For 4 CPU machines, each machine can have 1 dispatcher and 2 servers. So you can have up to 10 hosts, giving a total of 30 nodes with 10 dispatchers and 20 dispatchers.

If you have 8 CPU machines, you can have each host contain 1 dispatcher and 4 server nodes. This configuration allows you to have 6 hosts totaling 6 dispatchers and 24 server nodes, leaving the remaining 2 nodes for the central services instance.

Scale-Out Approach: Distributing Components

Figure 8-5 displays a typical distributed system. The most common design is to install the database on a different system and the central instance on a separate machine. Then, if you need to expand the system, you can add dialog instances, preferably on separate machines.

Each machine has only one dialog instance and hence only one Java dispatcher; this means that the same port can be used for the Java dispatchers across different machines. Each Java dispatcher can be associated with more than one server process, and the advantage is that each machine can be sized depending upon the number of server processes that are running.

Once you install dialog instances, you will have to consider *load balancing* the server processes using components such as SAP Web Dispatcher. In this scenario, it is possible to set up high availability solutions on the database. Performance is also improved because you have multiple systems with additional resources. However, the disadvantage with this setup is that implementing and maintaining it requires more effort.

Production Installation

For a production system, it is recommended that you install a *distributed system*, where you can have a separate host for the TREX server. Moreover, the portal database should be installed preferably on a separate host for a production system.

Do *Make sure that the operating systems of the portal server and the database are compatible.*

Figure 8-5 Distributed system

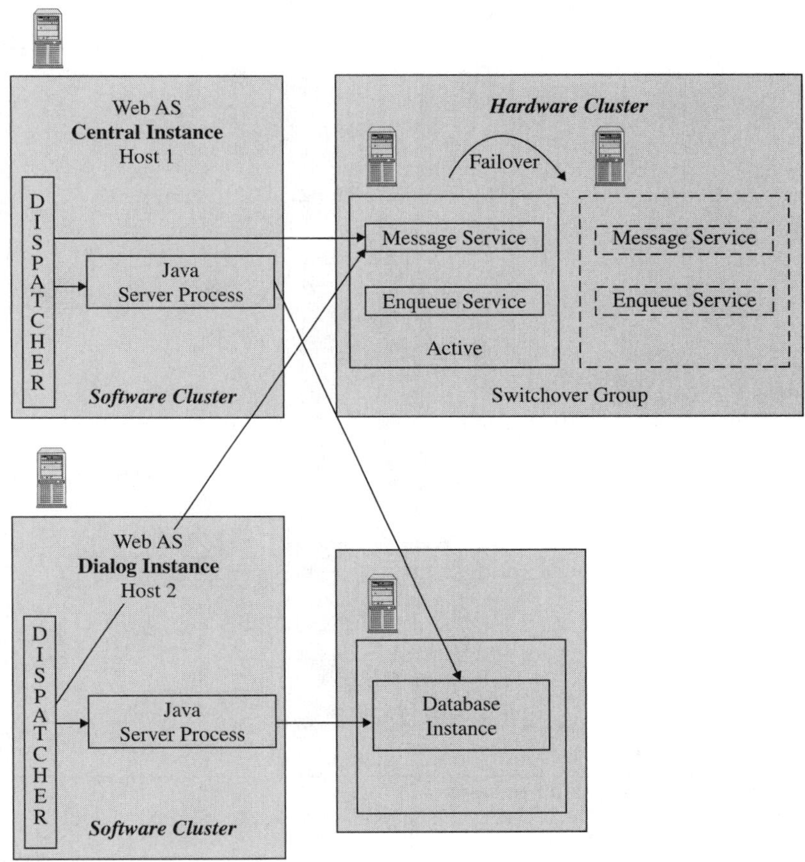

In the case of the distributed system shown in Figure 8-6, you can usually start with the database on a different system and the central instance on a separate machine. Then, when you need to expand the system, you can add dialog instances, preferably on separate machines.

With dialog instances, you will need to load balance the server processes, so you will have to use the SAP Web Dispatcher. In addition, when you have more than one server process, the J2EE application should be able to run on more than one server process—in other words, a clustered setup.

OSS notes

Following are OSS notes that can be accessed at http://service.sap.com/notes:

- **904620** Incorrect display of Quick Sizer entries
- **761489** TREX 6.1: Requirements and Recommendations

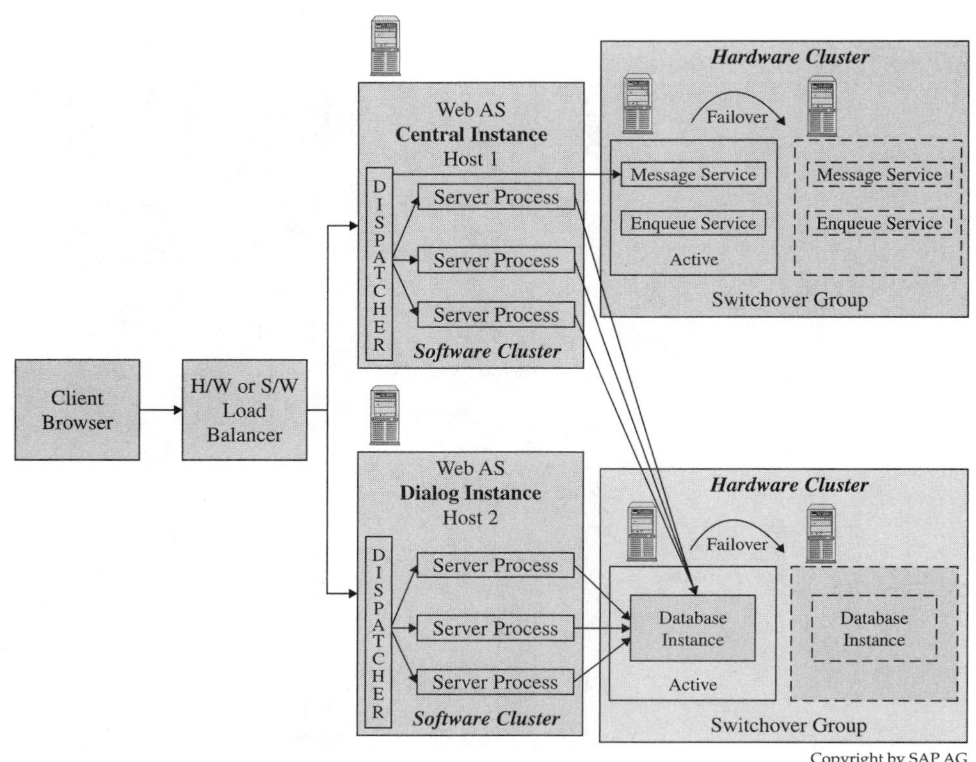

FIGURE 8-6 Production system: distributed setup

NOTE *For more details, refer to the sizing and scalability related resources listed in Appendix B.*

Summary

This chapter discussed the importance of scalability and the factors affecting scalability, including how to size the system so that the performance of the portal is not affected with increase in system load due to increased usage and new functionality on the portal. You learned about the different types of sizing and when to use them during the different phases of the portal implementation project. You read about different sizing techniques such as Quick Sizer, and concepts such as SAP Portal Performance Benchmarks based on SAPS that can be used for sizing. You also learned how to use the Quick Sizer for sizing in the Enterprise Portal scenario. The chapter also looked at how to measure scalability and finally explored different vertical and horizontal scaling techniques that can be adopted when planning the portal infrastructure for scalability and performance.

9

CHAPTER

Web Infrastructure Components

This chapter discusses the various components of the web infrastructure and analyzes how you can design these components while keeping in mind such design aspects as session stickiness, load balancing, and encryption. After reading this chapter, you will learn how implementing session stickiness and load balancing conflicts with encryption. You will also take a look at the SAP Web dispatcher and learn how to install it.

Technical Requirements of Web Infrastructure

Web infrastructure deals with the components such as the web server, load balancer, SAP Web Dispatcher, and the reverse proxy that resides between the client browser and the portal server. These Web infrastructure components are the first point of contact with the public Internet. They shield the portal server and the other backend systems from the outside world. As a result of their unique position in the system architecture, while designing the technical infrastructure for the portal, you need to consider a number of factors such as the following:

- **High Availability** High availability (HA) of the web infrastructure components
- **Load Balancing** Load balancer should be easily configurable and should support HA solutions
- **Encryption** Encryption is required, which often conflicts with load-balancing techniques
- **Session Stickiness** Business transactions demand the need for session management
- **Performance** The Web infrastructure components should have enough CPU processing power to support enterprise class web applications
- **Web Content** Web content handling, most of which is dynamic information
- **Application and Network Security** Both application and network security should be carefully designed considering that these components are located between the public Internet and the company's secure backend systems

- **Network architecture** Use of HTTP/HTTPS, reverse proxies, and firewalls should be reviewed taking into consideration the company's security policy
- **Integrate-ability** Integration of the web components into the existing infrastructure
- **Cost** Cost of installing web infrastructure components

Session stickiness, load balancing, and encryption are the most important among these considerations. Chapter 42 deals with network security. Part VII deals with security in detail, addressing authorization, authentication, and SSL topics. Let us now see how these three factors interplay with each other.

Session Stickiness

Because the user session is stored on a particular application server or dialog instance, session stickiness must be maintained. *Session stickiness* ensures that the requests are routed to the same application server for a specific user session so that the application server will have access to all the data relevant to that user when processing across multiple requests for a given user session. Session stickiness is an important requirement, especially for business class enterprise applications, such as B2B and CRM, that are web enabled.

Techniques for Session Stickiness

Session stickiness can be based on session ID, such as the following:

- URL session IDs (jsessionid)
- Logon ticket or cookie parameters
- IP address of the client
- Cookies inserted by the load balancer into the client requests

Issues with Implementing Session Stickiness

Several issues and challenges are associated with implementing session stickiness using techniques mentioned earlier. Implementing session stickiness often conflicts with the other requirements of the web infrastructure, such as high availability, performance, encryption, and load balancing. A better understanding of these conflicts will help you when choosing the right combination of web infrastructure components during the technical infrastructure design phase so that your specific business requirements like high availability, performance, security, and so on are adequately met.

Cookie Method When you implement the Secure Sockets Layer (SSL), you need to encrypt and decrypt the request, and this will interfere with implementing session stickiness. For example, the cookie method for implementing session stickiness does not work with SSL, because you cannot read the cookie information as it is encrypted.

TIP *Using the cookie method for implementing session stickiness conflicts with SSL.*

Client IP Address When using the client IP address for tracking a user session, SSL works fine. However, the problem with using a client IP address for session tracking is that it is not scalable, as the number of users connected using the same proxy server increases. All the users connecting through the same proxy server, which is often the case with intranets, will be treated as having the same IP address and hence will be routed to the same application server. This means that the load-balancing functionality completely fails.

TIP *Using a client IP address for session stickiness interferes with load-balancing functionality.*

If an Internet service provider (ISP) uses load balancing across multiple proxy servers, the same client will be accessing the portal server through multiple IP addresses of the proxy servers, even for the same user session. In such cases, this technique will fail. Another issue is that the load balancer cannot distinguish between requests arriving for stateful or stateless applications.

TIP *SSL can affect portal performance due to the need for encryption. You should assess the possibility of using* SSL accelerators.

Third-Party Authentication Solutions When authentication techniques using third-party solutions such as Netegrity SiteMinder or Entrust GetAccess are used, you should ensure that the session management and data encryption in the application are not compromised. Sometimes, it may be necessary to implement early authentication using third-party solutions before the request reaches the portal server. In such cases, you may have to terminate SSL by decrypting the request so that authentication can proceed.

TIP *Using third-party authentication techniques may result in SSL termination.*

End-to-End Security Proper design may necessitate including a DMZ setup when the portal is accessed from the public Internet. Load-balancing solutions act as terminators for SSL, meaning the request needs to be decrypted for the load balancer to route the requests to the appropriate dialog instance or application server. Sometimes the load balancer may be used to authenticate the user against a corporate LDAP, which also requires that the request be decrypted. This can result in the communication between the load balancer and the server to be non-encrypted in pure text form.

In order to implement end-to-end security, the communication channel between the client browser and the server should be encrypted. However, this is not the case when a load balancer is used because this results in SSL termination, as discussed above. This conflicts with the concept of end-to-end security.

Load Balancing

When you have multiple application servers, you need a device that provides a single point of access to all those servers. This single point of access is the load balancer. The clients can then access the load balancer using a single IP address or URL. This also results in reduced maintenance because one server certificate installed on the load balancer is sufficient to enable SSL.

Load-Balancing Options

When implementing load balancing, you can either implement the *client-side* or the preferred *server-side* load balancing method. You should also explore the need for *functional load balancing* based on a URL. While discussing load-balancing techniques, you should make the choice between "SAP Web Dispatcher" and external load-balancing solutions such as Cisco.

Message Server–Based Client-Side HTTP Load Balancing

As shown in Figure 9-1, the client requests are directed to a particular message server by including the port. The message server receives the URL and redirects it to a dialog instance.

NOTE *This is not a preferred method and is included here for the sake of completeness.*

The message server chooses the appropriate application server based on the load on the application server and the number of users who are logged on. The message server also chooses the ABAP or the Java instance based on the type of application for which the request has been made.

If the user bookmarks the site, and then tries to access the site using that bookmark, the site may appear down if that dialog instance is down, even though other dialog instances are still available. It may also be confusing to the users when they see that the URL is different from the one that they entered initially.

Because now the user can access the individual application servers, you need to install a server certificate on every individual application server, which adds to the cost and administrative efforts.

If firewalls are used, the redirection will not work unless the reverse proxy is configured appropriately.

It is likely that the message server may get overloaded with increasing client requests, while its primary job is to manage the cluster within the Web Application Server (WAS).

However, this type of load balancing is easy to implement. This solution is more suited for an intranet setup.

SAP Web Dispatcher–Based One-Level Load Balancing

As shown in Figure 9-2, the load balancer is placed in front of the WAS. Unlike the previous scenario, the client requests are submitted to the load balancer and not the message server. So the load balancer redirects the incoming client requests to the appropriate dialog instances and the central instance based on the processing capability of the instances.

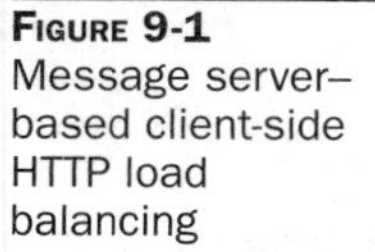

FIGURE 9-1 Message server–based client-side HTTP load balancing

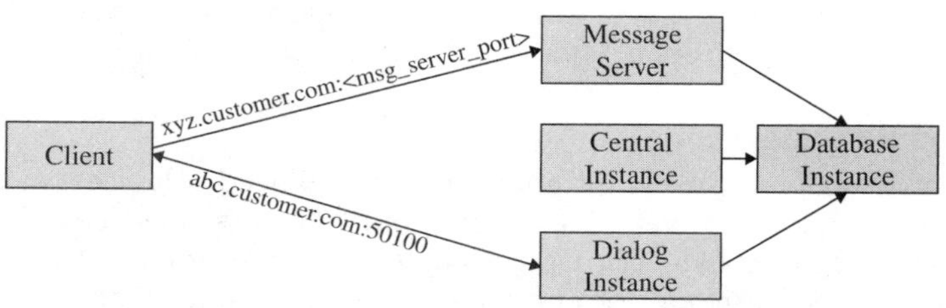

Client accesses portal using xyz.customer.com:<msg_server_port>, but the message server redirects it to abc.customer.com:50100 based on the load

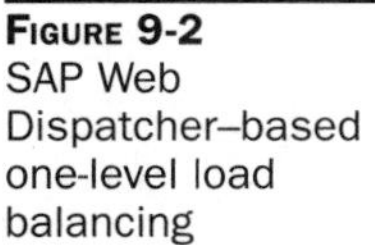

Figure 9-2 SAP Web Dispatcher–based one-level load balancing

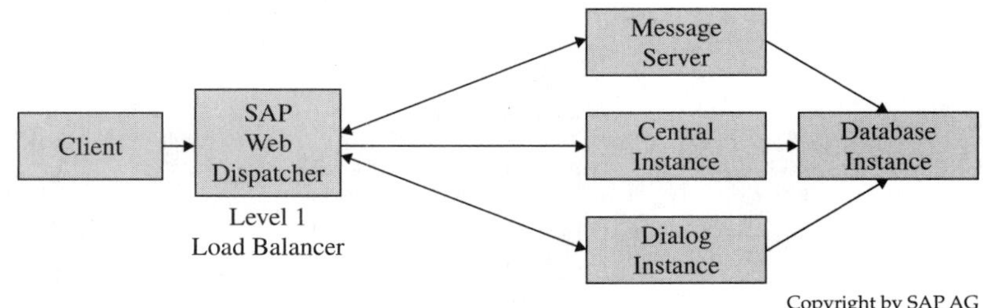

If SAP Web Dispatcher is used as the load balancer, it uses the message server for retrieving the configuration and system administration data of the cluster and forwards the request to the appropriate application server.

SAP Web Dispatcher SAP Web Dispatcher is delivered free of charge by SAP. It supports cookie and URL rewriting features for session handling. It supports re-encryption if SSL termination occurs and supports end-to-end security. The job of the SAP Web Dispatcher is to send the HTTPS request to the appropriate application server based on a session cookie. If the request contains a session cookie, it sends the request to the correct application server based on the cookie content. If there is no session cookie, it compares the URL prefix with the URL mapping table.

Note *SAP Web Dispatcher is a software load balancer that supports up to 3000 hits per second.*

The SAP Web Dispatcher uses a profile file for startup and other configuration parameters. It needs the following information for its operation:

- The port at which it should receive the HTTP(s) requests (icm/server_port_<x>)
- The host at which it should receive the HTTP(s) requests (rdisp/mshost)
- The port at which it can access the message server (ms/http_port)

It is not recommended that you install the SAP Web Dispatcher on the central instance, because it could result in a heavy load on the system due to SSL termination. Moreover, the central instance must always be available to the client. One way to avoid this issue is to install SAP Web Dispatcher as a high availability solution. This is discussed in a subsequent section "SAP Web Dispatcher" in this chapter.

URL-Based One-Level Functional Load Balancing

As shown in Figure 9-3, load balancing is accomplished based on the functionality requested in the URL. For example, if the request is for application A, the load balancer will direct the requests to particular server nodes or dialog instances, and if the request is for application B, the request is directed to a different set of dialog instances.

Functional load balancing can be achieved by using SAP Web Dispatcher with respective login groups or by using third-party solutions such as Cisco. The load balancer should be able to read the incoming request, and if SSL is used, it must be able to decrypt the message. This results in SSL termination at this point.

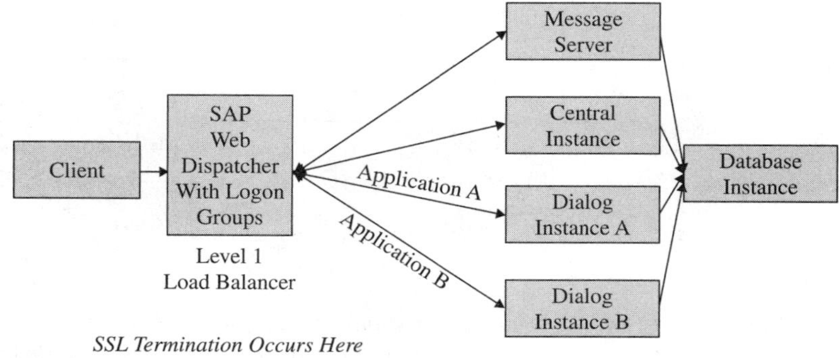

FIGURE 9-3 URL-based one-level load balancing

If SAP Web Dispatcher were the load balancer, it would determine a group of servers that could handle the request based on the detail from any application server. Once it determines the server, it would then dispatch the request to the Internet Communication Manager (ICM) of that application server.

Reverse Proxy–Based One-Level Load Balancing

You can have a reverse proxy included along with the one-level load balancing, as shown in Figure 9-4. This may be needed for security reasons such as the need for setting up a DMZ-based architecture and the need for hiding the actual URLs from the end user. It may also be needed because of authentication methods that are in use.

NOTE *Reverse Proxy enables setting up a DMZ-based architecture and hides actual URLs from end user.*

Advantages of Using a Reverse Proxy The *reverse proxy* helps to separate the LAN from the WAN. To the user, the reverse proxy represents the site itself and helps to prevent the user from accessing the Enterprise Portal (EP) directly. The idea is that instead of allowing the

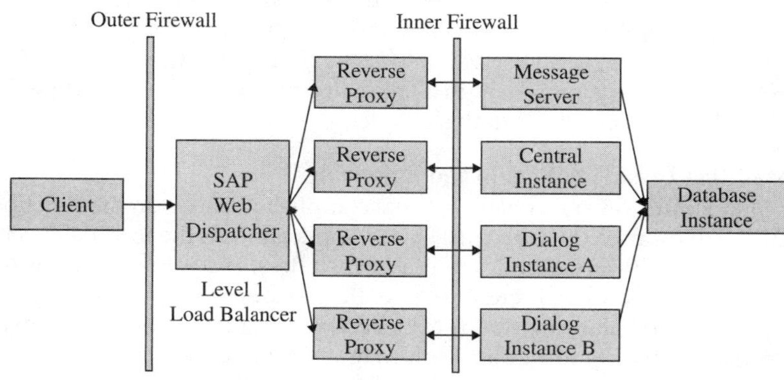

FIGURE 9-4 Reverse proxy–based one-level load balancing

user to access the portal directly, you place the reverse proxy in the DMZ and then allow the reverse proxy to access the EP and other backend servers. The inner firewall ensures that only the reverse proxy can access the EP and the backend servers. The difference between the forward proxy and reverse proxy is that the forward proxy is a proxy to the client, while a reverse proxy is a proxy to the server.

Another advantage is that you only need to open port 80 for the users to access the portal, because they will now be accessing the reverse proxy. Even if the backend servers or the host names of the backend servers are changed, you need not change or add more ports in the inner firewall, because the changes are managed in the proxy rules or mappings.

NOTE *The reverse proxy acts as the single point of access to the backend servers.*

The reverse proxy forwards the request to the different backend servers based on the URL content. This makes it possible to access more than one server under one host name.

Another advantage of a reverse proxy is that you can cache content, both static and non-static, on the reverse proxy server. Reverse proxy functionality can be implemented using SAP Web Dispatcher, SQUID, Apache, IIS, and Novell iChain.

NOTE *SAP Web Dispatcher is not a fully reverse proxy because the response does not go through the SAP Web Dispatcher.*

The IIS Proxy was often used as a reverse proxy, but SAP will not support it in the future, so SAP Web Dispatcher or Apache is preferred. Internet Information Services (IIS) uses an Internet Server API (ISAPI) filter called IISProxy for providing the reverse proxy functionality. The reverse proxy authenticates the user and adds the NTLM authentication header to the request. The IISProxy can be downloaded from the service marketplace. It can be used in Windows-based NTLM authentication.

The Apache Web Server can be used as a reverse proxy by editing its configuration file (httpd.conf) to include the mod_rewrite and mod_proxy modules in the LoadModule and AddModule entries. Using Location tags, we can set up rules for the list of applications that the Apache web server should redirect the request to. The mod_rewrite module re-writes the URL received by the Apache web server and creates a new URL that redirects the request to one of the backend applications. The mod_proxy module modifies the response from the backend application so that it appears as if the response was sent from the Apache server and not from the backend application.

Disadvantages of Using a Reverse Proxy Now that you have seen the advantages of using a reverse proxy, let's address some of the disadvantages.

SSL terminates at the reverse proxy, so you can use only plain text inside the LAN, even though SSL can be used outside the LAN. Another disadvantage with a reverse proxy is that it can be a single point of failure in the system. Moreover, firewalls and proxy translations could potentially slow down system performance.

TIP *Reverse proxy can be a single point of failure and can slow system performance.*

Reverse Proxy–Based Two-Level Load Balancing

Figure 9-5 displays two-level load balancing with reverse proxy and SAP Web Dispatcher. This setup provides the following benefits:

- Session stickiness can be implemented at the level 1 load balancer
- The reverse proxy hides the actual URL from the end user
- The SAP Web Dispatcher allows implementing functional load balancing
- Increased security for external users due to the DMZ-based architecture

NOTE *For more details, refer to the Web Infrastructure concepts for SAP Web Application Server document available at http://sdn.sap.com.*

Installing the SAP Web Dispatcher

In this section, you will learn how to install the SAP Web Dispatcher.

The SAP Web Dispatcher can be installed on the SAP WAS or separately in the DMZ zone. Installing it on the SAP WAS may result in overloading the system and may also pose security risks.

TIP *It is recommended that you install the SAP Web Dispatcher in the DMZ layer.*

Scenarios Using SAP Web Dispatcher

You should be aware of some implications for SSL when using the SAP Web Dispatcher. You can set up the SAP Web Dispatcher for three scenarios:

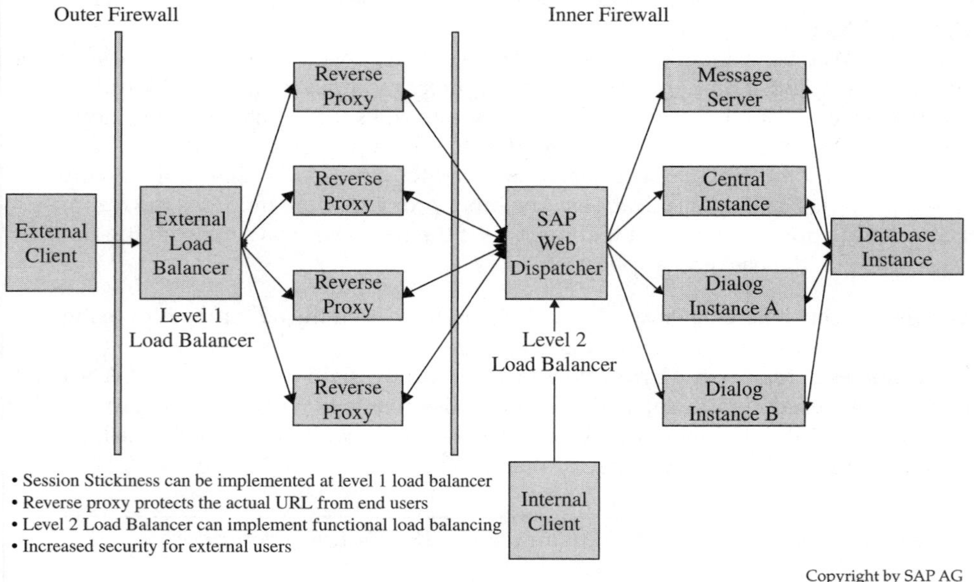

FIGURE 9-5 Reverse proxy–based two-level load balancing

- SSL termination
- SSL re-encryption
- End-to-end SSL

In *SSL termination*, the SAP Web Dispatcher decrypts the incoming request, accesses the session cookie information, and hence is able to forward the request to the correct application server using the proper load balancing techniques. However, because the SAP Web Dispatcher needs to decrypt the incoming request to read the cookie to implement full-fledged load balancing, SSL is terminated at the point of the SAP Web Dispatcher. SSL is not used between the Web Dispatcher and the application server. This setup also requires more CPU resources due to the need for decrypting the incoming request.

In the *SSL re-encryption* method, the SAP Web Dispatcher re-encrypts the request after decrypting the request. Hence the communication between the Web Dispatcher and the application server remains SSL. The fact that the communication between the SAP Web Dispatcher and the application server is SSL implies it is stateful and hence the sessions can be reused and need not be created again. This leads to reduced need for CPU resources when compared to the SSL termination scenario.

In *end-to-end SSL*, SSL is employed right from the client to the application server. In this setup, the SAP Web Dispatcher simply forwards the incoming request to the appropriate application server based on the client IP address. It does not have any information regarding the contents within the incoming request and hence full-fledged load balancing is not possible. Because of this less than optimal load distribution, the application servers are not fully utilized, which results in poor CPU performance.

High Availability for SAP Web Dispatcher

When the SAP Web Dispatcher fails, the whole portal is inaccessible to the user. To prevent this, you can install the SAP Web Dispatcher in a *switchover cluster.* Another solution is to install multiple SAP Web Dispatchers behind the network load balancer (NLB), as shown in Figure 9-6. The NLB should take care of the load balance of web dispatchers. The NLB need not implement session stickiness, because the SAP Web Dispatcher will take care of the load balancing on the SAP WAS and session stickiness.

Since the SAP Web Dispatcher also supports re-encryption, you can allow SSL termination on the NLB. This setup, however, has major limitations as far as maintaining end-to-end SSL is concerned, because the load balancer should now be capable of sending the request to the appropriate web dispatcher and this implies that the request needs to be decrypted.

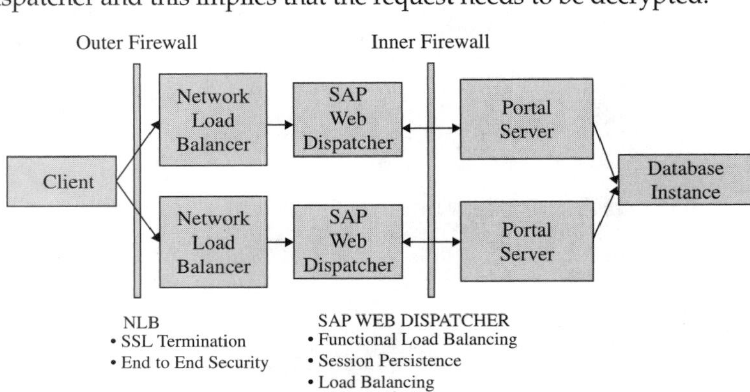

Figure 9-6 SAP Web Dispatcher in high availability mode

Installing the SAP Web Dispatcher

To install the SAP Web Dispatcher, do the following:

1. Copy the sapwebdisp.exe and icmadmin.SAR files from *<drive>*:\usr\sap\J2E\SYS\exe\uc\NTI386 or *<drive>*:\usr\sap\SID\JCxx*exe folders*.
2. Extract the icmadmin.SAR file using the SAPCAR program (located on the SAP Service Marketplace).
3. Open the SAP Management console and open the Process List under the central services instance.
4. Right click the message server process and choose Developer Trace, as shown next.

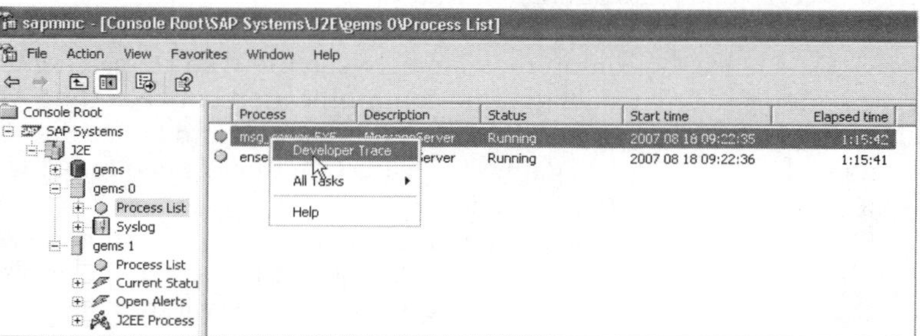

Copyright by SAP AG

5. In the resulting developer trace, check for the HTTP port on which the message server is listening, as shown next.

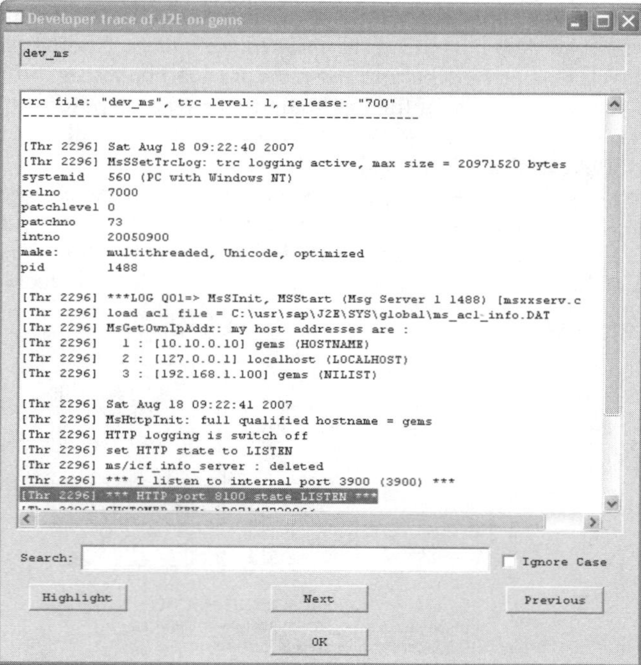

Copyright by SAP AG

6. Open a command prompt, and then navigate to the folder where the SAR files were extracted. To install the SAP Web Dispatcher, enter the command **sapwebdisp –bootstrap** to see the screen shown next.

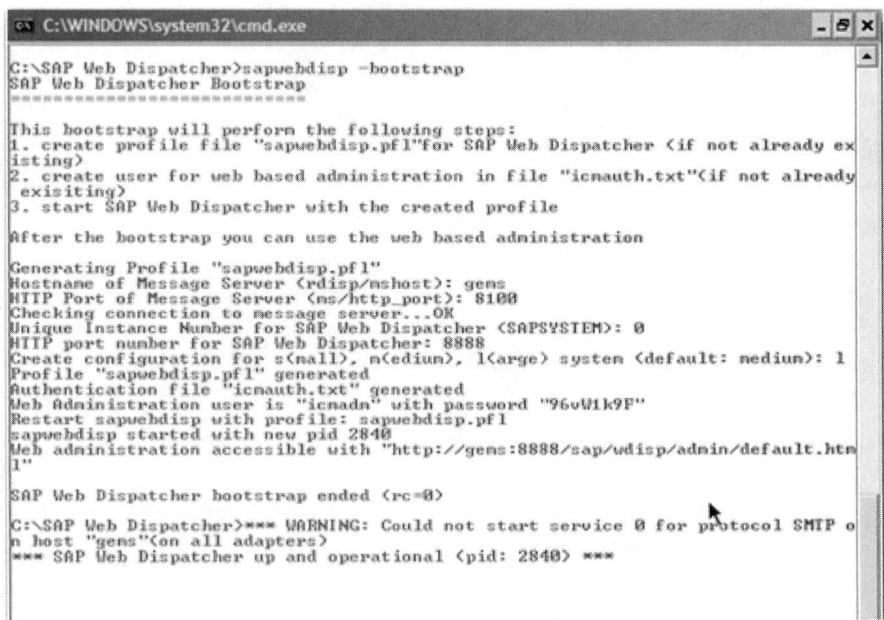

C:\WINDOWS\system32\cmd.exe
C:\SAP Web Dispatcher>sapwebdisp -bootstrap
SAP Web Dispatcher Bootstrap
==============================
This bootstrap will perform the following steps:
1. create profile file "sapwebdisp.pfl"for SAP Web Dispatcher (if not already existing)
2. create user for web based administration in file "icmauth.txt"(if not already exisiting)
3. start SAP Web Dispatcher with the created profile
After the bootstrap you can use the web based administration
Generating Profile "sapwebdisp.pfl"
Hostname of Message Server (rdisp/mshost): gems
HTTP Port of Message Server (ms/http_port): 8100
Checking connection to message server...OK
Unique Instance Number for SAP Web Dispatcher (SAPSYSTEM): 0
HTTP port number for SAP Web Dispatcher: 8888
Create configuration for s(mall), m(edium), l(arge) system (default: medium): l
Profile "sapwebdisp.pfl" generated
Authentication file "icmauth.txt" generated
Web Administration user is "icmadm" with password "96vW1k9F"
Restart sapwebdisp with profile: sapwebdisp.pfl
sapwebdisp started with new pid 2840
Web administration accessible with "http://gems:8888/sap/wdisp/admin/default.html"
SAP Web Dispatcher bootstrap ended (rc=0)
C:\SAP Web Dispatcher>*** WARNING: Could not start service 0 for protocol SMTP on host "gems"(on all adapters)
*** SAP Web Dispatcher up and operational (pid: 2840) ***

7. Enter the value for HTTP Port of Message Server (ms/http_port): In this case, the message server port is 8100.
8. Enter the following values:

   Unique Instance Number for SAP Web Dispatcher (SAPSYSTEM): **0**

   HTTP port number for SAP Web Dispatcher: **8888**

   Create configuration for s(mall), m(edium, l(arge) system <default: medium>: **1**

9. Jot down the Web Administration user and password details as well as the URL for administering the SAP Web Dispatcher over the Web.

As shown in the next illustration, you can display the process in the Task Manager. Note that the SAP Web Dispatcher is running as a process with ID 2840.

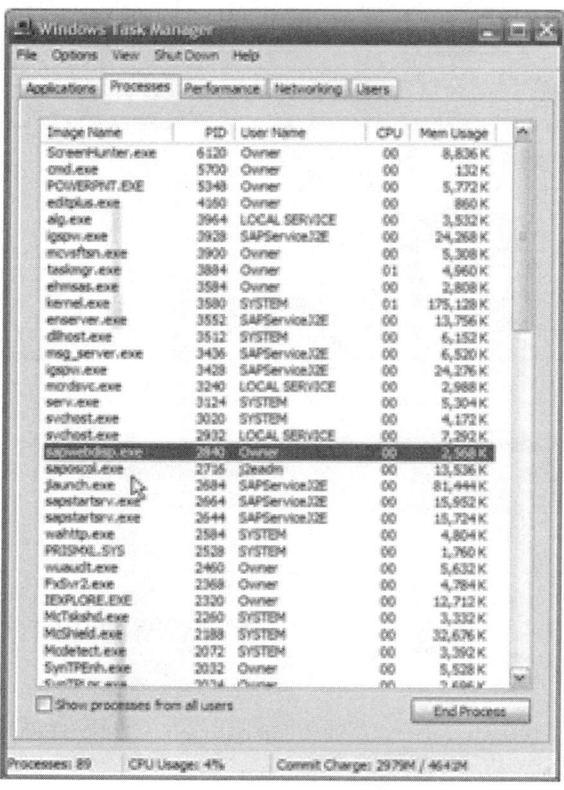

Displaying the SAP Web Dispatcher Profile

After installing the SAP Web Dispatcher, to check the SAP Web Dispatcher version, enter **sapwebdisp –V** in the command prompt, as shown next.

```
C:\WINDOWS\system32\CMD.exe

C:\Documents and Settings\Owner.YOUR-B280B1E83B>cd \

C:\>cd SAP Web Dispatcher

C:\SAP Web Dispatcher>sapwebdisp -v

SAP Web Dispatcher Version 7.00.7, multithreaded, Unicode, 32 BIT


kernel information
------------------

system name      =
kernel release   = 700
database library =
compiled on      = NT 5.0 2195 Service Pack 4 x86 MS VC++ 13.10
compile time     = Mar  9 2006 20:43:31
update level     = 0
patch number     = 47
source id        = 0.048

supported environment
---------------------

operating system
  Windows NT 5.0
  Windows NT 5.1
  Windows NT 5.2

patch comments
--------------

  (  0) ( 0.001) Provide option to preserve Unicode chars in HTML Escape (note 8
32220)
  (  1) ( 0.004) CST patch collection 15 2005 (note 834501)
  (  2) ( 0.007) CST patch collection 21 2005 (note 845887)
  (  3) ( 0.011) CST patch collection 24 2005 (note 851195)
  (  4) ( 0.011) VM Patch Collection 2 (note 853183)
  (  5) ( 0.014) CST Patch Collection 28 2005 (note 860319)
  (  6) ( 0.014) CST Patch Collection 28 2005 (note 860319)
  (  7) ( 0.018) CST Patch Collection 31 2005 (note 867690)
  (  8) ( 0.020) Optimization of VMC session storage (note 871988)
  (  9) ( 0.021) Enhanced SAP encoding methods (note 866020)
  ( 10) ( 0.023) CST Patch Collection 36 2005 (note 874665)
  ( 11) ( 0.023) CST Patch Collection 37 2005 (note 877058)
  ( 12) ( 0.023) VMC Patch Collection 6 (note 865932)
  ( 13) ( 0.026) CST Patch Collection 39 2005 (note 884266)
  ( 14) ( 0.030) CST Patch Collection 41 2005 (note 888245)
  ( 15) ( 0.033) CST Patch Collection 45 2005 (note 895230)
  ( 16) ( 0.034) ICM Patch Collection (V) (note 851852)
  ( 17) ( 0.036) CST Patch Collection 49 2005 (note 904777)
  ( 18) ( 0.041) CST Patch Collection 1 2006 (note 913187)
  ( 19) ( 0.046) CST Patch Collection 06 2006 (note 921223)
  ( 20) ( 0.047) CST: Missing content length in content server upload (note 9253
27)
  ( 21) ( 0.047) CST Patch Collection 06 2006 (note 921223)
  ( 22) ( 0.047) Corrections within the SAP content of filter (note 925602)
```

Accessing the Portal Through the SAP Web Dispatcher

After installing the SAP Web Dispatcher, you can access the SAP Portal using the URL http://<host>:8888/irj/portal. The following illustration shows how the client request is dispatched to the SAP Web Dispatcher instead of reaching the message server directly.

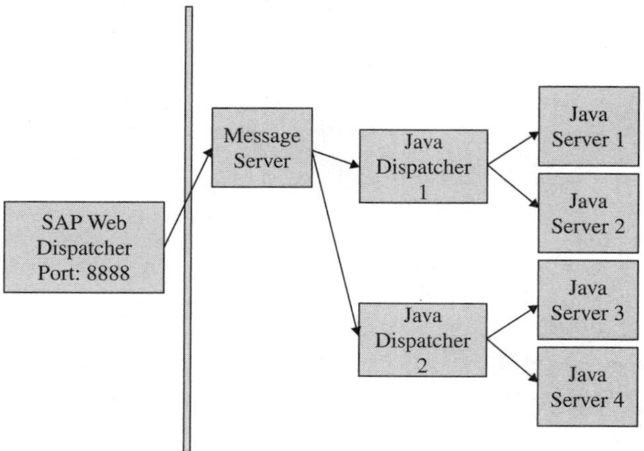

Starting / Stopping the SAP Web Dispatcher

To stop the Web Dispatcher, enter the command **sapntkill –INT <PID>**.

If you need to run the Web Dispatcher again, use the following command from command prompt: **sapwebdisp pf=sapwebdisp.pfl**.

Install the SAP Web Dispatcher as a Service

To install as a service, enter this command:

ntscmgr install SAPWebdispatcher -b <*drive*>:\usr\sap\SID\JCxx\exe\sapwebdisp.exe -p service pf=sapwebdisp.pfl

Or enter this command:

ntscmgr install SAPWebdispatcher -b C:\usr\sap\J2E\SYS\exe\uc\NTI386\sapwebdisp.exe -p service pf=C:\usr\sap\J2E\SYS\exe\uc\NTI386\sapwebdisp.pfl

If this command doesn't work properly, do the following:

1. Edit the registry entry by running the program regedit.
2. Do a search for *SAPWebdispatcher* and change the `ImagePath` to where your sapwebdisp.exe is currently residing.

3. Navigate to the folder <*drive*>:\usr\sap\J2E\SYS\exe\uc\NTI386>, and enter the following command, as shown in the next illustration:

   ntscmgr install SAPWebdisp -b c:\usr\sap\J2E\SYS\exe\uc\NTI386\sapwebdisp.exe -p "service pf=sapwebdisp.pfl -shm_attach_mode 6"

```
C:\>cd C:\usr\sap\J2E\SYS\exe\uc\NTI386

C:\usr\sap\J2E\SYS\exe\uc\NTI386>ntscmgr install SAPWebdispatcher -b c:\usr\sap\
SID\JC01\exe\sapwebdisp.exe -p service pf=sapwebdisp.pfl
CreateService SUCCESS

C:\usr\sap\J2E\SYS\exe\uc\NTI386>_
```

Once you have installed the Web Dispatcher as a service, open Control Panel | Services and check whether the SAP Web Dispatcher is indeed running as a service.

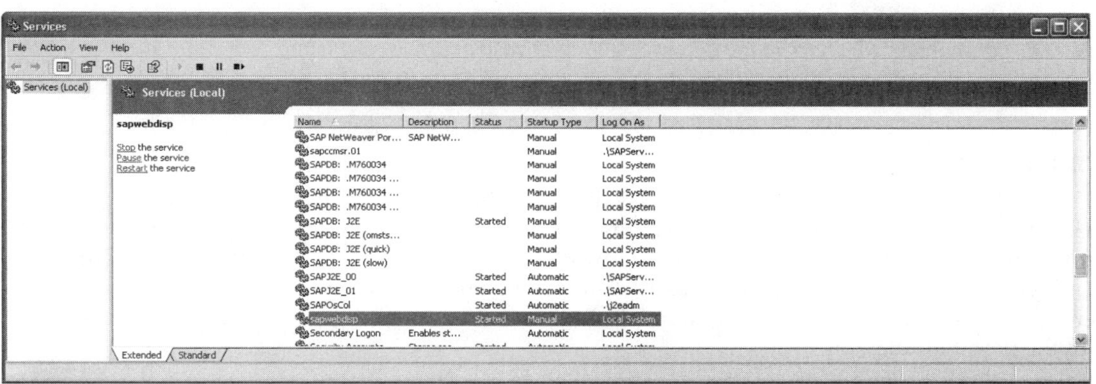

TIP *Sometimes, the Web Dispatcher service may not be running, in which case you may simply have to restart the SAP Web Dispatcher.*

Removing the SAP Web Dispatcher

To remove the service, enter the command **ntscmgr remove sapwebdisp**.

Redirecting the URL

To redirect the user from http://WEBDISP_HOST:PORT to a different URL—such as http://WEBDISP_HOST:PORT/irj/index.html—you can edit the sapwebdisp.pfl file by adding the following parameter:

```
# SAP Web Dispatcher Web Administration
icm/HTTP/redirect_0 = PREFIX=/, TO=/irj/index.html
```

After making the change, restart the SAP Web Dispatcher.

OSS Notes

Following are some useful OSS notes that can be accessed at http://service.sap.com/notes:

- **953784** SAP Web Dispatcher Connection Pooling
- **834184** Installing the SAP Web Dispatcher in an MSCS Environment
- **709482** Virtual hosts and SAP Web Dispatcher
- **870127** Security note for SAP Web Dispatcher
- **908097** SAP Web Dispatcher 7.00: Importing patches
- **552286** Troubleshooting for the SAP Web Dispatcher
- **538405** Composite SAP Note on the SAP Web Dispatcher
- **768691** SAP Web dispatcher and workload distribution load balancing
- **561885** Generation of URLs (SAP Web Dispatcher/Reverse Proxy)
- **1040325** HTTP load balancing: Message Server or Web Dispatcher?

NOTE *For more details, refer to the document 'Web Infrastructure concepts for Web Application Server' and over web infrastructure related resources listed in Appendix B.*

Summary

This chapter and the previous two chapters discussed how you proceed with planning for a technical infrastructure, keeping the following in mind: high availability using switchover solutions, scalability using distribution of software and hardware, sizing for better performance and scalability, and a robust web infrastructure that balances between session management, encryption, and load balancing requirements. In the next few chapters, you'll learn how to plan for the portal installation.

PART

Portal Installation

CHAPTER 10

Preparing for Portal Installation

This chapter discusses some useful tips that can be followed to ensure a successful implementation of the portal, such as referring to installation guides, documentation, OSS notes, maintaining installation cookbooks, quicklinks, installation DVDs, release restrictions, and installation tips.

Planning

Devoting enough time and effort during the planning phase will ensure a smoother portal installation and efficient operation of the portal after Go-Live.

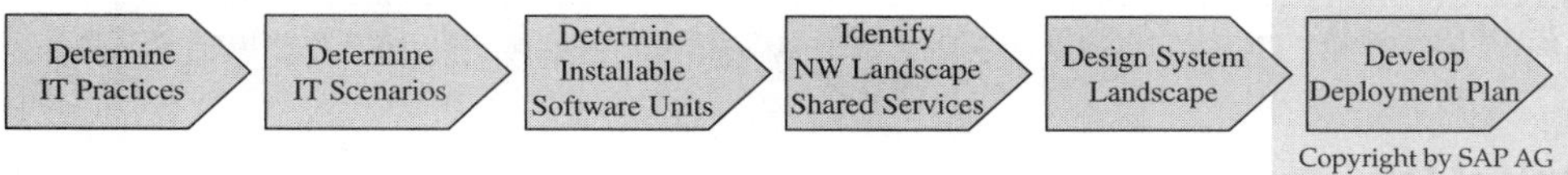

Copyright by SAP AG

It is good practice to develop a list with the following details in the portal planning phase:

- Determining the required IT practices based on business requirements—for example, User Productivity Enablement
- Determining the required IT scenarios—for example, Running An Enterprise Portal (EP)
- Determining the required software units, namely, the usage types, the standalone engines, and the clients—for example, usage types such as EP, Application Server (AS) Java, and Business Intelligence (BI); standalone engines such as TREX, and clients such as the SAP GUI
- Determining the need for system-wide, shared components such as Solution Manager, Computing Center Management System (CCMS), Solution Manager Diagnostics, System Landscape Directory (SLD), NetWeaver Administrator (NWA), and so on, for implementing a SAP NetWeaver landscape

- Including the SAP release strategy, maintenance, and support strategy in planning
- Determining the system landscape—decide how many systems are required and how they are deployed for development, quality assurance (QA), and production (PRD)
- Determining the system hardware requirements based on sizing techniques such as Quick Sizer
- Using the Product Availability Matrix for identifying platform support for operating systems, database systems, client systems, Java development kits (JDKs), and so on
- Creating the deployment plan by mapping the systems, shared system-wide components, and standalone engines to actual physical hosts

Master Guide Document: A Must Read

It is important that you read the SAP documentation in detail and plan for the installation fully before embarking on the actual installation using the installation CDs. Read the master guide and other documentation and prepare a checklist of steps needed specifically for a portal installation.

The master guide contains detailed information regarding the various technical implementations of IT scenarios (such as "Running an Enterprise Portal") and helps you plan for integration with other systems. It also helps you plan for the overall system landscape by including system-wide, shared components such as Solution Manager, CCMS for centralized monitoring, and administration of the SAP NetWeaver landscape. It also provides information on other useful documents that may be required during the installation process.

Do *Read the master guide, which provides a starting point for the installation planning process.*

Technical Infrastructure Guide

The next important documentation is the *Technical Infrastructure Guide – SAP NetWeaver 7.0* (or whichever version you plan to implement). This guide provides information on the following:

- How to distribute the various usage types across hardware systems
- Available options for clustering to implement high availability
- Other distribution options to implement scalability, performance, stability, and security
- Aspects of network infrastructure

Service Marketplace Documentation Download

To download the manuals, go to http://service.sap.com/instguides as shown in Figure 10-1 and select SAP NetWeaver | SAP NetWeaver 7.0(2004s) | Installation. Here you can access the *Master Guide, Technical Infrastructure Guide, Planning Guide – System Landscape Directory, Media List for SR1/SR2, Installation Guide – SAP NetWeaver 7.0 SR1/SR2*, and other documents.

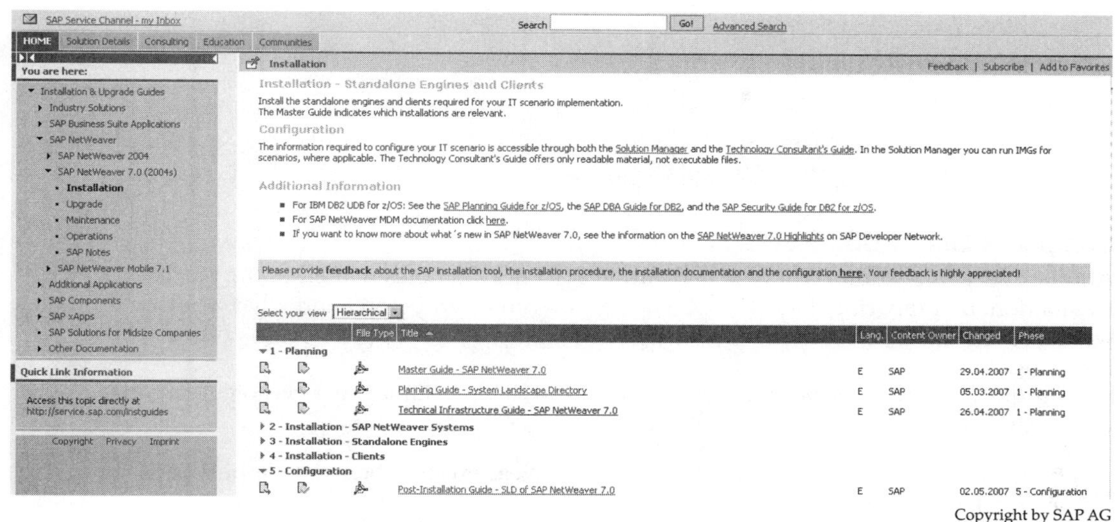

FIGURE 10-1 SAP Service Marketplace installation guides download

You can also find documentation for System Copy; documentation for installation of standalone engines such as TREX, Web Dispatcher, and so on; and documentation for installation of clients such as SAP Developer Workplace, SAP NetWeaver Developer Studio, and so on.

Platform-Specific Guides

As can be seen on the SAP Service Marketplace, a number of platform-specific guides are available for different combinations of operating systems and databases, such as the following:

- SAP NetWeaver 7.0 SR1 Java on Windows: Oracle
- Media List for SAP NetWeaver 7.0 Support Release 1
- System Copy for SAP Systems based on SAP NetWeaver 7.0 SR1 Java
- Planning Guide for System Landscape Directory

Service Marketplace Quicklinks

Refer to the following *quicklinks* for information regarding the platform support, OSS notes, and other documents:

- http://service.sap.com/platforms
- http://service.sap.com/pam
- http://service.sap.com/sapnotesnw70
- http://service.sap.com/installnw70

- http://service.sap.com/ha
- http://service.sap.com/security
- http://service.sap.com/sizing
- http://service.sap.com/sp-stacks
- http://service.sap.com/solutionmanager

Compile a List of OSS Notes

Another very important activity is to compile a list of OSS notes related to the portal installation. By preparing the list of OSS notes, you can know beforehand what works and what does not work and hence avoid any potential unpleasant surprises in the future while installing.

The quicklink http://service.sap.com/sapnotesnw70 has a number of OSS notes categorized under various headings, such as the following:

- General notes that include information on release restrictions and support package stack guides
- Installation-related notes that include information on checking for prerequisites, notes arranged by combinations of operating system and database, as well as product release version
- Database related notes
- System copy related notes
- Upgrade to SAP NetWeaver 7.0 related notes
- Maintenance notes
- Operations, configuration, and administration notes
- Usage type related notes for IT scenarios and scenario variants

---

CAUTION *This information is constantly changing, so you are recommended to refer to the Service Marketplace for current information.*

Some important OSS notes are listed here:

- **864172** SAP NetWeaver 7.0 Documentation
- **707730** Release restrictions for SAP NetWeaver '04
- **852008** Release restrictions for SAP NetWeaver 7.0
- **803018** Central Note for NetWeaver04 High Availability Capabilities
- **933402** Pilot Projects: J2EE inst. on heterogeneous landscape NW04/04s
- **855498** Installation Prerequisite checker
- **836198** Additional information on upgrading to SAP NW 7.0 Java
- **894170** NW04s (700) Central Note for User Management Engine (UME)
- **894958** NW04s (700) Central Note for Security

- **656711** Deploying Support Packages with SDM
- **657763** Installing SAP J2EE Engine Support Packages (SAP Web AS 6.30)
- **919106** SAP NetWeaver 7.0 SR1 Installation on Windows: Oracle
- **675938** SAP Web AS 6.40 ABAP Installation on Windows
- **676072** SAP Web AS 6.40 Java Installation on Windows
- **875322** J2EE engine installation on heterogeneous architectures
- **711093** Release restriction note for Web AS 6.40

Caution *OSS notes keep changing due to their dynamic nature and hence you are always requested to visit the SAP Service Marketplace for the latest information.*

Installation Media

The media shipped by SAP for both installation and upgrade is also important to consult. For installing SAP NetWeaver 2004 SR 1, the required installation media is subdivided into the following:

- **Initial media for installation or upgrades** For initial installation, the DVD name for NW2004SR1 is Installation Master NW2004sSR1 and the DVD for upgrade is known as Upgrade Master NW2004sSR1.
- **Media for specific operating system and databases** OracleOnNW2004sSR1, MaxDBOnNW2004sSR1, MSSQLOnNW2004sSR1, and DB2UDBOnNW2004sSR1. The SAP NetWeaver 2004s SR1 kernel DVD is also available for different operating systems.
- **Media for the installable units of SAP NetWeaver:**
  - **DVDs for usage types** Depending on the usage type identified during the planning phase, you must choose the appropriate DVD. For example, for Application Server Java, you should choose JavaComponent NW2004sSR1 and Kernel NW2004sSR1 DVDs.
  - **For standalone engines** Search and Classification NW2004sSR1 DVD for TREX, Kernel NW2004sSR1 for Web Dispatcher, and Presentation NW2004sSR1 for Content Server.
  - **For client installation** Presentation NW2004sSR1 DVD for SAP GUI for Windows, SAP GUI for Java, Adobe LifeCycle Designer, and Business Explorer (BI); Developer Studio NW2004sSR1 for installing NW Developer Studio; and Kernel NW2004sSR1 for SAP NetWeaver Developer Workplace.

Platform-Specific Installation Guide

Refer to the relevant installation guide for combinations of operating systems and databases. For example, if you want to install SAP NetWeaver Application Server (WAS) Java on a Microsoft SQL Server database in Windows, you would refer to the *Installation Guide – SAP NetWeaver 2004s SR1 Java on Windows: MS SQL Server*. To access this guide, go to http://service.sap.com/nw70 and then click on the link SAP NetWeaver 7.0 SR1–Installation Guides. Then choose your relevant database, which this case will be MS SQL Server and

PART III

then click on the Java link corresponding to the Windows operating system. The installation guide is a comprehensive document that deals with the following:

- Installing the usage types, standalone engines, and clients
- Distributing usage types such as Enterprise Portal and Exchange Infrastructure to various hosts
- Designing the system configuration for high performance
- Deciding on the basic SAP system parameters such as SAP system ID, database ID instance number, and other details related to Adobe LifeCycle Designer, SAP Solution Manager, and Development Infrastructure

Release Restrictions

Identify the *release restrictions* before implementation to avoid any surprises during or after the portal installation. For example, a number of release restrictions exist for SAP NetWeaver 2004s at the time of writing, such as the lack of SAPinst support for HA setups and uninstall. Some important OSS notes that contain info on release restrictions are listed here:

- **852008** Release restrictions for SAP NetWeaver 2004s
- **853507** Release Restr.: Usage Type BI of SAP NetWeaver 2004s
- **853509** Release Restr.: Usage Type EP of SAP NetWeaver 2004s
- **853571** Release Restr.: Usage Type AS-ABAP of SAP NetWeaver 2004s
- **853572** Release Restr.: Usage Type AS-Java of SAP NetWeaver 2004s
- **853725** Rel. Restr.: SAP NW 2004s - Search and Classification (TREX)
- **853770** Rel. Restr.: SAP NW 2004s - SAP NetWeaver Developer Workpl.
- **883948** NW 7.0(2004s): Inst.Add.Java Usage Types/Software Units

Installation Tips, Tricks, and Pitfalls

Following are some of the typical issues and aspects to watch for during the installation process.

Required Skill Sets

Before proceeding with the installation, you must ensure that sufficient system administrators and Java developers know how to troubleshoot Java-related issues and to read log files in Java.

Ensure that proper communication and coordination exist between the portal architects, network administrators, project manager, and portal developers. This is required for designing an effective technical infrastructure and proceeding with the installation process. For example, in a typical project, help should be obtained from portal architects regarding the design of the architecture, business analysts regarding the functional requirements, Java developers for troubleshooting log messages, project managers for details regarding the project progress, and network engineers for setting up firewall security.

TIP *To ensure a successful portal installation, skilled resources such as Java developers, basis administrators, portal architects, and network administrators are required.*

Proper Sizing: Avoid Shared Systems

Another potential pitfall is trying to install a portal on a shared environment that hosts other usage types such as Exchange Infrastructure (XI), BI, and so on. It is important to size the hardware properly before the actual installation. You should take into consideration all the business functionality requirements and identify all the portal components such as knowledge management and collaboration, and TREX that are required.

If you choose to install Enterprise Portal along with other usage types, there will be a number of issues that you have to consider. In the future, if you want to scale your Enterprise Portal due to increasing load on the system, you will expend lot of effort to migrate the different usage types to two different systems. You may be left with the only option of adopting measures like adding multiple dialog instances, database clustering techniques, and other hardware-based solutions to implement scalability.

The other drawback is that you may not be able to upgrade the portal without upgrading the other usage type. There could be patch dependencies that may force you to upgrade the other usage type also. In some cases, an existing functionality may not function properly after the upgrade. At least it demands that you test all possible test case scenarios in the second usage type to ensure that there is no loss in existing functionality or incorrect behavior after the upgrade.

You may also face constraints in system administration activities such as Backup and Recovery, System Copy, Monitoring, Security, and so on.

DON'T *Avoid installing a portal on a shared environment.*

Installation Cookbook: Document Comprehensively

It is good practice to develop a "cookbook" that captures in detail all the installation steps, the OSS notes, the configuration parameters that were used, the references to various technical documentation, and the log file locations used for troubleshooting. Keeping track of these changes will help when you need to troubleshoot issues as well as when planning for upgrades, installing support package stacks, and so on.

SAP's Patching Strategy

You should understand common installation errors and the various tools offered by SAP. Many changes have occurred surrounding SAP's new patching strategy, and these are important to know during the post-installation process.

As a part of installation planning, you should use the new Support Package Stacks (SPS) concept from SAP to simplify the process of applying patches across different NetWeaver components on ABAP and Java stacks. SPS can be used to identify the required patches for various components and helps to identify the required tools for installing them. It is now important that you check for dependencies between support packages and be careful because of the potentially large number of combinations that are possible.

DO *It is good practice to install the SPS and follow it up with the manual installation of minor patches.*

Knowledge of Installation and Troubleshooting Tools

A number of installation tools have been provided by SAP such as SAPinst, the Visual Administrator, the NetWeaver Administrator, Software Delivery Manager (SDM), and the JSPM.

SAPinst is the front-end tool for installing all SAP NetWeaver components and usually comes with the installation DVDs. Visual Administrator is the GUI tool that can be used for configuring and administering the cluster and the cluster nodes, the services, and the managers. J2EE config tool can be used for configuring the J2EE engine when it is in offline mode. SDM is a tool that can be used for deploying software applications, support packages, and business packages. From NetWeaver 7.0 onward, you should use the JSPM for installing support package stacks and Java support packages, instead of SDM.

Check Installation Prerequisites

Before proceeding with the installation, ensure that you have met all the hardware requirements such as the RAM and disk space requirements. Ensure that your network requirements such as setting up the firewall rules, assigning ports, and setting up Web Dispatcher have been met. You may encounter issues with the SAPinst installation, because sometimes the port 21200 that it uses has not been allowed through the firewall.

Typical Installation Issues

Some typical problems that you may face during installation are missing environment variables for the JDK and using the wrong version of the JDK.

Sometimes you may not be able to log on to the Visual Administrator because the J2EE engine is not running. Right after the installation, the portal takes a substantial amount of time to start due to the intensive startup process.

Another reason could be that the wrong password was used for the Admin user or that the user was locked out due to repeated invalid attempts. It is also possible that the connectivity parameters were set up incorrectly due to wrong port number or transport layer protocol. Finally, if the Visual Admin is not accessible, it may be required to activate the SAP Emergency user to gain access.

NOTE *For more details, refer to the installation related resources listed in Appendix B.*

Summary

This chapter discussed some useful tips that you can follow to be prepared for the installation. Although this is not a complete list, it will hopefully provide you with a hint of what to look for.

11 CHAPTER

Portal Installation

This chapter addresses some of the steps that can be required in a portal installation. This information will introduce you to what is expected during a typical portal installation. However, your portal installation may have aspects that differ from those discussed here due to various factors such as the IT scenarios you choose, the technical infrastructure design considerations, software release versions, and so on. This chapter walks you through the steps involved in installing the portal using NetWeaver 7.0.

NOTE *Appendix A contains instructions on installing SAP NetWeaver 7.0 (2004s) – Java Trial Version, which includes the Application Server Java, NetWeaver Portal, and Content Management and Collaboration.*

Pre-Installation Planning

Before proceeding with the installation, you should prepare a checklist with the following details:

- Your decision on which NetWeaver solution version you plan to install based on considerations such as SAP release strategy, maintenance strategy, support strategy, product availability matrix (PAM), and so on.
- List of IT practices, IT scenarios, and the required or optional software units such as usage types, standalone engines, and standalone units such as the Application Sharing Server.
- List of required and optional usage types such as Application Server Java, Enterprise Portal Core, Enterprise Portal, Development Infrastructure, and so on.
- List of required and optional portal functionalities such as Guided Procedures, Universal Worklist, Knowledge Management and Collaboration, TREX, and so on.
- Choice between the central, distributed, and high availability systems.
- Choice between the AS Java verses AS ABAP and AS Java installation.
- Choice of databases such as IBM DB2 for Linux/Unix/Windows, IBM DB2 for z/OS, MaxDB, MS SQL, and Oracle for installing the SAP systems.

- High availability and scalability design requirements such as Microsoft Cluster Service, Enqueue Replication Server, database clusters, additional dialog instances, and so on.
- Technical infrastructure design with details on how the various software units will be distributed to different hosts.
- List of system hardware requirements for the various hosts based on sizing results.
- Choice between different User Management Engine (UME) data sources such as J2EE database, SAP R/3, and Lightweight Directory Access Protocol (LDAP).
- Network layout design, including information on whether reverse proxies such as Apache and load-balancing solutions such as SAP Web Dispatcher are required.
- List of OSS notes, release restrictions, and so on.
- List of required support packages and patches.
- List of required installation DVDs.

This checklist is prepared in addition to the list obtained at the end of the planning phase, which was discussed at the beginning of Chapter 10. Before installing the portal, refer to the following:

- Master Guide – NetWeaver 7.0
- Technical Infrastructure Guide – SAP NetWeaver 7.0
- SAP NetWeaver Java on Windows: MS SQL Server
- Developer Workplace for SAP NetWeaver 2004s SR1 / Developer Workplace for SAP NetWeaver 7.0 SR2

Installation Options

Before proceeding with the actual installation, you must make design considerations such as the following:

- Central, distributed, and high availability system
- SAP system based on AS ABAP, AS Java, or both AS ABAP and AS Java

A central system is preferred when you want to install all the mandatory instances of the SAP system such as the central services instance Java, database instance, and central instance on a single host. You can also choose to install one or more dialog instances on the same host or on a different host.

During the installation, the system will prompt you to choose the required software units at one point. The software units relevant for the portal scenario are NetWeaver Enterprise Portal Core Components (EPC) and the Enterprise Portal (EP). To install the EP Core usage type, the AS Java usage type is sufficient. To install the EP, you need the EP Core usage type and the AS Java usage type.

If you do not choose the right combination of software units (usage types), the system will not let you proceed to the next step in the installation process. To install Business Intelligence (BI) Java, you need AS Java, EP, and EP Core usage types. The Development Infrastructure (DI) usage type requires only the AS Java usage type.

NOTE *The AS ABAP usage type is required only if you are installing NetWeaver Mobile Infrastructure (MI) and NetWeaver Process Integration (PI).*

If you choose to install a distributed system, the mandatory instances such as central services instance Java, database instance, and central instance can be installed on separate hosts. You may also choose to install additional dialog instances on a separate host, but that would be an optional step. A central system is preferred for development systems and distributed system is preferred for production systems. Refer to Chapters 6, 7, and 8 to learn how these factors can affect the design of the system.

When installing a SAP system, three system variants are possible:

- Based on AS ABAP and AS Java
- Based on AS Java
- Based on AS ABAP

The system variant based on AS ABAP and AS Java was formerly known as ABAP+Java system or the double stack system. It contains both the ABAP application server and the J2EE engine. The system variant based on AS Java is also known as the Java system or the Java standalone system and the system variant based on AS ABAP is known as the ABAP system or the ABAP standalone.

Installing an SAP system with the instances distributed on multiple hosts involves the following three steps:

1. Install a central services instance (SCS) and prepare the host as an SAP global host.
2. Install a database instance after the first step is completed. The AS Java and AS ABAP have their own database schema in the same database.
3. Install the central instance. During this step, other usage types based on AS ABAP and AS Java are also installed.

Choosing a Local or Domain Installation

During the installation, the system will prompt you to choose either a local installation or a domain installation.

A local installation is suited for a single-host installation, which is the case when you choose a central system option without installing any dialog instances. You need to be the local administrator on the host on which you plan to install the central system. In such a scenario, the account and user information are not visible to other hosts. This is therefore *not recommended* for a distributed installation. If you decide to go ahead with a distributed installation with a local administrator, you need to take some additional steps such as using the same passwords for users, such as *<SID>adm* and *SAPService<SID>*. Problems may arise with the transport directory. You should ensure that all hosts belong to the same workgroup.

If you choose a domain installation, you need to be the domain administrator of the domain. If not, you should have a domain user with local administrator rights. Domain installation is the preferred option for a distributed installation. You should ensure that all machines belong to the same domain so that the user information that is stored centrally on the domain controller can be shared across these machines.

PART III

TIP *Local installation is preferred for single-host installation, and domain installation is preferred for distributed installation.*

SAP System Parameters

You should decide what the desired values are for the SAP System parameters beforehand and capture these values in the cookbook for future reference. A number of SAP system parameters are required for the installation:

- **SAP system ID** This ID is three alphanumeric characters, all uppercase letters, which identify the entire SAP system and are unique throughout the organization. Note that the first character should be a letter.
- **Database ID** This ID can be different from the SAP system ID and identifies the database instance.
- **Instance number** This number is unique within the host and can have a value from 00 to 97. This number is used for technical identification of the process.
- **Messaging service port** This port is unique for the SAP system on all hosts and is required for the message service, which is installed in the SCS instance host. The messaging service port uses the parameter *rdisp/msserv_internal* with the default value *39<nn>*, where *<nn>* is the instance number of the messaging service instance.
- **Operating system users** SAPinst creates *<SID>adm* and *SAPService<SID>* users. *SAPService<SID>* is the user used by the Java Startup and Control Framework at the operating system level to launch the various J2EE processes such as message service, enqueue service, and so on.

NOTE *The maximum length of the host names of servers running SAP software with release 4.6 or higher is 13 characters.*

UME Configuration: Choosing the Datasource

You must choose between storing User Management Engine (UME) data in the Java database, the Lightweight Directory Access Protocol (LDAP) database, or the ABAP database. If you decide to have the Java database as the UME data source, the UME Web Admin and SAP NWA tools can be used for user administration. If you decide to have LDAP as the UME data source, you can use the same user administration tools, but you need to configure the LDAP after the NetWeaver AS Java installation. The users for accessing the J2EE database are named *Administrator* for the Administrator role and *Guest* for the guest user role. Guest users have read-only access and belong to the Authenticated Users group.

INFO *The UME Web Admin tool can be accessed at http://<j2ee_host>:5<j2ee_instance_number>00/useradmin. The SAP NetWeaver Administrator (NWA) can be accessed at http://<j2ee_host>:5<instance_number>00/nwa.*

If you decide that the ABAP database should be the UME data source, you can use transaction *SU01* for user administration in the SAP R/3 system after the installation.

In order to use the UME Web Admin and SAP NWA tools for administering users in the SAP R/3 system, the communication user used for connecting to the SAP R/3 ABAP system from the J2EE system should have the required authorization rights in the R/3 system. The communication user should be created manually in the SAP R/3 system with the user ID *SAPJSF_<JAVA_SYSTEM_ID>*. This user should be a communications type user (not a dialog user) and should have the role SAP_BC_JSF_COMMUNICATION to allow the ability to create, change, and delete users. Note that the role SAP_BC_JSF_COMMUNICATION_RO only provides display access. The connection parameters that are required when configuring the ABAP database as the UME data source are the application server number, application server host name, and communication user (SAPJSF_*<JAVA_SYSTEM_ID>*).

Other users to be created in the ABAP system are as follows:

- Administrator user for the J2EE engine: J2EE_ADMIN_*<SID>* with role SAP_J2EE_ADMIN
- Guest user for the J2EE engine: J2EE_GUEST_*<SID>* with role SAP_J2EE_GUEST

Pre-Installation Steps

Before proceeding with the actual installation, you need to carry out certain preliminary steps such as the following:

- You must ensure that the Windows file system you are using is the NTFS type. For this, right-click the root directory in Windows Explorer and select Properties in the context menu.
- If you are using a domain installation, you should ensure that the SAP or the database instance is not installed on the domain controller.
- You must ensure that the host names are not longer than 13 characters.

Downloading the Installation DVDs

You need the following software installation DVDs:

- For installing the central services instance, central instance, and the dialog instance, you will need the Installation Master DVD, NetWeaver Java DVD, and the kernel DVD.
- For installing NetWeaver 2004s SR1 with the Microsoft SQL Server, you will need the Installation Master NW2004sSR1, JavaComponent NW2004sSR1, and Kernel NW2004sSR1, respectively.
- For installing NetWeaver 2004s SR2 with the Microsoft SQL Server, you will need the Installation Master NW2004sSR2, JavaComponent NW2004sSR2, and Kernel NW2004sSR2, respectively.
- For installing the database instance, in addition to the above DVDs, you will need the RDBMS DVD (MSSQLOnNW2004sSR1 for installing NetWeaver 2004s SR1 / SR2 with Microsoft SQL Server).

NOTE *Starting from SAP NetWeaver 7.0 SR2, the Enterprise Portal is available as two separate usage types, namely, the EP Core (EPC) and the Enterprise Portal (EP). The EP Core contains the core portal components such as Portal Platform, Guided Procedures (GP), and Universal Worklist (UWL). EP contains other portal add-on functionalities such as Knowledge Management, Collaboration, .Net PDK, Web DynPro extension, and Visual Composer (VC).*

Note that the preceding list of DVDs and their content is shown only for illustration purposes. The actual details are always changing and vary for your installation depending upon the versions used. SAPinst reads the LABEL.ASC file to verify the DVD's contents. The Installation Master DVDs can also be downloaded from http://service.sap.com/swdc, provided you have the necessary license and authorizations. Navigate to Downloads | Installations and Upgrades | Entry By Application Group | SAP NetWeaver (choose your solution) | SAP NETWEAVER | SAP NETWEAVER 7.0 (2004s) (release of your solution) | Installation And Upgrade | Windows Server (choose your operating system) | MS SQL SERVER (choose your database).

You can identify the relevant DVDs by looking at the solution name in the Title of the downloadable object in the Service Marketplace web page. For example, if you are looking for NetWeaver 2004s SR2 DVDs, the title is likely to start with *NW 2004s SR2*. You must ensure that you have downloaded all the relevant Installation Master, Java Component, Kernel, and the RDMBS objects. The downloadable objects have a *<material_number>_<sequence_number>* format.

After downloading the relevant objects to a download directory on the host where you intend to run the SAPinst, you must extract the objects starting with the one that has the lowest number—for example, 51032246_1, and then 51032246_2, and so on. To extract the downloaded files, you must use the SAPCAR version 700 or SAPCAR 640 with patch level 4 or higher. Refer to Chapter 12 on how to use SAPCAR to extract the files.

Check the Hardware and Software Requirements of Hosts

Check that the central system host meets the hardware and software requirements. For this, refer to the installation guide for the particular combination of SAP NetWeaver version and database you are using.

If you are installing a distributed system, you must check the hardware and software requirements for the central services instance, database instance, central instance, and dialog instance hosts individually. Again, refer to the installation guide for the requirements checklist. If you install multiple instances on a given host, you must add up the individual requirements for those instances.

First check the disk space:

1. From the Control Panel, open the Administrative tools icon.
2. Double-click Computer Management.
3. Choose Disk Management from the list on the left.
4. Right-click the installation drive and choose Properties.

Next, check the RAM. From Windows Explorer, choose Help | About Windows. Yc see the screen shown in Figure 11-1, which displays the physical memory available to Windows operating system.

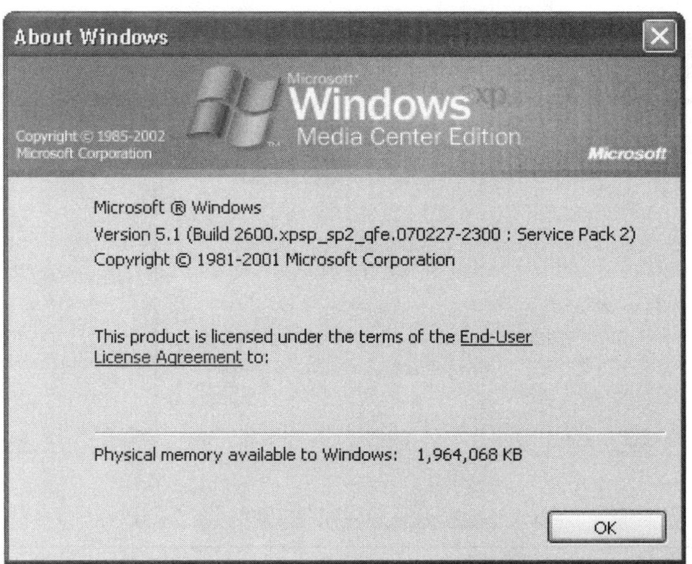

Figure 11-1 Available RAM for Windows

Next, check the paging file size:

1. From the Start menu, right-click My Computer and choose Properties.
2. In the System Properties window, open the Advanced tab. Under Performance, click the Settings button.
3. In the Performance Options window's Advanced tab, in the Virtual Memory area, click Change. You'll see the screen shown in Figure 11-2, which shows the paging file sizes. Figure 11-2 shows that currently 2877 MB RAM have been allocated to the C: drive.

Running the SAPinst for Prerequisites Check

Optionally you can run the Prerequisites checker using the SAPinst tool in a standalone manner. To run the prerequisites checker in standalone mode, do the following:

1. Click sapinst.exe in the installation master DVD.
2. When the SAPinst Welcome screen appears, navigate to SAP NetWeaver 2004s Support Release 2 | Additional Software Life-Cycle Tasks | Additional Preparation Tasks | Prerequisites Check. Then click Next twice.

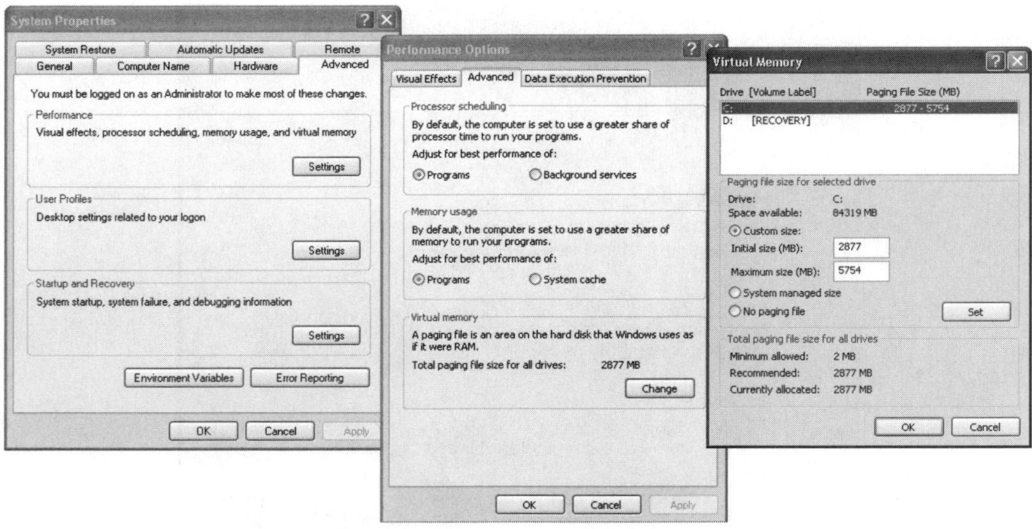

FIGURE 11-2 Paging file sizes for Windows

3. In the Prerequisites Checker | Services screen, you must select instances you plan to install on that host, as shown in the following dialog box. Click Next.

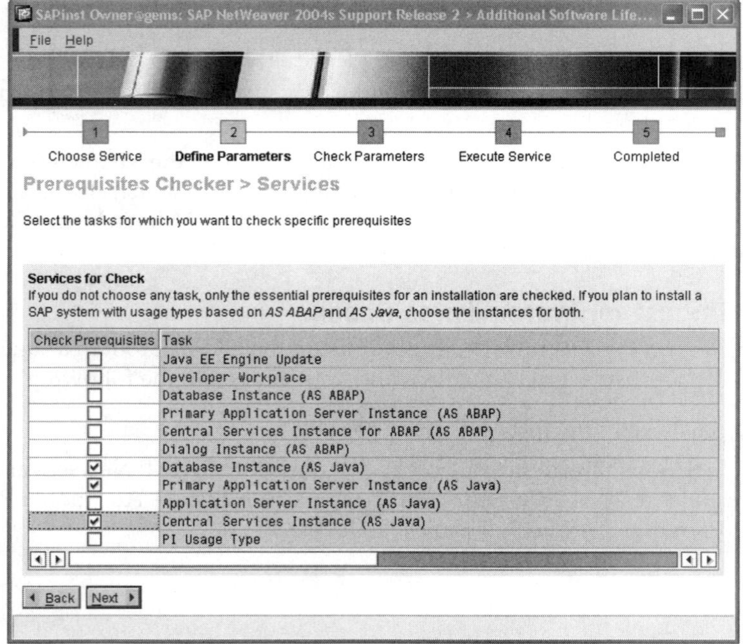

4. If you have selected the database instance, the system will prompt you to select the database type. Select the database, click Next, and then click Start.

INFO *The Prerequisites check is also carried out during the installation process by SAPinst.*

The prerequisite checker checks for the operating system version, swap size, domain controller, RAM size, and host name requirements. Note that these are basic minimum requirements and if these requirements are not met, you may have problems after installation. Note that for a production system, you should also rely on the sizing results in addition to these.

Install and Configure Sun Java SDK 1.4.2_0

To check the installed JDK version, go to the Add or Remove Programs screen from the Control Panel. Scroll through the list of installed programs and you will be able to identify the different versions of the JDK that have been installed. Following are the steps for installing and configuring the Sun Java SDK 1.4.2_0 (versions higher than 1.4.2_06 and less than 1.5):

1. Go to http://java.sun.com/products/archive/j2se/1.4.2_09/index.html. Then click the Download J2SDK link to download j2sdk-1_4_2_09-windows-i586.exe, as shown in Figure 1-3.
2. From the Control Panel, click the System icon, and in the System Properties window, choose the Advanced tab. Then click Environment Variables.
3. Click New to open the Edit System Variable dialog box, shown in Figure 11-4.
4. In the Variable Name field, type in **JAVA_HOME**, and in the Variable Value field, type **c:\j2sdk1.4.2_09**. During installation, SAPinst will check for the `SAPINST_JRE_HOME` environment variable; if it is not found, it will check for the `JAVA_HOME` variables.
5. Repeat Step 3.

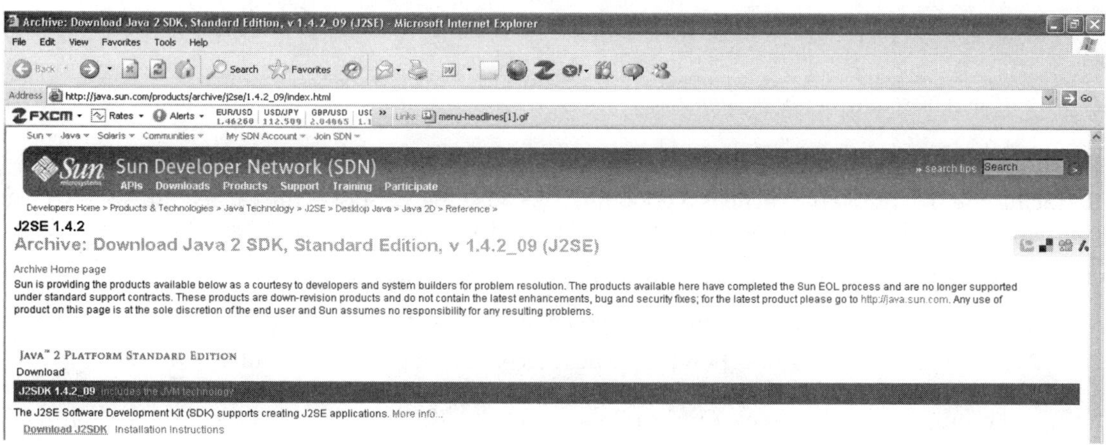

FIGURE 11-3 Download page on Sun for J2SE SDK 1.4.2

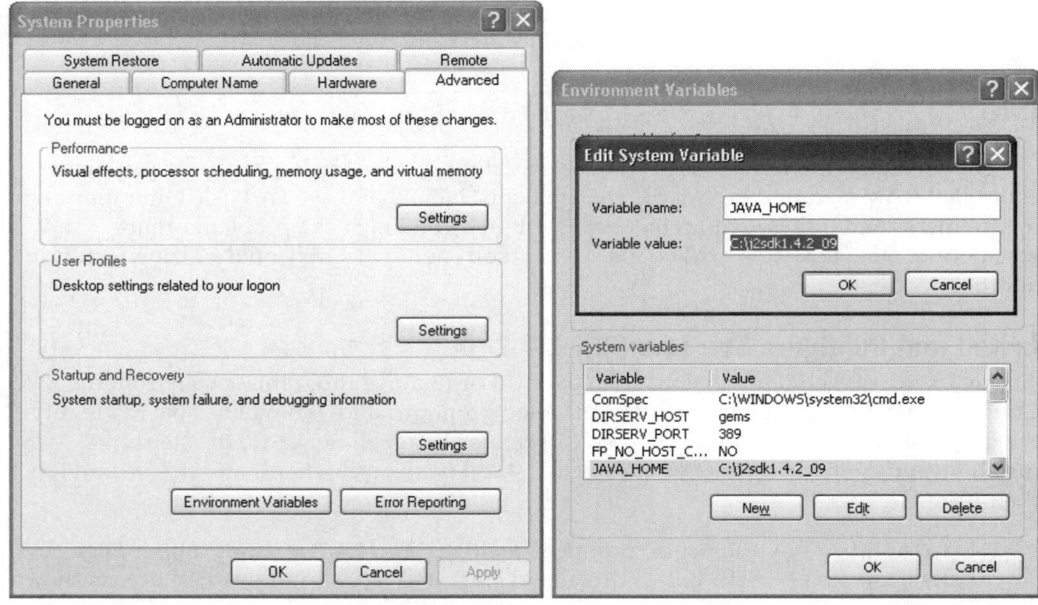

FIGURE 11-4 Setting up the environment variables

6. In the New User Variable dialog box, enter **PATH** in the Variable Name field and in the Variable Value field, enter the bin folder—for example, c:\j2sdk1.4.2_09\bin. Click OK.
7. To download Java Cryptography Extension (JCE) policy files, go to http://java.sun.com/j2se/1.4.2/download.html, and download jce_policy-1_4_2.zip (Java Cryptography Extension [JCE] Unlimited Strength Jurisdiction Policy Files 1.4.2).

DON'T *The JDK should not be version 1.5.x.*

Reducing the File Cache Size

Reducing the size of the file cache is a good idea, because the Windows file cache will compete with SAP programs for memory. Here's how to do this:

1. From the Control Panel, open the Network Connections window.
2. Right-click Local Area Connection and choose Properties.
3. In the Local Area Connection Properties screen, choose File and Printer Sharing for Microsoft Networks and choose Properties. Then choose Maximum Data Throughput for Network Applications and click OK.

Install and Configure Microsoft SQL Server

Once you have completed all the pre-installation steps, your next step is to install the required database, which, in this case, is Microsoft SQL Server. For SAP NetWeaver 7.0 SR1 and SR2, you can install either Microsoft SQL Server 2000 or SQL Server 2005. Though it is recommended that the SQL Server 2005 be installed, the installation steps have been included here for both the SQL Server versions. You can install the SQL Server either manually or automatically using the SQL4SAP.VBS script. If you want to use the automatic option, refer to OSS note 377430 for SQL Server 2000 and OSS note 896566 for SQL Server 2005. The following sections discuss how to install the SQL Server manually.

NOTE *You cannot use the automatic option to install the SQL Server if you plan to set up a high availability environment.*

Install and Configure Microsoft SQL Server 2000

If you have an existing SQL Server installation that is older than the one you plan to install, uninstall it and delete the folder C:\program files\sql server. Restart the computer, and then start the SQL server installation. Then do the following:

1. Double-click autorun.exe file in the x86\SQL2000 folder that contains the MS SQL Server software.
2. Select the SQL Server 2000 components.
3. In the Install Components Microsoft SQL Server 2000 Enterprise Edition dialog box, choose Install Database Server.
4. In the Welcome screen, click Next.
5. In the Computer Name screen, choose Local Computer. Then click Next.
6. In the Installation Selection screen, choose Create A New Instance Of SQL Server, or install Client Tools. Then click Next.
7. In the User Information dialog box, enter your Name and Company. Then click Next.
8. In the Software License Agreement screen, choose Yes after reading the license agreement.
9. In the Installation Definition screen, select the Server And Client Tools radio button. Then click Next.
10. In the Instance Name dialog box, select the Default checkbox, if possible, or enter an instance name. Then click Next.

11. In the Setup Type dialog box shown next, choose Custom, and then click Next.

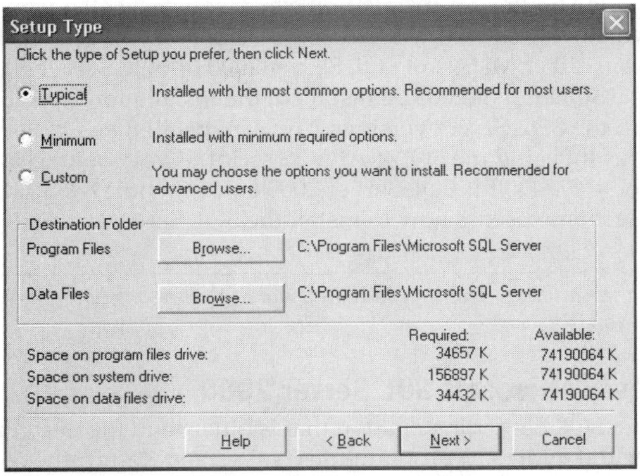

Setup Type

Click the type of Setup you prefer, then click Next.

Typical — Installed with the most common options. Recommended for most users.

Minimum — Installed with minimum required options.

Custom — You may choose the options you want to install. Recommended for advanced users.

Destination Folder

Program Files — Browse... — C:\Program Files\Microsoft SQL Server

Data Files — Browse... — C:\Program Files\Microsoft SQL Server

	Required:	Available:
Space on program files drive:	34657 K	74190064 K
Space on system drive:	156897 K	74190064 K
Space on data files drive:	34432 K	74190064 K

Help — < Back — Next > — Cancel

12. In the Select Components screen, click Next.
13. In the Service Accounts dialog box, choose Use The Local System Account, and then click Next.
14. In the Authentication Mode screen, choose Mixed Mode. Enter a password for a login and then click Next.
15. In the Collation Settings screen, choose SQL Collations. From the drop-down list, choose Binary Order, for use with the 850 (Multilingual) Character Set. Then click Next.
16. In the Network Libraries screen, click Next.
17. In the Start Copying Files screen, click Next. The installation will now proceed. Once the installation is complete, click Finish.

SQL Server 2000 is now installed.

Install SQL Server Service Pack 4

You must always install the latest service pack for the MS SQL Server because it includes all the changes in the previous service packs. As of this writing, the latest service pack levels for SQL Server 2000 are SP4 and SP2 for SQL Server 2005.

NOTE *You need not install each of the SQL Server service packs individually.*

Here's how to install SQL Service Pack 4:

1. Go to http://www.microsoft.com/downloads/details.aspx?familyid=8E2DFC8D-C20E-4446-99A9-B7F0213F8BC5&displaylang=en.

2. In the Change Language field, select English.
3. Click the Download Files Below link.
4. Assuming you have a 32-bit Windows platform, download the SQL2000-KB884525-SP4-x86-ENU.EXE file to your local folder (choose the appropriate .exe file that suits your architecture).
5. Double-click the SQL2000-KB884525-SP4-x86-ENU.EXE file.
6. In the Open File–Security Warning dialog box, click Run.
7. In the InstallShield Wizard screen, note the folder location where the files will be extracted and click Next. Then click Finish.
8. Ensure that the SQL Server is not running.
9. Navigate to the folder where the files are unpacked and double-click setup.bat.
10. In the Welcome screen, click Next.
11. In the Software License Agreement screen, click Yes.
12. In the Instance Name dialog box, choose the instance name.
13. In the Connect To Server screen, choose The SQL Server System Administrator Login Information (SQL Server Authentication) radio button. Enter the password you entered for SA user during the SQL Server installation and click Next.
14. In the SQL Server 2000 Service Pack 4 Setup screen, choose Upgrade Microsoft Search and Apply SQL Server 2000 SP4 (required) checkbox and then click Continue.
15. In the Error Reporting screen, click OK.
16. In the Start Copying Files screen, click Next.
17. In the Setup screen, click OK.
18. In the Setup Complete screen, click Finish to restart your computer and complete setup.

Service Pack 4 is now installed. If you have problems during the installation of the service pack, refer to the OSS note 417089.

Apply the SQL Server Hotfix

It is important that you apply the latest SQL Server hotfix (also known as QFEs) for a given service pack release as it can avoid potential issues in functionality.

NOTE *The latest Hotfix that is available for the SQL Server 2000 Service Pack 4 is SQL Server 2000 Build 2187.*

Here's how to apply the SQL Server hotfix:

1. Go to https://websmp109.sap-ag.de/swcenter-3pmain. At this location, you can download the patches for various database systems including the MS SQL Server.
2. Navigate to Database Patches | MS SQL Server | SQL Server 32 bit | SQL Server 2000.

PART III

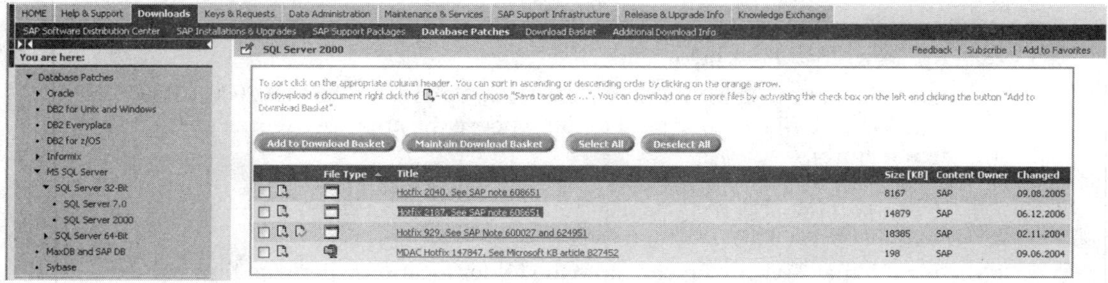

Copyright by SAP AG

FIGURE 11-5 SAP Service Marketplace download page for SQL Server hotfix

3. Click the link Hotfix 2187, See SAP Note 608651, shown in Figure 11-5. Figure 11-5 displays the location in the SAP Service Marketplace where the database patches and support tools provided by third-party vendors can be obtained.
4. Click Save to store the file SQL2000_8_00_2187_x86x64.exe in your local folder.
5. Double-click SQL2000_8_00_2187_x86x64.exe. Click Run.
6. In the Software Update Installation Wizard screen, choose Next.
7. In the License Agreement screen, choose I Agree and click Next. Then choose the instance and click Next.
8. In the Authentication Mode screen, choose SQL Server Authentication and enter the SA password. Then click Next.

The SQL Server hotfix is now installed.

Apply the Collation Fix

During the SQL Server 2000 installation, you chose the value Binary Order For Use With The 850 Multilingual Character Set for the Collation Setting. This option creates the databases and table columns with the SQL_Latin1_General_CP850_BIN collation setting. However, this collation setting does not sort the Unicode data properly for SAP systems that use Java components. Therefore, you need to change the collation setting from SQL_Latin1_General_CP850_BIN to SQL_Latin1_General_CP850_BIN2 using the steps mentioned next. Since SQL Server 2005 already uses the SQL_Latin1_General_CP850_BIN2 collation type, these steps are not required during SQL Server 2005 installation.

Here's how to apply the collation fix:

1. Go to http://service.sap.com/notes.
2. Enter **600027** in the Number field and click the arrow button next to the field. A new window will appear with the details of the OSS note.
3. Scroll down the page and download the instcoll_i386.zip (or choose the zip file that suits your architecture). Save instcoll.exe to the C: drive.

4. Double-click instcoll.exe. Then Enter **y** in the y/n prompt. Look for the following entries in the command prompt:

```
Default collation successfully changed.
Recovery Complete.
SQL global counter collection task is created.
```

5. Close the Command prompt window. The collation fix has been applied.

TIP *If you encounter any problems, refer to the OSS note 600027 for help.*

Install and Configure Microsoft SQL Server 2005

To install Microsoft SQL Server 2005 software, you must ensure the following:

- You are a local administrator.
- At least 2GB hard disk space is available for a 32-bit machine.
- Ensure that the Microsoft Distributed Transaction Coordinator service is running.

Following are the steps required to install the software:

1. Double-click the setup.exe file in the Servers folder for the 32-bit platform.
2. In the End User License Agreement screen, choose the checkbox to accept the licensing terms and conditions, and click Next.
3. In the Installing Prerequisites screen, click Install. This step installs the required Microsoft SQL Native Client and the setup support files. Click Next to proceed.
4. In the System Configuration screen, you can check the required configuration and view, and save the report to a file. Click Next to proceed.
5. In the Registration Information screen, enter the personal details and the product key. Click Next.
6. In the Components To Install screen, select the SQL Server Database Services and the Workstation components, Books Online, and development tools checkboxes. Then click Advanced.
7. In the Feature Selection screen, expand Database Services, click Replication, and select Entire Feature Will Be Unavailable to deselect replication. In a similar manner, expand Client Components and deselect Business Intelligence Development Studio. Click Next.
8. In the Instance Name screen, choose the Default Instance and click Next. To view a list of installed instances, you can click Installed Instances.
9. In the Service Account screen, choose Use The Built-In System Account For Each Service and select Local System. Ensure that the SQL Server and SQL Server Agent are selected under Start Services At The End Of Setup.
10. In the Authentication Mode screen, choose Mixed Node (Windows Authentication And SQL Server Authentication). Enter the password for SA in accordance with your system's password policy.

11. In the Collation Settings screen, choose SQL Collations (Used For Compatibility With Previous Versions Of SQL Server) and choose Binary Order Based On Code Point Comparison, For Use With The 850 (Multilingual) Character Set. Choose Next.
12. In the Error And Usage Report Settings screen, click Next.
13. In the Ready To Install screen, click Install. To view the log files during the install, you can click the Setup Finished link under the Status column. Click Next.
14. In the Completing Microsoft SQL Server 2005 Setup screen, click Finish.
15. To finalize the configuration, navigate to the Start menu, then click All Programs | Microsoft SQL Server 2005 | Configuration Tools | SQL Server Configuration Manager. On the right pane, check whether the Named Pipes and TCP/IP are enabled. If not, right-click each one and click Enable in the context menu.
16. Complete the installation by restarting the SQL Server.

SAPinst

Now that you have installed the SQL Server, your next step is to install the SAP NetWeaver AS Java, and along with it the other usage types such as Enterprise Portal Core and Enterprise Portal. To install the AS Java and Enterprise Portal, you must start the SAPinst SAP software installation tool.

Before Starting the SAPinst Installation Tool

SAPinst uses the SAPinst GUI and a GUI server. When SAPinst is started, both the SAPinst GUI and the GUI server also start. SAPinst GUI connects to the GUI server and the GUI server in turn connects to SAPinst. Before starting the SAPinst, ensure the following:

- Check whether the `TEMP` environment variable is set to a suitable value. During the installation, a sapinst_instdir\\<*installation_directory*> folder gets created under the Program Files folder for storing the log files. If it cannot be created under Program Files, the folder gets created in the location set in the `TEMP` variable.
- Ensure that you have local administrator rights, if you are doing a local installation. If you are doing a domain installation, you should either have domain administrator rights or be a domain user with local administrator rights on the host.
- Ensure that you have at least 130MB of free space in the installation directory and 60 to 200MB of free space for SAPinst executables.

Starting the SAPinst Installation Software

Insert the Installation Master DVD and navigate to <*DVD_Drive*>:\IM_WINDOWS_I386 folder. Double-click sapinst.exe to start the SAPinst tool. A SAPinst software installation screen similar to the one shown in Figure 11-6 will appear.

TIP *During installation using SAPinst, it is useful to check the sapinst_instdir folder for troubleshooting. In addition, the SAPinst self-extractor log file dev_selfex.out contains useful information if an error occurs.*

Setting the Port for SAPinst

During installation, port 21200 is used for communication between SAPinst and the GUI server, while port 21212 is used for communication between the GUI server and the

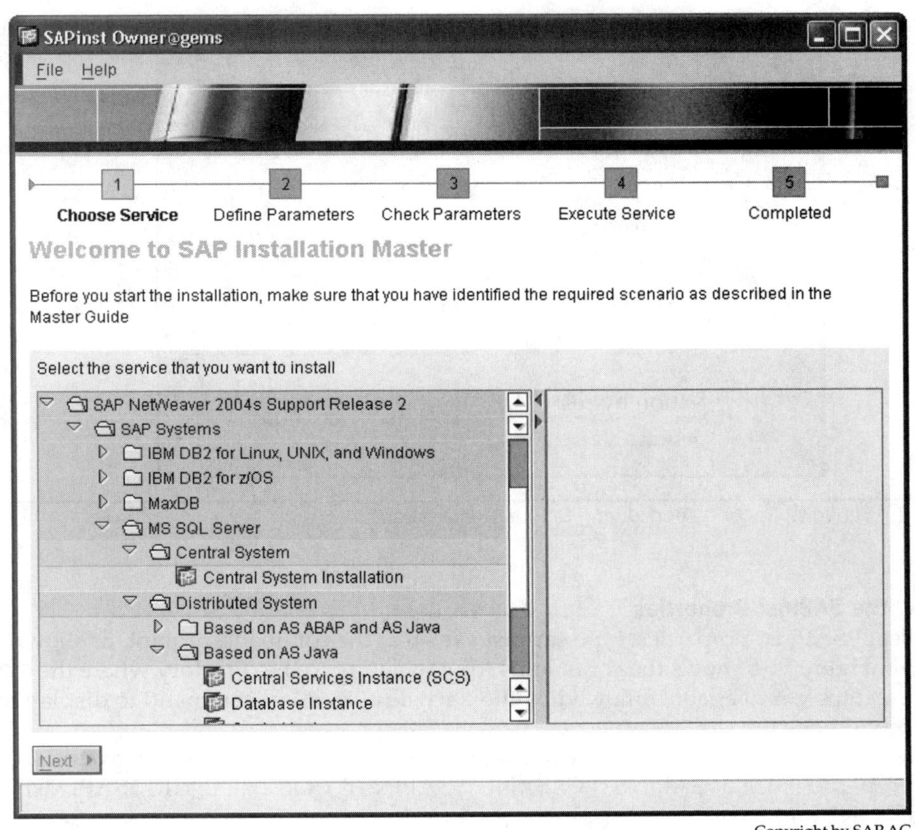

FIGURE 11-6 SAPinst install screen for NetWeaver installation software

SAPinst GUI. If SAPinst is used by another port, use the command prompt to go to the required directory where sapinst.exe exists and enter the following:

```
sapinst.exe SAPINST_DIALOG_PORT=<free_port_number_sapinst_gui_to_gui_server>
GUISERVER_DIALOG_PORT=<free_port_number_gui_server_to_sapinst_gui>
```

In this command, replace the placeholders *<free_port_number_sapinst_gui_to_gui_server>* and *<free_port_number_gui_server_to_sapinst_gui>* with ports other than 21200. This command will execute the SAPinst on a port other than 21200.

TIP *Sometimes SAPinst installation may not proceed if the firewall restricts the 21200 port.*

Sometimes, if the Windows firewall is active, you may see the screen as displayed in Figure 11-7. Click Unblock to proceed.

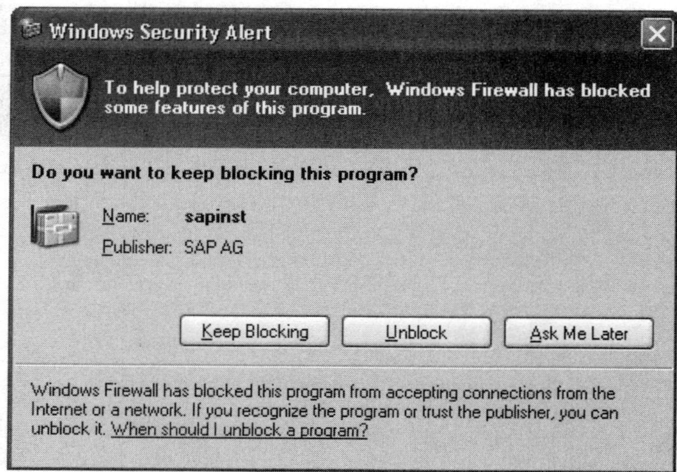

FIGURE 11-7 Windows Security Alert during SAPinst installation

Retrieving the SAPinst Properties

To get a list of SAPinst properties, type **sapinst.exe –p** at the command prompt, as shown in Figure 11-8. Figure 11-8 shows the commands for navigating to the directory where the SAPinst executable is available followed by the `sapinst.exe -p` command to display the SAPinst properties.

Figure 11-9 shows the output after entering the command. The output displays some SAPinst properties such as SAPINST_CLEANUP, SAPINST_CONTROL_URL, SAPINST_DIALOG_PORT, and so on.

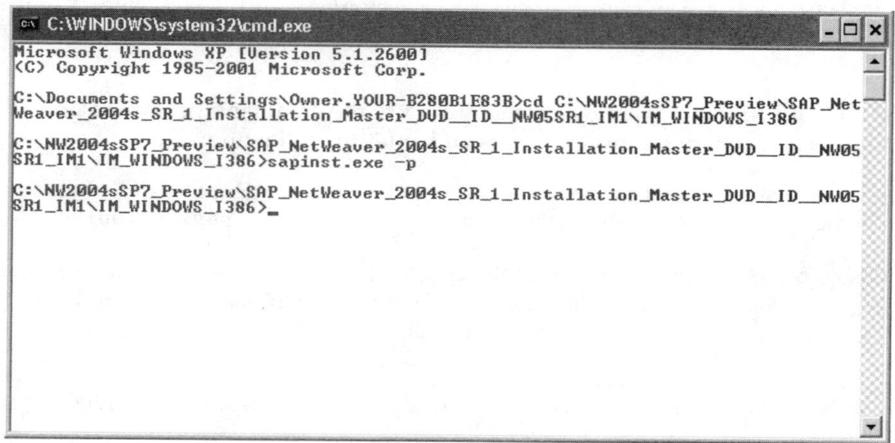

FIGURE 11-8 Command prompt screen showing command

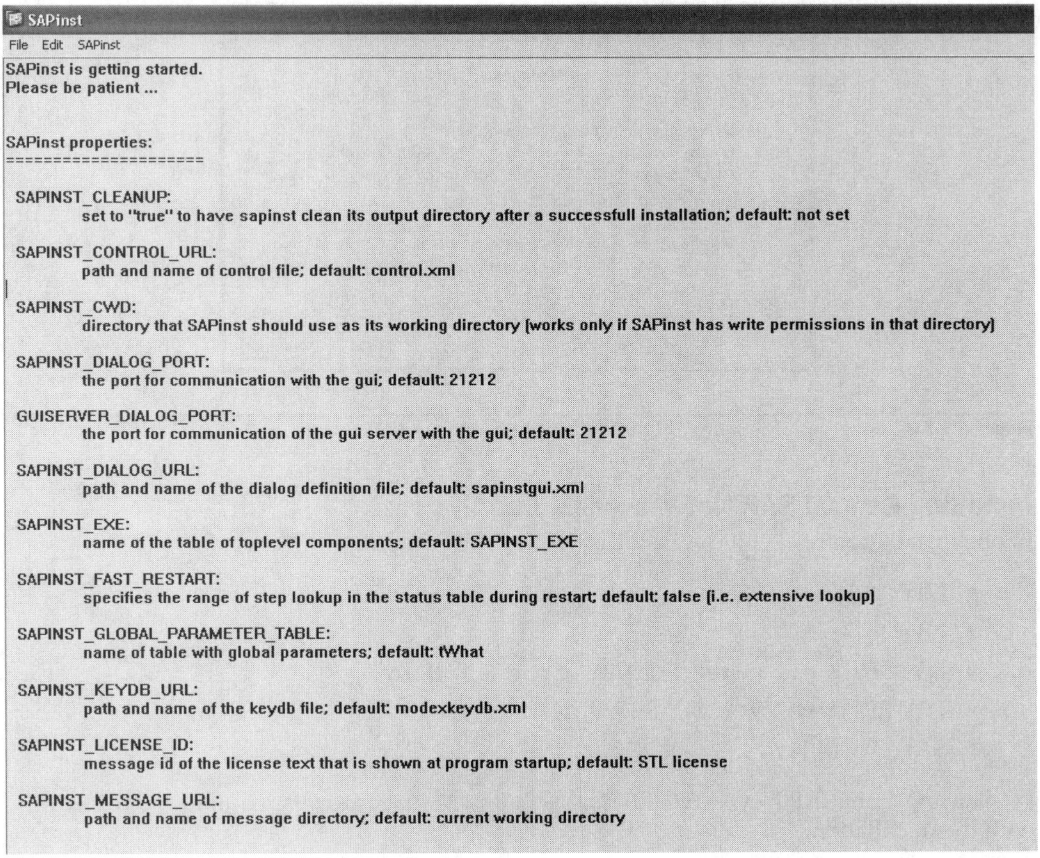

SAPinst

File Edit SAPinst

```
SAPinst is getting started.
Please be patient ...


SAPinst properties:
=====================

 SAPINST_CLEANUP:
         set to "true" to have sapinst clean its output directory after a successfull installation; default: not set

 SAPINST_CONTROL_URL:
         path and name of control file; default: control.xml

 SAPINST_CWD:
         directory that SAPinst should use as its working directory (works only if SAPinst has write permissions in that directory)

 SAPINST_DIALOG_PORT:
         the port for communication with the gui; default: 21212

 GUISERVER_DIALOG_PORT:
         the port for communication of the gui server with the gui; default: 21212

 SAPINST_DIALOG_URL:
         path and name of the dialog definition file; default: sapinstgui.xml

 SAPINST_EXE:
         name of the table of toplevel components; default: SAPINST_EXE

 SAPINST_FAST_RESTART:
         specifies the range of step lookup in the status table during restart; default: false (i.e. extensive lookup)

 SAPINST_GLOBAL_PARAMETER_TABLE:
         name of table with global parameters; default: tWhat

 SAPINST_KEYDB_URL:
         path and name of the keydb file; default: modexkeydb.xml

 SAPINST_LICENSE_ID:
         message id of the license text that is shown at program startup; default: STL license

 SAPINST_MESSAGE_URL:
         path and name of message directory; default: current working directory
```


FIGURE 11-9 SAPinst properties output

Additional Software Lifecycle Tasks

In the SAPinst installation tool are options for Additional Software Life cycle Tasks such as Active Directory Configuration, Operating System Users and Groups, and conducting Prerequisites Check for hardware and software. Other installation services are included for creating additional dialog instances on an already existing system, conducting a system copy, and uninstalling an SAP system. Depending upon the version you are using, these options could vary.

Exit, Stop, and Continue Buttons

Clicking F1 on any input parameter displays a Help dialog box. Choose File | Exit to display a dialog box with two buttons: Stop and Continue, as shown in Figure 11-10. Clicking Stop will stop the installation, but you can continue again later. Choosing File | Logoff will stop the SAPinst GUI, but the SAPinst and GUI server continue to run. You can reconnect later on.

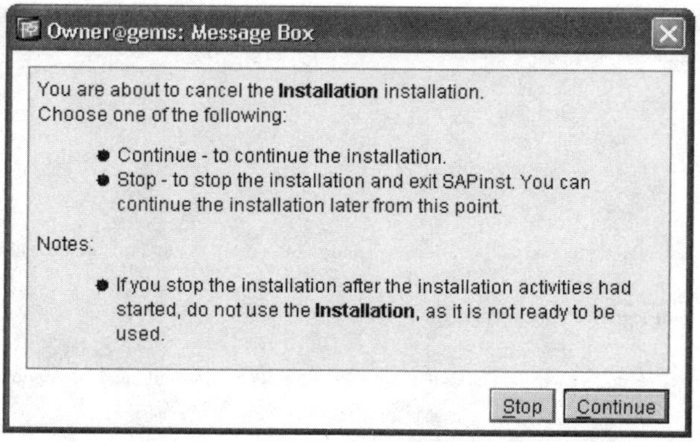

Copyright by SAP AG

FIGURE 11-10 Stop and Continue buttons during the SAPinst install

Installing Central SAP NetWeaver AS Java System

In one installation run, you can install all of the following for NetWeaver 2004s(7.0):

- NW AS Java
- NWDI
- NW EP Core (Core functionality of portal platform)
- NW EP—KMC, VC, WD, .Net PDK
- SAP NW BI Java

Starting from SAP NetWeaver 2004s, a Solution Manager Key is required to proceed with the installation.

TIP *Refer to OSS note 811923 on how to generate the Solution Manager Key.*

Following are some of the steps involved when installing a SAP NetWeaver AS Java system using default values. Note that the steps for you may differ depending upon a number of factors specific to your installation:

1. Launch the SAPinst tool by double-clicking the sapinst.exe file in the IM_WINDOWS_I386 folder for the 32-bit Windows operating system.
2. Navigate to SAP Systems | <*your database*> | Central System | Central System Installation.
3. In the What Do You Want To Do screen, select the Run A New Installation radio button and click OK.
4. In the Parameter Mode | Default Settings screen, leave the Parameter Mode set to Typical and click Next.
5. In the SAP System | Software Units screen shown in the following illustration, select the AS Java usage type as well as the Portal related usage types—namely, EP Core and EP. Deselect AS ABAP and click Next to proceed.

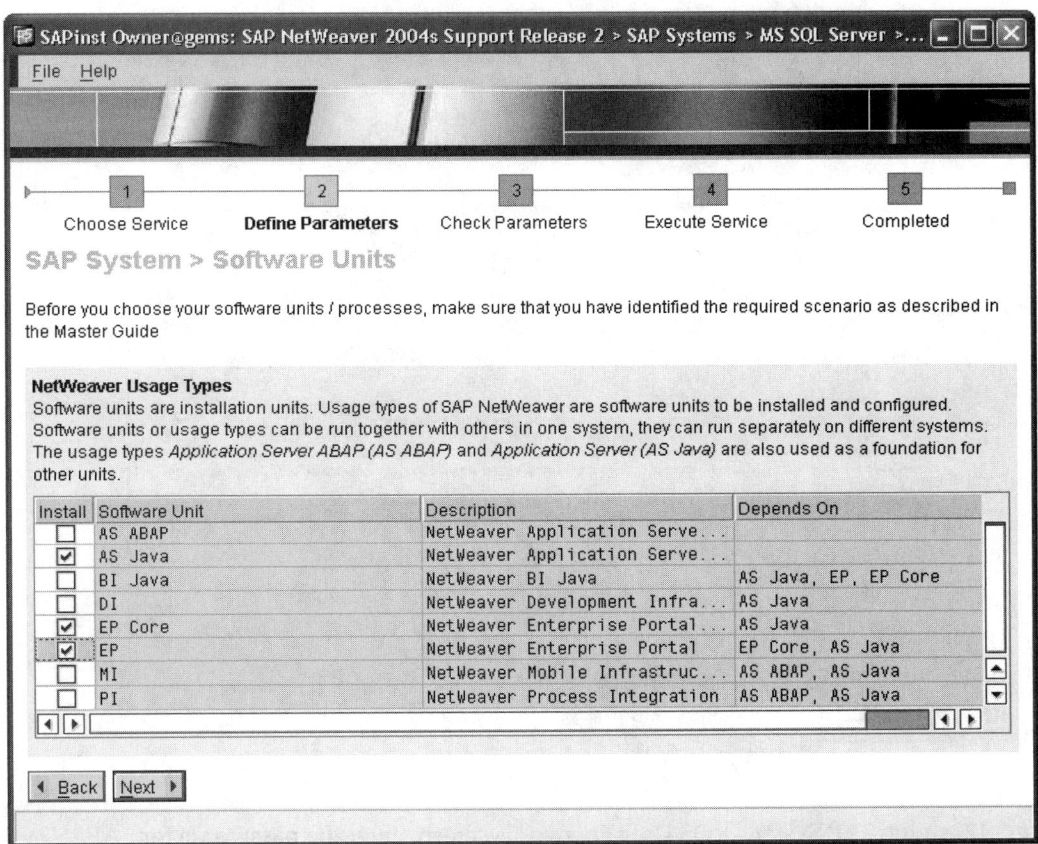

6. In the Media Browser | Software Package Request screen, click the Browse button to select the location where the Java Component software DVD (Java Component NW2004sSR2) is located. Click OK.
7. In the SAP System | Java Development Kit screen, enter the location of the JDK directory. Click Next.
8. In the SAP System | JCE Unlimited Strength Jurisdiction Policy Archive screen, click Browse to select the JCE Unlimited Strength Jurisdiction Policy zip file that was downloaded when installing the Sun Java SDK 1.4.2_0 (refer to step 7 in the section "Install and Configure Sun Java SDK 1.4.2_0"). Click Next.
9. In the SAP System | General Parameters screen, enter the SAP system ID, preferably J2E, in the SAP System ID (SAPSID) field. Click Next.
10. In the SAP System | Master Password screen, enter the master password that will be used for all users that SAPinst creates during the installation process. Click Next.
11. In the SAP System | Windows Domain screen, select Local Installation in the Domain Model field as shown next. Click Next.

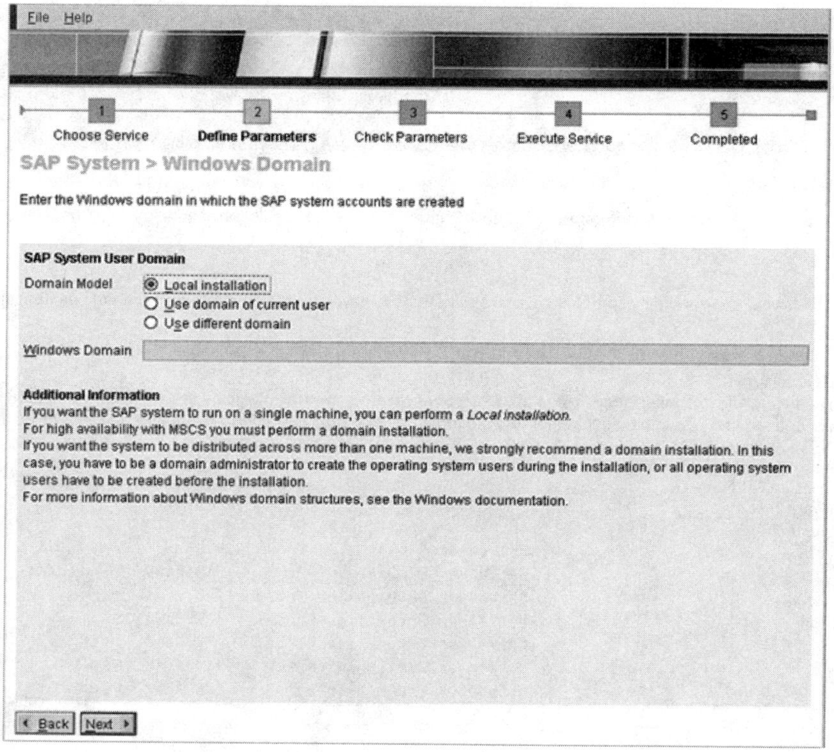

File Help

1 Choose Service 2 Define Parameters 3 Check Parameters 4 Execute Service 5 Completed

SAP System > Windows Domain

Enter the Windows domain in which the SAP system accounts are created

SAP System User Domain

Domain Model
- Local installation
- Use domain of current user
- Use different domain

Windows Domain

Additional Information

If you want the SAP system to run on a single machine, you can perform a *Local installation*.
For high availability with MSCS you must perform a domain installation.
If you want the system to be distributed across more than one machine, we strongly recommend a domain installation. In this case, you have to be a domain administrator to create the operating system users during the installation, or all operating system users have to be created before the installation.
For more information about Windows domain structures, see the Windows documentation.

Back Next

12. In the SAP System | OS User Passwords screen, enter the passwords for SAP System Administrator and SAP System Service User. Note down these passwords for future reference as shown next. Click Next.

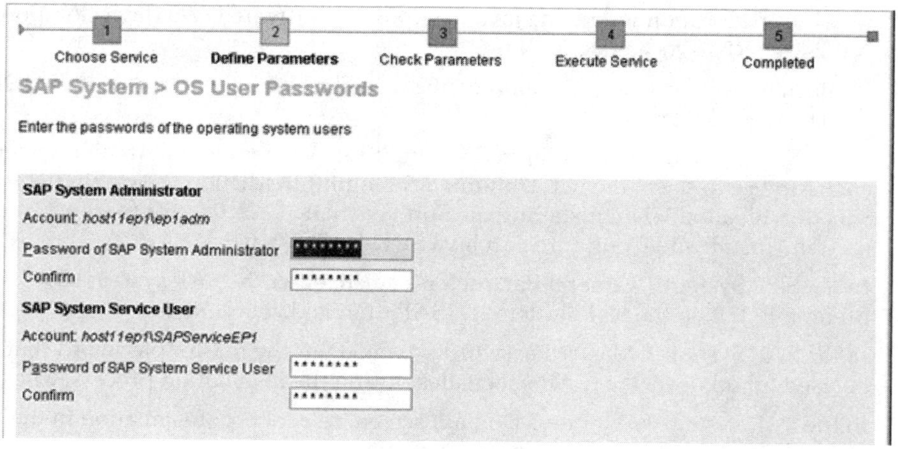

1 Choose Service 2 Define Parameters 3 Check Parameters 4 Execute Service 5 Completed

SAP System > OS User Passwords

Enter the passwords of the operating system users

SAP System Administrator

Account: *host11ep1\ep1adm*

Password of SAP System Administrator ********

Confirm ********

SAP System Service User

Account: *host11ep1\SAPServiceEP1*

Password of SAP System Service User ********

Confirm ********

13. In the SAP System | Database Parameters screen, enter the Database ID (DBSID). Click Next.
14. In the next few screens, enter the database parameters such as password for database schema, database server drives, and database users.
15. In the SAP System | Secure Store Settings screen, enter a Key Phrase (8 to 30 characters). Click Next.
16. In the SAP System | Central and SCS Instance screen, enter the Central Instance Number and the SCS Instance Number as **00** and **01**, respectively, as shown next. Click Next.

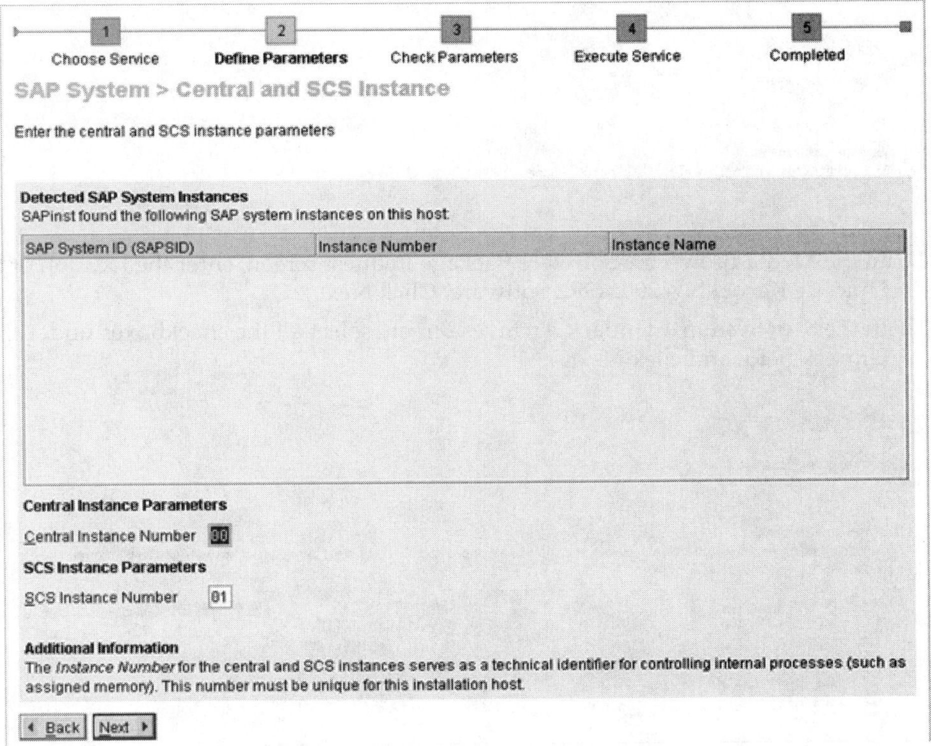

Copyright by SAP AG

17. In the Media Browser | Software Package Request screen, click Browse to select the location of the Kernel software DVD (UC Kernel NW2004sSR2) and then click OK.
18. In the SAP System | Central Instance screen, leave the default values for Host with Transport Directory and Internal SCS Messaging Service Port and click Next.
19. In the SAP System | UME Configuration screen, leave the default selection for UME Configuration as Use Java Database (default).

PART III

20. In the SAP System | Java UME screen shown next, in the J2EE Engine Connection section, enter the Administrator User, Password For Administrator User, and Guest User name. Under the SDM Connection section, enter the SDM Password.

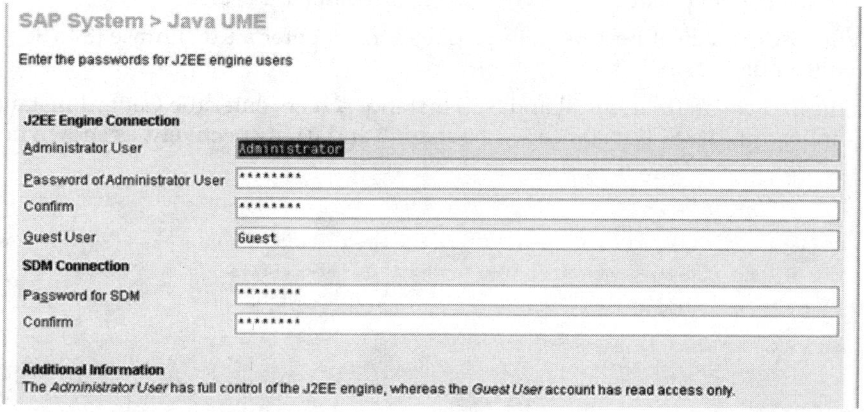

SAP System > Java UME

Enter the passwords for J2EE engine users

J2EE Engine Connection

Administrator User: Administrator

Password of Administrator User: ********

Confirm: ********

Guest User: Guest

SDM Connection

Password for SDM: ********

Confirm: ********

Additional Information

The *Administrator User* has full control of the J2EE engine, whereas the *Guest User* account has read access only.

21. In the Media Browser | Software Package Request screen, enter the location of the Unicode Kernel NW2004sSR2 Software. Click Next.
22. In the SAP System | Unpack Archives screen, select all the checkboxes under the Unpack field, and click Next.

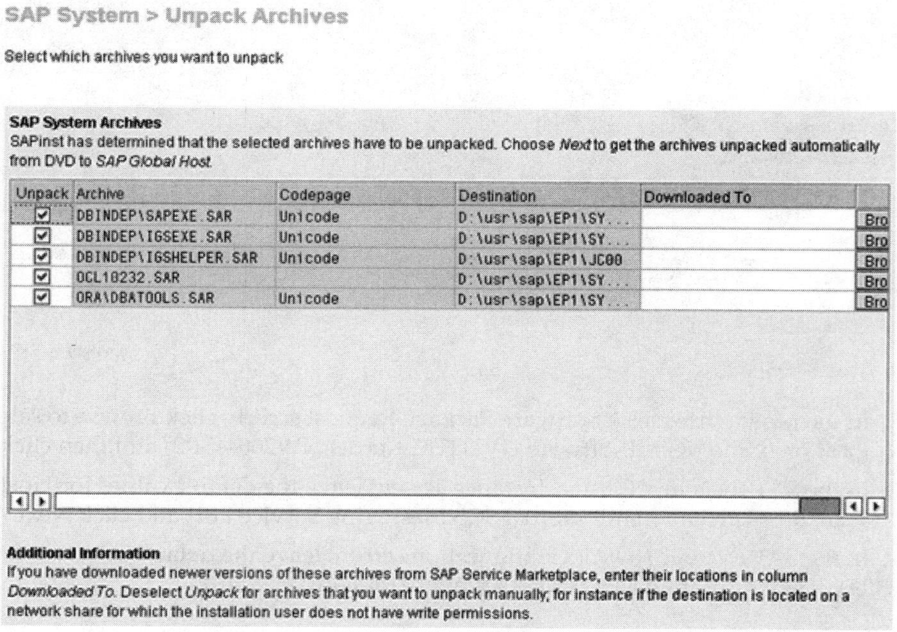

SAP System > Unpack Archives

Select which archives you want to unpack

SAP System Archives

SAPinst has determined that the selected archives have to be unpacked. Choose *Next* to get the archives unpacked automatically from DVD to *SAP Global Host*.

Unpack	Archive	Codepage	Destination	Downloaded To	
☑	DBINDEP\SAPEXE.SAR	Unicode	D:\usr\sap\EP1\SY...		Bro
☑	DBINDEP\IGSEXE.SAR	Unicode	D:\usr\sap\EP1\SY...		Bro
☑	DBINDEP\IGSHELPER.SAR	Unicode	D:\usr\sap\EP1\JC00		Bro
☑	OCL10232.SAR		D:\usr\sap\EP1\SY...		Bro
☑	ORA\DBATOOLS.SAR	Unicode	D:\usr\sap\EP1\SY...		Bro

Additional Information

If you have downloaded newer versions of these archives from SAP Service Marketplace, enter their locations in column *Downloaded To*. Deselect *Unpack* for archives that you want to unpack manually; for instance if the destination is located on a network share for which the installation user does not have write permissions.

23. In the SAP System | NWDI Landscape screen, leave the Prepare SAP System For NWDI Integration unchecked. Click Next.
24. In the SAP System | System Landscape Directory screen, select No SLD Destination and click Next.
25. In the SAP System | ADS Administrator screen, enter the password for ADS Administrator and click Next.
26. In the Parameter Summary screen shown below, review the settings and click Start to proceed with the installation.

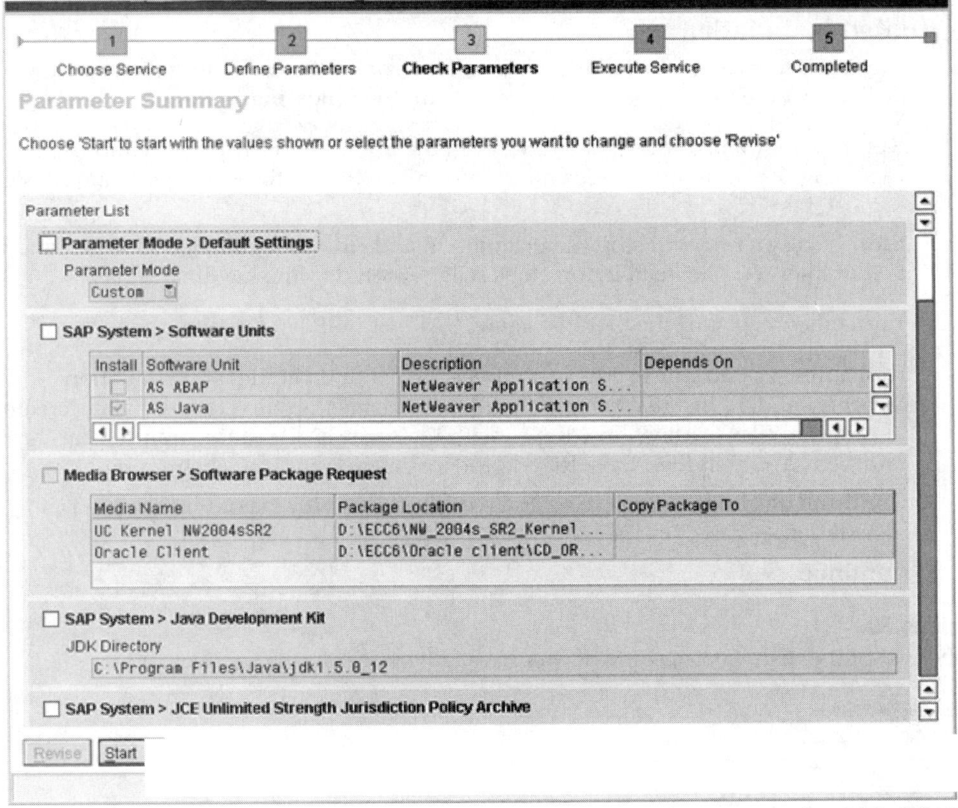

27. In the SAP System | SAP Solution Manager screen, enter the Solution Manager Key and click Continue.

NOTE *Starting with SAP NetWeaver 2004s, a Solution Manager Key is required to proceed with the installation. Refer to OSS Note 811923 on how to generate the Solution Manager Key.*

Web AS Post-Installation Activities

After the installation, try to log into the Web AS Java system (J2EE engine) using the following users:

- For NW AS Java and AS ABAP, use Administrator and Guest users. In the AS ABAP system, these users are mapped as J2EE_ADMIN and J2EE_GUEST, respectively.
- For AS Java System, the users on the J2EE engine are the same, but the corresponding users in the J2EE database are also known as Administrator and Guest.

To log on to the J2EE engine, enter the URL *http://<hostname>:5<instance_no>00.*

Interrupted Installation

The system can interrupt the installation due to an error, or the user can stop it by choosing Exit in the SAPinst menu. A dialog box appears with the following options:

- **Retry** Commences the installation from the point of interruption without repeating previous steps; steps are stored in keydb.xml file in the program files\sapinst_instdir\..\...
- **Stop** This option will stop the installation and close both the SAPinst GUI and the SAPinst server. The installation steps will be stored in the keydb.xml file.

Later on, when you start the SAPinst again, SAPinst will display two options:

- **Run a new installation** SAPinst moves the contents of the old installation directory and all installation-specific files to the backup directory, which is created in program files\sapinst_instdir\.... with the name as log_date_month_year_hrs_min_secs. You will then have to redo the installation from the beginning.
- **Continue old installation** SAPinst will continue with the old interrupted installation.
- **Continue**

Services File

At the end of the installation, some new entries will appear in the services file:

```
<drive>\windows\system32\drivers\etc\services
sapdpXX = 32XX/tcp
sapdpXXs = 47XX/tcp
sapgwXX = 33XX/tcp
sapgwXXs = 48XX/tcp
```

Here, XX is the instance number. There can be more than one entry for a port number.

Directory Structure After Install

Figure 11-11 shows the directory structure of folders that will be created after the installation. The details of the important folders such as SAP kernel files and transport directory are presented next.

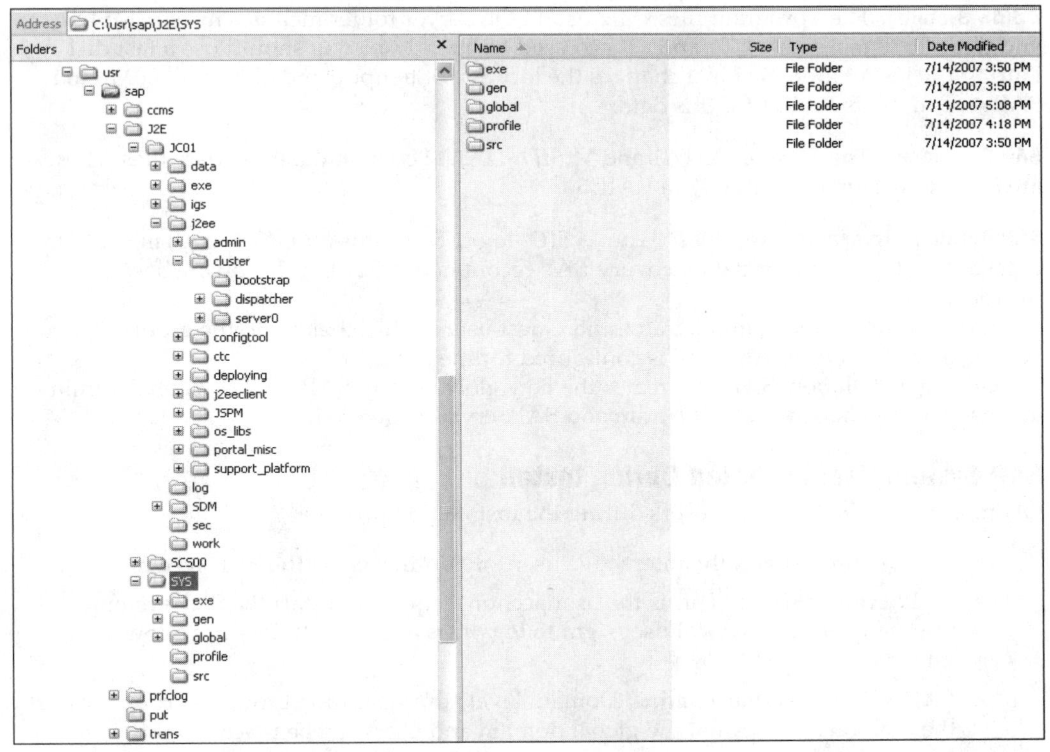

FIGURE 11-11 Folder structure displaying contents in the SYS folder

SAP System First are SAP kernel and related files:

- **\usr\sap** Created on the global host (CSI host); shared with the name sapmnt; contains the following files under \usr\sap\<*SID*>\SYS, where <*SID*> stands for the SAP System ID (default value for SAP Web AS Java is J2E):
  - **global** Contains global data
  - **profile** Contains profile information for all instances
  - **exe** Contains executable kernel programs
- **\usr\sap** Created on the local host; shared with the name saploc; contains local instance specific data; all the exe files under saploc are loaded from the global host during the startup using the program called sapcpe.

Then the SAP transport directory:

- **\usr\sap\trans** Transport directory that contains SAP software for the transport of SAP objects; can be stored outside the global system; usually the global host is also the transport host; you can specify a different host during installation.

DBMS System The \program files\Microsoft SQL Server folder includes master, MSDB, and tempdb database files. Tempdb is accessed frequently, so you should use a fast disk. During the installation, SAPinst changes the location of tempdb and allocates 300MB to it. SAP recommends RAID1 for this data.

SAP Database The \\<*SID*>DATA1 and \\<*SID*>DATA2 contain database data files. These are preferably stored separately in RAID5.

SAP Database Transaction Log Files The \\<*SID*>log<*N*> records all the changes made to the database and is useful for data recovery. SAP recommends RAID 1 (hardware based mirroring).

SAPinst creates the Administrator and Guest users, which belong to the group Authenticated Users, when UME is configured for the Java DB.

During installation, SAPinst creates the new global group SAP_<*SID*>_GlobalAdmin and assigns two new users <*SID*>adm and SAPService<*SID*> to it.

SAP System Users Created During Install

SAPinst creates the following users during the installation process:

- **<*SID*>adm** This is the interactive user for administering the SAP system.
- **SAPService<*SID*>** This is the user account required to start the SAP system internally. It has the local user right to log on as a service. It does not allow interactive logon.
- **SAP_<*SID*>_GlobalAdmin** Domain level administration group to group users at the domain level so that the global domain and users can be placed in the appropriate local groups.
- **SAP_<*SID*>_LocalAdmin** Local administrator group available only in the local machine. Contains the global administrator group of the domain to which the system belongs.
- **SAP_LocalAdmin** Members belonging to this group have full control of the usr/sap/trans folder. <*SID*>adm and SAPService<*SID*> are members of this group.

OSS Notes

Following are some useful OSS notes that can be accessed at http://service.sap.com/notes:

- **852008** Release Restrictions for SAP NetWeaver 2004s
- **982502** Portal Usage Types EP and EPC
- **855498** Installation Prerequisite Checker
- **821875** Security Settings in the Message Server
- **883948** NW 7.0(2004s): Install Additional Java Usage Types/Software Units
- **611361** Hostnames of SAP Servers
- **805390** SAP Solution Manager Is Required for SAP Software
- **737368** Hardware Requirements of Java Development Infrastructure

- **153641** Swap Space Requirement for R/3 64-Bit Kernel
- **62988** Service Packs for Microsoft SQL Server
- **608651** SQL Server 2000 Most Recent Hotfix
- **600027** Installing the Corrected MS SQL Server Collation
- **709140** Recommended JDK and VM Settings for the Web AS630/640/7.0
- **212876** The New Archiving Tool SAPCAR
- **19466** Downloading SAP Kernel Patches
- **828978** SDM Cannot Write SCA Component Information in CVERS

NOTE *For more details refer to the installation related resources listed in Appendix B.*

Summary

This chapter looked at some of the important steps involved during the portal installation. It discussed the central versus distributed options, local versus domain installation, choice of UME data store, and deciding upon the SAP system parameters such as system ID. It then walked you through the various installation steps for Sun JDK, Microsoft SQL Server 2000, SQL Server Service Pack 4, SQL Server Hotfix, SAP Web AS, and NetWeaver Portal. It also discussed how to use the SAPinst software: starting the SAPinst software, checking the SAPinst log files for troubleshooting, changing the port for SAPinst if necessary, retrieving the SAPinst properties, conducting prerequisites check using SAPinst, and how to proceed with an interrupted installation. You also glanced at the system users that were created and the directory structure after the portal install.

12

CHAPTER

Post-Installation Steps

This chapter discusses the steps you must take after the initial default installation of the SAP portal so that it can run with good performance and stability. Post-installation steps such as the following are covered here:

- Troubleshooting SAPinst-related issues
- Troubleshooting the portal installation
- Logging on to the Web AS and portal
- Running the System Analyzer and support platform
- Installing the portal license
- Deleting the portal log files
- Configuring using the Template Installer
- Configuring the J2EE engine
- Applying the patches
- Making a system backup
- Uninstalling the portal, if required

NOTE *More information on fine-tuning the SAP NetWeaver Application Server (NWAS) and the portal are available in Chapter 33.*

Troubleshooting During Installation

Following are some hints on how to proceed when you encounter issues while installing the portal.

SAPinst Troubleshooting

Following are recommendations for SAPinst-related issues:

- Check the log and trace files in the <*user profile directory*>\.sdtgui\ directory for errors, as shown in the following illustration (for example, in C:\Documents and Settings\<*logged in admin user*>\.sdtgui).

Address C:\Documents and Settings\Owner.YOUR-B280B1E83B\.sdtgui

Name	Size	Type
server.1.trc	1,429 KB	TRC File
server.2.trc	1,250 KB	TRC File
server.3.trc	1,252 KB	TRC File
server.4.trc	1,230 KB	TRC File
server.5.trc	1,367 KB	TRC File
server.6.trc	1,381 KB	TRC File
server.7.trc	7,719 KB	TRC File
server.8.trc	1,416 KB	TRC File
server.9.trc	1,283 KB	TRC File
server.err	0 KB	ERR File
server.out	0 KB	OUT File
gui.err	0 KB	ERR File
gui.out	0 KB	OUT File
sdtserver	1 KB	Text Document
server.trc	530 KB	TRC File

- Check sdtstart.err in the user profile directory for SAPinst startup errors.
- Ignore SDM-related errors that state that components are missing—see OSS Note 828978.
- To restart the SAPinst GUI after you have logged out, open a command prompt, navigate to the directory where the startinstgui.bat file is installed by entering the appropriate path, and enter **sapinstgui.bat** at the command prompt. Alternatively, you can double-click the sapinst.exe file. If the SAPinst and the GUI server are both running on the local host, the SAPinst GUI will start.
- If SAPinst is installed/running on a different host, a dialog box appears, as shown in the following illustration, where you enter the host name where SAPinst is running.

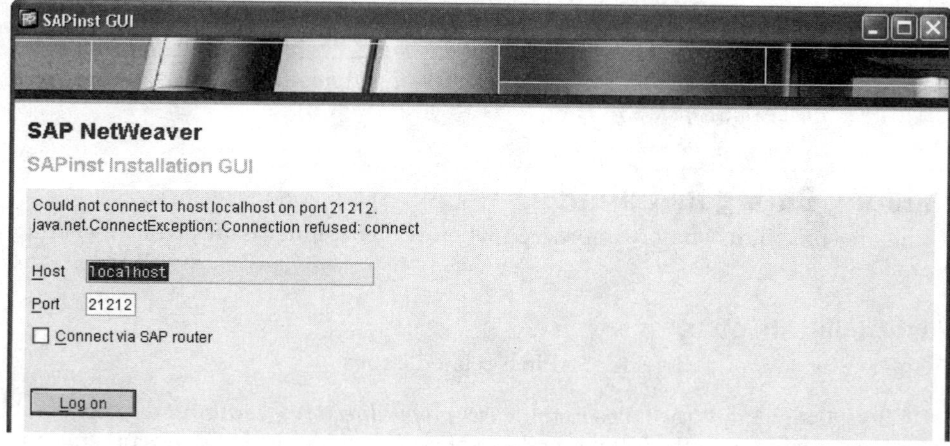

- You can also use `sapinstgui.bat -host <hostname>` to start SAPinst remotely.
- To see a list of options to start the SAPinst GUI, use `sapinstgui.bat -h` in the command prompt, as shown here:

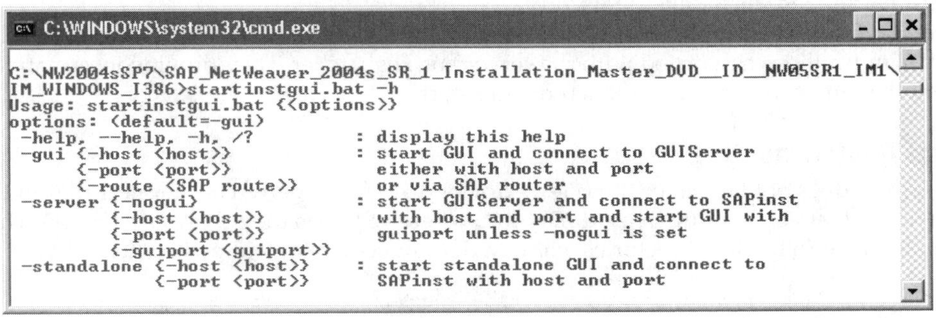

```
C:\WINDOWS\system32\cmd.exe

C:\NW2004sSP7\SAP_NetWeaver_2004s_SR_1_Installation_Master_DVD__ID__NW05SR1_IM1\
IM_WINDOWS_I386>startinstgui.bat -h
Usage: startinstgui.bat {<options>}
options: (default=-gui)
 -help, --help, -h, /?          : display this help
 -gui {-host <host>}            : start GUI and connect to GUIServer
      {-port <port>}              either with host and port
      {-route <SAP route>}        or via SAP router
 -server {-nogui}               : start GUIServer and connect to SAPinst
         {-host <host>}           with host and port and start GUI with
         {-port <port>}           guiport unless -nogui is set
         {-guiport <guiport>}
 -standalone {-host <host>}     : start standalone GUI and connect to
             {-port <port>}       SAPinst with host and port
```

- Click View Logs. After solving the problem, you can either start the installation from the point where it was stopped or restart the entire installation from the beginning.

PART III

Troubleshooting with J2EE Engine Log Files

Following are some of the log files that can be checked when you encounter problems with the SAP J2EE engine startup after the installation.

Default Trace Files

These files are located at \usr\sap\J2E\JC01\j2ee\cluster\server0\log folder. They are useful for troubleshooting application-related startup issues after the JControl has successfully started.

Bootstrap Files

A number of bootstrap-related files are located in the \usr\sap\<*SID*>\JC<*instance_number*>\work directory. These files can help you identify issues with the bootstrap mechanism during startup. A bootstrap file exists for the instance as well as for each node. In addition, other bootstrap developer trace files exist, such as dev_bootstrap, bootstrap log files from JVM such as std_bootstrap.out, and bootstrap JVM output files such as jvm_bootstrap.out.

dev_jcontrol File

This file is located in the \usr\sap\<*SID*>\JC<*instance_number*>\work directory. It is the trace file for the JControl process. It provides information on where the Java Control and Startup framework have failed.

dev_server and dev_dispatcher Files

These files are located in the \usr\sap\<*SID*>\JC<*instance_number*>\work directory. These are trace files for the JLaunch process associated with the server and dispatcher. These files can be used to troubleshoot at which stage the startup failed during the server and dispatcher startup processes. They provide information on the JVM configuration for the server and dispatcher processes. These files can also be used to identify problems due to incorrect memory settings.

std_server and std_dispatcher Files

These files are located in the \usr\sap\<*SID*>\JC<*instance_number*>\work directory. These are JVM output logs associated with the server and dispatcher. They provide information on whether any core service has failed during startup.

Portal Troubleshooting

If the portal does not launch or the iViews do not display properly, check for.err files in the following folders by logging in as <*SID*>adm, where <*SID*> is the AS Java system ID. Then navigate to the following directories, namely, deployment, pcd, and pcdContent:

```
\usr\sap\<sid>\JC<instance_no>\j2ee\cluster\server0\apps\sap.com\irj\servlet_jsp\
irj\root\WEB-INF\deployment
\usr\sap\<sid>\JC<instance_no>\j2ee\cluster\server0\apps\sap.com\irj\servlet_jsp\
irj\root\WEB-INF\deployment\pcd
\usr\sap\<sid>\JC<instance_no>\j2ee\cluster\server0\apps\sap.com\irj\servlet_jsp\
irj\root\WEB-INF\deployment\pcdContent
\usr\sap\<sid>\JC<instance_no>\j2ee\cluster\server0\apps\sap.com\irj\servlet_jsp\
irj\root\WEB-INF\deployment\pcdContent\no_overwrite
```

If present, rename the files as .ept or .par files. Restart the J2EE engine and check whether the files have been renamed as .bak.

Another good troubleshooting tool is to check the default.trc file in the <*drive*>\usr\sap\<*SID*>\JC<*instance_no*>\j2ee\cluster\server0\log folder. You should check the default Trace.trc file that has the latest timestamp on it:

Address C:\usr\sap\J2E\JC01\j2ee\cluster\server0\log

Name	Size	Type
applications		File Folder
archive		File Folder
libraries		File Folder
services		File Folder
sqltrace		File Folder
system		File Folder
applications.0	473 KB	Text Document
applications.1	10,241 KB	Text Document
applications.2	10,241 KB	Text Document
applications.3	10,241 KB	Text Document
applications.4	10,241 KB	Text Document
config_audit.0	6 KB	Text Document
defaultTrace.0.trc	10,241 KB	TRC File
defaultTrace.1.trc	10,241 KB	TRC File
defaultTrace.2.trc	586 KB	TRC File
sat.0.trc	2,097 KB	TRC File

Post-Installation Activities

If the system is not properly tuned, you may encounter issues with performance, J2EE engine crashes, and other system problems that are often difficult to troubleshoot. You may also have gaping holes in security that need to be fixed. The system may not have been sized correctly, the J2EE engine may not be adequately tuned, and the logging settings that are configured by default may be undesirable for production.

As a part of the post-installation steps, you must ensure that the installation finished successfully. Some of the key areas that may need attention are as follows:

- HTTP request logging
- Garbage collection settings
- System Landscape Directory (SLD) configuration
- J2EE application logging
- Timeout settings
- User security
- Database upgrades
- Support patches
- Web application server tuning
- Portal server tuning

Post-Installation Steps for Portal

Follow these steps as a part of initial technical configuration of the portal.

Copy the Import Filter File

The CMS_MAPPING.properties file is the import filter file stored in the Portal Content Directory (PCD) that helps to filter objects when migrating EP 5.0 business packages to run on later versions. The import filter contains two kinds of objects, those that need to be skipped when importing into the later versions and those that need to be mapped from EP 5.0 to later versions so that they can be used in the later versions. You will have to copy this file from /usr/sap/<*SID*>/JC<*xx*>/j2ee/cluster/server<*x*>/apps/sap.com/irj/servlet_jsp/irj/root/WEB-INF/portal/system/pcd/Migration/mapping to a target location that is defined in the PCD configuration property `PCD.Migration.Path.Mapfile`.

To check the location, go to top level menu and select System Administration | Support Portal. Then select Portal Content Directory | PCD Configuration in the content area and scroll to the Parameters For Portal Content Migration section. Check for the property PCD.Migration.Path.Mapfile.

INFO *The current value for the PCD.Migration.Path.Mapfile property is /usr/sap/<SID>/SYS/global/pcd/Migration/mapping.*

Activate the Initial Permissions on the Portal

The next step is to activate the initial permissions on the portal. It is important that you carry out these steps to ensure that the correct permissions are assigned to the users. Note that in a cluster environment, this needs to be done only on the central instance. The other server nodes are synchronized automatically during the restart of the J2EE engine. Follow these steps:

1. Rename the initialPermissions.xml.template as initialPermissions.xml in the usr/sap/*<SID>*/JC*<xx>*/j2ee/cluster/server*<x>*/apps/sap.com/irj/servlet_jsp/irj/root/WEB-INF/portal/system/xml/acl folder.
2. Rename the initialPermissionsKMC.xml.template file as initialPermissionsKMC.xml in the usr/sap/*<SID>*/JC*<xx>*/j2ee/cluster/server*<x>*/apps/sap.com/irj/servlet_jsp/irj/root/WEB-INF/portal/system/xml/acl folder.

Logging on to J2EE and Portal

Once the installation is complete, you should determine whether you can access the J2EE engine and the portal. Here's how to calculate the port for HTTP and HTTPS:

- J2EE engine HTTP port = 50000 + (100 × instance number)
- J2EE engine HTTPS port = 50000 + (100 × instance number) + 1

To access the SAP J2EE engine, go to http://<host><http-port>/irj. Use the J2EE admin user ID and password to log in.

NOTE *After installing for the first time, it takes about 30 minutes to start the J2EE engine and log in to the portal successfully. The initial starting duration for the portal is high due to the fact that the portal components and services are loading for the first time into the portal runtime environment.*

Checking Whether the Installation Is Complete

Once the installation is completed, you need to verify that it was successful. This can be done by running the Support Platform. Starting from NetWeaver 2004 SP13, you can use the Support Platform instead of the System Analyzer. To start the Support Platform, go to http://*<hostname>*:*<port>*/sp.

The Support Platform uses plug-ins that let you conduct tests and generate reports. Plug-ins are small Java programs that can be created for any task. Standard plug-ins are available for checking the system configuration and verifying the permissions, system data, and so on.

The main work area contains options such as the following:

- Configure a plug-in
- Run a plug-in on a single node or all the nodes
- View the results
- Save the results
- Export the results into a spreadsheet

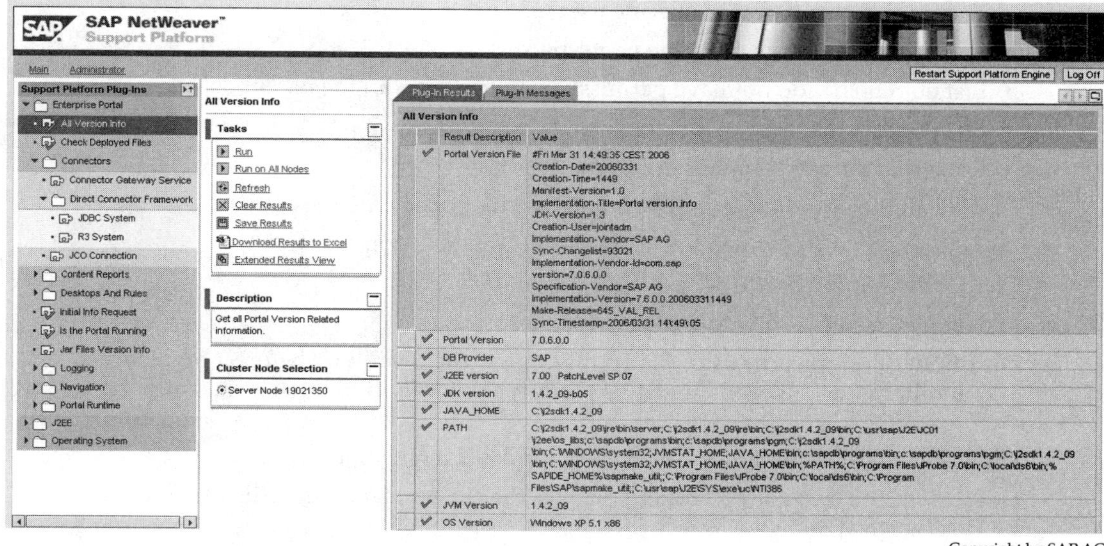

FIGURE 12-1 Support Platform for verifying portal installation

Figure 12-1 displays the various plug-ins that are available for the EP. On the right side of the screen, under the Plug-In Results tab, you can view the details regarding the EP version by clicking Run under the Tasks section in the middle pane.

TIP *The Support Platform has a number of features to check the EP, J2EE, and operating system configurations.*

The Plug-In Results tab contains the results generated by the plug-in, and the Plug-In Messages tab contains the messages generated by the plug-in.

Under the Enterprise Portal plug-in, you can check the following:

- Version
- Status of deployed files by verifying whether all the PAR files have a .bak extension
- Status of the connector gateway service for checking the connectivity of the various system objects
- Status of the JDBC and the SAP R/3 system connectivity
- Content reports:
  - Broken delta links for a Portal Content Directory (PCD) location
  - Track changes to the objects in a PCD location during a specified time period
  - Track changes to the objects in a PCD location by a specific user

    - Track objects created by a specific user
    - List objects that have the same namespace
    - List objects that do not have permissions inherited from the parent object
    - PCD objects that are not assigned to a role
    - Roles that are not assigned to a user
- Display all the portal display objects and the rule collections
- Initial Info Request: Retrieves all the logs and creates a .zip
- Check whether the portal is running
- List of deployed JAR files and their versions
- For troubleshooting purposes, send a message to the default.trc before a problem and another after the problem; helps identify the location in the log file for debugging
- Under navigation, configure the levels of top-level navigation
- Get cluster info data for PRTBridge, such as the cluster elements, J2EE, OS, and PRTBridge versions
- Get the PRTBridge info such as the PRTBridge status and cluster communication diagnostics
- Ping PRTBridge on other server nodes

Under the J2EE Engine Section, you can check the following:

- JVM system properties and version
- Log controller properties and information about logging
- The stack traces of the servers
- J2EE version and JDK version

Figure 12-2 displays the various plug-ins available for the J2EE engine.

You can also check the operating system environment variables, available hard disk space, availability of the `javac` command via the command line, operating system version for the Java Virtual Machine (JVM) system, RAM details, and finally the Windows privileges such as whether the following are assigned to the Administrators group:

- Act as part of the operating system
- Replace a process-level token
- Adjust memory quotas for a process

While testing the plug-in, when you click the Plug-in properties editor, you can configure the plug-in by entering the required parameter values for testing. The following illustration shows how to test the Java Connector (JCO) connection plug-in in by entering the parameters

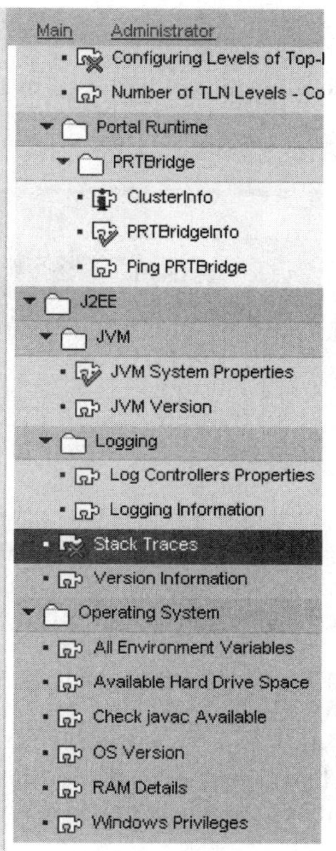

FIGURE 12-2 Plug-ins available for J2EE engine in support platform

for a JCO connection such as user, password, language of the backend system, application server host name, client number, and system number:

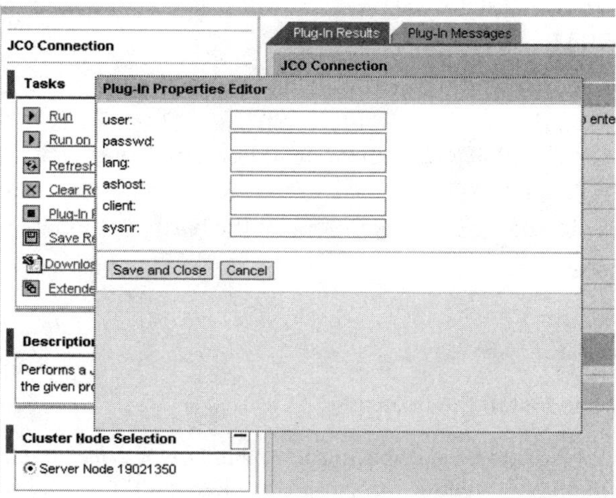

The Administrator section, accessible by clicking the Administrator link in the upper-left corner of the Support Platform screen, allows you to upload a plug-in, download the plug-in, and remove the plug-in, as displayed in the following illustration:

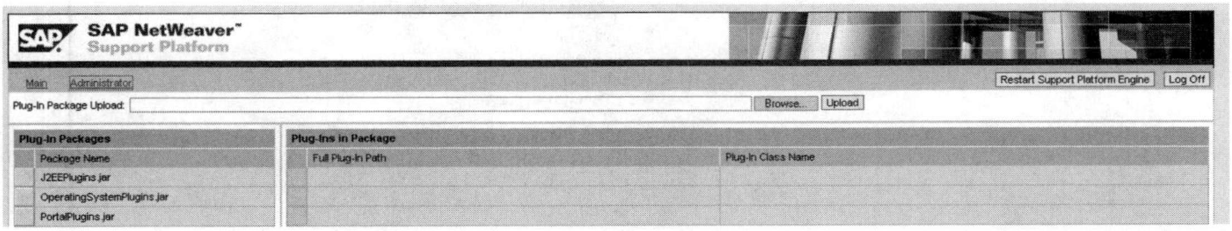

TIP *The Support Platform can be downloaded from the SAP. See OSS Note 812688.*

Install the EP License

The EP temporary license is valid for only one month. To obtain a license key from the Service Marketplace (http://service.sap.com/licensekeys), a license key request authorization is needed. Prior to SAP NetWeaver 2004, single products were installed separately and each had its own license key. As of SAP NetWeaver 2004 SP1 (including SP9.0), no separate license key is required for the portal because the license key is obtained as part of obtaining the license key for the NetWeaver AS ABAP stack or the NetWeaver AS Java stack. For obtaining a license for a high availability system, refer to OSS Note 181543.

When a permanent license key expires, you can install a temporary license within four weeks before the permanent license key expires again. The following details are required for obtaining the license:

- Installation number: 10-digit number provided by SAP
- System ID
- System type: production or test
- SAP Product: SAP NetWeaver
- Product version: SAP NetWeaver 7.0 (2004s)
- License type: *Standard* is used for EP 6.0 SP 9 and above installed on an ABAP stack; *J2EE* is used for EP 6.0 SP9 and above installed on a Java stack; *Portal* is used for EP 6.0 systems SP 8 and lower
- Hardware key: 11-character value unique to the hardware where the portal is installed
- Operating system
- Database
- Technical usage for NetWeaver

Follow these steps to install the license:

1. Start the Visual Admin by navigating to <*installation_drive*>:\usr\sap\J2E\JC<*instance_number*>\j2ee\admin, and double-click the go.bat file.

2. In the Connect To SAP J2EE Engine, select the Default connection, and click New to create a new connection.
3. In the Create A New Connection window, enter a suitable name in the Display Name field. Select the Direct Connection To A Dispatcher Node radio button and click Next.
4. In the Create A New Connection window, enter a suitable user name, host name, and port 5*NN*04, where *NN* is the instance number. Note that the user should have Administrator access to the J2EE engine. Leave the Transport Layer as Default. Click Save. Now you have created a new connection, which you can use to connect to the Visual Administrator.
5. To log in to the Visual Administrator, choose Connect | Login. The Connect To SAP J2EE Engine appears. Select the newly created connection and click Connect. Enter the correct password and click Connect.
6. Navigate to Cluster | Server | Services | Licensing Adapter and note the hardware key, as shown in the next illustration, which displays a list of available services for the SAP J2EE server on the left.

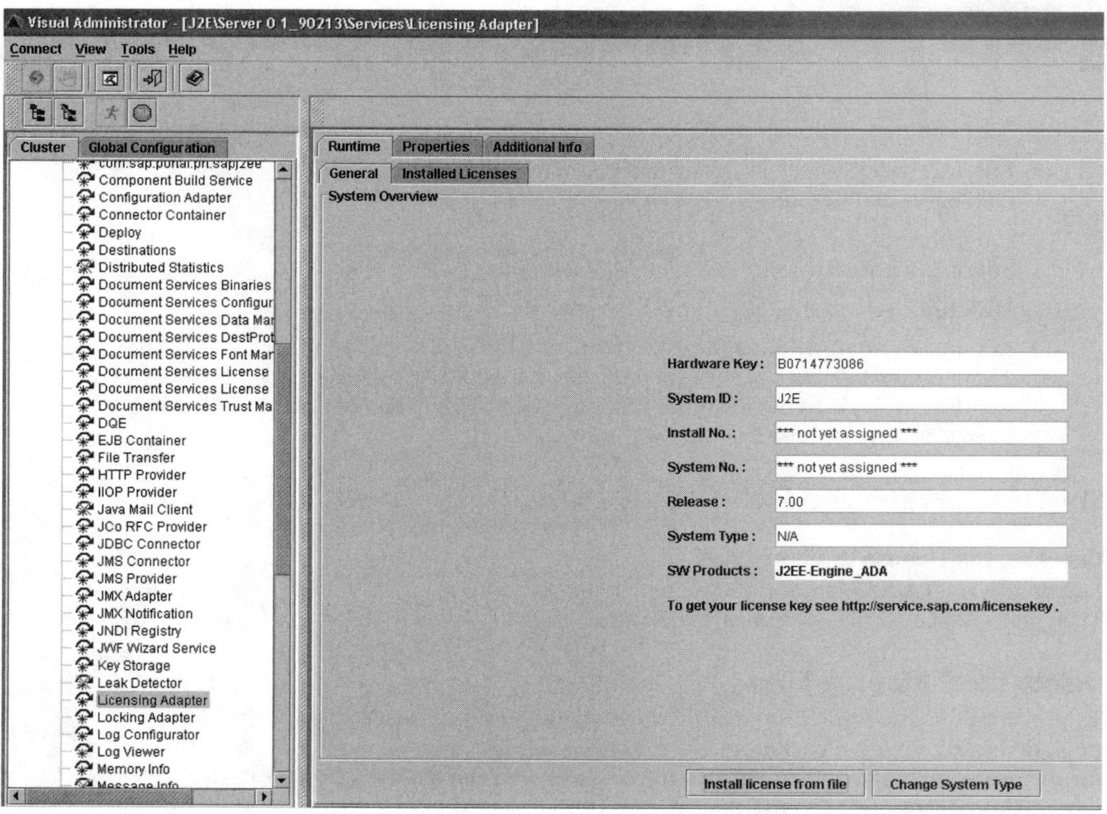

Do *A new license key should be obtained if the installation number, system ID, database, or hardware key changes.*

7. Go to www.service.sap.com/licensekeys. Then click Request License Key under the Service Corner, as shown in the following illustration. This page on the SAP Service Marketplace is where the licenses for SAP software can be administered for your organization.

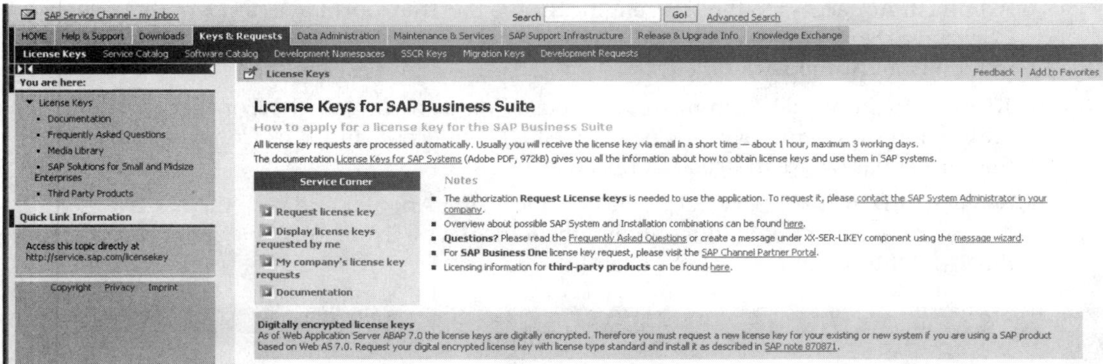

Copyright by SAP AG

8. Select an installation and choose New System or Change Details for System.
9. Enter the details such as Software Product, SW Product Release, Basis Release, Database, or Operating system.
10. Enter the Hardware Key that you noted in step 6. Click Save New Item and click Submit Request to SAP.
11. Wait until you receive your key; then save it as a text file.
12. Log in to Visual Admin again. Navigate to Cluster | Services | Licensing Adapter. Then, on the bottom of the right pane, click Install License From File. In the Open window, browse to the location where the key file was saved and click Open. The license is now installed.

Tip *The license key generated is unique to a system and cannot be used for a different system.*

Checking the License Validity Period

Log on to Visual Administrator, and then navigate to Server | Cluster | Services | Monitoring. Then go to Root | Kernel | Licensing Manager | License Validity Period | *Software Product*.

Delete the Portal Log Files

To prevent the passwords used during the installation process from being exposed, you must delete all the log files. For added security, you can simply change the passwords used for the users. Navigate to the log files stored during the installation process in the directory <*drive*>:\program files\sapinst_instdir\NW04SR1<*your version*>\EP. You can also delete the files under the directory %userprofile%\.sdtgui\. The %userprofile% usually points to <*installation directory*>\Documents and Settings\<*user*>\ for a Windows system.

Use the Template Installer

After installing the J2EE engine and the portal application, you should configure the system for the portal scenario using the SAP Server Template Configuration Tool. Using the Template Installer, you can configure the technical settings for the EP scenario.

Do *Run this tool* only once *after the installation for each J2EE instance.*

For a cluster, run the installer first on the central instance and then run it on the other dialog instances. If you don't run it on all instances, configuration inconsistencies may arise.

Don't *You cannot use the Template Installer after the upgrade, add-in install, or when implementing new scenarios.*

Ensure that at least 2GB of memory are available on the installation before applying this tool. Refer to OSS Note 739788.

The following steps are involved in running the SAP Server Template Configuration Tool:

1. Run the cfgtemplategui.bat file under usrsap\\<*SID*>\\SYS\\global\\TemplateConfig. Click Next in the Welcome screen.
2. Click the Apply radio button in the Choose Action screen of the SAP Server Template Configuration Tool wizard, as shown next. The Restore Previous Backup option is helpful when you want to reverse the changes in situations when the changes made to your J2EE engine configuration using the template tool result in improper operation of the system. You can use this option only if you have taken a backup in the first place, when you first used the template configuration tool (refer to step 8 below):

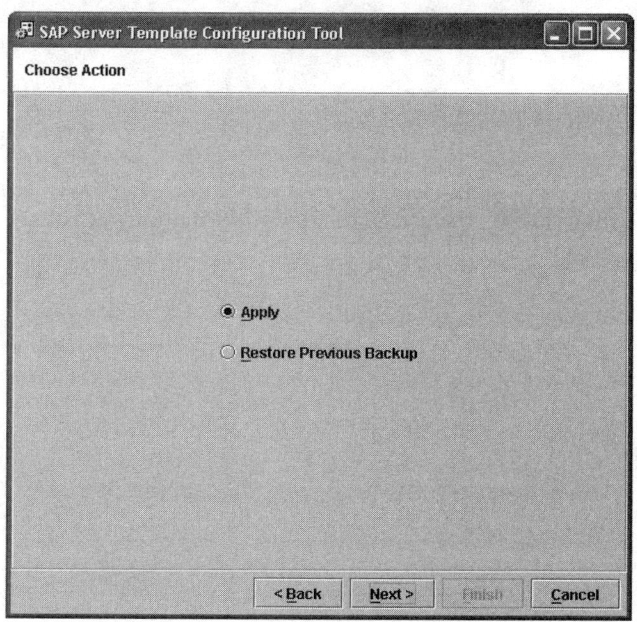

PART III

3. Select the portal_1CPU.zip file located under the usr\sap\<*SID*>\SYS\global\TemplateConfig\templates folder for the template filename.
4. Select the working folder under usr\sap\<*SID*>\SYS\global\TemplateConfig for the working directory. This is usually selected by default.
5. In the Initial Data screen of the Template Configuration tool, select the instance folder—for example, usr\sap\<*SID*>\JC<*xx*>, where *xx* is the instance number. The following illustration displays the paths for the portal configuration template file, working directory of the template configuration tool, and the J2EE instance directory.

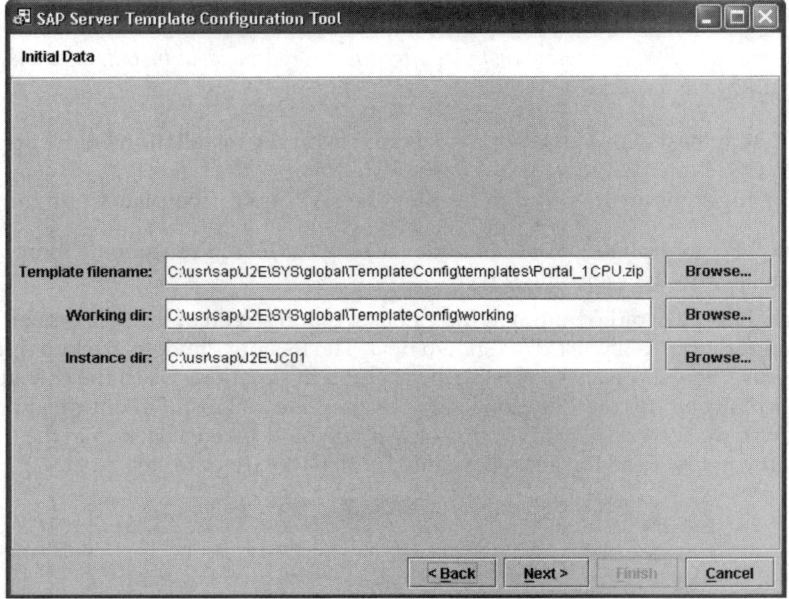

6. Click Next. An Edit System Dependencies screen showing the existing system settings appears, as shown next. The screen displays information such as the instance number,

OS platform, SAP System ID, JDK home directory, central services instance number, central instance host name, and message services port.

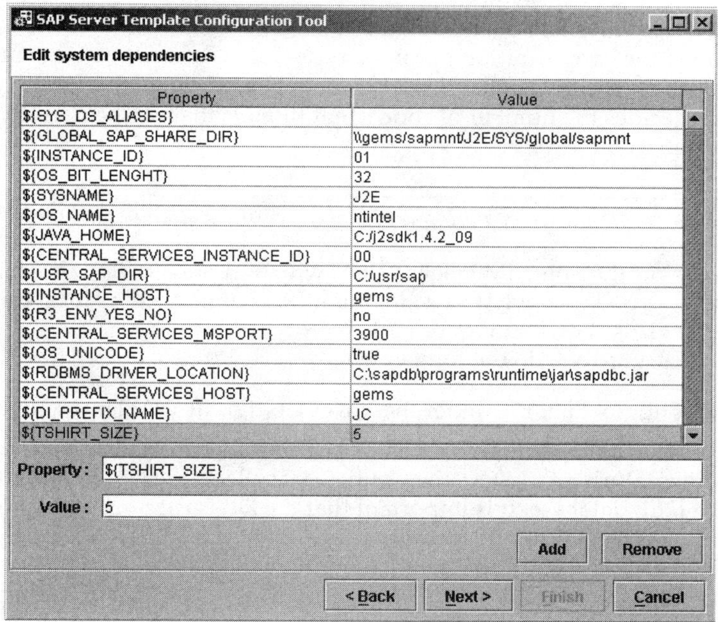

Copyright by SAP AG

7. Click Next. An Edit Hardware Dependencies screen showing the current hardware settings is displayed, as shown next. One of the settings displays the current memory. You may change this value after taking into account the memory the other applications may use.

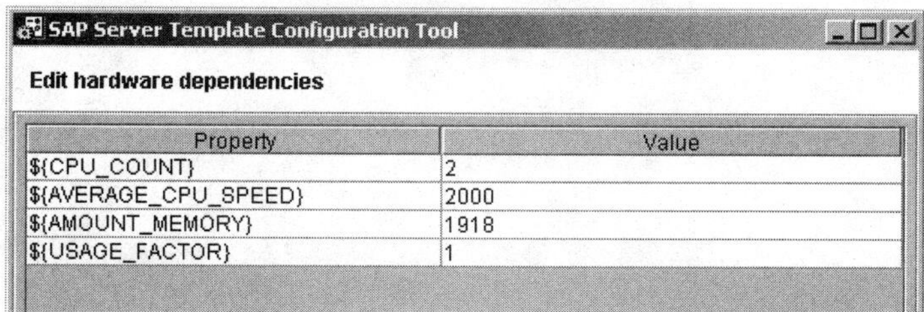

Copyright by SAP AG

8. In the Advanced Options screen, select Backup Option if desired, and then click Next.
9. In the Preview Component screen, select the component, and then click Next.
10. In the Completing The SAP Template Configuration Wizard, click Finish.

Configuring the J2EE Engine

Now let's take a look at some of the steps needed to configure the J2EE engine.

Configuring the Dispatcher and Server Thread Manager

If required, change the configuration parameters such as `ChangeRQSizeStep` and `MaxRQSize` values for the dispatcher thread manager based on your specific requirements. The `MaxRQSize` decides the number of concurrent threads that can be used to serve the incoming requests.

CAUTION *Exercise caution when changing J2EE engine configuration parameters.*

On the server side, the ThreadManager values will most often need to be changed. Do not change these unless you know what you are doing. To change these values, use the J2EE engine's Config Tool, as shown in Figure 12-3.

To access the Config Tool, do the following:

1. Run the configtool.bat file under the \usr\sap\J2E\JC01\j2ee\configtool folder.
2. In the Connection Settings screen, click Yes under Do You Want To Use The Default DB Settings. During this step, the Config tool collects the latest configuration data from the J2EE database. It is important that the DB is running at this time. If not, you will receive an error. In such situations, use the SAP Management Console to restart the database and then start the Config tool again.
3. Navigate to Cluster-data | Instance | Server | Managers and select ThreadManager, as shown in Figure 12-3.

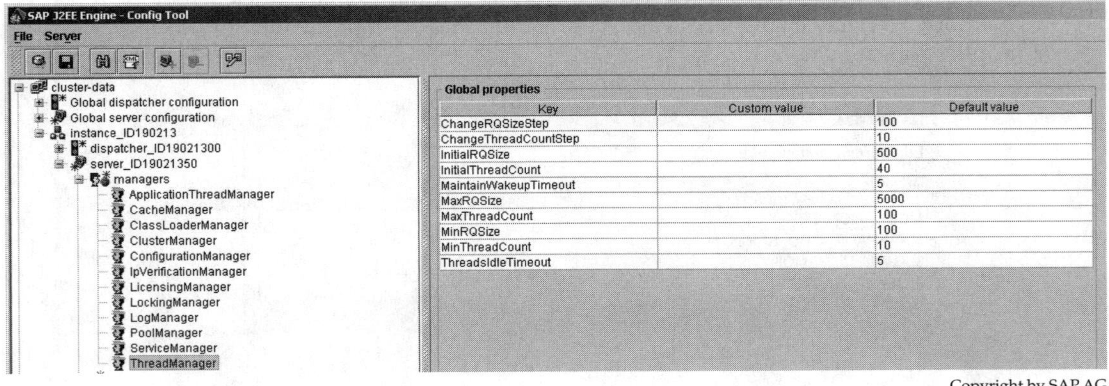

FIGURE 12-3 Configuring the server ThreadManager

4. To change any of these properties, select the property under the Global Properties section in the right pane.
5. Replace the old value with the new value in the Value field at the bottom of the right pane. Click Set.
6. Click the Save button in the top toolbar. Click OK in the Logs window.
7. A Config Tool window appears, stating that for the change to take effect, the Java cluster must be restarted. Click OK in the Config Tool window.

Figure 12-3 displays the different properties, such as InitialThreadCount, MaxThreadCount, and so on. The actual values for these properties would depend on the specifics of the installation, but some of the suggested values are listed here. Needless to say, these should be used with caution:

- **ChangeRQSizeStep** 200 (the request queue is increased in `ChangeRQSizeStep` increments until the `MaxRQSize` is reached while serving incoming requests)
- **MaxRQSize** 10000 (maximum size of the request queue; if reached, the next starting thread is blocked until a request is completed)
- **InitialRQSize** 1000 (initial size of the request queue until which the threads can be used to process the requests)
- **InitialThreadCount** 100 (initial number of threads in the thread pool, which are in the `waitQueue`, until a `RunnableObject` uses it for processing)
- **MaxThreadCount** 200 (maximum number of threads available for processing; required to avoid overload due to a large number of threads serving requests)
- **MinThreadCount** 100

Configuring the ConnectionsManipulator Manager

You must also identify whether tuning can be done for the ConnectionsManipulator Manager, Service Manager, HTTP service, and the JDBC Connector service.

The ConnectionsManipulator is available only for the dispatcher and is used to configure the number of client connections to the cluster. To access it, you must navigate to Cluster | Dispatcher | Managers | ConnectionsManipulator in the Config Tool. The `MaxParallelUsers` property of the ConnectionsManipulator Manager defines the number of users that can be processed simultaneously by the dispatcher. This value would depend upon the `MaxHeapSize` of the J2EE engine. The dispatcher property `GetStreamsSoTimeout` decides the timeout before which the dispatcher should create a connection. Shown next is the list of properties under the HTTP Provider

PART III

service of the server. You can see in the illustration that a number of useful http properties can be configured, such as AlwaysCompressed, CacheControl, CacheSize, CacheTimeout, NeverCompressed, SAPCacheControl, FileBufferSize, and so on.

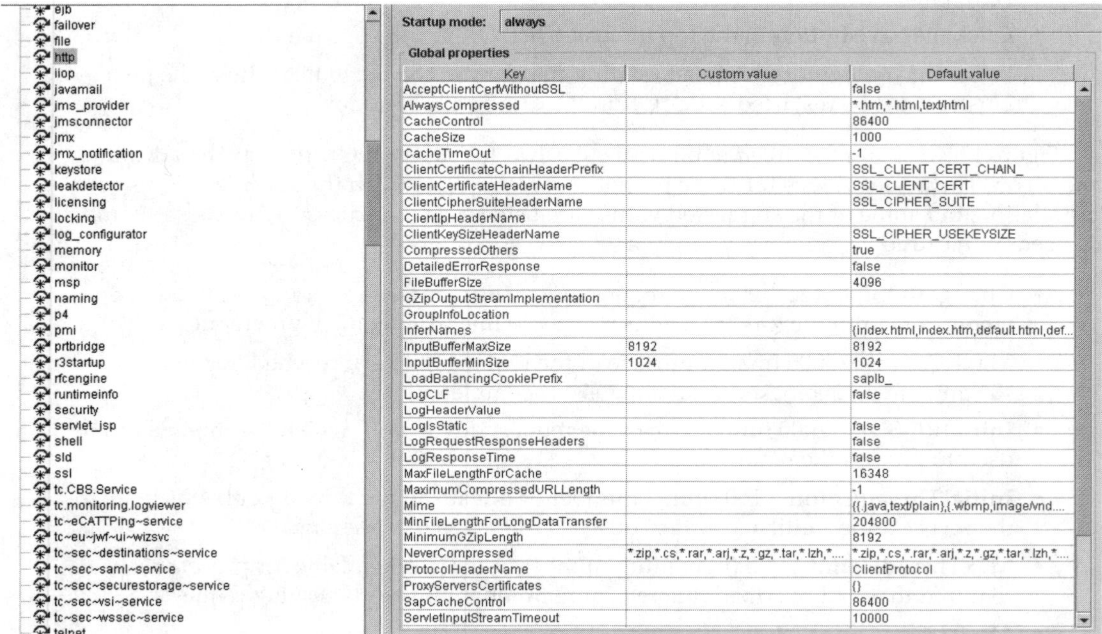

Configuring the SLD

The document *Post-Installation Guide – SLD of SAP NetWeaver 7.0* contains the steps required to configure the SLD. The SLD is installed by default with the installation of the Web AS Java usage type. No additional installation or configuration steps are required because the SLD is already configured during the installation process. To configure the data suppliers of the systems that are connected to the SLD, you simply specify the SLD address.

NOTE *Chapter 44 discusses how to configure the SLD.*

Apply Patches

To apply the patches, first go to http://service.sap.com/patches. Then do the following:

1. Navigate to Entry By Application Group | SAP NetWeaver | SAP NetWeaver | SAP NetWeaver 7.0(2004s) or choose <*your version*> | Support Package Stacks | Support Package Stacks.
2. Under Step 1 of 3, Choose Your Source And Target Stack, enter your current and target stack info. Select the relevant usage types under Usage Selection section. Click Next Step.

3. In the Step 2 of 3, Choose Configuration Page, you must choose all the OS-independent and -dependent configurations, DB independent, and dependent configurations for the previously chosen usage types. Proceed by clicking the arrow before each entry under the ConfigTree. Click Next Step.
4. In the Step 3 of 3, Downloadable Support Packages, to install using Java Support Package Manager (JSPM), click Save As File. In the Choose The Kind Of File You Want To Download window, right-click on Save This Table As A XML File and choose Save Target As to save it in your local folder.
5. To install using SDM, click the Add To Download Basket button. Then click the Download Basket button.
6. Using the SAP Download Manager, download these objects into your local folder. Then use the SDM to deploy these packages. Note that it is recommended that you use the JSPM instead of the SDM to deploy support packages. JSPM uses the SDM to deploy the software components. The advantages of using JSPM are discussed in Chapter 23.

NOTE *Refer to Chapter 23 for information about how to use the JSPM.*

PART III

Download SAPCAR

SAPCAR is a compress utility provided by SAP to compress/decompress files delivered by SAP. It was previously known as CAR, but starting from the R/3 release 4.6C, SAP improvised upon the CAR tool and called it SAPCAR. The files compressed by the CAR utility were known as .CAR files and those compressed by SAPCAR are known as .SAR files. Note that the CAR tool can decompress only .CAR files, but the SAPCAR tool can decompress both .CAR and .SAR files. To download SAPCAR, go to http://service.sap.com/patches. Then do the following:

1. Navigate to Entry By Application Group | SAP Technology Components | SAPCAR | SAPCAR 7.00 | SAPCAR 7.00/. Then go to Windows Server on IA32 <or choose your operating system>.
2. Select the checkbox for the SAPCAR .exe file and choose Add To Download Basket. Use the SAP Download Manager to download this file to your local folder.
3. Add the .SAR file to the folder where the sapcar.exe file was stored.
4. Go to the Command Prompt, and navigate to the folder where the SAPCAR.exe file was downloaded in step 2.
5. Enter **sapcar –xvf 'name of sar file.sar'**.
6. All the files will be extracted to the sapcar folder. Create a new folder and save the extracted patch files to the newly created folder.

TIP *You need at least SAPCAR 700 or SAPCAR 640 with patch level 4. Read OSS Note 212876 for information.*

Using SDM to Install Patches

SDM stands for Software Deployment Manager, which, as the name implies, is used for deploying J2EE applications on NetWeaver AS Java. It can also be used to deploy software patches from SAP including the Software Component Archives (SCA) and the Software Deployment Archives (SDA). Note that to install the Support Packages, you should use the JSPM.

1. Go to \usr\sap\J2E\JC01\SDM\program and double-click StartServer.bat to start the SDM server.
2. To start the SDM client, double-click RemoteGUI.bat in the same folder in step 1. Choose SDMI Gui | Login from the menu.
3. In the Enter Login Information For SDM Server dialog box, enter the SDM password (this is the password that was given during install) and click Login.
4. After logging in successfully, you will see four tabs at the top of the screen: SDM Repository, Deployment, Undeployment, and Log Viewer. To deploy, click the Deployment tab. The Step 1 of 4, Choose SCAs/SDAs To Be Deployed, screen will appear.
5. Choose the Add SCA/SDA To Deployment List (Local File Browser) - Alt+A button. An Open window will pop up for you to choose the downloaded SDA patch files that you want to deploy. Choose the patch file that you want to deploy.
6. To expand the options, click the down arrow located in the lower-right corner of the Deployment tab. In the Deployment Configuration area at the bottom half of the screen, select the Update Deployed SDAs/SCAs That Have Any Version radio button in the Settings For Updating SCAs/SDAs section, as shown in the following illustration. Click Next.

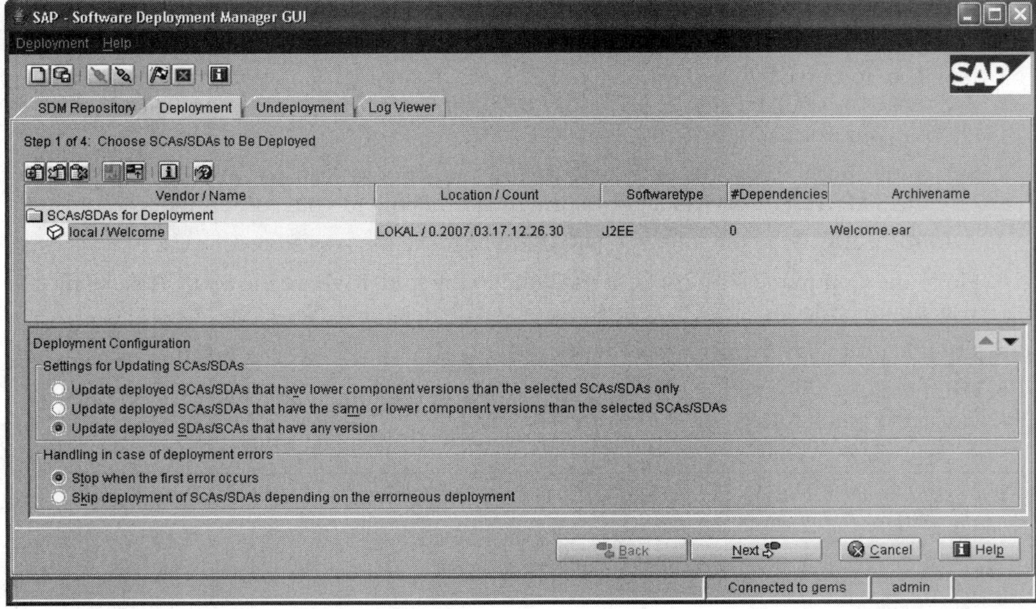

7. In the Step 3 of 4, SDM Is Ready To Deploy - Start Deployment, screen, click Start Deployment.
8. In the Step 4 of 4, Deployment Completed Successfully - Confirm, screen, click Confirm, which updates the J2EE database with the deployment details.

System Backup

Creating a system backup is an important step; if you encounter any problems after installation, you can potentially use the backup to restore the system to its initial state.

Do *You should create a backup right after the installation.*

Take the following steps to back up the system registry, the system state data, SAP data, and database data:

1. Save the registry. Choose Start | Programs | Accessories | System Tools | Backup. Sometimes the backup tool may not function properly because the Removable Storage service is not running in the host. In such situations, go to the Start | Control Panel | Administrative Tools | Services and start the Removable Storage service.
2. Choose Emergency Repair Disk and then choose Also Backup The Registry To The Repair Directory in the Emergency Repair Diskette window.
3. To save the system state data, choose Start | Programs | Accessories | System Tools | Backup again.
4. Choose Backup Wizard (Advanced) and then click Next in the Backup Wizard welcome screen.
5. Choose Only Back Up The System State Data as shown next. Click Next.

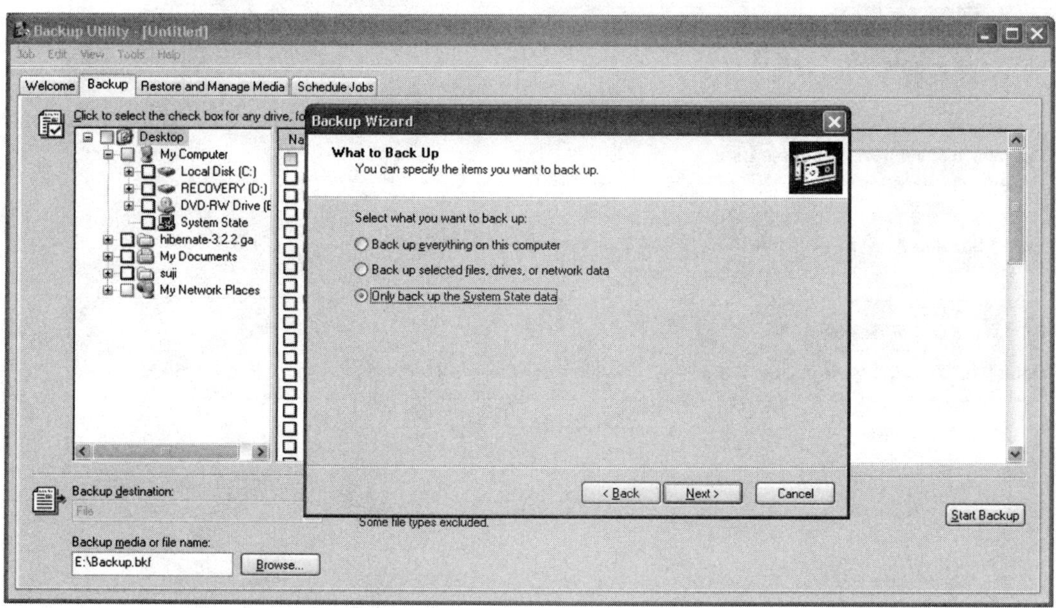

6. In the Backup Type, Destination And Name, window, choose a location in the Choose A Place To Save Your Backup and enter a suitable name for the backup in the Type A Name For This Backup field.
7. In the Completing the Backup Wizard, click Finish to save the system state data.
8. To save the SAP related data, repeat steps 3 and 4.
9. Choose Back Up Selected Files, Drives Or Network Data. Then click Next.
10. In the Items To Backup window, select the relevant SAP, database, and windows directories such as \usr\sap, <*root_directory*>:\windows, home directory for j2eadm, installation directory for the database such as SQL Server (<*installation directory*>:\Program Files\Microsoft SQL Server\, and so on.
11. In the Backup Type, Destination And Name, window, in the Choose A Place To Save Your Backup field, choose a location and in the Type A Name For This Backup field, enter a suitable name for the backup.

Uninstalling the SAP J2EE System

One option to delete the SAP instance is to double-click the startUnistall.bat file in the <*drive*>:\usr\sap\J2E\JC01\j2ee\portal_misc\uninstall folder. Enter the required details, as shown in the next illustration, and then click OK. This will delete the portal installation on that particular instance, which in this case is the JC01 instance.

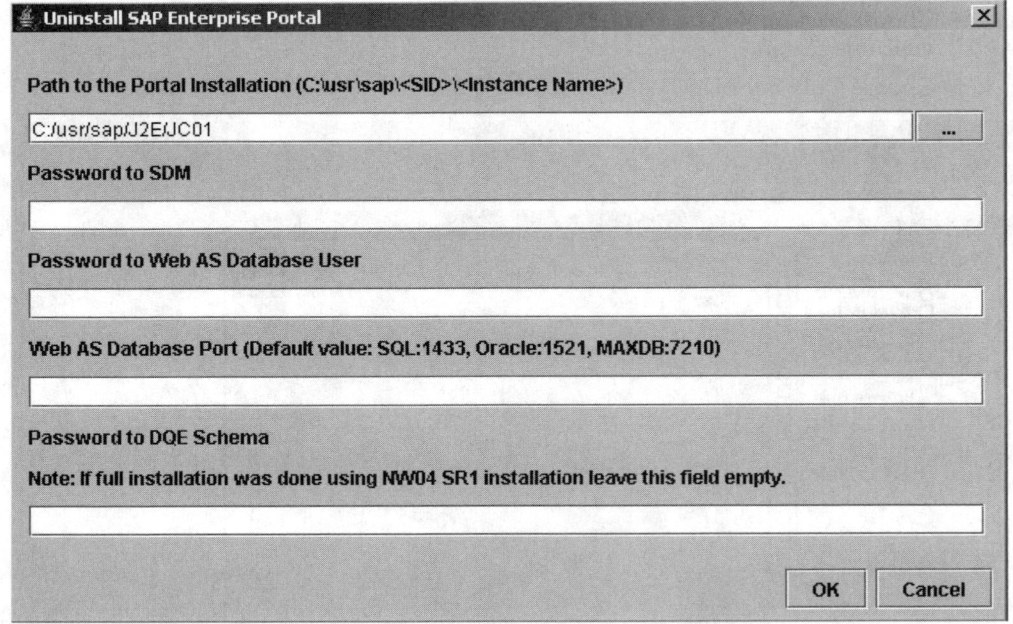

Copyright by SAP AG

Using SAPinst to Uninstall the SAP J2EE System

You can use SAPinst to uninstall the SAP system. This section addresses the steps involved in uninstalling a central as well as a distributed SAP system.

Uninstalling the Central SAP System

You can uninstall the entire central system in one run of the SAPinst. To uninstall an SAP central system, start the SAPinst tool and do the following:

1. In the Welcome screen, navigate to SAP System | Additional Software Life-Cycle Tasks | Uninstall | Uninstall - System / Standalone Engine / Optional Standalone Unit. Click Next.
2. In the What Do You Want To Do screen, select the Run A New Installation radio button and click OK.
3. In the SAP System | General Parameters screen shown next, click Browse to select the SAP system's profile directory, which is at <*installation directory*>:\usr\sap\<*SID*>\SYS\profile. Click Next.

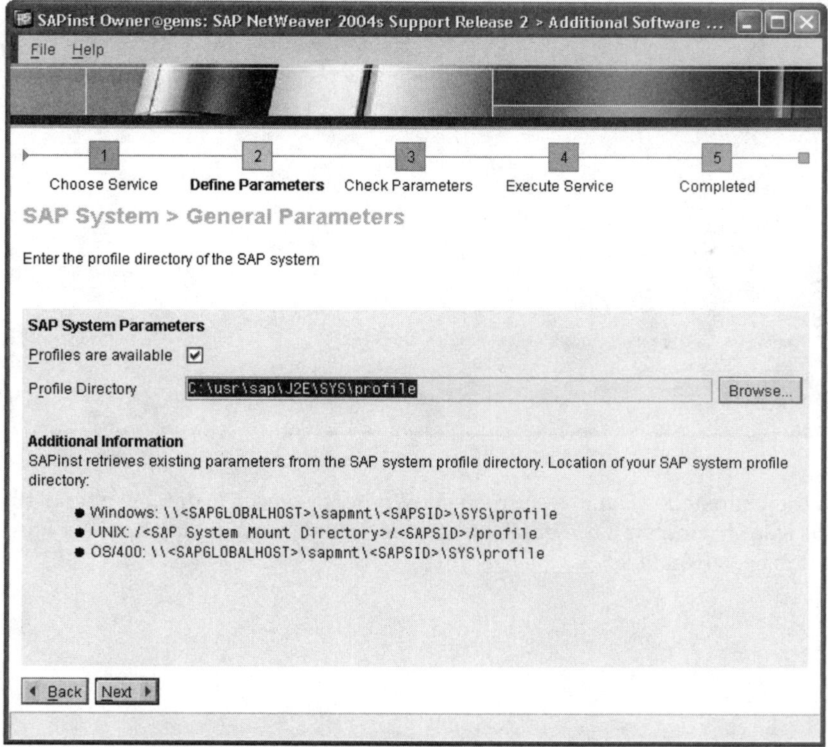

INFO *The profile directory contains both a default profile (DEFAULT.PFL) and other instance-specific profiles that provide configuration information for the instances.*

4. In the Uninstall | SAP System or Standalone Engine screen, select the instances to uninstall as shown in the next illustration. To select the instances, you must deselect the Remove All Instances Of The SAP System Or Standalone Engine On This Host checkbox. Select the Remove OS Users Of SAP System Or Standalone Engine On This Host checkbox if you want to delete OS users belonging to the SAP J2EE system. Then click Next.

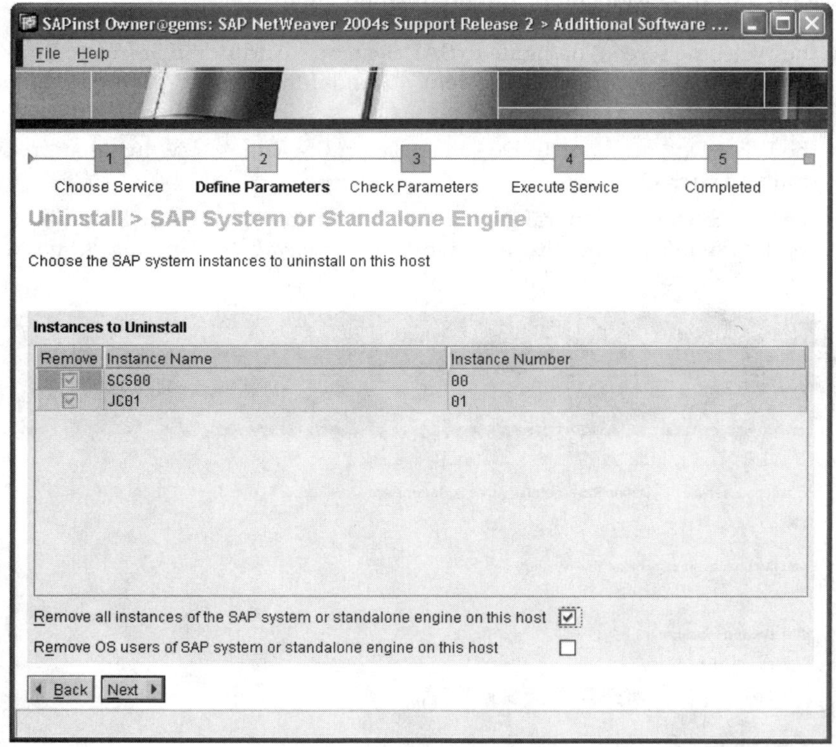

5. In the Uninstall | Database screen shown next, select the database type. If you do not want to uninstall the database, deselect the Uninstall Database (or Parts of the Database) checkbox.

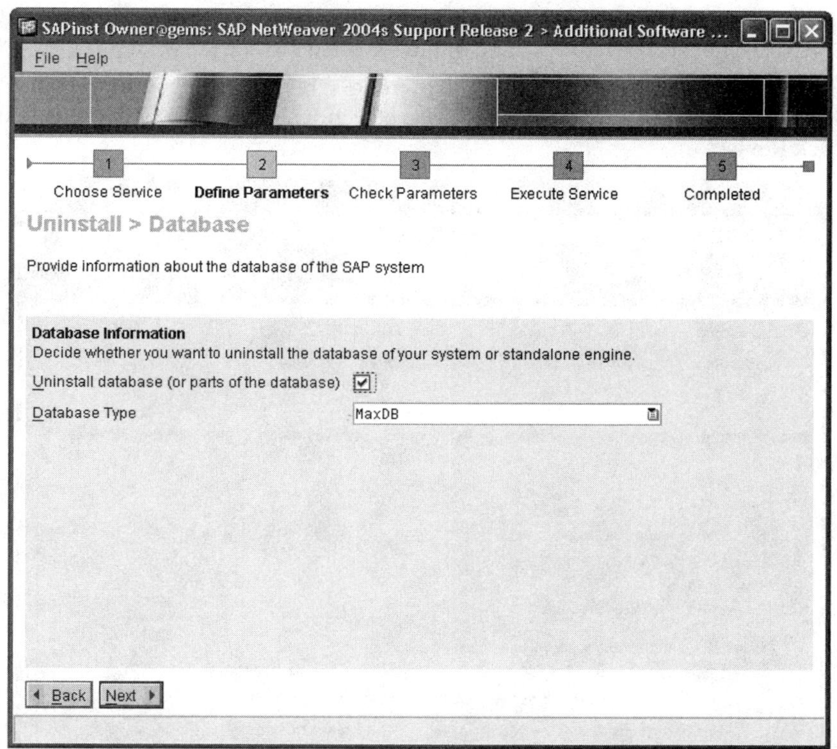

6. In the SAP System | Database Parameters screen, enter the database parameters such as the database ID and the host name.
7. In the MaxDB | Database Users screen, enter the passwords for the Database System Administrator account named *superdba* and the Database Manager Operator account named *control*. Click Next.
8. In the MaxDB | Drop Schema Or Database screen, select the Drop The Whole Database checkbox to delete all the data and the related database files. Click Next.

9. In the MaxDB | Remove Database Software screen, select the Remove Database Software checkbox to remove the database software. Click Next.
10. In the Parameter Summary screen shown next, review the entries and click Start. If you want to change any of the previous selections, select any of the checkboxes and click Revise.

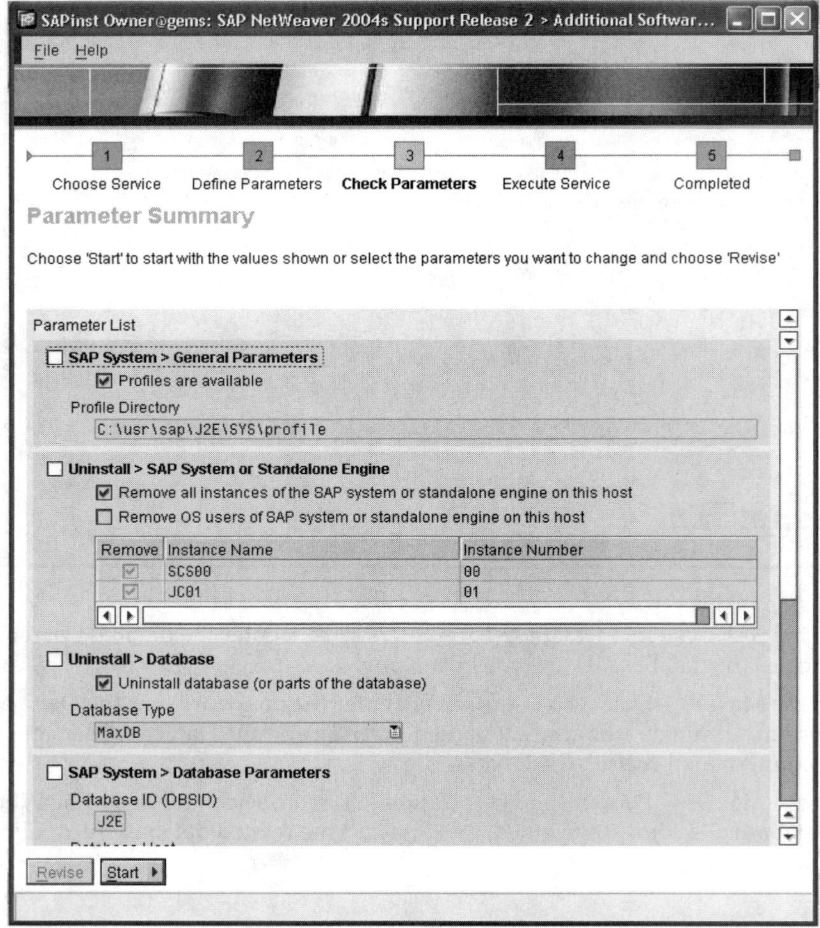

11. Delete the SAP_<*SID*>_LocalAdmin local group.
12. To delete the database software itself, use the Add/Remove Programs applet from the Control Panel.
13. Delete the \usr\sap\trans directory manually.

Uninstalling a Distributed SAP System

To uninstall an SAP system that has a distributed setup, the SAPinst has to be run locally on each individual host in the sequence presented here:

1. Delete the dialog instances locally on each host.
2. Delete the database instance. Make sure that all remaining instances are stopped.

NOTE *When deleting the database instance during a distributed SAP system uninstall, stop the message server instance only after all the database instance parameters are entered.*

3. Delete the central instance.
4. Delete the central services instance.
5. Delete the SQL Server using the SQL Server Uninstaller.
6. Delete the local user group SAP_<*SID*>_LocalAdmin.
7. Delete the directory \usr\sap\trans folder.

Performance Tuning and Content Administration

Once all the post-installation activities are completed, you may need to implement certain basic performance tuning activities on the portal platform components, the SAP J2EE engine, and the Web infrastructure components. For more information on this topic, refer to Chapter 33.

The project then moves into the next phase, which is usually the content management phase. For more information, refer to Chapters 13 to 20.

NOTE *For more details, refer to the installation related resources listed in Appendix B.*

Summary

In this chapter, you learned some useful tips on how to troubleshoot a portal installation when it fails or when it does not complete successfully. You learned how to look for SAPinst-related issues as well as portal troubleshooting in general. You learned how to use the System Analyzer as well as the Support Platform to check whether the portal installation is complete. You then learned how to install the portal license, delete the portal log files, use the template installer to configure the portal scenario, configure the J2EE engine dispatcher and server thread managers, uninstall the SAP system, apply patches, and create a system backup.

PART IV

Content Administration

CHAPTER 13

Developing Content and Assigning Permissions

This chapter discusses aspects related to developing initial content and assigning permissions. You'll learn about the different types of SAP and custom-developed portal content. This chapter also takes a look at the Portal Content Directory, the portal content object model, and various content object types such as iViews, pages, roles, and worksets. You'll learn how to use the Content Administration Tool of Portal Content Studio and how to administer content using delta links, templates, and namespaces.

Creating Initial Content

Content administration is one of the administrator's first activities during the portal installation process. As part of the initial implementation, the content administrator may be required to implement some of the business packages and the content developer may create portal content objects such as iViews, pages, roles, and worksets.

Content administrators must create some custom administration roles, depending on the business requirements gathered during the initial phases of the project. They also must assign initial permissions to content objects as well as implement delegated content administration, if required.

Initial permissions can be assigned to content objects using *access control lists* (ACLs), which are a combination of users or user groups and the list of actions that are possible for those users or groups of users. By assigning an ACL to a content object, you can define whether a user or group of users can create an object, change that object, delete that object, run that object during runtime, or even assign permissions to that object.

In subsequent chapters, you will learn the importance of permissions and security zones for administering portal content. You will learn about delegated content and user administration and how to implement delegated content and user administration. Chapters 24 and 25 deal with how to implement delegated content and user administration. Chapter 34 discusses the various authorization models available in the portal like security zones, UME actions, and permission models.

As an administrator, you can customize the look and feel of the portal to meet the global branding requirements of your organization. You will learn how to customize portal themes, create display rules, and customize default framework pages. Chapter 17 discusses this in detail.

Types of Initial Content

After you install the portal, the initial content you create can be composed of the following:

- Content provided by SAP
- Custom-developed content
- Business packages

Initial Content Provided by SAP

If the portal is implemented for the first time, SAP provides some out-of-the-box content by default. This content is required for the portal to run the first time, and some of this content can be customized during the implementation. All content in the portal can be accessed from the portal content catalog, which is organized as a tree structure and can be accessed by clicking Content Administration on the first-level menu, clicking Portal Content in the second-level menu, and Portal Content under the Browse tab. The SAP-provided content can be found in the Portal Content Catalog page, by clicking the Portal Content folder under the Browse tab and then clicking the Content Provided by SAP folder, as shown in Figure 13-1.

DON'T *The content objects found in the Content Provided by SAP folder should* never *be modified under any circumstances. If you change the content, you run the risk of losing the custom changes made to the SAP content when you upgrade the portal, because they will be overwritten by the new changes after you upgrade to the latest version.*

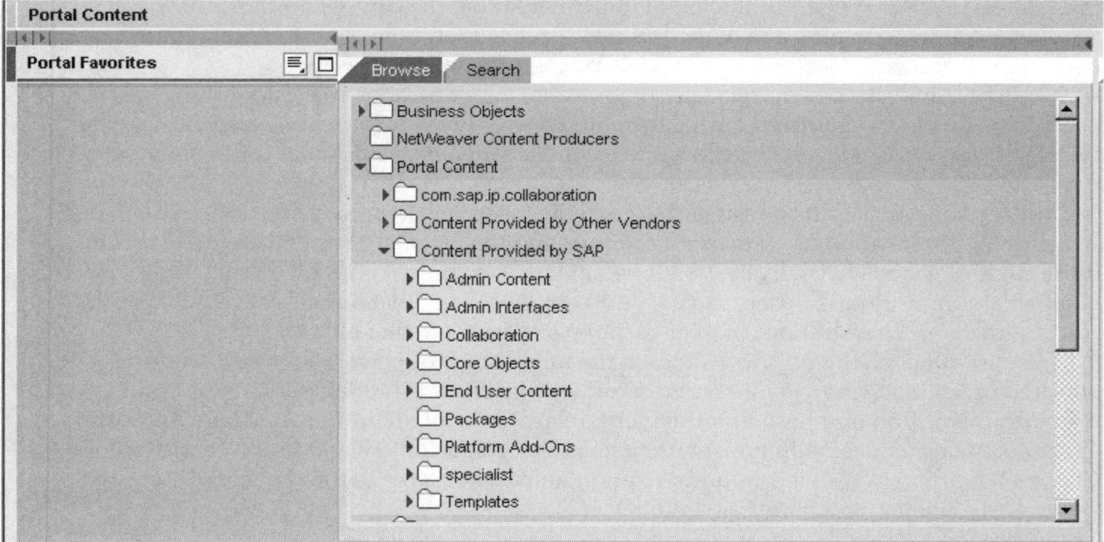

FIGURE 13-1 Accessing content provided by SAP

The Content Provided by SAP of the portal content catalog contains initial content for administrators, end users, and specialists. The initial content for administrators can be accessed at Content Administration | Portal Content | Content Provided by SAP | Admin Content as shown below. In the illustration, under the Admin Content folder, the initial administrator content is integrated with the pre-configured roles such as System Administrators, Content Administrators, Collaboration Administrators, and User Administrators. You can notice from the following illustration that the Super Administrator role contains content from System Administrator, Content Administrator, and User Administrator roles. The Super Administrator role has portal permissions for all initial portal content.

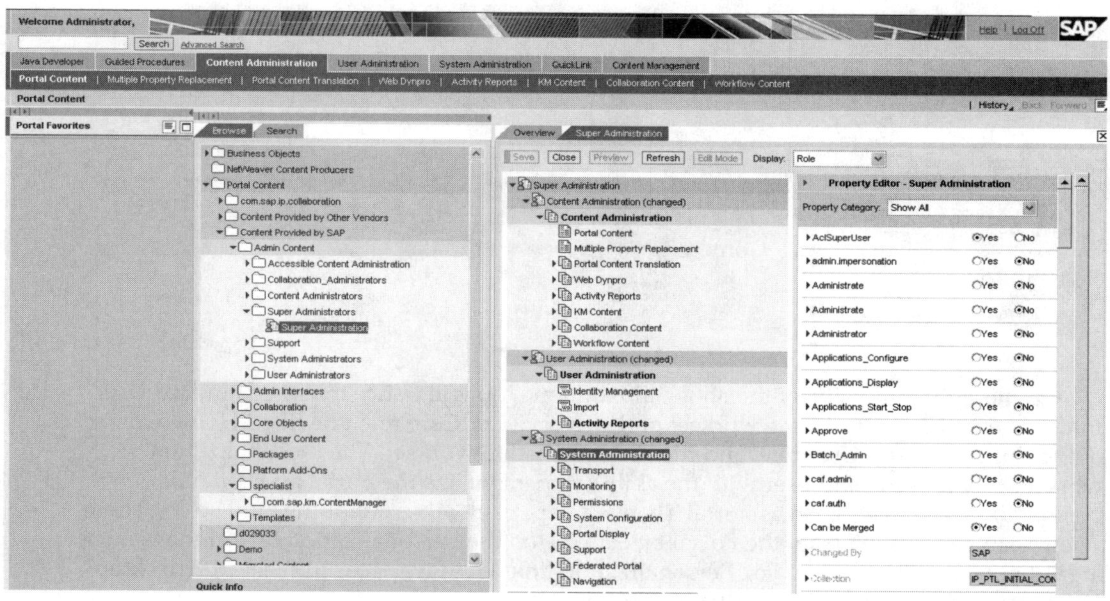

Copyright by SAP AG

The initial content for non-administrative portal users, also known as end users or every user, is available at Content Administration | Portal Content | Content Provided by SAP | End User Content.

INFO *The end user content is integrated into three out-of-the-box every user roles such as Control Center User role, Every User Core role, and Standard User role.*

The Control Center User role contains a Home workset that provides content for carrying out daily business activities such as Top News, Inbox, Daily Calendar, Discussions, Team Rooms, and so on. The Control Center User role requires KM components to be installed. The Every User Core role contains personalization iViews and an empty Home workset. The idea of an empty workset is that it provides you with the flexibility to merge iViews from other roles such as the Control Center User role that have Home worksets (but with functional iViews) using Merge IDs (you will learn how to use Merge IDs in Chapter 15).

In the following illustration, the Control Center User folder contains the Control Center User role and the Standard Portal Users folder contains the Every User Core role and the Standard User role.

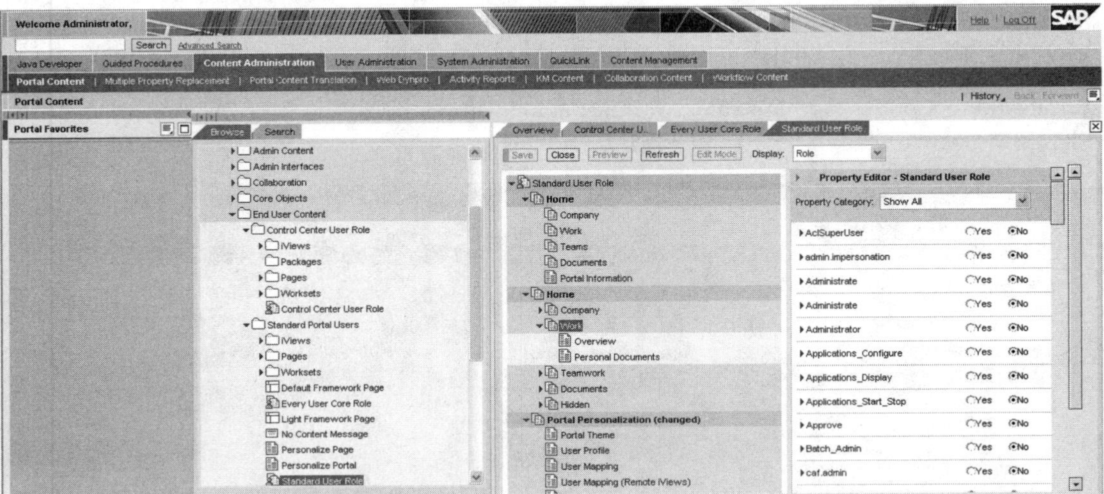

Copyright by SAP AG

On the right-hand side of the above illustration, you will notice that the Standard User role contains the empty Home workset of the Every User Core role, the filled Home workset of the Control Center User role, and the personalization workset. The personalization workset provides the end user with the ability to personalize the portal and contains personalization iViews such as Portal Theme, User Profile, User Mapping, and so on. These iViews can be accessed from the Portal by clicking on the Personalization link in the header area of portal user interface. The Personalization link will not appear in the portal desktop unless the user is assigned to the standard user role.

Custom Development: Delta Links to SAP-Provided Content

In order to reuse the content provided by SAP in your custom development, you must navigate to Portal Content | Portal Administrators for administrator content and Portal Content | Portal Users for end user content. While the contents in these paths are similar to those under the Content Provided by SAP directory, these can be modified because they do not belong to the SAP namespace and hence are not affected during a portal upgrade or support package install. Figure 13-2 displays the contents of the Portal Administrators folder. SAP provides delta links to all objects in the Portal Administrators and Portal Users folders; to avoid overwriting SAP content, you should either modify these SAP-provided delta link objects or create delta links of these objects and include them in your custom-created folders for modification.

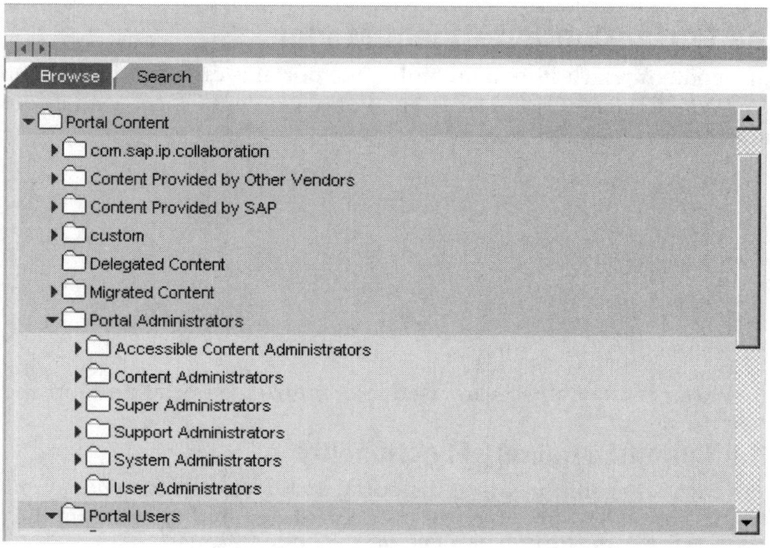

FIGURE 13-2 Content available in the Portal Administrators folder

DON'T *SAP does not provide a warning when you try to modify standard SAP content, so you need to be very careful not to change these objects.*

Business Packages

Another type of SAP-provided business content is the *business packages*, which provide a jumpstart for an implementation by providing various ready-to-use worksets, roles, iViews, and pages. The business packages are categorized by user group:

- Business packages for *user*
- Business packages for *manager*
- Business packages for *specialist*

The *user packages* can be accessed by the end users to check travel information, weather information, and other such information. The *manager packages* provide the worksets, roles for checking budget-related data, and team-related information for managing teams and employees. Managers can use the budget-related data to check the latest status on training and travel budgets. The *specialist packages* are required for some specialized roles in an organization, such as sales representatives, sales managers, customer service representatives, and customer service managers. These are more complex packages because they can span multiple backend systems and may require connectivity and additional configuration steps.

NOTE *For more information on installing business packages, refer to Chapter 16.*

Using the Portal Content Object Model

All the content relevant to maintaining the portal is organized into a model structure known as the *Portal Content Object Model*. The Portal Content Object Model consists of portal content objects such as these:

- iViews
- Pages
- Worksets
- Roles
- Layouts

These portal content objects are used to organize the portal desktop and the user interface.

Portal Content Directory Functionality

One of the main components of the portal architecture is the *Portal Content Directory*, first shown in Figure 13-1, in which all the content required to maintain the portal is stored and maintained. The Portal Content Directory is the central place to

- create various content objects
- administer them by assigning permissions and changing their properties

In fact, the Portal Content Directory is a form of directory structure in which all the content objects are stored in the form of a hierarchy. All the portal content objects are stored in the portal database, which is known as the *Portal Content Directory database.*

Following are some of the basic functionalities allowed in the Portal Content Directory:

- Delta links
- Relationships between objects
- Transport mechanism
- Personalization
- Object notification
- Versioning
- ACLs
- Filters

TIP *To view the Portal Content Directory, the user must have been assigned the Content Administrator role or the Super Administrator role.*

Portal Content Object Types

Now let's take a look at the various content objects that are available in the portal.

iView: A Container for Retrieving Data

The *iView* is the basic component used to retrieve both *dynamic data* as well as *static data* from the various backend systems that are available in an organization. The various backend systems could be the following:

- R/3 systems such as Business Information Warehouse (BW) and Customer Relationship Management (CRM)
- Database systems such as Oracle and Microsoft SQL Server
- Web content from various intranet and Internet websites
- Content management systems and knowledge management systems
- E-mail systems such as Lotus Notes and Microsoft Outlook
- File systems

NOTE *The iView is like a container for data that are retrieved from the various backend systems and displayed on the portal desktop.*

Personalization of iViews Personalization is the mechanism by which an end user can change some of the properties of the iViews during runtime. End users can change only those properties of the iView that the content administrator has allowed.

Some examples of the iView properties that can be changed are the following:

- Color of the iView
- Height and width of the iView
- Positioning of the iView within a page

Personalization is different from *configuration* in the sense that configuration is usually done by an administrator, and the changes that the administrator has implemented are applicable for the whole portal and not just to one individual user. With personalization, the user changes only his or her own portal.

Page: A Container for iViews

The page is the next highest level object in the portal. Unlike the iView, which cannot contain any other object inside it, the page can contain another page or another iView.

The page includes information on the different iViews it contains as well as how the iViews are arranged inside it. The arrangement of iViews within the page is known as the *layout* of the page. Some of the layouts available in the portal are T layouts, three-column layouts, and wide-narrow-wide layouts. End users can personalize a page and choose from among the layouts that have been assigned to the page by the content administrator during design time.

The end users can also move the iViews around from one container to another within a given layout. However, they cannot change the arrangement of the containers themselves. If the content administrator had assigned only one layout for the page at design time, then the end users will not be able to choose any layout for personalization at runtime.

NOTE *For more information, refer to Chapter 14.*

Workset: A Container for Day-to-Day Activities

The next highest level object on the Portal Content Object Model is the *workset*, a collection of both pages and iViews. The workset helps you collect all the related pages and iViews in one location.

The workset should be designed so that it enables a particular person in an organization to conduct his or her day-to-day activities. For example, the requirements for a customer service representative in an organization include being able to place sales orders, check the status of sales orders, and verify data related to a customer account. So the content administrator could create a workset that contains iViews for creating sales orders, checking the order status, and checking customer account data.

TIP *Worksets can be reused in different roles in an organization, and this avoids the need for re-creating the pages and iViews for various roles.*

Role: Enables Navigation and Personalization

The next highest object on the portal is the *role*, which performs the same functionality as the workset in terms of bringing all the pages and iViews together. The pages and iViews are required for a person in an organization to conduct his or her day-to-day activities. The difference between a role and a workset is that a *role can also be assigned to a user or a group of users.*

Roles and Navigational Capability By assigning the role to a group of users or to a user, you can provide navigational capability to the user or group of users on the portal. *Navigational capability* refers to the user's ability to navigate through the portal using the top-level navigation menus (including the first-level and second-level menus) and the detailed navigational menu that appears in the left side of the Portal Content Studio interface.

What appears in the top-level menu and in the tree structure in the detailed navigation area depends on the roles added to the user profile. The role also decides the sequence or order in which the various tabs on the first-level menu are displayed.

TIP *Sequencing of menus in the portal desktop depends on a role property called* sort sequence.

Positioning Content Within the Role The role decides which pages and iViews a user can view based on what content has been assigned to that role. Also, whether a page or an iView is displayed at the top-level menu or in the navigation area depends on where that page or iView has been assigned to that role. If the page or iView under consideration is very important, it can be assigned to the role either at the top-level menu or as a link in the navigation area.

To show the iView on the top-level menu, you must assign iViews directly to the role. Or, if that iView or page does not contain critical content, you can include it in the navigation area by assigning the iView to some subfolder within that role.

In a way, the role also provides a navigational structure and some form of access control, even though other means of setting up permissions for content objects, such as User Management Engine (UME) actions, security zones, and permissions, exist, as you will see in Chapter 34.

Folder: Organizing Content

An iView can be assigned to a page, a workset, or a role. It is the smallest possible component, and no other content object can be assigned to it. A page can be assigned to another page or to a workset or a role. Worksets can be assigned to another workset or to a role, and a role can be assigned to another role. You can also create folders and subfolders, thus creating folder hierarchy in the Portal Content Directory. The relationship between objects basically denotes the ability to assign one content object to another—for example, the ability to assign an iView to a page, a page to workset, and a workset to a role.

NOTE *No other portal content object can be assigned to an iView.*

Folders help you organize the portal content objects for easier maintenance and administration. In fact, a folder hierarchy can be used later on for delegated content administration, wherein certain administrators will be allowed access only to certain folders and objects contained within those folders. The folder hierarchy can be created based on the organizational structure, type of content, or any other criteria. Folders can also be assigned to various roles, and thus the folders can be used to provide the navigational structure on the portal.

Portal Content Studio: Content Administration Tool

The Portal Content Studio provides the programmer's equivalent of NetWeaver Developer Studio for developing and administering content. Figure 13-3 displays the Content Administration tool for administering page content.

NOTE *The Portal Content Studio can be used to develop the portal content objects.*

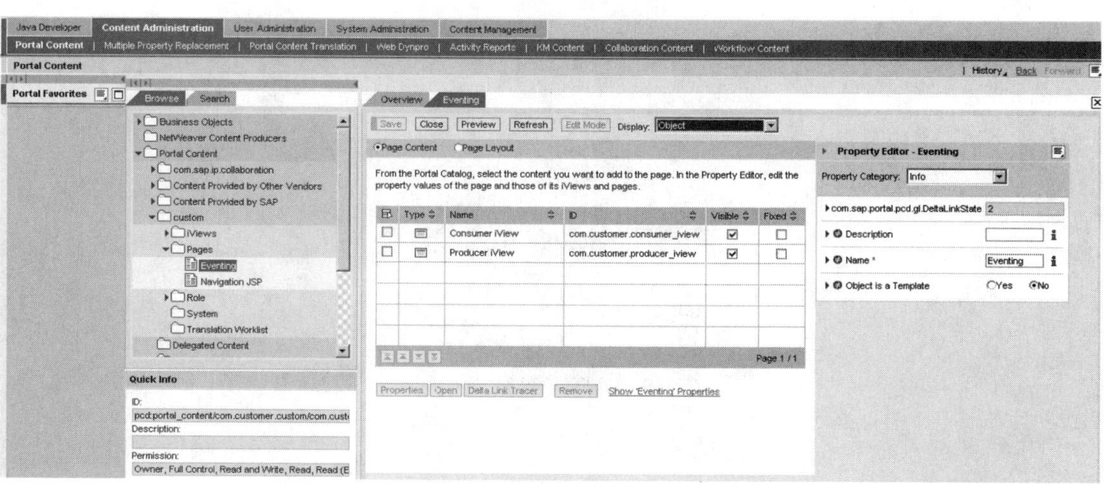

FIGURE 13-3 Portal Content Studio Content Administration tool interface

Portal Content Catalog

Figure 13-4 displays the portal catalog section of the Portal Content Directory (PCD). It contains two tabs, one for browsing through the content hierarchy and the other tab for searching using keywords and filter mechanisms. Below the Browse tab is a tree structure of the portal catalog, which contains all the objects that are stored in the PCD. Below the portal catalog tree is the Quick Info section, which contains information on the current object's ID, description, and available permission levels.

Search Filters

The PCD offers a filter mechanism that you can use while searching for content objects with the search functionality. Figure 13-5 displays the search portion of the PCD, which can be accessed by clicking the search tab. You can restrict the search using filters by choosing the appropriate values in the Search In and Object Type dropdown fields shown in Figure 13-5. The Search In field restricts the search area within the Portal Content Catalog, and the Object Type field restricts the search by object type such as folders, iViews, roles, and so on.

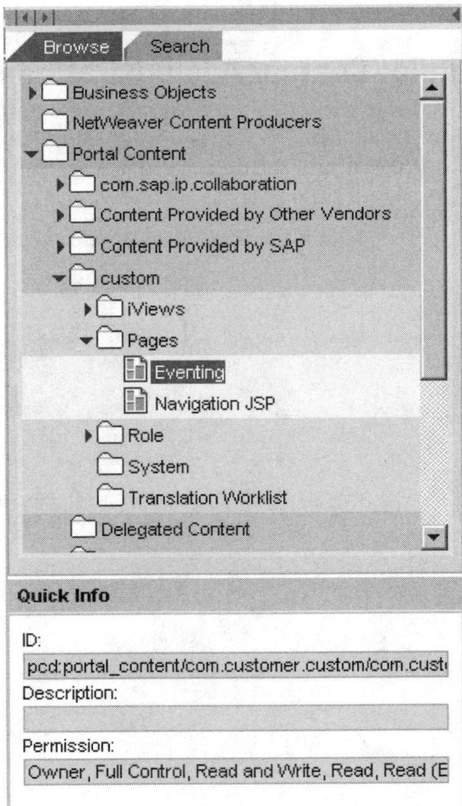

FIGURE 13-4 Tree structure of content objects

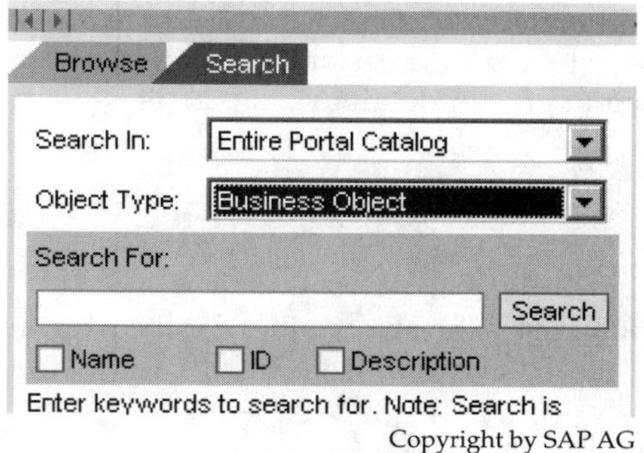

FIGURE 13-5 Search criteria in the PCD Search tab

Page Editor

To the right of the portal catalog is the editing area for the page. Figure 13-6 displays the editing area for a page named Eventing.

In Figure 13-6, at the top of the page editor area is the Object tab—in this case, the object being viewed is the Eventing page. You can toggle among objects while working with various objects that are currently open in the Portal Content Studio. The Object tab is useful if you work on various content objects at the same time; it helps you to focus on a particular content object—such as a role object, an iView, or a page—by clicking the relevant Object tab.

Object Editor Tools

Below the Object tab are the object editor tool buttons, such as Save, Close, Preview, Refresh, and Edit Mode. The following illustration shows the page editor tool buttons.

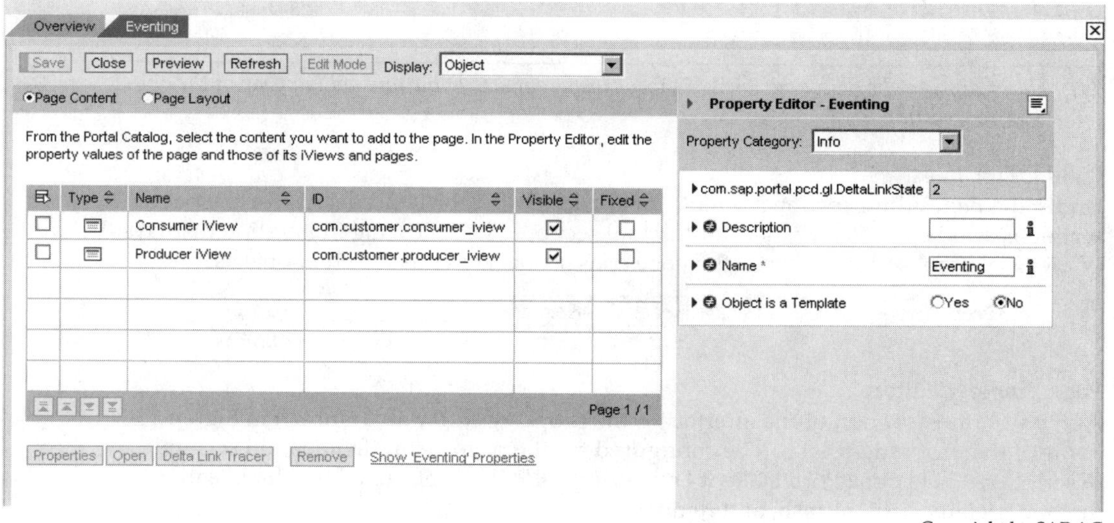

FIGURE 13-6 Page editor area

The Display dropdown field provides the ability to toggle between different views of the editor such as Object view, Permissions view, Related Links view, and so on. The page editor is discussed in greater detail in Chapter 14.

Copyright by SAP AG

This illustration shows the object editor for the page, with radio buttons available to switch between Page Content and Page Layout:

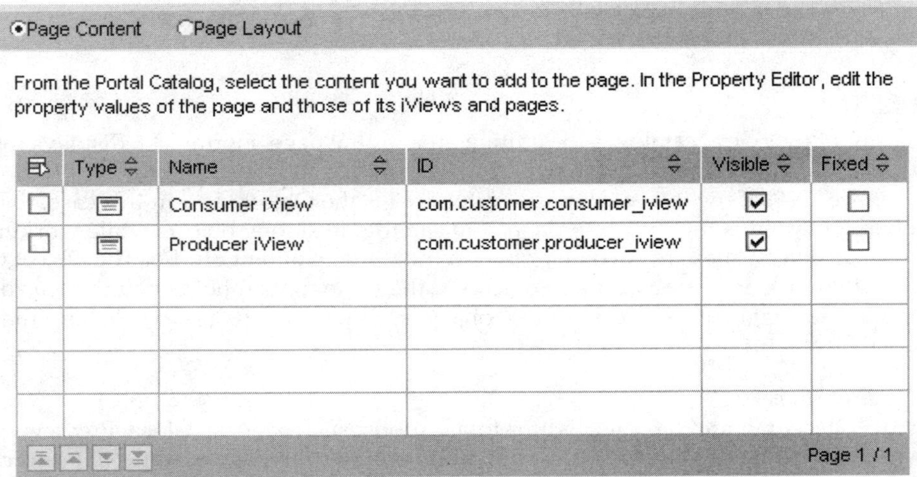

Copyright by SAP AG

TIP *Depending on the object currently in focus, different sets of buttons will appear in the object editor tool section.*

Child Editor Tools

Under the page editor section are tools for working with the child objects for the page. This section is referred to as the Child Editor Tool section. The following illustration displays the iView editor tool section because the page consists of iViews as the child objects.

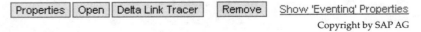

Properties | Open | Delta Link Tracer | Remove | Show 'Eventing' Properties

Copyright by SAP AG

Page Property Editor

At the rightmost section of the interface is the property editor area, shown in Figure 13-7. Some of the properties that can be configured for the page are authentication scheme, description, Enterprise Portal Client Framework (EPCF) levels, fixed height, isolation method, details, help, refresh, and remove.

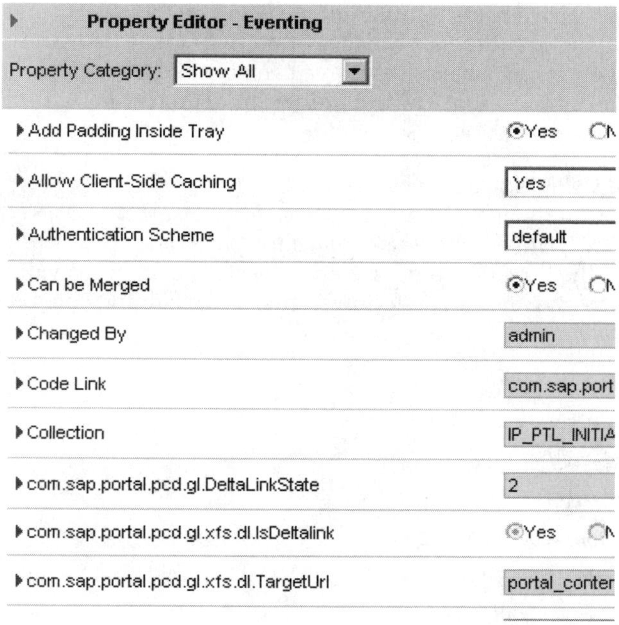

Figure 13-7
Page property editor

Copyright by SAP AG

TIP *Properties can be used either for* configuration *during design time by the administrator or for* personalization *during runtime by either the admin or the end user.*

Object Naming Convention

Every object on the portal uses a *naming convention*. The object name is composed of three elements:

- **Object ID** The folder path in the PCD where the object is located; this can be identified in the property field called PCD Location for any given portal content object.
- **Namespace prefix** Optional; for SAP objects, it has the value *com.sap.portal* or *com.sapportal.**. In the case of custom-created objects, the namespace prefix usually includes the company name, such as *com.companyname*.
- **Base name** The actual name of the object that has been created in the PCD—for example, *content_admin_role*. The base name can be used while searching for objects with the search functionality on the PCD.

The complete object name is the concatenation of the object ID, the namespace prefix if any, and the base name of the object—such as *pcd:portal_content/administrator/content_admin/com.sap.portal.content_admin_role*.

TIP *The namespace is similar to the concept of packages in Java and development classes in Advanced Business Application Programming (ABAP) programming.*

The namespace helps to differentiate between the objects that may have the same name but may belong to different packages or namespaces. The namespaces can also be used to differentiate between objects that have been created by various units or development teams within your organization. These naming conventions can be applied not only to various portal content objects, but also to folders.

Example of Using Namespaces

Here's an example of a namespace: *<domain>.<company>.<object_type>.<region>.<package_name>.<role>.<software_product>.<content_type>.<name>.*

Usually the domain, company, and object type are fixed values. A typical example of a content object name (if you followed the above naming convention) is *com.customer.pcd.us.custom.admin.sap_crm.iview.google*, where:

com – domain

customer – company name

pcd – object type

us – region

custom – package name

admin – role

sap_crm – software product

iView - content type

google- iView name

Copying Objects

You can copy a content object into another content object—for example, you can copy an iView from another iView—in three ways:

- Create a simple copy
- Create a *delta link*
- Use a *template*

Simple Copy

When you create a target iView from a source iView using a simple copy, the target iView has *no dependency* on the source iView. When any property on the source iView changes, that property on the target iView does not change. You can create simple copies for all kinds of objects.

Delta Link

When you copy a source iView into a target iView using a delta link, the target iView will *inherit the properties* of the source iView. So if any property (for example, the height of the iView) on the source iView changes, the corresponding property on the target iView will also change. On the other hand, the source iView is not dependent on the target iView—so if any property on the target iView changes, the corresponding property on the source iView will not change.

Delta links have several benefits. First, delta links provide the benefit of *reusability*; you can reuse the source object as instances of multiple target objects and you do not have to replicate any changes that occur in the source object to all the target objects. The changes made to the source object are automatically propagated to all the target objects provided a given property was not changed in the target object.

TIP *The reusability feature of delta links enables easy maintenance of all the portal content objects.*

Another useful benefit of the delta link feature is that when you create custom portal content of the original SAP content objects using delta links, you can upgrade the portal in the future, and the changes that were made to those original SAP objects are automatically transferred to the custom objects that have been created based on the SAP objects.

TIP *When using delta links, unchanged parts of custom code inherit the latest changes made to SAP objects.*

Template

Objects can be created by copying them from a *template*; this option is available only for iViews, pages, systems, and layouts. The template offers reusability. Using a template means you don't have to define the properties of an object when you create it. The target object that was created based on the template automatically *inherits* all the properties defined for the template; this saves a lot of effort during the creation of the target object.

Figure 13-8 shows the iView Wizard that lets you create an iView from a template.

Figure 13-9 shows the Page Wizard that lets you create a page using a template.

Chapter 14 discusses how to create pages and iViews using the page and iView editors in the Portal Content Catalog.

Inserting an Object into a Source Object

A target object can also be inserted into a source object—for example, you can insert an iView into a page or a page into a workset. When you insert an iView into a page, you are creating a *relationship* between the page and the iView.

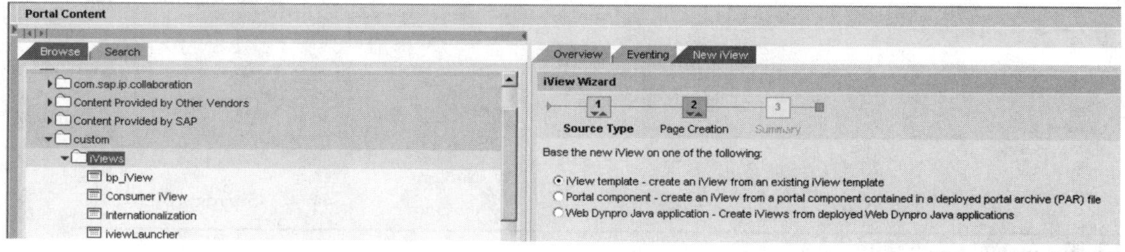

FIGURE 13-8 iView Wizard

Overview | Eventing | New iView | New Page

Page Wizard

1 Page Properties — 2 Page Template — 3 Page Layouts — 4 Summary

This wizard guides you through the steps required to create a portal page based on an existing template.
Specify general properties for the new object (page).

Page Name: *

Page ID: *

Page ID Prefix (Example: com.companyname):

Master Language *
English

Description:

Copyright by SAP AG

FIGURE 13-9 Page Wizard

The action in Figure 13-10 adds an iView to a page.
The action in Figure 13-11 adds a page to a page.

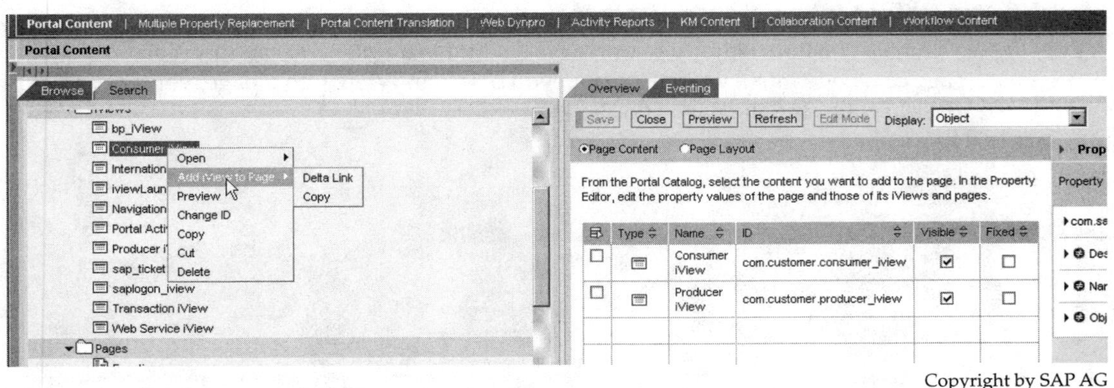

Copyright by SAP AG

FIGURE 13-10 Adding an iView to a page

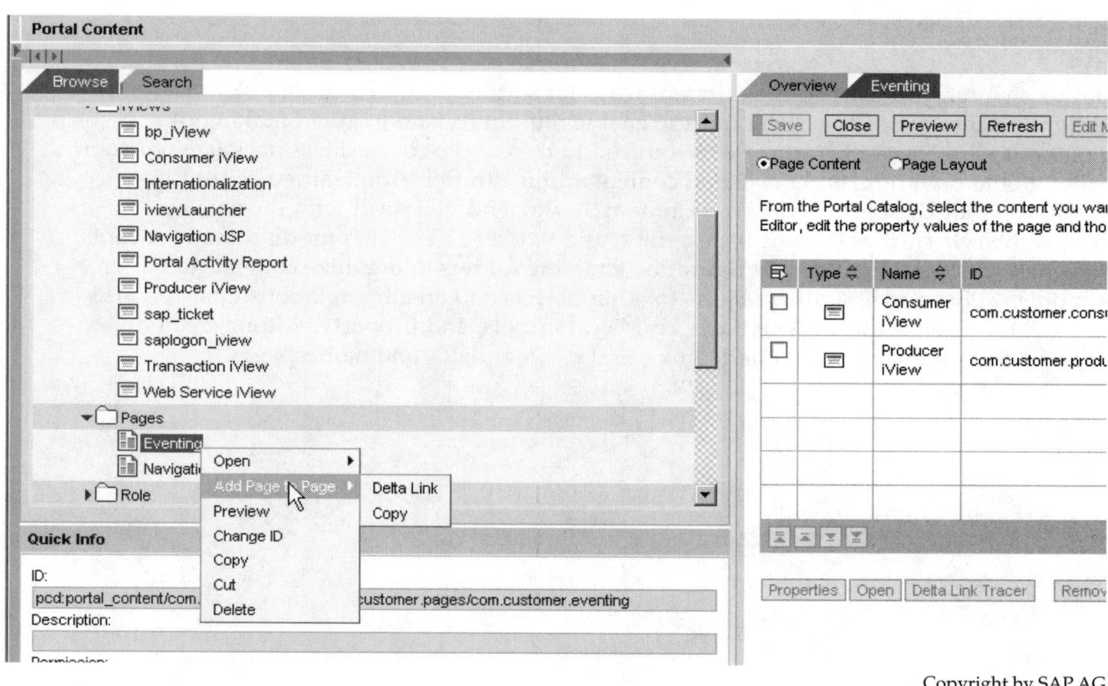

FIGURE 13-11 Adding a page to a page

Using Chained Objects

You can create objects that are linked together in a chain so that changes made to one source *object* (iView, page, or workset, for example) affects other target objects to which that source object is linked as well as other objects to which the target object is linked; in other words, if you make a change to object 1, and it is linked to object 2 and object 2 is linked to object 3, then that change is propagated to objects 2 and 3 because of this chain relationship.

NOTE *For more details, refer to the content administration related resources list in Appendix B.*

Summary

In this chapter, you learned the different ways for setting up initial content. You learned the importance of creating delta links to enable reusability and to avoid making direct changes to SAP content. You were introduced to the concept of business packages, custom roles, global branding, and delegated content administration. You learned about the Portal Content Directory and Portal Content Studio, and you dealt with the various content objects such as iViews, pages, roles, and worksets. The chapter discussed concepts such as personalization and configuration, creating folders to organize content for easier administration, and assigning objects to other objects and creating relationships. You also learned how to use the object editors, child editor tools, and property editors; create copies using simple copy and delta links; and use templates and namespaces.

14

CHAPTER

Developing iViews and Pages

This chapter discusses how to use the iView Property Editor and Page Editor to create and edit iViews and pages. You will learn how to create a URL iView, pass URL parameters to the URL iView, and use the URL parameter for end-user personalization. You will learn about the various property categories and properties of iViews and pages that affect their runtime behavior. You will be introduced to the editor tools such as delta link tracer and child object tools. You will also learn about sub properties and how they can be used for personalization of iViews and pages.

Using iViews: The Fundamental Building Blocks

iViews are the fundamental building blocks of the portal. Due to the numerous ways in which an iView can connect to backend systems, many types of iViews can be used. iViews are a bit complex to configure when compared to other portal content objects.

One of the most common iViews are transaction iViews that connect to a backend system such as SAP R/3, Customer Relationship Management (CRM), or Business Information Warehouse (BW) systems. The other most common iViews are those that connect to an SQL database or other relational database system. A number of knowledge management–related iViews, Web Service iViews, and other types of iViews can also be used.

TIP *To connect to these backend systems, you would have to create system objects under the System Configuration menu on the portal. This is discussed in Chapter 18.*

You can create an iView in three ways, as shown in the following illustration:

- **Using an iView template** SAP provides a number of standard templates for creating iViews that you can use to create the iView.
- **Using a portal component** Portal components can be custom-created and deployed on the portal as a PAR file, which can then be used to create an iView.
- **Using Web DynPro applications** iViews can be created based on Web Dynpro Java applications deployed on the AS Java system.

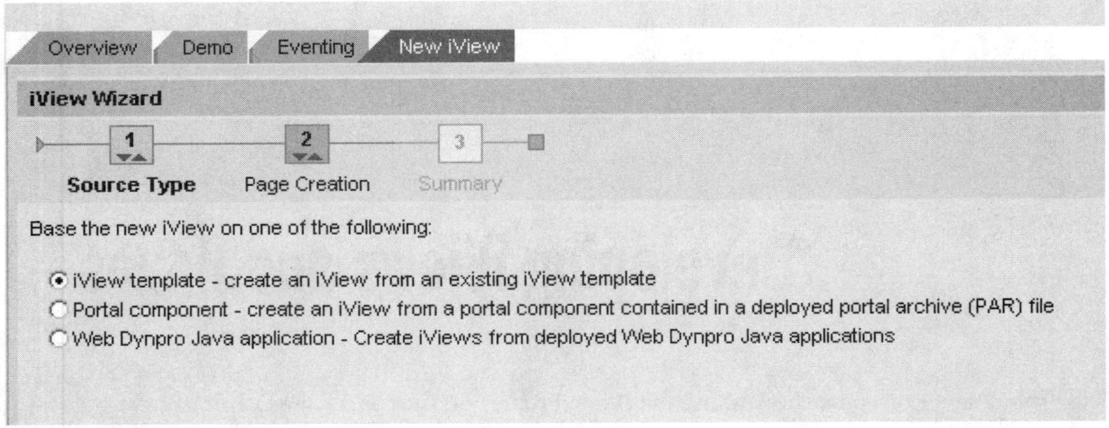

Creating a URL iView

Here's how to create an iView:

1. Open the Portal Content Studio by clicking on Content Administration | Portal Content.
2. If you have not created your own custom folder for storing development objects, do so by right-clicking on Portal Content. Select New | Folder from the context menu.
3. In the General Properties screen of the Folder Wizard, in the Folder Name field, enter a suitable name such as **Custom Development** and in the Folder ID field, enter a corresponding ID such as **custom_development**. If required, enter a suitable description in the Description field. Click Finish.
4. Right click the newly created folder in which you want to create the iView and choose New | iView, as shown next.

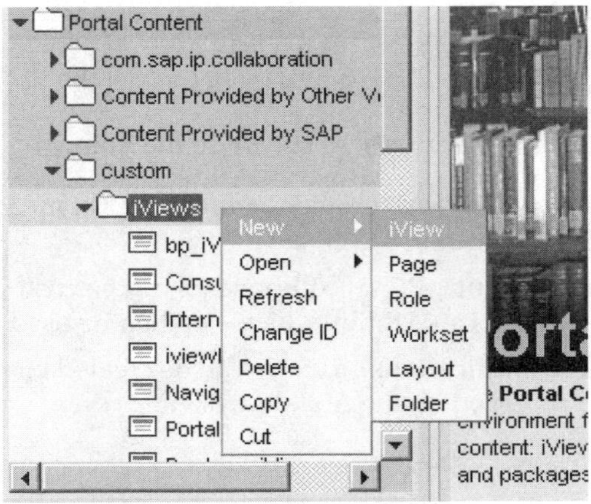

5. In the iView Wizard, select the first option, iView Template, and then click Next. The template selection screen of the wizard will appear, as shown next.

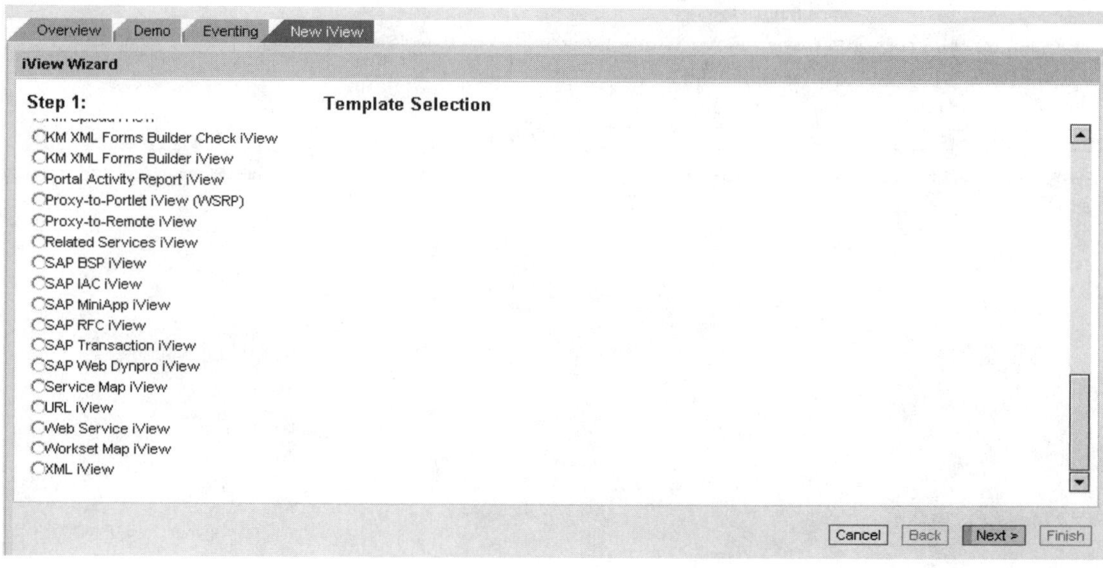

Copyright by SAP AG

6. The above illustration displays a number of SAP-provided iView templates such as SAP BSP iView, SAP IAC iView, SAP Transaction iView, SAP Web Dynpro view, Web Service iView, XML iView, and so on. Since the simplest form of iView is a URL iView, choose the URL iView radio button in the Template Selection screen (step 1) of the iView Wizard. Then click Next.
7. In the General Properties screen (step 2) of the iView wizard shown on the next page, enter the general properties for the iView such as iView Name, iView ID, iView ID prefix, Master Language, and Description. Note that the iView ID prefix and description fields are optional. Then click Next.

TIP *The iView ID prefix can be named in com.company_name format. This naming convention helps to identify portal content objects belonging to certain organizational units, and administer them differently.*

8. In the Define Source URL (step 3) of the iView Wizard, Enter **http://www.google.com/search** in the Enter URL field, as shown on the next page. Click Next.

PART IV

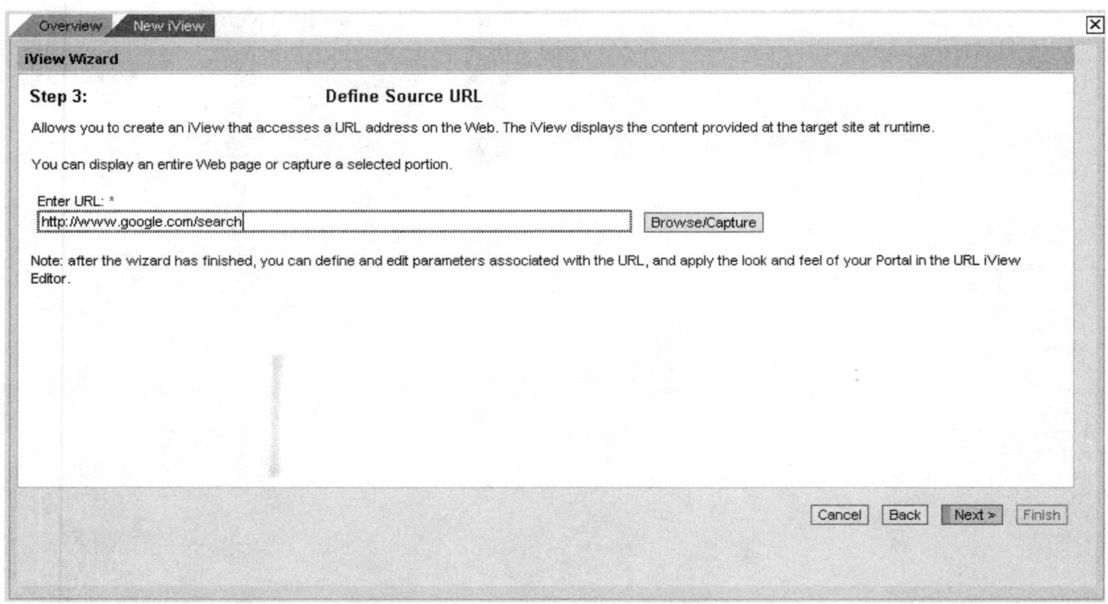

Copyright by SAP AG

9. Click Finish in the Summary screen of the iView wizard. The URL iView editor will now appear as shown in Figure 14-1. In the URL iView Editor, you can perform the following activities:
   - Pass in URL parameters
   - Capture third-party page content, either in part or in full
   - Configure the URL parameter for personalization at runtime
   - Change the URL iView properties
10. In the URL iView Editor, click Preview. The Google home page will appear.
11. Collapsing the left navigational panel will provide more space to work with. To collapse the navigation panel, click the arrow, as shown here:

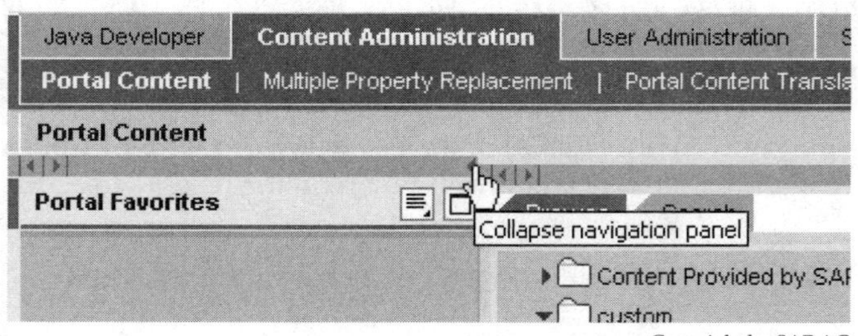

Copyright by SAP AG

FIGURE 14-1 URL iView Editor

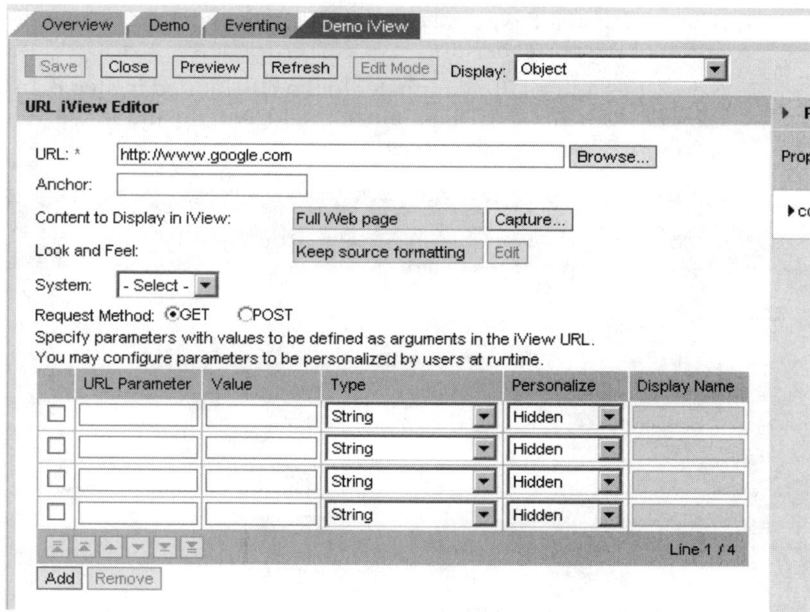

12. You can enlarge the width of the portal catalog by clicking the arrow, as shown on the right.
13. To collapse the portal catalog, click the arrow, as shown here:

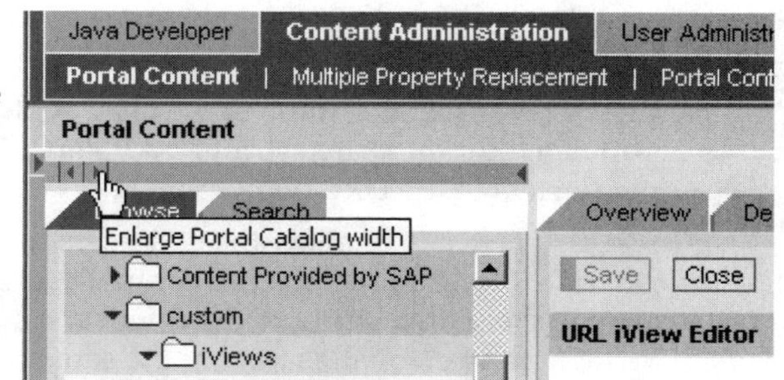

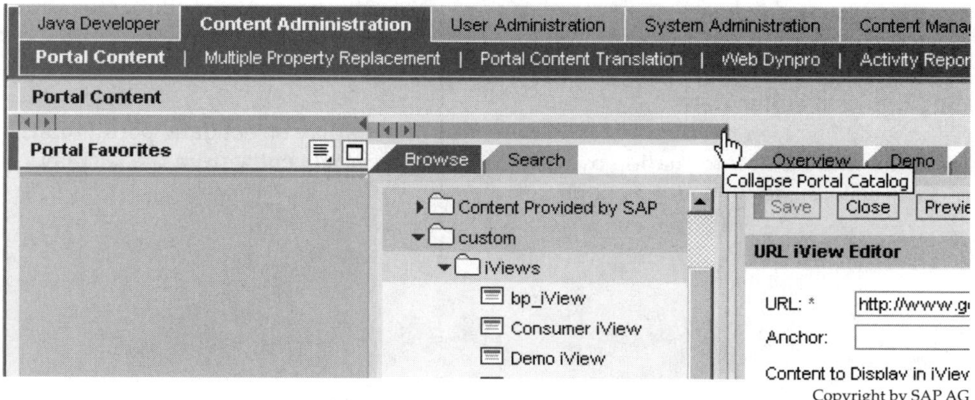

14. After collapsing the portal catalog, the iView Editor screen will cover the entire width of the portal desktop.
15. Now let us add a URL parameter to the URL added in step 8. In the URL iView Editor screen, in the URL parameter field, enter **q** and in the Value field, enter the string **SAP Portal** as shown next.

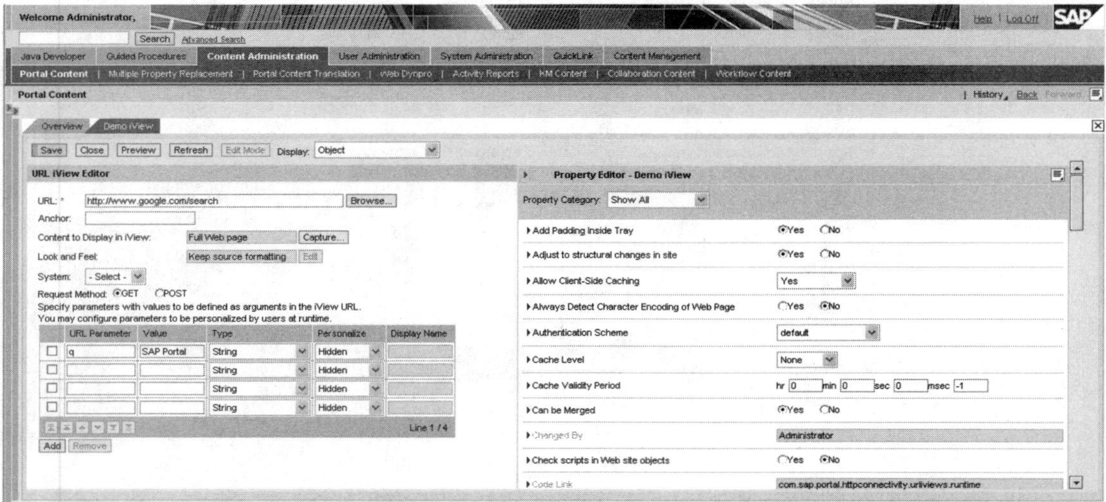

16. Click Preview again. You will see the Google page open with search results pre-populated for the search string "SAP Portal." This step proves how we can add URL parameters to the URL iView.
17. It is also possible to allow the end users to personalize the URL parameter at runtime. For example, we can configure this iView such that the end user can change the search string to the iView at runtime. In order to do that, select Read/Write in the Personalize field in the same row where you entered the URL parameter in step 14. Enter the string **Search String** in the Display field. This value will appear to the end user at runtime for personalization. Click Save. In the section titled "How Personalization Works" of this chapter, we will demonstrate how personalization works.

Toggling Between Editor Views

You can toggle between the views of the iView Editor to display object data, permissions, related links, and other information by selecting an appropriate entry from the Display drop-down list, as shown on the next page.

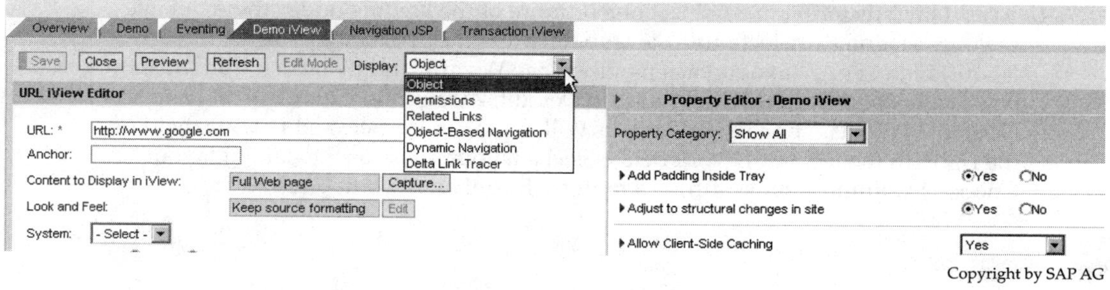

Creating a Page

Here's how to create a page in the Page Wizard:

1. In Portal Content Studio's portal catalog, right click the folder in which you want to create the page and choose New | Page.
2. In the Page Properties screen of the Page Wizard shown below, enter the Page Name, Page ID, the Page ID Prefix, and a Description, if any, and then click Next.
3. In the Page Template screen of the Page Wizard shown below, choose the Default Page Template and click Next.

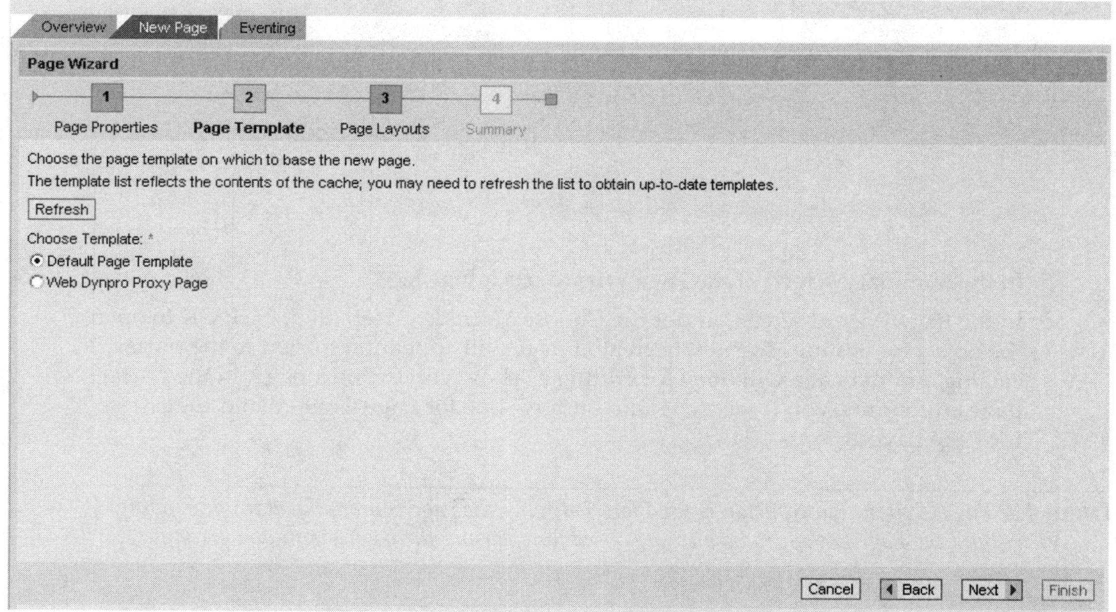

PART IV

4. To add layouts to the page, select one or more of the layouts under the Available Layouts section (to select multiple layouts, press the CTRL key as you select each layout) in the Page Layouts screen of the Page Wizard, and then click Add, as shown below. Choose 1 Column (Full Width) - Default, 2 Columns (Equal Width), and the Double T layouts. The selected layouts will appear in the Selected Layouts field on the right. In the Default Layout field, select a layout to use as the default layout. Choose 1 Column (Full Width) - Default as the default layout. Click Next.

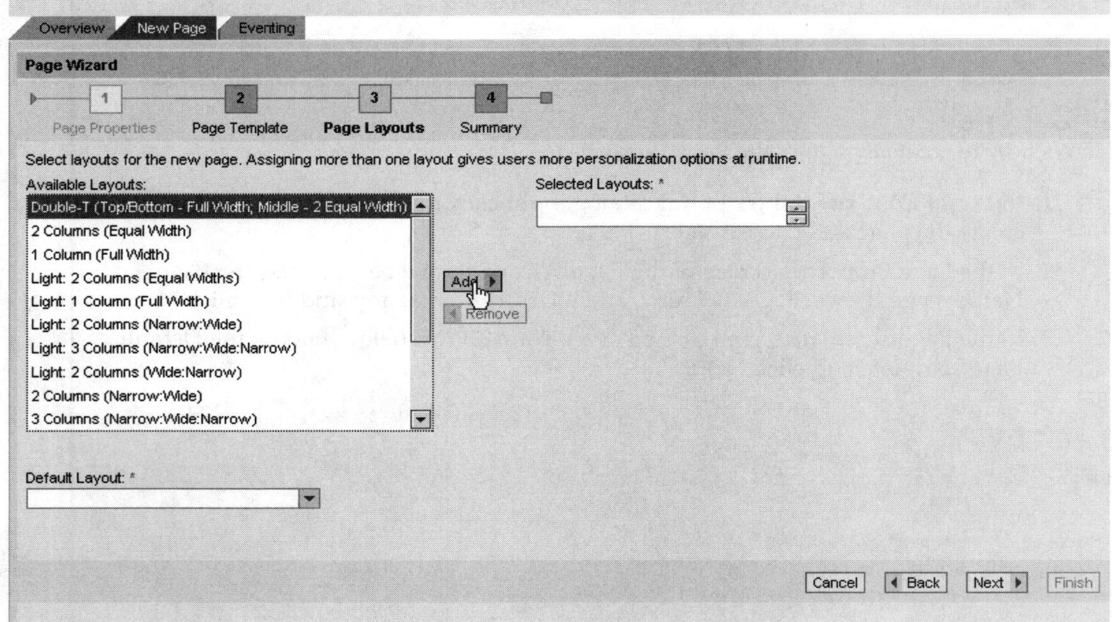

5. In the Summary screen of the Page Wizard, click Finish.
6. In the Page Wizard screen, under the Choose Your Next Step field, click OK to open the object for editing. The newly created page will appear on the left in the portal catalog and the page will open for editing as shown on the next page. In the Portal's page editor area, you'll see two radio buttons, one for Page Content and the other for Page Layout.

INFO *The Page Content radio button is used for modifying the page content by adding/removing iViews, and the Page Layout radio button is used for choosing the page layout and arranging the iViews.*

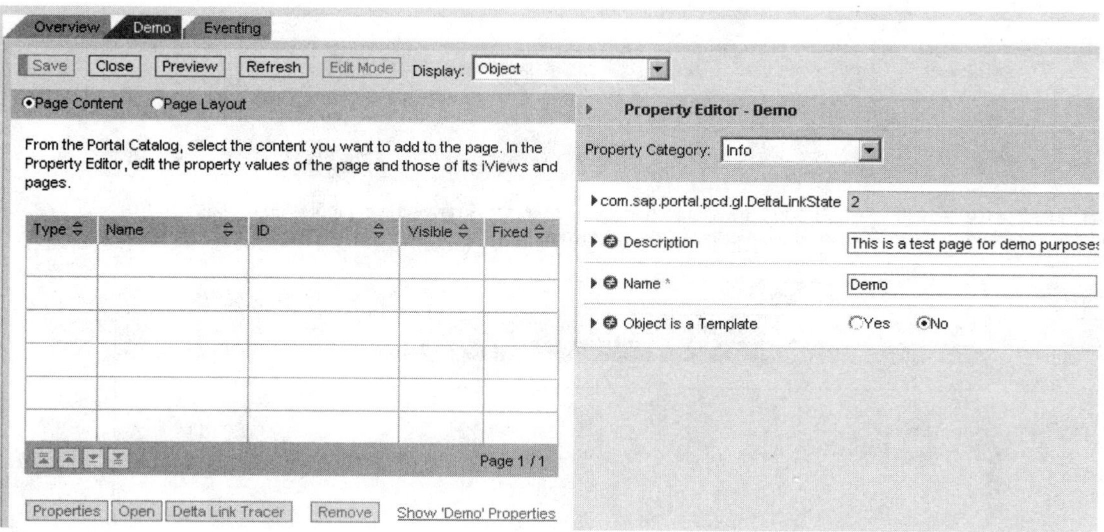

Assigning Content to the Page

One of your first steps in creating a page is to assign content to the page by adding iViews. To add an iView to the page, do the following:

1. Keep the target page open in the Object Editor section of the portal. If the target page is not opened already, navigate to the page in the Portal Content Catalog and right click to select Open | Object.
2. Navigate to the iView that you created in this chapter in the portal catalog.
3. Then right click the iView and choose Add iView To Page | Delta Link Or Copy. If you choose Delta Link, any changes made to the iView will be carried over to the iView in this page. If you chose Copy, then there will be no link between the original iView and the iView copied into the target page. The iView is now added to the page. Repeat step 2 for the remaining iViews that need to be added to the page. For simplicity's sake, let us just add one iView, the one we created in this chapter.
4. Once the page content has been added, click the Page Layout radio button.
5. Choose the desired layout by selecting one of the values on the drop-down list in the Show Layout field, as shown in Figure 14-2.
6. If you have multiple iViews, drag and drop the iView in the required container of the layout, and then click Save.

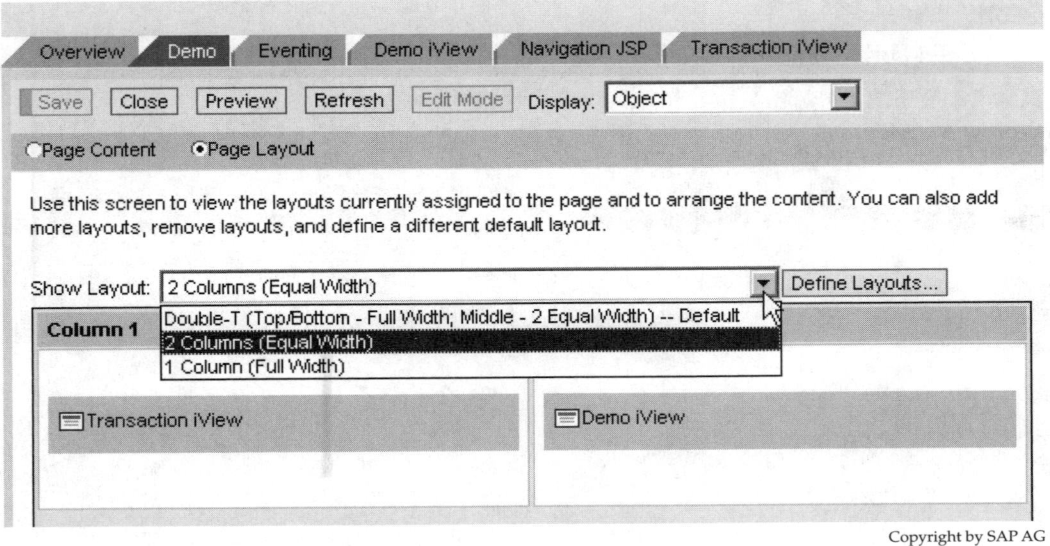

FIGURE 14-2 Page Layout

7. Click Preview to view the page during design time. The page will appear as shown next. You will notice that the Google iView does not cover the full length of the page and that there is a scrollbar on the right.

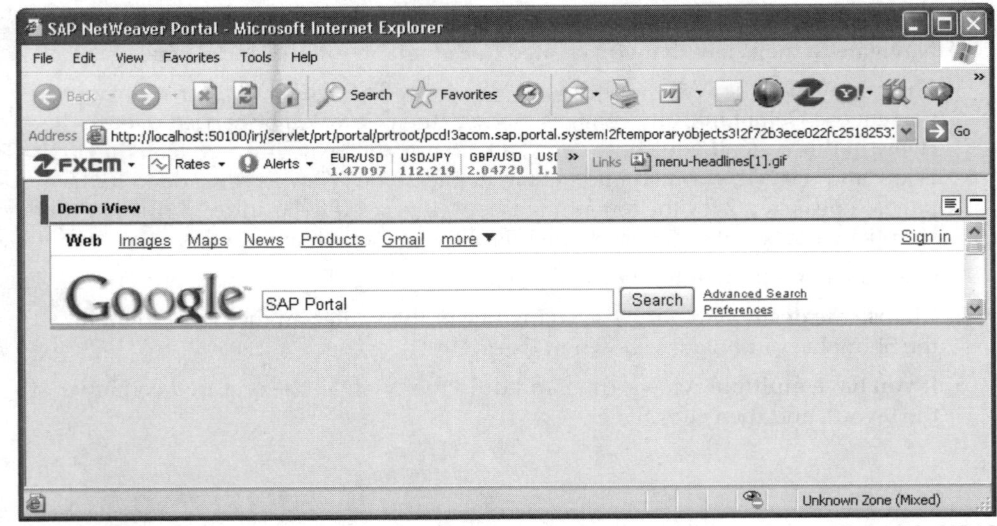

8. To rectify the issue, change the Height Type property of the iView to FULL LENGTH. Preview the page again. The iView will now cover the full page.

Page Layout Templates

Figure 14-3 displays the list of page layout templates provided by SAP in Enterprise Portal 7.0.

In EP 6.0, only five layout templates were available. While adding iViews to the page in the Page Content view of the Page Editor, any number of iViews can be added to a container.

TIP *In EP 7.0, you can create our own custom layouts.*

Delta Link Tracer

Clicking the Delta Link Tracer for the child object, which in this case is the Demo iView, opens a screen that provides info on the delta link sources and the dependents for that iView. For the Transaction iView, there are no dependents, but the source objects are displayed, as shown in Figure 14-4.

Here, the SAP Transaction iView is the standard SAP transaction iView template located at Portal Content | Content Provided by SAP | Templates | iView Templates | SAP Transaction iView. The custom iView named Transaction iView is based on the SAP transaction iView and is included in the Demo page.

Child Object Tools

The Child Object Tool section of the Demo page contains buttons for the following:

- **Properties** View the properties of the iViews
- **Open** Open the iViews
- **Delta Link Tracer** Check the Delta Links Tracer for the iViews
- **Remove** Remove iView

Initially these buttons are grayed out; they become active once the iViews are selected in the Page Content view.

FIGURE 14-3 Page layout templates

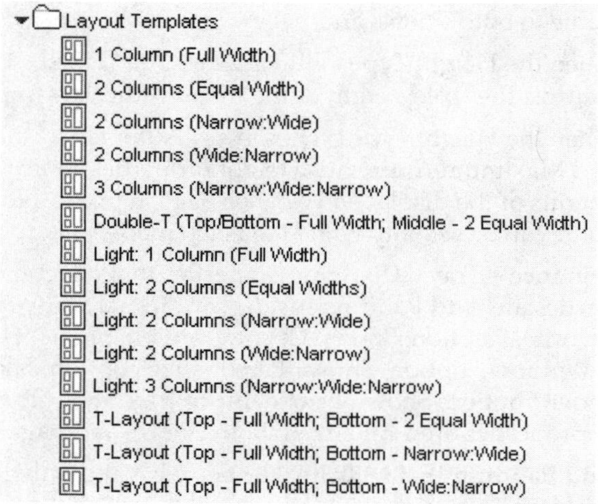

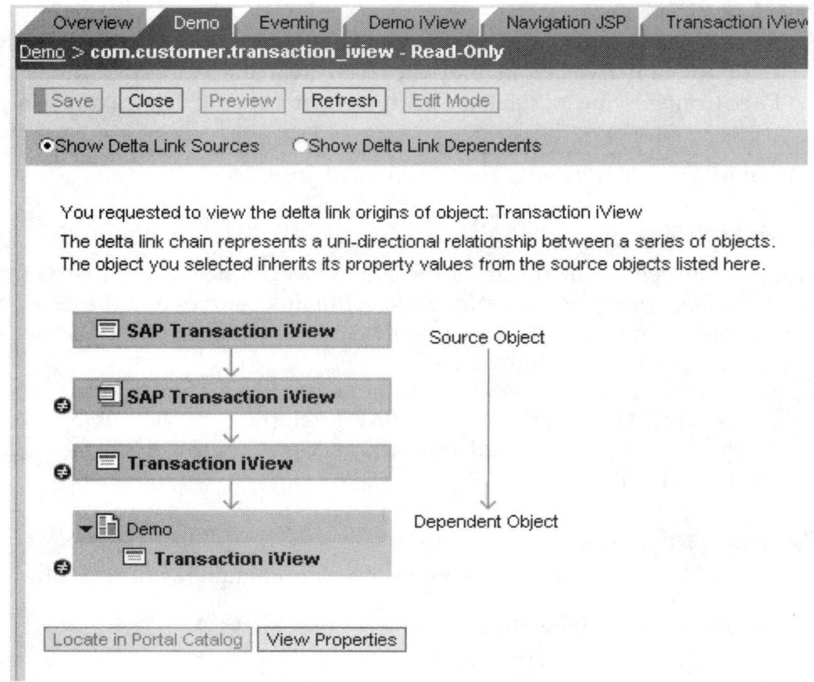

FIGURE 14-4 Delta Link Tracer for iView

iView / Page Property Categories and Properties

Let us discuss a few iView property categories and properties.

- **Appearance – Size** Contains properties such as Fixed Height, Height Type, Max Automatic Height, and Minimum Automatic Height. Note that these properties are available to both iViews and pages.
  - When the Height Type value is chosen as "Fixed," the Fixed Height property controls the fixed height of the displayed iView or page in pixels.
  - When the Height Type is chosen as "Automatic," the Minimum Automatic Height and Maximum Automatic Height properties control the minimum and maximum heights of the displayed iView or page in pixels. Note that, for an iView, this value can be set only when the Fetch mode is set to Server-side.
- **Appearance – Tray** Contains properties that affect the appearance of the tray. The properties are Add Padding Inside Tray, Initial State – Open Or Closed, Show "Add To Favorites" option, Show "Details" option, Show "Help" option, Show "Open in New Window" option, Show "Personalize" option, Show "Refresh" option, Show "Remove" option, Show object name in tray, Show Tray, and Tray Type. Note that these properties are available to both iViews and pages.
  - **Add Padding Inside Tray** Property is valid only if the Show Tray property is enabled. This controls if spacing is required between the tray and the iView, when the iView is displayed inside a tray.

- The Initial State - Open or Closed property controls whether the iView will be opened or closed when displayed initially.
- Show "Add To Favorites" option, Show "Details" option, Show "Help" option, Show "Open in New Window" option, Show "Personalize" option, Show "Refresh" option, Show "Remove" option, based on whether the value is Yes or No, these options appear in the options menu of the page or iView. This is demonstrated in a subsequent section titled "Options Menu" of this chapter.
- Show Object Name In Tray shows or hides the page name or iView name in the tray.
- Show Tray controls whether the tray should be displayed or not around the page or the iView.

- **Availability** contains properties such as Supported User Agents and Unsupported User Agents that provide information about supported browsers. Note that these properties are available to both iViews and pages.
  - The Supported User Agents property defines the combination of browsers, browser versions, and OS platforms that are supported. One possible option is (MSIE, >=5.5, *). This implies that all IE browsers that are greater than 5.5 are supported on all OS platforms.
- **Drag & Relate** contains properties such as Main Object and Name Of External Window that are required for Drag & Relate functionality. Note that these properties are available to both iViews and pages.
  - Main Object refers to the actual target object, usually a database table, for a given drag and relate operation.
  - Name Of External Window is relevant when the Launch in Property is set to "Display in Separate Window."
- **Information** contains properties that provide information. These properties are Changed By, Collection, Created By, Description, Domain, Family, Forced Request Language, Last Date Changed, Master Language, Name, Object Is A Template, Object Type, PCD Location. Changed By, Collection, Created By, Domain, Master Language, Object Type, and PCD Location are read-only properties. All these properties, except the Family property, are available to both iViews and pages.
  - Collection is a property meant for SAP's internal use and it defines the translation worklists. You will learn about translation worklists in Chapter 22. The value "IP_PTL_INITIAL_CONTENT" denotes initial portal content.
  - Domain defines the general application area such as EP for Enterprise Portal. This is used internally by SAP for translation.
  - Family denotes a particular category to which the iView belongs. Examples of Family are Branch, Business, Department, Industry, Personal, and so on.
  - Master Language denotes the original language in which the iView / page was written and maintained.
  - PCD Location helps to identify the path where the iView or page is stored in the portal content catalog. An example is pcd:portal_content/custom_development/DEMO, where custom_development is the ID of the custom folder that was created and DEMO is the ID of the iView in that custom folder.

- **Load** contains properties that affect the loading behavior of the page or iView. The properties are Allow Client-Side Caching, Cache Level, Cache Validity Period, and Work Distribution Topic. Note that these properties are available to both iViews and pages.
  - The Allow Client-Side Caching property controls whether the system uses the browser's cache when loading the page or iView.
  - Caching Level controls the caching behavior on the portal. Cache content can be shared across by everyone, user, browser session, or none at all. Possible values are Shared By Everyone, User, Session, or None.
  - Caching Validity Period controls for how long the cache remains valid before it is refreshed again.
- **Monitoring** contains the Monitor Hits property used for monitoring. If set to Yes, the data collection service will monitor the number of hits on this iView. The default value is Yes. This property is available to both iViews and pages.
- **Navigation** contains properties relevant for navigation. Properties are Can Be Merged, Default Entry For Folder, Entry Point, Height Of External Window, Initial State Of Navigation Panel, Invisible In Navigation Areas, Launch In New Window, Merge ID, Merge Priority, Quick Link, And Sort Priority, Width Of External Window, Window Features, and Workset Map Pictogram. Note that these properties are available to both iViews and pages.
  - The Can be Merged, Entry Point, Merge ID, Merge Priority, and Sort Priority properties are discussed in Chapter 15.
  - Default Entry For Folder. If there are multiple iViews in a folder, the first iView in the hierarchical structure will display by default. If this property is set to Yes on another iView, then that iView displays when the folder is opened.
  - The Initial State of Navigational Panel property controls whether the detailed navigational panel is displayed open or closed when the iView / page is accessed at runtime.
  - The Launch In New Window property controls whether the iView is displayed in the portal content area, a separate browser window, a separate portal window with header, or a separate portal window without the header area. The Height of External Window and Width of External Window properties control the height and width of the external window, respectively.
  - The Invisible in Navigation Areas property disallows the iView / page to be displayed in the navigational areas such as Top Level menus and the Detailed Navigational menu. The default value is No.
  - The Window Features property helps to enter the typical JavaScript properties of a popup window, e.g., toolbar=yes, width=100.
  - The Workset Map Pictogram property can be used to include a picture for the iView in a workset map page.
  - Quick Link is a shortcut to a page or iView. It is added to the portal URL e.g., http://<host>:<port>/irj/portal/Google, where Google is the name of the quick link for an iView that opens up the Google page.

- **Web Page Area** properties are used to control the behavior of URL iViews during runtime. These properties do not apply to pages. These properties are Adjust To Structural Changes In Site, Always Detect Character Encoding Of Web Page, Check Scripts In Web Site Objects, Force Detection Of Character Encoding, Maintain Web Site Functionality, Open iView Links In New Window, and Remove Client Events From Web Site Content.

CAUTION *Web Page Area properties control the behavior of URL iViews. They should be used cautiously as they can impact iView performance.*

    - The Adjust To Structural Changes In Site property is used when the iView displays a captured area of a source web page and the web page contains dynamic data.
    - The Always Detect Character Encoding Of Web Page property is used by the portal to check the character encoding of the target web page in URL iView. The default value is No and this property is valid only when the Fetch Mode property is set to server-side. This property is used when you use the capture feature. The portal displays the target web page in a UTF-8 character encoding set. Setting this property ensures that if the target web page is not in UTF-8 format, the portal converts it into UTF-8.
    - The Force Detection Of Character Encoding property applies when the Always Detect Character Encoding Of Web Page is set to No. Again, the Fetch Mode property should be set to server-side. This property ensures that the character encoding is checked the next time the iView / page is previewed in the Object editor. This can be used when the page displays unintelligible text.
    - The Check Scripts In Web Site Objects property ensures that any potential Javacript in the web page displayed by the iView is suppressed before displaying.
    - The Maintain Web Site Functionality property is used when you want to disable the scripts used in the web page displayed in the URL iView by setting this property to No. The default is Yes.
    - Open iView Links In New Window enables the hyperlinks in the web page to be opened in a new window.
    - The Remove Client Events From Web Site Content property is set to Yes, if you want to disable client events such as OnClick in the web page displayed in the URL iView.
- Other properties such as Authentication Scheme and Code Link for both iViews and pages:
    - The Authentication Scheme property of the iView is used to define the minimum logon authentication scheme required for accessing the iView.
    - The Code Link property defines the portal component upon which the iView or the page is based.

Isolation Method Property

This property can contain a value of Embedded or URL Isolated and determines the behavior of the pages when the iView is refreshed or loaded.

When this property has the value as "embedded," the source code of the iView becomes a part of the source code of the overall page in which it is located. As a result, when the iView is refreshed, the portal page is also refreshed at the same time, along with the other iViews that may be present in that page. After the refresh, the navigation area iView is refreshed as well. As a result, the information regarding the point at which the user clicked in the navigation tree is lost.

When this property has a value "URL Isolated," the IFrame belonging to the container in which the iView is located is treated independently from that of the other IFrames. So when the IFrame is reloaded, only that IFrame is reloaded, independent of the other IFrames on that page.

Fixed and Visible Properties for iViews in a Page

In the following illustration, the Fixed checkbox is selected in the Page Content area for the Demo iView. During runtime, the end user will not be able to remove the Demo iView from the page.

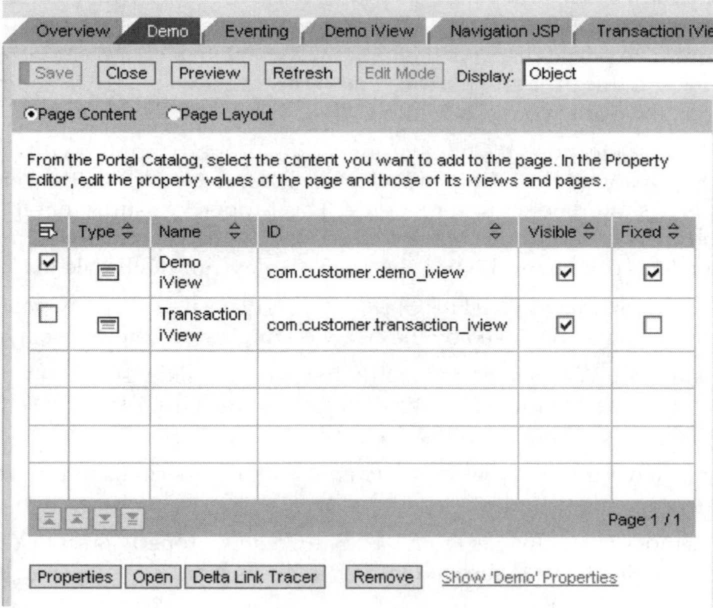

Figure 14-5 shows that the Remove From Page option does not appear in the Options menu when the Fixed checkbox is selected.

In addition, if the Visible checkbox is unchecked, the iView will not be visible in the page during runtime. This functionality may be helpful when you want to implement some hidden activity on the page through an iView without having to display the iView during runtime.

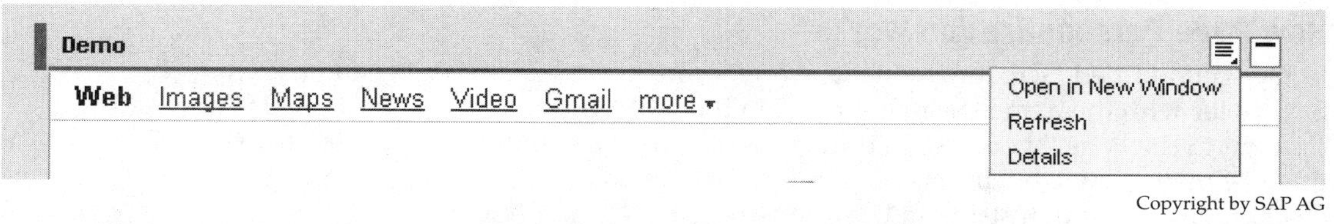

FIGURE 14-5 iView during runtime with Remove from Page option

Subproperties

Every property of an iView has a set of subproperties, such as the following:

- Property ID
- Inheritance
- End-User Personalization
- Property Description

Figure 14-6 displays the subproperty for the `Allow Client-Side Caching` property that appears when you click the arrow next to the property name. The Inheritance property decides whether the `Allow Client-Side Caching` property can be changed in the target iView that was created by copying from the source iView. In this case, because Can Be Edited In Target Objects appears in the Inheritance field, it will be possible to change this property in the target iView during runtime.

The End-User Personalization property controls whether the `Allow Client-Side Caching` property can be changed during personalization at runtime by the end user. If Hidden is selected, the `Allow Client-Side Caching` property will not appear in the Personalization dialog box. To make it possible to change this property during runtime, the value Read/Write should appear in the End-User Personalization field.

INFO *Some properties such as the pcdLocation property cannot be changed in the Property Editor. The End-User Personalization field is grayed out to indicate that this property is read only.*

▾Allow Client-Side Caching Yes
Property ID ALLOW_BROWSER
Inheritance Can be Edited in Target Objects
End-User Personalization Hidden
Property Description Specifies whether or not the portal uses the cache of the client's browser
Reset

FIGURE 14-6 Subproperty for ALLOW_BROWSER property

How Page Personalization Works

In the section titled "Creating an URL iView," you created a URL iView and passed a URL parameter with the name "Search String" in the URL editor. In the section titled "Assigning Content to the Page," you assigned the iView to the page that was created in the section titled "Creating a Page." In this section we see how an end user can personalize the iView by changing the search string in the iView.

1. Navigate to the page in the portal content catalog and open it for editing by clicking Open | Object from the context menu.
2. Click Preview in the Page Editor to view the page. A page will appear with the name of the iView in the top left of the page in the tray area that surrounds the iView.
3. Now click on the Options menu on the top-right corner of the iView as shown below.

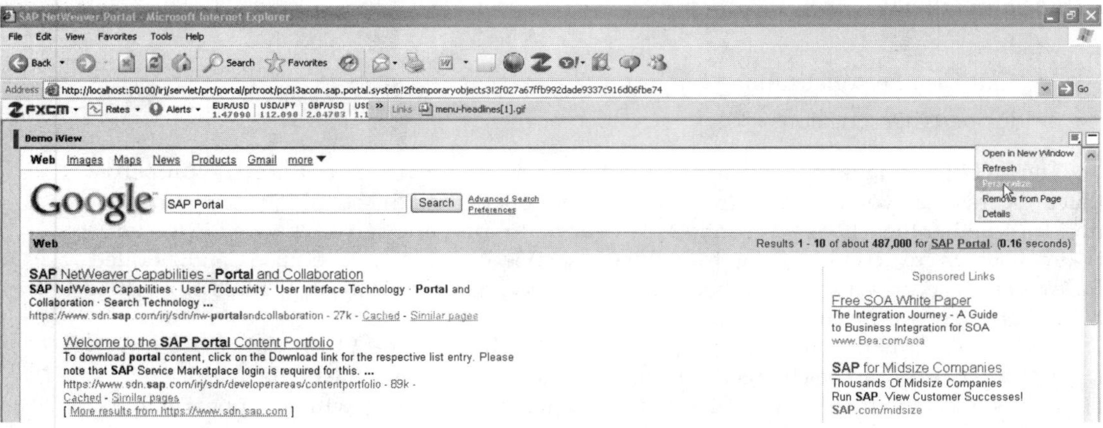

Copyright by SAP AG

4. A Personalization popup box will appear with a field named Search String, which you entered when creating the URL iView. Change its value from "SAP Portal" to "SAP Portal Guide" as shown below and click Apply.

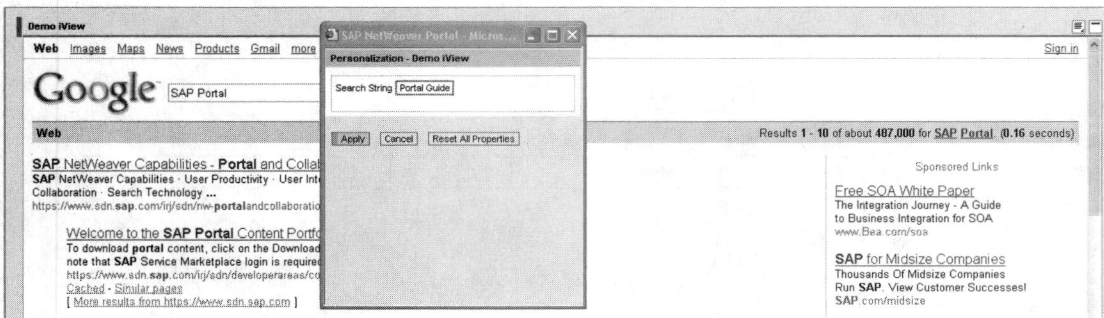

Copyright by SAP AG

5. The Google page will load again with the results for the newly entered search string.

Note that this search string will be active only for the user who changed the value. The search string value will remain as "SAP Portal" for the remaining users, unless they changed the value as well. Also note that this URL parameter was configured as Read/Write when the URL parameter was added to the URL iView. If it was set to "Read," then the search string will appear as a read-only field.

The other iView properties can be personalized in the same way. As was mentioned in the section titled "Subproperties," the End-User Personalization subproperty for a given property should be maintained as Read/Write for it to be personalized at runtime. The default value for this subproperty for all properties is hidden and hence they do not appear in the personalization dialog box when the end user clicks on Personalize in the Options menu.

NOTE *For more details, refer to the content devlopment related resources listed in Appendix B.*

Summary

In this chapter, you learned how to create an iView using an iView Wizard. You created a URL iView using an iView template. You glanced through different iView / page property categories and properties and reviewed the importance of subproperties. You learned how to use page editors and created a page using the Page Wizard. You added iViews to the page using the Page Content section and chose different layouts in the Page Layout section of the Page Editor. You learned how to use the Delta Link Tracer, child object tools, and how to customize the Options menu. You also learned about subproperties and their role in end-user personalization.

15

CHAPTER

Developing Roles and Worksets

This chapter covers roles and worksets and how to create them. You will learn how to assign roles to users and how to design them for portal navigation.

Benefits of Roles

One of the benefits of using the portal is role-based personalization. Roles let you allow different users to view different content depending upon the role that has been assigned to their user profiles. For example, a sales manager will be able to look only at the sales-related iViews that have been assigned to his or her role. In the same way, a customer service representative may look at only those iViews that have been assigned to his or her role.

Another advantage in using roles is that whenever a new user is created on the portal, you do not have to add content for that user from scratch. You can simply add the necessary roles to that user and all the content belonging to those roles is automatically displayed for that user when the user logs in.

TIP *Roles enable easy maintenance of users and the content they need to access.*

Organizing Content Using Worksets

iViews and pages are assigned to a workset, which is assigned to a role. Worksets are simply a collection of iViews and pages that can be used to organize content.

These iViews and pages are organized relative to a person's day-to-day activities in an organization. For example, consider a customer service representative. On a daily basis, this representative may need access to information such as customer contact details, sales order information, customer service–related information, and knowledge base information. All sales order–related information could be stored under one workset, all service-related information could be stored on a different workset, and so on.

Content can be reused for different roles. After assigning the roles to one set of users or groups of users, you can assign the same content to different users or groups of users. For example, suppose a sales representative requires access to a workset used by the customer service team—such as the sales order–related workset. That workset could be added to a role created for the sales representative.

Roles

You can assign other portal content to roles, create worksets, change role properties, and assign permissions to roles. The role is the largest semantic object in the portal, while the iView is the smallest semantic object in the portal. A role can contain another role, so you can create a hierarchy of roles. A role can also contain any other content object in the portal such as iViews, pages, and worksets.

Roles, Worksets, and Navigational Structure

The workset is structured to accommodate the day-to-day activities that a user needs to conduct in a particular role. Worksets contain reusable content that can be used in multiple roles, and a role can contain multiple worksets. Thus, a role and a workset have a many-to-many relationship.

Considering that you can also create a hierarchy of worksets, and a workset can be included in a role, you can manipulate the navigational structure on the portal simply by modifying the hierarchy of worksets.

TIP *The role is usually structured according to the organizational structure in your organization and the informational needs of the users.*

Roles and worksets also have Permission Editors. To access them, simply click the Permission drop-down menu in the Display field of the Role Editor or right click the role object and choose Open | Permissions, as shown next:

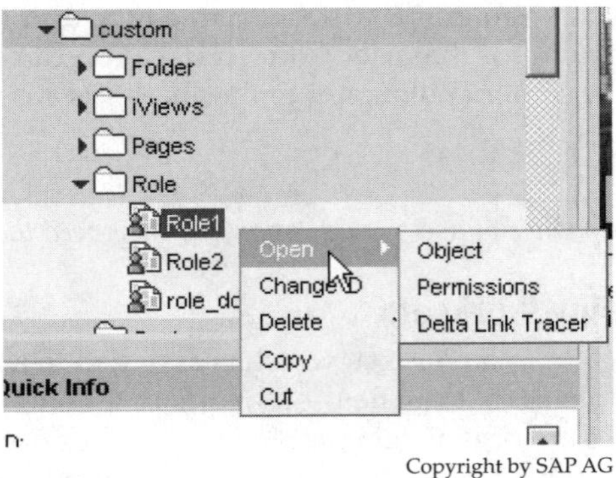

Figure 15-1 displays the list of permissions that have been assigned to the role named Role1. You will notice that the super administrator role has the highest level of permission such as owner permission and end user permission as well as role assigner permission for the role named Role1. Also, it is not possible to change the permission levels for the super administrator.

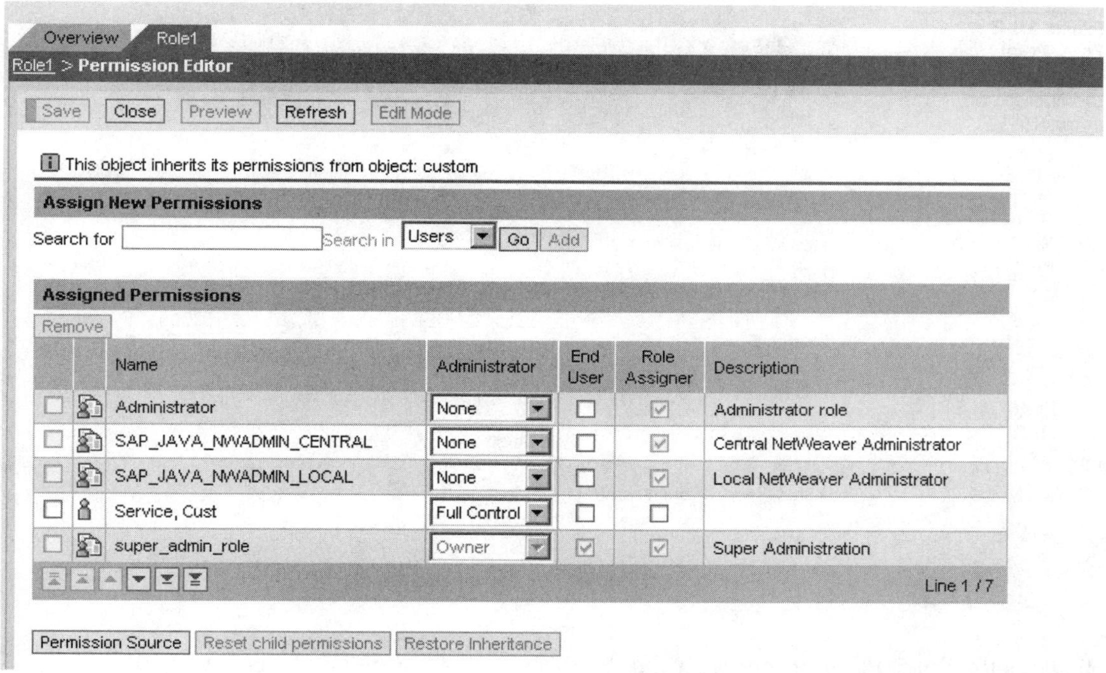

Overview Role1

Role1 > Permission Editor

Save Close Preview Refresh Edit Mode

This object inherits its permissions from object: custom

Assign New Permissions

Search for [ ] Search in Users Go Add

Assigned Permissions

Remove

Name	Administrator	End User	Role Assigner	Description
Administrator	None	☐	☑	Administrator role
SAP_JAVA_NWADMIN_CENTRAL	None	☐	☑	Central NetWeaver Administrator
SAP_JAVA_NWADMIN_LOCAL	None	☐	☑	Local NetWeaver Administrator
Service, Cust	Full Control	☐	☐	
super_admin_role	Owner	☑	☑	Super Administration

Line 1 / 7

Permission Source Reset child permissions Restore Inheritance

FIGURE 15-1 Permissions assigned for role

Role Properties

Role properties are categorized in the following way in Enterprise Portal (EP) 7.0:

- **Information** Changed By, Created At, Created By, Description, Last Date Changed, Master Language, Name, PCD Location, Person Responsible
- **Navigation** Can Be Merged, Entry Point, Invisible In Navigation Areas, Leaf Folder, Merge ID, Merge Priority, Pictogram, Show Add To Favorites Option, Sort Priority
- **User Management Permissions** AclSuperUser, Administrate, Administrator, Configure, Developer, and so on

These user permissions are automatically assigned to the user who has been assigned to a particular role, if the value for the User Management Engine (UME) permission for the role has been set to Yes in the Role Property Editor. For more details on user management permissions, refer to Chapter 34.

Entry Point Property

In the Property Editor, the Entry Point property needs to be set to Yes for the role to appear in the navigational structure of the portal. After assigning the role to the user, if the Entry Point property has not been set for the role, the role will not show in the top-level navigational menu. This is a common mistake made by beginners. Figure 15-2

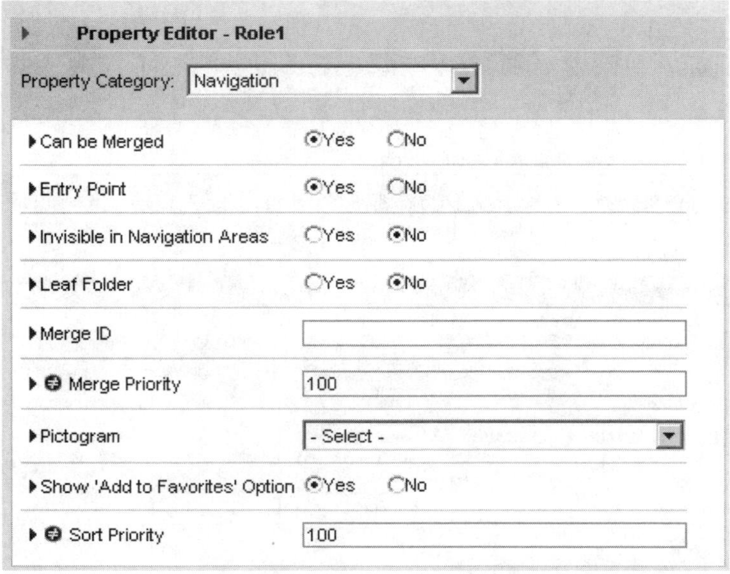

FIGURE 15-2 Entry Point property under the Navigation category

displays the Entry Point property for the Role1 object. Figure 15-2 also displays the various properties available for the role object under the Navigation property category. To access the Property Editor, right click Role1 and choose Properties.

TIP *Entry Point is an important property to note during role creation.*

Permissions and ACLs

Although permissions are discussed in Chapter 34, you should know that permissions can be assigned to content objects using access control lists (ACLs), a collection of permission levels, and the users assigned to those levels. Permission levels are classified into two major categories: administrator permissions and end user permissions.

The administrator permissions come into play during design time when a content administrator tries to create, change, delete, or assign permissions for content objects. The administrator permissions that are available are Owner, Full Control, Read/Write, Read, and None.

The end user permission levels are considered during runtime. They decide whether an end user can access the content object during runtime according to a value of Yes or No.

Folder Structure

At the time of implementation, before any serious development effort takes place, it is helpful to create folders to organize custom development objects to facilitate easier maintenance. This helps you differentiate custom objects from standard SAP-provided content and prevents the possibility of unknowingly modifying standard SAP content.

By organizing the content into folders, you can also implement delegated content administration easily. Each folder comes with its own set of properties and permissions, and by assigning the correct permission levels, you can enable or disable users and administrators from viewing content during runtime as well as reading, creating, deleting, assigning permissions, and performing other tasks during design time. For more on delegated content administration, see Chapter 24.

TIP *To implement delegated content administration, folders can be organized according to the organizational hierarchy or type of content.*

Folders within the Roles

You can create folders within roles. You can create a hierarchy of folders within the roles, similar to the hierarchy of worksets. After creating the folder, you can move the folder within the role structure.

You can create a folder in two ways, as shown in the following illustrations:

- Right-click the role name and select New Folder.

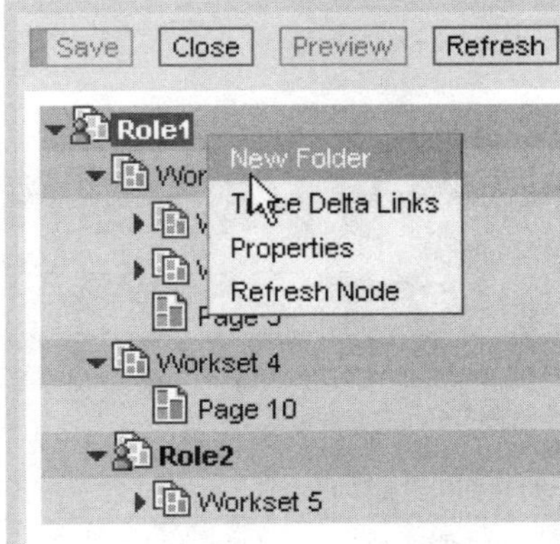

Copyright by SAP AG

- Click New Folder from the Child Object Tools section.

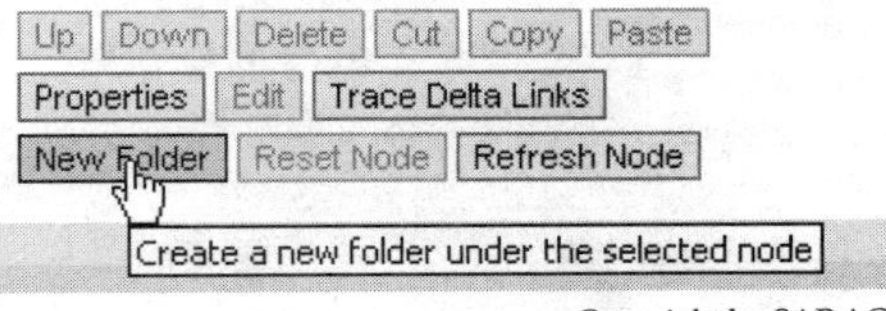

Copyright by SAP AG

The folder can be created at any level within the role content hierarchy by selecting the appropriate node under which you want to create the folder. You can also move the created folder up or down by selecting the Up or Down button in the Child Object Tools section.

The Role1 structure shown in Figure 15-3 will display on the portal when assigned to a user, as shown in Figures 15-4 and 15-5.

PART IV

FIGURE 15-3 Content assigned to a role

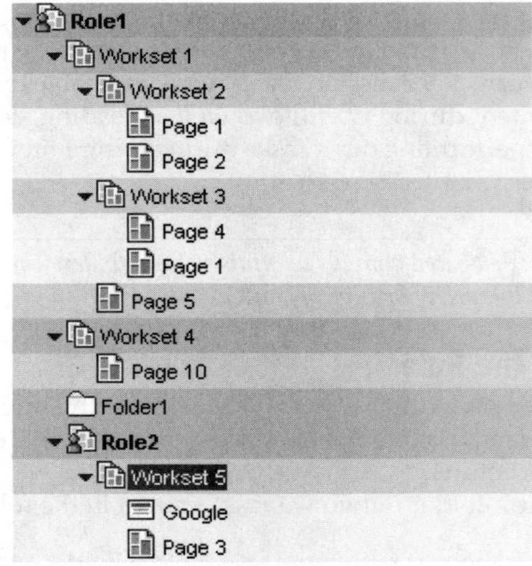

FIGURE 15-4 Portal desktop after assigning the role to a user

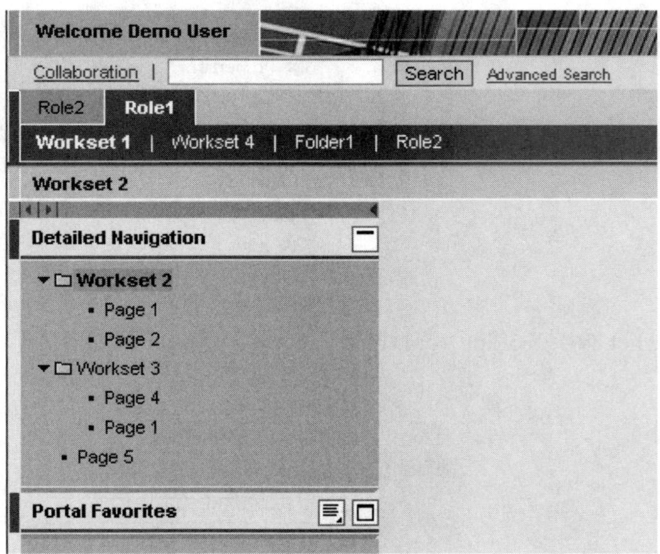

FIGURE 15-5 Portal desktop after assigning the role to a user

Copyright by SAP AG

As a demonstration, let's create a role and assign content such as iViews, pages, and worksets to the role.

1. Right click the folder in which you want to create the role and choose New | Role:

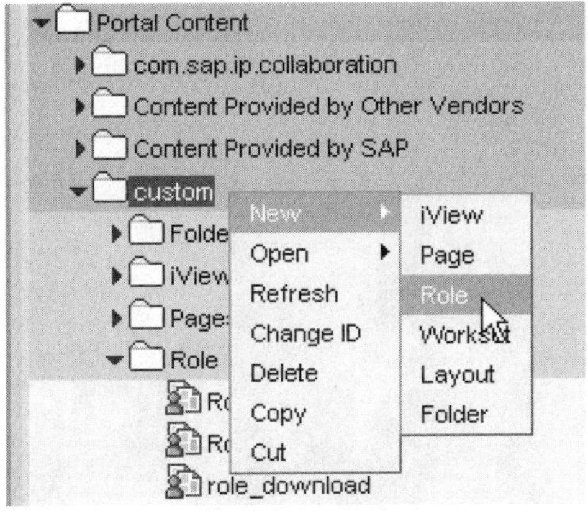

Copyright by SAP AG

2. In the General Properties sheet of the Role Wizard, enter the Role Name, Role ID, Role ID prefix (optional), and Description (optional) as shown next.

Overview Role1 New Role
Role Wizard
Step 1: General Properties
Role Name: *
Role3
Role ID: *
role3
Role ID Prefix (Example: com.companyname):
com.customer
Master Language: *
English
Description:
This is a demo for creating a role object.
Cancel Back Next > Finish

Copyright by SAP AG

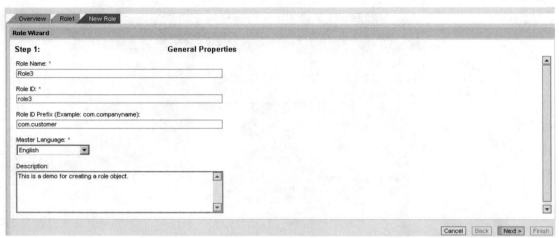

3. In the Summary screen, review your settings and click Finish.

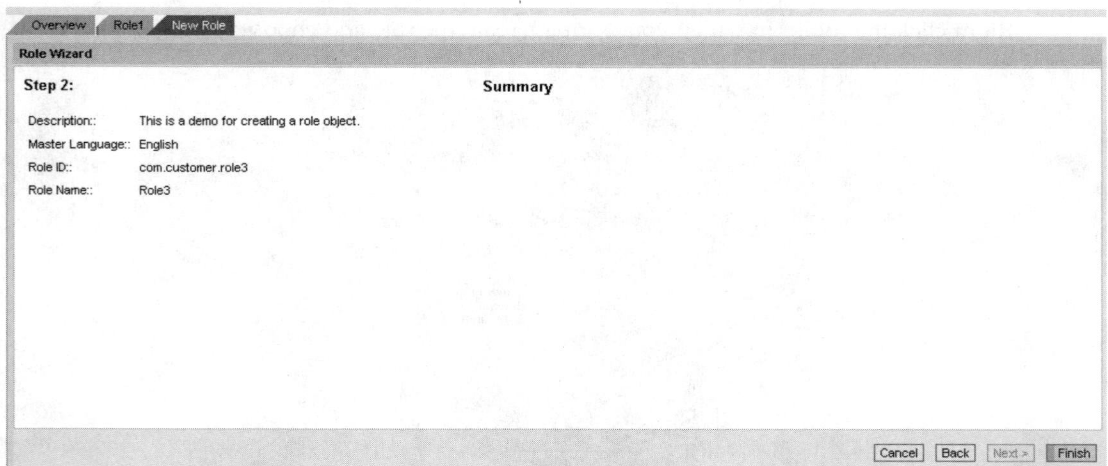

Copyright by SAP AG

4. In the Choose Your Next Step screen, click OK. The role object appears in the Content Editor section:

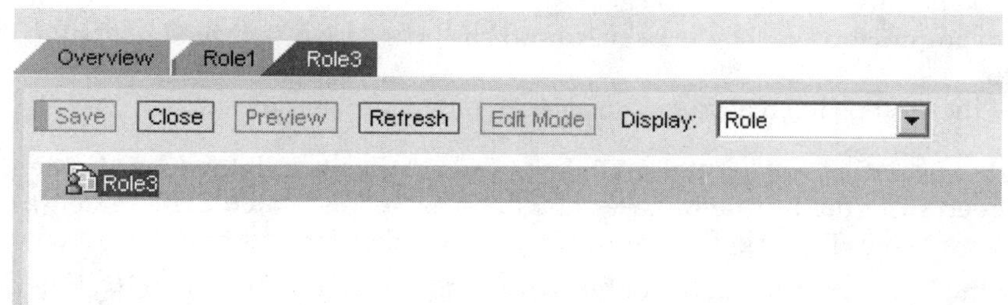

Copyright by SAP AG

5. Right click the Demo iView object from the Portal Content catalog that needs to be added to the role, and choose Add iView to Role | Delta Link, as shown in the following illustration. The Demo iView is added to the Role3 role.

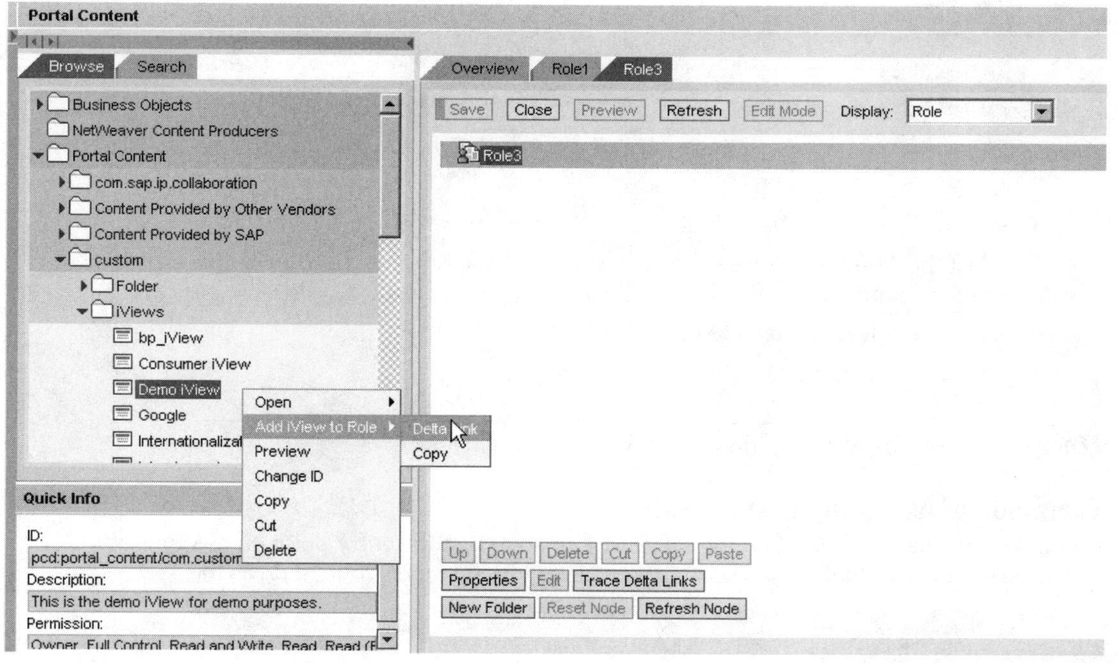

Copyright by SAP AG

NOTE *You cannot assign folders using this procedure. The procedure works only for iViews, pages, and worksets.*

PART IV

Assigning a Role to a User

Once the role has been created, you can assign the role to a user. After logging into the portal as an administrator, choose User Administration | Identity Management in the top-level menu.

Follow these steps to create a new user and assign a role to the user:

1. If the user does not exist, you'll need to create the user. In the Identity Management screen's Get field (in some cases, it will be named as Search Criteria field), enter the user's name. Then click Create User, which is the third button in the second row.
2. In the Details section at the bottom of the screen, enter the Logon ID. Enter the password details in the Define Password and Confirm Password fields.
3. Enter the user name in the Get field, leave the default option set as User, and click Go. If the user exists, his or her name will show in the Results section:

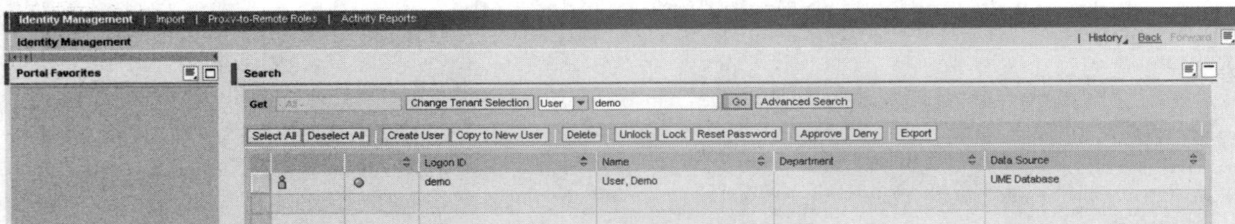

4. Select the user and click Modify in the Details section of the screen.
5. Select the Assigned Roles tab and in the Available Roles section, enter the required search parameters for the role to which you want to add the user.
6. Select the roles that need to be added and click Add.
7. Save the user by clicking the Save button.

HINT *To select multiple roles, press the CTRL key while clicking the roles.*

Examples of Assigning Entry Points

If you remove the entry point on the role and instead assign the entry point on the page, and if you assign the role to the user, you will see the following when you log on as the user:

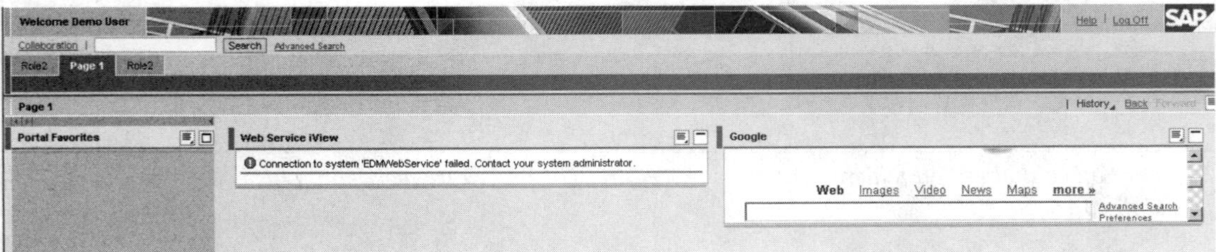

The reason why Role2 appears twice in the tabs across the top of the screen is because this user has been assigned two roles: Role1 and Role2. Role1 in turn is composed of Role2. If this occurs, you have not set the entry point as Role1; instead, you have set the entry point as Role2 and page1, which is contained in Role1. When you log on as the demo user, you will see Role2 first, and then you will see page1 instead of Role1 because Role1 is not set as the entry point. And now, since Role1 also contains Role2, Role2 is displayed again.

This trivial example shows the impact of not setting up the entry point and the location at which the entry point is set. It is also possible to sort the order in which the top-level menu is displayed, and you can remove redundant entries in the hierarchy structure—for example, Role2, which is displayed twice.

To order menus, use the Sort property in the Property Editor, and for removing redundant content, use the Merge property. Before you move on to using these two properties, you should be aware of the impact of activating the entry point at Role1. The impact is the same irrespective of whether the entry point on the page is set to Yes or No, because the entry point on the topmost object in the hierarchy always takes effect. The entry point on the page is ignored because the entry point is set at the Role1 role.

In the following illustration, page1 is missing across the top of the screen and is moved inside Workset2, which is part of Role1.

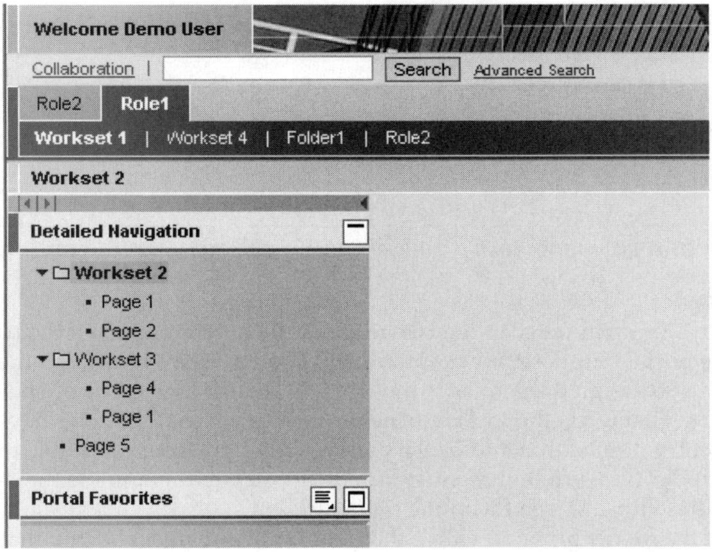

Copyright by SAP AG

HINT *Even though it is possible to set up the entry points on pages and iViews, it is not recommended that you do so. Pages and iViews should be part of the worksets or folders contained within the roles, so setting up the entry points on pages and iViews should be avoided.*

Sort Property

This property is a number that can be assigned to the entries on the top-level menu. In our example, Role2 is shown first, followed by Role1.

Suppose that your requirement is to show Role1 first, followed by Role2. You can assign the Sort property for both Role1 and Role2 so that the property value for Role1 is lower than the value for Role2. The role with the lowest Sort property will be arranged at the far left at the top of the screen.

HINT *Any changes to the Sort property affect the display for all the users and are not user specific.*

To access the Property Editor, right click on the role in the Portal Content Catalog and choose Properties. The Sort property for Role1 has a default value of *100*. Change it to *99* in the Property Editor, and then log in as demo user and you will see that Role1 now appears at the far left.

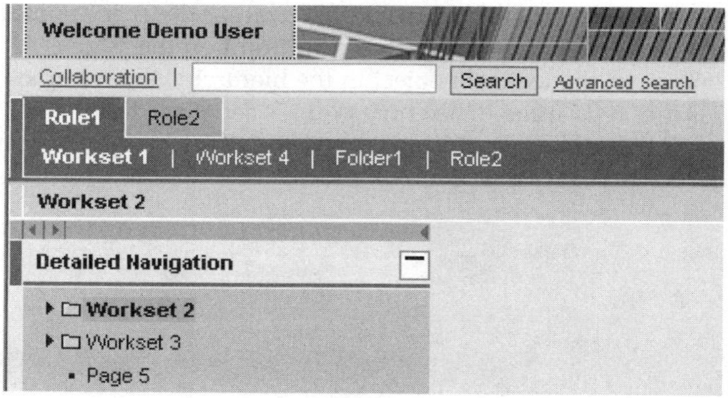

TIP *The Sort property can range from a value of 0 to 100 and can take on decimal values as well.*

Merge Property

You can use the Merge property to remove redundant content objects in the navigational structure of the portal. Suppose, for example, that you have two roles with the same workset. When you assign these roles to a user and the user logs in, he or she will have these worksets available via the top-level menus (assuming that the roles have been configured as entry points). It could be very confusing to the user to be able to access the same content under two different menu options. So you could eliminate the duplicate worksets by setting up a Merge ID on the two worksets.

You can set the Merge property either at the role or at any nodes within that role. If the Merge property is set at the level of the role, the two roles are merged into one. The contents inside the role are merged, which means the content from one role is added into the other role and displayed on the portal. Which role and contents are displayed first depends on the Merge ID. The role with the lowest value for the Merge ID will be displayed first on the menu.

If, on the other hand, the Merge ID is set at the level of a particular node within that role, then only the content within that node is merged between those roles.

If the two roles have the same content, such as worksets, during merging, the two worksets will appear twice. In such cases, you need to eliminate them by setting up the Merge IDs at the level of the worksets.

Here's an example to demonstrate. Following are two roles, Role3 and Role4, attached to a user with duplicate Workset 5. Role3 contains Workset 5 and Role4 contains Workset 5 and Workset 4:

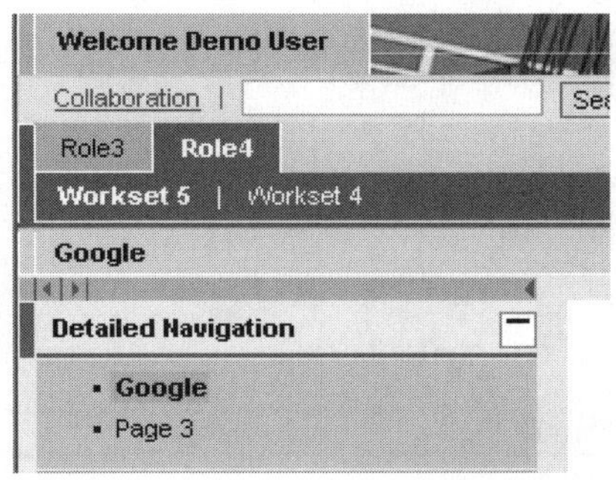

Copyright by SAP AG

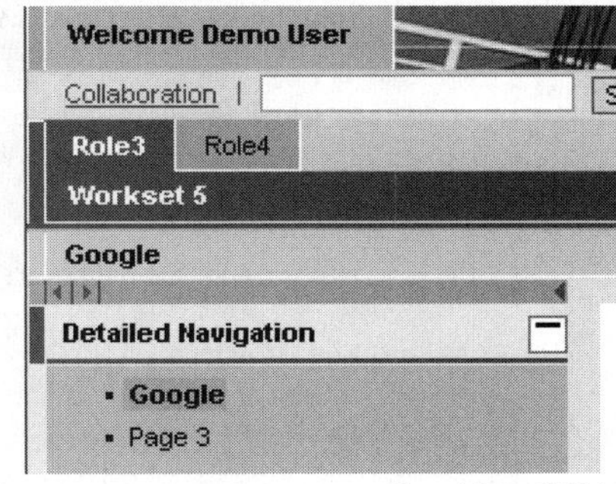

Copyright by SAP AG

Here is the result after setting up the Merge ID property for Role3 and Role4 with a value of *100* and leaving the Can Be Merged property for the two roles set at the default value of True:

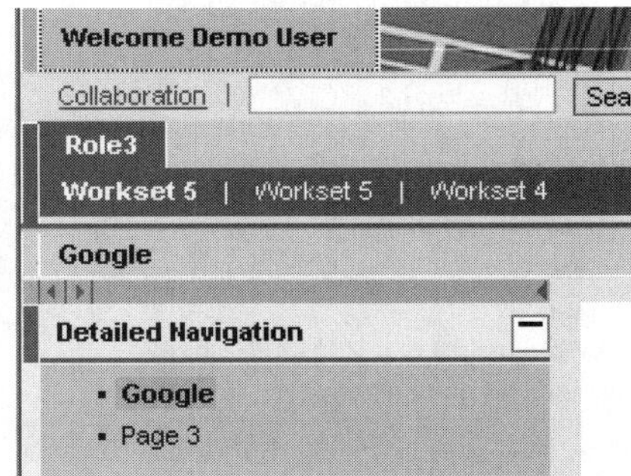

Copyright by SAP AG

You can see that Role4 has been eliminated, and the contents within Role4, in this case Workset 5 and Workset 4, are simply added to the contents displayed under Role3. However, duplicate Workset 5 entries appear. To fix this, set the Merge ID property on Workset 5 in Role3 and the Merge ID property of Workset 5 in Role4 to the same value.

To change the Merge ID property for Workset 5 in Role3, open the Role3 object, right click Workset 5, and then choose Properties. The Property Editor will open on the right. Change the Merge ID property to *100*, as shown in Figure 15-6. Then repeat the same steps for Role4 and Workset 5.

HINT *You can identify which property editor has been opened by looking at the title on top. For example, in the screen displayed on the next page, you know from the title that you are working on a workset named as Workset 5.*

PART IV

Figure 15-6 Changing the Merge ID

Copyright by SAP AG

After making this change, only one Workset 5 appears:

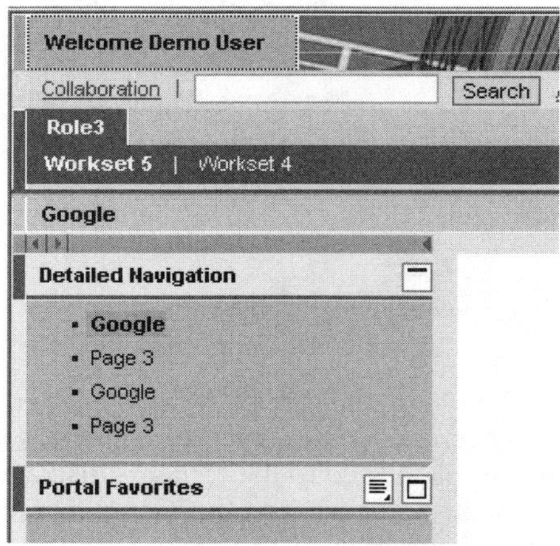

Copyright by SAP AG

However, now the contents within Workset 5 are repeated twice. So you have to set the Merge IDs in the same way for pages Google and Page 3.

Content Development Tips

Several tips can prove to be useful for ensuring good performance.

From a content developer standpoint, the home page should be well designed for better performance. In addition, considering that the home page is the first page that the user sees, the overall user perception of the site performance can be influenced by the home page. Following are some guidelines for developing the home page:

- Use static content as much as possible and a limited number of iViews on the home page.
- Use content that can be shared by all the users. Disallow personalizations at the page level that control which iViews should be displayed on the page and what content should be displayed on the iView.
- Avoid iViews that fetch data from backend systems or those that use Java Connector/J2EE Connector architecture (JCO/JCA) and web services. If JCO is used, use connection pooling techniques to reuse connections.
- Use iViews that are embedded (not isolated) on the page. Use URL isolation on the page.
- Where possible, caching should be used for the pages and iViews and should have shared values.
- In the Portal Content Directory (PCD), when creating new folder structures, ensure that not more than 50 objects are placed under each folder. In addition, the size of the images and JavaScript should be reduced as much as possible to enable quick rendering.
- Client-side eventing should also be used as much as possible when dealing with selection models such as drop-downs, so that only the iViews are affected and not the page itself.
- Using a limited number of roles will also help increase performance. The number of roles should be in the range of tens and not hundreds. Also, merging the roles/worksets will help to simplify the navigation hierarchy.

NOTE *For more datails, refer to the content development related resources listed in Appendix B.*

Summary

This chapter focused on the benefits of using roles, organizing content using worksets and folders, and using roles for enabling portal navigation. It discussed important role properties such as Entry Point, Merge ID, Merge, and Sort. It covered assigning permissions to roles, creating new users, and assigning roles to users. It also discussed some good content development tips such as designing the home page, reducing the size of images and JavaScript, and using a limited number of roles.

CHAPTER 16

Using Business Packages

This chapter discusses business packages, which are predefined content developed by SAP or third-party vendors that serves particular business requirements. Business packages are a collection of roles, worksets, pages, or iViews that have been professionally developed in confirmation with SAP's design guidelines. In this chapter, you will learn about different business packages, and the factors you must consider before choosing to deploy a business package. You will also learn how to download, import and uninstall business packages in the portal.

By deploying a business package, you can save costs, time, and efforts during implementation. Because it is created by either SAP or third-party vendors, a business package does not require much development time, which results in cost savings. Usually, no costs in licensing are involved for importing a business package as long as the customer has purchased licenses for the portal system and the backend system with which the business package will be integrated.

In addition, while deploying the business package, you can either deploy the whole business package or only a portion of it, depending on the customer's requirements.

A business package helps you integrate with SAP content in the back end. For example, if you have already implemented the SAP Human Resources Application (HR), SAP Sales and Distribution (SD), and SAP Business Information Warehouse (BW), you can install the business package and quickly integrate with the back end to create transactions through the Web.

You can install three types of business packages:

- Business packages for end users
- Business packages for managers
- Business packages for specialists

A business package can consist of the following:

- **Portal content objects** The roles, worksets, pages, iViews, business objects, and system objects.
- **PAR files** Portal Archive (PAR) files include Java applications or configuration files required for content management, plus collaboration modules and universal worklists.
- **Web Dynpro applications** Web Dynpro applications can be run in an iView.
- **Other objects** Transport packages, Visual Composer PAR files, Repository Manager PAR files, and collaboration room templates can be included.

Portal Content Portfolio

To access the business packages developed by SAP, go to http://www.sdn.sap.com/irj/sdn/developerareas/contentportfolio. Note that when you try to download the business package, you are actually redirected to the SAP Service Marketplace most of the time. In other words, the SAP-developed business packages are delivered from http://service.sap.com/swdc. In order to download the business package, you will need the required license relevant for that particular business package. Figure 16-1 displays the Portal Content Portfolio, where the business packages have been made available under the three major categories, namely, Business Packages For Every User, Business Packagers For Managers, and Business Packages For Specialists. Figure 16-1 displays the business packages available for every user such as Employee Self Service, Design Collaboration, and so on.

To access business packages developed by third-party vendors, you must do the following:

1. Access the Partner Solution directory at http://www.sap.com/ecosystem/customers/directories/SearchSolution.epx.
2. In the Partner Information Center: Search page, select EP-BP 6.0 - SAP NetWeaver Portal Business Packages 6.0 in the Third-Party Defined Integration Scenarios field.
3. In the Certification Category field, select the Enterprise Portal iViews. To select multiple iViews, click the CTRL key. Click Search.
4. In the Partner Information Center: Search Results page, after identifying the business package that meets your needs, you must contact the vendor directly to download the business package.

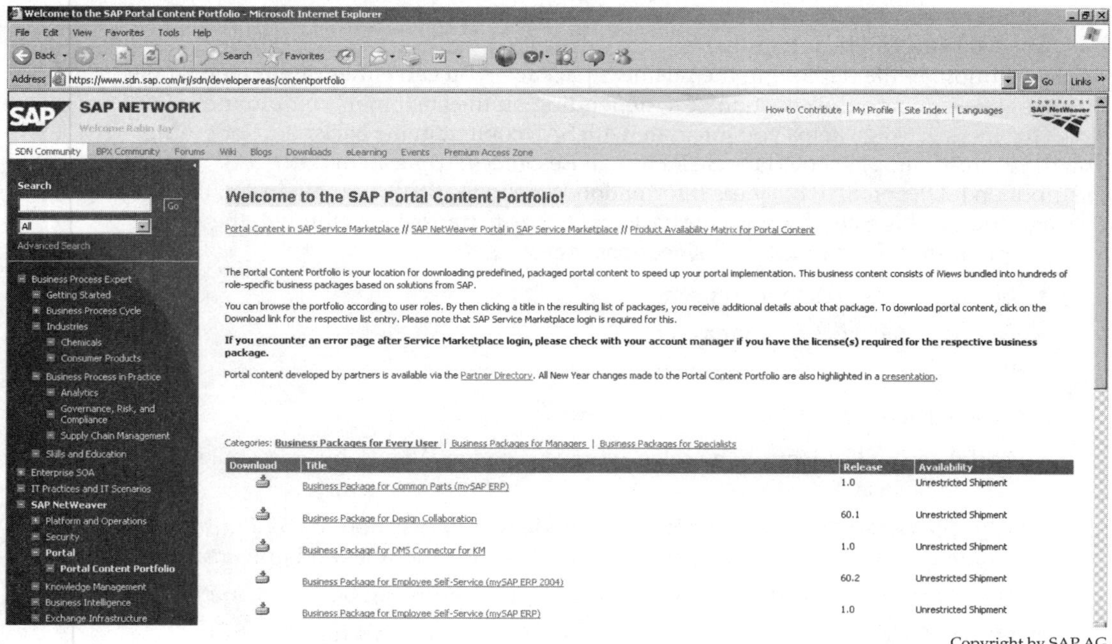

FIGURE 16-1 Portal Content Portfolio

Business Packages for Every User

If you need to implement generic functionality for and users, the Business Packages for Every User is the choice. The Business Packages for Every User category offers packages that can be applied to the employees in the organization. Following are some examples of these packages:

- Business Package for Employee Self-Service
- Business Package for Learning
- Business Package for Projects

Business Package for Employee Self-Service

The Business Package for Employee Self-Service contains content that can be used by the employee to maintain his or her own data in the portal. For example, the content can be related to processing benefits; displaying salary statements; recording working time; career-related activities such as maintaining skill sets; and maintaining personal data such as bank information, travel management, and life events.

Business Package for Learning

The Business Package for Learning contains content that is geared to meet an employee's learning needs. To install this package, a license is required for the SAP learning solution as well as the licenses for mySAP HR, mySAP Enterprise Resource Planning, or mySAP Business Suite. The content is built on Business Server Pages (BSP) and the required backend system is SAP R/3 4.7.

Business Package for Projects

The Business Package for Projects contains content for enabling groups of users to work together on projects. Currently, the focus is on displaying project-related information such as project structure, milestones, billing data, documents, and BW reports.

NOTE *For more information on licensing and technical requirements, refer to the SDN website.*

Business Package for Managers

To implement portal functionality for business managers, you should implement Business Package of Managers. The content is aimed at line managers, team and project leaders, and department heads. The worksets for this package are grouped broadly into two areas: My Staff and My Budget. To install the Business Package for Managers, at least a limited professional user license is required for either mySAP Business Suite or mySAP ERP.

My Staff Content

The My Staff content is geared toward helping managers carry out HR-related activities for team members—from recruiting employees, to annual reviews, to compensation planning. Some of the worksets under My Staff are Attendance, Employee Review, Personnel Change Requests, Recruitment, and Compensation.

My Budget Content

The My Budget content is aimed at managing budgets, including planning, monitoring, and cost analysis. Some of the worksets under My Budget are Cost Centers, Assets, Internal Orders, Projects, Profit Centers, and Cost Center Planning.

Business Packages for Specialists

The Business Packages for Specialists category includes packages geared for skilled segments and industry segments. Here are some examples of the packages included:

- Business Packages for Assets
- Business Packages for Channel Management in Customer Relationship Management (CRM) High Tech
- Business Packages for Financial Services
- Business Packages for High-Tech Channel Management
- Business Packages for Intellectual Property Management
- Business Packages for mySAP CRM – Business Productivity Pack
- Business Packages for Sales
- Business Packages for CRM
- Business Packages for SRM

Administering the Business Packages

Administering a business package includes performing all the tasks related to the installation and management of business packages. Business package administration activities can span the whole gamut of content administration, user administration, and system administration.

Before Installing the Business Package

Following several steps can help you identify whether a business package is suitable for installation. You can open the business package documentation by clicking the link containing the name of the business package in the Portal Content Portfolio. The business package documentation will appear as shown in Figure 16-2.

In Figure 16-2, the business package documentation provides information such as General Information, Documentation, System Availability, Business Context, and License Information. The General Information section provides basic information such as the package functionality, the release, and the availability status.

BP Naming Convention

The Portal Content Portfolio page on SDN provides information on the BP release and the BP availability such as unrestricted shipment, restricted shipment, and so on. When you click on the download icon to the left of the business package title, you will be taken to the software download page in the SAP Service Marketplace. In the download page, click on the BP ESS 4.6C-4.7 50.4 link and then click on #OS Independent link. An additional tab named Downloads will open up and under the Download Objects column you will notice the physical name of the business package file, for example, BPESS46C504 0-20000613.ZIP. The business package name includes naming conventions that contain important information such as the following:

- Name of the package (BPESS, which stands for Business Package for Employee Self-Service)

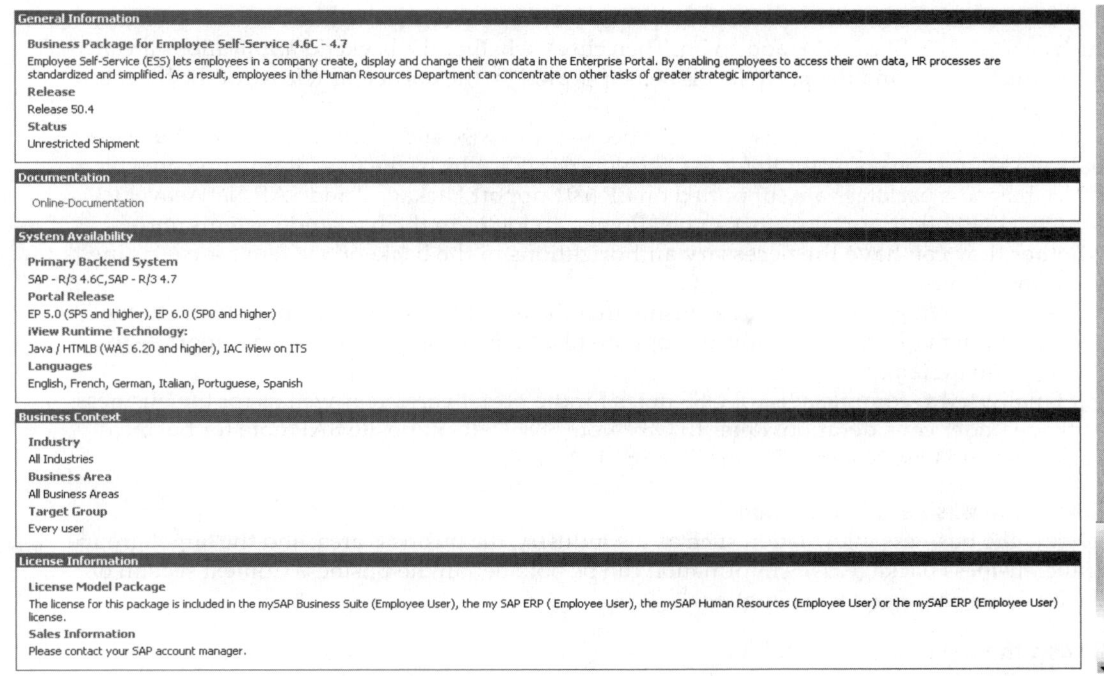

General Information
Business Package for Employee Self-Service 4.6C - 4.7
Employee Self-Service (ESS) lets employees in a company create, display and change their own data in the Enterprise Portal. By enabling employees to access their own data, HR processes are standardized and simplified. As a result, employees in the Human Resources Department can concentrate on other tasks of greater strategic importance.
Release
Release 50.4
Status
Unrestricted Shipment
Documentation
Online-Documentation
System Availability
Primary Backend System
SAP - R/3 4.6C,SAP - R/3 4.7
Portal Release
EP 5.0 (SP5 and higher), EP 6.0 (SP0 and higher)
iView Runtime Technology:
Java / HTMLB (WAS 6.20 and higher), IAC iView on ITS
Languages
English, French, German, Italian, Portuguese, Spanish
Business Context
Industry
All Industries
Business Area
All Business Areas
Target Group
Every user
License Information
License Model Package
The license for this package is included in the mySAP Business Suite (Employee User), the my SAP ERP (Employee User), the mySAP Human Resources (Employee User) or the mySAP ERP (Employee User) license.
Sales Information
Please contact your SAP account manager.

Figure 16-2 Business package documentation

- Major release (504, which stands for 50.4) - 50 is the major release, which stands for the Enterprise Portal release, and 4 is the minor release that identifies the Business Package release
- Support package
- Patch level (optional; in this example, the patch level is 0) - Usually cumulative, which means that patch level 3 will contain patch levels 1 and 2. The latest patch level is available in the SAP Service Marketplace for download (for example, BP for CRM 5.0 SP1 Patch 2)

Review the Technical Information

Review the technical information, such as the system requirements related to the backend systems and the portal itself, before installing the business package. This information is available in the System Availability section of the business package documentation.

Don't *Do not proceed with the installation of a business package without reviewing the technical information.*

Ensure that the business package can be implemented for the existing backend systems, such as SAP R/3, BW, CRM, and so on. Then check whether the backend applications are at the correct release and the patch levels are supported by the particular release of the business package.

Check whether the portal itself has the necessary release and patch levels for the business package to function correctly. Refer to OSS Note 642775, which contains information on which EP 5.0 business packages are supported on EP 6.0 Support Package 2 and SAP NetWeaver 04.

Check whether portal users can be allowed to log in to the backend systems and whether they can have the necessary authorizations in the backend system for executing the transactions.

If you are planning an upgrade, ensure that the new BP version is compatible with the backend systems, because usually an upgrade to a BP is accompanied with an upgrade to the backend systems.

Finally, try to compile a list of OSS notes for the portal version as well as for the business package under consideration. Refer to OSS Note 588665 (Composite SAP note for business packages) and OSS Note 642775 for EP 6.0SP1/NW04.

Review the Business Information

Review the business information such as the industry, the business area, and the target group of the business package. This information can be obtained in the Business Context section of the business package documentation.

Review the Online Documentation

Review the online documentation (help.sap.com) by clicking the Online Documentation link on the business package documentation page shown in Figure 16-2. Check whether the business package meets all the functional requirements of the organization. The online documentation also contains technical information on the iViews, worksets, and other objects included in the package. Information is also available for each iView regarding the runtime technology used for the iView, the technical name (such as com.sap.pct.isht.nfp.cm.sellin), the portal release for which the iView is supported, the data source for the iView, languages supported, the application component to which the iView belongs (you can use this information to create an OSS message under that application component, for example, EP-PCT-IHT-CMC BP High Tech Channel Management 5.0), and the visibility information that defines the location and role under which the iView can be displayed.

Read the instructions on how to configure the backend system. Sometimes the backend system may need to support single sign-on (SSO), and for this the SAP Security Library (SAPSECULIB) may need to be installed.

In some cases, the package may be dependent on objects shared from other business packages. In such cases, the referenced business package must be installed first before you deploy this referencing package.

Review the License Information

Review the license information so that the required license can be procured, if necessary. The license information is located in the License Information section of the business package documentation.

Check whether the backend system has the necessary license to support the increased number of users that may arise due to the increased number of portal users accessing the back end.

The business package may have **different licensing models**. For example, the package may require an Enterprise Portal license. Or it may require a license for the backend system—for example, the mySAP HR license may be required to install a mySAP HR package.

Download the Business Package

Once all the prerequisites have been met, you can download the package by clicking the download icon (Figure 16-3).

Download the file by clicking the Add To Download Basket button or by clicking the link under the Download Object column.

Back Up the Business Package

Ensure that the business package is still under release maintenance. This is important because the support for the business package usually lapses in the following situations:

- The backend R3 system is no longer supported
- The portal release is no longer supported
- Only the latest two business package releases are supported
- Only the latest two support package levels for the portal are supported

Do *Make a backup of the local copy of the business package, because the package could be replaced with a later version.*

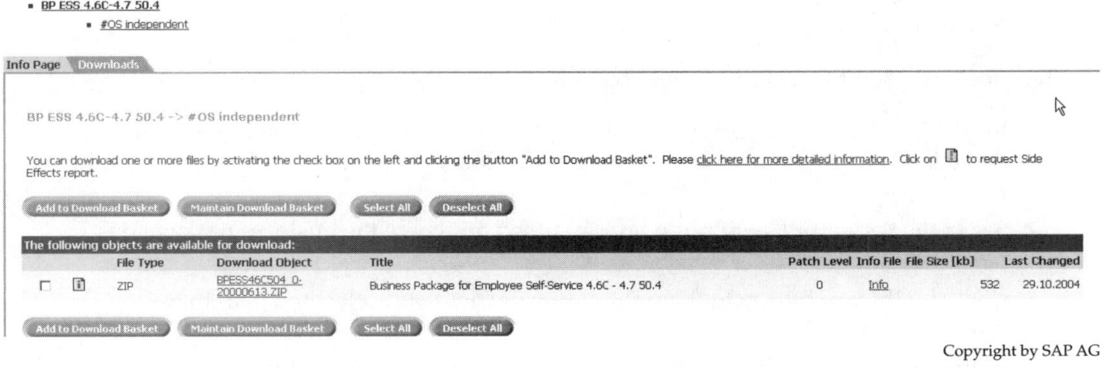

Figure 16-3 Download information page

File Types for Business Packages

Enterprise Portal 5.0 required that you use a <*pkg_name*>.pkg file. The .pkg file can be considered similar to a linked list that contains pointers to all the other objects within the package and ensures that all the dependent objects are imported. In versions earlier than EP 6.0 SP2, the <*pkg_name*>.epa file is a condensed file that contains all the objects belonging to the package.

For business packages running on Net Weaver 04 or higher, the packages are in the Software Deployment Archive (SDA) or Software Component Archive (SCA) format, so the Software Deployment Manager should be used.

For business packages greater than Net Weaver 04s, the Java Support Package Manager can be used.

Importing the Business Packages

When importing a business package, it's best to import it into a sandbox instead of a development system, because it is not possible to uninstall the package automatically after it is imported. Adequate testing should be done before the import, to avoid any issues later on during the development phase or after deployment in a production environment. You should also create a backup of the portal server environment before the import so that the system can be restored to its original state if necessary.

Note that, starting from EP 6.0 SP3, business packages are also available in the Software Component Archive (SCA) and Software Deployment Archive (SDA) formats. The Software Deployment Manager can be used to deploy such business packages.

NOTE *When uploading or importing into the portal, the whole package should be imported. This takes care of any dependencies that may exist between objects such as pages within a workset or iViews within a page.*

To import the downloaded business package, do the following:

1. In the Portal, navigate to System Administration | Transport in the top-level menu and click Transport Packages | Import in the detailed navigation menu as shown in Figure 16-4.
2. Select the Server or Client radio button, based on where the business package has been stored.
3. Click the Browse button to the right of the File field and select the path to the business package.
4. In the Content to be Overwritten field, select the appropriate value, based on whether you want pre-existing content for this business package, if any, to be overwritten.
5. Click Import.

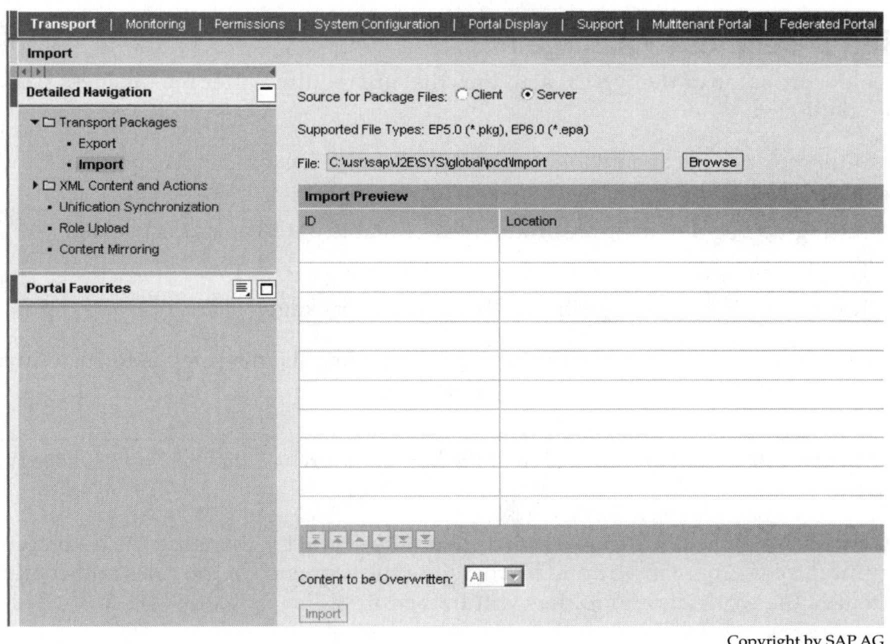

Copyright by SAP AG

FIGURE 16-4 Importing the business package

The objects in imported packages are stored in the following folders in the PCD, depending on the EP version. For EP 5.0, they are stored at Content Provided by SAP | Content for Line Manager, Specialists or Every User. For EP 6.0, they are stored at Migrated Content | EP 5.0 | *Object type* (iViews, Pages, Roles, and so on).

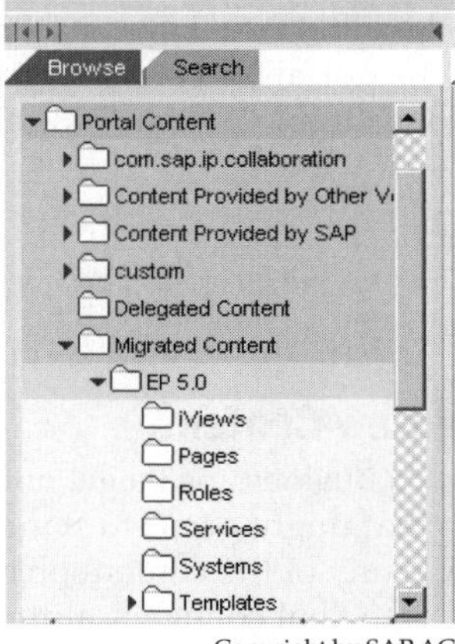

Copyright by SAP AG

PART IV

Customizing a Business Package

Given below are some of the typical activities that are required after the business package has been deployed:

- Setting up the backend connectivity by creating a system landscape object in the portal. This is discussed in detail in Chapter 18.
- Setting up users with appropriate roles available in the business package.
- Test the connectivity to the backend systems.
- Test the business functionality of the business package.

Once the initial prototype testing has been completed, the next step is to customize the package to suit your specific business requirements.

NOTE *Customization can be accomplished at the level of the organization, the roles, or the iViews or pages.*

You can change the navigational structure on the portal by changing the delivered worksets and roles. This can be done by changing the sequence of the roles and changing the content of the worksets and folders within the roles.

At the organizational level, you can change the company's look and feel by using a custom theme to reflect the organization's branding requirements.

The iViews and the layouts on the delivered pages can be changed, deleted, or added; in the same way, you can add the delivered pages and iViews to your own custom-developed pages, worksets, and roles. Changing the properties of those objects can change the behavior of the iViews and pages.

Business Package and Backend Configuration

The backend SAP R3 system must also be configured properly. For example, if you need to implement the BP for Financial Services, it is important that the Finance (FI) module has been configured properly in the backend SAP R/3 system. Proper system objects should be created in the system landscape on the portal for connecting to the backend R/3 systems—these include ERP, CRM, and BW, for example. When using SAP BW, pay special attention to fine-tuning the SAP BW system.

NOTE *Detailed instructions for configuring the business packages are available in the "Technical Description" section of the iViews.*

Using Delta Links for Creating New Content

When creating new content based on a business package, you should create it as *delta links*. This protects you from any changes that might occur to standard content during an upgrade of the business packages. Moreover, if any of the content objects on which the delta link was created changes in the business package, that change is automatically propagated to the custom content.

Upgrades vs. New Installation

When installing a newer version of the business package, you should identify whether it results in new objects or simply updates already installed objects. The system will create new objects if the technical names of the objects in the installation differ from those already stored on the system. If the objects use the same technical names in the two business packages, the system simply overwrites the older content objects with the new versions.

If new objects are created, you need to remember to create delta links for them. The custom changes to the delta-linked objects are not overwritten. However, the changes to the standard content are propagated to the unmodified content of the delta-linked objects.

Note that the functionality available in an older version of the portal may not be supported when you upgrade. For example, the BP for Portal Users exists in EP 5.0, but we do not have an equivalent business package in EP 6.0/NW'04. However, a number of iViews from BP for Portal Users are included in SAP Enterprise Portal 6.0/NW'04 as Initial Content. Hence you cannot upgrade from EP 5.0 to EP 6.0/ NW'04. So you need to take some extra steps for migrating from BP for Portal Users to EP 6.0/NW'04 Initial Content. For more info, refer to OSS Note 642827.

NOTE *When changing content of objects that are based on PAR files, the source code for the PAR files is not be available.*

Pilot Testing

After the necessary configuration and the entire unit test have been completed, the software should be pilot tested for user acceptance. During the pilot testing, you should analyze the installation to decide whether the package installation is successful. Success depends on a number of factors, such as the business goals met, technical issues if any, the functionality available, the look and feel, navigation issues, backend configuration issues, content ownership, end user training, and change management.

Portal Adoption

Finally, the installation of the business package should not be treated as a pure technical exercise. Rather, it should be mixed with a balanced approach that involves bringing together various stakeholders who will be developing, maintaining, and using the applications.

NOTE *Installing business packages is not just a pure technical exercise; it must be a collaborative effort involving business users.*

A team should be created, consisting of business package users and representatives from every level in the organizational hierarchy possible so that the changes can be implemented smoothly and with support. A capable technical team should be constituted to develop portal content both from standard and custom content.

Finally, because user adoption is extremely important after the portal goes live, sufficient time and attention should be paid to train users in portal personalization and general usage. Constant monitoring and motivation are keys to driving the portal usage to its maximum potential.

Uninstalling the Business Packages

It is not possible to uninstall some business packages using any standard tool. Starting from NW'04, you can use SDM to undeploy business packages that are in the SCA / SDA format. You can do the following to uninstall business packages:

- Remove the roles assigned to the users that are relevant to the business package.
- Delete the working folder where the custom changes have been created.
- Delete all the iViews in the PCD where the imported business package is stored.
- Delete the roles, the pages, the worksets, and the templates and then the systems related to the business package. While deleting these objects, be careful not to delete the KM-related objects such as the Content Manager role, the KM related pages, worksets, and so on. KM-related objects can be identified by checking for the prefix com.sap.km.* in the name.

CAUTION *When uninstalling a business package, you must be careful not to delete portal content objects in that package that are referenced in other business packages.*

NOTE *For more details, refer to the business packages related resources listed in Appendix B.*

Summary

You learned about the importance of using business packages, the different types of packages, and how to administer them. You also walked through a few steps involved in reviewing the technical and functional requirements for the business package. Finally, you looked at how to import the business packages and addressed the issue of uninstalling, if required.

17 CHAPTER

Changing Portal Look and Feel: Branding

After implementing the portal, one of your first steps is to customize the look and feel of the portal to meet the branding requirements of the organization. When the user logs in, he or she sees a portal desktop—a collection of user interface components. In this chapter, you will learn how to customize the portal desktop.

Changing the User Interface

The user interface components are responsible for providing the layout for navigation and displaying content with a certain look and feel. You can create different portal desktops that provide different layouts as well as look and feel. The different layouts are made possible using portal framework pages, and a different look and feel may be obtained by using portal themes. Different combinations of portal framework pages and portal themes can result in multiple portal desktops. These multiple portal desktops can then be assigned to different user groups, such as departments, subcompanies, or business partner segments, by creating desktop rules. Figure 17-1 illustrates how different portal desktops can be assigned to different users based on portal display rules. Portal desktop A contains framework page A and theme A, while portal desktop B contains framework page B and theme B. Portal desktop A can be assigned to internal employees, business partners, and field sales representatives based on roles or groups using portal display rules. Similarly, portal desktop B can be assigned to dialup users based on bandwidth using portal display rules.

NOTE *Multiple framework pages and multiple themes can be assigned to multiple portal desktops during design. A particular portal desktop can be assigned to a user, group, or role using portal display rules.*

Why Use Different Portal Scenarios?

Portal scenarios can be typically classified into internal users, external users, and a mixture of the two. Of course, you can have any number of classifications of users depending on the business requirements for the organization.

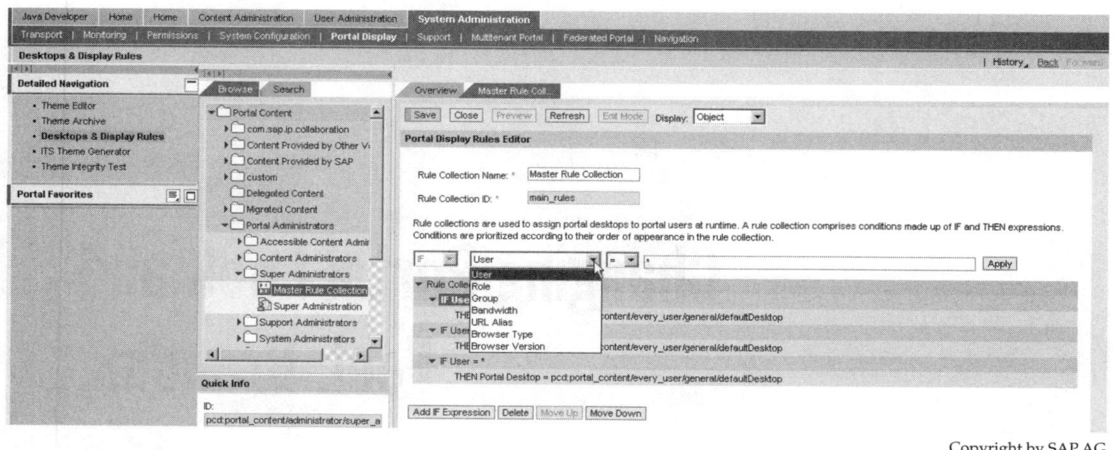

Copyright by SAP AG

FIGURE 17-1 Assignment of different portal desktops to users based on portal display rules

Internal users are the most knowledgeable and professional users. They can be trained and hence can cope with complex designs such as drag and relate, different backend systems, web services, and so on. Because of the huge amount of information that needs to be displayed, a deep hierarchy of content often needs to be created by making use of the detailed navigation panel.

On the other hand, external users are relatively less portal savvy and may not require more than two levels of navigation. These users are often short-term, first-time users of the portal and often tend to be impatient. Some typical examples of such users are suppliers, customers, and other business partners. They could also be anonymous users who may not be required to log into the portal.

The third scenario is a combination of scenarios: Some users could log on to the portal to access special content, while others may be guest or anonymous users who are required to log in.

You should be able to design different portal user interfaces for different users based on different criteria. This is accomplished by creating different portal desktops and assigning them to various user populations with desktop rules.

Components of the Portal Display

Let's first take a look at some of the components that make up the portal display.

Framework Page

The framework page is responsible for the overall layout of the portal desktop. A portal desktop is a collection of framework pages and portal themes. At design time, a portal desktop can have more than one framework page and more than one portal theme. However, at runtime, only one framework page and portal theme are assigned to the portal desktop using a concept called portal display rules. These rules are created by Content Administrators at design time.

The framework page determines the navigational structure, layout, and content for a portal desktop. It contains typical components of a page such as header area iView, top-level navigation iView, detailed-level navigation iView, and content area. You can create multiple framework pages by copying the default framework page that comes as part of the initial content and customizing the layouts to cater to different user scenarios. Examples of user scenarios are dialup users, field-sales representatives who use mobile laptops, internal employees, and external business partners.

Note that SAP provides a default desktop with a default framework page and default portal theme. You are not supposed to modify the SAP-provided objects because they get overwritten during an upgrade and you will lose your custom changes.

DON'T *Do not change the SAP-provided default framework page.*

The framework pages can be accessed under Content Administration | Portal Content in the top-level menu.

Portal Theme

The portal theme covers the overall look and feel of the portal by allowing you to change the color, font size, and other visual aspects of the various user interface elements such as buttons, labels, and so on. You can even choose your own company logo. Portal themes do not affect the navigational structure, layout, or content of the portal desktop. That job is done by the framework page.

SAP provides standard themes, but you can also create custom themes. To be able to change the themes, you must have either a System Administrator or Super Administrator role. A Content Administrator role will not help. End users can have the ability to change the look and feel of the portal by changing the portal theme at runtime.

HINT *End users can select themes from a predefined list during runtime.*

To access the portal theme editor, choose System Administration | Portal Display on the top-level menu and Theme Editor in the detailed navigation menu.

Portal Desktop

The portal desktop is the overall container that holds together the framework page and the portal theme as one unit. Using the portal desktop, you can create portal desktop rules to assign directly to various users, user groups, or role-based scenarios. Instead of assigning the individual framework pages and portal themes to the users, you can assign the portal desktop to the users. The portal comes with a default portal desktop, which is displayed to all the users by default. Deleting this will result in problems for the logged in user.

To access the portal desktop editor, choose System Administration | Portal Display in the top-level menu and Desktops And Display Rules in the detailed navigation menu.

Rule Collection

Rule collection is a collection of portal desktop display rules. The portal desktop rules can be used to define how different portal desktops are assigned directly to different users, groups, or roles. Different portal desktops can also be assigned indirectly to a user based on platform-specific criteria such as bandwidth, browser version, browser type, or URL using the portal desktop display rules.

Portal Desktop Display Rule

Each portal desktop display rule is nothing but a condition built using IF-THEN expressions. A single condition can have multiple, nested IF expressions and one THEN expression. The IF expression can have parameters such as users, groups, roles, bandwidth, browser version, browser type, and URL. The THEN expression can have two parameters, namely, portal desktops and rule collections. Thus one example of a portal desktop rule could be

IF (Group = ABC) OR IF (Browser Type = MSIE), THEN Portal Desktop = portal_desktop_A, where ABC could be the name of a group of users who use a dialup connection, MSIE stands for Microsoft Internet Explorer, and portal_desktop_A is the name of a custom-developed portal desktop created specially for dialup users.

Master Rule Collection (main_rule)

After you create these rule collection objects based on your business and technical requirements, you must assign them to a default rule collection object known as the Master Rule Collection (main_rules).

NOTE *The Master Rule Collection object is used by the portal at runtime to determine the default portal desktop for the logged in user.*

To access the rules collection editor, choose System Administration | Portal Display in the top-level menu and Desktops And Display Rules in the detailed navigation menu.

Customizing the Portal Desktop

The following steps are used to customize the portal desktop:

1. Create the navigation iViews.
2. Build the navigation pages using the iViews created in step 1.
3. Create the page layout.
4. Create the framework page using page layout and the navigation page.
5. Create the portal themes.
6. Create the portal desktop using the portal themes and the framework page.
7. Change the Master Rule Collection to include the newly created portal desktop.

Creating the Framework Page

Figure 17-2 displays a typical portal *framework page,* which consists of three major components: header area, navigation panel, and the content area. The header area consists of the masthead iView, tools area iView, and top-level navigation iView. Below the header iView is the page title bar iView. The Navigation panel is the left-hand area under the page title bar iView and it contains navigational iViews such as Detailed Navigation, Dynamic Navigation, Drag & Relate Targets, Related Links, and Portal Favorites. The content area consists of pages, and iViews along with the layout containers for arranging the iViews and pages.

NOTE *A portal desktop can be assigned to any number of framework pages and portal themes.*

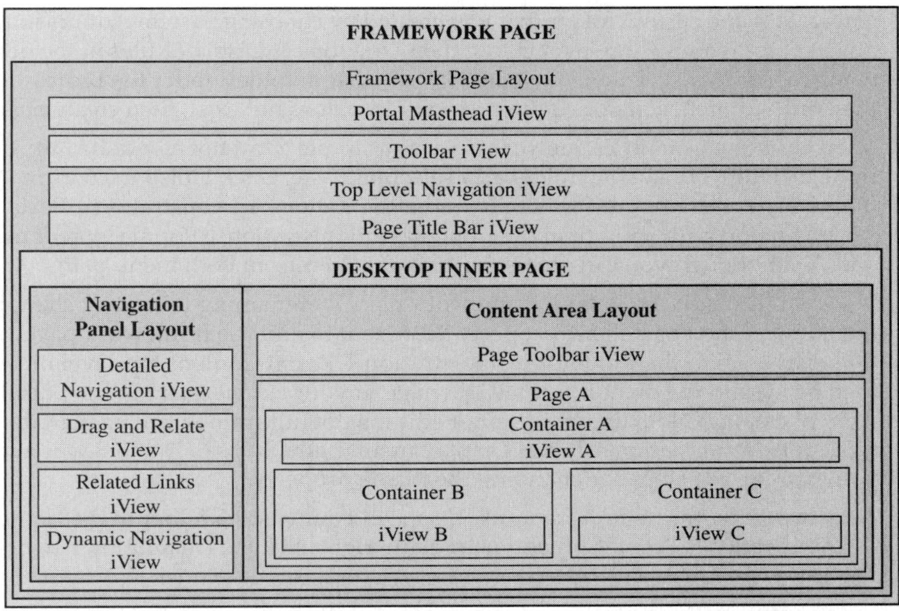

FIGURE 17-2 Components of a portal framework page

Follow these steps to create and then edit a framework page:

1. Navigate to System Administration | Portal Display in the top-level menu, choose Desktops & Display Rules in the left navigation panel, and then choose Portal Content | Portal Users | Standard Portal Users in the Portal Content Catalog.
2. Right click Default Framework Page and choose Copy, as shown next.

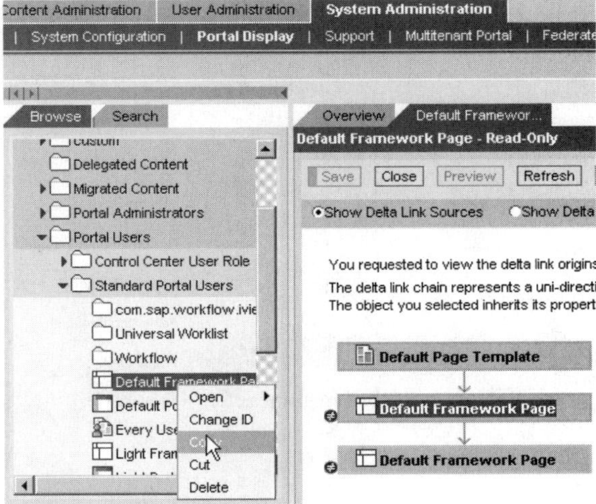

3. Navigate to the custom folder that you created by choosing System Administration | Portal Display in the top-level menu, then Desktops & Display Rules in the detailed navigation panel, and then navigate to your custom folder under the Browse tab in the Portal Content Catalog. If the custom folder does not exist, then create one.
4. Then paste the Default Framework Page as a simple copy, not as a delta link, by right clicking your custom folder and selecting Paste. Click Finish to confirm. Note that you can carry out this task only under the System Administration | Portal Display menu path and not in the Content Administration | Portal Content menu path, even though you can access the custom folder from both menu paths.
5. Now you can edit the default framework page by renaming it, first by changing the name in the Page Name property. Note that to edit the framework page, you must navigate to the Content Administration | Portal Content top-level menu and then browse to the default framework page in your *custom folder* in the portal content catalog. Note that you cannot edit the default framework page in the System Administration | Portal Display menu path. Steps 6, 7, and 8 will guide you through the steps for changing the Name property.
6. After accessing the default framework page in your custom folder in the Content Administration | Portal Content menu path, right click the Default Framework Page and choose Open | Object.
7. In the Property Editor section of the Framework Page screen, select Show All in the Property Category drop-down list. Scroll down to the Name property.
8. Change the Name property by entering a suitable name.
9. To edit the framework page, make sure the Page Content radio button is selected. Select the checkbox next to Page Title Bar and click the Properties button at the bottom of the Page Content Editor, as shown next.

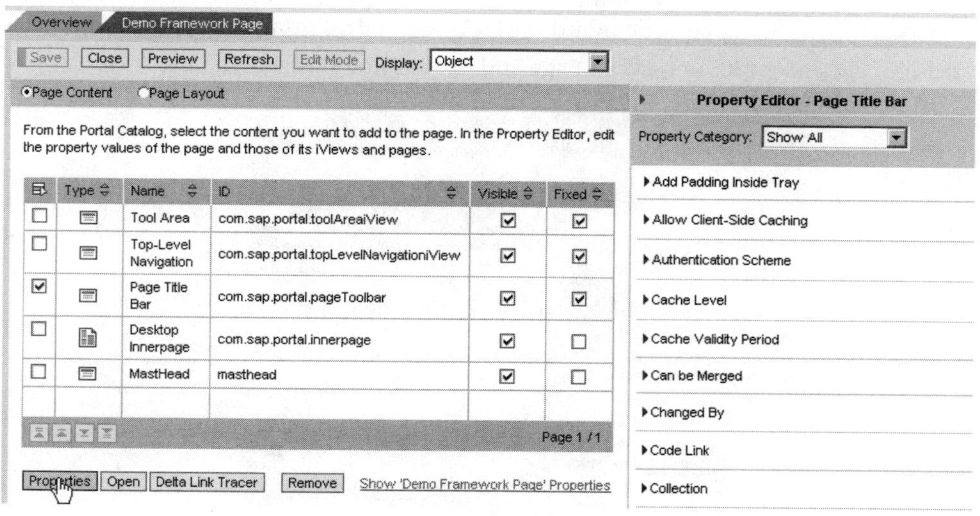

10. Click Yes to save the changes you have already made to the Name property. Now the page editor for the default framework page will reload with the new name appearing in the Object tab. The property list on the right will now display the properties for the Page Title Bar iView. Choose Show All under the Property Category drop-down list, and then change the property Show History List from Yes to No. Then click Save.

Now you have created a new default framework page with the history link disabled in the page title bar.

Modifying the Portal Theme

You can modify the color, font size and type, or company logo in the portal theme.

NOTE *It is not possible to save the theme with the same name as the SAP-provided themes. However, you can save it under a different name using Save As.*

To modify an SAP-provided portal theme, do the following:

1. Go to System Administration | Portal Display in the top-level menu and choose Theme Editor in the detailed navigation menu. The screen shown next will appear.

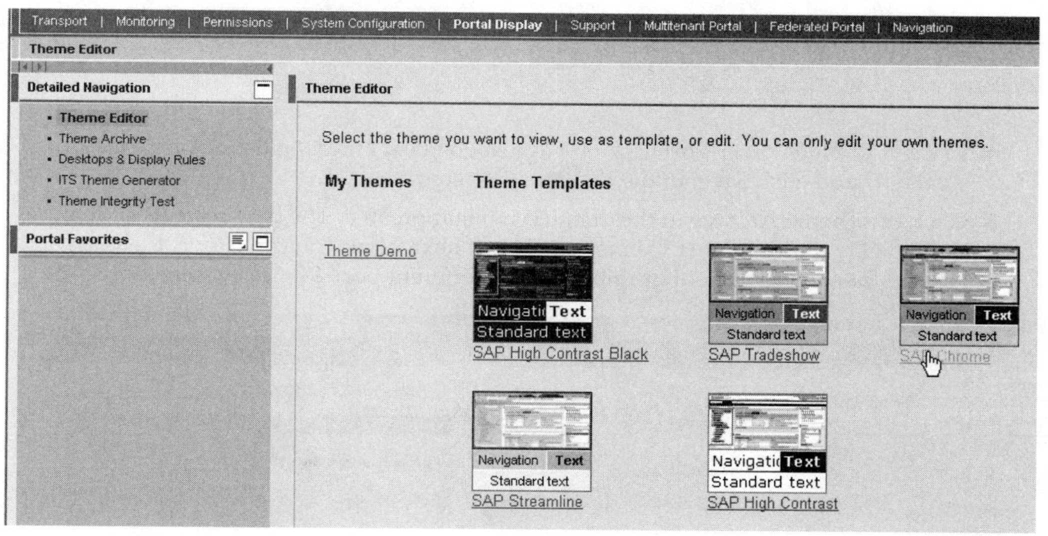

Copyright by SAP AG

2. The above illustration displays a number of themes such as SAP High Contrast Black, SAP Tradeshow, SAP Chrome, SAP Streamline, and SAP High Contrast. Select one of the SAP themes. A Current Theme: <theme name>[Read-Only] will appear.
3. In the Current Theme: <selected theme name>[Read-Only] screen, you will notice that on the left-hand side, you have a list of user interface elements that you can select to modify the look and feel. On the right-hand side, there is a Preview section

PART IV

at the top, where you can preview the user interface element selected on the left. At the bottom right-hand side, there is a Styles section, where you can change the parameters for the user interface element that was selected to change the look and feel of the selected user interface element. Hover your mouse over the Border Width of Masthead, as displayed next. You can see that the corresponding region, which in this case is the masthead, gets highlighted in the Preview section. In the Styles: Portal Masthead section, enter **10px** in the Border Width Of Masthead field and click Save As.

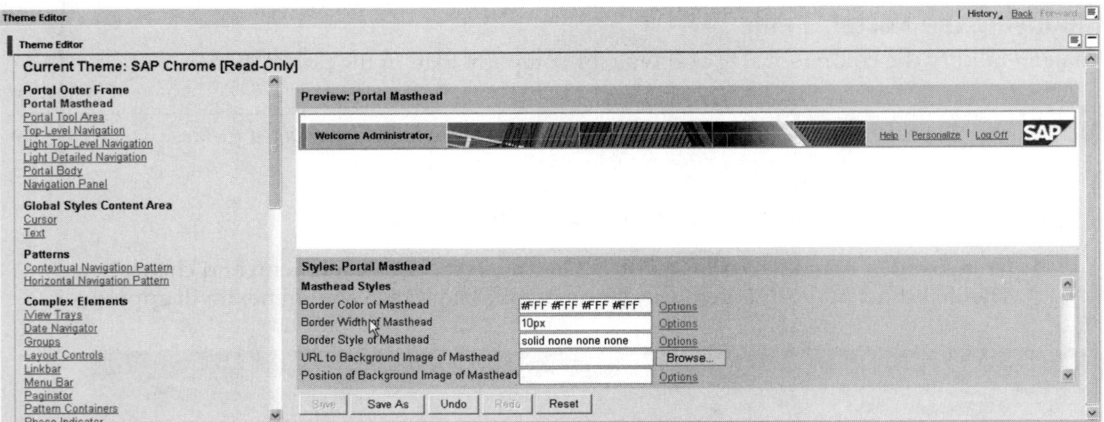

Copyright by SAP AG

4. In the SAP NetWeaver Portal - Web Page dialog box, enter the theme name and theme ID and click Save. In the Be Patient screen, click OK.
5. Click the Theme Archive in the detailed navigation area. The newly created theme will display under Export Themes, as shown next. Now you can export the newly created theme into a client or import it to a different portal in the system landscape.

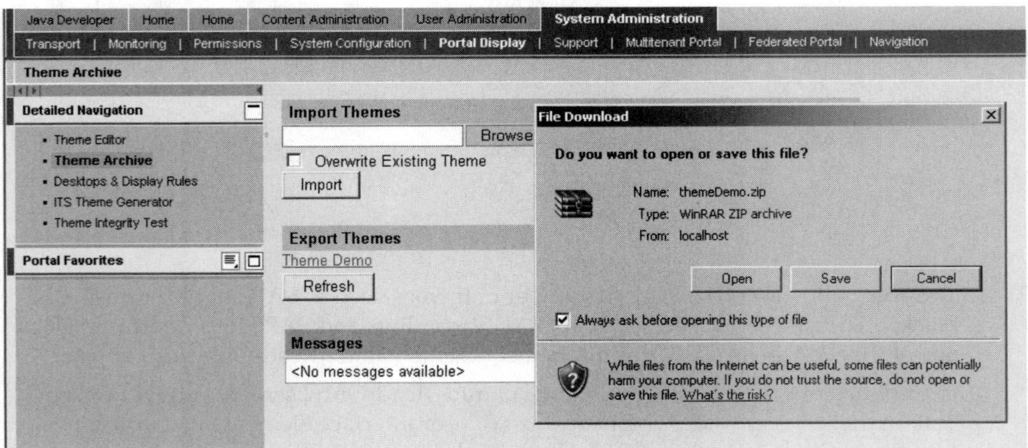

Copyright by SAP AG

Exporting and Importing a Theme

To export a theme, click on the newly created theme. A File Download window will appear as shown in the previous illustration. Click Save to save the theme to your local folder.

You can make the necessary changes to the theme in the development portal system, and then, after the changes have been fully tested and accepted by the users, you can export them and import them into the other servers.

TIP *You can send the theme in ZIP format to a third-party vendor who could make the necessary changes and send it back to you.*

The newly created theme, named Theme Demo in the following illustration, is stored in the Themes folder along with the other SAP-provided themes in the Portal Content Directory (PCD):

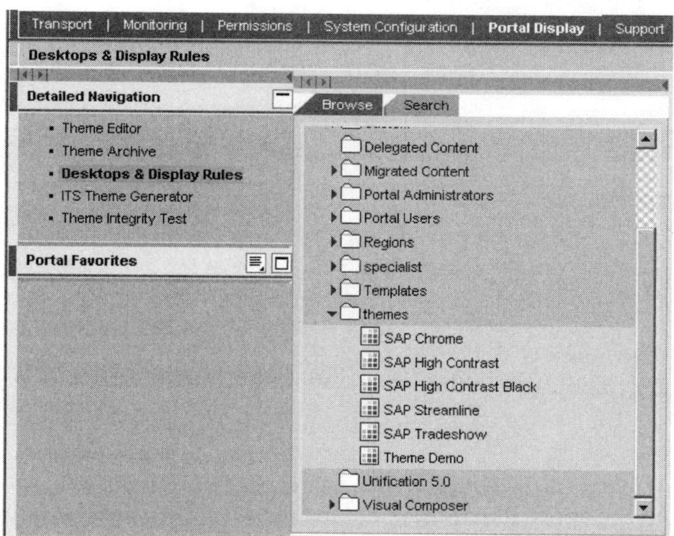

Trying to delete an SAP-provided theme results in an error, as shown here.

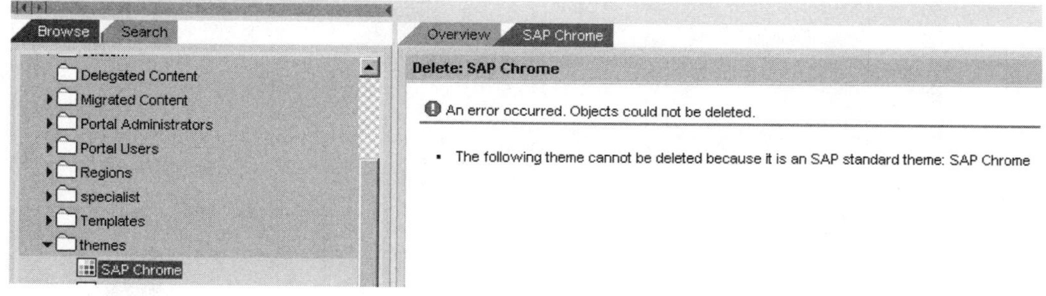

PART IV

Adding the Theme to the Portal Desktop

After you have created a custom theme, you can add it to the default portal desktop and make the theme the default. Here's how:

1. Navigate to System Administration | Portal Display in the top-level menu, then click on Desktops & Display Rules in the detailed navigation menu.
2. In the Portal Content Catalog, navigate to Portal Users | Standard Portal Users. Right click on Default Portal Desktop and select Open | Object from the context menu. The following screen will appear:

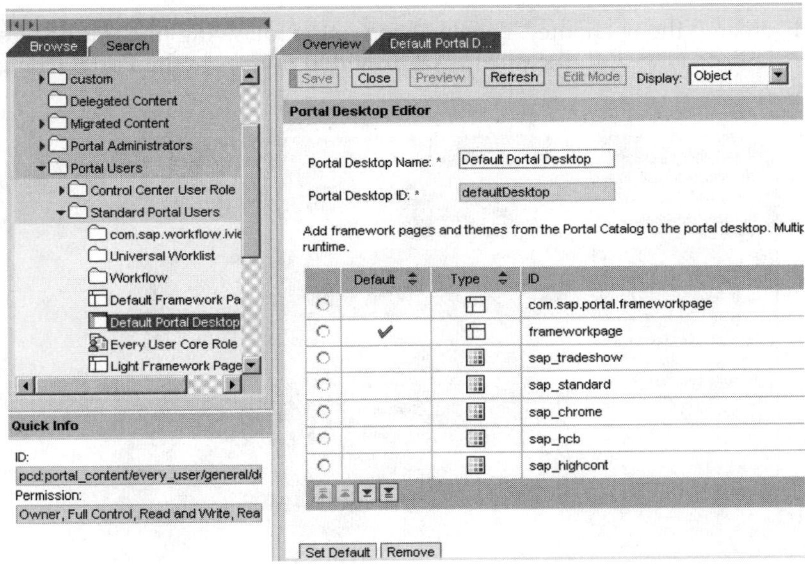

Copyright by SAP AG

You can see from the above illustration that in the Portal Desktop Editor on the right, the default portal desktop contains a framework page and the SAP themes added to it. The end user can select any of these themes during personalization. If you want to include the custom theme to the portal desktop, you should navigate to the theme in the PCD, right click the theme name, and choose Add Theme To Portal Desktop, as shown here:

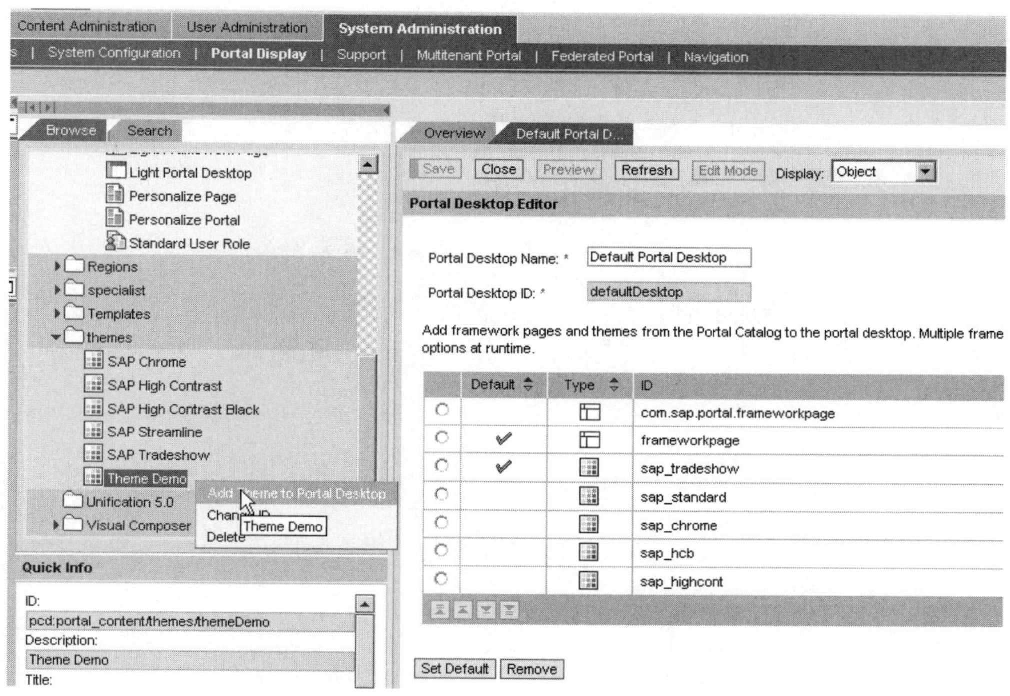

Copyright by SAP AG

When trying to add the custom theme to the portal desktop, remember to keep the Default Portal Desktop open for editing, as shown in the above illustration. To make the newly added custom theme the default, select the radio button next to the theme name and click the Set Default button, as shown in Figure 17-3. Then click Save.

Creating a New Portal Desktop

The following procedure shows how to create a new portal desktop:

1. Go to System Administration | Portal Display in the top-level menu and click Desktops & Display Rules in the detailed navigation menu.
2. Navigate to the custom folder where you would like to store the new portal desktop. Right click that folder and choose New | Portal Desktop, as shown next.

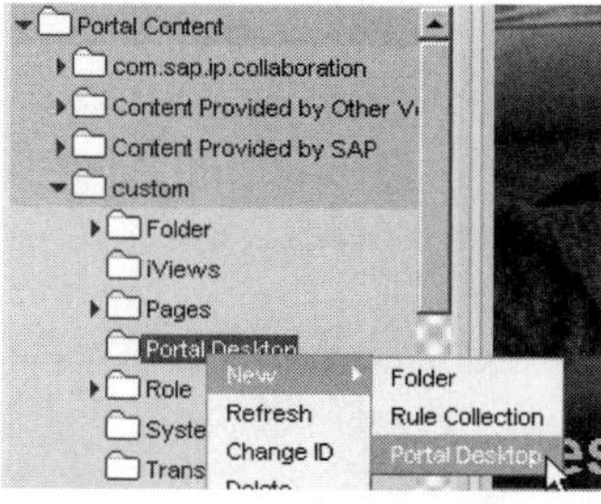

Copyright by SAP AG

Copyright by SAP AG

FIGURE 17-3 Setting up the newly created portal theme as the default

3. In the two fields in the Portal Desktop Editor screen on the right, enter a Desktop Name and Desktop ID.
4. Navigate to System Administration | Portal Display in the top-level menu and click Desktops & Display Rules. Then browse to Portal Content | Custom | Pages. Now add the newly created framework page to the portal desktop by right clicking the framework page and choosing Add Framework Page to Portal Desktop, as shown next.

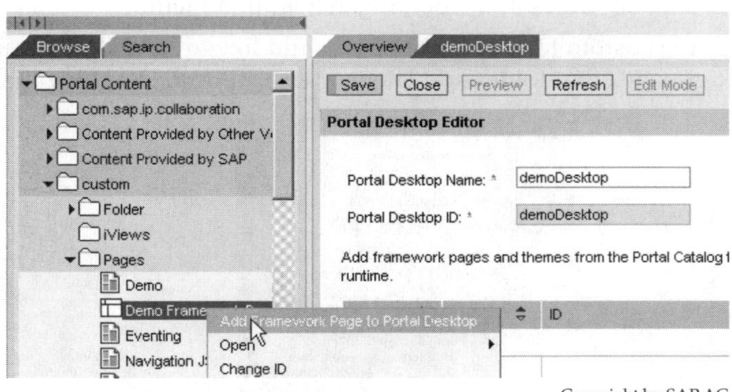

Copyright by SAP AG

5. Now open the Themes folder under Portal Content, right click a theme name, and choose Add Theme to Portal Desktop, as shown next. End users can select any themes you've added during runtime personalization.

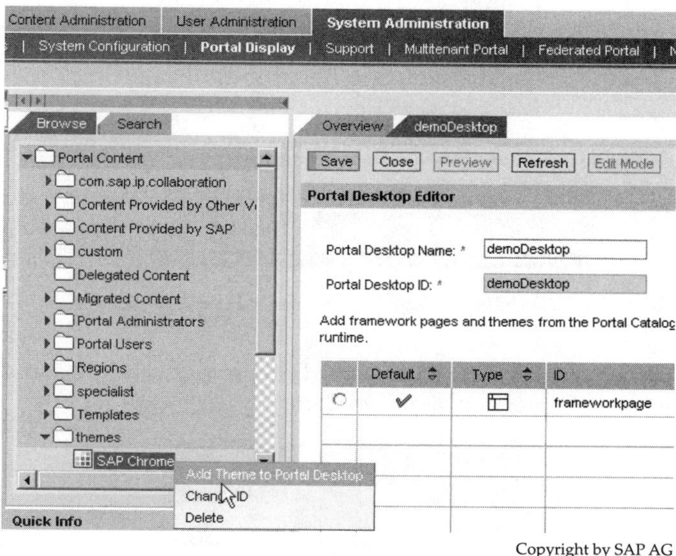

6. Make sure that you select one theme as the default, and click Save.

You have now successfully created a portal desktop and assigned the newly created framework page and a theme to it. You can add more framework pages and themes to the desktop, if required, which will provide more personalization options at runtime.

Creating the New Rule Collection

To create the New Rule Collection, first navigate to System Administration | Portal Display in the top-level menu and then choose | Desktops & Display Rules.

1. Right click the custom folder where you want to store the display rules and choose New | Rule Collection.
2. In the Portal Display Rules Editor, enter the name and ID for the rule collection.

3. Select the THEN statement, as shown next:

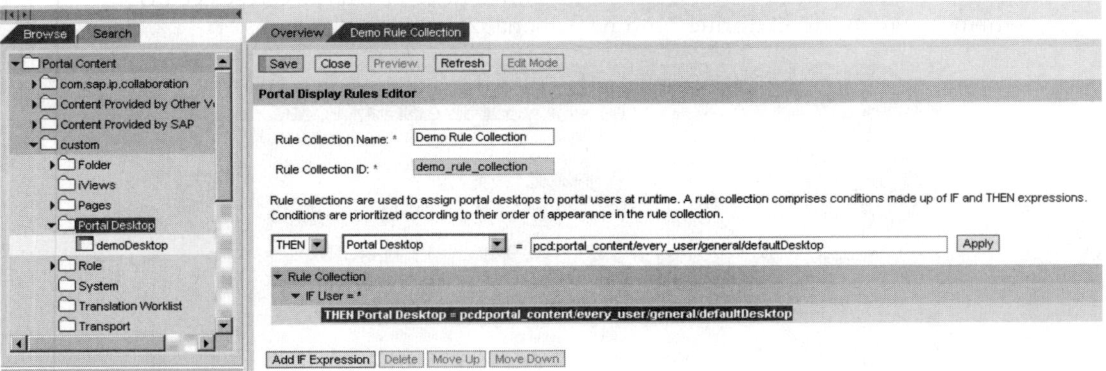

Copyright by SAP AG

4. Navigate to the portal desktop you created earlier, right click it, and choose Add Portal Desktop to Expression, as shown here:

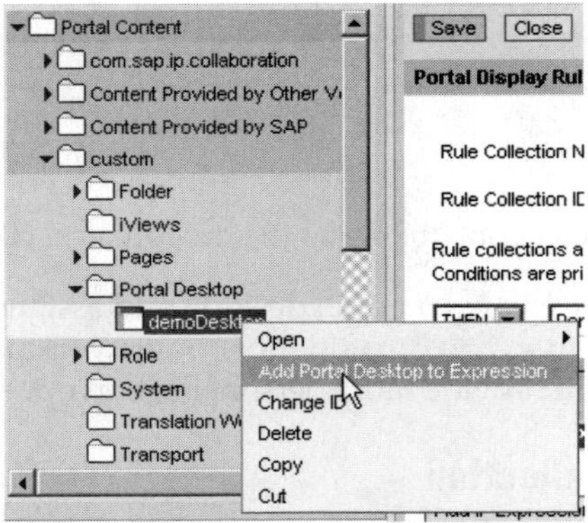

Copyright by SAP AG

5. Click Apply. The rule now displays the newly added portal desktop added to the THEN statement.
6. Click Save. The newly added rule will now display in the navigation area:

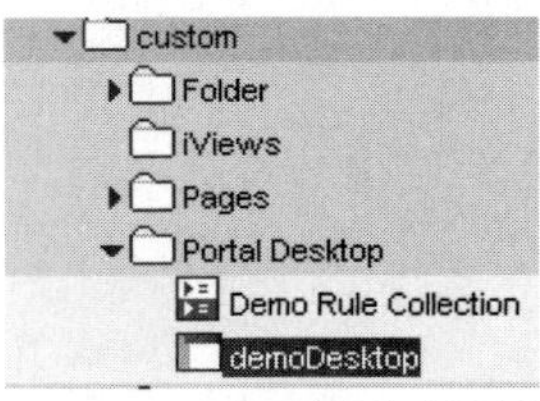

Copyright by SAP AG

NOTE *All rules must be added to the Master Rule Collection.*

Working with the Master Rule Collection

The Master Rule Collection is a set of rules that help define which user gets which portal desktop at runtime. Usually, one rule is used as a catch-all expression, such as *user=**. This rule defines that all users are assigned the default desktop.

You can modify a rule collection by defining additional rules or expressions so that users belonging to different groups or roles can be assigned to different portal desktops.

You can create portal desktops in addition to the default desktop and assign them to different portal themes and framework pages. Then, when users log into the portal, they will see different portal desktops depending on the department (role), browser type, connection bandwidth, external or internal users (groups), and so on, to which they belong.

DON'T *Be careful not to delete the Master Rule Collection. If it's deleted, the portal will not be able to assign the portal desktop to the user at runtime.*

Here's how to change the rule collection:

1. Navigate to System Administration | Portal Display in the top-level menu and choose Desktops & Display Rules in the detailed navigation menu.
2. Then, in the Portal Content Catalog, go to Portal Content | Portal Administrators | Super Administrators. Right click Master Rule Collection and choose Open | Object. The Portal Display Rules Editor page will open in the content area on the right, as shown next:

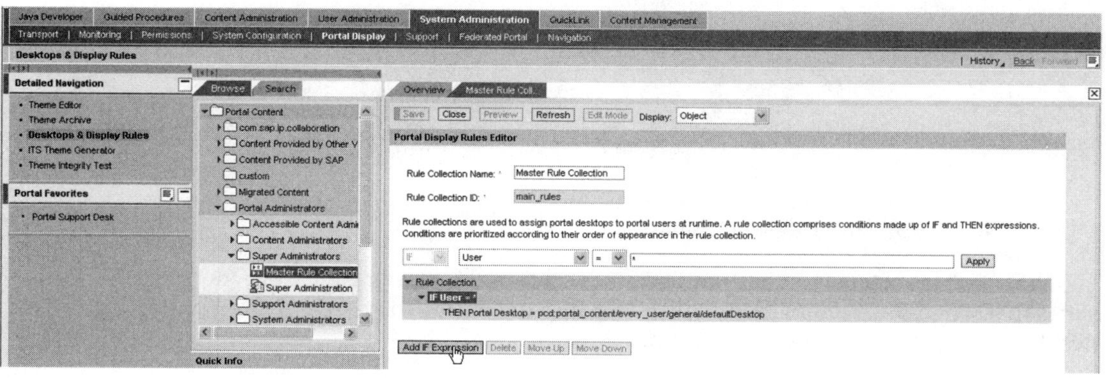

Copyright by SAP AG

3. Click the Add IF Expression button at the bottom of the page. The ADD IF Expression button is highlighted in the previous illustration. The newly added IF expression will appear as the first statement in the rule collection with the default values.

PART IV

4. Select the newly created, first IF expression under Rule Collection. At the top of the rule collection, you will notice a row of fields such as a grayed-out drop-down field with an IF entry, another drop-down field for selecting the parameters for the IF expression, a third drop-down field with = and NE choices, an empty field with * entry, and an Apply button, as shown next:

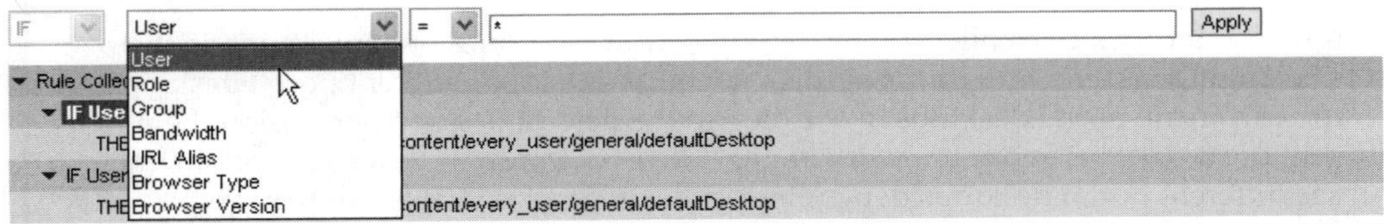

5. In the above illustration, you can notice that you can set up display rules for various criteria such as user, role, group, bandwidth, URL alias, browser type, and browser version. Choose User in the drop-down list and then type the user name in the field next to the field with a drop-down with value =. Click Apply. The first rule in the rule collection will change from User=* to User=Administrator, where Administrator is the name of the user entered in this step.
6. Choose THEN in the first rule collection. Right click the newly created desktop in the navigation area and choose Add Portal Desktop to Expression, as shown next.

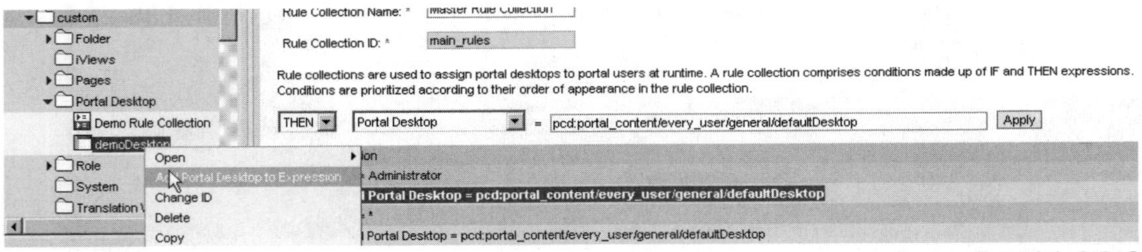

7. Click Apply and then click Save.

Now, in this section, you have added a new rule to the Master Rule Collection which states that when the Administration user logs into the portal, the newly created portal desktop will appear to the administrator.

Test the Changes

Now log out and log in as the user to test the changes.

You'll notice that after changing the Master Rule Collection, the look and feel of the portal has changed because the newly created portal desktop has a different theme than that of the default desktop. Moreover, in the far right of the page title bar, only the Back and Forward links appear; the History List link does not appear since you changed the framework page, as shown here:

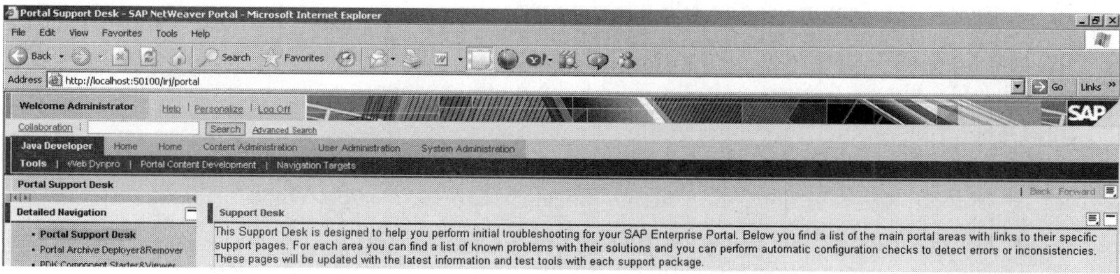

Copyright by SAP AG

Through this trivial example, you have learned how to create a new rule in the Master Rule Collection, and assign the newly created portal desktop to the new rule in the Master Rule Collection. As a result of this new rule, when the user logs in, he or she views the newly created portal desktop instead of the default portal desktop.

TIP *Sometimes, if the changes were made incorrectly, you can receive an error message such as this: "Error occurred while trying to access desktop: pcd:portal_content/……, the object does not exist or you are not authorized to access it…". This could be because the user does not have the required READ permissions to the default portal desktop or because no desktop rule was created for that user. Of course, you may also receive this error if the portal desktop itself was deleted.*

To remedy the permission issue, go to System Administration | Portal Display in the top-level menu and then browse to Portal Content | Portal Users | Standard Portal Users | Default Portal Desktop and verify that the Everyone group has READ permission for the default portal desktop.

If the portal desktop has been deleted, you can recover it. Navigate to System Administration | Portal Display in the top-level menu, choose Desktops & Display Rules in the detailed navigation, and browse to Portal Content | Content Provided by SAP | End User Content | Standard Portal Users. Then copy the default portal desktop as a delta link to the folder Portal Content | Portal Users | Standard Portal Users.

Transporting the Portal Desktop

The portal desktop can be transported in two ways: You can export and then import the themes from one system into the other using the menu path System Administration | Portal Display | Theme Archive. Or you can create a transport package and include the portal desktop in it. You should then export the package and re-import the package in the other system. Remember to uncheck the box Include All Objects On Which The Exported Objects Depend. Chapter 22 discusses portal transports in detail.

Using the ITS Generator

Using the Internet Transaction Server (ITS) theme generator, you can change the look and feel of SAP transactions, Internet Application Components (IACs), and ITS services so that they are in line with the look and feel of the custom objects that were created in the portal. This can be achieved by creating the ITS stylesheet for the theme used on the portal by using the ITS generator. The ITS generator should also be used when a higher ITS patch release is installed so that the ITS stylesheet is updated.

To use the ITS generator, use the following steps:

1. Navigate to System Administration | Portal Display in the top-level menu and then click ITS Theme Generator in the detailed navigation menu.
2. Depending on the ITS version, enter the following:
   - For ITS 6.20 and lower, in the Select Theme For ITS Stylesheet Generation screen, in the ITS Server field enter **http://<server>:<port>/<scripts/wgate**.
   - For ITS 6.40, in the ITS Server field, enter **http://<server>:<port>/sap/bc/gui/sap/its**.
3. Enter the user and password credentials for the ITAS 6.40 version. No user/ password is required for ITS 6.20 and lower.
4. In the ITS Preview Service field, enter the ITS service or the IAC for which you want to generate the stylesheet. Or you can leave the default value sap_preview service, which contains all the elements required for ITS images.
5. In the Portal Theme field, enter the custom-created portal theme for which you want to generate the ITS stylesheet.
6. This opens up the ITS Theme Generator page, which has a preview section at the top and an editable section at the bottom. Change the images, if required, in the editable section and click Generate. This generates the ITS stylesheets for the selected theme, as shown here:

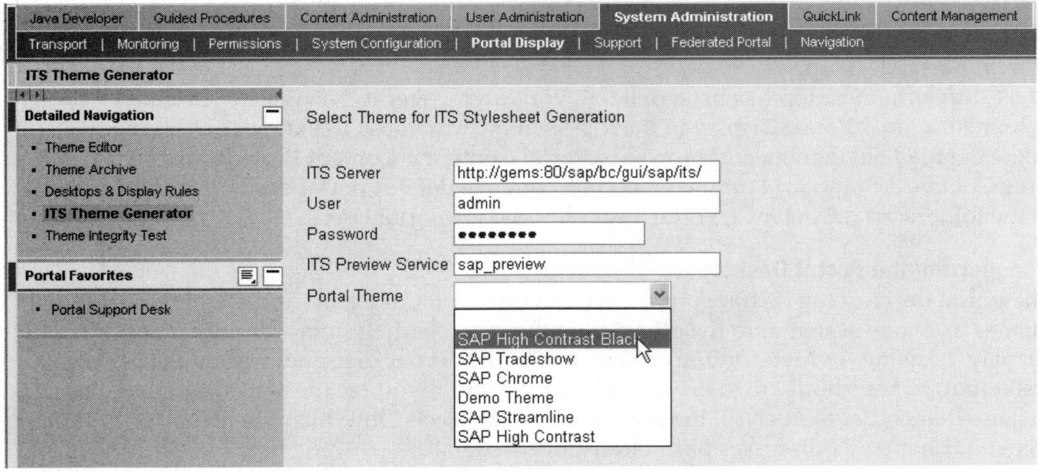

Using Theme Integrity Tests

Theme integrity tests can be used to test for errors in the portal theme and can be used for several scenarios. The theme integrity test can be used to conduct the server-side URL connection test, the personalization test, and the PCD test.

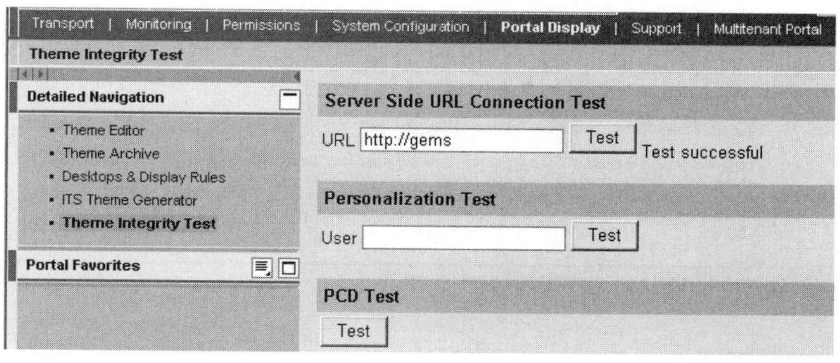

FIGURE 17-4 Testing the server-side URL connection

Server-Side URL Connection Test

The server-side URL connection test is specially developed for Netscape and can be used to check whether the resources are available in the portal server. You can also use this test if you are using a release prior to EP 6.0 SP2 Patch 27 and if you have difficulty previewing the theme editor. To conduct the server-side URL connection test, do the following:

1. Navigate to System Administration | Portal Display on the top-level menu and click Theme Integrity Tests in the detailed navigation menu.
2. In the Server Side URL Connection Test field, enter the URL for which you want to test the connectivity from the portal.
3. Click the Test button against the URL field. The result will appear as shown in Figure 17-4. It will display an HTTP error in case of a connectivity issue.

Personalization Test

The personalization test helps to identify the portal theme that was personalized by a user. To conduct the personalization test, enter the user ID in the User field under the Personalization Test section of the Theme Integrity Test page and click Test. The results will appear as shown in Figure 17-5. In this example, the user admin has used sap_tradeshow as the theme.

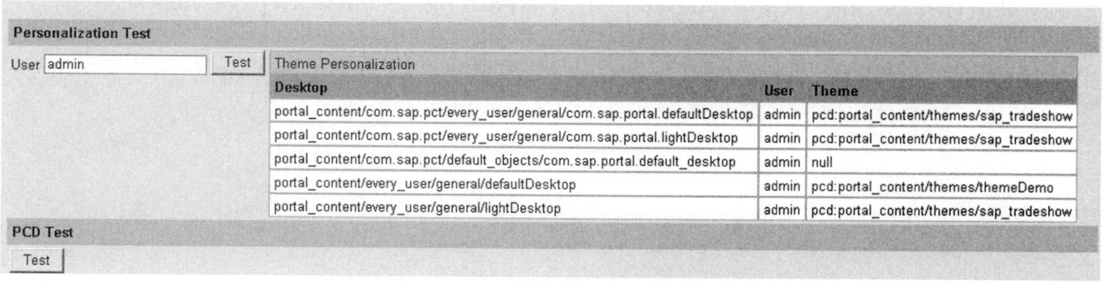

Personalization Test

User admin Test

Theme Personalization

Desktop	User	Theme
portal_content/com.sap.pct/every_user/general/com.sap.portal.defaultDesktop	admin	pcd:portal_content/themes/sap_tradeshow
portal_content/com.sap.pct/every_user/general/com.sap.portal.lightDesktop	admin	pcd:portal_content/themes/sap_tradeshow
portal_content/com.sap.pct/default_objects/com.sap.portal.default_desktop	admin	null
portal_content/every_user/general/defaultDesktop	admin	pcd:portal_content/themes/themeDemo
portal_content/every_user/general/lightDesktop	admin	pcd:portal_content/themes/sap_tradeshow

PCD Test

Test

FIGURE 17-5 Test for checking the personalization settings of the user

PCD Test

Test	Subtest	Result
	Get PCD Service user (doPrivileged)	Test successful
	Access PCD without user	Access denied (Object: portal_content/themes/sap_standard) com.sapportals.portal.pcd.gl.PermissionControlException: Access denied (Object: portal_content/themes/sap_standard) at com.sapportals.portal.pcd.gl.PcdFilterContext.filterLookup(PcdFilterContext.java:421) at com.sapportals.portal.pcd.gl.PcdProxyContext.basicContextLookup(PcdProxyContext.java:1095) at com.sapportals.portal.pcd.gl.PcdProxyContext.basicContextLookup(PcdProxyContext.java:1101)

FIGURE 17-6 Connection test to the PCD or database

PCD Test

When creating or editing themes in the Theme editor, the portal should be able to connect to the database or PCD. To conduct this test, click the Test button under the PCD Test section of the Theme Integrity Test page. Figure 17-6 displays the test results.

Useful OSS Notes

- **687485** Changes to Default Framework Page have no effect
- **861452** NW'04 upgrade to >=SP11 Theme Editor missing themes
- **869690** Error occurred while trying to access desktop
- **856865** Error occurred while trying to access framework page
- **823210** Full-Control permissions required to edit Rule Collection
- **715307** Cannot log in: "No portal desktop defined for this user"

NOTE *For more details, refer to the branding related resources listed in Appendix B.*

Summary

This chapter discussed the need for different portal user interfaces for different user groups. It discussed the various components of the Portal Framework page and the importance of portal themes, the portal desktop, and rule collection. You walked through the various steps involved in customizing the portal desktop, such as creating a framework page, creating a portal theme, creating a new portal desktop using the newly created portal theme and the portal framework page, creating a new rule collection and assigning it to the master rule, and finally testing the new portal desktop changes by logging on as the user.

CHAPTER 18

Connecting to SAP and Non-SAP Backend Systems

When you consider a portal system landscape, you realize that it is nothing but a collection of systems. To connect to those systems, you need to create a system object on the portal. A *system object* is simply a convenient way of representing the external or backend application using a collection of properties, so that by maintaining those connection properties, you can connect to those systems.

Once you have created the system object, you can then include this system object as an iView property for fetching data from the backend system. One of the important steps in configuring a business package after it has been deployed on the portal is to create the required system objects so that the iViews in the business package can connect to the appropriate SAP backend systems such as SAP R3, SAP CRM, and SAP BW. This chapter discusses how to connect to various backend systems.

Creating System Objects

The set of properties that define the system is contained in an XML file called portalapp .xml, which is part of a Portal Archive file (PAR). The portalapp.xml file contains the definitions for a number of systems and the connection properties required to connect to those systems.

A system object can be used to connect to a backend system and to retrieve data from the backend system. The system object can be created from either of the following:

- PAR file
- System template

TIP *It is also possible to create a template from a PAR file and then use that template to create a system.*

It is not possible to add to or delete properties from a system object. To add properties, you should define a new system with additional properties, as shown here:

1. Make a copy of the system object's PAR file.
2. Open its portalapp.xml file and then add the new properties.
3. Redeploy the PAR file.
4. Create the new system.

To make sure that the iViews that were using the old system object continue to use the new one, remove the system alias from the old system object and attach it to the new system object. To prevent the system object from being overwritten during an upgrade, remember to create the new system under a different path other than Portal Content | Content Provided By SAP.

Creating a system requires the following steps:

1. Define the system properties.
2. Edit property attributes, if required.
3. Define a system alias.
4. Define user mapping.
5. Test the connection to the backend application.

System Properties

The following properties are common to all system objects:

- System name
- System type

In Figure 18-1, saplogon is the name of the system object, and SAP_R3 is the name of the system type.

System Aliases

A system can be accessed only through its alias, which is created as a part of the system creation process. The system alias does not appear in the Portal Content Directory (PCD); it can be accessed only through the System Alias Editor by selecting System Aliases under the Display dropdown as shown next:

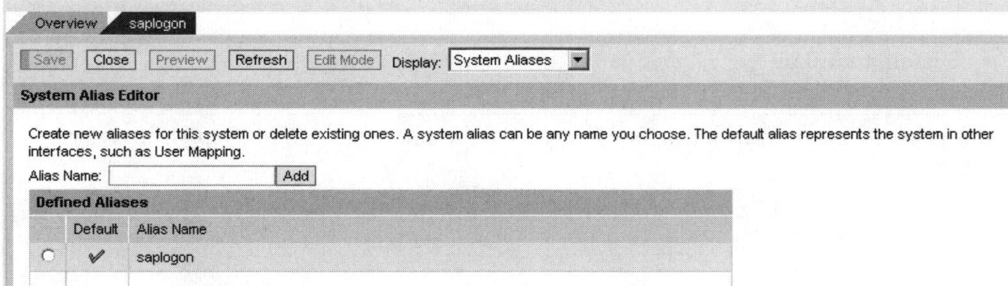

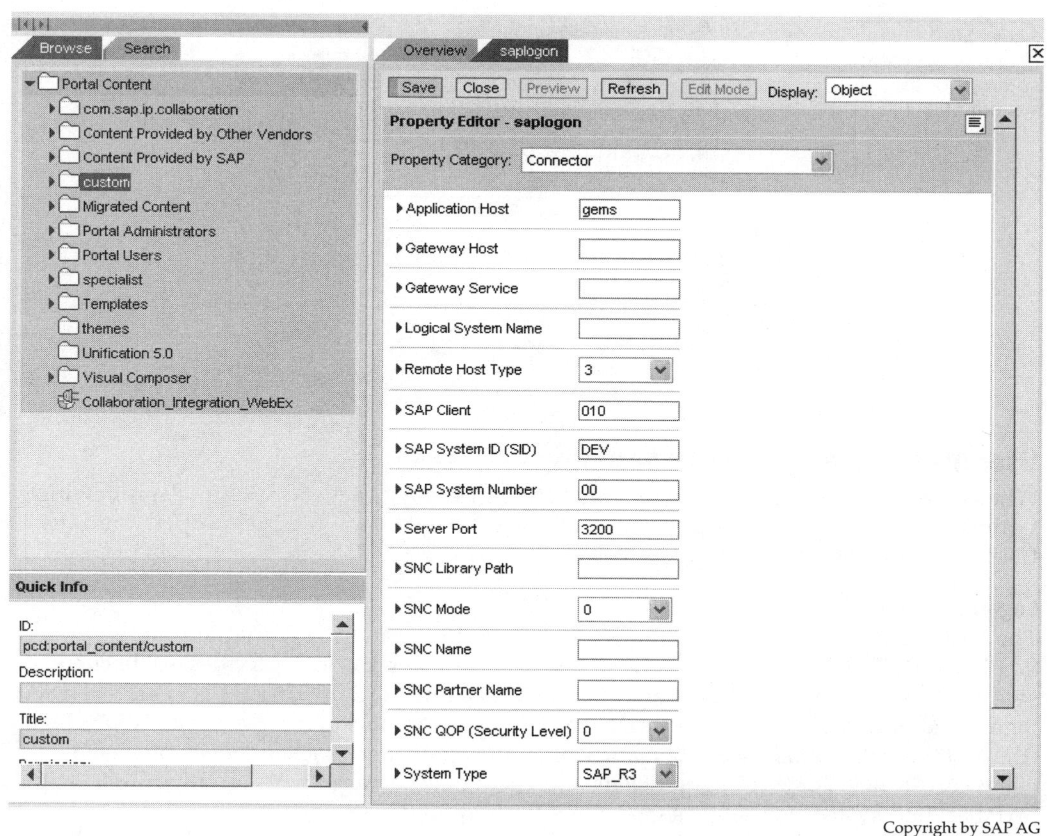

FIGURE 18-1 Property Editor showing saplogon as the system object name and SAP_R3 as the system type

The portal installation software includes a set of predefined system templates for all the connectors it provides. They can be accessed by choosing System Administration | System Configuration in the top-level menu, choosing System Landscape in the detailed navigation menu, and browsing Portal Content | Templates.

NOTE *Changing the template will change the system objects that are based on this template via the inheritance behavior.*

A system should have at least one alias, which can refer only to one system at a time. However, you can have any number of aliases for a given system. When transporting content, the system aliases do not get transported. So the alias should be defined again in the new system to which the content was transported.

When defining the system alias for SAP systems, you should use the same name for the same value that was used for the logical system name in the SAP system to which the connection is being made. The logical system name is maintained in the table T000 in the SAP system.

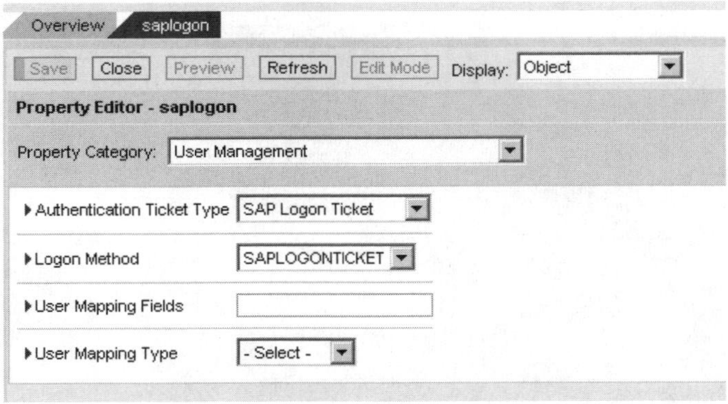

FIGURE 18-2 User Management settings for the system object

User Management Category Settings

When creating the system objects for connecting to an SAP backend system, the following settings are used for the User Management category: the Logon Method property and the User Mapping Type property.

Logon Method

The Logon Method property, as shown in Figure 18-2, can be set to UIDPW, SAPLOGONTICKET, or X509CERT. UIDPW is used when the logon to the SAP backend system uses a user ID and password as credentials. SAPLOGONTICKET is used when SAP logon tickets are used for authenticating against the SAP backend system, and X509CERT (the X.509 certificate) is used when authentication against the backend system is using client certificates. For SAP logon tickets and client certificates to work, configuration of the SAP backend system for single sign-on (SSO) is required.

TIP *The preferred method is to set up the connectivity with the backend system using the UIDPW and verify the connectivity. You can then change it to an SAP Logon ticket.*

User Mapping Type

The possible values for this property are Admin, User, and Admin/user. User Mapping Type defines who can maintain the user mapping for the system. If admin is selected, only the administrator can maintain the user mapping. The administrator conducts user mapping using the user administration tool. If User is selected, only the end user can maintain the user mapping. The user can implement user mapping using the personalization option in the header area after logging on as a user. If Admin/user is selected, both the administrator and the end user can maintain the user mapping.

Creating an SAP System

Two templates are available for creating an SAP system:

- SAP system with load balancing
- SAP system that uses a dedicated application server

The settings required for creating an SAP system can be broadly defined under the property categories in Connector and User Management. Settings under Internet Transaction Server (ITS) and Web Application Server (WAS) are required for displaying SAP transactions and Business Information Warehouse (BW) reports, respectively.

Under the connector properties are three types of connector settings:

- Application server connection for a single dedicated application server
- Message server connection when load balancing is used
- Connection string connection for connecting using connection string template

Connecting Using a Dedicated Application Server

Figure 18-3 displays the Property Editor screen used for maintaining the connector properties to an SAP backend system.

Following are some of the properties required for connecting to the SAP backend system using a dedicated application server:

- **Application Host** Host name or IP address of the application server
- **Gateway Host** Host name of the gateway server
- **Gateway Service** Service name or port number of the gateway server
- **Logical System Name** Concatenation of System ID + *CLNT* + Client number (for example, XYZCLNT030)
- **SAP Client** Client number of the SAP backend system, such as 001

FIGURE 18-3 Typical connector properties for connecting to SAP backend system

- **SAP System ID** Three-digit system ID, such as D11
- **SAP System Number** Instance number of the SAP backend system, such as 01
- **Server Port** Port number of application server: *32* + SAP System Number (for example, 3201)
- **System Type** Type of SAP system, such as SAP_R3, SAP_BW, or SAP_CRM

NOTE *The gateway host and service properties can be maintained here when the R/3 gateway host and port number or service are not maintained in the C:\WINNT\system32\drivers\etc\services file or if the values are incorrectly maintained from the actual R/3 gateway values.*

Following are the steps involved for creating a system object when connecting to the SAP R/3 backend system using the dedicated application server:

1. In the top-level menu of the portal, navigate to System Administration | System Configuration and select System Landscape in the detailed navigation menu.
2. Navigate to the custom folder where you want to store the custom object. If the custom folder has not been created, create a new one.
3. Right click the custom folder and choose New | System (from template).
4. In the Step 1: Template Selection screen of the System Wizard, choose the SAP System Using Dedicated Application Server radio button as shown below. Then click Next.

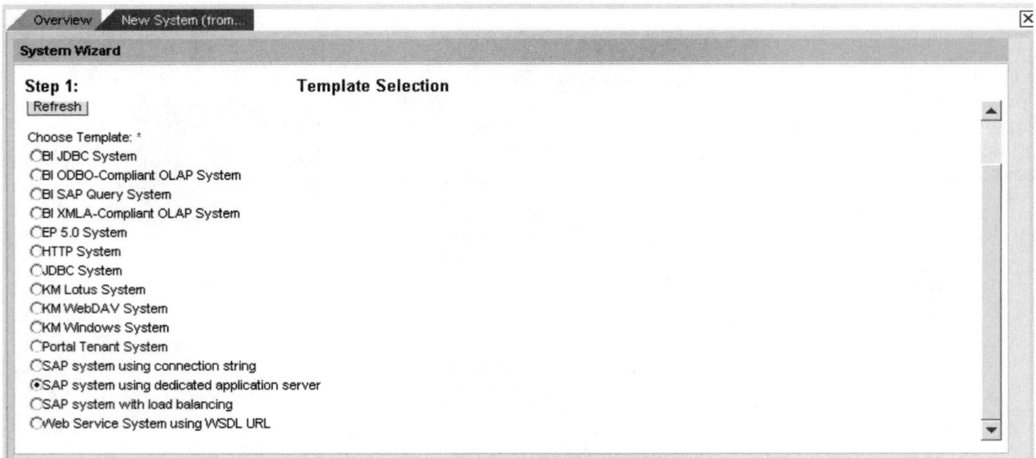

Copyright by SAP AG

5. In the Step 2: General Properties screen of the System Wizard, enter the System Name, System ID, and System ID prefix (optional). Then click Next.
6. Click Finish in the Step 3: Summary screen.

7. Click OK to open the system object for editing.
8. In the Property Editor screen, select Connector from the Property Category drop-down list, and enter the following values:
   - Application Host: gems <enter your application server host name>
   - Remote Host Type: 3 <choose '3' for R3 system, 'E' for an external system>
   - SAP Client: 010 <enter your SAP client number>
   - SAP System ID: DEV <choose your SAP system ID>
   - SAP System Number: 00 <enter your SAP system number>
   - Server Port: 3200 <port number of your application server>
   - SNC Mode: 0
   - SNC QOP (Security Level): 0
   - System Type: SAP_R3
9. In the Property Editor screen, select User Management from the Property Category drop-down list. Enter the following values:
   - Authentication Ticket Type: SAP Logon Ticket
   - Logon Method: UIDPW
   - User Mapping Fields <leave this empty; required only if you use additional fields for user mapping purposes>
   - User Mapping Type: admin, user
10. Click Save.
11. In the Property Editor screen, select System Aliases from the Property Category drop-down list.
12. Enter the Alias Name as SAP_R3.
13. Click Add. Click Save and then click Close.

If the portal user is not the same as the SAP backend user, you must set up User Mapping as shown next:

1. Navigate to User Management | Identity Management in the top-level menu of the portal. Enter the user you are going to use for connecting to the backend system.
2. Click Go.
3. Select the checkbox next to the user. Click Modify, and navigate to the User Mapping For System Access tab in the User Details screen.
4. In the System Selection screen, select the system object created in the previous steps and enter the user details such as Mapped User ID and Mapped Password. These user credentials are passed on to the backend system for validation, when the portal user tries to access an iView that fetches data from the backend system.

INFO *Single sign-on to the backend system can be achieved by mapping the portal user ID to the backend user ID. This is achieved by maintaining the Mapped User ID and Mapped Password for the portal user in Identity Management.*

Now you can test the connection to the backend application:

1. Select Connection Tests from the Display drop-down. Three types of system connection tests are available, as shown next:

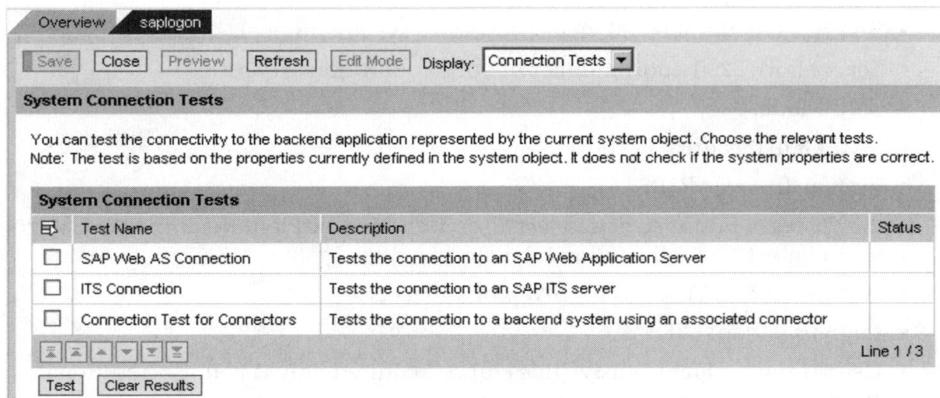

2. Select the checkbox Connection Test For Connectors to test the connection with the SAP R/3 backend system.
3. Click Test.

Message Server Connection with Load Balancing

Following are some of the properties required for connecting to the SAP backend system using a message server with load balancing:

- **Logical System Name** Concatenation of System ID + *CLNT* + Client number (for example, XYZCLNT030)
- **SAP Client** Client number of the SAP backend system
- **R/3Name/System ID** Three-digit system ID
- **Server Port** Any value for a port used by the message server
- **Message Server** Host name or IP address of the server with the central instance
- **System Type** Type of SAP system (for example, SAP_R3, SAP_BW, SAP_CRM)

The system object is created such that it connects to the message server rather than connecting to the application server, as was the case in the preceding example. Following are

the steps for creating a system object to connect to the SAP backend system using the load-balancing approach:

1. Run the System Landscape Wizard by navigating to System Administration | System Configuration in the top-level menu and choosing System Landscape in the detailed navigation menu.
2. Navigate to the custom folder where you want to store the custom object. If the custom folder has not been created, you may create one now.
3. Right click the custom folder and choose New | System (from template).
4. In the Step 1: Template Selection screen of the System Wizard, choose the SAP System With Load Balancing radio button. Click Next.
5. In the Step 2: General Properties screen of the System Wizard, enter the System Name, System ID, and System ID prefix (optional). Then click Next.
6. Click Finish in the Step 3: Summary screen.
7. Click OK to open the system object for editing.
8. In the Property Editor screen, select Connector from the Property Category drop-down list, and enter the following values. You must maintain a different set of properties as compared to the dedicated application server scenario.
   - Message Server: gems <enter name of the message server host>
   - Remote Host Type: 3
   - SAP Client: 010 <enter your SAP client number>
   - SAP System ID: DEV <choose your SAP system ID>
   - Server Port: 3600 <port number of your message server>
   - SNC Mode: 0
   - SNC QOP (Security Level): 0
   - System Type: SAP_R3
   - Trace Mode: 0 < a value of '0' implies that RFC trace is disabled>
9. In the Property Editor screen, select User Management from the Property Category drop-down list and enter the following values:
   - Authentication Ticket Type: SAP Logon Ticket
   - Logon Method: UIDPW
   - User Mapping Fields <leave this empty; required only if you use additional fields for user mapping purposes>
   - User Mapping Type: admin, user
10. Click Save.
11. In the Property Editor screen, select System Aliases from the Property Category drop-down list.
12. Enter the Alias Name as SAP_R3.
13. Click Add. Then click Save and Close.

If the portal user is not the same as the SAP backend user, you must set up User Mapping, as shown next:

1. Navigate to User Management | Identity Management in the top-level menu of the portal. Enter the user name for connecting to the backend system.
2. Click Go.
3. Select the checkbox next to the user. Click Modify and navigate to the User Mapping For System Access tab in the User Details screen.
4. In the System Selection screen, select the system object created in the previous steps and enter the user details such as Mapped User ID and Mapped Password. These user credentials are used by the user ID when logged on to the portal for connecting to the backend system.

Now you can test the connection to the backend application:

1. From the Display drop-down menu, select Connection Tests.
2. Select the checkbox Connection Test for Connectors to test the connection with the SAP R/3 backend system.
3. Click Test.

Connecting Using a Connection String Template

Following are some of the properties required for connecting to the SAP backend system using a connection string.

If you're using a connection string to an application, you can use either a connection string to a dedicated server or a message server. If you're using a connection string to a dedicated server, you can use /H/*<host>*/S/*<port>* (the port is *32* + *<system number>*). If you're using a connection string to a message server, you can use /M/*<message server host name>*/S/*<message server port>*/G/*<logon group>*.

- **Logical System Name** Concatenation of System ID + *CLNT* + Client number (for example, XYZCLNT030)
- **Client** Client number of the SAP backend system
- **R3Name/System ID** Three-digit system ID
- **SAP System Number** Instance number of the SAP backend system
- **System Type** Type of SAP system (SAP_R3, SAP_BW, SAP_CRM)

Connecting to an ITS System

ITS settings are maintained for displaying SAP transactions. Figure 18-4 displays the properties to be maintained for the system object under the Internet Transaction Server (ITS) category.

FIGURE 18-4 ITS settings for the system object

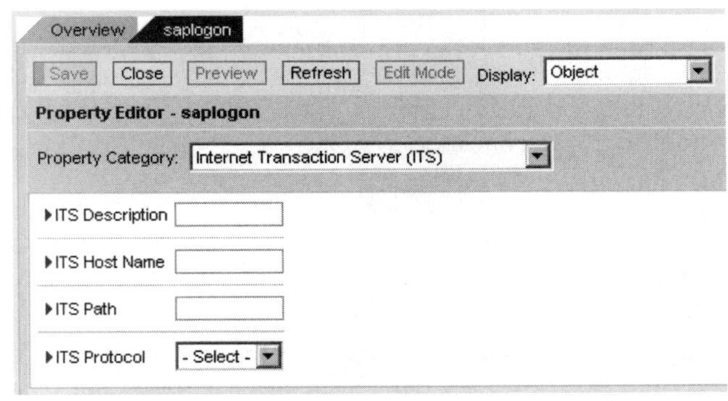

The system object in this is created such that it connects to the Internet Transaction Server. Following are the steps for creating a system object for connecting to an ITS system:

1. Run the System Landscape Wizard by navigating to System Administration | System Configuration in the top level-menu and choose System Landscape in the detailed navigation menu.
2. Navigate to the custom folder where you want to store the custom object. If the custom folder has not been created, create one now.
3. Right click the custom folder and choose New | System (from template).
4. In the Step 1: Template Selection screen of the System Wizard, choose the SAP System Using Connection String radio button. Then click Next.
5. In the Step 2: General Properties screen of the System Wizard, enter the System Name, System ID, and System ID prefix (optional). Then click Next.
6. Click Finish in the Step 3: Summary screen.
7. Click OK to open the system object for editing.
8. In the Property Editor screen, select Internet Transaction Server (ITS) from the Property Category drop-down list, and enter the following values. You must maintain a different set of properties as compared to the dedicated application server scenario.
   - **ITS Description** Any description
   - **ITS Host Name** <host> 8002 (this value can be found under transaction SMICM: choose Go To | Services and find the host and port for the HTTP service)
   - **ITS Path** /scripts/wgate for the ITS 6.20; should be left blank for ITS 6.40
   - **ITS Protocol** HTTP or HTTPS
9. In the Property Editor screen, select System Aliases from the Property Category drop-down list.
10. Enter the Alias Name as SAP_R3.
11. Click Add. Then click Save and Close.

If the portal user is not the same as the SAP backend user, you must set up User Mapping as shown next:

1. Navigate to User Management | Identity Management. Enter the user name for connecting to the backend system.
2. Click Go.
3. Select the checkbox next to the user.
4. Click Modify and navigate to the User Mapping For System Access tab in the User Details screen.
5. In the System Selection screen, select the system object created in the preceding steps and enter the user details such as Mapped User ID and Mapped Password.

Now you can test the connection to the backend application:

1. From the Display drop-down menu, select Connection Tests.
2. Select the checkbox ITS Connection to test the connection with the ITS backend system.
3. Click Test.

Connecting to a Web Application Server for CRM and BW Scenarios

Web AS settings, shown in Figure 18-5, are required for displaying BW reports and for BSP applications in CRM. The system object is created such that it connects to the Web Application Server, which is used by the BSP applications in SAP CRM systems. The Web AS connection is also required for connecting to the SAP BW system for generating reports using the SAP Business Explorer.

1. Run the System Landscape Wizard by navigating to System Administration | System Configuration in the top-level menu of the portal and choose System Landscape in the detailed navigation menu.

FIGURE 18-5 Web AS properties for the SAP system object

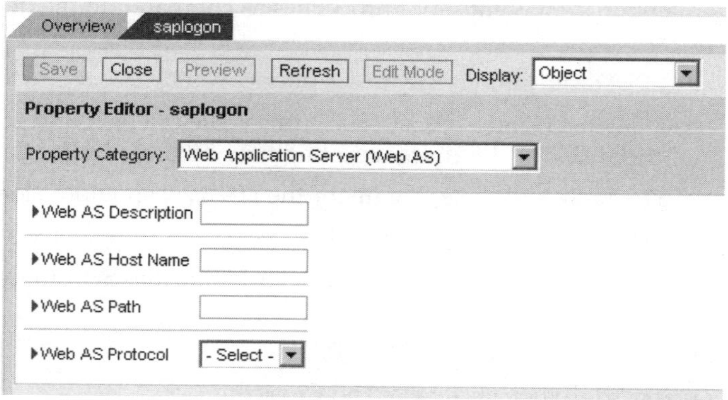

Copyright by SAP AG

2. Navigate to the custom folder where you want to store the custom object. If the custom folder has not been created, create one now.
3. Right click the custom folder and choose New | System (from template).
4. In the Step 1: Template Selection screen of the System Wizard, choose the SAP System Using Dedicated Application Server or SAP System With Load Balancing radio button. Click Next.
5. In the Step 2: General Properties screen of the System Wizard, enter the System Name, System ID, and System ID prefix (optional). Then click Next.
6. Click Finish in the Step 3: Summary screen.
7. Click OK to open the system object for editing.
8. In the Property Editor screen, select Web Application Server (WAS) from the Property Category drop-down list, and enter the following values:
   - **WAS Description** Any meaningful description for the Web AS system
   - **WAS Host Name** <host> 50060 (this value can be found under transaction SMICM: choose Go To | Services and find the host and port for the HTTP service)
   - **WAS Path** This could be sap/bc/bsp/sap for CRM applications and sap/bw/bex for BW applications; to check for this value, go to transaction code SICF in the SAP system
   - **WAS Protocol** HTTP or HTTPS
9. In the Property Editor screen, select System Aliases from the Property Category drop-down list.
10. Enter the Alias Name as SAP_R3, SAP_CRM, or SAP_BW—or anything you prefer.
11. Click Add. Click Save and then click Close.

If the portal user is not the same as the SAP backend user, you must set up User Mapping as shown next:

1. Navigate to User Management | Identity Management in the top-level menu. Enter the user name for connecting to the backend system.
2. Click Go.
3. Select the checkbox next to the user. Click Modify and navigate to the User Mapping For System Access tab in the User Details screen.
4. In the System Selection screen, select the system object created in the previous steps and enter the user details such as Mapped User ID and Mapped Password.

Now you can test the connection to the backend application:

1. From the Display drop-down list, select Connection Tests.
2. Select the checkbox SAP Web AS Connection to test the connection with the Web AS backend system.
3. Click Test.

Configuring a JDBC System

When configuring a JDBC system, you need to provide the connection properties for the backend JDBC system, as shown in Figure 18-6. The two most important properties are

- Connection URL
- Driver Class Name

The JDBC driver is also installed as part of the portal installation. This driver is capable of connecting with MS SQL, Oracle, and DB2 backend systems.

For the MS SQL Server, you'd use the following values:

- **URL** jdbc:sap:sqlserver://<*server*>:<*port*>;DatabaseName=<*database_name*> (for example, jdbc:sap:sqlserver://localhost:1433;DatabaseName=Northwind)
- **Driver** com.sap.portals.jdbc.sqlserver.SQLServerDriver

For the Oracle database system, use these values:

- **URL** jdbc:sap:oracle://<*server*>:<*port*>;SID=<*sid*> (for example, jdbc:sap:oracle://localhost:1521;sid=xyz)
- **Driver** com.sap.portals.jdbc.oracle.OracleDriver

For the DB2 server, use these values:

- **URL** jdbc:sap:db2://<*server*>:<*port*>;DatabaseName=<*database_name*> (for example, jdbc:sap:db2:// localhost:5916;DatabaseName=J2E)
- **Driver** com.sap.portals.jdbc.db2.DB2Driver

TIP *If the connection does not work, try replacing the DatabaseName=*<database_name> *with Location=*<database_name> *in the URL.*

You can also use your own JDBC driver, but this requires some configuration steps. First of all, the JDBC driver should be deployed and registered in the Web AS system. Second, the JDBC connector should reference the driver and the portal component that is connecting to the backend system. For more information, refer to OSS Note 773401.

FIGURE 18-6 Connection properties for JDBC system

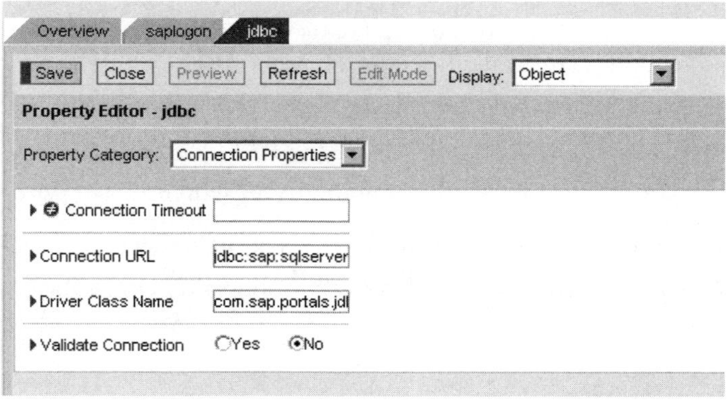

Connectors

Sometimes the portal application may require a middleware component called a *connector* to connect with the backend application. Connectors are basically resource adapters deployed on the Web AS stack and are responsible for managing the connectivity with the backend system. SAP provides an SAP connector and a JDBC connector for the purpose.

iWay Connectors

SAP also has partnered with iWay to provide connectors to PeopleSoft and Siebel from the NetWeaver portal. The iWay connectors can be downloaded from the service marketplace at www.service.sap.com/swdc. Choose Download | Installations and Upgrade | Entry by Application Group | Adapters | for SAP NetWeaver 04 (Portal Edition). The iWay connectors are supported from NetWeaver 04 SPS13 onward.

TIP *Refer to OSS Note 913483 for more information on iWay connectors.*

Testing R/3 Connectivity from an iView

Several tools are available for testing the connectivity to the backend R/3 system.

Connectivity Testing Tool

Navigate to <*drive*>:\usr\sap\J2E\JC01\j2ee\cluster\server0\apps\sap.com\irj\servlet_jsp\irj\root\WEB-INF\deployment\temp folder. Rename the com.sap.portal.unification.connection.tester.par.bak file by removing the .bak extension.

You must log on to the portal as an administrator. The administrator ID should have adequate user mapping and permissions on the corresponding SAP backend system.

Using the portal archive uploader, deploy the PAR file and then access the tool using the following URL: http://<portal_host>:<port>/irj/servlet/prt/portal/prteventname/HtmlbEvent/prtroot/com.sap.portal.unification.connection.tester.TestingConnection. This tool contains four tests, as shown in Figure 18-7.

The following tests can be used:

Connector Gateway Service The Connector Gateway Service can be used to test the connectivity using the system objects that were created in the System Administration menu. This test uses the Connector Gateway Service to connect to the backend system. The Result section provides the complete details of the error or success message. Here is a sample error message for a failed connection:

```
com.sapportals.connector.connection.ConnectionFailedExceptionoccured:Linked
Exception: Connection Failed: Nested Exception. Failed to get connection......
- - - - - -
Nested Exception. Failed in creating the JCO Connection. |Connect to
SAP gateway failed Connect_PM  TYPE=A ASHOST=xyx SYSNR=01 GWHOST=xyz
GWSERV=sapgw01 PCS=1 LOCATION    xyz:sapgw01' not reached TIME
Sat Jun 16 19:51:53
```

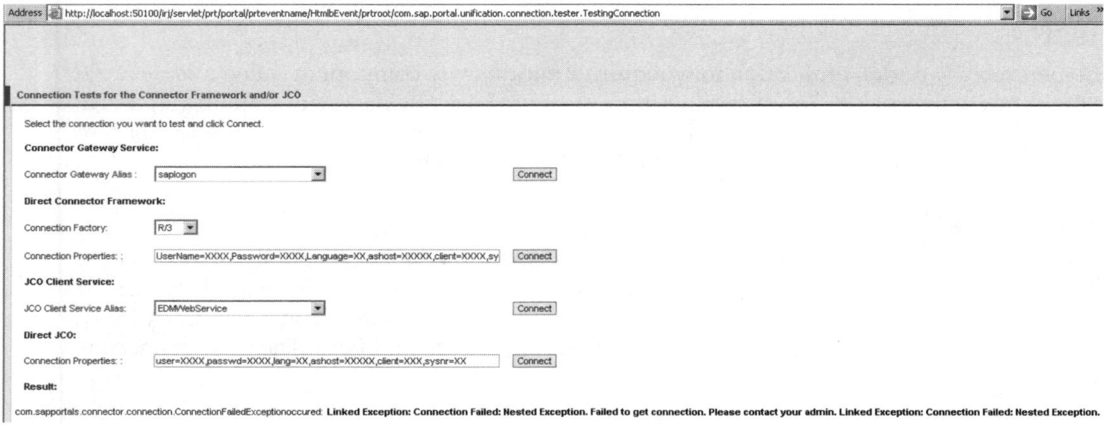

Figure 18-7 Connection tests

Direct Connector Framework This helps you test the connectivity directly with the backend SAP or with the Java Database Connectivity (JDBC) system by passing on the connectivity parameters directly. For an SAP system, you will need to use the following Connection Properties setting:

UserName=XXXX,Password=XXXX,Language=XX,ashost=XXXXX,client=XXXX, sysnr=XX,SystemType=SAP_XX.

For a JDBC system, you will use the following setting:

driver=com.sap.portals.jdbc.sqlserver.SQLServerDriver,url=jdbc:sap:sqlserver://XXXX; DatabaseName=XXXXX,UserName=XXXX,Password=XXXX

JCO Client Service This test is similar to the first test, but it uses the Java Connector (JCO) client service to connect to the backend system.

Direct JCO This test helps to connect to the R/3 system using the JCO client. The following Connection Properties are required:

user=XXXX,passwd=XXXX,lang=XX,ashost=XXXXX,client=XXX,sysnr=XX

Support Platform Tests for Connectivity

The connectivity testing functionality is also available in the Support Platform under Enterprise Portal | Connectors. The support platform can be accessed at http://<host>:<port/sp. Connectivity to the backend systems for system objects that were created in the system landscape editor can be tested. The system objects use the Connectivity Gateway Service for connecting to the backend system. You can also test connectivity to JDBC systems, R3 backend systems, and native JCO connectivity. To test these connections, click the Plug-In

Properties Editor link and enter the connection parameters in the Plug-In Properties dialog box shown next. Click Save And Close and then click Run to test the connectivity:

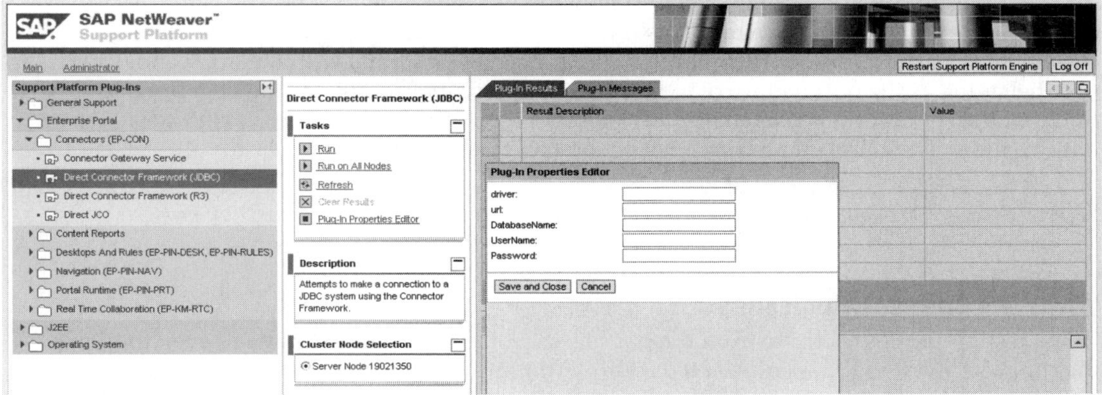

Copyright by SAP AG

Enabling Logging and Tracing for Connectors

Starting with NetWeaver 04 SP9, the default trace file contains error information for the SAP, JDBC, and Web Service connectors. For additional information that may help in troubleshooting, you can change the trace level in the Log Configurator Service in the Visual Admin. After launching the Visual Administrator, navigate to cluster | server | services | Log Configurator. On the right-hand pane, click on the Locations tab under the Runtime tab and navigate to com | SAP | Portal | Connectors. Change the severity from Error to Debug, as shown next:

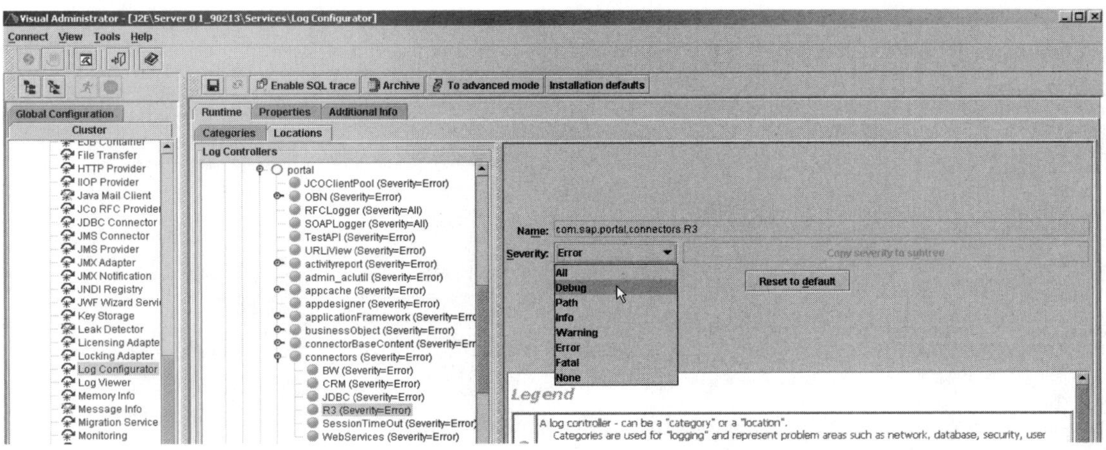

Copyright by SAP AG

Connectivity Issues

Now let's discuss some of the potential issues you may face when setting up the connectivity with the backend systems.

PART IV

Validate Connection Property

This property is useful for situations in which the backend system is behind a firewall. This property tries to validate a physical connection, identifies whether it is broken, and tries to create a new connection if required. This is useful for scenarios in which the firewall may close a connection after a certain amount of time. This will interfere with the JCO connection pool behavior, as the portal may try to reuse an existing connection from the pool but may find that the connection is broken. If this property is set to True, the portal may try to remove the existing broken physical connection and create a new valid one.

NOTE *Because this validation process is very time consuming, the Validate connection property should be set to True only if this is really needed.*

WAS/ITS Connectivity Issues

When testing the connectivity from the portal server, the connectivity may fail even though the connectivity from the iView succeeds during runtime. This could be because during runtime, the client browser's proxy settings may be used, but while testing the system object in the portal, the portal server's proxy settings may be used. Alternatively, the test succeeds simply because the backend system was successfully reached even though the user is not successfully authenticated in the SAP backend system.

To resolve the proxy setting issue on the portal, set up the proxy setting on the portal side under System Administration | System Configuration in the top-level menu and choose Service Configuration in the detailed navigation menu. Then navigate to Applications | com.sap.portal.ivs.httpservice | services | proxy, as shown next. Right click on proxy and choose Configure. In the screen shown next, enter the appropriate values for the proxy server through which the portal should be accessed. In the HTTP - Enable Proxy Setting field, enter 'true' for working through a proxy. In the HTTP Proxy Host and HTTP Proxy Port fields, enter the name or IP address and the port of the proxy server, respectively:

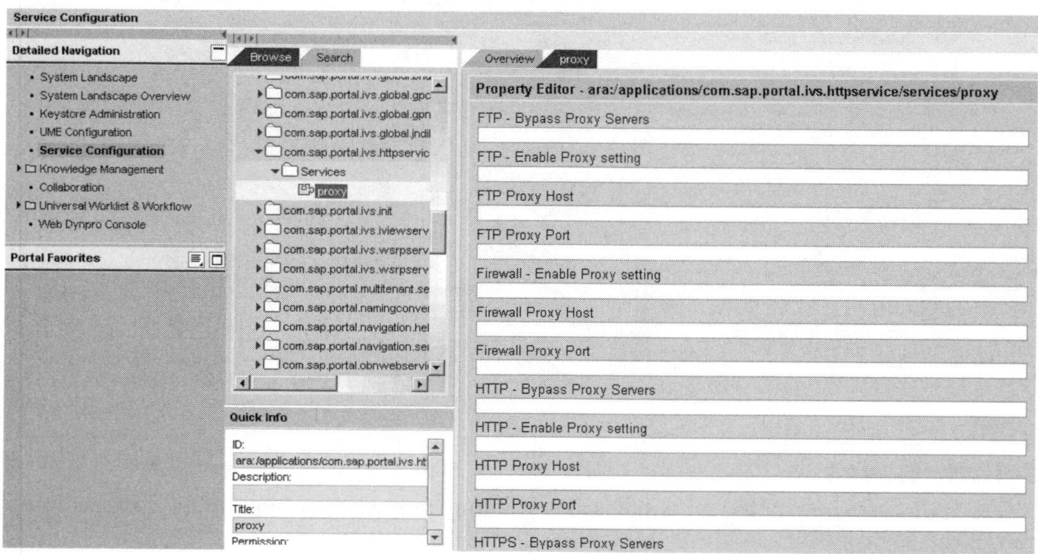

End User Permission

The system object in the portal is used to connect to a backend system and retrieve data from the backend. To retrieve the data, the system object should be assigned with end user permission for that particular user, role, or group that needs to access the backend. In the next screen, shown below, the End User permission for the saplogon system object is assigned for the content_admin_role. This allows the user who has been assigned the content_admin_role role to view the data from the backend system that the system object named saplogon represents.

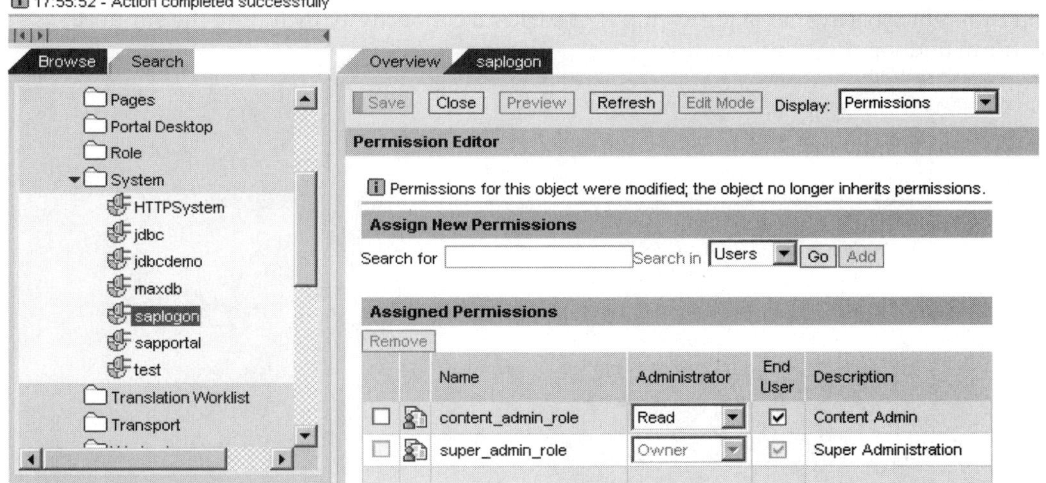

Useful OSS Notes

Following are some useful OSS notes that can be accessed at http://service.sap.com/notes:

- **929093** How to get a traced R/3 connection
- **939588** Combo box is invisible in ACL editor - System and Permission
- **986641** Access denied: Missing 'End User' permission for system
- **1004550** Identity Management applications with poor performance
- **944095** ITS/WAS connection test fails
- **1004116** Wrong behavior of inverse user mapping in specific scenario

NOTE *For more details, refer to the system administration related resources listed in Appendix B.*

PART IV

Summary

In this chapter, you learned about the importance of system objects, the portalapp.xml file, system properties, and system aliases. You learned the various steps involved in defining a system object to connect to an SAP system and a JDBC system. You discovered the three different ways to connect to an SAP backend system and walked through the different properties to be maintained for each one of the connection types—namely, a dedicated SAP application server, a load balanced SAP system, and connection using string template. You also learned about setting up the User Management settings, ITS settings, and WAS settings for connecting to SAP CRM and SAP BW. You learned about the typical connectivity issues and different tools available for testing R/3 backend connectivity including the support platform and logging configuration.

CHAPTER 19

Implementing Federated Portals

The increasing trend toward globalization has spurred a proliferation of portals as well as multiple ownerships that are created to serve various departments and geographical regions. As a result, users must maintain logins to a number of portals to access a variety of content. By implementing a federated portal network, you can help increase the user productivity by providing a central login to all the portals in the system landscape. This chapter discusses some of the benefits of federated portals and covers some of the steps required to configure them. You will also learn about the different methods such as remote role assignment, remote delta links, remote application integration, and WSRP-compliant content integration for implementing federated portal networks.

You can implement a global portal in different ways. Prior to NetWeaver 2004s, you could create one central portal that connects to all the required backend systems. This is the simplest form of global portal because it consists of only one portal.

Beginning with NetWeaver 2004s, the *Federated Portal Network* (FPN) allows more than one portal installation to share content. Two options are available to implement the FPN: *Content Federation* and *Portal Federation*.

Content Federation

With Content Federation, centralized access is available to the portal network, but the content can be produced and maintained in more than one portal installation. The portal accessed by users to log on centrally is known as the *consumer portal*, which redirects the incoming requests to the *producer* portals, where the required content is available. The benefit of Content Federation is the separation of application execution from that of content rendering. Content reuse is made possible due to the possibility of creating remote roles and remote iViews that are compliant with Web services for remote portlets (WSRP).

Portal Federation

With Federated Portal, a centralized logon is not provided, but every portal installation can behave as a consumer as well as producer portal. The user can log on to any of the portals in the network and access local content in the portal as well as global content available in the other portals.

NOTE *Federated Portal setup is useful in the case of mergers and acquisitions so that both the portals can continue to coexist while still allowing the users to access the content from the counterpart portal.*

Advantages of Federated Portal Network

By using the Federated Portal Network, you need not maintain content redundantly and no content synchronization or transporting content is required from one portal installation to another. An FPN also reduces administrative requirements resulting from consolidation, reuse of portal content, and delegation of portal administration, which leads to reduced Total Cost of Ownership (TCO). You can increase user productivity by providing a single logon to the central portal.

TIP *It is possible to reuse content from non-SAP portals as well, as long as they are WSRP-compliant.*

Content Sharing Modes—Reusing Remote Content

Portal content on the remote producer portal can be reused in the consumer portal using methods such as remote role assignment, remote delta links, remote application integration, and WSRP content sharing. The type of method used to integrate the remote portal content will depend upon on how much portal content needs to reside on the consumer or producer portal as well as whether the content needs to be administered on the consumer or producer portal. Note that both the producer and consumer portals should be running for the FPN to function properly.

NOTE *Content from producer portals that belong to releases prior to SAP NetWeaver 7.0 SPS 09 cannot be used to form a Federated Portal Network.*

Remote Role Assignment

Reusing portal content is made possible by implementing remote role assignment in the local portal installation. Starting with SAP NetWeaver 7.0 SPS09, you can use the conventional User Management Engine (UME) tool to assign remote roles. The role and the role content are maintained in the producer portal. This option is ideal when you do not want to change the content provided by the producer portal. The content is maintained and executed on the producer portal itself. The only content administration activity you would want to carry out on the consumer portal is to merge the remote roles with the local roles on the consumer portal. You need to assign the users on the consumer portal to the remote roles that exist on the producer portal.

NOTE *Starting from SAP NetWeaver SPS 13, it is possible to transport remote role assignments.*

Remote Delta Links

The other option available to share content is the *remote delta links* method, which is available since SAP NetWeaver 7.0 SPS 10. Remote content copy involves copying the content provided by a producer portal and localizing it for use in the consumer portal. Using this method, iViews, pages, worksets, and roles can be shared from the producer portal. The administrator in the consumer portal can easily navigate through the Portal Content Directory (PCD) of the producer portal and copy it into the PCD of the consumer for future customization. The copied content is created as a delta link, so any changes to the content in the producer portal are automatically transferred to the content in the consumer portal, provided the content was not modified on the consumer portal. Thus, this content can be reused when you want to include a mix of content both locally maintained as well as globally under one role.

NOTE *Unlike the remote role assignment option, using remote delta links, you can also copy over the role content such as iViews, pages, and worksets from the remote, producer portal into the consumer portal.*

Remote Application Integration

The remote application integration method is basically an extension of the application integrator functionality and is available starting from SAP NetWeaver SPS 13. It is available currently for integrating BI Java applications and reports from the producer portal. The BI application running on the producer portal can be integrated into the consumer portal by creating iViews based on standard SAP templates. Content such as iViews, pages, worksets, and roles continue to be created and administered in the consumer portal. Note that both the producer and consumer portals should be on SAP NetWeaver SPS 13.

WSRP Content Sharing

WSRP content sharing involves creating iViews based on portlets offered by a WSRP 1.0-compliant SAP or non-SAP producer. This functionality is available as of SAP NetWeaver 7.0(2004s) SPS06. The WSRP content continues to run on the producer portal and hence the producer portal should continue to be running for rendering the content. The look and feel of the iView are adapted to the theme of the consumer portal.

NOTE *WSRP content sharing applies only to iViews and cannot be applied to business packages, roles, worksets, pages, and so on. In addition, this can be applied only to basic Java-based iViews and cannot be used for ABAP or Web Dynpro-based iViews.*

Usage Scenarios for FPN

A federated portal network can be composed of multiple producer portals and multiple consumer portals. It can be used in a number of business scenarios such as discussed below.

Business units such as sales, human resources, and finance can maintain their own autonomous portals. Users can log on to a central consumer portal where content from the autonomous portals is integrated as shown in Figure 19-1.

Each business unit can have its own autonomous portal. Whenever users access central content, they can be redirected to a producer portal where the central content is maintained.

Critical and non-critical content can be maintained in different producer portals, so that you can maintain different service-level agreements (SLAs) for the producer portals. The producer portal with critical applications must have higher availability when compared to the producer portal with non-critical content. The consumer portal, however, must be fully available.

You can share content between SAP and non-SAP WSRP-compliant portals. The SAP NetWeaver Portal can be used either as a consumer or a producer.

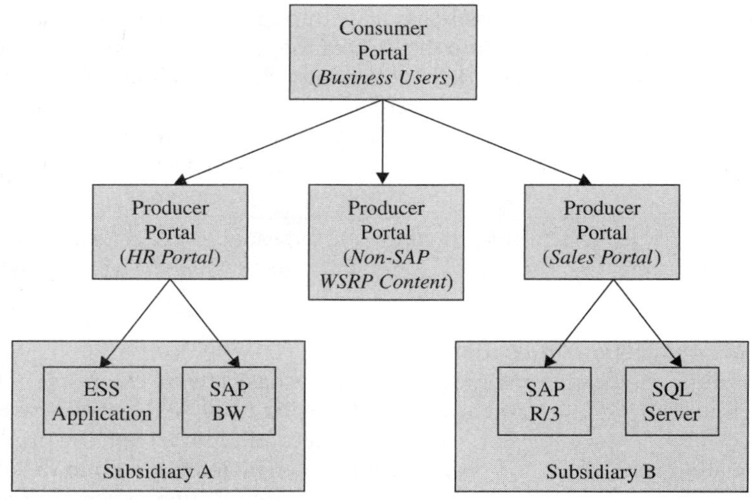

FIGURE 19-1 One-to-many federated portal

In some cases, you may be forced to use different versions of business packages because you need to implement functionality from both versions. In such situations, you can have producer portals with content from the different business packages.

NOTE *For more information, refer to the central OSS Note 880482 for Federated Network Portal (SAP Net Weaver 7.0).*

You can have a single producer portal, where all global content such as corporate-level content can be maintained centrally. This content can then be accessed by other divisions of the company using their own portals as shown in Figure 19-2.

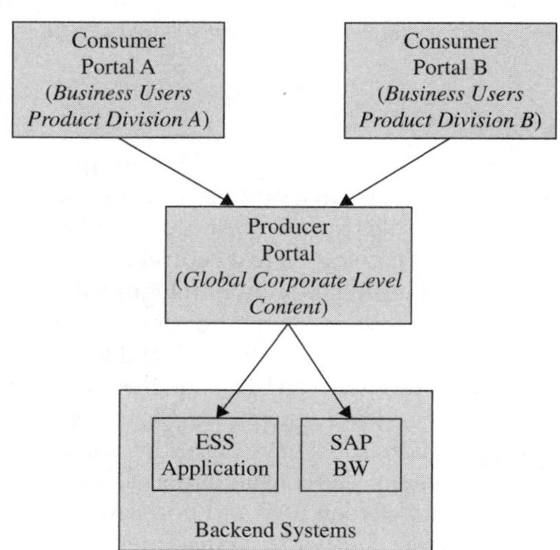

FIGURE 19-2 Many-to-one federated portal

Configuring a Federated Portal

Several configuration steps are required for setting up a federated portal before content sharing can occur between the producer and the consumer portals. Setting up a trust between the producer and consumer portals and registering the consumer are some of the basic configuration steps required.

Setting Up a Trust Between the Producer and the Consumer

First of all, you need to set up a trust between the producer and the consumer so that the users on the consumer portal can be authenticated against the producer portal when accessing content. Note that the user IDs should exist on both the consumer and producer portals and they should be the same. The user IDs should be same because FPN uses SAP logon tickets for authentication between the producer and consumer portals. Also note that when using SAP logon tickets, you may run into problems if you have portals belonging to different subdomains. In those situations, you will have to configure the DNS to address the same portal with different domain names or configure the portal to send logon tickets for different domains to the browser. Refer to OSS notes 654982 and 654326 as well as SAP Help documentation for help on configuring logon tickets for multiple domains.

When implementing remote content sharing using the remote role assignment technique, you will need to establish a two way trust between the producer and consumer. This ensures that content sharing can occur in both directions. For example, when you delete the producer role in the producer portal, the remote role assignment on the consumer portal for the users is also deleted automatically.

TIP *This trust is important only for transferring content between SAP portals.*

Download the Portal Server Certificate from the Consumer Portal The portal server certificate file (verify.der) should be downloaded from the consumer portal and must be imported into the producer portal. Figure 19-3 shows how to download a portal server certificate.

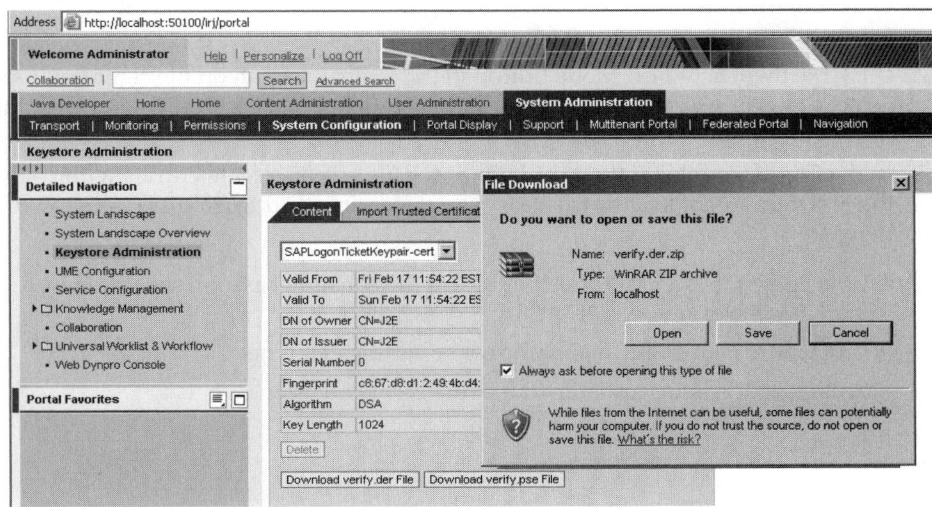

FIGURE 19-3 Downloading a portal server certificate

As shown in Figure 19-3, in the Content tab, click Download verify.der File button and save the verify.der.zip file into your local folder.

Import the Portal Server Certificate into the Producer Portal After you have downloaded the portal server certificate from the consumer portal, log on to the producer portal to import the certificate. Navigate to System Administration | System Configuration in the top-level menu of the producer portal and select Keystore Administration in the detailed navigation menu. Select the Import Trusted Certificate tab and click Browse to select the verify.der file downloaded from the consumer portal, and click Upload, as shown next:

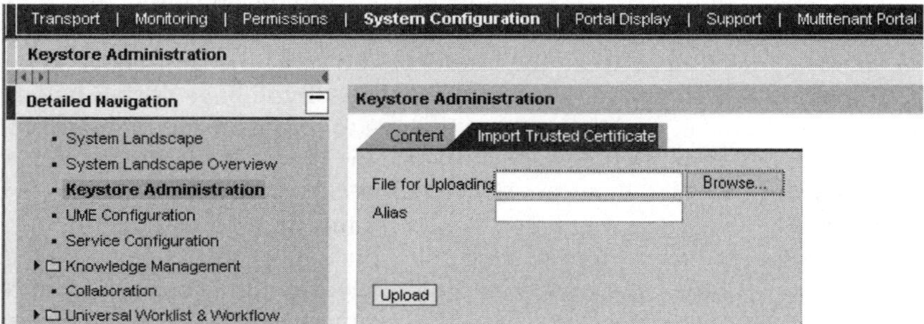

Configure the Trust on the Producer Portal To configure the trust on the producer portal, do the following:

1. Log on to the Visual Administrator belonging to the producer portal.
2. Navigate to Cluster | Server Node | Services | Security Provider.
3. Open the Runtime and then Policy Configuration tabs. Select Ticket from the Components list.
4. Click the Switch To Edit Mode button in the toolbar section on the right-hand side. Select com.sap.security.core.server.jaas.EvaluateTicketLoginModule and click the Modify button.
5. In the Options table on the Edit Login Module screen, create entries with the appropriate values for trustedsys1, trusteddn1, and trustediss1, as shown here:
    - trustedsys1: System ID and client ID of the consumer portal, separated by a comma (for example, C2D, 000)
    - trusteddn1: Distinguished name of the certificate owner
    - trustediss1: Distinguished name of the certificate issuer

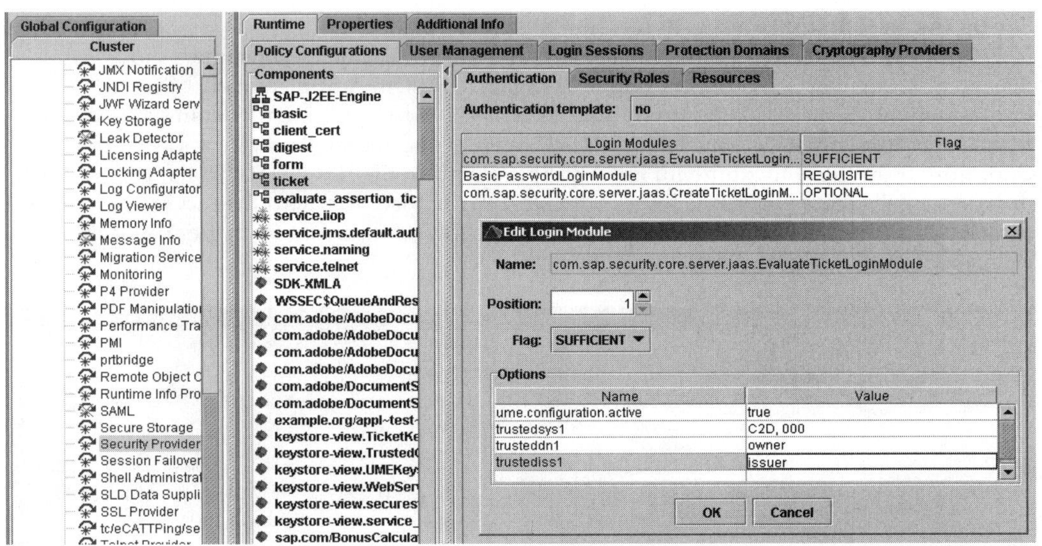

HINT *If more than one consumer exists, enter values for trusteddn2, trustediss2, trustedsys2, and so on.*

Configuring the User Persistence Stores

The users that exist on the consumer portal should also exist on the producer portal. The best way to accomplish this is to use the same central user store for the consumer and the producer portals. Another alternative is to ensure that the user data are duplicated in the different user stores to which the portals point. Using SAP logon tickets to log on to the different portals is a recommended approach to achieving single sign-on (SSO) between the portal systems.

HINT *If the user stores are of different persistence types—for example, LDAP, ABAP, and so on—refer to OSS Note 880482.*

Configure the Proxy Settings

If you are using a proxy server that manages the traffic that leaves your company firewall, you may need to configure the proxy server settings for both the consumer and the producer portals.

To do this, go to System Administration | System Configuration | Service Configuration. Navigate to the com.sap.portal.ivs.httpservice application in the portal catalog. Then open the proxy service, enter the proxy details, and save and restart the service. To restart the service, right click on com.sap.portal.ivs.httpservice application and choose Administrate. In the Application Details screen, click on the Restart link.

NOTE *Before implementing a federated portal network, ensure that the version of the consumer portal is either higher or equal to the version of the producer portal. When you try to implement client-side eventing, if the latest API is not available and if the functionality implemented in that missing API is called, you may run into problems.*

Set Up the Registration Password for the Consumer Portal

If you want increased security, you can register a password that all the consumers should enter when registering with the producer portal. Navigate to System Administration | System Configuration | Service Configuration, and then navigate to Applications | com.sap.portal.ivs.wsrpservice application | Services. Right click AutoGenProducer1_0 service and select Configure from the context menu. Enter the password in the REGISTRATION_PASSWORD property, as shown next. Save, close, and restart the service. To restart the service, right click on com.sap.portal.ivs.wsrpservice application and choose Administrate. In the Application Details screen, click on the Restart link.

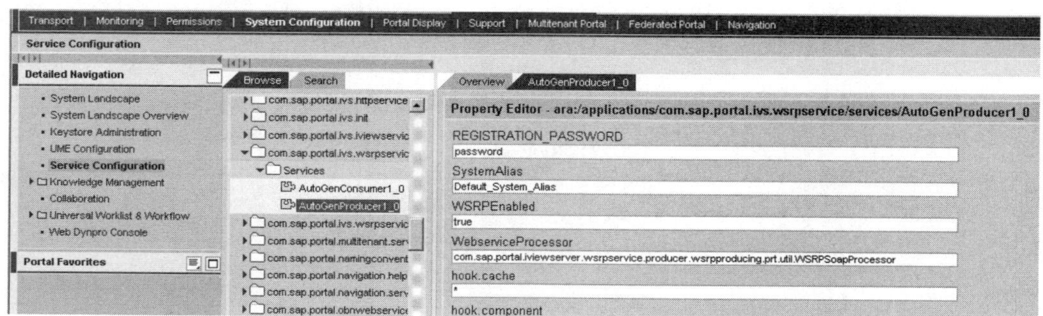

Copyright by SAP AG

Configure Caching on the Consumer Portal

Enabling caching on the consumer portal can help reduce the traffic between the consumer and the producer portals. Caching can also occur on the producer portal, but you have no control over it.

To enable caching, do the following:

1. Go to System Administration | System Configuration | Service Configuration.
2. Navigate to Applications | com.sap.portal.ivs.global.gpcache application | Services. Right click on FederatedPortalCache and select Configure. Edit the cachePersistency, maxCacheSize, and maxValidityPeriodInSec properties of the FederatedPortalCache service, as shown next.

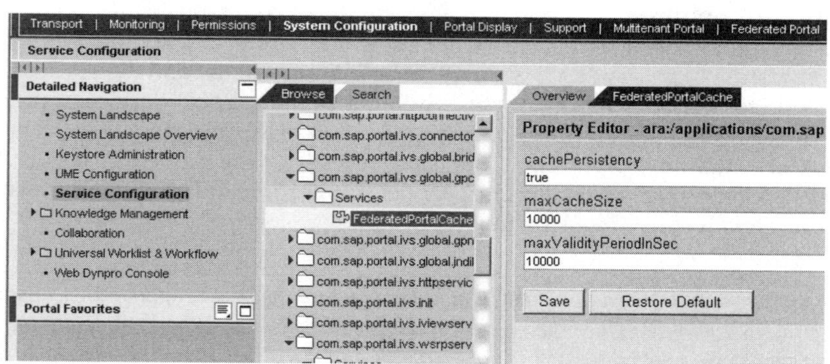

Copyright by SAP AG

If the content in the producer portal is dynamic, reduce the maxValidityPeriodInSec value. Setting the cachePersistency to true means caching data are stored in both the memory and the database. If cachePersistency is set to false, only memory caching is active. Retrieving cache data from a database may impact performance.

3. Save, close, and restart the service. To restart the service, right click on com.sap .portal.ivs.global.gpcache application and choose Administrate. In the Application Details screen, click on the Restart link.

TIP *Since the cache properties are set manually, you should be careful to ensure that the portal performance is not impacted due to improper settings.*

To update the cache lifetime property, do the following:

1. Go to System Administration | Federated Portal in the top-level menu of the consumer portal. Select Myself as Content Consumer | Configure My Consumer Profile in the detailed navigation menu.
2. Define the Validity Period for Objects Cached in the Portal Catalog (seconds) property. If the value is negative or 0, the setting in the maxValidityPeriodInSec takes over; if not, the value entered here will be effective.
3. You may need to clear the remote role assignment cache due to changes made on the producer portal. To do so, click Clear Cache.

When you are using remote role assignment, the role and its navigation structure are cached on the consumer. When using remote delta links, the shared portion of the PCD in the producer portal is cached. At the same time, the producer caches the remote delta link content that was modified on the consumer to reduce the round trips between the consumer and the producer portals.

Optimizing the Consumer Profile

To improve the performance even more, you can optimize the consumer profile by configuring the OptimizerC service of the com.sap.portal.ivs.global.jndibridge application. In the Property Editor - ara:/applications/com.sap.portal.ivs.global.jndibridge/services/OptimizerC screen, enter the value for the Languages To Be Retrieved By The Application field, such as en;enUS. Then enter the full URL of the portal under the My Portal Address property. Activating this service enables caching to occur on the consumer portal instead of the client browser.

Setting Up Permissions for the Content

As a part of the configuration steps, you should provide the appropriate administrator and end user permissions on the portal content objects, depending on the type of content sharing techniques used. In the case of remote role assignment (RRA), the administrators should be provided with role assigner permission for roles. For the users to view iViews during runtime, the end user permission should be enabled for the iViews, pages, and layouts.

If the business user displays an iView that connects to a backend system, that system object should be assigned end user permission for that business user.

In the case of remote delta links, the business user should be assigned with end user permission for all the portal objects on the producer for which the delta links need to be created. The content administrator should have read permission to the remote content so that he or she can create remote delta links.

In the case of WSRP application sharing mode, the business user should have end user permission for the portal component on the producer that gets executed by the proxy-to-portlet iView on the consumer. The iView or the folder containing the iView should have administrator read permission for the portal content on the producer so that the administrator can create proxy-to-portlet iViews based on them. The administrator should have end user enabled so that he or she can preview the iViews.

Registering the Consumer

Suppose role A exists in the producer portal with all the necessary content added to it. Your objective is to add this role into the consumer portal so that you can assign remote roles to the users to access the content in the producer portal. To do that, you need to create a connection from the consumer to the producer portal.

1. Log on to the Consumer Portal and navigate to System Administration | Federated Portal in the top-level menu. Navigate to Myself as Content Consumer | Manage My Producers.
2. Right click NetWeaver Content Producer and select New | NetWeaver Content Producer, as shown next:

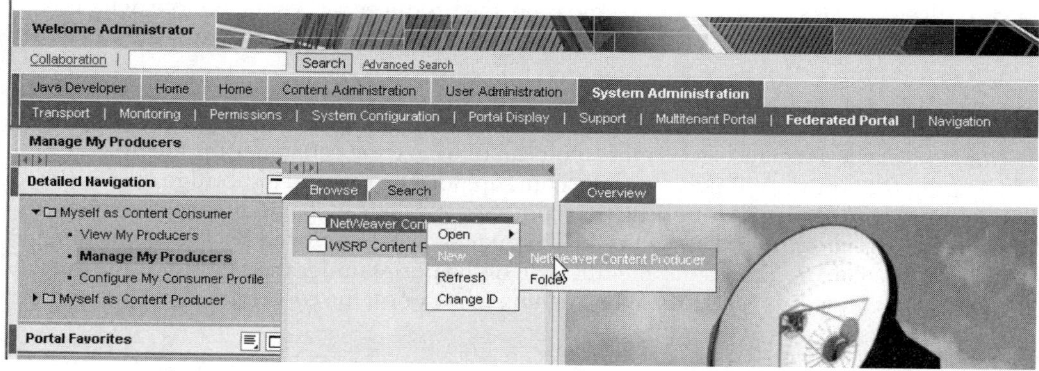

Copyright by SAP AG

3. Enter the required parameters such as Protocol, Host Name of the producer portal, Port as shown next, and then click Next and then Finish.

Overview | New SAP Producer

Producer Wizard

Step 2: **Define Producer URL**

Specify the full URL of the NetWeaver content producer. The URL must point to the WSDL definition file of the Web Services for Remote Portals (WSRP) service exposed by the producer you are connecting to.

Either enter the protocol, host name, and port (the wizard will construct the URL by inserting these parameters before the path of the WSDL definition file) or enter the entire URL yourself.

(•) Enter connection parameters for wizard to construct full URL to WSDL file

Protocol: * http

Host Name: * gems

Port: 50100

Path to WSDL Definition File: /irj/portalapps/com.sap.portal.ivs.wsrpservice/wsdl/wsdl.html

Edit | Reset Default

( ) Enter full URL to WSDL file of NetWeaver content producer

Full URL to WSDL Definition File:

Cancel | Back | Next > | Finish

4. In the Display drop-down, choose Connection Tests to test the connection to the producer portal from the consumer portal. Choose the checkbox and click the Test button:

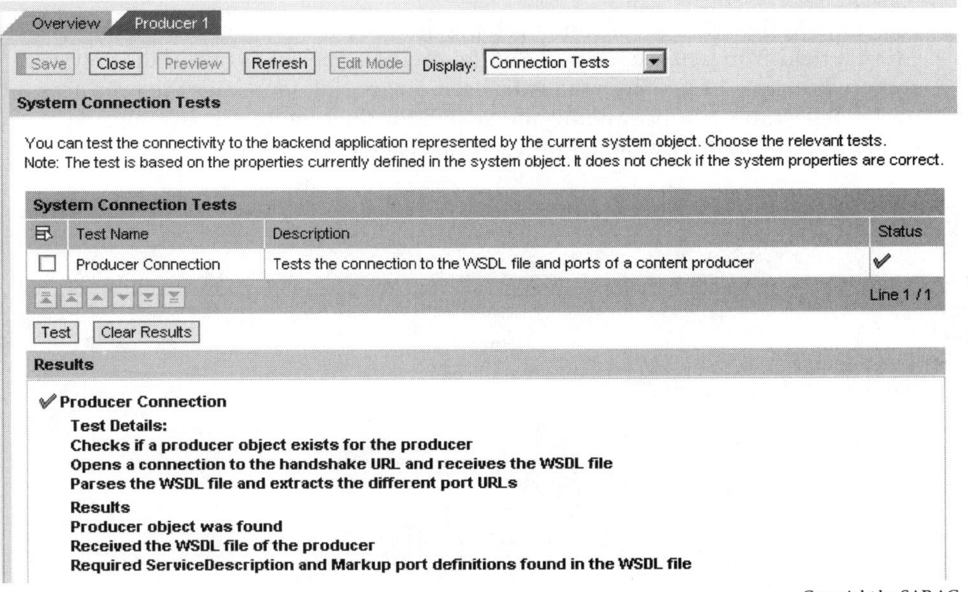

5. Once the connection to the producer has been tested successfully, you can register the consumer with the producer. Then choose Producer Registration from the Display drop-down, as shown here:

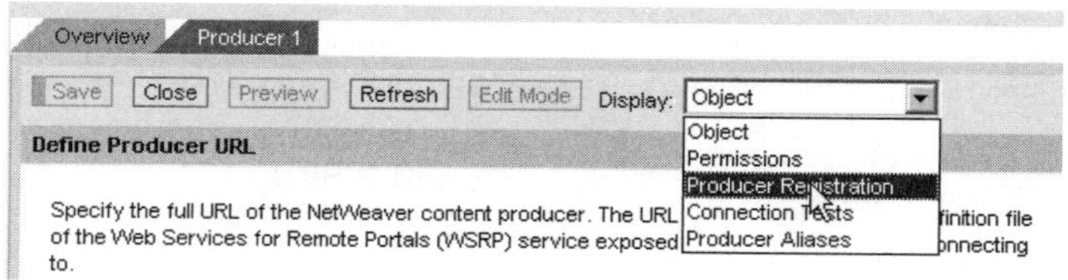

Copyright by SAP AG

6. Enter suitable values in the Your Consumer Name and Your Consumer URL fields and click Register. The Status message 'You are registered on the producer' will appear if registration was successful.

Remote Role Assignment to the User in the Consumer Portal

The next step is to assign the remote role to a user in the consumer portal. You can use similar steps to those you normally use to assign a role to the user.

1. Go to User Administration | Identity Management in the top-level menu of the consumer portal, enter the user name, and click Go.
2. When the user name appears, select the user by clicking on the leftmost cell in the row and click Modify.
3. Select the Assigned Roles tab and click the dropdown menu against the Search Criteria field. You will see the name of the producer portal as one of the entries as shown in Figure 19-4, where the entry 'remote_portal' identifies the producer portal. Select the producer name and search for the remote role by entering a suitable value in the Available Roles section. Then click Go.

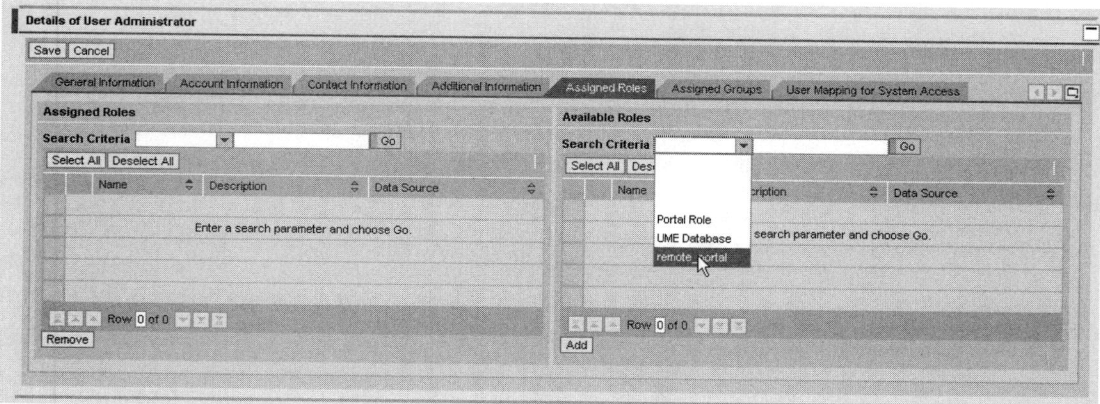

Copyright by SAP AG

FIGURE 19-4 Displays the producer object entry in the dropdown for role source

4. Once the required role is found, click the Add button in the Available Roles section and then click the Save button in the Details section to save the user profile.
5. Log on as the user who has the new role assigned, and check whether you are able to access the content from the remote portal.

Create a Remote Delta Link to Content on the Producer Portal

To be able to create remote delta links, you must have read permission on the producer objects located in the NetWeaver Content Producers and WSRP Content Producers folders.

1. To assign the required permission, navigate to System Administration | Permissions on the top-level menu of the consumer portal and Portal Permissions in the detailed navigation menu. Navigate to NetWeaver Content Producers, right click the Producer for which you want to assign the required permission, and select Open Permissions from the context menu. You can then add the required user and assign the appropriate administrator permission in the Permission editor.
2. You should also assign the required end user permission in both the producer and consumer portals for the producer object and the portal contents (folder, iView, and so on) that are remotely shared.
3. Administrator read permissions should be assigned for administrators in both the producer and consumer portals for the portal content so that they can view the remote content from the producer portal and work with the remote content in the consumer portal.
4. To create the remote delta link, navigate to Content Administration | Portal Content in the top-level menu of the consumer portal. Then navigate to NetWeaver Content Producers | <Producer Object> | Portal Content and continue till you reach the portal content (folder, iView, and so on) you want to copy. Right click the portal content object and select Copy as shown in Figure 19-5, where Remote Portal is the producer object and Remote Content is the remote content available in the producer portal.

PART IV

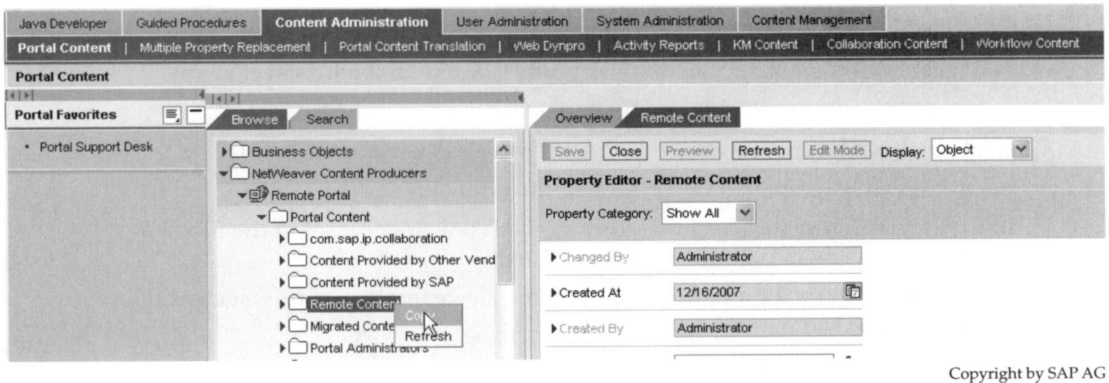

FIGURE 19-5 Displays the Producer Portal and Producer Content

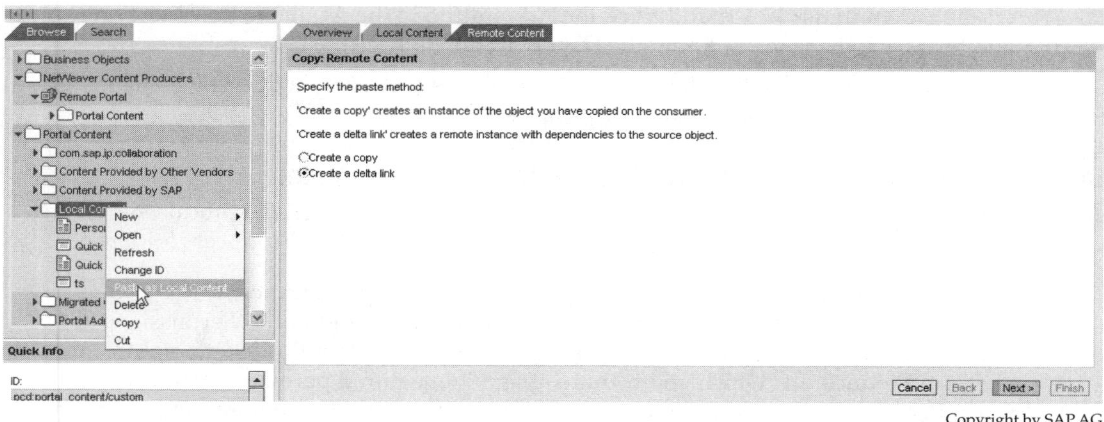

FIGURE 19-6 Displays copying of remote content into consumer portal's custom folder

5. Navigate to the custom folder in the Portal Content Catalog where you want to paste the remote content and select Paste As Local Content from the context menu as shown in Figure 19-6, where Local Content is the custom folder in the consumer portal into which the Remote Content folder from the producer portal is pasted as a delta link.
6. In the Copy: Custom screen, select the Create A Delta Link radio button and click Next.
7. In the Delta Link Confirmation screen, click the Finish button to create the remote delta linked iView.

Creating a Remote Application Integration iView

SAP has provided a standard iView template for creating remote iViews for integrating BI reports into the portal. To create a remote integration iView, do the following:

1. Navigate to Content Administration | Portal Content in the top-level menu.
2. Navigate to the custom folder in the Portal Content Catalog.
3. Right click on the custom folder and select New | iView to create an iView.
4. Select the iView template radio button in the iView Wizard.
5. In the Step 1: Template Selection screen of the iView Wizard, select the BEx Web Application iView radio button and click Next.
6. In the Step 2: General Properties screen, enter the general properties such as iView Name, iView ID, and so on, and click Next.
7. Select the SAP NetWeaver BI radio button in the Step 3: Version of BEx Web Application screen shown next. Click Next.

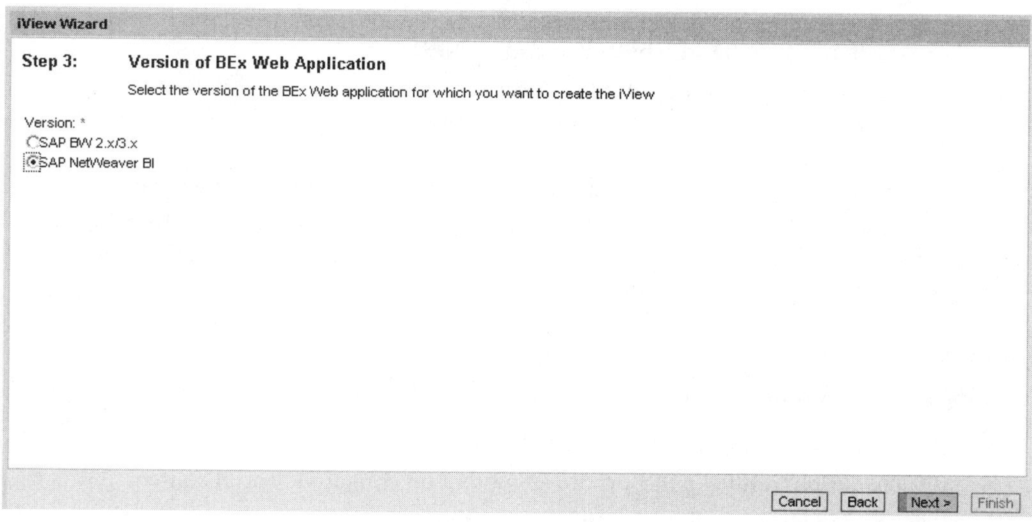

Copyright by SAP AG

8. In the Step 4: BEx Web Application Parameters screen of the iView Wizard, enter the query string for the URL in the BEx Web Application Query String field and click Next.
9. Click Finish in the Summary screen. Click OK to open the object for editing.
10. Click Preview to preview the iView.

Creating Remote Content from a WSRP Producer

Now let's see how to create content from a WSRP producer.

1. Go to System Administration | Federated Portal in the top-level menu and navigate to Myself As Content Consumer | Manage My Producers.
2. Right click WSRP Content Producers and choose New | WSRP Content Producers.
3. In the Step 1: General Properties screen of the Producer Wizard, enter the producer name, ID, and so on, and then click Next.
4. In the Step 2: Define Producer URL screen of the Producer Wizard, enter the URL of the WSDL file—for example, http://wsrp.bea.com/portal/producer?wsdl, in the Full URL To WSDL Definition File field. Click Next and then click Finish. Click OK to open the producer object for editing.
5. From the Display drop-down, choose Producer Registration. Then enter the consumer name and click Register.
6. After you've registered, go to Content Administration | Portal Content.
7. Open your custom folder and right click to select New | iView from the Context menu.
8. In the iView wizard, Select the iView Template radio button and click Next.

9. In the Step 1: Template Selection screen of the iView Wizard, select the Proxy-to-Portlet iView (WSRP) radio button and click Next.
10. In the Step 2: Select The Content Producer screen of the Proxy-To-Portlet iView Wizard, select the content producer created previously for the WSRP content and click Next.
11. In the Step 3: Select Portlets screen, select the portlets and then click Finish.
12. Go to the folder in Content Administration again and you will see that the iViews for the various portlets that you selected have been created automatically. Click Preview to view all the iViews.

Useful OSS Notes

Following are some useful OSS notes that can be accessed at http://service.sap.com/notes:

- **880482** Central Note: Federated Portal Network (SAP NetWeaver 7.0)
- **1105800** FPN: Can't expand producer content on consumer portal content
- **1100834** Inconsistent FPN-Runtime Exception
- **1017308** Federated Portal Network - RRA Permission Problem
- **1076893** Problems with Session Management
- **863837** Central Note for "Multitenant Portal" Scenario (SAP NW2004s)
- **1033804** Blank Page error when trying to login by user with RRA
- **654982** URL requirements due to Internet Standards
- **654326** Domain restrictions in a portal environment
- **701205** Single Sign-On using SAP Logon Tickets

Note *For more details, refer to the federated portal related resources listed in Appendix B.*

Summary

In this chapter, you learned about global portals and the benefits of using the federated portal network. You also learned the two methods available to implement a federated portal network and the differences between the content federation and portal federation methods. Potential scenarios for which federated portal networks can be used were identified, and then the configuration steps required for setting up an FPN were covered. You learned the different techniques available to integrate remote content into the portal such as remote role assignment, remote delta links, remote application integration, and WSRP content integration. You also learned in detail the steps required to implement remote content integration using these techniques.

20

CHAPTER

Implementing External-Facing Portals

External-facing portals are web portals and other Internet portals, such as business-to-business (B2B) and business-to-consumer (B2C) portals, that expose information over the Internet to customers, partners, and employees. When you configure SAP NetWeaver Portal as a public website with better performance and easy-to-use features, it is known as an external-facing portal. In this chapter, you will learn some of the salient features of an external-facing portal and some of the configuration steps involved in setting up and external-facing portal.

Portals were originally created to serve the needs of a company's internal users, but eventually their usefulness became obvious for B2B and B2C Internet scenarios. These expanding portal needs introduced some unique requirements such as performance, security, website-like behavior, and customization. The external-facing portal can be used to implement public web portals that provide anonymous content and self-registration capability to users, and they perform well even in low-bandwidth situations. External-facing portal functionality is available starting with SAP NetWeaver 2004 SPS 14 and SAP NetWeaver 7.0 (2004s) SPS 06.

Features of an External-Facing Portal

An external-facing portal provides some benefits such as improved performance, easy-to-use features, and improved customizability. When compared to a standard portal implementation, an external-facing portal offers improved performance due to the following features:

- *Server-side caching* of navigation hierarchies and nodes eliminate additional server roundtrips.
- The use of *shorter URLs* for a specific navigation node results in reduced network traffic. The shorter URLs are identified by short GUIDs instead of the long, complete navigation path.
- The use of *light framework pages* with lighter navigation iViews and a single frame instead of multiple frames. The light navigation iViews do not use HTMLBusiness for Java (HTMLB) or client-side eventing functionality and hence the large

resource files associated with such functionality are not required to be downloaded. This results in improved performance. Light framework pages can be assigned by administrators using desktop rules at design time.

- A *smarter page builder* downloads only the required libraries when client-side eventing or HTMLB is used.

An external-facing portal offers website-like behavior that puts first-time and one-time users at ease due to the following:

- Lighter framework pages contain only one frame and provide website functionality such as Back, Forward, and Refresh buttons.
- The use of standard, fixed URLs to identify the pages allows the Internet search engines to index the pages. Refer to OSS Note 933452, which discusses how to change the iView's User Supported Agents property so that it allows the user agent of the search engine to access the page for indexing.
- *Quick links* allow you to navigate directly to a specific page on the website. Refer to OSS Note 893855 for information on how to resolve quick link–related issues for anonymous users.
- You can *store a URL as a favorite* and e-mail it to others.

An external-facing portal offers easy customizability of its look and feel due to the following:

- *JSP Navigation tag libraries* help in developing top-level and detailed-level navigation iViews.
- *Layout tag libraries* can be used for developing custom layouts and iView trays.
- *Framework tag libraries* are used for developing masthead and page title bar iViews, creating functions such as logging off, help, and so on.

In addition, an external-facing portal offers a single-portal infrastructure for both internal and external users, resulting in reduced total cost of ownership (TCO) and increased return on investment (ROI). It allows access to the portal under low-bandwidth conditions and using dialup connections, thus providing the ability to serve a larger customer population. Finally, it offers the ability to serve both anonymous and registered users.

Implementing an external-facing portal is not without limitations, however; consider the following:

- Backend sessions may not terminate even if the user logs off from the portal or the application.
- Work protect mode functionality, which detects whether the user has entered any data in the form and whether those data should be saved when the user navigates away from the form to a different location, may not work.
- SAP Web Dynpros, SAP transaction iViews, and business packages that use the Enterprise Portal Client Manager (EPCM) WorkProtect feature may not work properly.
- Remote Role Assignment functionality in Federated Portal Networks may not work.
- Since event handling is not supported, object-based navigation and relative navigation may not work.

- Anonymous users may not be able to access certain pages when short URLs are used. Refer to OSS Note 913367. This issue has been resolved as of NetWeaver 2004 SPS 16 and NetWeaver 2004s SPS 7.
- Collaboration rooms are not supported.
- Other restrictions apply when using KM, related links, personalization iViews, application integrator, and so on.

Due to these limitations , it is not recommended that you use external-facing portals for intranet scenarios.

TIP *Refer to OSS Notes 916545, 709354, 877188, and 853509 for the latest updates.*

Implementing an External-Facing Portal

When implementing an external-facing portal, you should be focused on enabling improved performance and easy-to-use features:

1. The user administrator sets up anonymous logon and self-registration scenarios if required. Refer to the relevant chapters in this book for information on setting up these scenarios.
2. The developer develops light content specifically for use in the external-facing portal. Content created for the external-facing portal should be of static nature as much as possible. Avoid using HTMLB, client-side eventing, out-of-the-box KM iViews, and related links for pages and iViews.
3. The system administrator assigns that content to the users, groups, or roles.
4. The system administrator configures the navigation cache by changing the appropriate J2EE parameter.
5. The developer creates or modifies the light framework page to suit the company requirements for branding, look, and feel.
6. The content administrator customizes the light framework page by replacing the standard navigation iViews with the custom-developed navigation iViews.
7. The system administrator customizes the styles using the Theme Editor.
8. The system administrator assigns the light framework page to the users, groups, or URL alias for accessing light portal using desktop display rules. The users who use the URL for light portal (http://*<host>*:*<port>*/irj/portal/light) will be assigned the light framework page and the users who use the default portal URL will be assigned the default portal desktop.
9. You can implement the relevant network performance improvement techniques mentioned in the guide "Optimizing Network Traffic in EP 6.0."

HINT *When implementing an external-facing portal, you are not required to execute all these steps. You can implement just a few steps and still reap the benefits of an external-facing portal.*

Let's now proceed and set up some of these steps.

PART IV

Configuring the Navigation Cache

The *navigation cache* is a new feature used for caching the set of navigation nodes that have already been accessed by a user. When the next user tries to access the same navigation node, the navigation hierarchy is retrieved from the cache instead of being generated.

Whenever a new entry point is added to the role or when changes are made to the navigation nodes, the navigation cache is deactivated. To view the design-time changes during runtime, you must clear the cache. If you are concerned about performance issues due to clearing the cache, you can synchronize the cache with the Portal Content Directory (PCD) after the change is made.

NOTE *By default, the navigation cache is turned off.*

Log on to Visual Administrator as the J2EE administrator, and navigate to Global Configuration | Server | Services. Then choose the com.sap.portal.prt.sapj2ee service. You can view three properties to configure the navigation cache, as shown in Figure 20-1:

- portal.navigation.cache.enable (should be set to TRUE)
- portal.navigation.cache.lifetime (in minutes)
- portal.navigation.cache.maxsize (number of objects)

Then log in to the portal as a super administrator and choose System Administration | Navigation. You can view the navigation cache settings. To clear the cache, click Clear Cache.

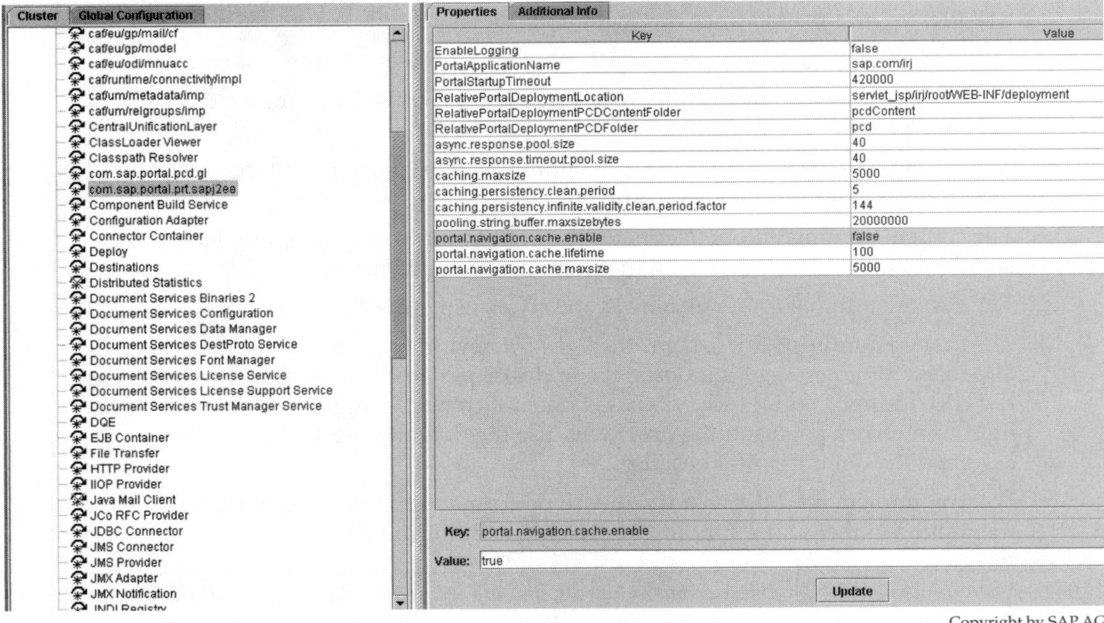

FIGURE 20-1 Viewing properties of the navigation cache

TIP *At present, it is not possible to clear the cache for specific connectors, so clearing the cache could be a performance drag.*

Configuring the Short URL

Choose System Administration | Navigation and set Use Short URLs to TRUE. Then click Save Configuration.

In Figure 20-2, you can see the full URL and the corresponding short URL. Using the short URLs, you can access the portal instead of using the full URLs. The advantage with using the short URLs is that you can hide internal content structure and it reduces network traffic.

NOTE *Because the URL is short, you can use the HTTP GET request.*

This URL, http://*<server>*:50100/irj/portal?NavigationTarget=navurl://b7be7ee0ab511df519aaf1189868954f, can be used instead of this URL, http://*<server>*:50100/irj/portal?NavigationTarget=navurl://ROLES://portal_...ws/com.sap.portal.monitoring/portal.

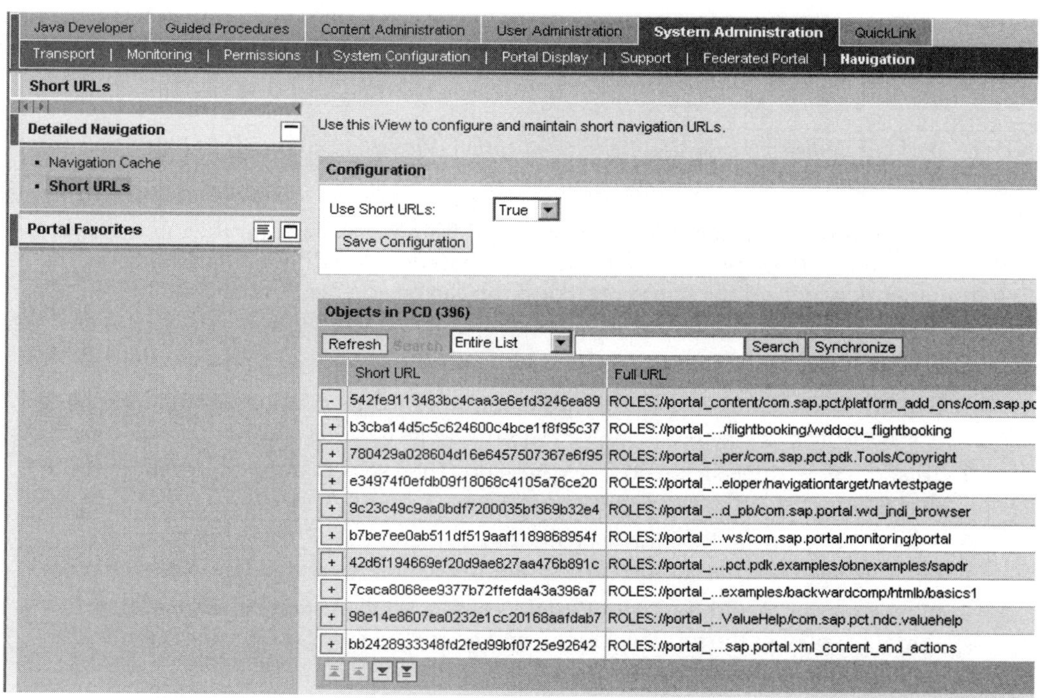

FIGURE 20-2 Full and short URLs

Simply copying the short URL for monitoring from the screen shown in Figure 20-2 displays the portal screen for monitoring, as shown here:

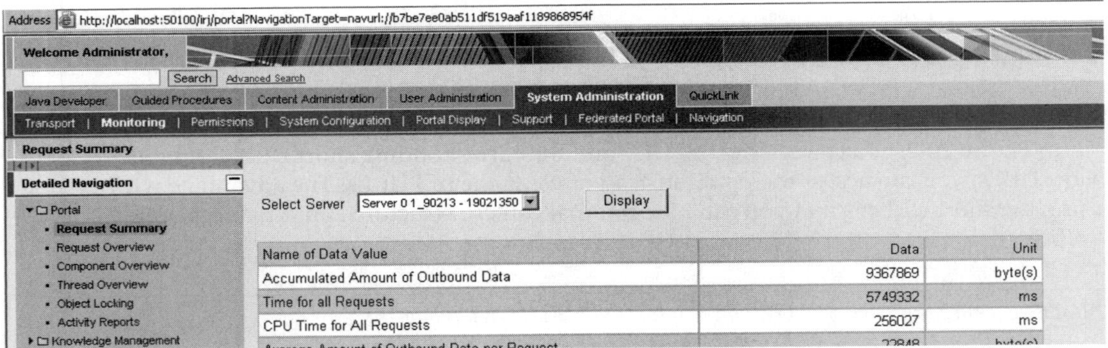

Copyright by SAP AG

Configuring the Light Framework Page

You must try to use the light framework page is provided by SAP for the external-facing portal scenario. The advantage in using a light framework page is that, unlike the standard framework page, it uses a single frame. Because there is only one single frame, there is no client-side event framework (and consequently client-side JavaScript) involved for enabling communication between multiple frames.

NOTE *The light framework page uses lighter navigation iViews that do not use HTMLB and client-side eventing JavaScript.*

Using desktop rules, you can assign a standard framework page for the internal users and a light framework page for the external users based on the different URL aliases. The light framework page and the light portal desktop can be accessed under System Administration | Portal Display in the top-level menu and Desktops & Display Rules in the detailed navigation menu.

1. Expand Portal Content | Portal Administrators | Super Administrators. Right click Master Rule Collection and choose Open | Object.
2. To add a new rule, click Add IF Expression. Then select Group under the second drop-down list and enter **Anonymous Users**. Choose Apply.
3. Select THEN Portal Desktop = pcd:portal_content/every_user/general/defaultDesktop. This should correspond to the newly created IF expression.
4. Now, in order to add the Light Portal Desktop, go to System Administration | Portal Display in the top-level menu and select Desktops & Display Rules in the detailed navigation menu.
5. Go to Portal Content | Content Provided by SAP | End User Content | Standard Portal Users. Right click Light Portal Desktop and choose Add Portal Desktop to Expression.

6. Click Apply and then Save.
7. Using this same procedure, add another rule for using the light portal desktop for the URL alias with value portal/anonymous, as shown next:

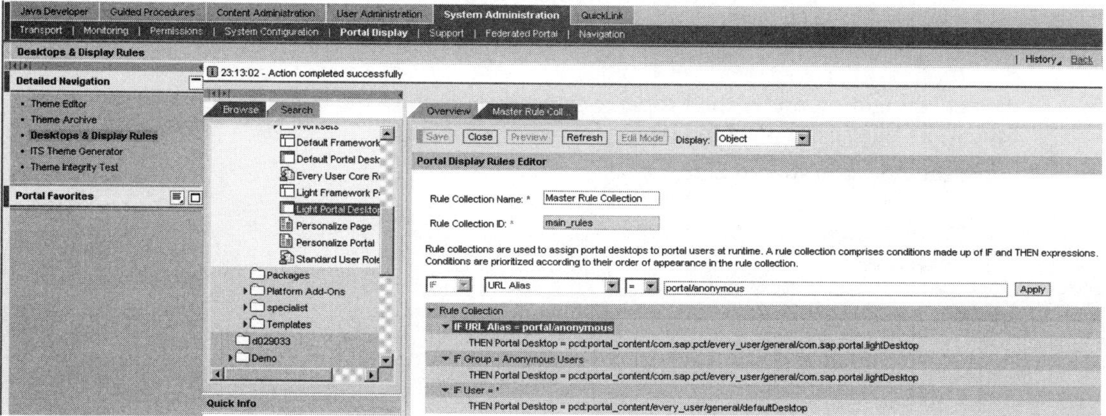

Now when the anonymous user logs on, the light portal desktop will be displayed for the user. Note that once the user logs on to the portal, the portal desktop cannot be changed at runtime. If you want to display a different portal desktop that contains heavy content such as HTMLB or client-side eventing functionality, you must have the user log off and log on using a different username or URL alias. You may, however, configure your portal such that the light portal desktop is displayed for anonymous users and a portal desktop made of a standard framework page is displayed after the user logs on.

Modifying the Light Framework

Using SAP NetWeaver Developer Studio, you can change the masthead and top-level navigation iViews, and then deploy them into the portal. You can then assign these iViews to the light framework page. This customization of the navigation iViews may be required to change the look and feel of the portal to align with the public website.

Setting Up Quicklinks on the Portal

You may use quick links to navigate directly to a page or iView on the portal just as you would do in a web portal. Quicklinks are created by maintaining the *Quick Link* property of an iView or a page. For example, if you created a quicklink called *help*, you could access that quicklink by adding it to the URL as shown here:

http://<host>:<port>/irj/portal/help

Tip *If more than two quicklinks with the same name are attached to two navigation nodes, only the quicklink attached to the first navigation node of the user's navigation tree will appear.*

Now to attach the quicklink to an iView:

1. Go to Content Administration | Portal Content in the top-level menu and then navigate to Portal Content | your custom folder | iViews (assuming you have created an iView folder to store iView objects).
2. Select any iView. Right click on the iView and choose Open | Object for editing the iView.
3. Select Navigation under the Property category and enter the name of the quicklink—for example, **Google**.
4. Save the iView as shown here:

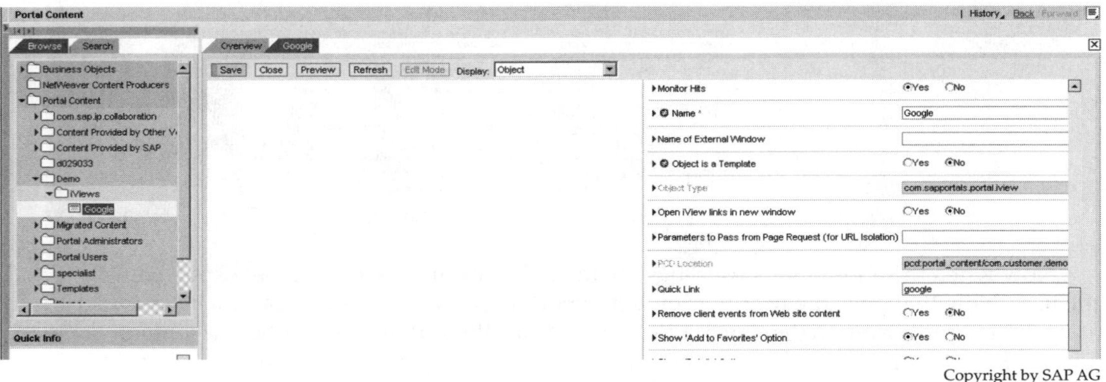

Copyright by SAP AG

To test the iView, enter **http://<*host*>:<*port*>/*irj*/*portal*/*name_of_the_quicklink***. If required, log on to the portal.

NOTE *In order to display the iView, the iView should be a part of the role to which the user has been assigned. The role should be available as an entry point so that the iView is displayed as part of the user's navigation tree.*

Setting Up Anonymous Content to Anonymous Users

Another activity that you can do to set up an external-facing portal is to set up anonymous content for the anonymous users. This can be content that anyone visiting the site can access without authentication. This is typically the case for public websites.

Two types of anonymous setups are possible: using *named anonymous users*, which is the default configuration, and *simple anonymous logon*.

When using simple anonymous users, you cannot assign any roles or groups to the anonymous users. Also, because there is no named user involved in the case of simple anonymous users, personalization functions are not possible. For the same reason, no SAP logon tickets can be issued.

Named anonymous users are physical users stored in the user data store and hence you can assign them to the group Anonymous Users. You can then assign the roles to the Anonymous Users group.

To set up anonymous content, you need to configure the J2EE engine using the config tool, as shown next. The following changes need to be made, depending on whether it is a simple or named anonymous user. To make the changes, go to the config tool, navigate to Global Configuration | Server | Services, and choose the com.sap.security.core.ume.service service. Maintain the properties as shown next. The default value for the ume.logon .anonymous_user.mode property is 0, which is the simple anonymous users scenario. To configure the named anonymous users scenario, you should maintain it as 1.

ume.logon.anonymous_user.mode=1 Named anonymous users.

ume.logon.anonymous_user.mode=0 Simple anonymous users.

ume.login.guest_user.uniqueids

- The default value is anonymous.
- You can maintain a list of comma-separated user IDs.
- Required only if *ume.logon.anonymous_user.mode=1*.
- Administrator must create these users in the user data store with passwords that meet the UME requirements.
- The passwords need not be known.
- When accessing anonymous content through a portal URL, you can pass the named user to the *j_user* parameter (for example, http://<*host*>:<*port*>/irj/portal?j_user=<*named_user*>).

ume.login.guest_user.defaultid If the *j_user parameter* is empty, the named user maintained here is used as the default named user when accessing the portal. If this field is left empty, the first user in the unique ID list above is used.

1. The first step is to create the anonymous users that were used in the previous section. This refers to the case where *ume.logon.anonymous_user.mode* was set to 1. You should create the users mentioned in *ume.login.guest_user.uniqueids* or *ume.login .guest_user.defaultid*.
2. After creating the necessary pages and iViews, you should set up the *Authscheme* property of the pages and iViews to anonymous.
3. Then create a role specifically for containing anonymous content.
4. Assign the pages and iViews to the role.
5. You can assign the role either to the individual anonymous users or the Anonymous Users group.
6. Then you should create a new iView based on the standard portal launcher component called *com.sap.portal.navigation.portallauncher* and set the *AuthScheme* to anonymous.
7. You can then access the anonymous content by invoking the above iView.

Accessing Anonymous Content

Following are some of the options you can use to access the anonymous content:

- Directly call the Portal Launcher iView after creating the iView as mentioned in the previous section:

  http://*<server>:<port>*/irj/servlet/prt/portal/prtroot/pcd!3aportal_content!2AnonFolder!2fiViews!2fanon.PortalLauncher
- Modify the portal's initial logon page: Edit the index.html file in the location …\cluster\server\services\servlet_jsp\work\jspTemp\irj\root and change the *location.replace* parameter to a similar value as shown here:

  <body onload="location.replace('portal' + document.location.search)"></body> to <body onload="location.replace('servlet/prt/portal/prtroot/com.sap.portal.navigation.portallauncher.anonymous' + document.location.search)"></body>
  Note that a portal restart is required.
- Pass the named anonymous user to the URL parameter *j_user* to view that particular named user's content (for example, http://*<server>*:*<port>*/irj/portal?j_user=*<named_anonymous_user>).*
- Call any iView with *Authscheme* set as anonymous and with end user permission assigned using the URL shown here:

  <http/https>://*<server>:<port>*/irj/servlet/prt/portal/prtroot/pcd!3aportal_content!2f*myfolder*!2f*myiView*, where *myfolder* and *myiView* are custom folders and iViews, respectively.
- By having different anonymous users, you can have different roles assigned and thus have different URLs and thus maintain different anonymous content.
- Once the *ume.login.guest_user.uniqueids* is maintained, the content can be accessed using *<http/https>*://*<server>:<port>*/irj/portal/anonymous. You will be logged on as the first user in the list.
- You can also access anonymous content using this URL:

  <http/https>://*<server>:<port>*/irj/portal/anonymous?guest_user=*anon2*, where *anon2* is the named anonymous user.

HINT *The difference between* guest users *and* anonymous users *is that for guest users, the content has* Authscheme *as guest and not anonymous. While simple anonymous users cannot receive SAP logon tickets, guest users can.*

If Knowledge Management is used, some restrictions are involved. Refer to the following OSS notes:

- **709354** Restrictions on KM with anonymous logon
- **837898** How to set up anonymous logon for KM
- **728106** Using a release prior to NetWeaver 2004 SPS 12 with KM and anonymous logon

Changing the Default Portal URL

Another change that you can implement that can mimic a public website is to change the URL port from 50100 to 80. Another change is to implement the redirect feature so that when you access the server through the URL, it gets redirected from the J2EE engine to the portal URL.

1. Log on to the Visual Administrator, and go to Cluster | Dispatcher | Services | HTTP Provider.
2. Choose Ports and change the ports for HTTP and HTTPS by entering the following: **(Port:80, Type:http)(Port:81, Type:ssl)**.
3. Click Update and then Save. You can now access the portal at http://<*server*>:80/irj/portal instead of http://<*server*>:50100/irj/portal.
4. To change the irj/portal entry for the portal URL, in Visual Administrator, go to Cluster | Server | Services | HTTP Provider.
5. In the Start Page field, enter **/irj/portal** as shown here:

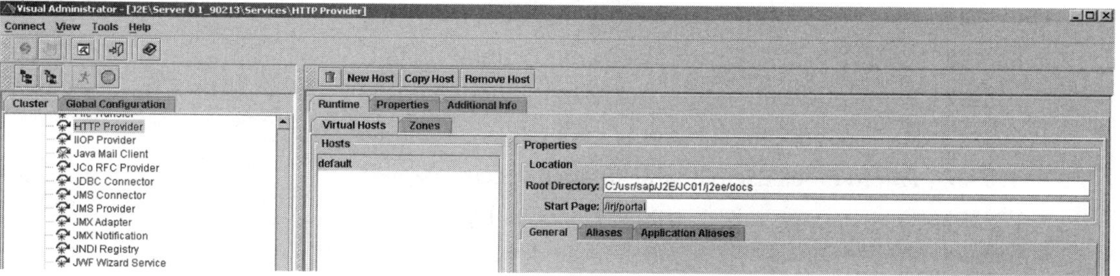

6. Choose Save Properties and restart the service.

After this change, if you try to access the J2EE engine's home page at http://<*server*>:<*port*>, you will be redirected to the portal at http://<*server*>:<*port*>/irj/portal.

Changing the Portal Page Title

You can change the portal title from the default value of *SAP Enterprise Portal 7.0* to something more meaningful to the portal implementation. This feature is also helpful when the users try to bookmark a page for later use.

Rename the prtCentral.properties.bak file to prtCentral.properties in the folder <*installation_drive*>:\usr\sap\J2E\JC01\j2ee\cluster\server0\apps\sap.com\irj\servlet_jsp\irj\root\WEB-INF\portal\system\properties. Change the value under *portal.html.head.title* to a more meaningful value. Save and close the file, and then restart the J2EE engine.

Removing the Options Menu in the iView or Page

You can remove the Options menu from appearing in the iView or page so that the page looks like a typical page in a public website. Here's how to do this:

1. Navigate to Content Administration | Portal Content in the top-level menu of the portal and browse to the iView or page for which you want to remove the Options menu.
2. Right click the iView or page and choose Open | Object.
3. From the Property Category drop-down, select the Appearance - Tray option.
4. Select the Yes radio button for the Show Tray property and click Save.

Useful OSS Notes

Following are some useful OSS notes that can be accessed at http://service.sap.com/notes:

- **870247** Using Named Anonymous Users
- **916545** Central Note for External-Facing Portal (NW 7.0)
- **877188** Central Note for External-Facing Portal (NW 04)
- **933452** External-Facing Portal and Search Engine Indexing
- **893855** EFP – Hotfix for support of Quicklinks for anonymous user
- **913367** Anonymous users unable to open specific pages
- **709354** Restrictions on KM with anonymous logon
- **837898** How to set up anonymous logon for KM
- **728106** Using a release prior to NetWeaver 2004 SPS 12 with KM and anonymous logon

NOTE *For more details refer to the external-facing portal related resources listed in Appendix B.*

Summary

This chapter discussed the need for and the benefit of using external-facing portals. It looked at some of the salient features and limitations of an external-facing portal. It then walked through some of the potential configuration steps that can be followed when implementing an external-facing portal.

V

PART

System Administration

21

CHAPTER

Portal Backup and Restore

Backup refers to the copying of files and data for the entire system, such as the portal system, or for just a few components under consideration, such as the portal database or the file system, to another storage system. *Restore* refers to the process of retrieving the previously backed up files and data. This chapter discusses in detail the backup and restore options available for the portal.

A backup and restore is usually required to prepare for the following eventualities:

- Hardware or file system failure
- Damage due to viruses
- Issues during installation of software patches and upgrades
- Potential human mistakes, such as accidentally deleting some files or changing configuration
- Loss of system or data due to theft

Full-System vs. Partial Component Backup

You need to consider a number of factors before deciding between a *full-system* (*consistent landscape*) backup and a *partial component* backup. One of the driving factors in adopting a consistent landscape backup strategy is the interdependency between the portal configuration and the portal components.

In a *consistent landscape backup*, all systems are backed up so that the data are consistent between all systems. In this case, all replicated data are identical between the systems and the non-replicated data are restored. With consistent system backup, however, you cannot restore the system to a specific point in time—such as the point at which the system crashed. This is because some changes could have been made between the time the backup occurred and the time the system crashed.

Consistent landscape backup is an option for disaster recovery or for test systems, or it can be used before upgrading systems. It is usually impossible to restore a system completely, and some data loss usually occurs. Service-level agreement (SLA) requirements must also be considered. Consistent landscape backup is a time-consuming process.

A *partial component backup* can be adopted depending on the type of data storage involved and the ease with which the backup can be accomplished. In most cases, it is often easier to create a backup of only the portal database and Web Application Server (AS) database.

On the other hand, for an *individual system backup*, you can recover the system up to the point of the crash. This is possible especially for database systems. However, for non-database systems such as configuration files and software files, you need to create a backup and restore strategy.

Portal Backup Strategy

Figure 21-1 illustrates some of the important steps involved when devising a portal backup strategy. Devising the portal backup strategy consists of three main steps:

- Conduct preliminary tasks, such as analyzing the system landscape.
- Design a strategy that includes all procedures or steps involved.
- Conduct a final verification process that confirms the success of the strategy.

Taking an Inventory of the System Landscape

Before drafting a portal backup strategy, you need to take an inventory of the various critical components in the system landscape. The system landscape can consist of both portal-specific components and components that are not an intrinsic part of the portal.

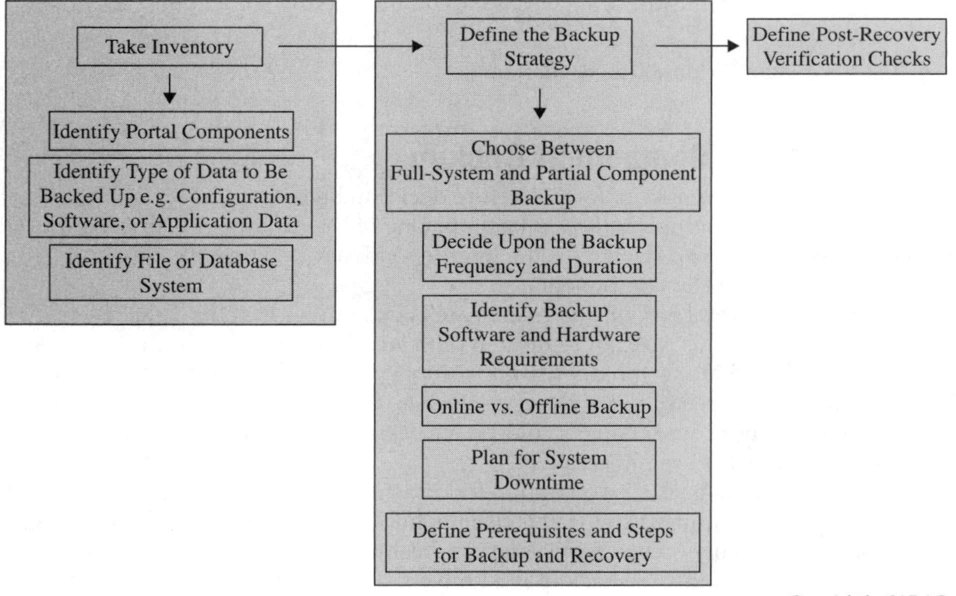

FIGURE 21-1 Steps Involved In a portal backup and restore strategy

Identify Critical Portal Components

The following critical portal components need to be backed up:

- J2EE engine cluster
- Portal platform
- RDBMS database system
- User Management Engine (UME) persistence store
- Portal Archive (PAR) files created by SAP and custom PAR files
- iView templates
- Personalization data

Note that the RDBMS database is particularly critical because it consists of Portal Content Directory (PCD) objects such as role definitions, page-to-role relationships, PAR files, iView templates, and other personalization data. The UME persistence store is also critical; this could be a Lightweight Directory Access Protocol (LDAP) or R/3 system, or a database, depending on the UME configuration.

Identify Critical Non-Portal Components in the System Landscape

Other critical non-portal components in the overall system landscape include the following:

- Web servers
- Java-based applications and their related configuration
- RDBMS databases used by those applications and their data
- Other native applications that are critical to the organization

Identify Leading System

When more than one system is involved, you should identify the *leading system*—the one in which the master data are up to date and the transactions are maintained in this system. The changes are then replicated from the leading system to the other systems.

Identify Specific Requirements for NetWeaver Landscape

It is important that you also identify which NetWeaver landscape system components should be backed up. Data consistency between system components is extremely important, because often some form of data transfer takes place between the systems. So when the backup occurs, some data are held up in the queue. If this queue information is not captured properly, valuable data can be lost. This is a common scenario when the portal speaks to a backend Customer Relationship Management (CRM) system, which in turn replicates sales order information to a backend R/3 system. After the systems are recovered, it should be possible to restart the queues so that the replication of data from the CRM system to the R/3 system can commence again.

Identify SAP Web AS Java Cluster Components

In the SAP Web AS Java cluster, much configuration data related to the startup framework, the Server Central Services (SCS) instance, the central instance, and the dialog instance should be backed up.

Considering that the data are distributed across both the file system and the database, you should take care to ensure that the backup of both the file system and the database data is taken at the same time to avoid inconsistencies.

TIP *The database software should also be backed up along with the configuration data to maintain consistency of data.*

Identify Software Delivery Manager Components

The SDM contains information about applications that have been deployed into the J2EE engine (applications themselves are stored as PAR files in the file system), and software deployment parameters stored in the file system. The configuration data related to the Internet Graphics Service (IGS) are stored in the file system as well.

DON'T *The SDM should not be running at the time of backup to avoid any inconsistencies that may arise because of someone trying to deploy an application at the time of backup. Every time a deployment occurs through the SDM or the SAPINST, the SDM-related information will change.*

During deployment, some files may be opened and may interrupt the backup. It is therefore important that you schedule a period of inactivity with both administrators and end users to avoid any inconsistencies such as missing transports.

Identify Content Management and Collaboration Components

If Content Management and Collaboration is installed, the configuration and the software application data are stored in both the file system and the database.

TIP *If external systems are connected, the connectivity details should also be backed up.*

The other major component is the UME persistence database that contains data related to external systems such as LDAP, servers, or databases. If TREX has been installed, the configuration and the software application data should be backed up.

NOTE *OSS Notes 915673 and 975965 contain information on how to conduct online data backup and restore for TREX 6.1 and TREX 7.1, respectively.*

Identify File Structure for Backup

The following file structure information can help you identify the folders that need to be backed up:

- **Java central instance folder,** ***usr/sap/<SID>/JC00*** Contains subfolders such as data, exe, j2ee, log, SDM, sec, and work. The SDM folder contains deployment-related data in the file system.
- **System Central Services Instance folder,** ***usr/sap/<SID>/SCS01*** Contains subfolders such as data, exe, log, sec, and work.

- **System folder,** ***usr/sap/<SID>/SYS*** Contains the executables, profiles, and configuration files for the J2EE engine, plus subfolders such as exe, gen, global, profile, and src. The global folder contains the transport packages for EP content and XML Forms Builder related data.
- **J2EE cluster folder,** ***usr/sap/<SID>/j2ee/cluster*** Contains subfolders such as bootstrap, dispatcher, and server information.
- **Dispatcher folder,** ***usr/sap/<SID>/j2ee/cluster/dispatcher*** Contains subfolders such as bin, cfg, dtd, log, and temp; contains data that are synchronized from the database during the bootstrap mechanism at startup.
- **Server folder,** ***usr/sap/<SID>/j2ee/cluster/server*** Contains subfolders such as apps, bin, cfg, dtd, log, META-INF, and temp; contains data that are synchronized from the database during the bootstrap mechanism at startup.

NOTE *The bootstrap Java program creates a property file, which describes the Java instances.*

Back up Software and Configuration Files

As far as software is concerned, you can install the system again, but the configuration parameters change with every new modification to the system functionality. The recommended option is to take a backup of the installed software after the installation or upgrade.

Configuration files, on the other hand, should be backed up more frequently in a regular manner and especially after changes in configuration settings.

A file system backup could be either incremental or a full backup. The best option would be to take a full file system backup and a Windows registry backup for backing up software, configuration data, and log files.

Computing Center Management System Agents

If the CCMS system was installed, the SAPCCMSR and the SAPOSCOL agent data must be backed up. The configuration data related to these agents are stored in the file system as well as the database. The RDBMS system contains data related to the configuration as well as software systems.

Devise a Backup Strategy

The next step is to devise a backup strategy that considers several factors, including scheduling considerations, backup frequency, backup duration, type of data to be backed up, system availability, people to involve in the process, software and hardware involved, and contingency plans for potential errors and missteps.

How soon the backup can be completed and how long it takes to recover the system fully are important considerations. If the system needs to be recovered fully up to the point of crash, the backup/restore procedure may take a little longer. The timeframe for the backup/restore process may also be dictated by the system availability requirements listed out in the existing SLAs. It may not even be possible to shut down the system during a backup, another important consideration when choosing between an offline and on online backup.

While designing the system backup strategy, all the required stakeholders, such as system administrators and developers, should be included in the planning. The system backup strategy should be finalized before any backup procedures occur. It can take weeks to prepare a strategy, and it is important that adequate time is devoted to this process, including trying out various options practically to iron out any uncertainties or issues related to authorization, client certificates, LDAP, connectivity and network issues, and other issues.

You should take an inventory of the available backup software and hardware. You should capture in detail the backup procedures that have been finalized for each and every component in the landscape. The backup procedure should also take into account the backup schedule depending upon the volume of data and the sensitivity of the data. The backup procedure should be inclusive of the development and quality assurance systems. Enough controls should be in place to ensure that the success or failure of the backup process can be adequately verified. This is especially important when restoring from an online backup.

NOTE *Refer to OSS Note 779708 for more information on online backup and restore of portal for SAP NetWeaver 04 and NetWeaver 2004s.*

You should also consider various error scenarios that are likely to occur when restoring/ recovering the system. You must be prepared with alternatives if the recovery does not complete properly. All the dependencies that exist between various steps should be captured, such as restoring the file system after a database is restored.

Dependencies between the data stored in the PCD database and the data stored in the UME database should also be considered.

TIP *Aspects such as creation of users, configuration of network, and others should be properly identified and well coordinated during the recovery operation.*

Additional measures should also be considered, such as building up hardware redundancy using some of the following techniques:

- RAID protection of disks
- Redundant hardware path for accessing data
- Maintain offline copies of data
- Use devices for database logs
- High Availability (HA) solutions

To enhance database consistency, log mirroring should be implemented on different disk controllers. Storing log files twice on disk and twice on tape should be explored.

Choose the Backup Method

Depending on whether the type of data storage is file-based or database-based, corresponding backup methods should be selected. The combination of system components, data types, and the data storage types will often drive the type of backup methods chosen.

Online Backup The advantage of using an online backup strategy is that the systems can be in running mode. However, the disadvantage is that a complete backup may not be possible because open files may not be copied during an online backup of the files and the database. For example, files could be opened at the time of deployment using SDM or when import / export activities are carried out on the portal. It should be ensured that no configuration changes are done to the EP applications, J2EE engine, and KMC system during an online backup. Starting from NW 2004 SPS 10, SAP officially supports the online backup of the components.

Offline Backup When an offline backup is chosen, the J2EE engine, the database processes, and the TREX processes should be stopped. All the services on the application servers should also be stopped.

During offline backup, all the files can be quickly copied into a storage device such as a tape. Hardware that can take snapshots of the hard disk is useful for offline backup.

It is important to keep the downtime at a minimum by starting the portal immediately after the files are copied. Offline backup can be used to take a full backup of the system, whereas the online backup works only for individual components. It is possible to obtain a consistent restore when using offline backup. Offline backup should be done at least once after the initial install and then before or after an upgrade. After that, you can create an offline backup once a week.

NOTE *Offline backup cannot be done on a daily basis due to system availability constraints.*

Restoring the J2EE Engine

When restoring the J2EE engine, the following steps are required:

1. Restore the Java instances either by using SAPINST to install the new Application Server (AS) Java system or by restoring the file system from the offline backups.
2. Restore the database by using the vendor-specific tools.
3. Restore the Software Delivery Manager (SDM).
4. Restore the applications by overwriting the /usr/sap/<SID> folder.
5. Restart the J2EE engine.

Assuming that the portal host was restored using this procedure for the J2EE engine, the subsequent steps for restoring the portal components are as follows:

1. The PCD and the portal server files should be restored from the file backup after recovering the portal host.
2. The portal LDAP should be restored.
3. The portal repository database should be restored from the backup.

Recovery Strategy

Another aspect to consider for the backup strategy is the recovery strategy. You need to address the important question as to whether the system needs to be restored from the point of crash or whether the system should be restored from the most recent backup.

If the second option is chosen, you will lose data collected between the time when the crash occurred and when the last backup was done. You need to address the question of whether the data loss arising out of the second option is acceptable. If other interconnected systems are involved, can the data be recovered from those systems also?

Suppose, for example, that you have two systems that communicate with each other, and you are able to recover data from one system until the point of crash, but you can restore data from the latest backup for the second system. Because data from one system could be dependent on the data from the other system, since they are not in sync after the point of recovery, inconsistency issues will exist. You need to consider whether it is possible for operations to continue with inconsistent data.

Post-Recovery Checks

After the recovery process is complete, your next step is to conduct post-recovery checks to verify that the backup and restore strategy was successful. The check involves starting the portal components one after the other to ensure that they are running properly. If you encounter a problem, you should check the logs and the OS processes. If necessary, you can use some monitoring tools such as Computing Center Management System (CCMS), SAP Solution Manager Diagnostic tools, and others.

Once the components are fully started, ensure that they are working properly. For example, you can check the portal URL, log into the portal, and conduct some basic functionality tests to check that everything is working as expected.

Useful OSS Notes

Following are some useful OSS notes that can be accessed at http://service.sap.com/notes:

- **779708** Online backup and restore for portal – NW 04 and NW 2004s
- **1064468** EP 6.40 / 7.00: PRT properties files – Upgrade consideration
- **975965** TREX 7.0/7.1: Data backup (online) and recovery
- **915673** TREX 6.1: Data Backup (Online) and Restore

Note *For more details, refer to references related to Backup and Restore in Appendix B.*

Summary

This chapter looked at the need for backup and discussed how to devise a backup and restore strategy. It compared the merits and demerits of taking a full system backup and a partial component backup. It then took an inventory of the portal system landscape that needs to be backed up and addressed aspects such as backup recovery time, contingency plans, backup methods, restore and recovery procedures, and post-verification steps.

CHAPTER 22

Transporting Portal Content

This chapter focuses on the import/export functionality of the portal. It discusses the need for transporting portal content, describes the transport process, and establishes the need for process controls. You will learn about creating transport packages for portal content, personalizing data, working with system objects and template objects, and configuring export settings. You'll also learn about the options available for importing content into the portal.

Transporting Content

Once the development of portal content is completed and tested, your next step is to transport the content into the QA and production (PRD) systems. You should have a proper transport and change management system to ensure that only the right content is transported to the right systems, in the right order, and at the right time.

A number of options are available for transporting content between systems. The SAP Enterprise portal provides an import/export functionality for this purpose. Another option is to transport content using the NetWeaver Development Infrastructure (NWDI), which is often used for transporting Java-based, custom-developed objects. Starting from SAP NW SPS 13, the Change and Transport System (CTS) used for transporting ABAP workbench objects has been enhanced to transport non-ABAP objects such as Java, Enterprise Portal, and Web Dynpro objects.

NOTE *With subsequent releases of NetWeaver, the portal transport mechanism has been integrated with the NWDI infrastructure–based SAP Java Software logistics mechanism.*

Transport Package

Once the development environment has been fully tested, You must include the entire relevant portal content into a *transport package*. The transport package can then be exported into a file system so that it can be imported into the relevant QA system in the portal landscape. The QA system should then be functionally tested, verified, and approved for transport into the PRD system. If, during the testing in QA, errors are identified, they must be reworked in the development environment and transported again into QA using the transport package mechanism.

TIP *By re-importing the transport package into QA and overwriting the PCD object again, you can rectify any error-prone PCD objects.*

Transporting packages may result in the following:

- Creating a PCD object if it does not already exist in the target system
- Overwriting a PCD object if already exists
- Creating the necessary linkages for an object that contains relationships—for example, importing an iView may also result in updating the relationships between that iView and the page in which it is included
- Creating the PCD hierarchical structure in the target system

Transport Process Controls

You can deduct from the preceding process description that it is paramount that you come up with some process discipline to ensure that the various steps are well coordinated and tracked to avoid errors or mistakes. You can consider the following to help improve the overall manageability of the transport mechanism:

- Which system administrator does the import?
- What is the order of importing packages?
- What are the storage locations of the packages?
- How do you maintain the versions of the transport packages?
- Do you track the success/failure of the imports?

Exporting Transport Packages

The export process, in and of itself, is a simple process, but you should follow certain guidelines and best practices to ensure the most successful export functionality:

- Create a custom administration role for export.
- Create transport packages based on roles that contain end user content.
- Keep the number of objects within the package to a minimum.
- Avoid potential content overlap between transport packages.
- Adopt proper naming conventions for transport packages.
- Implement export reporting to check for export status.

Create a Custom Administration Role for Export

Content administrators are usually responsible for exporting content and creating transport packages. It may be helpful to create a custom role with only transport-related iViews and assign that role to content administrators. To do this, you can create a delta link to the standard SAP-delivered system administration role, with all the content (except the transport-related iViews such as the export/import iViews) deleted from the copied system administration role.

TIP *Usually, developers will have the Transport Admin role in the development environment and the administrators will have the Transport Admin role in the QA and PRD environments.*

In addition, make sure that the administrators have the following permissions in the portal content catalog:

- at least read access to the content that needs to be included in the transport package
- at least read/write access to the folder where the package is created

DO *If delegated content administration has been implemented, ensure that the delegated administrators can create and export the transport package.*

Define Roles as Units of Transport Packages

As far as possible, roles should be used as units of transport packages. In other words, you must add roles to the transport packages along with the content assigned to them. Having the transport package structured around the role also helps during testing.

By structuring along the roles, you will find it easier to test aspects such as these:

- Navigation on the portal
- User interface of iViews and pages
- Accessing backend content
- Functionality related to the user role

NOTE *To access the backend content, remember to create the system alias for the newly imported system object in the target system.*

Limit the Number of Objects in a Package

Changing the role often means an iView, page, or workset has been changed. So this leaves you with two options when creating transport packages: you can create packages just for the changed objects, or you can create packages for the entire role and its content.

Each option has its pros and cons. Transporting only the changed objects has these benefits:

- Transport packages are smaller in size
- Shorter amount of time required to import
- Easier to isolate the problem packages when an issue occurs

On the other hand, including the entire role and its content may result in large transport packages and hence longer import times. However, fewer errors may occur because there is less chance of missing links in the content, and relationships between the role and the other objects are intact.

Avoid Content Overlap Between Packages

Extra precautions must be taken to ensure that the same content does not exist in multiple transport packages. Overlapping content can result in overwriting of newer content by older versions of that content. One way to avoid this is to create smaller and well-defined transport packages. It is also a good idea to ensure that the transport packages are imported in a proper sequence by using time stamps as part of the package names. You should also use the ACL mechanism to ensure that only a limited number of administrators can import the transport packages in the PCD folders of the target system.

Adopt Proper Naming Conventions

You should adopt proper naming conventions that uniquely identify the packages as well as the objects that are included in the package. The typical convention for naming packages is shown here:

- Domain name, such as *.com*
- Company name, such as *com.customer*
- Organizational unit or department name, such as *com.customer.sales*
- Project or user name, such as *com.customer.sales.john*
- Type of object, such as *com.customer.sales.john.iView*
- Object name, such as *com.customer.sales.john.iView.salesOrderIview*

Implement Export Reporting to Check for Status

After creating a transport package, you must check the export report files that are created under the default location maintained in the PCD property Pcd.TransportApplication .ProcessReportDir. For more information, refer to the section "Configuring Report Directory for Exports" in this chapter. The export report file contains information on the state of the included objects in the transport package. You must check if any of the objects have an error state, in which case, the transport package should be stored in a different location. The error in the transport package must be corrected and should be finally used for import only when the errors have been eliminated.

Export Settings

It is possible to control what objects are included in a transport package based on the export settings discussed below.

Resolve References Property

You can access the Resolve References property for a transport package in the Property Editor under the Export Settings property category (see Figure 22-1). You should ensure that the system includes dependent objects in the transport package. A value of Yes for Resolve References will ensure that dependent objects are included.

References Filter Property

You can use the References Filter property to filter out dependent objects based on the included namespaces. For example, in Figure 22-1, only objects belonging to the namespace com.customer.* will be exported because the value com.customer.* has been maintained for the References Filter property.

FIGURE 22-1 Choose Yes to ensure that dependent objects are included

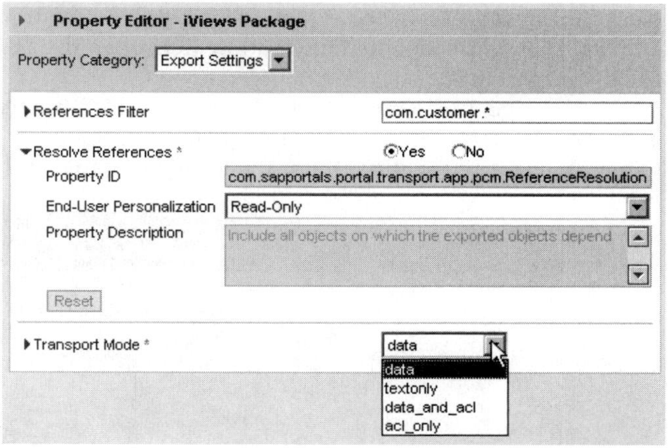

Copyright by SAP AG

Transport Mode Property

The Transport Mode property determines what can be transported. You can select one of the following:

- **data** Content, including the default value; all content objects, including the languages, are transported
- **textonly** Text only; transports only language-specific texts
- **data_and_acl** Content and permissions, including the ACLs assigned to the content objects in the export package
- **acl_only** Permissions only; contains only the ACLs without the content objects

---

TIP *You should try to avoid using the data_and_acl and acl_only because the ACLs are often system-specific and users are not usually the same in the target systems.*

Creating EPA Transport Packages

In Enterprise Portal 6.0, the transport package is an Enterprise Portal Archive (EPA) file and the objects within the transport package are in the Enterprise Portal Transport (EPT) format. The packages in the EP 5.0 are .pkg files, which include the business packages that are also in .pkg format. The objects within the EP 5.0 .pkg file have their own object-specific formats.

An EPA transport package archive is created in the following order:

1. Create the transport package.
2. Add content objects to the package.
3. Check the export objects.
4. Maintain permissions for the package.
5. Start the export.
6. Check the export results.

To access the package export editor, go to System Administration | Transport in the top-level menu, and then in the detailed navigation area, open the Transport Packages folder and choose the Export link.

To create a package, navigate to the folder under which the transport package should be created in the Browse tab; right click the folder, and select New | Transport Package, as shown in the following illustration. Enter the transport name and ID and click Finish.

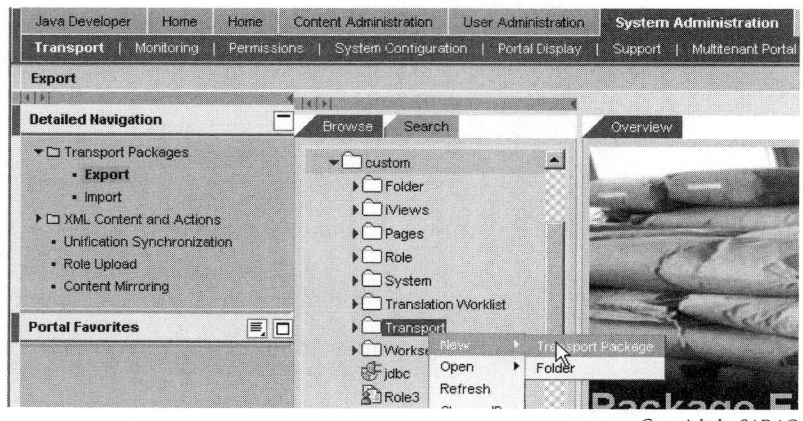

NOTE *Transport packages and folders with or without content can be added to the transport package.*

To add an iView to the transport package created in the previous step, navigate to that iView (in the illustration below, a custom iView called Transaction that was already created is used for demo purposes), using right click that iView, and choose Add Object To Transport Package, as shown next.

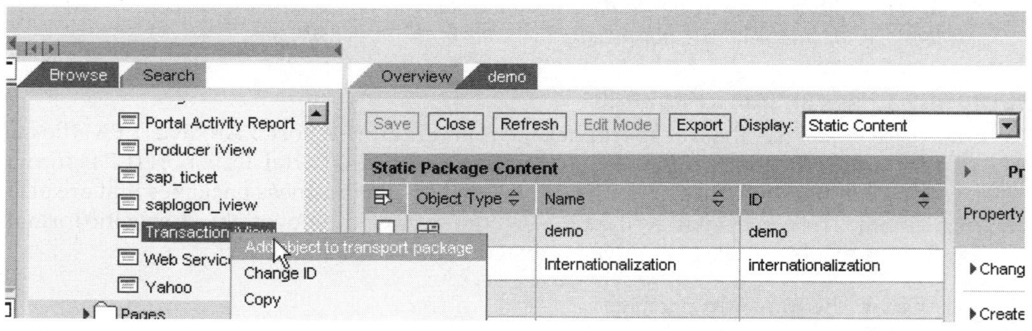

To add a folder to a transport package, navigate to the folder you want to add, right click the folder, and choose Add Object To Transport Package, as shown next:

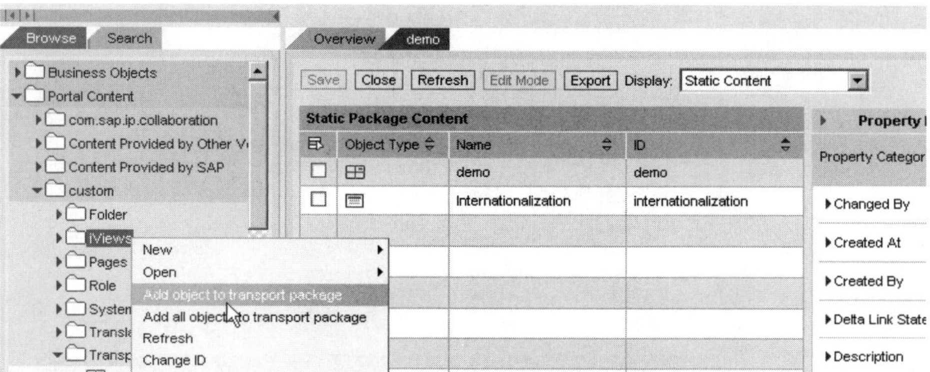

Copyright by SAP AG

Transporting Personalization Data

Personalization data that are related to the various iViews and pages can be transported using the export and import packages.

TIP *To transport personalization data, the user must exist in both the source and the target systems.*

Choose Personalization Transport from the Display drop-down menu. In the Available Personalization Data section of the Personalization Transport Settings screen, enter the user name in the Search For field after selecting Users from the Search In drop-down. Click Add. If the user exists, the user will now appear in the Results section. Select the checkbox before the User name and choose Add to include the user for which the personalization data should be transported, as shown in Figure 22-2. Choose the Export button. The Export preview screen appears as shown in Figure 22-3. If no personalization data are found for the user, the value Not Found is displayed in the Export preview page during the export.

To create the transport package, choose the Start Export button in the Export Preview screen. If necessary, you can change the file name or target destination where the package should be stored. The Export Status screen appears displaying the status of the transport. You can also download the .epa transport package to your local folder by clicking the Download Export File link.

TIP *You cannot choose partial personalization data for a particular user for export.*

Transporting System Objects

When transporting *system* objects, note that the system aliases are *not* transportable. The system aliases should be maintained in the target systems. Remember that iViews often contain references to the system aliases as a part of their properties. It is therefore important that you create system aliases in the target systems with the same names as those used in the iViews when transporting system objects.

FIGURE 22-2 Personalization transport settings

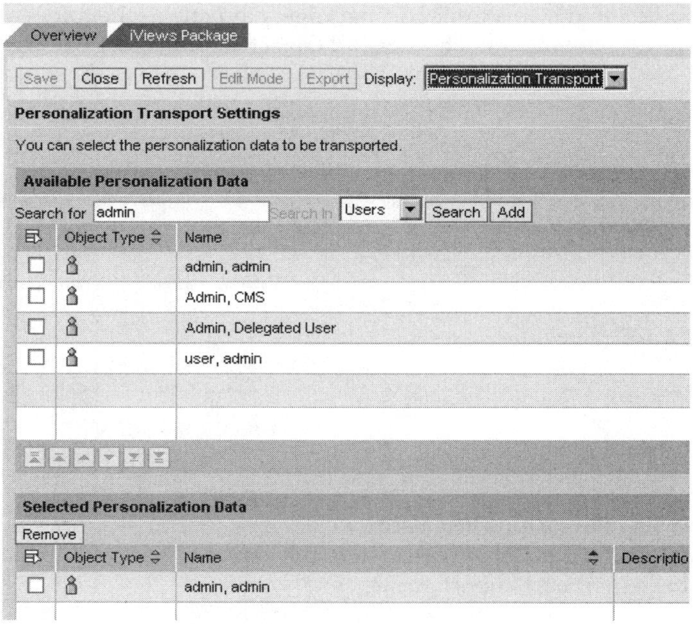

Copyright by SAP AG

FIGURE 22-3 Export Preview screen for portal transports

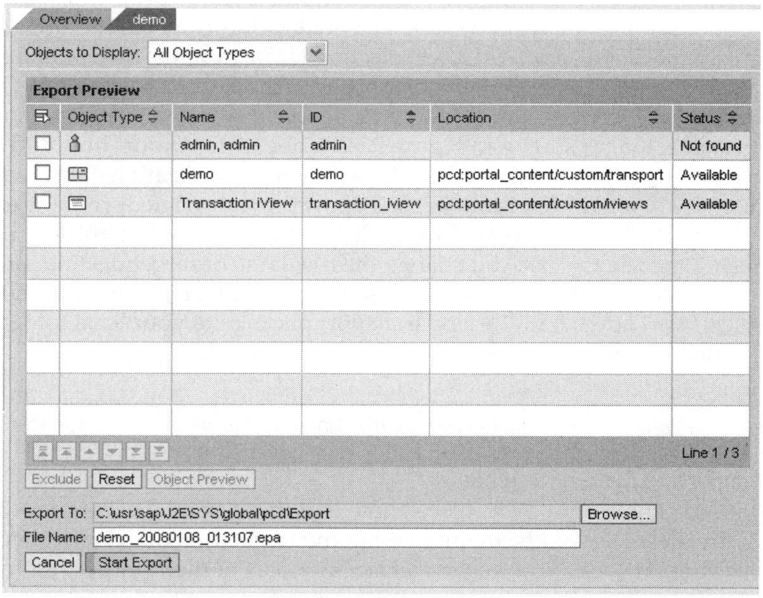

Copyright by SAP AG

Transporting Template Objects

When transporting *template* objects, take care to ensure that the template is first transported before the objects referencing the template are transferred. Also, to prevent the template from being used by unintended users, implement an ACL for the template objects.

Creating Language Transports

You can create language transport packages that contain only text objects, but no content objects. These texts could come from the PCD database for various content objects such as iViews, pages, and roles, or they could be resource bundles extracted from the PAR files during their deployment and stored as a separate object in the portal.

The resource bundles are automatically included in the transport package when exporting an iView or when including the dependent objects. You cannot transport text objects unless their parent objects are available in the target system. Figure 22-4 shows the Language Transport Settings window, where you select languages when transporting text objects.

NOTE *During the deployment of the PAR file, the resource bundle is extracted from the PAR file and is stored as a separate object in the portal.*

Role User Assignments

Importing the role content does not in any way modify the existing user role assignments in the target system. In fact, the role user assignments will vary between the different systems in the system landscape and hence they should be maintained separately in all three systems as part of the initial setup.

While testing in QA, if the uploaded role is a new one, the role should be assigned to the test user. However, for subsequent role imports, the user assignment remains intact and no action is required.

Configuring the PCD for Exports

It is possible to configure the PCD to manage the transports. To check the PCD configuration, go to System Administration | Support. Then click Portal Content Directory in the content

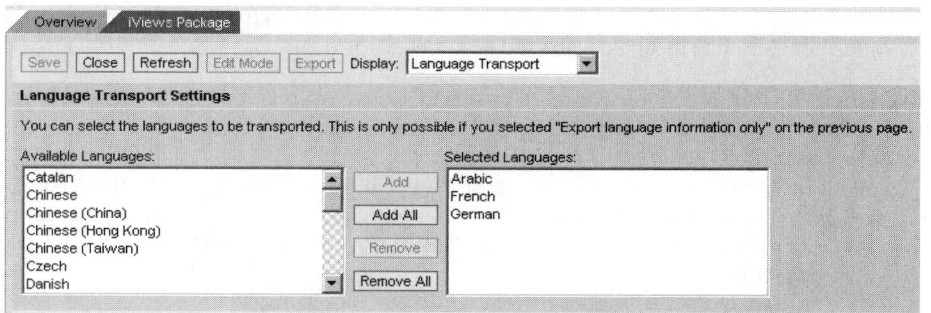

FIGURE 22-4 Selecting languages for transporting text objects

PART V

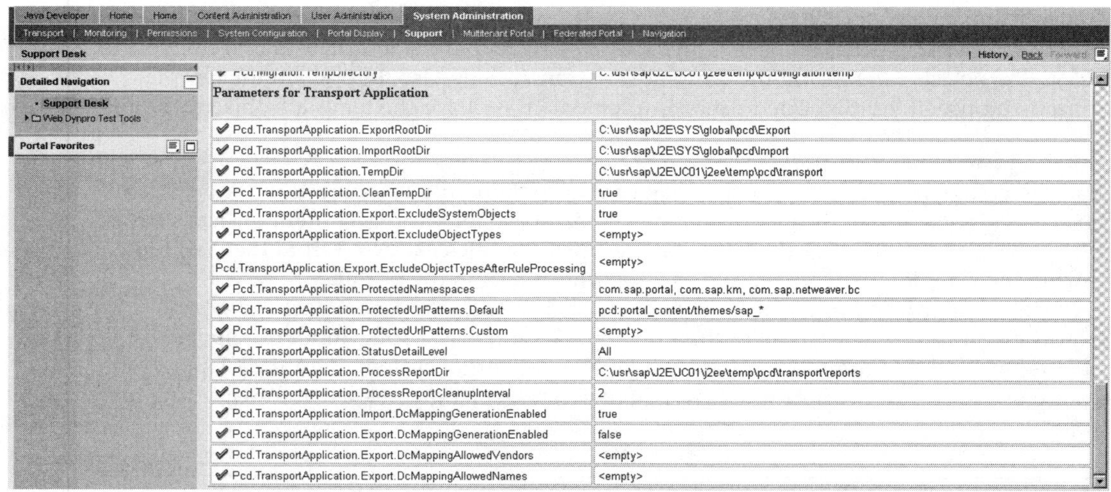

FIGURE 22-5 PCD configuration properties

area and choose PCD Configuration in the Test And Configuration Tools section of the Portal Support Desk: Portal Content Directory screen. Figure 22-5 displays the PCD configuration properties.

The following properties are relevant for export:

- **Pcd.TransportApplication.ExportRootDir** Defines the directory where the transport files are located.
- **Pcd.TransportApplication.Export.ExcludeSystemObjects** Decides whether the system objects should be excluded from the transport package; the default value is *true* and should not be changed.
- **Pcd.TransportApplication.Export.ExcludeObjectTypes** Defines the object types that can be excluded from the package.
- **Pcd.TransportApplication.Export.ExcludeObjectTypesAfterRuleProcessing** Defines whether dependent objects should also be exported.

To change the PCD configuration, go to the PCDStartup.properties file available in the global directory for the PCD, whose default location is defined in the PCD.Home system property as /usr/sap/<*Instance*>/sys/global/pcd.

To prevent any change to the PCD data or their configuration, log on to the Visual Admin and go to Global Configuration | Server | Services and select com.sap.portal.pcd.gl service. On the right-hand pane, change Pcd.Pl.WriteProtectedActivated to *true*. Then click Update, and start the service again.

Configuring Report Directory for Exports

An XML log is created every time an export package is created. The location can be configured using the Pcd.TransportApplication.ProcessReportDir parameter, whose default value is

C:\usr\sap\J2E\JC01\j2ee\temp\pcd\transport\reports. A similar file is also created for the transport packages that have been imported. The file contains information such as the following:

- **User** Who created the export file
- **startTime, endTime** Start time and end time for the whole package
- **totalObjects, processedObjects, errorObjects** How many objects were included in the package, how many were processed successfully, and how many objects resulted in error
- **state** Final state of the process: FINISHED, CANCELED, or ERROR
- **packageUrl** Location in the PCD
- **file** Name and location in the file system
- **object details:** url (location in the PCD); type (type of the included object); state (state of the included object—such as OK, ERROR, NO_PERMISSION, NOT_FOUND, NOT_TRANSPORTABLE)
- **startTime, endTime** Start and end times for the included object

Following is a sample XML log generated during a transport created for export:

```
<?xml version="1.0" encoding="utf-8"?>
<TransportReport version="1.0">
  <Process id="EXPORT-0313_231945_796_d9ca1109f173076d" type="Export"
state="FINISHED" user="Administrator" startTime="2007-03-13T23:19:46.750-05:00"
endTime="2007-03-13T23:19:47.609-05:00" totalObjects="3" processedObjects="3"
errorObjects="0" packageUrl="portal_content/com.customer.custom/transport/test"
file="C:\usr\sap\J2E\SYS\global\pcd\Export\test_20070313_104125.epa">
    <Object url="pcd:portal_content/com.customer.custom/transport/test"
type="com.sapportals.portal.transport.TransportPackage" state="OK"
startTime="2007-03-13T23:19:46.765-05:00" endTime="2007-03-13T23:19:47.375-05:00"/>
    <Object url="pcd:portal_content/com.customer.custom/com.customer.iviews/
com.customer.demo_iview" type="com.sapportals.portal.iview" state="OK"
startTime="2007-03-13T23:19:47.375-05:00" endTime="2007-03-13T23:19:47.453-05:00"/>
    <Object url="pcd:portal_content/com.customer.custom/role/role_download"
type="com.sapportals.portal.role" state="OK" startTime="2007-03-13T23:19:47.453-05:00"
endTime="2007-03-13T23:19:47.531-05:00"/>
  </Process>
</TransportReport>
```

NOTE *The process report gets cleaned up every few days, depending upon the PCD configuration Pcd.TransportApplication.ProcessReportCleanupInterval. The default value is 2 days.*

Configuring Protection from Overwriting System Objects

Two properties are responsible for protecting the SAP-provided initial content from being overwritten:

- **Pcd.TransportApplication.Export.ExcludeSystemObjects**: True
- **Pcd.TransportApplication.ProtectedNamespaces**: com.sap.portal, com.sap.km

By default, the first property ensures that the system objects are not included in the export. The second property ensures that com.sap.portal and com.sap.km objects are not included in the export as well as the import processes.

NOTE *Refer to OSS Note 618161 for information on how to avoid overwriting system objects.*

Importing Content

The import process is a manual process by default, though it can be automated. The import file directory is C:\usr\sap\<SID>\SYS\global\pcd\import, where the transport package that needs to be imported is stored.

TIP *To import the transport package, the system administrator will need write access to all the folders into which the objects are to be imported.*

It is important that strict import guidelines are used to prevent mistakes or errors during the import process. Potential possibilities include the following:

- Older content overwrites younger content
- The system administrator has no write permission for the folder into which the object needs to be created

Following are a few recommendations for importing content:

- By default, the overwrite option is enabled during the import, which results in the object being overwritten during an import.
- It is recommended that the import packages be imported from a central file share instead of a client.
- You should address whether many system administrators will have limited PCD access to certain dedicated folders or only a limited number of system administrators will have wider access to certain parts of the PCD tree and can import content.
- When multiple system administrators can import transport packages, it is recommended that the admin who does the transport is governed based on the transport naming prefixes.
- Transport packages must be imported based on time stamps, so that younger content is not overwritten by older content.
- Import packages during a scheduled maintenance window.

Import Options

You can display a list of deployed portal applications and test them with the Portal Anywhere application that can be accessed at http://<host>50100/irj/servlet/prt/portal/prtroot/PortalAnywhere.Go.

The following options are available for importing content:

- Import the PAR files using the cluster admin console http://<host><port> /irj/servlet/prt/portal/prtroot/com.sap.portal.runtime.system.console .ClusterAdminConsole as shown below. This application can also be accessed by choosing System Administration | Support on the top-level menu and Support Desk in the detailed navigation menu. Clicking Portal Runtime will display the Administration Console in the "Portal Anywhere" Admin Tools section. In the Archive Uploader section, click the Browse button to point to the par file that needs to be deployed onto the portal and click the Upload button:

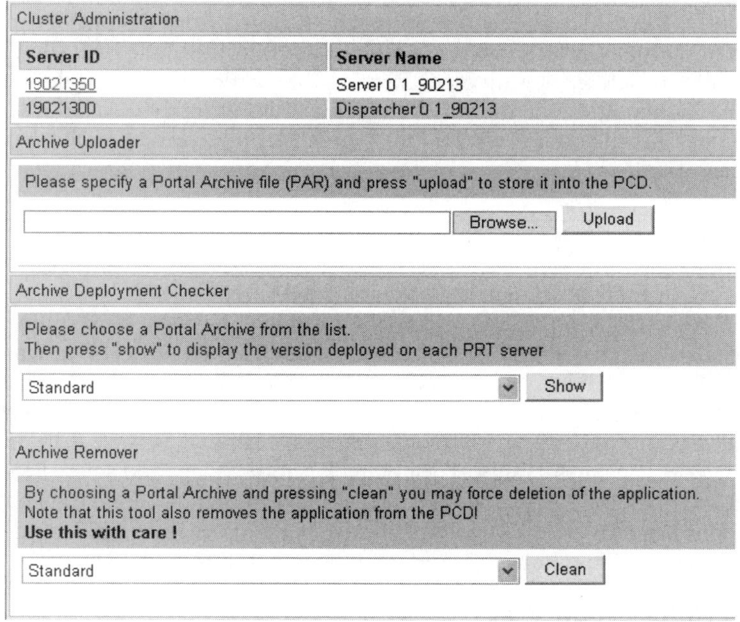

- Import the PAR files using the Package Import Editor on the portal
- Import the PAR files using the SDM GUI
- Import the PAR files using the SDM command-line interface
- Import the PAR files using the NWDS and NWDI

Exclude PAR Files from the EPA Archives for Export

By default, when deploying the portal content, the dependent objects are also included as part of the content. Since the PAR files are part of the dependent objects, they are deployed automatically along with other content objects. However, if you chose to separate the deployment of portal content objects and the PAR files, you must configure the PCD to exclude the PAR files when creating a transport package.

To do this, you should include the entry com.sapportals.portal.application .applicationrepository.Archive for the properties Pcd.TranportApplication.Export .ExcludeObjectTypes and Pcd.TranportApplication.Export.ExcludeObjectTypesAfterRule Processing.

Until Enterprise Portal 6.0 SP2, the PAR files were included as part of the transport package and were part of the EPA files. This is the recommended approach for situations in which the number of Java developments is very limited and hence the NetWeaver Development Infrastructure (NWDI) infrastructure is not used as such. However, if a large number of custom portal developments and J2EE applications such as Web Dynpro exist that necessitate a NWDI infrastructure, the recommended approach is to convert the PAR files into EAR files and then deploy them using the SDM tool.

When using SDM, you should try to separate the PAR file from the portal content objects. The portal content objects will continue to be part of the EPA files. The PAR file usually requires other content such as logging configuration that is required for deployment using SDM, which is not available in a typical EPA file. Thus, removing the PAR file from the EPA file and creating an EAR file on its own for subsequent deployment using SDM helps to prevent deployment issues.

NOTE *For additional help, refer to OSS Note 725797.*

Prevent Users from Uploading Transport Packages from Client

The Enable File Upload from the Client property of the delta linked standard Import Transport iView should be changed from Yes to No. To access the delta linked Import iView, select Content Administration | Portal Content and navigate to Portal Content | Portal Administrators | System Administrators | System Admin. Right click System Admin role and select Open | Object. In the role editor on the right, navigate to System Admin | System Administration | Transport | Transport Packages | Import. Right click Import iView and select Properties from the context menu to open the iView's property editor on the right. Change the Enable File Upload from Client property from Yes to No. This prevents users from uploading transport packages from the client. This change should be done in both QA and PRD.

Convert the EPA Files into SDM Files

The last three options (using SDM GUI, SDM command-line interface, NWDS and NWDI) involve converting the PAR files into an EAR file and the EPA files into SDA files.

Converting the EPA files into an SDA file basically includes adding some software logistic metadata that are required for deployment using the SDM tool.

Finally, an SCA file can be created that includes all the SDA files and the EAR files, thus bundling all the portal applications and the portal content together. Figure 22-6 illustrates this.

Here's how to create the SDA file for EPA and EAR files:

1. Download the sapmake_util.zip file from the OSS Note 696084 attachment and extract it to the installation directory of SAP NetWeaver Developer Studio. If the NWDS is installed in C:\Program Files\SAP\JDT, extract the files into C:\Program Files\SAP.
2. Change the environment variable `SAPIDE_HOME`, if it already exists, from C:\Program Files\SAP\JDT to C:\Program Files\SAP. Add a new variable, if it does not exist already.

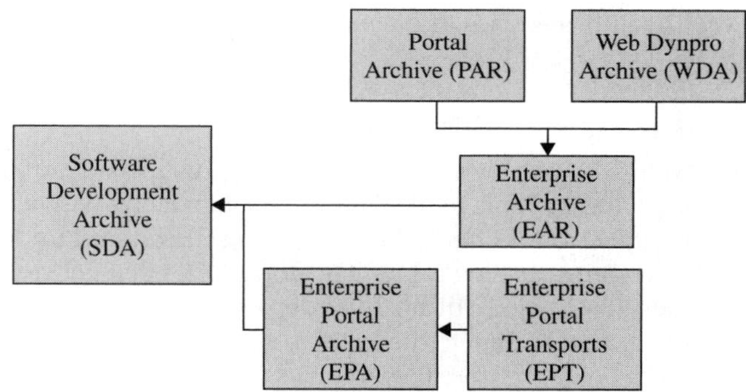

EPA + Software Logistics Metadata = SDA

SDA + EAR = SCA

Using SAP Make Utility, we can convert the following
par2sda – PAR file to SDA file
epa2sda – EPA file to SDA file
SDA to SCA file

FIGURE 22-6 Bundling of EPT, PAR, WDA, and EAR, EPA into SDA and SCA files

3. Change the `PATH` variable to include %SAPIDE_HOME%\sapmake_util.
4. Add a vendor ID with a length lesser than 20 characters in the sapmake .properties file. Navigate to the sapmake.properties file and change the `vendor=unspecified` to `vendor=`*XYZ*, where *XYZ* is the name of the vendor.

```
# Unique identifier for the company/organization which created the
software
# This property is part of SCA and SDA identifiers - it helps to avoid
naming conflicts
# of software from different vendors.
# not longer than 20 characters
# Recommendation: use the internet domain name of your company/
organisation,
# e.g. mycompany.com
#
vendor=customer
# The release of a software component
# This property is part of software component versions (major version).
#
release=0
```

5. To create an SDA file out of a PAR file, navigate to the folder that contains the PAR file and use this command:

```
par2sda <name of PAR file> [results-dir]
```

6. To create an SDA file from the EPA file, use the command

```
epa2sda <name of EPA file> <development component name to be created>
[results-dir]
```

7. To create an SCA file from SDA files, use this command:

```
sca <name of directory containing sda files> <software component name
to be created> [results-dir]
```

Note that in all three cases, the result file is created in the current working directory by default.

Deployment Using the SDM Tool

Using the SDM tool for deployment provides some distinct advantages. All the deployments through the SDM are available in the SDM file system along with all the related metadata. The deployments can be troubleshooted using the log files stored under the /usr/sap/<sid>/<instance>/SDM/program/log folder. The import files that get created during a normal portal import continue to be created during SDM deployment. Moreover, any errors that occur during a portal import are also written to the system/server.log. The SDM prevents the same transport package files from being deployed again unless the option to deploy an older version is selected during the deployment.

Tip *Once the transport file is deployed, you cannot undeploy it using the SDM tool because it has no control over the PCD tables for undeployment.*

Another advantage in using the SDM is that you can automate the deployments using a script file that can be scheduled to run at certain times, and this can be used for multiple deployments. To use the script file, you run the SDM in a standalone mode using this command:

```
sdm jstartup "mode=standalone"
```

To coordinate multiple deployments, you must run the following command multiple times, pointing to the different files each time:

```
sdm deploy "file=<path>"
```

where *<path>* points to the location where the files to be deployed are available.

After the deployment is over, change the SDM to run in an integrated mode using the command

```
sdm jstartup "mode=integrated"
startserver.bat
```

Importing Using the Package Import Editor

To import content using the Package Import Editor, go to System Administration | Transport in the top-level menu and choose Transport Packages | Import in the detailed navigation menu. Then select either the Client or the Server radio button, and navigate to the directory that contains the EPA file. Click the Import button to import the transport package. Note that while importing, the objects belonging to the namespace com.sap.portal and com.sap.km are not imported.

Note *When importing, if only the individual objects are exported without the folder hierarchy, the corresponding hierarchy is also created in the target system, but only object IDs are used instead of folder names because the folder attribute information is missing.*

If only part of the hierarchy is exported and imported into the target system, the hierarchy is created for the part as usual and the hierarchy gets created for the other part also, but with IDs only instead of folder names.

Importing EP 5.0 Portal Content

You should consider several limitations when importing EP 5.0 content. The portal content in EP 5.0 is usually in a .pkg format if it was exported from an EP 5.0 system. The EP 5.0 content downloaded from SDN is already in a ZIP format.

DO *When trying to import from the client, the .pkg file should be wrapped in the ZIP format. On the other hand, if importing from a server, the ZIP file format cannot be used. So the ZIP file should be extracted and the included .pkg file should be used for importing.*

Read and write permissions are required for the export directory, import directory, the log file directory, and the PKG package. The message "ENDOFPROTOCOL" appears at the end of the log when the import is completed.

It is not possible to monitor the EP 5.0 import in the same manner as EP 6.0 content is monitored. All the imported content appears under Portal Content | Migrated Content | EP 5.0.

Import Reporting

A file similar to the report for the export is created for the import process as well. The location of the file is similar to that of the export file and is maintained by the PCD property Pcd.TransportApplication.ProcessReportDir.

Importing to Production

Once the imported changes in QA have been fully tested and approved, the changes can be imported into the PRD system. It is good practice to use different folders to store the transport package files.

TIP *You could name folders* in process, archive, *and* export *to help you identify each type of package file.*

The export folder in the development system can be mounted on to the QA import folder. You can create three folders in QA—the in-process folder, failed folder, and the archive folder. You can create one archive folder for the PRD.

Once the transport package is imported into QA and successfully tested, the transport package can be stored in the QA archive folder.

The export folder in QA is mounted to the import folder in PRD. Once the transport package is successfully imported into the PRD system, it is important to store the file in the archive folder maintained for PRD as a kind of backup.

NOTE *Refer to the central OSS Note 679516 for information about the Transport Package Editor.*

Useful OSS Notes

Following are some useful OSS notes that can be accessed at http://service.sap.com/notes:

- **696084** EP 6.0: How to create SDA files for EPA or PAR files
- **788265** EP6.0 How To transport a Portal Desktop
- **1003674** Enhancement for non-ABAP systems in CTS
- **972495** NW 7.10 Portal Export: references to GPAL objects
- **937074** EP6.0 NW04: cleanup interval for transport process reports
- **588913** Central note for Import and Export for EP 6.0
- **679516** Central Note for the Transport Package Editor
- **725797** EP6.0 NW04: Export of PAR files within EPA packages
- **914382** PCD deployment fails due to locked objects
- **827768** Comparison between Migration and Transport
- **690310** EP 6.0: logging and tracing for transport
- **618161** EP6.0 Export/Import: avoid overwriting of system objects
- **737448** EP6: Import does not update cached objects
- **991599** EP: Cluster synchronization for imported PCD objects fails
- **906120** Import error when trying to import NW'04s package in NW'04

NOTE *For more details, refer to the portal transport related resources listed in Appendix B.*

Summary

This chapter examined the need for portal transports and covered the steps involved in the transport process. It discussed some best practices when creating portal transports, such as creating a separate role for administrators to transport content, creating packages centered around roles, and limiting the number of objects in a package. It also discussed the importance of package properties such as resolve references, references filter, and transport mode. You learned how to create personalization data transport packages, language transport packages, and packages for system objects. You read about the report generated for exports and imports, setting up PCD properties for transports, and naming convention for exports. The chapter discussed the import process; the errors encountered during import, recommendations for import; and the different options available for import such as SDM, NWDI, Portal Anywhere application; the cluster admin console, and the Package Import Editor. Finally, the chapter discussed the importance of excluding the PAR files from EPA files for export, converting the EPA files into SDA files, and importing content using SDM and the Portal Import Editor.

CHAPTER 23

Installing Support Packages Using Java Support Package Manager

Java Support Package Manager (JSPM) is a software deployment tool that can be used for installing business packages, software components, and SAP kernel binaries. In this chapter, you learn about the prerequisites for installing support package (SP) stacks and support packages, and using the JSPM to install the SP stacks and support packages.

JSPM can be used for the following:

- Installing support package stacks and support packages for existing software components
- Installing or upgrading business packages
- Updating SAP kernel binaries, Software Delivery Manager (SDM), and Internet Graphics Service (IGS)
- Self-updating JSPM so that the latest version is used
- Deploying new SAP and non-SAP software components
- Installing additional usage types such as Enterprise Portal (EP) or Process Integration (PI)

Why JSPM Rather than SDM?

7.0 (2004s) Starting from SAP NetWeaver, the JSPM tool is recommended by SAP to install the support package stacks and support packages for SAP NetWeaver AS Java. Prior to NetWeaver 7.0 (2004s), tools such as SAPINST and SDM could be used for applying the support packages.

So the obvious question is why is JSPM now required and how is it superior to these other tools? When installing new support packages, support packages stacks, and new software components, JSPM ensures that the required prerequisites and dependencies are met.

In addition, JSPM uses the SDM to carry out the deployment in the background, so it automates some of the manual steps that you have to carry out during SDM deployment. The JSPM shares the same GUI (also known as *Software Delivery Tool*) as other tools such as SAPINST (used during installation) and SAPJup (used for upgrading Java instances) and is easy to use.

JSPM can be used to work in sync with the NetWeaver Development Infrastructure (NWDI) so that JSPM identifies the changed software component archive files in the DEV and CONS systems and transports them for deployment to the NWDI.

Installing the Support Packages

Java Support packages are the complete versions of the development components for an application. They can be delivered in the form of Software Component Archives (SCAs), JAR files, and SAR files. They can be delivered as a single component patch such as Patch 2 of support package 9. When installing Java support packages, you should install the latest support package level because they are complete versions of the development components. After installing the support packages. You should check for any OSS notes that identify any dependencies with other JSPMs.

When installing support packages, the JSPM checks whether the existing SP versions in the system are lower than the SP versions identified for deployment. It also checks whether the required software component versions are available for the support packages.

Installing the Support Package Stack

A *support package stack* is a collection of support packages for all the software components belonging to one product. It is a set of package versions that ideally work best together. It can consist of SCAs, SDM JAR files, Kernel SAR files (both database and database independent), SAPCAR files, and IGS SAR files. As the JAVA support package stack contains the kernal and SDM files, it can be used to update the SAP kernel, the SDM, and OS libraries.

When installing a complete support package stack, the JSPM uses a complete stack definition file that can be generated from the Service Marketplace at the time of downloading the support package stack. This is an XML configuration file that contains the details of the components within that SP stack, the SP levels, and the patch levels. It contains information regarding the OS and database used and is relevant for a particular installation only.

NOTE *The support package stack file ensures that the system is consistent by checking to determine whether the required prerequisites for all the software components in the system are met before deployment.*

Prerequisites for Installing SP Stacks and Support Packages

Following are some of the prerequisites required for installing SP stacks and support packages.

Back up the AS Java and Database Instance

Before installing the support package stacks or the support packages, you should take a backup of the Web AS Java instance and the database instance to avoid risks. The JSPM is going to modify the software components in the system, so a backup makes sense.

Check Names of EXE and Profile Folders

To start the JSPM, you must run the `start` command (`go.bat`) from the Windows command prompt as the <SID>adm user. Since the JSPM will refer to the /usr/sap/<SID>/SYS/exe and /usr/sap/*<SID>*/SYS/profile folders for kernel and profile parameters during startup, you must ensure that the names of these folders have not changed, especially after a previous backup. If so, the JSPM may not start.

Download Archives into the JSPM Inbox Directory

Ensure that the support package stack and the corresponding stack definition file or the support package have been downloaded into the JSPM inbox directory, whose default location is /usr/sap/trans/EPS/in.

TIP *Ensure that the <SID>adm user has read permissions to the /usr/sap/trans/EPS/in folder.*

To check the location of the JSPM inbox directory, open the command prompt in Windows, and change the working directory to the <drive>:\usr\sap\J2E\SYS\exe\uc\NTI386 location where the sappfpar executable is available. Then enter this command (see the illustration as well):

```
<drive>:\usr\sap\J2E\SYS\exe\uc\NTI386>sappfpar pf=<drive>:\usr\sap\<SID>\
SYS\profile\<SID>_<central_instance_name>_<host> DIR_EPS_ROOT
```

```
C:\usr\sap\J2E\SYS\exe\uc\NTI386>sappfpar pf=c:\usr\sap\j2e\SYS\profile\j2e_scs0
0_gems DIR_EPS_ROOT
\\gems\sapmnt\trans\EPS
```


Increase the SDM Timeout

During deployment, the SDM tries to start/stop the J2EE engine for SP6 and higher. For certain support package stacks, especially those that are related to EP, you should increase the SDM timeout to 2 hours from its default value of 30 minutes. Navigate to the folder *<drive>*:\usr\sap*<SID>**<instance_name><instance_no>*\SDM\program and execute `sdm j2eeenginestartstop mode=automatic timeoutmillisec=7200000` as shown in the following illustration:

```
C:\usr\sap\J2E\JC01\SDM\program>sdm j2eeenginestartstop mode=automatic timeoutmi
llisec=7200000
```


Synchronize the JSPM and the SDM Repository

Sometimes the JSPM does not update the versions of the deployed component in the database during the deployment, even though it has updated the SDM repository. To remove this inconsistency, do the following:

Stop the SDM server by running the StopServer batch file under the *<drive>*:\usr\sap*<SID>**<instance_name><instance_no>*\SDM\program folder and run the following commands in the Windows system:

```
sdm jstartup "mode=standalone"
sdm systemcomponentstate "mode=activate"
sdm jstartup "mode=integrated"
```

Start the SDM server by running the StartServer batch file and then restart the JSPM.

Check for Sufficient Free Space for the J2EE Engine

You must ensure that there is sufficient disk space before installing these components. For logging and storing data, you need at least 20 MB of free space in the /usr/sap/*<SID>*/*<central_instance_name>*/j2ee/JSPM. When patching a kernel or IGS, there must be at least three times the size of the downloaded archives free space in the /usr/sap/*<SID>*/*<central_instance_name>*/j2ee/JSPM/tmp folder. For SDM patches, there should be 10 MB of free space in the same folder. For deploying J2EE-related SCA components, there must be at least three times the size of the SCA files free space in the usr/sap/*<SID>*/*<central_instance_name>*/SDM folder.

Deploy the Required JSPM Support Package Level

Before installing a support package stack, support package, or a new software component of a given support package level, you must ensure that the JSPM is at the same level as the SP stack, support package, or the SP level of the software component, respectively. To update the JSPM, you must deploy it as a single support package.

TIP *To deploy business packages using JSPM, you must update the JSPM to the highest available support package level as a single support package.*

Starting the JSPM

Let's now proceed by starting the JSPM.

1. Navigate to the /usr/sap/*<SID>*/*<central_instance_name>*/j2ee/JSPM folder and double click go.bat. If you are not running as the <SID>adm user, you will see the following error:

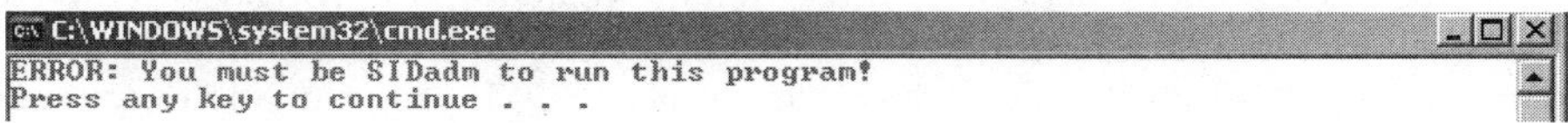

2. Choose Start | Programs | Accessories, right-click Command Prompt, and choose Run As, as shown next.

3. Enter the <SID>adm user, as shown next. The command prompt will then appear.

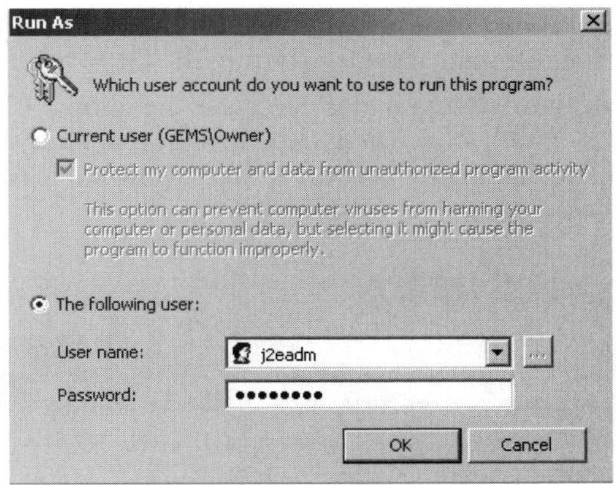

4. Change the working directory by entering
   `cd /usr/sap/<SID>/<central_instance_name>/j2ee/JSPM`
   in the command prompt, and then press ENTER. Then enter **go.bat** and press ENTER. The Log On screen for JSPM will appear, as shown here:

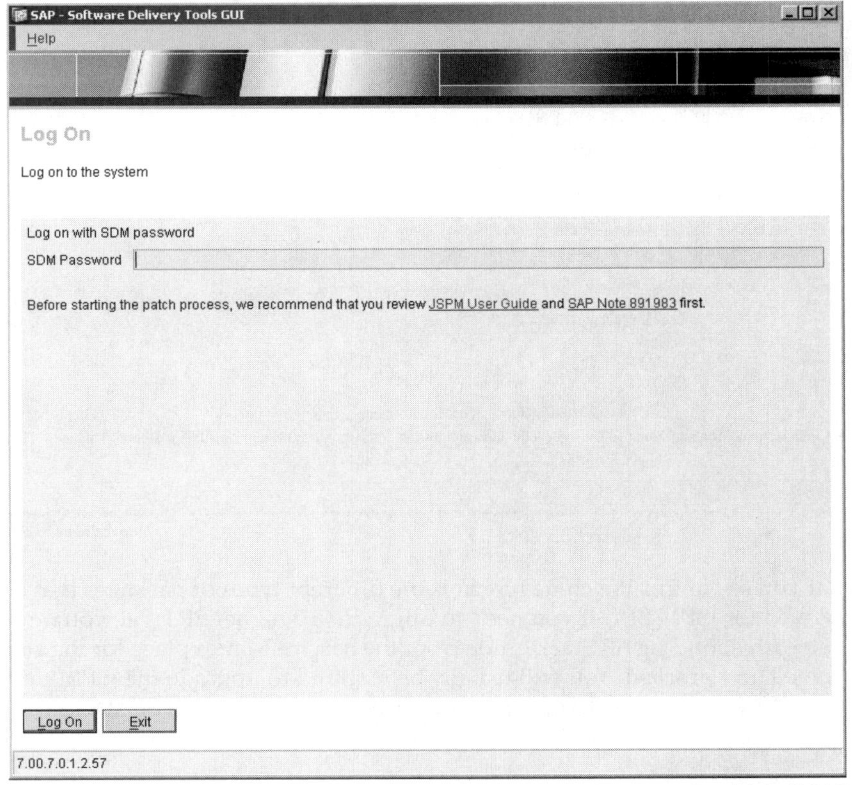

If the Log On screen does not appear, ensure that the SDM, J2EE server, dispatcher, and the database are running. Then try starting the JSPM again.

5. Enter the SDM password. (Note that if you enter the wrong SDM password three times, the SDM server will stop. You'll have to start it again and log in.) Enter the correct password and be patient, because it takes quite some time to log on. The GUI appears as shown next:

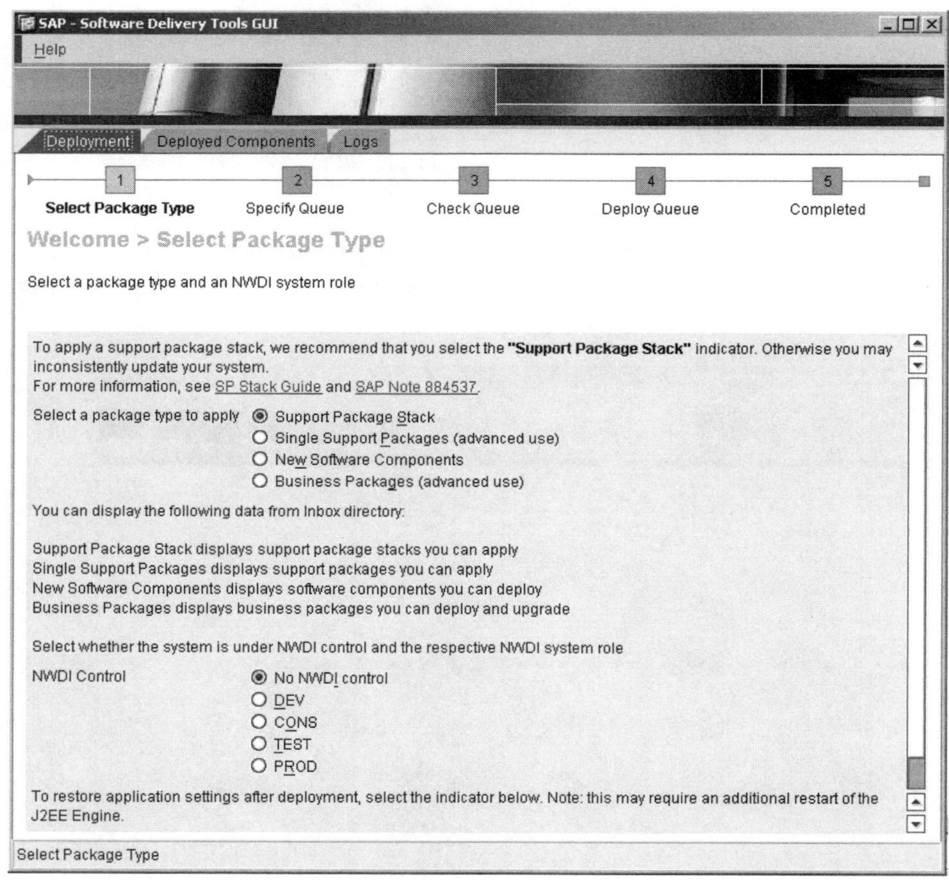

What you see in this Welcome screen is the different types of packages that can be deployed for JSPM SP7. If you need to upgrade to a higher SP level, you must refer to the corresponding SP Stack guide from the Service Marketplace for the steps involved and proceed. You will usually be required to upgrade the JSPM first to the latest SP level and then deploy the other support packages and SP stacks.

Installing the Latest JSPM Support Package

In this section, we'll install the latest version of JSPM, which at this time is SP12.

1. Download the JSPM along with the other support package stacks for the different usage types that are already installed in the system. To do this, go to http://service.sap.com/sp-stacks, click the Downloads tab, then click SP Stack Download, as shown next:

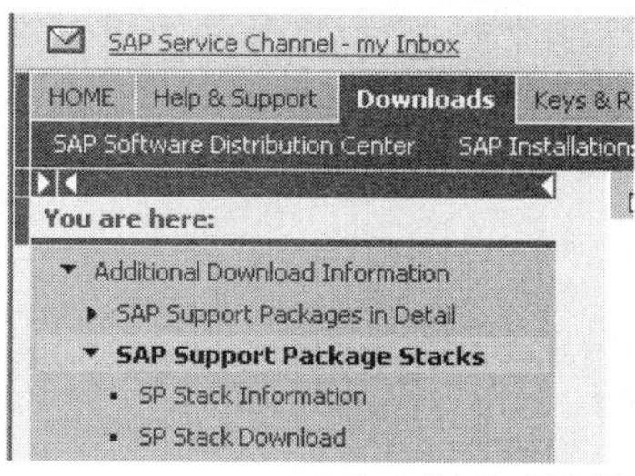

Copyright by SAP AG

2. Select SP Stack SAP NetWeaver 2004s, as JSPM is part of the Usage type Java. The following Support Package Stack Downloads screen appears:

Copyright by SAP AG

3. Ensure that the SP levels are the same for all the usage types that have already been installed. To check for the installed usage types, go to http://*<hostname>*:*<port>* for the J2EE engine and then click System Information.

TIP *Forgetting to upgrade even one usage type that was already installed in the system will result in inconsistencies.*

PART V

4. Click the All Components link, as shown next:

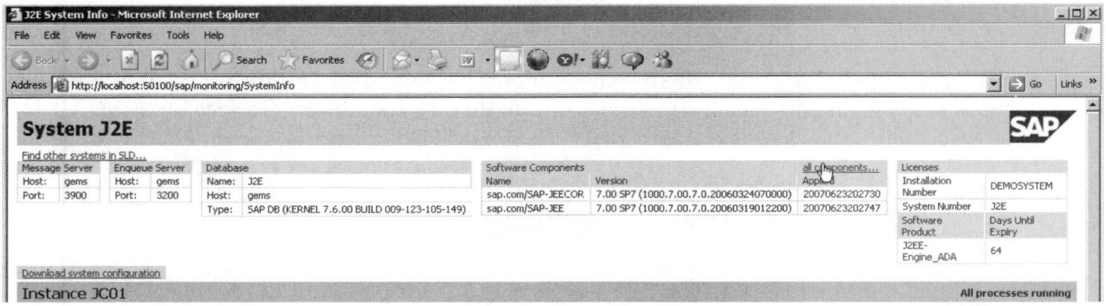

Copyright by SAP AG

The next screen displays the list of software components, vendor names, versions, and the component names, from which you should try to infer the usage types installed.

TIP *Refer to OSS Note 883948 to identify the list of software components for various usage types.*

Note that after installing the new usage type, you must follow it up with some initial configuration steps, as outlined in the installation guide, because unlike SAPinst, JSPM does not carry out these steps.

5. Once you have identified the usage types in step 4, select those usage types in the Usage Selection section of the Step 1 of 3 - Choose Your Source And Target Stack screen; then select the Source Stack, if known, and click Next Step.
6. In the Choose Configuration step, select both the database and operating system configurations that apply to your installation. Also do not forget to select the database and operating system–independent support packages. Choose the appropriate 32- or 64-bit configuration for the Windows system. Click Next Step.

   The list of downloadable support packages will appear in the Step 3 of 3 - Downloadable Support Packages screen as shown next:

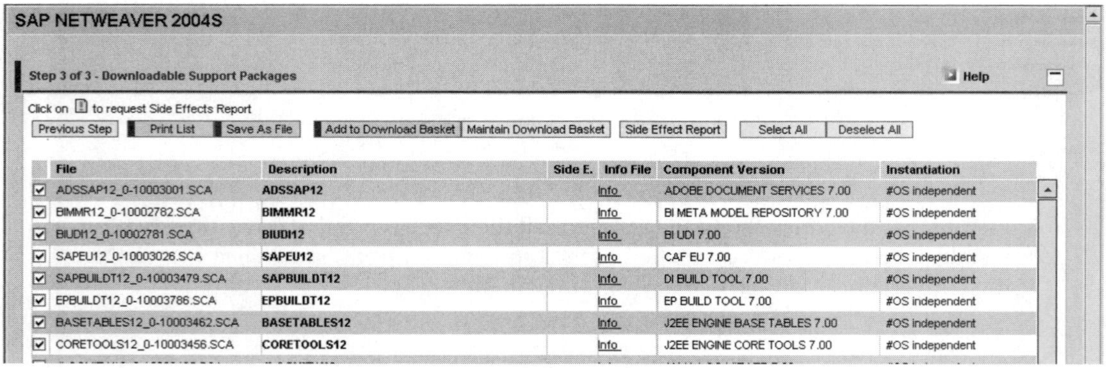

Copyright by SAP AG

7. Make necessary changes, if any, and then click Save As File.
8. Right click and choose Save Target As (as shown next) to save the file as an XML file; save the file as SPSTab.xml under the <*drive*>:\usr\sap\trans\EPS\in folder. This is the support package stack XML configuration file that you referred to earlier. This XML file and the support packages should be stored in the same directory.

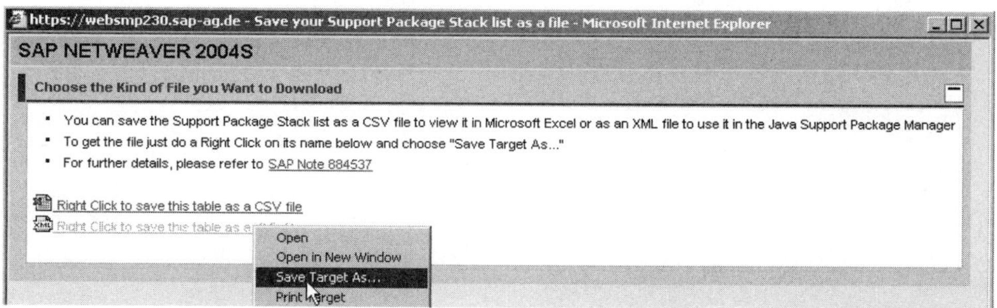

Copyright by SAP AG

Install SAP Download Manager

Now we'll install the SAP Download Manager.

1. In the Step 3 of 3 - Downloadable Support Packages screen, click Add To Download Basket. The following screen appears. Click Download Basket.

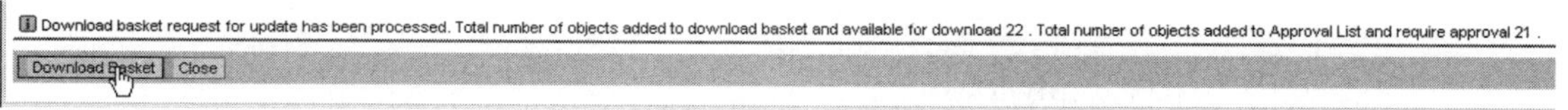

Copyright by SAP AG

The list of downloadable support packages appears, as shown next:

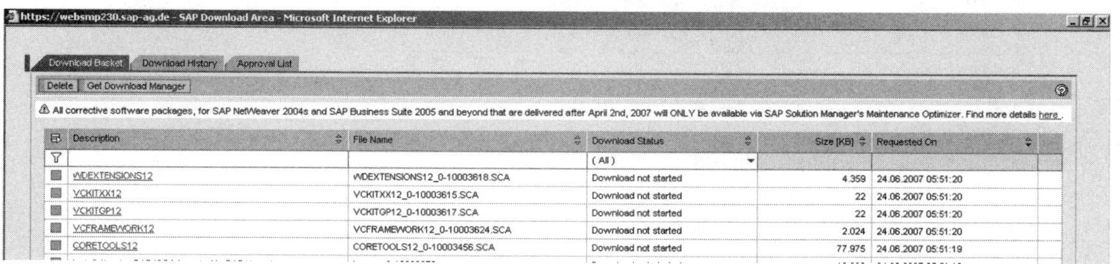

Description	File Name	Download Status	Size [KB]	Requested On
		(All)		
WDEXTENSIONS12	WDEXTENSIONS12_0-10003618.SCA	Download not started	4.359	24.06.2007 05:51:20
VCKITXX12	VCKITXX12_0-10003615.SCA	Download not started	22	24.06.2007 05:51:20
VCKITGP12	VCKITGP12_0-10003617.SCA	Download not started	22	24.06.2007 05:51:20
VCFRAMEWORK12	VCFRAMEWORK12_0-10003624.SCA	Download not started	2.024	24.06.2007 05:51:20
CORETOOLS12	CORETOOLS12_0-10003456.SCA	Download not started	77.975	24.06.2007 05:51:19

Copyright by SAP AG

PART V

2. To install the SAP Download Manager, click Get Download Manager, and then click Installing The Download Manager. Click the Microsoft Windows Installer link under the Installation Instructions for Microsoft Windows section, as shown next. Then click Run and proceed through the various steps in the Installation Wizard.

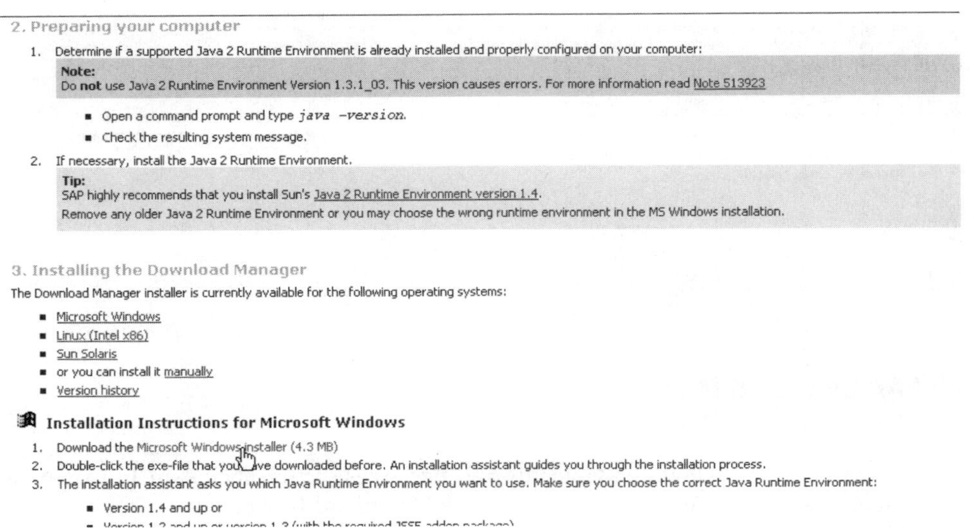

2. Preparing your computer

1. Determine if a supported Java 2 Runtime Environment is already installed and properly configured on your computer:

   Note:
   Do **not** use Java 2 Runtime Environment Version 1.3.1_03. This version causes errors. For more information read Note 513923

   - Open a command prompt and type *java -version*.
   - Check the resulting system message.

2. If necessary, install the Java 2 Runtime Environment.

   Tip:
   SAP highly recommends that you install Sun's Java 2 Runtime Environment version 1.4.
   Remove any older Java 2 Runtime Environment or you may choose the wrong runtime environment in the MS Windows installation.

3. Installing the Download Manager

The Download Manager installer is currently available for the following operating systems:

- Microsoft Windows
- Linux (Intel x86)
- Sun Solaris
- or you can install it manually
- Version history

Installation Instructions for Microsoft Windows

1. Download the Microsoft Windows installer (4.3 MB)
2. Double-click the exe-file that you have downloaded before. An installation assistant guides you through the installation process.
3. The installation assistant asks you which Java Runtime Environment you want to use. Make sure you choose the correct Java Runtime Environment:
   - Version 1.4 and up or

Copyright by SAP AG

3. Once the SAP Download Manager installation is complete, go to Start | All Programs | SAP Download Manager | Download Manager. The SAP Download Manager appears, as shown next:

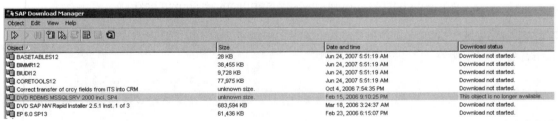

SAP Download Manager

Object Edit View Help

Object	Size	Date and time	Download status
BASETABLES12	28 KB	Jun 24, 2007 5:51:19 AM	Download not started.
BIMMR12	38,455 KB	Jun 24, 2007 5:51:19 AM	Download not started.
BIUDI12	9,728 KB	Jun 24, 2007 5:51:19 AM	Download not started.
CORETOOLS12	77,975 KB	Jun 24, 2007 5:51:19 AM	Download not started.
Correct transfer of crcy fields from ITS into CRM	unknown size.	Oct 4, 2006 7:54:35 PM	Download not started.
DVD RDBMS MSSQLSRV 2000 incl. SP4	unknown size.	Feb 15, 2006 9:10:25 PM	This object is no longer available.
DVD SAP NW Rapid Installer 2.5.1 Inst. 1 of 3	683,594 KB	Mar 18, 2006 3:24:37 AM	Download not started.
EP 6.0 SP13	61,436 KB	Feb 23, 2006 6:15:07 PM	Download not started.

Copyright by SAP AG

4. Choose View | Download Manager Configuration to open the screen shown next:

Copyright by SAP AG

5. Enter the SMP credentials and maintain the proxy, if relevant for your installation.
6. Select the objects you want to download. Then download all the selected objects by clicking the double right arrow, as shown here:

Copyright by SAP AG

7. Once all the support packages have been downloaded, proceed to the download store folder of SAP Download Manager and copy the packages into the EPS inbox folder, namely, <*drive*>:\usr\sap\trans\EPS\in. The location where the support packages are downloaded in SAP Download Manager is available in the Download Manager config, which can be accessed by choosing View | Download Manager Configuration | Download Store.
8. Now go back to the JSPM GUI and select Single Support Packages (Advanced Use). Before proceeding with the next step, ensure that all the manual steps, if any, as mentioned in the SP Stack Guide for the SP level under consideration, have been followed.
9. Under the NetWeaverDI Control section on the Select Package Screen, select No NetWeaverDI Control. If the DEV and CONS are selected, the JSPM does not apply the support packages on the modified software components. The JSPM then sends the standard service packages of the unmodified software components to the NetWeaverDI for modification adjustment. If TEST or PROD is selected, the JSPM does not apply support packages at all until the modification adjustment is completed. Click Next.

10. In the Specify Queue screen, select the sap.com/JSPM support package and click Show Details to display the following screen:

Select support packages to apply

Vendor/Name	Current SPLevel.PatchLevel	Target SPLevel.PatchLevel	Details
sap.com/JSPM	7.0	12.0	Show Details
com.sap/pdk-content	1.0	not found	Show Details

Archive file(s) location:\\gems\sapmnt\trans\EPS\in\JSPM12_0-10003470.SCA

Vendor/Name	Release	SP Level	Counter	Provider
List of DCs				
sap.com/JSPM	7.00	12.0	1000.7.00.12.0.20070507080400	SAP AG
sap.com/tc/sdt/app/jspm	7.00	12.0	7.0012.20070405133730.0000	
sap.com/tc/sdt/app/jspm/bootstrap	7.00	12.0	7.0012.20070405133730.0000	
sap.com/tc/sdt/app/jspm/ext	7.00	12.0	7.0012.20070405133730.0000	

11. Click Next to check whether the Software component, which in this case is JSPM, is deployable. Click Next again to deploy JSPM SP 12. The Status changes to SCHEDULED. Once the software component and its development components are deployed, the status will change to DEPLOYED.
12. Select the component and click Show Details for more information.
13. Exit the JSPM by clicking Exit, and start the JSPM again so that the new JSPM with the latest SP level is used.

Additional Deployment Support Packages

The new JSPM includes additional deployable support packages, as shown next:

To apply a support package stack, we recommend that you select the **"Support Package Stack"** indicator. Otherwise you may inconsistently update your system.For more information, see SP Stack Guide and SAP Note 884537.
For recommended Java VM settings, see SAP Note 723909.

The Inbox directory is \\gems\sapmnt\trans\EPS\in.

Select a package type to apply

- (•) Support Package Stack
- ( ) Java Support Package Manager (JSPM)
- ( ) Single Support Packages (advanced use)
- ( ) New Software Components
- ( ) Business Packages (advanced use)
- ( ) Install Additional Usage Type (advanced use)

As you can see, starting from Support Package Stacks (SPS) 12, you can install a JSPM Support Package as well as additional new Usage Types. Using this procedure, you can install new usage types such as Enterprise Portal, Business Intelligence Java, Mobile Infrastructure (MI), Development Infrastructure (DI), and JCRM.

HINT *You cannot install the Java add-in for an existing Advanced Business Application Programming installation (ABAP) or Process Integration (XI) usage type using the JSPM.*

Viewing Deployed Components

Clicking the Deployed Components tab displays the list of deployed software components, development components, and modified software components. It also displays the undeployed software components with a gray color. The legends for the various objects appear on the bottom of the screen. For each component displayed, you can obtain information regarding the release, SP level, counter, and the software provider name, as shown in Figure 23-1.

For example, in Figure 23-1, you can see that the software component sap.com/NET-PDK is not deployed yet, while the software component sap.com/RTC-STREAM has been deployed. And you can see that sap.com/com.sap.portal.dotnet.framework is a development component belonging to the software component sap.com/NET-PDK.

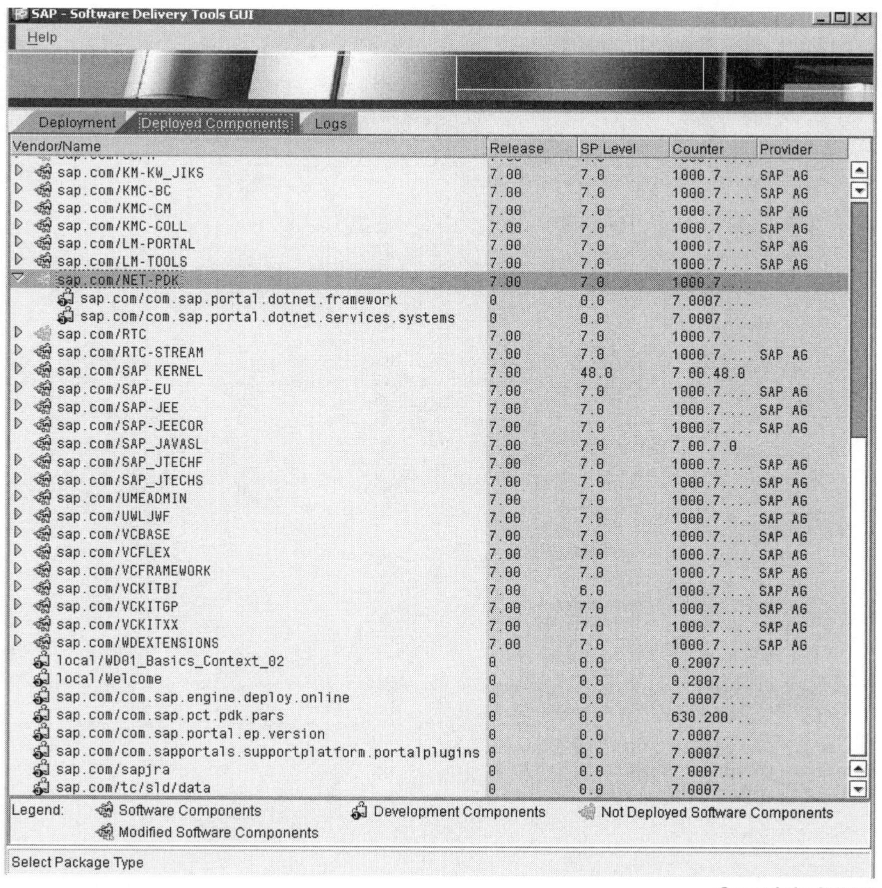

FIGURE 23-1 The Deployed Components tab

PART V

Viewing the Log Files

By clicking the Logs tab, you can see the JSPM Log Viewer, as shown in Figure 23-2. Even the SDM-generated log files are copied over to this directory.

Under Old Log Files, you can display the logs belonging to the previous sessions under each folder created for the purpose with its own timestamp. Following are some of the useful log files:

- **JSPM.LOG** Displays the JSPM GUI log
- **JSPM_PROCESS.LOG** Displays the JSPM process log
- **DETECT_SYSTEM_PARAMETERS.LOG** Displays the system parameters that were detected by the JSPM during startup

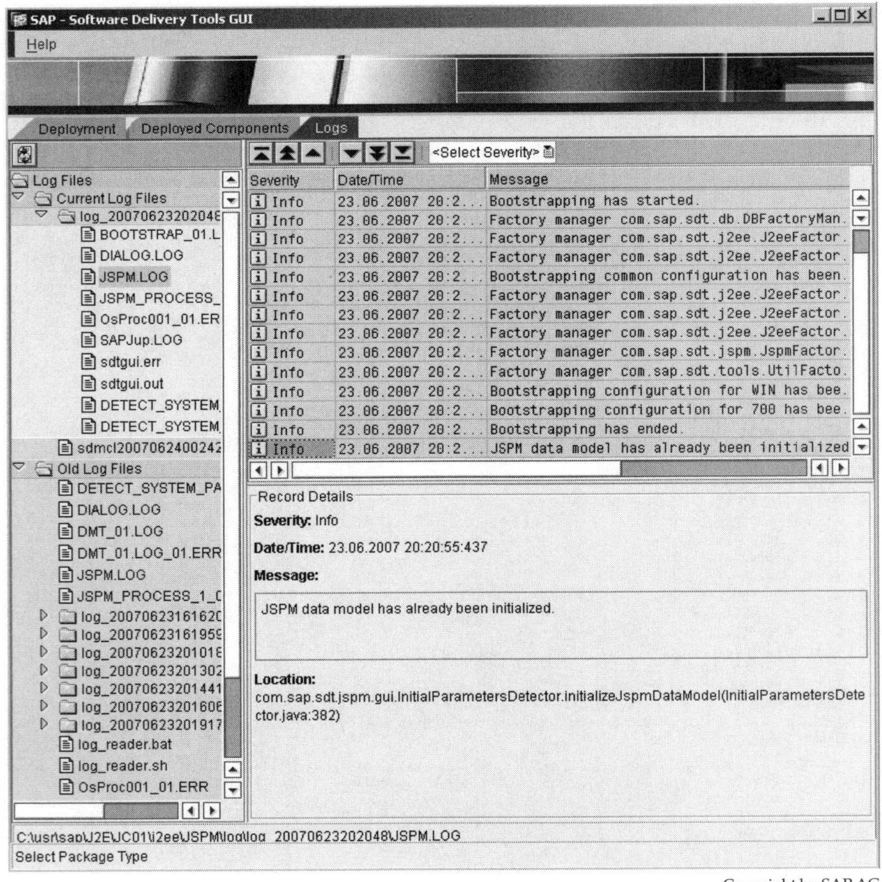

FIGURE 23-2 The JSPM Log Viewer

```
# Created by class com.sap.sdt.trace.SapLoggingAdmin on Fri Dec 03 15:00:59 EET 2004
### Set up logging and tracing format
formatter[Log] = ListFormatter
formatter[Log].pattern = %d [%5s]: %m
formatter[Trace] = TraceFormatter
formatter[Trace].pattern = %d [%s]: %-100l [%t]: %m

#### Set up tracing severity
com.sap.sdt.severity = ERROR

#### Set up logging severity
/System/Server/Upgrade.severity = INFO
```


FIGURE 23-3 Logging.properties file displaying the settings for logging and tracing

- **DETECT_SYSTEM_COMPONENTS.LOG** Displays the system components detected by the JSPM
- **sdm*.log** Displays the SDM log; available only for the current logs

The Record Details section contains the details of the log message such as the severity, date/time, the message, and location.

In the logging.properties file in the params folder, shown in Figure 23-3, the severity level for tracing is set to `ERROR` and logging is set to `INFO`. You can change the values for increased levels of debugging, if required.

DO *Remember to revert back to the default severity values once the change has served the purpose.*

JSPM Troubleshooting Issues

Following are some of the typical issues that can arise when using the JSPM.

When starting the JSPM, you may encounter issues due to the following:

- Not enough space in the disk
- JSPM GUI port 6240 is already in use
- /usr/sap/*<SID>*/*<central_instance_name>*/SDM/program/temp is missing

TIP *While troubleshooting, check the trace files in /usr/sap/*<SID>/< central_instance_name>*/ j2ee/JSPM/trc/JSPM<_xx>. for clues.*

Issues with Downloaded Files

Sometimes the downloaded files may not be visible in the JSPM for installing. The reason could be that the downloaded packages were created for older releases, or perhaps they belong to a lower or equal support package as compared to that already installed in the system. You can go ahead and download the correct versions.

TIP *After checking the queue, if the JSPM displays a revised status, the reason could be due to missing support packages or incorrectly named packages.*

PART V

Memory Issues

Sometimes you may encounter memory issues when the JSPM tries to store internal data in the XML files located in the usr/sap/<*SID*>/<*central_instance_name*>/j2ee/JSPM/data/variables folder. Refer to OSS Note 874123 to increase the JSPM JVM settings.

Because of insufficient SDM heap memory settings, the JSPM Wizard may hang at the Check Queue step.

TIP *If required, implement OSS Note 879377 to increase the SDM memory heap size.*

During deployment, if the status in the JSPM is NOT_DEPLOYED or DEPLOYED WITH ERROR, check the J2EE engine trace file for any out of memory errors. Implement OSS Note 723909 if necessary.

J2EE Engine Administrator Password Issue

Another reason for error could be that after an upgrade from SAP NetWeaver 2004 to SAP NetWeaver 2004s, the administrator was forced to change the password. This password change updates the UME and not the secured storage.

TIP *To change the password in the secured storage also, implement OSS Note 870445.*

JSPM Resources

You can access the JSPM User Guide in two ways as given below:

1. Go to www.help.sap.com, and navigate to SAP NetWeaver 7.0(2004s) and click the English link to open the SAP NetWeaver 7.0 library. Then click SAP NetWeaver By Key Capability | Solution Life Cycle Management by Key Capability | Software Life Cycle Management | Software Maintenance | Java Support Package Manager.
2. The NetWeaver 2004s Support Package Stack Guide can be accessed at http://service.sap.com/maintenanceNetWeaver70. Click the relevant SPS level and access the support package stack Guide – SPS*xx*, where *xx* is the SPS level.

Useful OSS Notes

Following are some useful OSS notes that can be accessed at http://service.sap.com/notes:

- **891983** The central note for JSPM
- **879289** The central note for the SP Stacks of SAP NetWeaver 7.0
- **884537** Information about the SP Stack Configuration XML file
- **723909** For Java VM settings
- **883948** On installing additional usage types
- **919105** SAP NetWeaver 2004s SR1 installation on Windows
- **874123** JSPM JVM memory settings

- **879377** Increase SDM JVM memory settings
- **870445** Update the password in the Secured Storage
- **764417** Troubleshooting the J2EE Engine

NOTE *For more details, refer to the JSPM related resources listed in Appendix B.*

Summary

In this chapter, you learned about the importance of JSPM and the various steps required before using the JSPM such as taking system backups, increasing the SDM timeout, ensuring free space in the J2EE engine, and upgrading the JSPM support package level. You read through an example for starting the JSPM, downloading the support packages from the service marketplace, and then installing the support packages. You also learned about some of the potential issues faced when using the JSPM, such as wrong passwords and memory issues.

24

CHAPTER

Implementing Delegated Content and System Administration

Delegated administration is an important feature of the portal that is especially useful in large-scale implementations that have global implications. Delegated administration can be used to delegate administrative activities related to

- managing content
- managing system configuration
- managing users

The delegated administration feature can be used to delegate some of the administrator activities to an administrator or a group of portal administrators. This chapter discusses how to implement delegated content and system administration.

How Delegated Administration Is Implemented

Delegated administration is made possible on the portal because of the structure in which the portal content catalog has been created. The portal content catalog contains a number of content objects such as iViews, pages, and worksets and system objects such as transports, system monitoring, and so on. Every one of those objects can be attached to an access control list (ACL).

The ACL is a combination of users and the actions that those users can perform on the content objects or system objects. By attaching an ACL to an object, you can provide various permission levels to different users and thus enable delegated administration. Since the portal content catalog can contain either content objects or system objects, you can delegate both content administration as well as system administration.

Delegated *user* administration, on the other hand, is a little different and is realized by using the *company* concept. Every user has an attribute or a property that can be attached to his or her profile, known as the *company*. By implementing delegated user administration, a delegated administrator can manage users who are attached to the same company to which they belong.

The company can be configured in different ways—for example, you can create a company for *internal users* and another company for *external users* and thus enable delegated user administration for internal and external users. Or an administrator could manage users belonging to different departments in the same organization. In that scenario, each department would be configured as an individual company.

Three factors enable delegated administration:

- Standard SAP roles
- Permission model
- Portal content catalog structure

Standard SAP Roles, Permissions, and Catalog Structure

When the portal is implemented for the first time, it contains standard SAP content out of the box, which you can customize for specific business purposes. The standard SAP content can be accessed by choosing Content Administration | Portal Content.

The portal content is delivered in the form of a folder hierarchy or a directory structure. The administrative roles have been provided in the folder content provided in SAP | Admin Content in the portal content catalog, displayed in Figure 24-1.

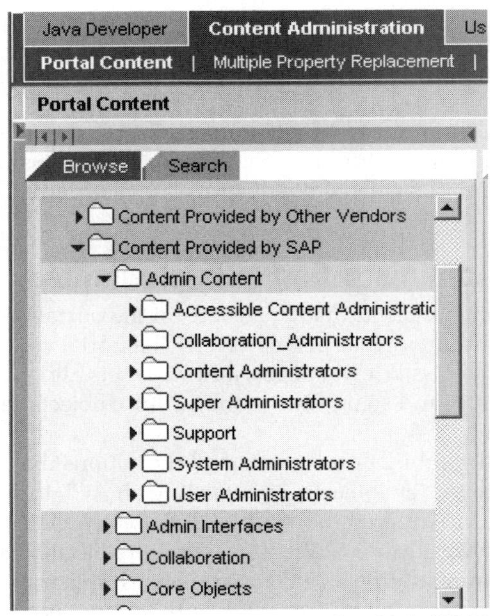

FIGURE 24-1 PCD displaying standard administrator roles

Four administrator roles are provided by SAP: *Content Administrator, System Administrator, User Administrator,* and *Super Administrator*, which is a collection of the first three roles. Since the Super Administrator is a collection of the other three roles, it does not contain a workset of its own.

You're also free to create your own custom versions of these roles and add whatever portal worksets that you deem necessary to those custom roles.

If you have trouble understanding the different icons presented in the Role Editor page, you can click the Overview tab and then view the meanings of the different icons (see Figure 24-2).

The Content Administrator role contains all the worksets that are related to managing content in the portal. Figure 24-3 shows the portal content objects such as worksets, pages, and iViews included in the Content Administrator role, which you can access via Content Provided By SAP | Admin Content | Content Administrators | Content Admin in the portal content catalog.

In the Figure 24-3, the Content Administrator role contains pages such as Portal Content and Multiple Property Replacement, followed by folders such as Portal Content Translation, Web Dynpro, Activity Report, and so on. These pages and folders related to this role are displayed as second-level menus at runtime. You can check this by choosing Content Administration | Portal Content in the top-level menu, as shown in the following illustration:

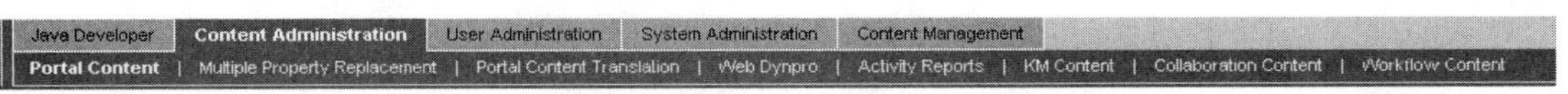

The System Administrator role contains the worksets displayed in Figure 24-4.

Figure 24-5 displays the contents of the User Administrator role.

The worksets in the User Administrator role appear as first-level menus and their content appears as second-level menus at runtime in the portal. Figures 24-4 and 24-5

Overview | Admin Content | Content Admin

The **Portal Content Studio** provides a central environment for developing and managing portal content: iViews, pages, layouts, worksets, roles and packages.

Icon Legend

Folder	iView (Hidden)
iView	Folder (Added to Delta Link Target)
iView Template	Folder (Changed in Delta Link Target)
Page	iView (Added to Delta Link Target)
Page Template	iView (Changed in Delta Link Target)
Workset	Portal Page (Added to Delta Link Target)
Role	Portal Page (Changed in Delta Link Target)
Page Layout	Workset (Added to Delta Link Target)
Unresolved Link	Workset (Changed in Delta Link Target)
Business Object	Business Object (Existing)
iView (Locked in Page)	Business Object Operation

FIGURE 24-2 Icons in the Overview tab display legends for content objects

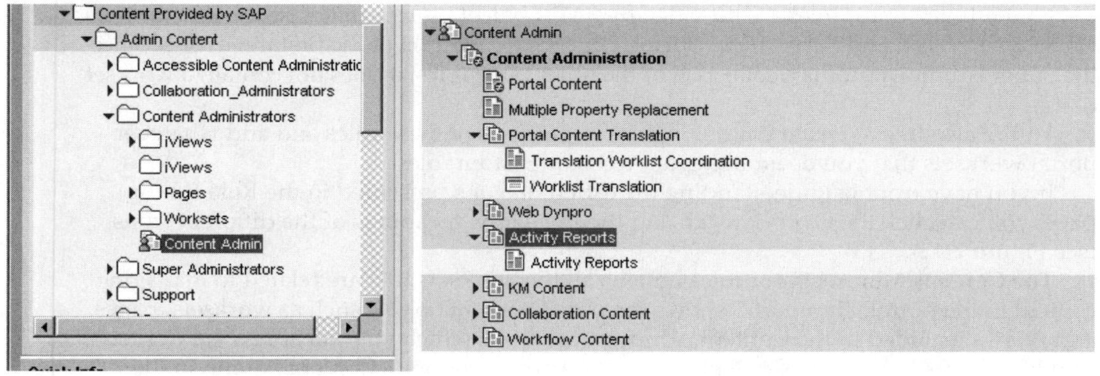

Figure 24-3 Worksets belonging to Content Administrator role

Figure 24-4 Worksets belonging to System Administrator role

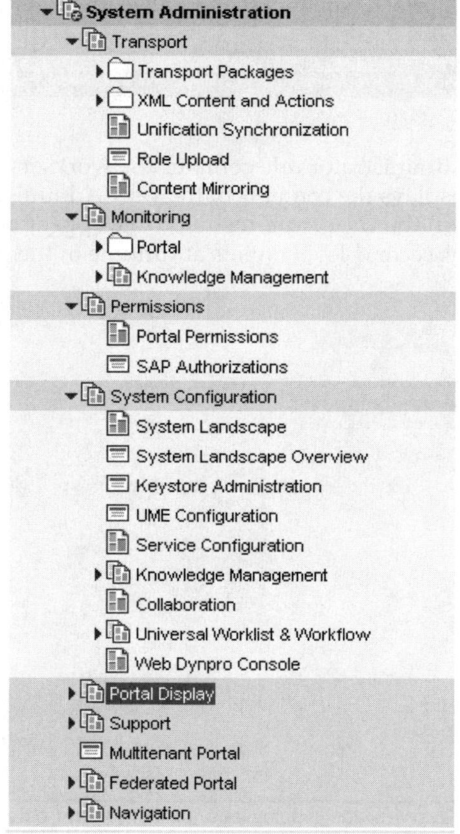

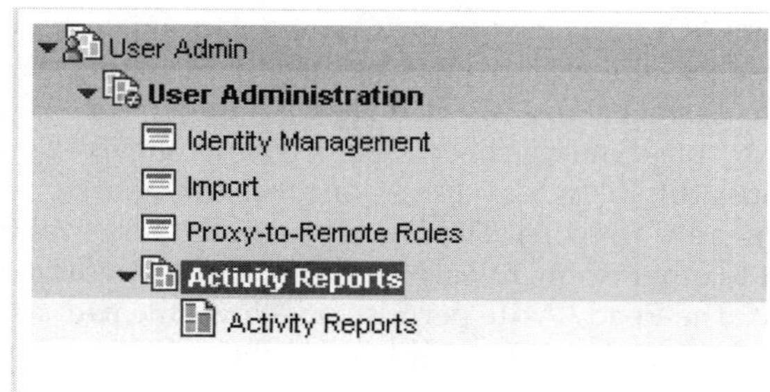

FIGURE 24-5 Worksets belonging to User Administrator role

display the contents under the System Administration and User Administration worksets, respectively. In Figure 24-4, the System Administration workset contains Transport, Monitoring, Permissions worksets, and so on. The System Administration folder appears as a first-level menu and its contents appear as second-level menus on the portal at runtime. The Transport workset, in turn, contains objects such as Transport Packages and XML Content And Actions folders, followed by a Unification Synchronization page and Role Upload iView. The content inside the Transport workset will appear in the detailed navigation menu. You may access the System Administration and the User Administration top-level menus in the portal to verify that the second-level menus under them correspond to the contents in the worksets displayed in Figures 24-4 and 24-5.

ACLs

Each of the content objects within each role is attached to an ACL. The ACL is a combination of the different actions that are possible to perform on the content as well as the users who are eligible to perform those actions.

Open the Permission Editor for the Content Administrator role object by right clicking the Content Administrator role in the portal content catalog and choosing Open | Permissions, as shown next:

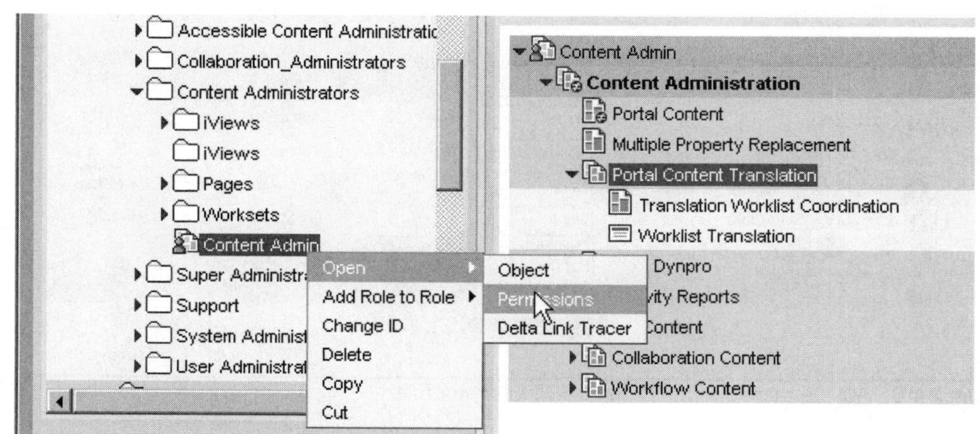

The various ACLs attached to the Content Administrator role are shown in Figure 24-6.

You can see that the ACL consists of three levels of permissions: Administrator, End User, and Role Assigner. You can also view a number of roles such as Administrator and content_admin_role that have been assigned different levels of permissions.

The various administrator permissions that can be assigned are Owner, Full Control, Read/Write, Read, and None. The Owner permission allows the user to assign permissions for this object to other users, roles, or groups. The Full Control permission lets the user delete content. The Read/Write permission allows the user to create/change this object, and the Read permission allows the user to view the object but not change it during design time in the portal content catalog.

The permissions can also be assigned to end users which controls behavior during runtime. Permissions are assigned by selecting the checkbox for End User. For the end user to be able to view any content object during runtime when logged in to the portal, the End User checkbox should be selected for that user in the ACL. This applies especially to iViews that need to be accessed by the end user during runtime.

Assigning Permissions

While assigning the ACL, you can assign the permissions to an individual user, a role, or a group, as shown next. You should generally avoid assigning permissions to individual

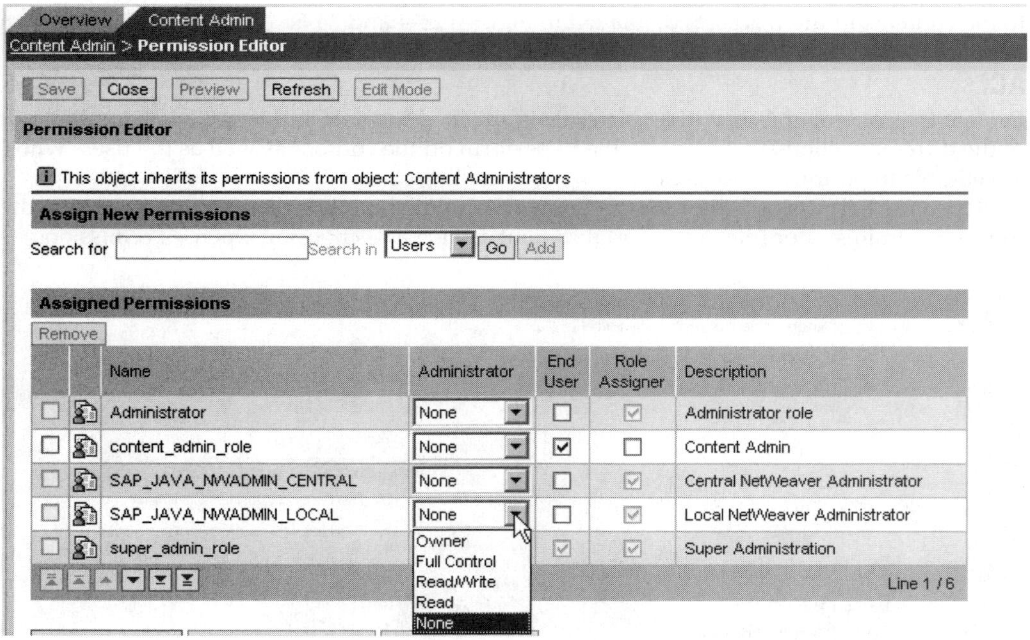

FIGURE 24-6 ACLs attached to the Content Administrator role

users, as this could turn into a potential maintenance nightmare. The most preferred way to assign permissions is to use roles.

Super Administrator All the standard SAP content, by default, offers an Ownership permission, End User permission, and the Role Assigner permission assigned to the Super Administrator. Nobody else can change the permission. Thus, an administrator with the Super Administrator role will be able to assign permissions to any object in the portal as well as view them during runtime.

Permission Inheritance Model Another important concept that enables delegated administration is the fact that all the contents within a particular folder automatically inherit the permissions that have been assigned to that folder. Consider an example that adds a user named *admin* in the portal content Permission Editor, as shown in Figure 24-7.

1. In the Permission Editor screen, search for the user by entering the user name in the Search For field and choose the Go button.

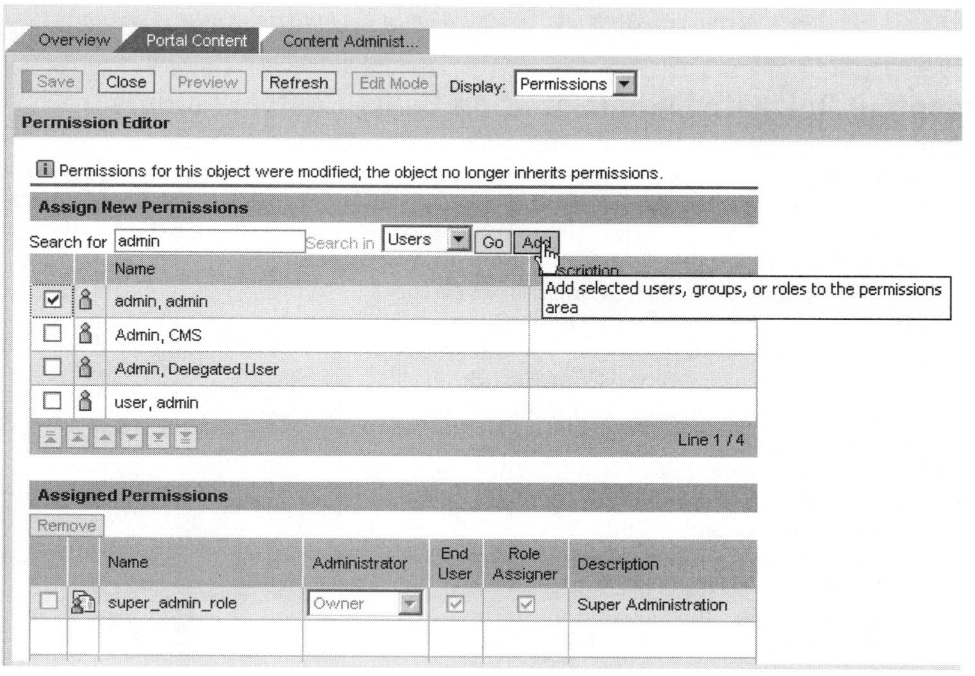

FIGURE 24-7 Portal content Permission Editor

2. Select the checkbox in front of the user in the Results section and click Add.
3. Click Save.
4. Open the Permission Editor for one of the objects under the Portal Content folder—let's use the Content Administrator role object. Notice that the newly added user also appears in the ACL of the Content Administrator object automatically due to the property of inheritance of permissions from higher level folders, which in this case happens to be the Portal Content folder.

Restore Inheritance If you change the permissions of the Content Administrator role, the inheritance link will be broken. So if you add one more entry in the ACL for the parent folder, that is, the Portal Content, that entry will not appear again in the child object, namely, the Content Administrator role. However, you can restore the inheritance behavior by clicking the Restore Inheritance button, which appears at the bottom of the Permission Editor Wizard, as shown next.

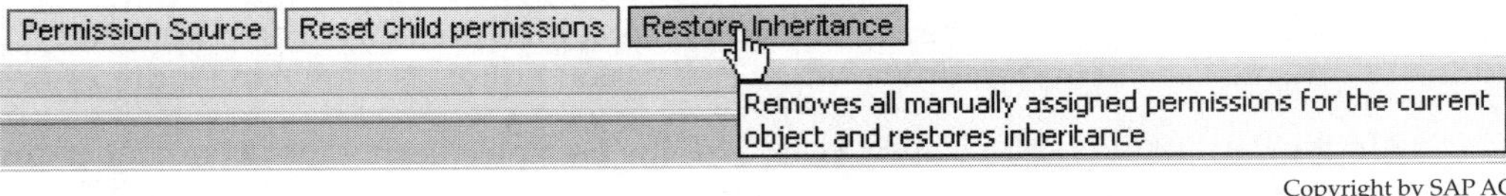

Copyright by SAP AG

NOTE *The Restore Inheritance button will be grayed out if the inheritance link is still intact.*

Implementing Delegated Administration Using Custom Folders

To implement delegated content administration, you can create custom folders based on the different criteria by which you want to delegate administration tasks. For example, if you want to divide the administration activities based on different regions, you could create custom folders for those different regions. You could create one folder for the North American region and another folder for the South American region.

You can then assign different permission levels for the users, roles, or groups for the two folders. For example, for the North America folder, you can assign the Read/Write permission for the Content_Admin_1 user and assign Read permission for the South America folder. And you can assign Read permission for the North America folder and assign Read/Write permission for the South American folder for a different user—say Content_Admin_2.

When logged in as a Super Administrator, you would see the screen on the right.

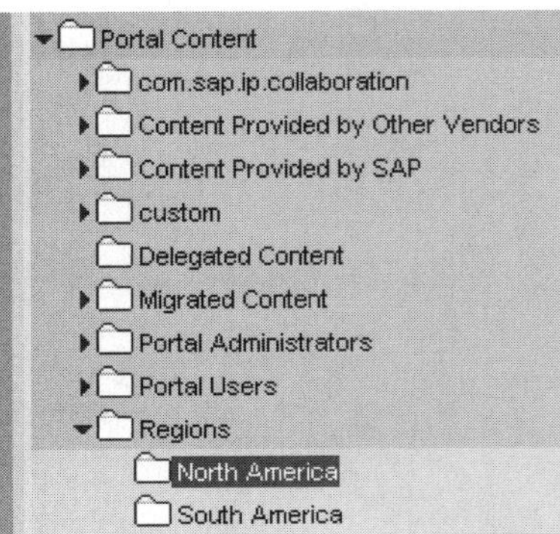

Copyright by SAP AG

Now you can assign the permissions to the Content_Admin_1 and Content_Admin_2 roles. In Figure 24-8, Read/Write permission for the North

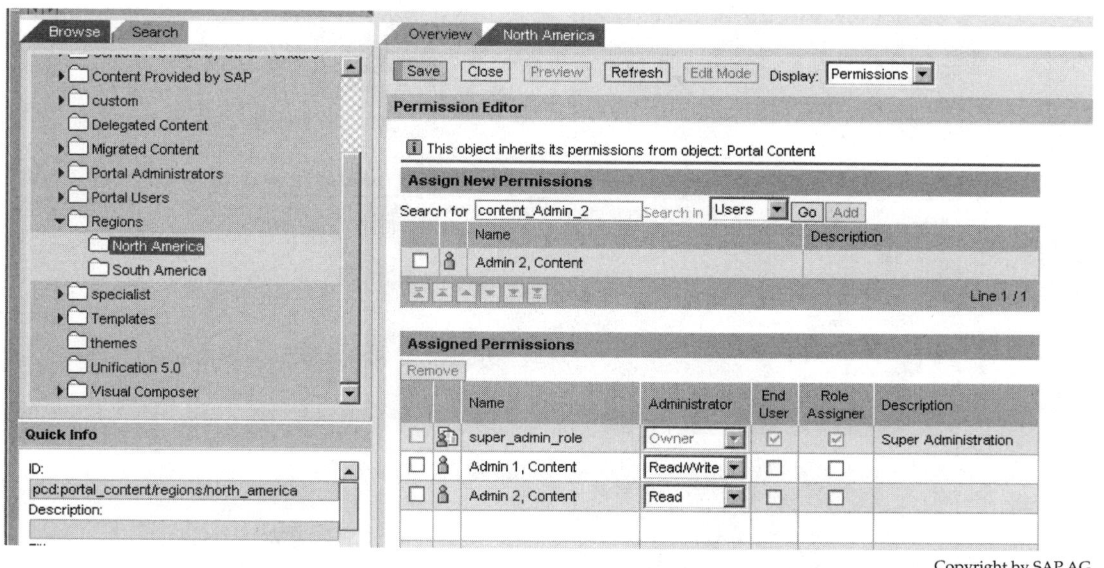

FIGURE 24-8 Assigned permissions for North America

America folder is assigned to the Content_Admin_1 user and Read permission is assigned for user Content_Admin_2.

In Figure 24-9, Read permission for the South America folder is assigned for the Content_Admin_1 user and Read/Write permission for Content_Admin_2 user.

Now, having assigned the appropriate permission levels to the North America and the South America folders for the Content_Admin_1 and Content_Admin_2 users, let us log in to the portal as those users and view the portal content catalog.

Logging in as Content_Admin_1 User

When you log in as the newly created Content_Admin_1 user, you cannot view the portal content catalog. This is because the portal content catalog ACL requires that the user have Super Administrator permission. So, in order for the Content_Admin_1 user to view the portal content catalog, you would need to add the user to the ACL list of the portal content catalog. The other option is to add the Content Administrator role to the user and add the Content Administrator role to the ACL list of the portal content catalog, as shown in Figure 24-10. Of course, adding the Super Administrator role to the Content_Admin_1 user will also do the trick, but that is not the intention here.

After assigning the Content Administrator role to the ACL of the portal content catalog and adding the role to the Content_Admin_1 user, you can view the Portal Content folder. Open the Regions folder and right click the North America folder. Then choose New and

Overview | South America

Save | Close | Preview | Refresh | Edit Mode | Display: Permissions

Permission Editor

Permissions for this object were modified; the object no longer inherits permissions.

Assign New Permissions

Search for content_admin_2 Search in Users Go Add

		Name	Description
☐		Admin 2, Content	

Line 1 / 1

Assigned Permissions

Remove

		Name	Administrator	End User	Role Assigner	Description
☐		super_admin_role	Owner	☑	☑	Super Administration
☐		Admin 1, Content	Read	☐	☐	
☐		Admin 2, Content	Read/Write	☐	☐	

FIGURE 24-9 Assigned permissions for South America

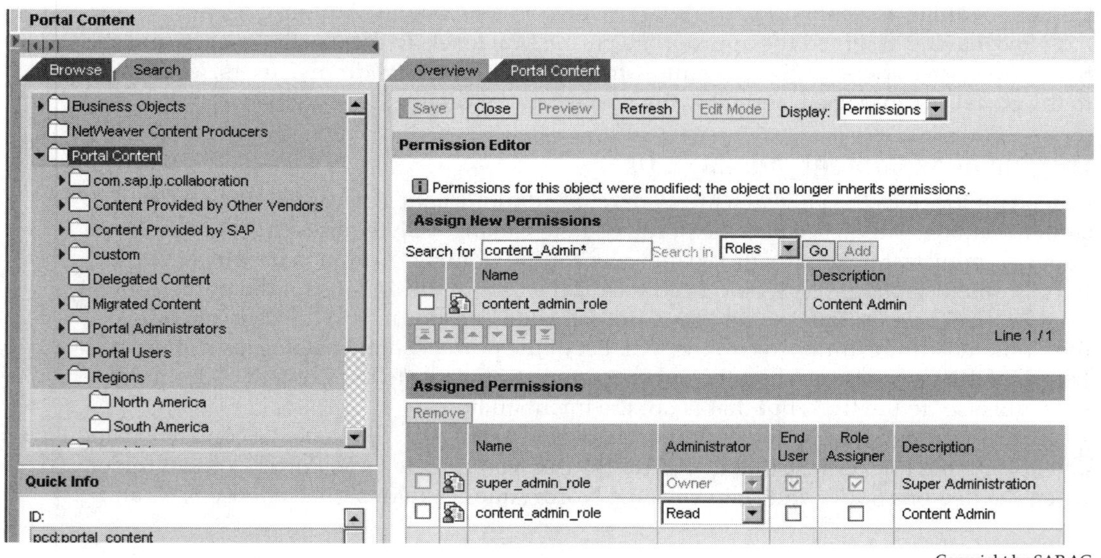

FIGURE 24-10 Adding roles

select whatever type of portal content object you want, such as iView, Page, or Role, as shown next:

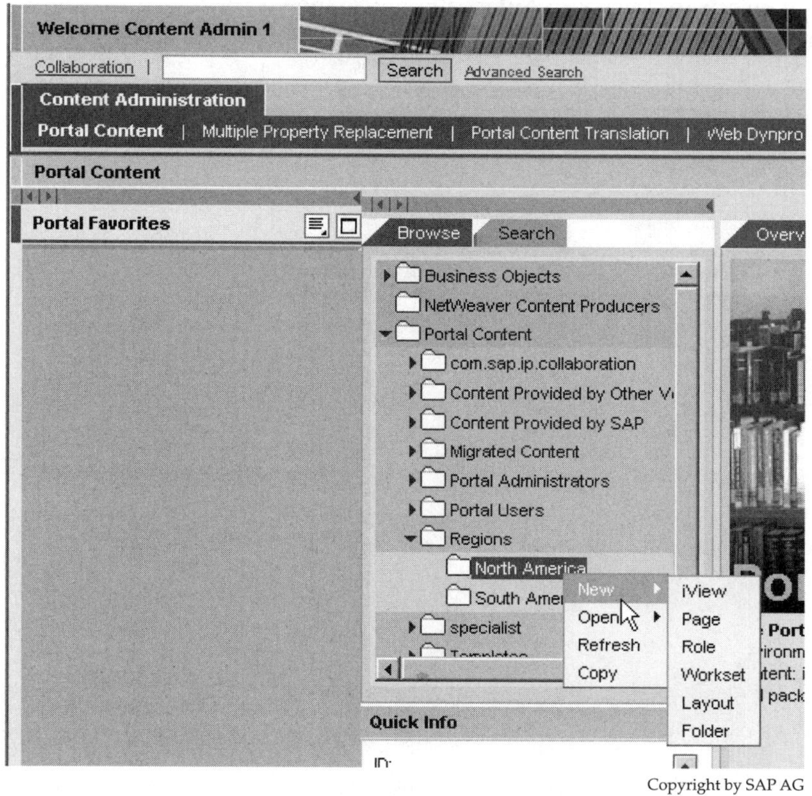

Copyright by SAP AG

Right click the South America folder to view the context menu shown next. You can only view the objects; you cannot create any of the portal content objects.

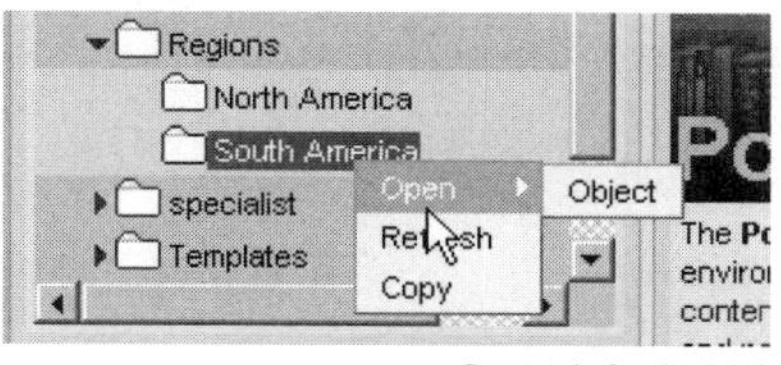

Copyright by SAP AG

PART V

Logging in as Content_Admin_2 User

Now log in as Content_Admin_2 user. You will find that the user has the ability to create new content objects for the South America folder as shown here:

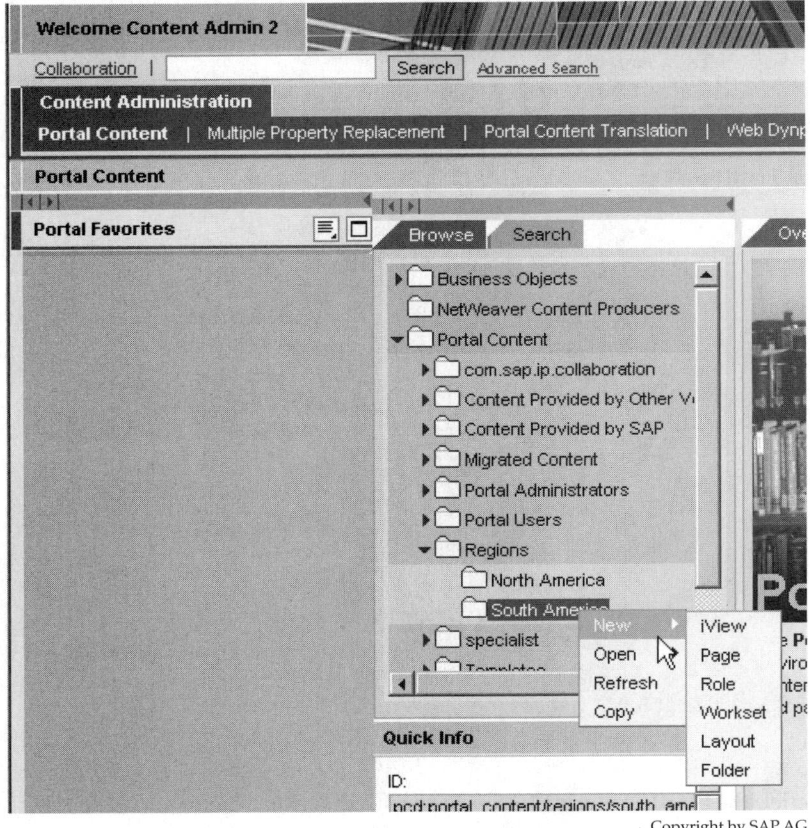

Copyright by SAP AG

However, the user can only view the objects under the North American folder, as shown next:

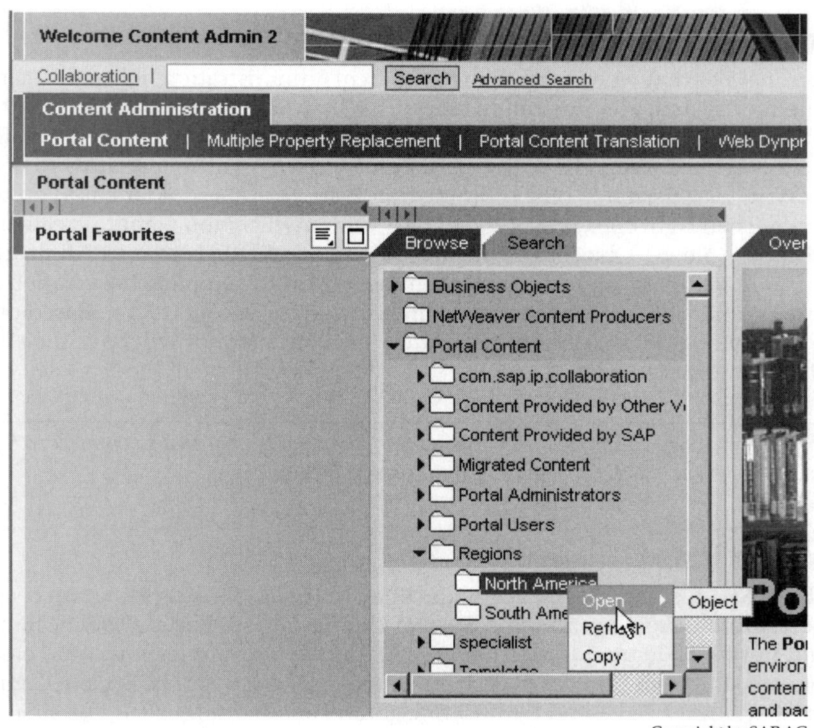

Copyright by SAP AG

You have implemented delegated content administration by assigning different ACLs for different folders to different users.

Now look at the Content_Admin_2 user. This user has only Read access to the North America folder, but he has Read/Write permission to the South America folder. This user has created a page named Page 1 under the South America folder.

Content_Admin_1 has created an iView under the North America folder. Now the Content_Admin_2 user can assign the iView belonging to the North American region to the Page 1 that was created under the South America folder, even though the user only has Read permission to the North America folder.

These kinds of delegation of responsibilities can be useful, for example, when you want to create several teams, such as one team named Development_Team that is responsible for the development of individual objects such as iViews and another team named Deployment_Team that is responsible for creating the pages, roles, and so on, and then assigning the iViews created by the Development_Team to the pages and roles. In our example, Content_Admin_2 would belong to the deployment team positioned in South America and Content_Admin_1 would belong to the development team positioned in North America.

Implementing Delegated System Administration

The same principles that were applied to the content administration delegation can be implemented for system administration delegation by using system objects.

Go to the Portal Content Catalog under System Administration | System Configuration. Create two folders and assign Read permission for a group of administrators to one folder and Read/Write permission to other administrators for the other folder based on your requirements. Then right click one of the folders under which you want to create the system object and choose New | Object to create the system object either from a PAR file or from a standard system template. Follow the steps in the wizard to complete the creation of the system object. Similarly, create another system object in the second folder. Based on which folder the system object has been created under, the administrator will have the ability to view or change the system object.

NOTE *The system object contains all the parameters that may be required to connect to the various backend systems such as R/3 systems or database systems.*

Creating Custom Roles

You can also create custom roles that provide different levels of access to system content such as Transport, Monitoring, Permissions, System Configuration, Portal Display, Support, Multitenant Portal, Federated Portal, and Navigation. For example, you could create one custom role called System Configurator that includes access only to the System Configuration, Multitenant Portal, and Federated Portal worksets and another role called Portal Support that contains only the Monitoring and Support worksets.

To create the System Configurator role, you must first create the role and then add the worksets corresponding to the System Configuration, Multitenant Portal, and Federated Portal. In order to locate the worksets, do the following:

1. First go to the System Configuration role under Portal Content | Portal Administrators | System Administration. Right click the System Administration role and choose Open | Object. The System Configuration workset will be available.

2. Right click the System Configuration workset and choose Trace Delta Links, as shown next:

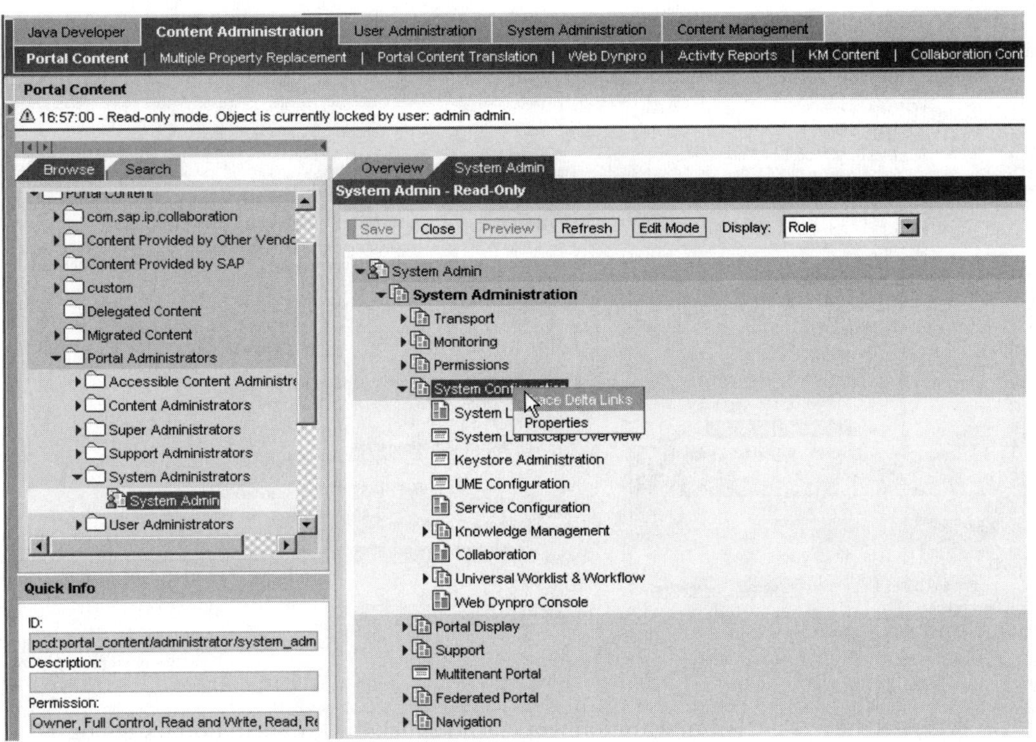

Copyright by SAP AG

3. The System Admin - Read-Only > Trace Delta Links - Read-Only screen appears as shown next:

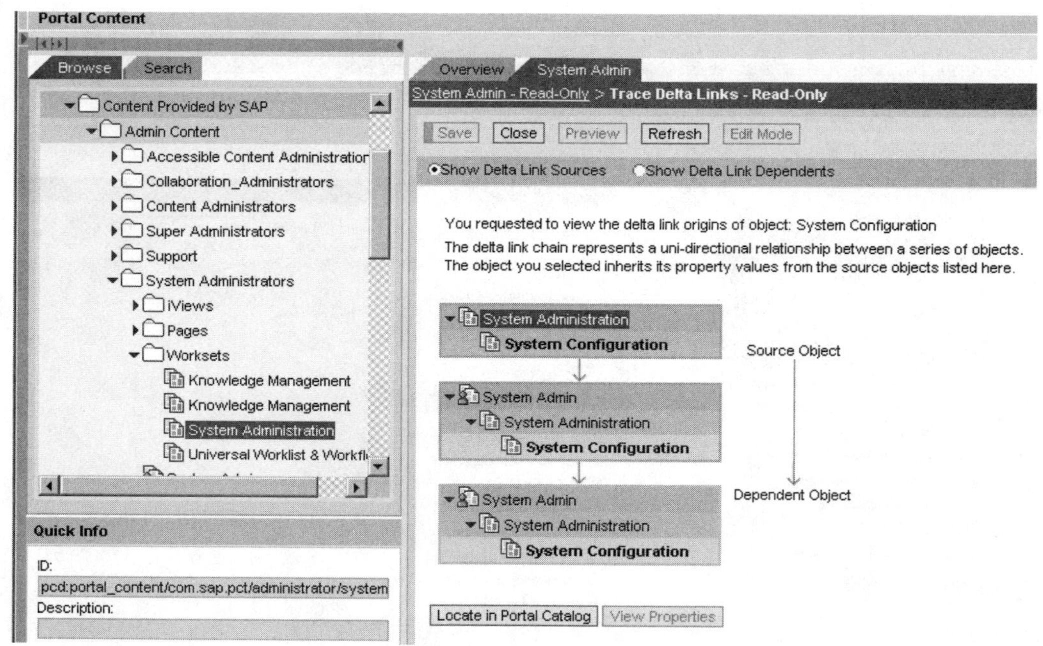

4. Select the System Administration workset and click the Locate in Portal Catalog button at the bottom of the screen shown in the illustration above. The system configuration workset will appear under the Portal Content | Content Provided by SAP | Admin Content | System Administrators | Worksets | System Administration.

5. Open the role you created for the System Configuration. Right click the System Administration workset, and choose Add Workset To Role | Delta Link to add the System Administration workset to the newly created role.

6. Since you need only the System Configuration, Multitenant Portal, and Federated Portal worksets, you can delete the other worksets. Because the custom role is the target object for the delta link, deleting the worksets will not impact the source object, which is the System Administration workset.

After completing these steps you can then assign this role to users who need the System Configurator role. In the same way, you can create the Portal Support role by creating a new custom role and adding the Transport, Monitoring, Support, and Navigation worksets to it.

The following illustration shows the user assigned to the System Configurator role. This user can access the System Configuration, Multitenant Portal, Federated Portal, and

Navigation menus. Because the System Configuration, Multitenant Portal, and Federated Portal worksets have been assigned to the System Configurator role, and because these worksets have their Entry point property set to Yes, these worksets appear as top-level menus on the portal as shown next:

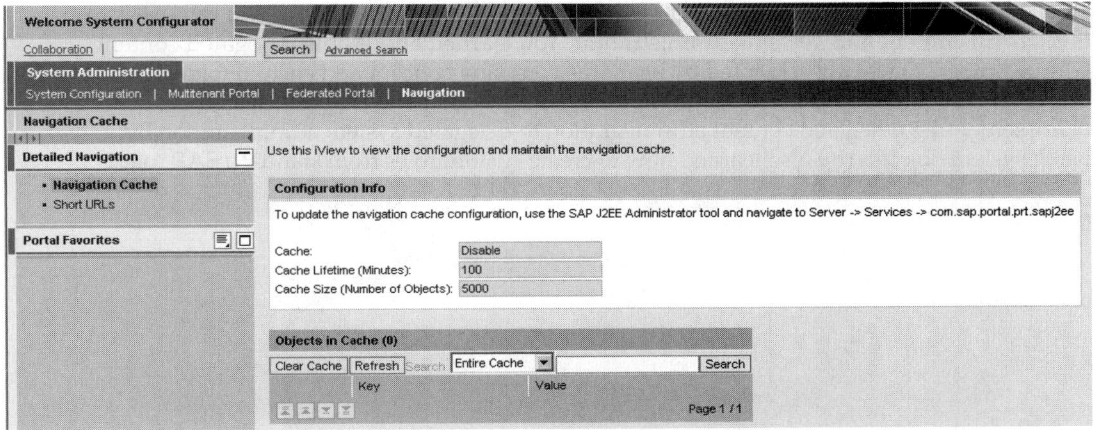

The next illustration shows the user assigned to the Portal Support role. This user can access the Transport, Monitoring, Support, and Navigation menus because this user is attached to the custom-created Portal Support role that contains the Transport, Monitoring, Support, and Navigation worksets. The worksets act as entry points in the top-level navigation menu on the portal.

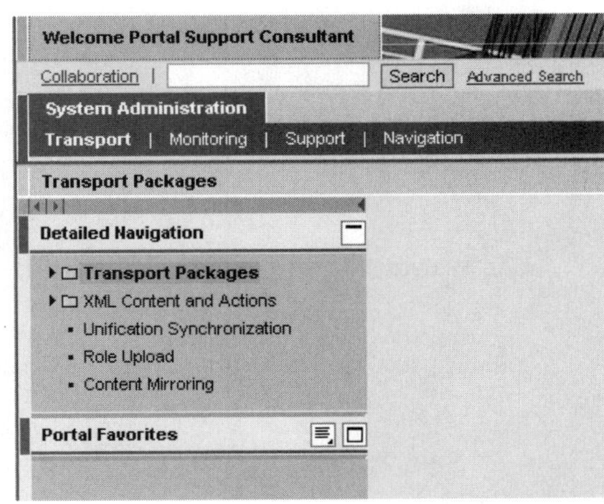

NOTE *For more details, refer to the delegated administration related resources listed in Appendix B.*

Summary

This chapter addressed the concept of delegated administration and how you can use it to implement content and system administration. You learned about how delegated content administration can be implemented by using the company concept and custom folders based on delegation needs, custom roles, and the permission model. The chapter covered the concept of implementing delegated content administration to delegated system administration by using system objects. You also learned how to create custom roles from standard SAP roles.

25

CHAPTER

Implementing Delegated User Administration

Delegated user administration is helpful when you want to delegate administration activities such as create, change, or delete users to different groups of administrators. It helps to streamline user administration activities by segmenting large user populations, especially in global portal implementations, into smaller, manageable groups based on criteria such as regions, departments, product divisions, and so on. The user groups can be set up by activating the company concept in the portal. The company concept can be activated by making some configuration changes in the J2EE engine—namely, the SAPUM .properties file. The delegated user administrator can only maintain users belonging to his or her company and only assign roles for which he or she has the permissions.

This chapter discusses how to implement delegated user administration and enable self-registration.

Delegating Administration Activities

You can store company details for a user in the attributes of the user's profile. A delegated user administrator can maintain only those users who belong to the same company to which he or she belongs. The delegated administrator is restricted in the nature of user administrative activities that he or she can carry out. Following are some of the activities that a delegated administrator cannot do, but an overall user administrator can do:

- Manage groups
- Manage roles
- Map users
- Import and export users
- Replicate a user to an external system

DON'T *Do not assign the administrative role to the delegated user administrator, because the delegated user administrator can then assign any other role and hence defy the very purpose of delegated administration.*

Conventional Groups vs. Company Groups

Every company maintained in the User Management Engine (UME) configuration is also a group by default, but such groups are not the same as the conventional groups. Unlike conventional groups, company groups are not stored anywhere and are instead determined dynamically.

Users and roles can be assigned to company groups, but conventional groups cannot be assigned to company groups. However, company groups can be assigned to conventional groups. Thus, a user can be assigned to a company group or to a conventional group to which the company group has been assigned.

Setting Up Company Groups

In a simple implementation with a small number of companies, companies can be maintained individually in the J2EE engine configuration using the property `ume.tpd.imp.class` in the SAPUM.properties file. The `ume.tpd.imp.class = com.sap.security.core.tpd.SimpleTPD` is enabled in the SAPUM.properties file. It is also possible to maintain company information in a backend system such as Supplier Relationship Management using TradingPartnerDirectory interfaces.

Using the Config Tool

To configure the company scenario, do the following:

1. Open the config tool by opening the *<drive>*/usr/sap/J2E/JC01/j2ee/configtool/configtool.bat file. Click Yes when you are asked whether you want to use the default DB settings:

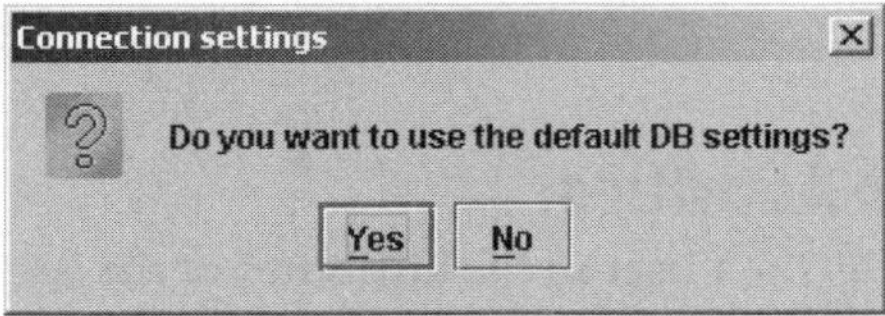

Copyright by SAP AG

After you click Yes, the config tool will update its files from the configuration values stored in the database. You may see the following error message:

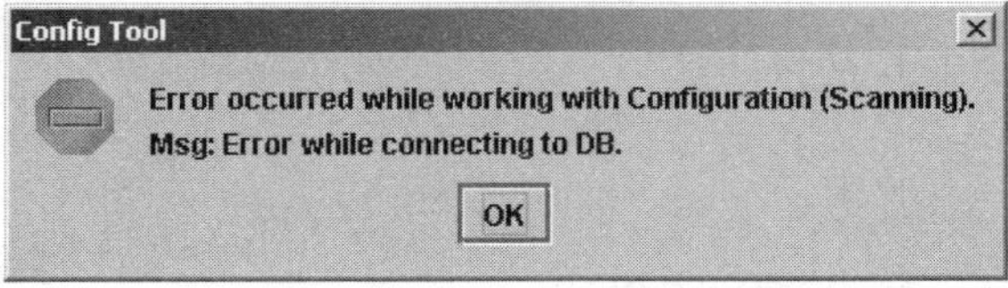

Copyright by SAP AG

This could indicate that the database is not running, as is evident here:

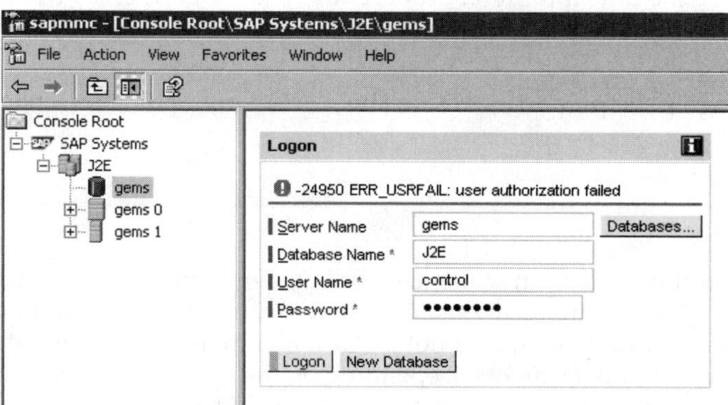

2. In this case, open the SAP management console and start your database. Click the database icon and enter the database login parameters. Then click Logon and then Online to start the database:

Your database should then start and display state information:

3. Now return to the config tool and choose File | Connect. Then click Load in the pop-up that appears.
4. Navigate to Cluster-data | Global Server Configuration | Services and choose the com.sap.security.core.ume.service.

5. Navigate to the property ume.tpd.companies and change it accordingly.
6. Also change the ume.tpd.prefix property by removing the entry *STPD_*. If this is not removed, the company groups will be created as STPD_sales, STPD_marketing, and so on.
7. After changing the properties, restart the J2EE engine so that the changes will take effect.

Business Scenarios

A delegated user administrator can manage users belonging only to one company, because the delegated user administrator cannot be attached to more than one company. This rule is in place for the same reason that you cannot create a hierarchy of administrators belonging to different companies or departments. Depending on the required business scenario, the company property can be used to represent users belonging to internal organizations or external users. It can also be used to represent various regions or departments within the organization.

Company Scenarios

Three company scenarios are possible. They can be activated by setting up the ume.tpd .companies property, as shown in Figure 25-1.

- **No companies scenario** If ume.tpd.companies = 0, then all the users do not belong to any company. This is used for internal scenarios, and the users become full users on self-registration. There is no need for an approval process.

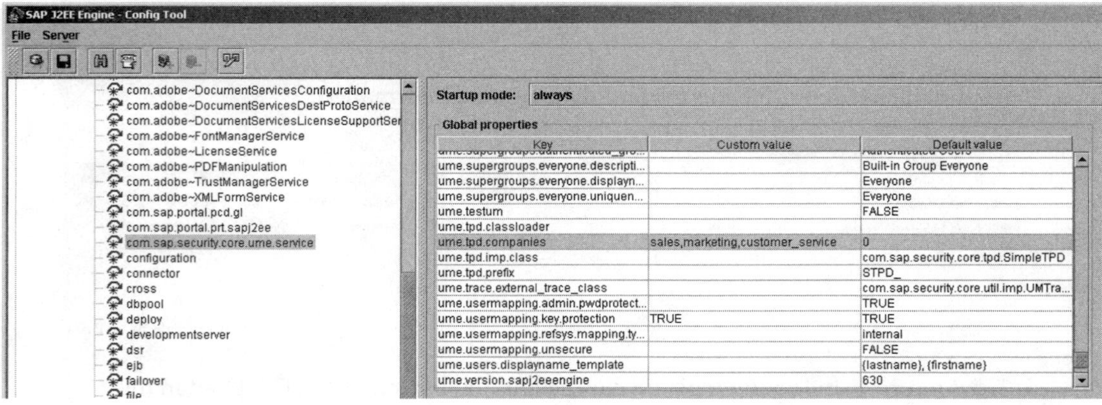

FIGURE 25-1 Activating a company scenario

- **Guest users and one company** If ume.tpd.companies = 1, then the users belong to one company. The self-registration and approval processes are now available. If the user is not approved, he is treated as a guest user. This scenario is usually employed for internal purposes.
- **Two or more companies and guest user** ume.tpd.companies = 2 or is set to a list of companies separated by a semicolon (;). This scenario is similar to the guest users scenario except that the users can belong to different companies, though they can belong only to one company at one point in time. If the users are rejected during the self-registration process, they are still treated as guest users. When the administrator creates a user using the user administration tool, and assigns the user to a company group, no approval is required. This scenario can be used to provide limited access to the external users.

NOTE *At the time of self-registration by the user, an e-mail is automatically sent to the user.*

Assigning Roles

To assign roles, the user must be able to use the Identity Management functionality available at User Administration | Identity Management in the top-level menu. To be able to use the Identity Management, the user must be assigned to a role that contains the role assignment iView. Examples of such roles are User Administrator, Super Administrator, and Delegated User Administrator. Two kinds of roles can be created:

- **Portal role** Created on the portal and used mainly for controlling the display of content in the portal. They act as containers for other portal content objects such as iViews, pages, and worksets. Considering that UME actions can be assigned to portal roles, it is possible that when portal roles are assigned to the user, the user may get some J2EE authorizations by virtue of the UME actions that have been assigned to the role.
- **UME role** A set of authorizations for J2EE applications that can be assigned to the user or group in the J2EE engine. Assigning a UME role will not provide the user the ability to view content in the portal. While the portal roles are stored in the PCD tables of the J2EE database, the UME roles are stored in the user management tables of the J2EE database.

UME.Manage_All Action

The UME.Manage_All action is attached to the Super Administrator and User Administrator roles, so they contain, by default, the role assigner permission for all portal roles. For other user administrators, they must have role assigner permission for the role that they want to assign to other users and groups. To access the standard User Administration role, go to Portal Content | Portal Administrators | User Administrators | User Admin, as shown here:

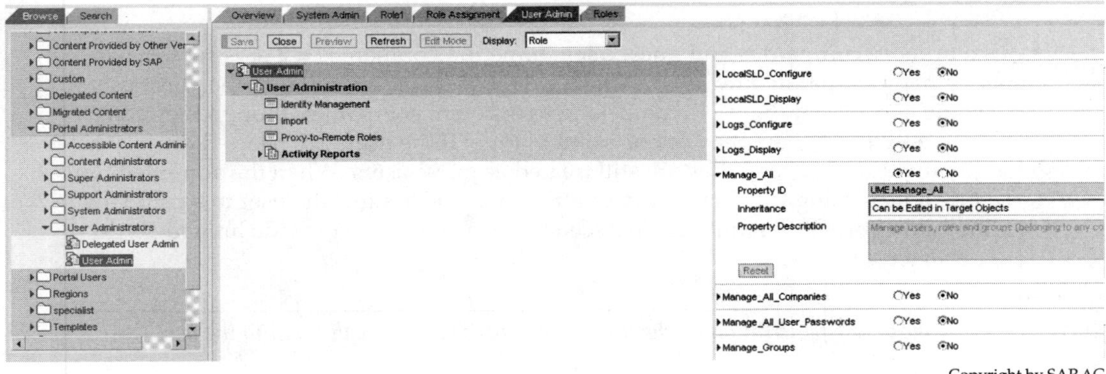

Copyright by SAP AG

TIP *Users belonging to the super administrator role or the user administrator role will be able to assign all portal roles to all users and groups.*

UME.Manage_Roles Action

To assign the UME roles to the user or group, you need either UME.Manage_All or UME.Manage_Roles action assigned to the role and this role should be added to the user administrator. It is not possible to assign role assigner permissions to the UME roles and hence the control as to who can assign is exercised using the UME.Manage_Roles action. As long as the user administrator is assigned to a role that contains the UME.Manage_Roles action, the user administrator can assign all UME roles to users and groups.

NOTE *Since NetWeaver 04 SP11, you do not need to use the UME.Manage_Users action to be able to assign the user to the roles.*

Do not assign the UME.Manage_Roles action to the delegated User Administrators, because this will allow them to assign the administrative roles to themselves and thus obtain full administration rights on the J2EE engine.

Creating a Delegated User Administrator Role

Now that you have enabled the company concept and activated the self-registration feature, you can create the delegated user administrators.

Create Delegated User Administrator

To create a delegated user administrator, you can either assign the user to a role that contains the UME.Delegated_Admin action or you can simply assign the user to the pcd:portal_content/administrator/user_admin/delegated_user_admin_role role.

TIP *The delegated user administrators should not have administrator or end user permissions, but they should have role assigner permission for the role that they will be required to assign to a user.*

A delegated user is shown in the following illustration; notice the Save Tenant Selection button:

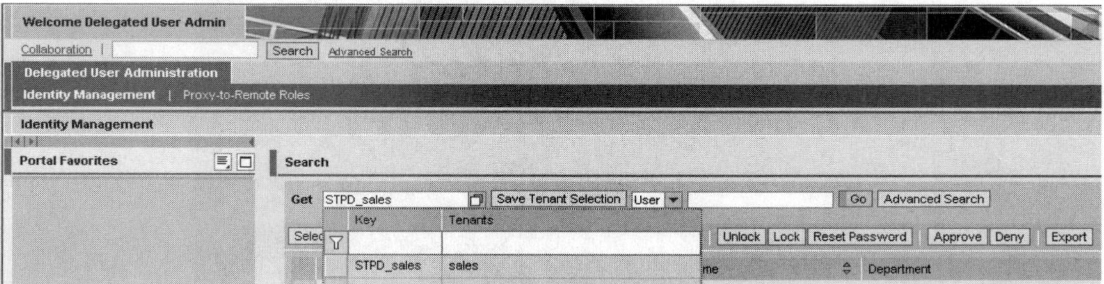

At the time of creation of the delegated user administrator, make sure that the user is attached to a company group. Notice that the delegated user administrator can manage only users belonging to the STPD_sales company group, even though other company groups are available in the portal. Also, if you click the choices for object type, only User and Role are available. The group will be missing because the delegated administrator cannot maintain groups.

Once the delegated user administrator has been created, your next step is to assign the delegated user administrator with the role assigner permission to the role that needs to be assigned to the users.

Enabling Self-Registration

To enable the self-registration property, the following properties should be set in the sapum.properties file:

- `ume.logon.selfreg=true`
- `ume.admin.selfreg_company=true`

While the first entry activates the self-registration process in general, the second property activates the self-registration process by company. You must use the steps similar to that outlined under the section using the config tool of this chapter to configure these properties.

TIP *If these two properties are not defined using the config tool, the self-registration link will not appear in the portal logon screen.*

Creating a Self-Registered User

Now let's create a self registered user.

1. In the Welcome screen, click the Register Now link:

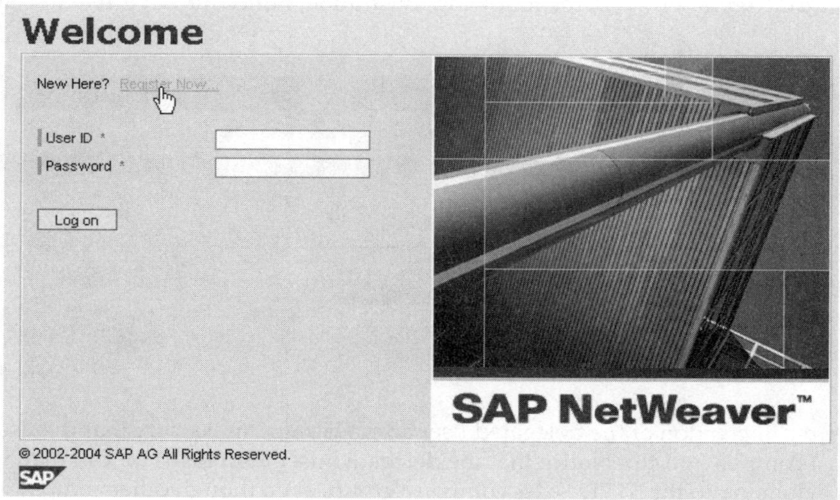

Copyright by SAP AG

2. Enter details for the self-registered user. Click the Search icon to the right of the Company field.

Welcome to User Registration

Registration of a New User

If you are a new user, use the form below for registration. Required entries are marked with *

User ID:* self_reg_user
Password:* ••••••••
Confirm Password:* ••••••••
Last Name:* User
First Name:* Self Registered
E-Mail Address:* sapportalguide@yahoo.com
Form of Address:
Language: -Select-
Company:
Activate Accessibility Features: (Screen reader required)

Submit Reset Cancel

Copyright by SAP AG

3. Enter an asterisk in the Company Name field and click Search.

4. Select a company group and then click Accept and then Submit.

Select Company

< No of Hits:3 Items Display 10 hits per page. This is page 1 of 1 pages >

	Company Name
(•)	sales
( )	customer_service
( )	marketing

< No of Hits:3 Items Display 10 hits per page. This is page 1 of 1 pages >

Accept | New Search | Continue as Guest User

Copyright by SAP AG

5. Enter any contact and additional information as required and click Submit. The self-registered user has now been created.

Assigning Content to the Self-Registered User

When you try to log on to the portal using the new self-registered user, an error will appear. This is because no content has been assigned to the role of the user. To assign the role to the newly created user, you must assign some roles to the group to which the user belongs. By default, the newly created user belongs to the Authenticated Users group, Everyone group, and the GUEST_USERS_COMPANY group. Proceed by assigning some role to the Everyone group:

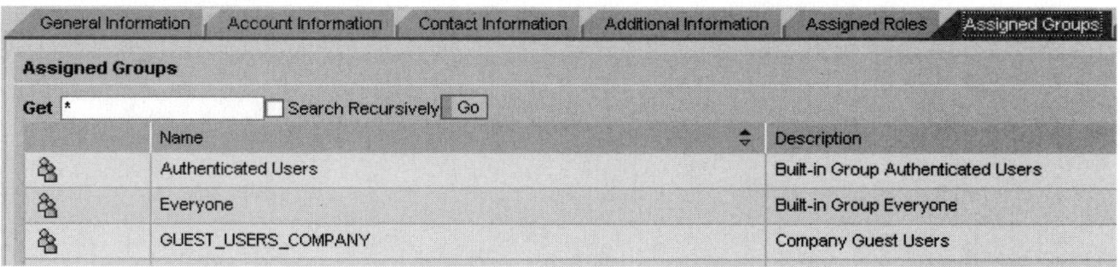

Copyright by SAP AG

Once the users have self-registered, they become guest users by default. To convert them into full users, the user administrator must approve or deny the guest users from the New User Requests link after navigating to User Administration | Identity Management in the top-level menu. If you have not activated the company concept, the self-registered users become full users upon registration.

NOTE *For more details, refer to the delegated administration related resources listed in Appendix B.*

Summary

In this chapter, you learned how to implement a delegated user administrator using the company concept. You learned about the different scenarios available using the company concept. Finally, you implemented self-registration on the portal and learned how to create a self-registered user.

VI

PART

Portal Troubleshooting

26

CHAPTER

Troubleshooting Portal Using Logs and Traces

This chapter covers such concepts as logging and tracing categories and locations. You will learn the various steps involved in enabling tracing and logging, configuring the Log Manager, and using the Log Configurator. You will also learn about the various types of log viewers and how to use them for troubleshooting.

Logging and Tracing

The logging functionality on the portal is based on the logging functionality of the J2EE engine, and the logging in the J2EE engine is based on the Central Logging system functionality of the J2EE engine provided by the SAP logging API.

The SAP logging API is composed of services such as the Log Manager, Log Configurator, and Log Viewer. The SAP logging framework offers the following advantages:

- No need to insert debug statements in code
- Eases use of the logging functionality
- Minimal impact on system performance due to logging

SAP Logging API

All the log information is stored in the following folders:

- *<server install folder>/server*/log/
- *<server_install_folder>/dispatcher*/log/

The SAP logging API enables logging and writes the log files either to the file system, the console, or another output destination based on the configuration.

The Java package used for SAP logging is com.sap.tc.logging. The SAP logging API provides two basic methods: logging and tracing. It is easy to make calls to these API methods as well as change the severity levels for logging without having to modify the source code.

Logging and Categories

Logging is based on categories, which help you classify the system into major logistic areas such as /System/Server, /System/Database, /Application/StatusPoint, and so on. Thus, using these logs, the system administrator can know right away if a problem lies with any major areas of the system.

Categories should be designed so that they are not tied to any software application, but rather classified based on administrative activities. The messages that are generated during logging are mainly related to a running system to ensure that it is running satisfactorily.

The error messages generated during logging are usually of the severity level ERROR or FATAL and not DEBUG or PATH.

Tracing and Locations

Tracing is based on locations and is used by developers who provide the trace information and help to identify any program bugs and flow logic issues.

NOTE *While logging is always switched on, tracing is usually switched off.*

The usual practice of the developers is to insert System.out.println statements or PrintStackTrace for exceptions as a way of debugging source code. After the program is completed and tested, the significant task of removing those statements begins.

Locations can be identified with package, class, or function names. The error messages generated during tracing are aimed at identifying any erroneous behaviors on the part of the software application. The error messages are usually of the severity type DEBUG or PATH. Error messages of severity level ERROR or FATAL must not be written to the traces. The syntax convention used for tracing is Location (Tracing) = com.sap.portal.<*logical_name_of_functionality*>—for example, com.sap.portal.*prt* -> is the entry point for all the trace information pertaining to the *portal runtime.*

Figure 26-1 displays how a log manager can be responsible for multiple log controllers, which in turn can contain multiple destinations, also known as logs. Logs in turn can contain multiple log records.

Log Manager

The Log Manager is the first manager started during system startup. It is used for the following:

- Stores system critical log files in the database
- Sets properties for switching the trace files on/off

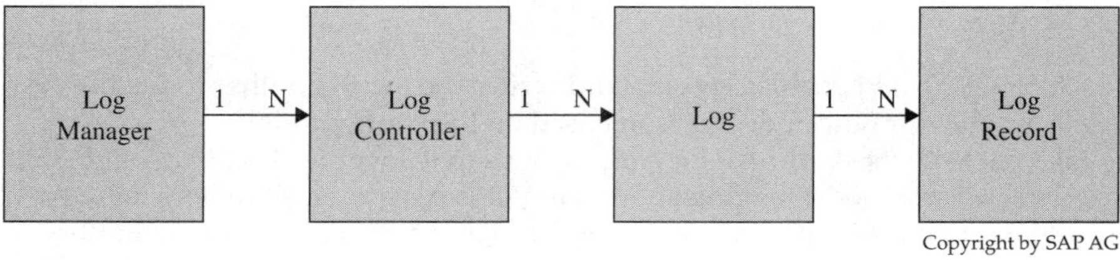

FIGURE 26-1 Relationship between a Log Manager, log controller, log, and log record

- Excludes locations from being written to a trace file
- Manages the *log controller*, an entity that represents the source area, namely, the location or the category

---

NOTE *Location and category are subclasses of the log controller class.*

The *log* is the destination where the file should be created, and *log record* represents the structure of the message. The *formatter* helps to format the log messages, and the *filter* is an optional functionality for screening out messages to be displayed.

Enabling Logging and Tracing

To enable logging or tracing, the following four conceptual steps are required:

1. *Identify the location or the category* for which you would like to generate the trace or log files, respectively. The developer usually does this when developing the source code.
2. *Assign the severity level* of the source.
3. *Define the output destination* where the log and trace files have to be created. This is usually the point of focus for the administrators or any user who wants to use logging or tracing.
4. *Insert messages and the corresponding severity levels* for which the message should be output to the log files.

Once these four steps are completed and the program is run, the logs are created.

Only those messages that have a severity level equal to or higher than that of the source will be output to the log files in the location specified in the output destination setting. Note that the actual task of creating and outputting the log files is separated from end user activities such as setting a severity level, managing the amount of logging, and changing the output destination.

Log Configurator

The configuration settings for logging and tracing can be changed using the Log Configurator service of the Visual Administrator and are stored in the Portal Runtime service.

The actual configuration for logging and tracing is available in the log-configuration .xml file. The log-configuration.xml file entries contain information on the following:

- Log destinations
- Type of destination
- Names of the log files
- Effective severity levels
- Count of log files that can be created
- Maximum size of the logs

It also contains information on log controllers, such as their effective severity levels and their associated destinations.

NOTE *Log controllers are simply definitions for the location or the category.*

You can assign severity levels to the following:

- Root node of the location or category tree
- Subtree
- Particular location or category node

Figure 26-2 displays the tree structure of a log controller on the left; on the right, you can see how a severity level can be assigned.

The function Copy Severity To Subtree assigns the severity level to all the child nodes belonging to that node. After making the change, click the Apply button to save the changes.

Advanced Mode

When you click the To Advanced Mode button, the view switches to the Advanced mode. In the Advanced mode, two more tabs, namely, Destinations and Formatters, will appear. To configure the format of the messages created by the existing destinations, click the Formatters tab. Here you can create, change, or remove formatters.

Types of Log Formats

Three different types of log formats are available for printing messages: *TraceFormatter, XMLFormatter,* and *ListFormatter.* The most common log format is the TraceFormatter, which is very user friendly and helps you understand the log quickly. It is possible to use placeholders, which help define how the messages are created.

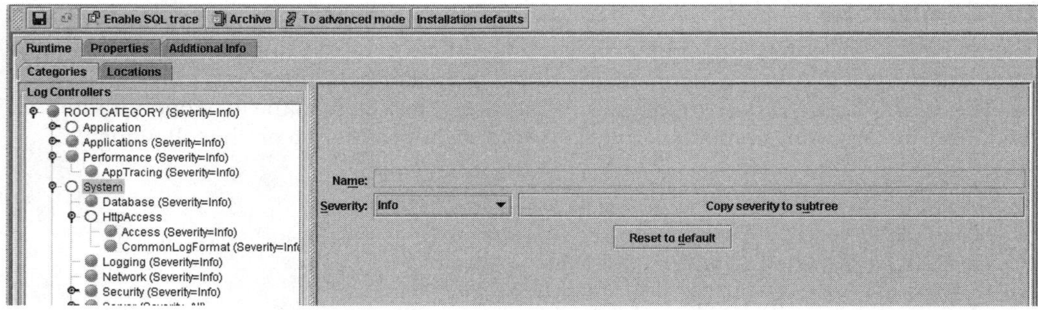

FIGURE 26-2 Tree structure of a log controller

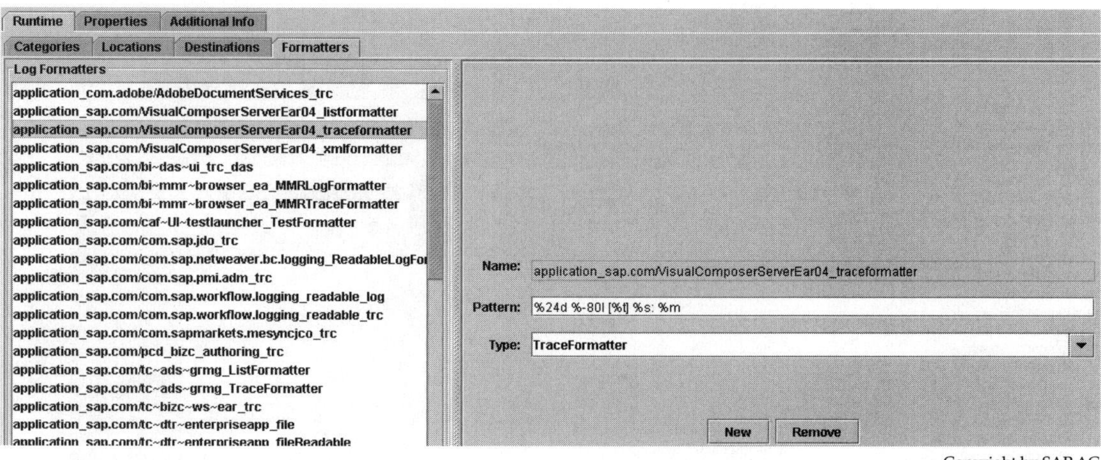

FIGURE 26-3 The Formatters tab

HINT *TraceFormatter cannot be used with the log viewer.*

The XMLFormatter creates the log records in an XML format, which can then be used in another application. The ListFormatter is used for creating log records in a format that can be used by the log viewer and the J2EE engine. It contains fields that are separated by hash signs.

Figure 26-3 shows how a Formatters tab contains information of the application, the type format, and the placeholders in the pattern field that define how the log messages are to be created.

Destinations Tab

In the Destinations tab, you can create, change, or remove the destinations. The tab contains the following information, as shown in Figure 26-4:

- *Log type* (FileLog or ConsoleLog)
- *Name of the log file* that needs to be created
- Number of *rotating files* that are created
- *Max size* of the logs
- *Severity level* of the messages that are created
- *Formatter* for the logs

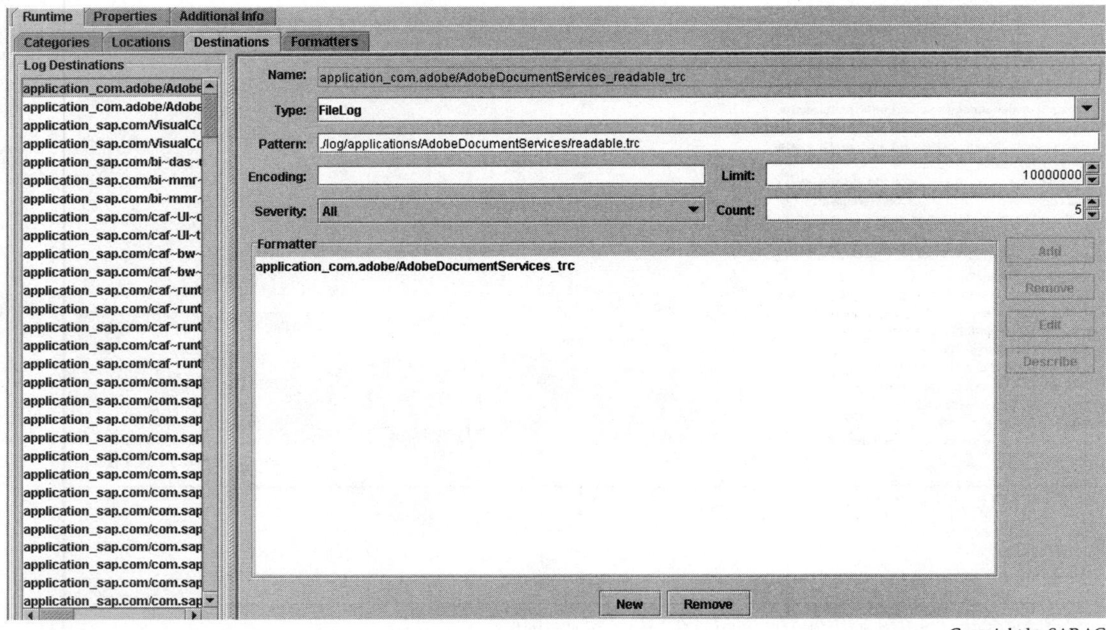

Copyright by SAP AG

FIGURE 26-4 The Destinations tab

Creating a New Controller

To create a new controller, go to the Categories or Locations tab, depending upon the type of the Controller, and click New.

NOTE *The log controller is a super class for the category or the location.*

Automatic Archiving

Setting the property `ArchiveOldLogFiles` to `ON` in the Log Configurator service can activate automatic archiving of log files at regular intervals.

The `ArchivesDirectory` property defines the location of the archives directory where archiving takes place. The default value is .log/archive folder.

TIP *Deleting the archive files is a manual process.*

Archiving Manually

You can also create an archive at any given point of time in the log destinations that you choose. In Figure 26-2, when you click the Archive icon on the top, a Log window appears, as shown next, where you can select the log destinations that you want to archive. After clicking OK, a dialog box appears with the details of the location (usually the *.log/archive* folder) where the archive was created.

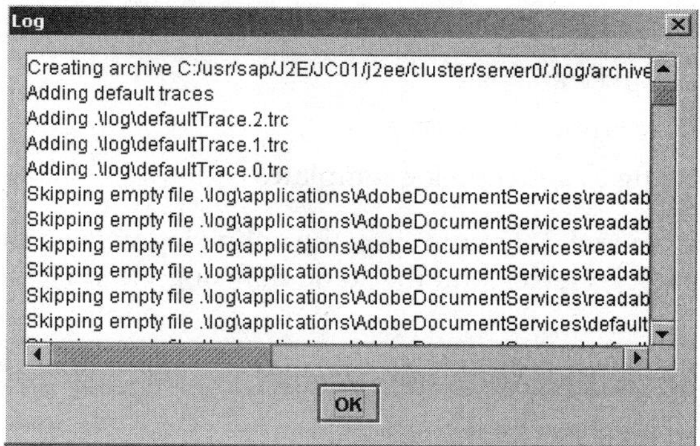

Copyright by SAP AG

Clicking the Installation Defaults button in Figure 26-2 completely replaces the entire log configuration.

Severity Levels

Depending on the severity level set, the log files are created. Following are the different severity levels that can be set in increasing order:

- DEBUG
- PATH
- INFO
- WARNING
- ERROR
- FATAL

For example, if the severity level is set at INFO, the log files include messages at the levels of DEBUG, PATH, and INFO. However, the messages at severity levels WARNING, ERROR, and FATAL are not created.

Log Viewer

NOTE *The log viewer is the runtime tool used to display both* system *and* application *log files.*

The log viewer displays the information available in the log files in a user-friendly manner and helps to search across multiple files and merge log files across servers, for example. By setting the severity level, you can control the amount of log data. The log viewer can be used for the following:

- To debug application issues
- To analyze system problems
- To analyze performance analysis
- To analyze SAT traces and SQL traces
- In CCMS monitoring to generate log templates

Log viewers come in several different types: the online log viewer, the integrated log viewer, the command line log viewer, and the standalone log viewer.

TIP *The logs and traces for the whole NetWeaver landscape can be analyzed using the SAP NetWeaver Administrator.*

Online Log Viewer

The online log viewer is available in the Visual Administrator as a Log Viewer service. The online log viewer is installed by default with the installation of the J2EE engine. This requires that the J2EE engine be running. The log viewer client accesses the log files on the NetWeaver AS directly without any additional configuration. The online log viewer is configured by default to generate five rotating log files with a size of 10MB each. Once all five log files have been created, the system overwrites the first oldest log file. But before doing that, the system creates a ZIP file of the five log files, which are now referred to as *archive* logs.

To log on to the online log viewer, you must first log on to the Visual Administrator by going to *<J2EE_installation_directory>*/admin/go.bat. After logging on, select any server node whose logs you want to analyze and then go to Services | LogViewer.

The Integrated Log Viewer

To log on to the Integrated Log Viewer, go to the *<j2ee_istallation_drive>*:\usr\sap\J2E\JC01\j2ee\admin folder and click the go.bat file. You must log on to the Visual Administrator using the P4 port. After logging on, open any server node and go to Services | LogViewer. The log viewer is then displayed along with all the log files that have been registered for that server.

The Command-Line Log Viewer

The command line log viewer is a command-line tool that can be used to convert the logs generated by the SAP logging API from a ListFormatter format into a TraceFormatter tool. In other words, it can be used to convert the log files into a human-readable format. The command-line log viewer can be used to display a single log or trace file, all log and trace files from a log directory, and a certain number of records in a log or trace file.

The Standalone Log Viewer

The standalone log viewer is used for central viewing of log files and requires two components: log viewer server and log viewer client. You can use the log viewer client to look at the logs centrally from all the servers provided a log viewer server runs in all those servers.

TIP *The standalone log viewer can be used to view logs whenever the J2EE engine is not running.*

The standalone log viewer is available in the folder *<j2ee_install_directory>/<SID>/JC<nr>*/j2ee/admin/logviewer_standalone. To start the log viewer, click the logViewer.bat file in the Windows system. In a UNIX system, you must click the logViewer.sh file. The standalone log viewer will appear, as shown in Figure 26-5.

The remoteserver.bat file can be used to connect from a remote system via an NI socket connection. The server should be configured to listen on an NI socket connection. The remoteserver.bat file is useful to view the logs on a remote machine, when the J2EE engine is shut down.

The user interface for the standalone log viewer and the integrated log viewer is common to both. The next few sections discuss the various activities that can be carried out, such as the following:

- Viewing the log files on multiple servers
- Merging log files from multiple servers
- Changing log severity
- Customizing columns
- Searching logs
- Adding new logs
- Sorting logs
- Viewing archived logs

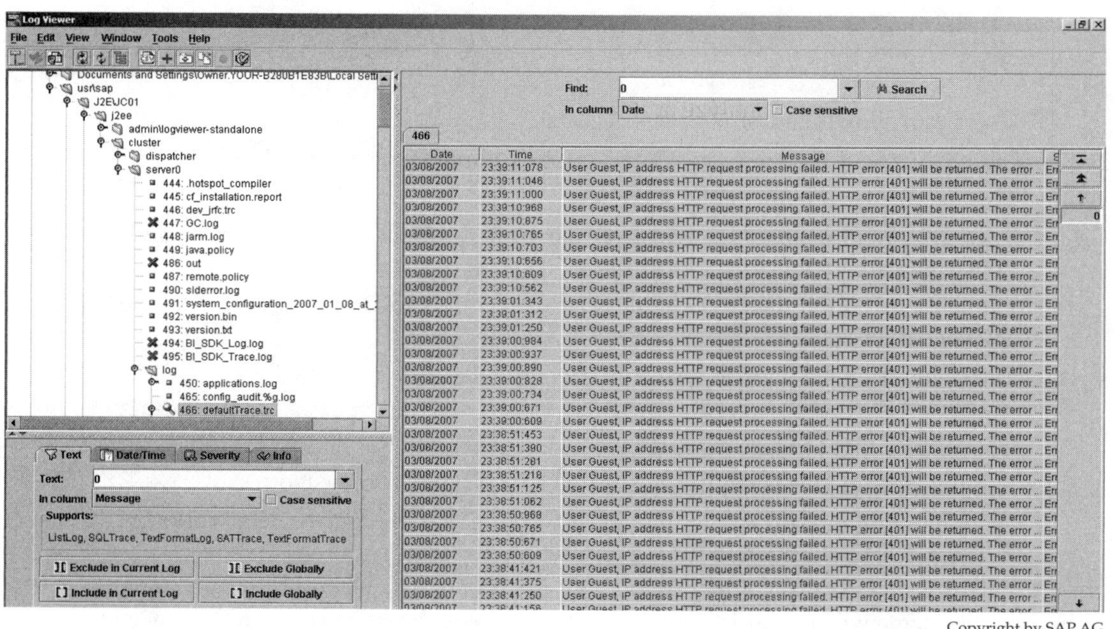

Copyright by SAP AG

FIGURE 26-5 The standalone log viewer

Configuring a Server for Log Viewing

Follow these steps to configure a server for log viewing:

1. Choose File | Configuration. In the Configuration dialog box, click Add to open the Add A Log Viewer Server dialog box:

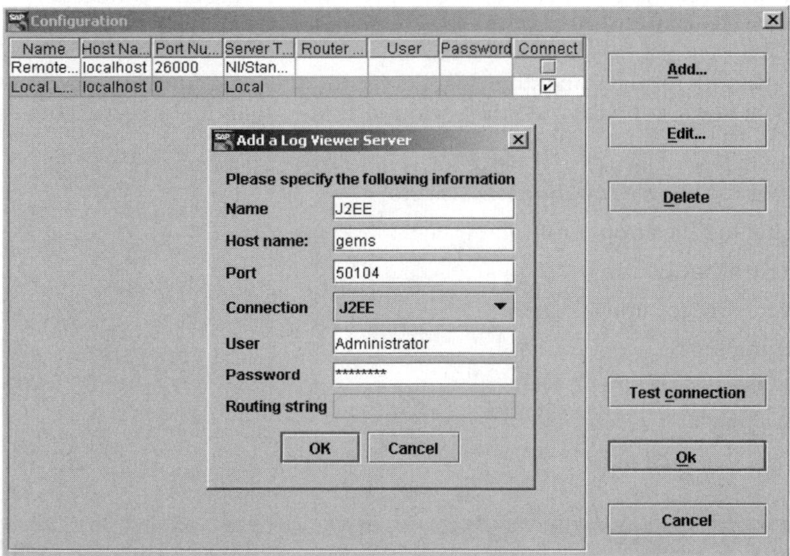

2. Enter the following information and click OK:

   Name: Name of the server to which you are trying to connect

   Host Name: Host name of the server

   Port: The default values are 5<*instance_no*>04 for a J2EE engine connection, and 26000 for a standalone log viewer server

   Connection: J2EE if the J2EE engine is running, NI/Standalone if the standalone log viewer server is used

   User: This is enabled when the connection type is J2EE. Enter the J2EE Administrator user

   Password: Enter the password for the user entered above

   Routing String: This is required for an NI socket type of connection

3. After entering the correct parameters, make sure that the connectivity works by clicking Test Connection in the Configuration dialog box.

4. Click OK to save the configuration. If the server connects successfully, the connected server name will appear in the left navigation menu. Sometimes, the test connection may not work. Make sure that the server is running for the J2EE connection type.

After the new configuration is saved, a file called BAMConfiguration.xml is created under the folder C:\usr\sap\J2E\JC01\j2ee\admin\logviewer-standalone\client. It contains the details of the servers connected to the log viewer.

Opening a Log File Individually

You can open a log file individually from the Windows file system:

1. Right click the log file and choose Open. Then select the program from the list shown in the Open With window:

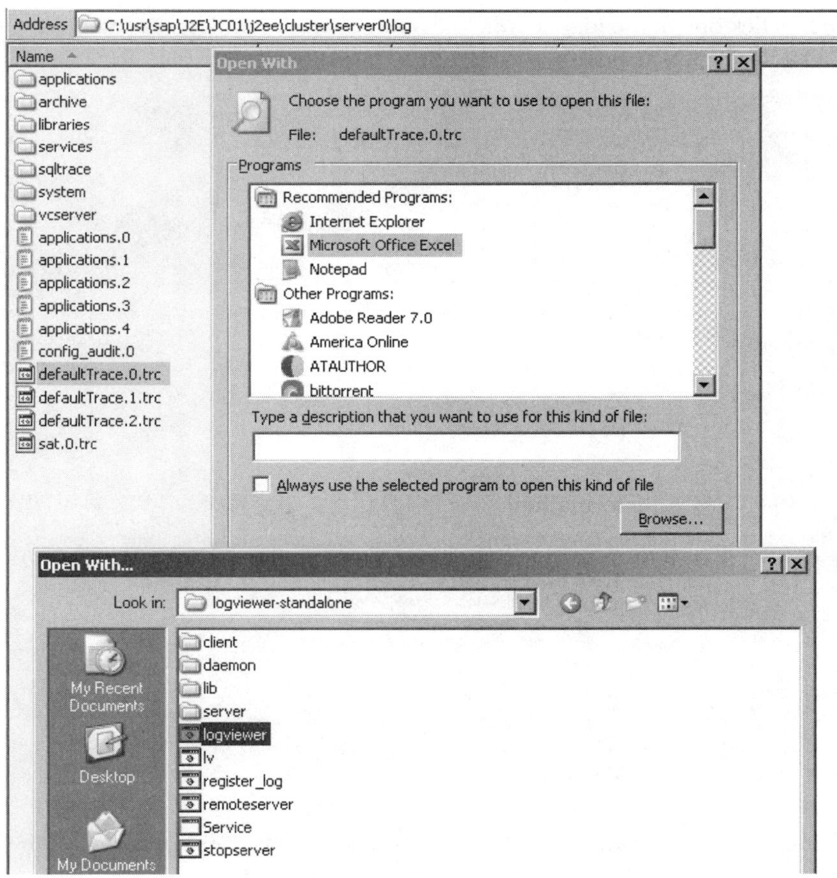

2. Click Browse and navigate to the folder where the log viewer.bat file is located (C:\usr\sap\J2E\JC01\j2ee\admin\logviewer-standalone) and select it. Then click OK.

The logs will now display in the log viewer, as shown here:

Copyright by SAP AG

3. Double-click one of the log records to display a detail window, as shown next. You can then click Additional Information for more details.

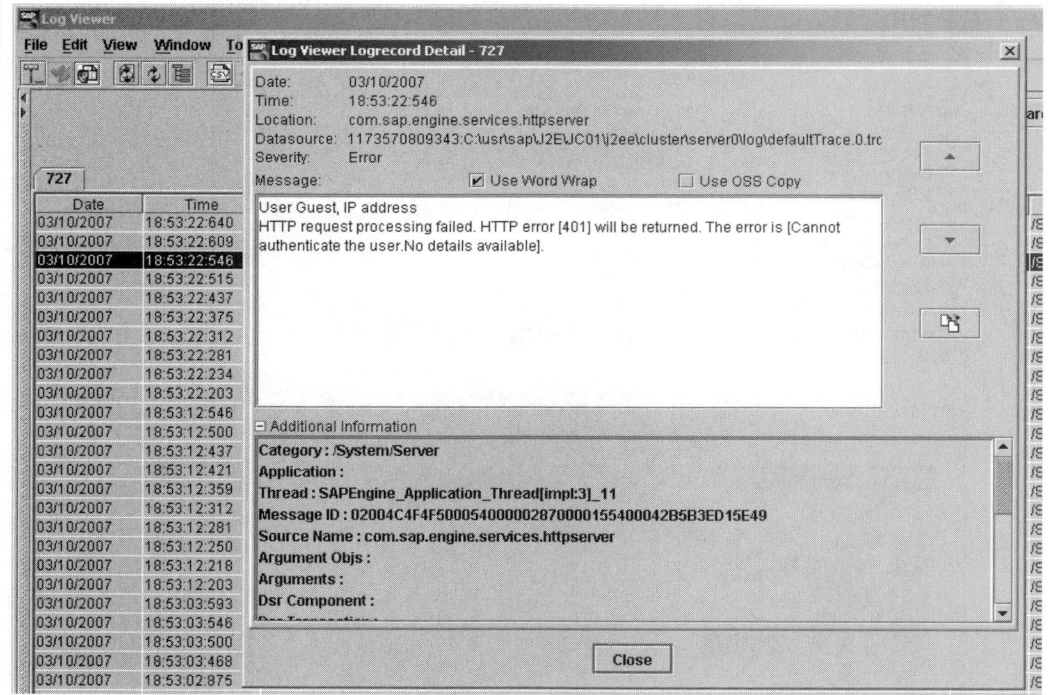

Copyright by SAP AG

4. Maximize this window and scroll down the log records. If the left pane of the log viewer appears in a collapsed mode, click the arrow to expand it:

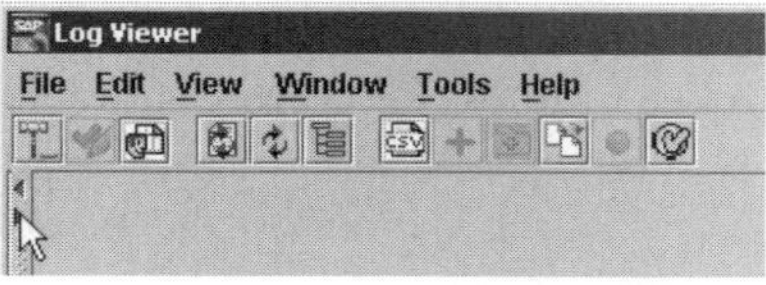

Copyright by SAP AG

5. The log files in the left pane can be viewed either as a table or as a tree by choosing View | View Logs as Tree or View Logs as Table, as shown next:

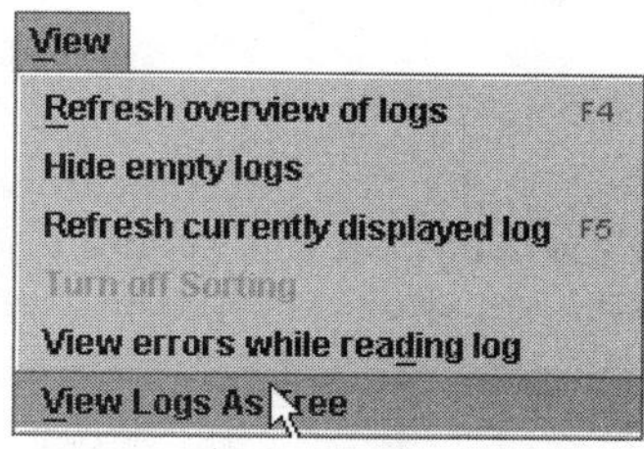

Copyright by SAP AG

Sorting

Sorting is possible in the table view. To sort the column in the table view, simply click the column. In the table view, the following columns are available:

- Server name
- Type of file
- State of the log files
- Name or path to the file
- Number of new records written since the session started
- Length of the files (-1 indicates the file does not exist)
- Date when the file was last modified

File Status

In the illustration to the right, you can see different icons next to the filenames in the log viewer navigation pane. These icons depend on the status of the files. Notice that the log file hotspot_compiler has a green checkmark next to it, which means it has been viewed. The log files logViewer_standalone_server.log and cf_installation.report show icons that indicate that they have not been viewed. The icon for GC.log indicates that there is no such log file.

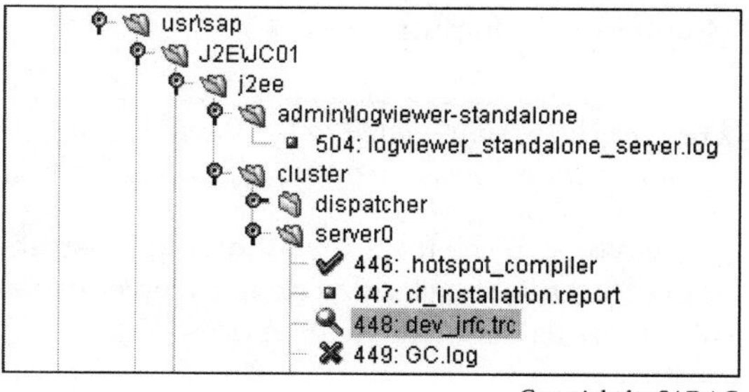

Copyright by SAP AG

After accessing the GC.log file, the icon will change color to red, as shown next, which indicates an error state:

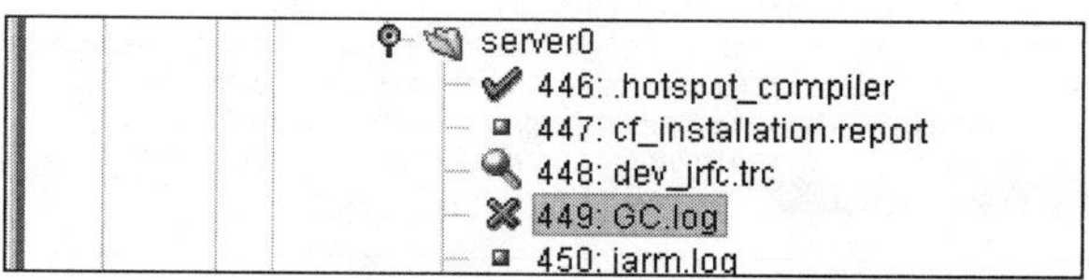

Copyright by SAP AG

PART VI

The drag and drop functionality lets you drag a log file and drop it in the left pane of the log viewer. The newly added file appears in the bottom of the tree and the log record details are shown on the right.

Undocking a File

You can undock a log file by clicking Undock on the context menu obtained by right clicking, as shown next. The log file will appear as a separate screen outside of the log viewer. Undocking may be helpful when you want to compare two log files using two separate windows.

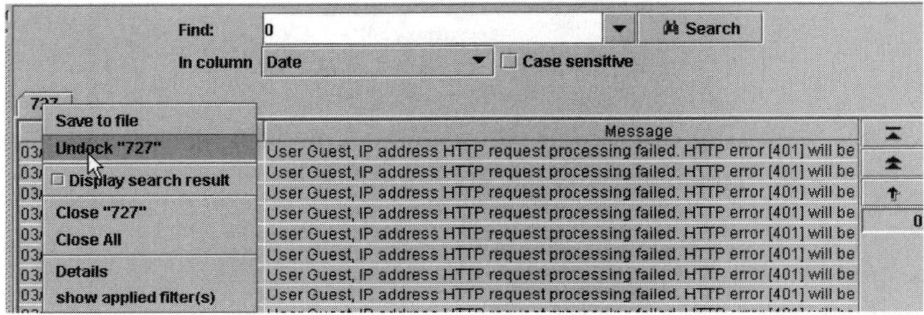

You can click the Dock icon on the separate screen to return to the original view.

Registering the Log File

By default, the log files that are displayed on the left pane overview of logs are registered on the J2EE engine and the standalone Log Viewer server.

To access the Log Viewer service, log on to the Visual Administrator, then navigate to Server | Services | Log Viewer | Properties. Check the setting for the Logviewer_ MonitorablePath property.

TIP *For the setting related to the standalone log viewer, go to the file* LogViewerServer.properties *under the folder C:\usr\sap\J2E\JC01\j2ee\admin\logviewer-standalone\server.*

As you can see from the following illustration, which is a section of the LogViewerServer .properties file, the standalone log viewer can add files belonging to the path usr/sap and its subfolders as denoted by three dots (...):

```
# MonitorablePath.
# For security reasons only the directories specified here can be
# used to "add" files.
# Specify directories, that can contain logfiles, which can be
# made available to the user. Usage: specify absolute path of each directory with a name of
# separated by the OS-specific path separator (Windows: ";", Unix: ":").
# Note: use \\ (double-backquote) or / in Windows and / in Unix as path separator.
# If the directory and all directories below it are specified you can use "...".
# Example (Unix): Logviewer_MonitorablePath=/usr/sap:/tmp:/usr/sap/C11/...
# Example (Windows): Logviewer_MonitorablePath=c:\\usr\\sap;c:\\tmp;c:/usr/sap/SDM/...
Logviewer_MonitorablePath=/usr/sap/...
```

To add files for viewing, right click the node where the log file exists and choose Add A Log File, as shown here:

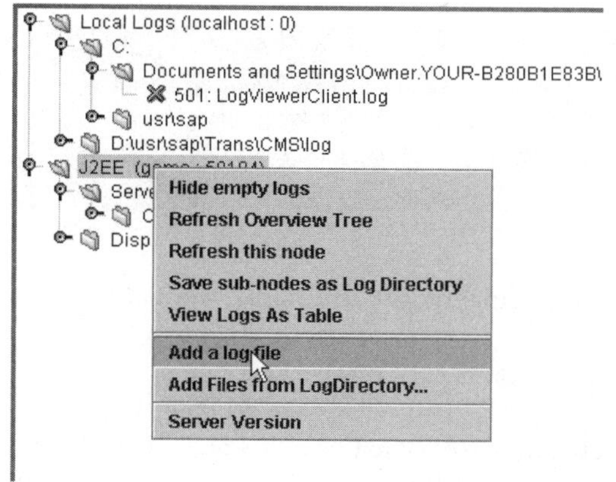

In the Add A file To Monitor window, shown next, browse to the log file that needs to be added, select the type of the log file and the format of the log file, and then click Add:

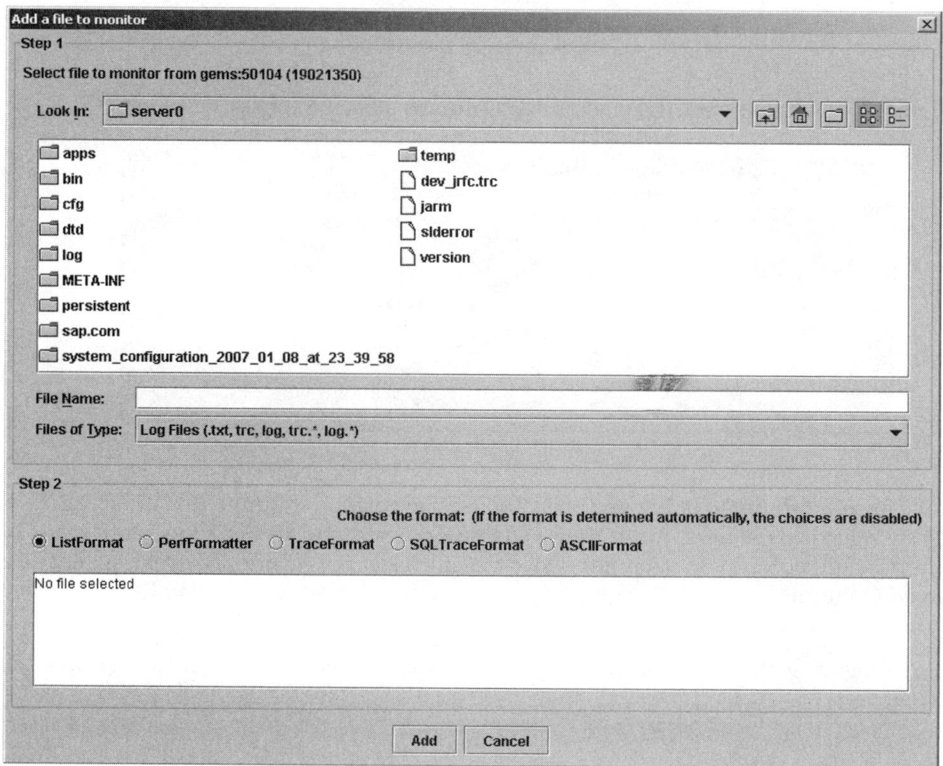

If you get the error message shown next, add the path to the file to the Logviewer_MonitorablePath property and then try adding the file again:

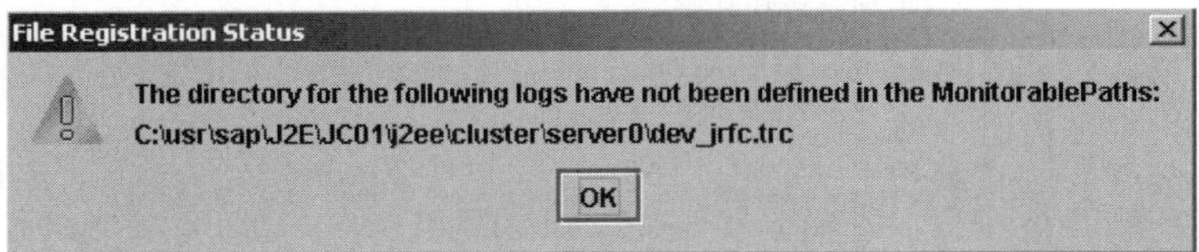

Copyright by SAP AG

To stop the standalone log viewer, click the stopserver.bat in Windows and stopserver.sh in UNIX.

Customizing Columns

You can add fields to the current display list of fields as well as change the position of the columns. The customization can also be done either by log type or for all log types.

To change by log type, choose the icon shown next in the toolbar of the log viewer:

Copyright by SAP AG

When you click that icon, the Customize Columns screen appears:

Copyright by SAP AG

You can select the type of log and then choose the various columns that are required for display by selecting the field under the Available Columns and then clicking Add to add fields to the right column. In a similar way, you can select the columns under Current Displayed Columns and click Remove to remove columns from the display list.

NOTE *Customizing columns in this way is specific to a user and is available for subsequent sessions for that user.*

To customize for all log types, right click the displayed column header and select/deselect the various columns, as shown next:

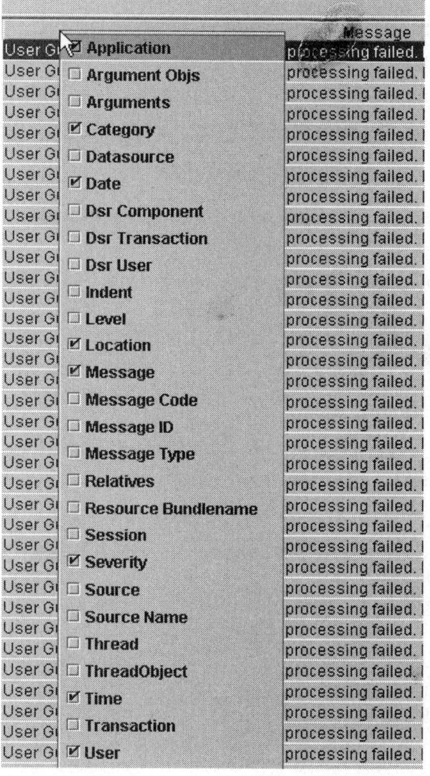

Copyright by SAP AG

You can also change the position of the columns simply by dragging and dropping the column header. To change the alignment of the content under a particular column, right click the column content and choose Align Right For Message, as shown here:

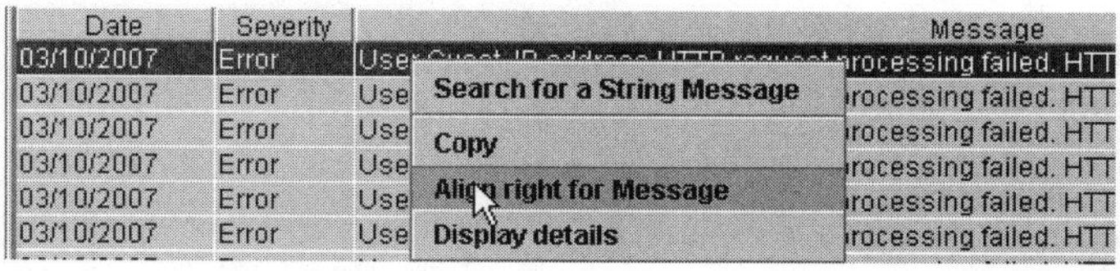

Copyright by SAP AG

NOTE *The changes to all log types shown above exist only for the current session.*

Searching Logs

Searching the log files is pretty intuitive. You can select the column in which you want to search and then enter the search parameter and click Search. Another option available to search is to right click the content of a column on which you would like to search and enter the search string, as shown here:

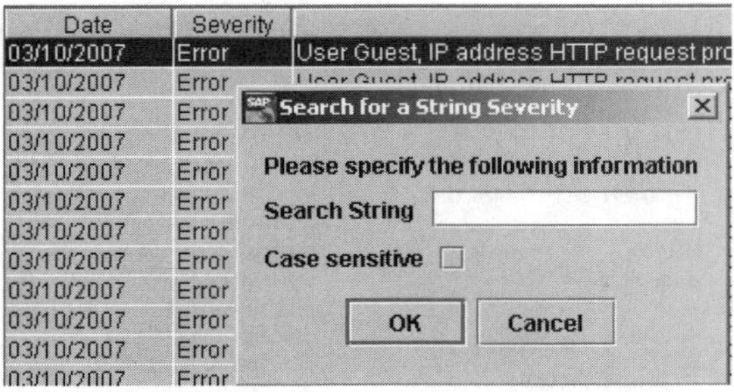

Copyright by SAP AG

Finally, it makes sense to save the log as a comma-separated values (CSV) file by clicking Save To File in the context menu obtained by right clicking, as shown next, and open it in Microsoft Excel to tap the analytical features of Excel.

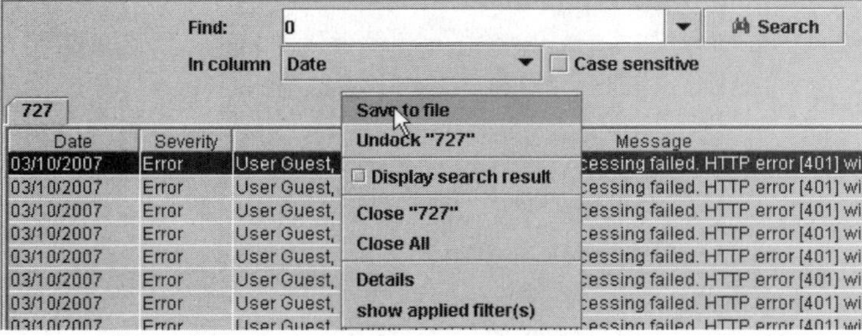

Copyright by SAP AG

Filtering Logs

Filters allow you to sort out particular records from the large number of log records available and help you fine-tune your analysis of the logs during troubleshooting. Filtering can occur based on text, date/time, and severity levels by entering the appropriate values in the bottom left half of the log viewer, as shown in the illustration on the right. Filtering can be applied either globally or to the current log file that is in display.

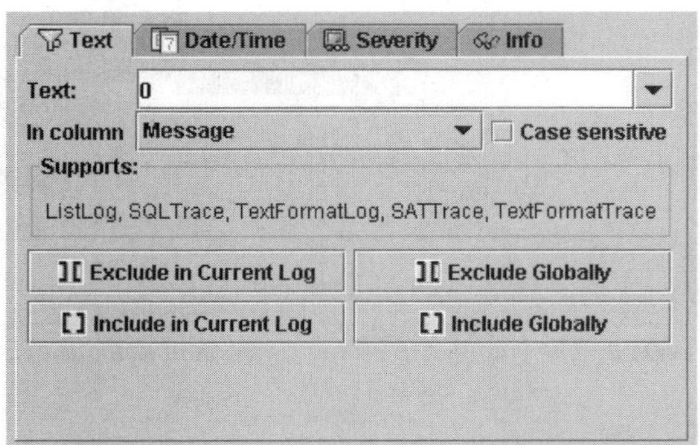

Copyright by SAP AG

Global filtering means the filter settings are applicable not only to the current log file, which is on display on the right of the log viewer, but it also applies to the log files that are likely to be opened in the future. Whenever new filters are added, they are added to the existing list of filters. The *Exclude* option implies all the records that do not satisfy the filter criteria are displayed on the right. Obviously the *Include* option implies the opposite.

Sorting Log Records

To sort the log records shown on the right in the log viewer, double-click the column and then click OK when the warning message appears, as shown next. The warning message notifies that no new records will be displayed when sorting is activated. If you want to sort by another column, double-click the column again. The sorting order should occur in such a way that the most important column is sorted last.

Copyright by SAP AG

Once the analysis is completed, you can disable the sorting by clicking the Turn Off Sorting icon in the toolbar:

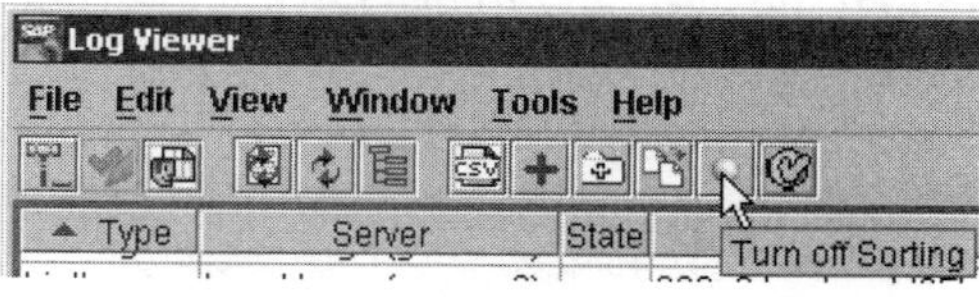

Copyright by SAP AG

Merging Log Files

Merging can be done for files both within the server and for files from across multiple servers. To merge the files, select multiple files by pressing the CTRL key as you click the files to be merged. Then select Merge Files And Display from the context menu obtained by right-clicking, as shown next:

Copyright by SAP AG

Displaying Archive Files

To display the archive files, simply navigate to the archive file in the left pane and double-click the archive log file to be displayed. Note that the archived logs are displayed as subnodes of the original log file.

Relevant OSS Notes

Following is a list of relevant OSS notes:

- **770853** Changing the trace level in the SAP J2EE engine
- **812776** SAP Log Viewer: Installation instructions
- **812683** SAP LogViewer Connection in remote support
- **718141** Standalone Log Viewer
- **781486** Standalone Log Viewer
- **737736** Tracing and Logging for SAP Connectors in NW04

NOTE *For more details, refer to the logging related resources listed in Appendix B.*

Summary

This chapter presented a detailed overview of the logging and tracing functionalities on the portal. Knowing how to use the log files can be very helpful during troubleshooting. Knowing how to configure logging and how to use the log viewers is a useful skill for an administrator as well as developer.

27

CHAPTER

Analyzing and Troubleshooting Portal Performance

This chapter covers performance analysis techniques and the strategies that can be used in performance analysis to identify portal performance issues. In this chapter, you will learn about the factors affecting performance as well as potential steps, tools and techniques you can adopt to analyze portal performance issues.

NOTE *For more details, refer to the* How to… Analyze Performance Problems *guide available at http://sdn.sap.com.*

Performance analysis includes such activities as testing, monitoring, analysis, and tuning. These activities form a closed loop throughout the lifecycle of the portal—that is, it is a continuous activity. Once the portal system has been tuned for optimum performance, you cannot leave the portal alone, because users are constantly added, applications are deployed, and portal system configuration can change, and all this necessitates further tuning. All these changes can have an adverse impact on portal performance; that's why it is important to constantly monitor performance, test performance, and tune it, as necessary.

NOTE *Performance tuning of the portal system is not a one-time activity.*

Factors Affecting Performance

A number of factors affect portal performance, and the interplay among these factors is often quite complex and conflicting in nature. It is important that you understand these constraints and realize that the overall performance of the portal is a sum total of the performance impact due to these individual variables in the portal architecture. Performance depends on a number of systems such as the portal server, the backend database, the application server, the network, the application itself, and the client.

Performance can be poor due to both *software components*, such as the database and the software load balancers, and *hardware components*, such as third-party interfaces and network connectivity components.

NOTE *Portal performance depends on both hardware and software components that constitute the portal infrastructure.*

The following factors can affect performance in the *portal layer*:

- Overhead due to authentication mechanisms and the consequent delay in login
- Time taken to connect with a back end
- Resources consumed due to logging
- Time taken to load home page
- Design of Java iViews

The following factors can affect performance in the *operating system layer*:

- Memory
- CPU consumption
- Network bandwidth
- Java Virtual Machine (JVM)
- The kernel

In the *J2EE layer*, you will have to deal with memory configuration, thread management, encryption, and session management issues. The application itself should be designed properly, giving due consideration to the Java garbage collection techniques, avoiding nested loops, not closing JDBC connections, and other factors. In addition, a sufficient number of threads should be made available for request processing, and it should be possible to create a sufficient number of concurrent sessions.

If the *database* is not tuned properly for performance, it can cause a very adverse performance impact. Even the database OS and the software should be tuned properly.

Other components that exist in the web infrastructure layer such as the *proxy server*, the *web server*, the *web dispatcher*, the *load balancer*, and the *routers* all play a role in the overall performance.

Performance Analysis

To get the most out of a portal system from a performance standpoint, you'll need to work on all the components—because, after all, a chain is only as strong as its weakest link. Even if you succeed in getting the most out of individual components, you can still experience very poor performance if any one of the components continues to be a performance bottleneck. A good performance strategy should therefore give due attention to every performance factor to be truly effective.

Before analyzing a performance problem reported in the portal, you should make sure that the following steps have been carried out:

- Ensure that all the basic administration and configuration tasks that are required during and after the implementation are completed.
- Ensure that the latest patches and hotfixes have been installed.
- Ensure that any other SAP recommendations such as the GoingLive Check analysis has been implemented.

Performing the Analysis

You could begin performance analysis by conducting a high-level analysis of the performance problem from an end user's standpoint. The idea behind conducting an end user analysis is to document and classify the issue thoroughly so that the subsequent analysis is pointed in the right direction. This can be done by asking the right questions and analyzing the logs. In addition, you should try to get a better handle on the problem by isolating the issue to a particular user, page, location, or time.

Once the initial end user analysis is completed, you can then decide whether to analyze the workload on the portal server or to proceed with client-side analysis for a single user. In conducting the workload analysis on the portal server, you need to collect all the required monitoring data. Then you can proceed by analyzing the operating system, portal workload, the JVM, and other factors. By analyzing the portal workload, you can isolate poor performance iViews. A single-user analysis can be accomplished using an HTTP trace, client-side analysis, network analysis, and backend analysis.

Gather Information

In this first step, you can ask the following questions to help you understand the problem:

- Is the problem related to a single user?
- Does the problem occur during heavy load conditions?
- Does the problem occur during specific times of the day or all the time?
- Does the problem occur only during a specific activity such as accessing a backend system or a database?
- Is the problem reproducible?
- Is the problem simply poor performance or is it also accompanied by incorrect results?
- Does the problem occur only during logon?
- Does the problem occur only during the first use?
- When did this problem start?
- Did anything change in the system, operating system, patches, or the application before or after the problem occurred?

Analyze the Logs

Your next steps after documenting the problem are to check the following:

- **Check the logging level of the logs and the traces that are created** To change the log level, refer to Chapter 26.
- **Check the size of the log files** The log file size should not increase more than 1MB under load.
- **Check for any errors in the log files** For example, check whether any error is being logged because of connectivity issues to any of the backend systems such as the content management server, database, or the SAP system.
- **Check the Windows Event Log for clues.**

Isolate the Problem

Your next step is to identify which component is responsible for the poor performance. Following are some of the techniques that you can use to isolate the location of the problem.

Web Infrastructure Issue: Connect to the Dispatcher Directly Try to connect directly to the dispatcher. If performance improves immensely, you have isolated the issue to the web infrastructure components.

Change the Portal Configuration Make the following changes and check the performance before and after:

- Connect to the portal using HTTP instead of HTTPS.
- Change the authentication requirements on the portal.
- Access static content and dynamic content.
- Disable any auxiliary services, monitoring processes, and other background processes that run on the portal such as, for example, the anti-virus program.

If the performance improves in any of the above scenarios tested, it could mean that the poor performance is due to some improper configuration on the portal server.

Client Location: Access from Intranet and Internet Check whether the performance varies when accessing the portal from within the intranet or from the public Internet. In such cases, conduct a network analysis to verify such aspects as network bandwidth, network latency, proxy configuration, and DNS server. Then follow with a comparison of the network configurations on the hosts involved.

TIP *The location of the client may also be responsible for poor performance.*

Compare the Portal Servers in the Cluster If a load balancer is used with more than one portal server host, it may be helpful to connect directly to the portal servers individually by bypassing the load balancer and then compare the performances.

HINT *If any of the portal servers show poor performance, it may be helpful to compare the configuration of that server with that of the other portal servers.*

Check the Browser Settings In some cases, poor performance may be due to caching on the browser or improper proxy settings. Clearing the browser cache and accessing the portal again may be of help.

Identify the Portal Content That Gives Poor Performance

It could be possible that the logon process itself is pretty time consuming or that a particular iView or page is taking a long time to download. To check for these problems, you can do the following.

Analyze the Logon Process and the Home Page IViews The logon process can be divided into a number of steps:

1. Log on; authentication against the User Management Engine (UME).
2. Download the default framework page that consists of the top-level menus.
3. Download the page consisting of the detailed navigation iView.
4. Download the content page and iViews.

The URL required for accessing the page or iView individually is http://<server>:<port>/irj/servlet/prt/portal/prtroot/com.sap.portal.navigation.portallauncher.default?NavigationTarget=MyPageName.

As you're trying to log on, if the default home page takes a long time to download, you should analyze whether an individual iView within that page is taking longer to download as compared to the other iViews using the URL provided.

Create a Dummy Page Create a dummy start page and try to access that page. If the page downloads quickly, the problem could be in accessing the UME for authentication. If accessing the page repeatedly does not result in improved performance, the problem could be in the caching configuration or in the number of roles assigned to that user. You can then assign a single role to the user and access the same page repeatedly. If the page downloads quickly at that point, you will know that the problem was due to the large number of roles that were assigned to the user.

TIP *Avoid assigning too many roles to a user as it can affect performance.*

Remove the IViews to Identify a Slow iView Remove iViews from a page with poor performance and then try to access the page until you can isolate a particular iView that is causing poor performance. Trying techniques such as enabling server cache for that iView or changing the isolation method may also be helpful. Subsequently, you can also adopt techniques such as user activity tracing, backend analysis, and thread dumps for further analysis.

Performance Monitoring

You should set up monitoring techniques that can be either operating system dependent or independent. You can use the tools provided by the portal server, the J2EE engine, or the JVM to collect such data as well as certain special techniques that SAP provides through its Solution Manager, such as the Computing Center Management System (CCMS) technology or Generic Request and Message Generator (GRMG) monitoring. In fact, even third-party monitoring tools can be used for collecting such data.

TIP *The monitoring data should be collected as far as possible not only on the portal server, but also from other systems such as the backend server, the database systems, and any other third-party systems that are connected to the portal.*

Persisting Monitoring Data and Analyzing Java Applications

Once the monitoring data are collected, they can be persisted to the file system for later analysis. Refer to OSS Note 766598 for information about persisting and analyzing Java monitoring data with the J2EE Engine 640. These analysis features are available starting from J2EE Engine 6.40 SP9. In order to persist the monitoring data and analyze the applications, you must carry out the following steps:

1. Trigger the collection of monitoring data and activate the persistency of monitoring data to a file system.
2. Access the monitored data using HTTP by deploying the Performance Viewer application for getting a detailed overview of the system.
3. Get a quick overview of the system by running the Performance Reporter application.

Trigger the Collection of Monitoring Data

Your first step is to start the config tool:

1. Start the config tool from *<drive>*:\usr\sap\J2E\JC01\j2ee\configtool.
2. Click Yes to connect to the default database.
3. Click Switch To Configuration Editor Mode, and then navigate to Cluster_data | Dispatcher | Persistent | Shell | Autorun.scr.
4. Double-click autorun.scr and click Download.
5. Edit the downloaded file to include the following entries:
   ```
   add monitor
   persist_monitoring_data -default
   ```
6. Click Switch Between View And Edit Mode icon in the toolbar and then click Yes in the Switch To Edit Mode dialog box. Double-click the autorun.scr file again.
7. Click Upload and upload the changed file from your local file system.
8. Repeat step 3 through 7 for the server by going to Cluster_data | Server | Persistent | Shell | Autorun.scr.
9. Click Switch Between View And Edit Mode to go back to view mode. Then click Switch To Config Tool Mode.
10. Click Apply Changes, and then choose File | Apply.
11. Choose File | Exit to exit the config tool.

Deploy the Perfviewer Web Application

Your next step is to deploy the web application:

1. Extract the ZIP file pviewer that was downloaded from the OSS note.
2. Convert the WAR file into an EAR file: Go to C:\usr\sap\J2E\JC01\j2ee\deploying\deploytool.bat, create a new project, and give it a name.
3. Click the Assembler tab, choose Assemble | Add Archive, and then point to the pviewer.war file. Then click OK.
4. Choose Assemble | Make ear, and give the EAR file a name.

Management of Performance Data
SAP J2EE Engine 6.40
Home page Logout

Activation of persistence of monitoring data
For Test Environment only!
Telnet connection is not secured!
Do not use in untrusted domains!

Telnet Connection settings
Telnet User
Telnet Password
Settings for persistence of Monitoring Data
Period forming one collection portion (minutes)
Interval between 2 j2ee counters collections (seconds) 60
Interval between 2 jarm data collections (seconds) 600
Number of weeks to keep history 2
Start Stop

Access and processing of collected monitoring data
Welcome
User:
Password:
Enter

Copyright by SAP AG

FIGURE 27-1 Logon screen

You can now deploy the EAR file using the Deploy tool. I prefer the Visual Admin tool for this, so let's go back to the Visual Admin tool.

1. Log on to Visual Admin, then navigate to Cluster | Services | Deploy | Runtime | Deploy and Start.
2. Click the Browse button and navigate to the EAR file. Then click OK, and click OK again twice. The deployment will begin.
3. Check in the Visual Administrator under the Deployed Components section to see if the sap.com/pviewer application is in running mode. You can access the Management of Performance Data logon screen at http://<*host*>:<*port*>/pviewer, as shown in Figure 27-1.
4. Now log on to the Management of Performance Data screen using the Administrator logon information. Figure 27-2 displays the home page of the Performance Viewer application.

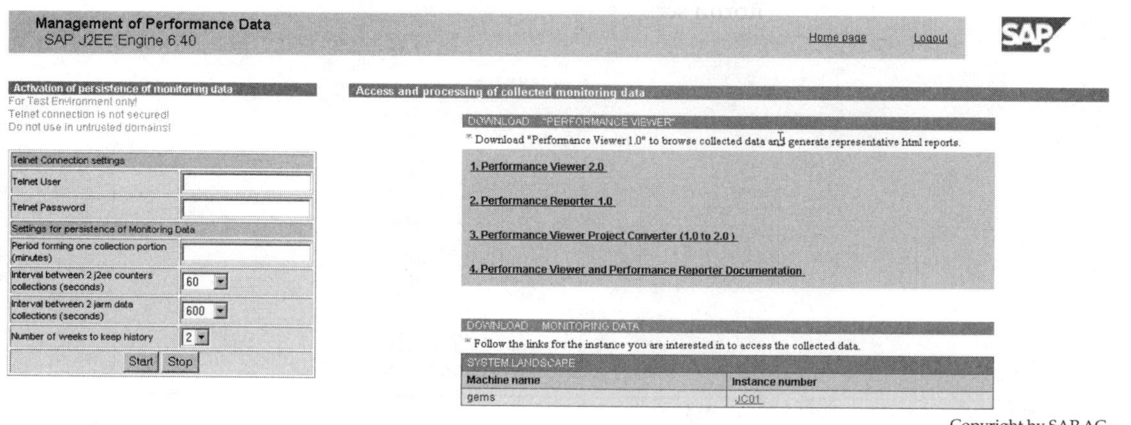

Copyright by SAP AG

FIGURE 27-2 Performance Viewer home page after logon

PART VI

Two tools are available for download: Performance Viewer and the Performance Reporter.

5. Extract the JAR file by clicking the Performance Viewer link.
6. After downloading, click the JAR file to start the Performance Viewer. The Performance Viewer can be used to browse the collected monitoring data and to generate new HTML files for performance analysis.

NOTE *Choose Help | Help from within Performance Viewer for more information on how to use this application.*

Activate Persistence and Launch Performance Viewer and Reporter

To activate persistency in the entire cluster log into the application using telnet, you'll fill in information into the fields on the left side of the Management window. Enter the required frequencies for collecting monitoring data and the days required to keep the data in history for analysis, as shown in Figure 27-3. Click Start when you're finished.

Once persistency is activated, a directory called MonitoringData is created under the C:\usr\sap\J2E\JC01\j2ee\cluster folder, where all the monitored data are stored. To conduct the analysis of the collected monitoring data, open the Performance Viewer application (Figure 27-4) and load the ZIP file by choosing Source Files | Load and browse to C:\usr\sap\J2E\JC01\j2ee\cluster\MonitoringData\<*node ID*>.

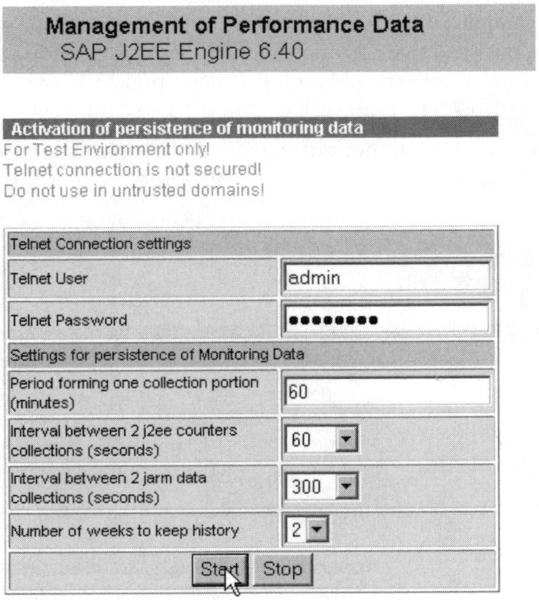

Management of Performance Data
SAP J2EE Engine 6.40

Activation of persistence of monitoring data
For Test Environment only!
Telnet connection is not secured!
Do not use in untrusted domains!

Telnet Connection settings	
Telnet User	admin
Telnet Password	••••••••
Settings for persistence of Monitoring Data	
Period forming one collection portion (minutes)	60
Interval between 2 j2ee counters collections (seconds)	60
Interval between 2 jarm data collections (seconds)	300
Number of weeks to keep history	2
Start Stop	

FIGURE 27-3 Activating persistence of monitoring data

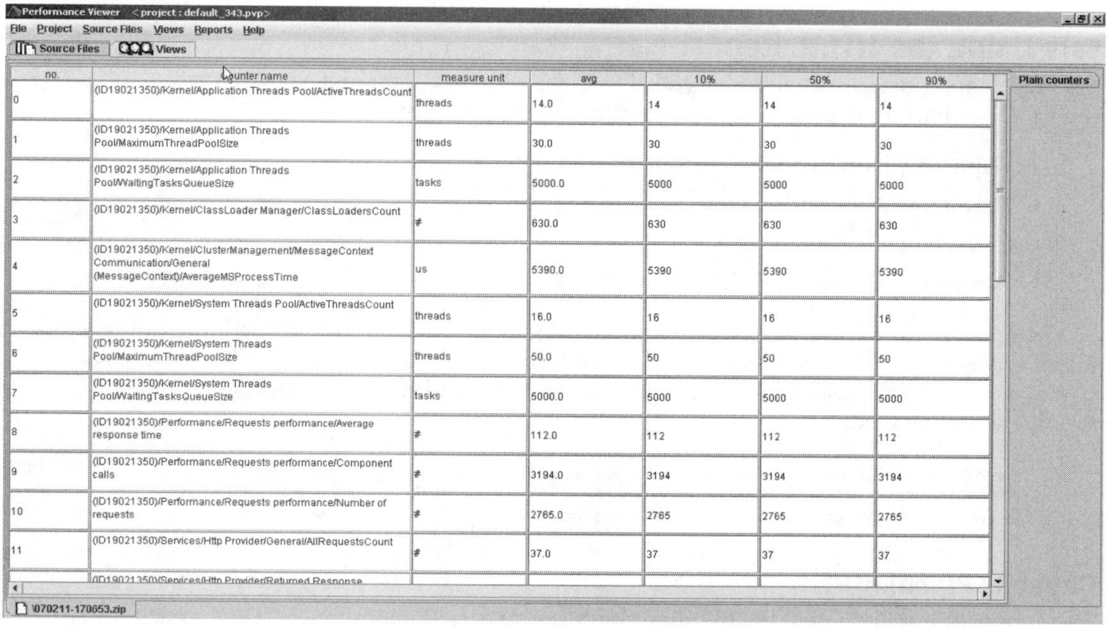

Performance Viewer <project : default_343.pvp>

File Project Source Files Views Reports Help

Source Files | Views

no.	counter name	measure unit	avg	10%	50%	90%
0	(ID19021350)/Kernel/Application Threads Pool/ActiveThreadsCount	threads	14.0	14	14	14
1	(ID19021350)/Kernel/Application Threads Pool/MaximumThreadPoolSize	threads	30.0	30	30	30
2	(ID19021350)/Kernel/Application Threads Pool/WaitingTasksQueueSize	tasks	5000.0	5000	5000	5000
3	(ID19021350)/Kernel/ClassLoader Manager/ClassLoadersCount	#	630.0	630	630	630
4	(ID19021350)/Kernel/ClusterManagement/MessageContext Communication/General (MessageContext)/AverageMSProcessTime	us	5390.0	5390	5390	5390
5	(ID19021350)/Kernel/System Threads Pool/ActiveThreadsCount	threads	16.0	16	16	16
6	(ID19021350)/Kernel/System Threads Pool/MaximumThreadPoolSize	threads	50.0	50	50	50
7	(ID19021350)/Kernel/System Threads Pool/WaitingTasksQueueSize	tasks	5000.0	5000	5000	5000
8	(ID19021350)/Performance/Requests performance/Average response time	#	112.0	112	112	112
9	(ID19021350)/Performance/Requests performance/Component calls	#	3194.0	3194	3194	3194
10	(ID19021350)/Performance/Requests performance/Number of requests	#	2765.0	2765	2765	2765
11	(ID19021350)/Services/Http Provider/General/AllRequestsCount	#	37.0	37	37	37
	(ID19021350)/Services/Http Provider/Returned Response					

Plain counters

\070211-170653.zip

Figure 27-4 Performance Viewer

Run the Performance Reporter Application

The Performance Reporter application is a good tool for identifying any configuration issues using an HTML report generated from the collected monitoring data. The HTML report contains views such as the Resource Consumption view and the Capacity Planning view based on information provided by counters such as memory, sessions, and threads. To run the Performance Reporter application, open a command prompt and then enter

```
Java -jar perfreporter.jar log1171229056375.zip test.html c
```

Here's the syntax:

Java -jar perfreporter.jar *<param1>* *<param2>* *<param3>* *<param4>*

The parameters are required in order:

- ***<param1>*** ZIP file or a folder of ZIP files containing monitoring data
- ***<param2>*** Name of the generated report
- ***<param3>*** Target folder for the generated report
- ***<param4>*** Template XML (optional parameter)

In the above example, test.html is the name of the generated report and c drive is the location of the target folder, where the generated report is located.

PART VI

Analysis Using the HTML Report

Two types of reports are included in the HTML report: a *line chart* and a *table formatted* report. Line chart reports are available for the following views:

- Capacity planning view
- Resource consumption view
- Error statistics view
- Applications activities view

To generate the HTML report, copy the ZIP file under the MonitoringData folder into the folder where the perfreporter JAR file is located and run the `java -jar perfreporter .jar <zip file name> report <drive>` command to run the app in the command prompt as shown next:

```
C:\Documents and Settings\Owner.YOUR-B280B1E83B\My Documents\Portal\04 Portal Pe
rformance>java -jar perfreporter.jar 070211-170654.zip report c

C:\Documents and Settings\Owner.YOUR-B280B1E83B\My Documents\Portal\04 Portal Pe
rformance>_
```

Capacity Planning View

The application will display the first line chart in Capacity Planning view. The Capacity Planning view consists of measurements of the following counters:

- Requests to SAP J2EE Engine services:

Reports

Capacity Planning View

Resource Consumption View

Error Statistics View

Applications Activities View

(ID19021350)Components by groups (JARM)

(ID19021350)Components Performance View (JARM)

(ID19021350)Requests Performance View (JARM)

(ID19021350)Users Activities View (JARM)

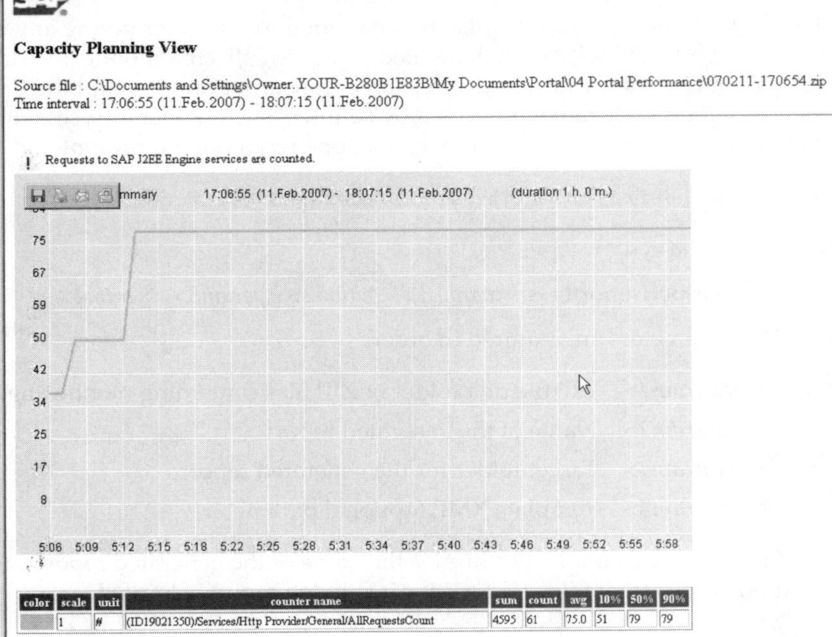

- Requests Summary statistic for the requests to applications that are instrumented with Java Application Response Time Measurement (JARM):

! For applications, which are instrumented with JARM, a "Requests Summary" stastic for the instrumented requests is available too.

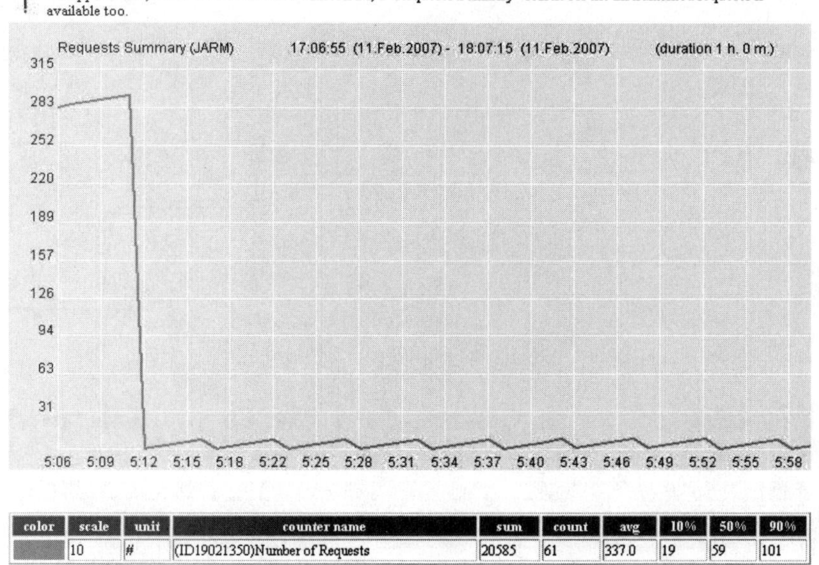

color	scale	unit	counter name	sum	count	avg	10%	50%	90%
	10	#	(ID19021350)Number of Requests	20585	61	337.0	19	59	101

- The average response time, measured on the J2EE Server node for applications instrumented with JARM:

! The average response time, measured on the J2EE Server node for applications instrumented with JARM.

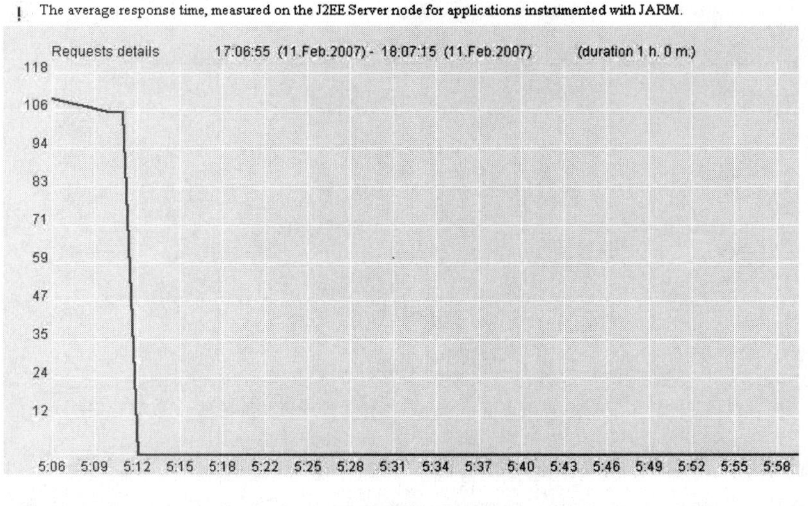

color	scale	unit	counter name	sum	count	avg	10%	50%	90%
	1	ms	(ID19021350)Average Execution Time of a Request (milliseconds)	646	61	10.0	0	0	0

PART VI

- Sessions and memory consumed by those sessions:

! Sessions and the memory, which they require.

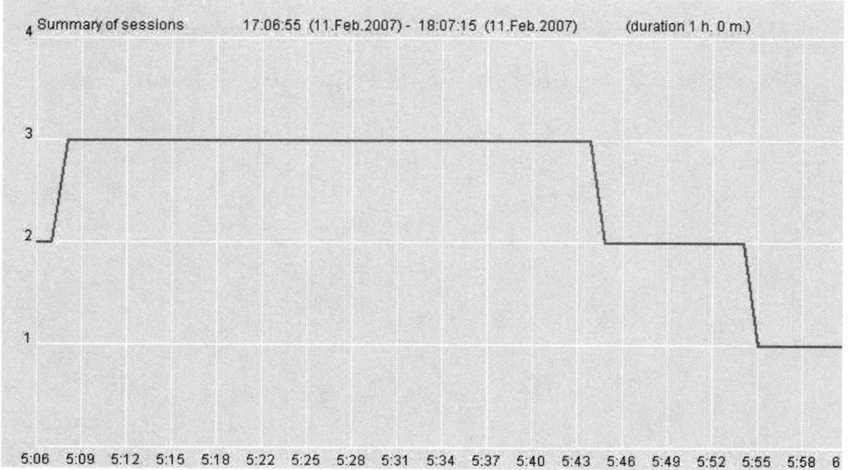

color	scale	unit	counter name	sum	count	avg	10%	50%	90%
	1	#	(ID19021350)/Services/Security/Aggregated Data/ActiveSessionsCount	143	61	2.0	1	3	3

Copyright by SAP AG

- Number of HTTP sessions and security sessions established on the J2EE Server node:

! Reports the number of http sessions and security sessions, established on the J2EE Server node.

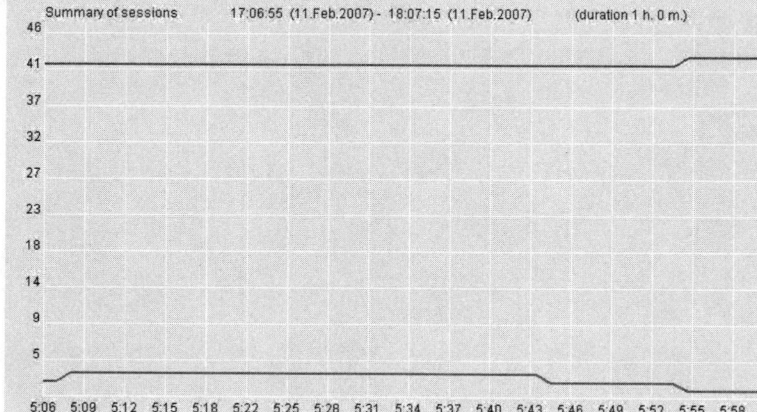

color	scale	unit	counter name	sum	count	avg	10%	50%	90%
	1	#	(ID19021350)/Services/Security/Aggregated Data/ActiveSessionsCount	143	61	2.0	1	3	3
	1	#	(ID19021350)/Services/Security/Aggregated Data/LoggedOffSessionsCount	2576	61	42.0	42	42	43

Copyright by SAP AG

Resource Consumption View

The resource consumption view consists of the following:

- Data for the memory usage inside JVM:

Resource Consumption View

Source file : C:\Documents and Settings\Owner.YOUR-B280B1E83B\My Documents\Portal\04 Portal Performance\070211-170654.zip
Time interval : 17:06:55 (11.Feb.2007) - 18:07:15 (11.Feb.2007)

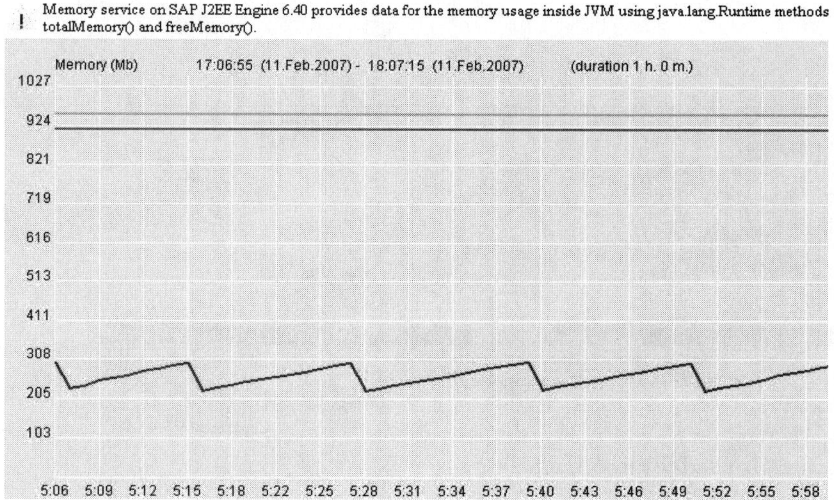

color	scale	unit	counter name	sum	count	avg	10%	50%	90%
	1	#	(ID19021350)/Services/Memory/AllocatedMemory	56059	61	919.0	919	919	919
	1	#	(ID19021350)/Services/Memory/AvailableMemory	58499	61	959.0	959	959	959
	1	#	(ID19021350)/Services/Memory/UsedMemory	16096	61	263.0	233	261	296

Copyright by SAP AG

- Application threads involved in the processing of customer requests—usually lower value preferred:

! SAP J2EE Engine 6.40 uses thread pools. Application threads are involved in processing of customer requests. In most of the cases smaller number of threads in this pool improves the performance.

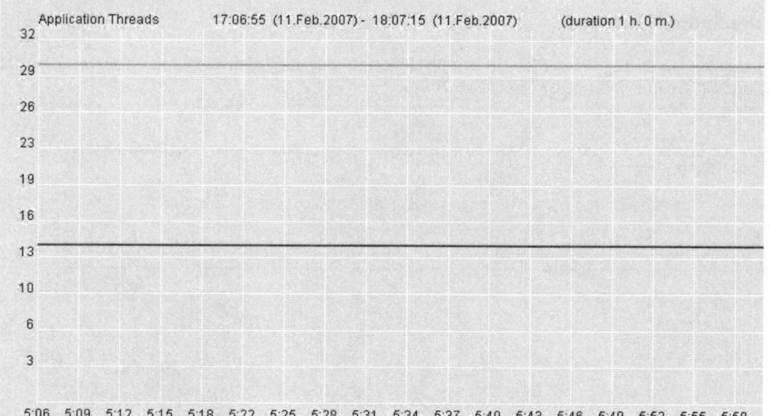

color	scale	unit	counter name	sum	count	avg	10%	50%	90%
	1	#	(ID19021350)/Kernel/Application Threads Pool/ActiveThreadsCount	854	61	14.0	14	14	14
	1	#	(ID19021350)/Kernel/Application Threads Pool/MaximumThreadPoolSize	1830	61	30.0	30	30	30

- System threads used for internal tasks:

! SAP J2EE Engine 6.40 uses thread pools. System Threads are used for internal tasks. If the System Threads are not sufficient the cluster node will block.

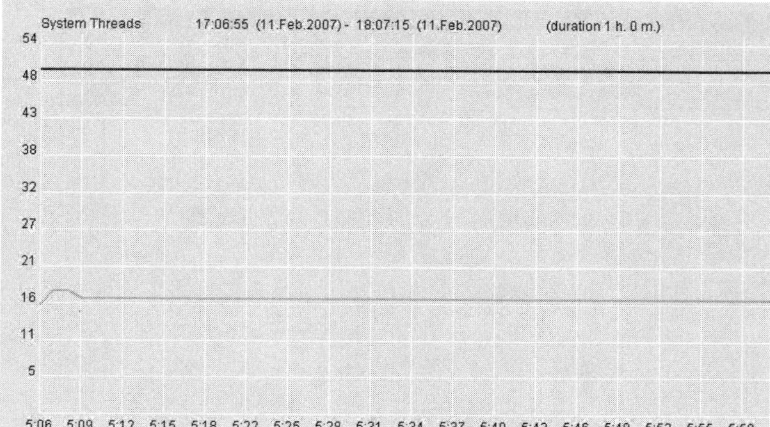

color	scale	unit	counter name	sum	count	avg	10%	50%	90%
	1	#	(ID19021350)/Kernel/System Threads Pool/ActiveThreadsCount	1038	61	17.0	17	17	17
	1	#	(ID19021350)/Kernel/System Threads Pool/MaximumThreadPoolSize	3050	61	50.0	50	50	50

Error Statistics View

The error statistics view consists of the following:

- Security errors:

Error Statistics View

Source file : C:\Documents and Settings\Owner.YOUR-B280B1E83B\My Documents\Portal\04 Portal Performance\070211-170654.zip
Time interval : 17:06:55 (11.Feb.2007) - 18:07:15 (11.Feb.2007)

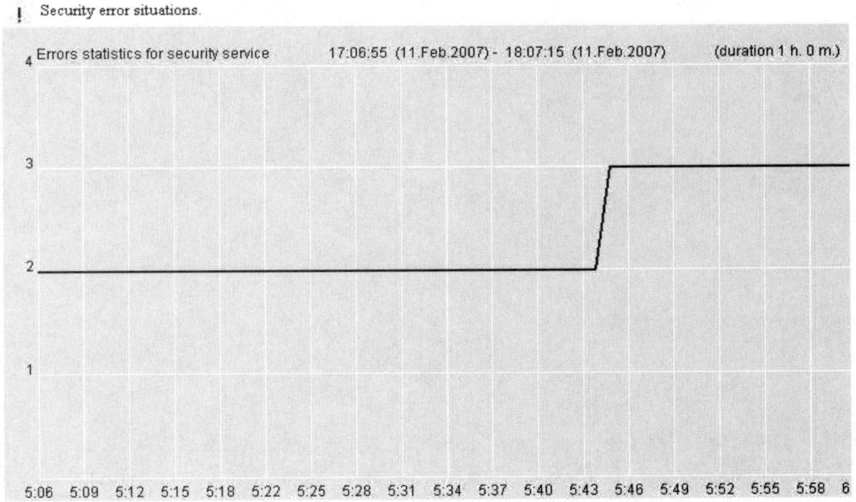

color	scale	unit	counter name	sum	count	avg	10%	50%	90%
	1	#	(ID19021350)/Services/Security/Aggregated Data/TimedOutSessionsCo unt	146	61	2.0	2	2	3

PART VI

- Timeout errors for sessions, transactions, and periodic tasks—the number of available system threads should be below the number of timeout errors:

! Timeouts for start of periodic tasks, expiration checks for sessions and transactions, other timeout based activities could be reason for unstability of the system in some cases. Important is that the number of timeouts in any moment do not exceed the number of available System Threads, otherwise there is formed a waiting queue. If there is high frequency rate the system has to be checked.

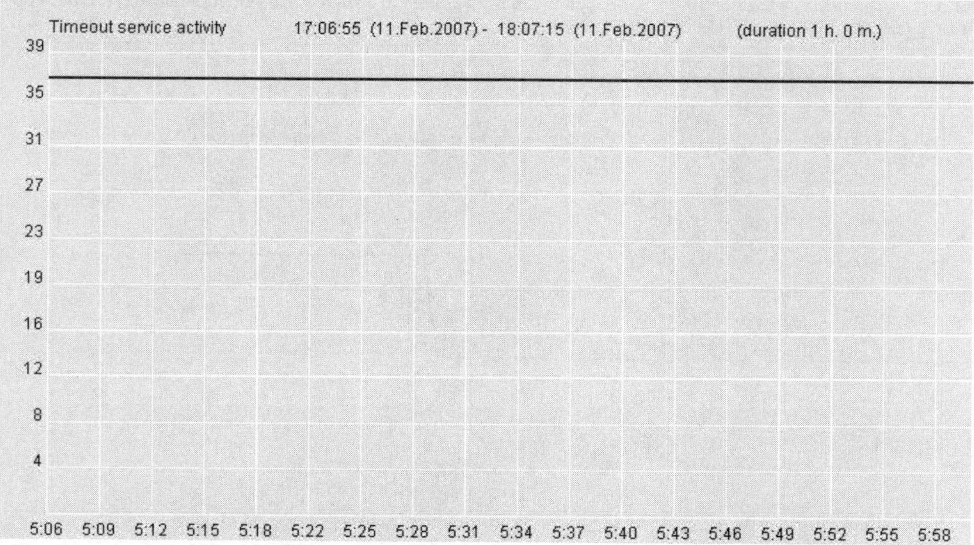

color	scale	unit	counter name	sum	count	avg	10%	50%	90%
	1	#	(ID19021350)/Services/Timeout/EstimatedFrequencyPerMinute	2257	61	37.0	37	37	37

- Number of class loaders—if the number of class loaders is very high, the memory consumption could be very high during the system idle state:

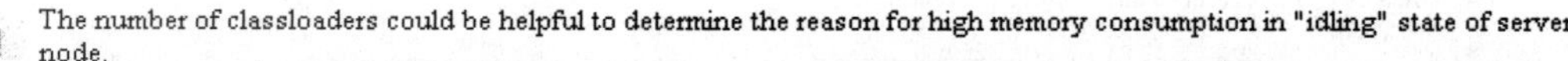

! The number of classloaders could be helpful to determine the reason for high memory consumption in "idling" state of server node.

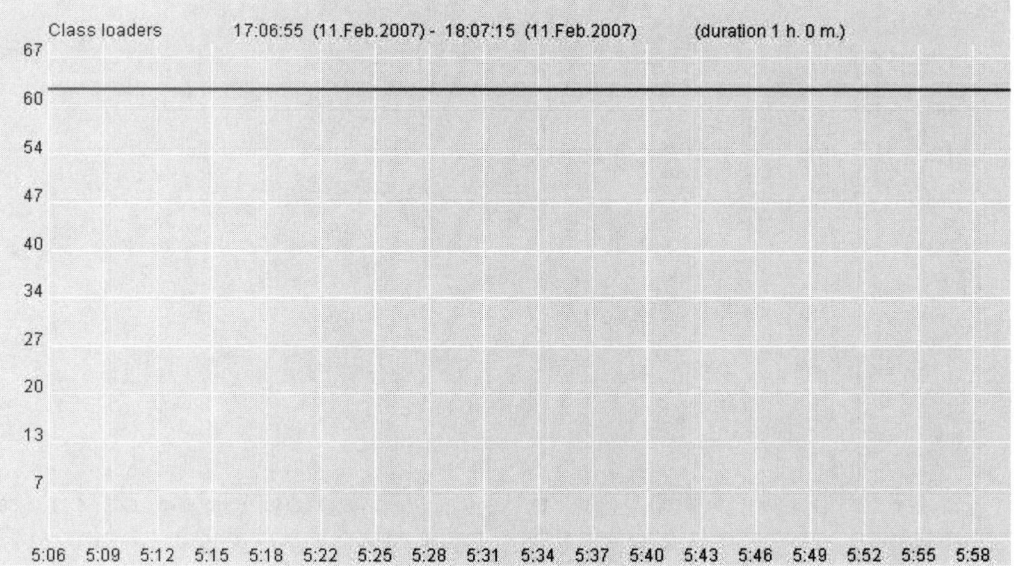

color	scale	unit	counter name	sum	count	avg	10%	50%	90%
	10	#	(ID19021350)/Kernel/ClassLoader Manager/ClassLoadersCount	38430	61	630.0	630	630	630

- Total log file size—the rate of increase should be low:

! In a smoothly running system the log files should not grow fast.Fast growing files means either misconfigured log level or some aften appearing or either looping exception.

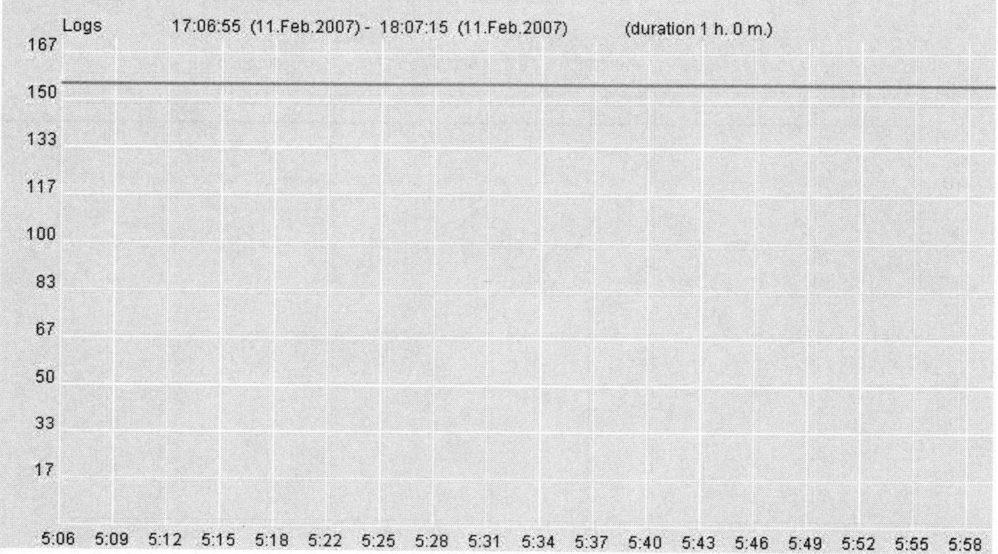

color	scale	unit	counter name	sum	count	avg	10%	50%	90%
	1000	bytes	(ID19021350)/Services/Log Configurator/General/TotalLogFilesSize	9551369	61	156579.0	156567	156582	156582

Applications Activities View

The Applications Activities view consists of the following:

- Number of component calls for all requests

- Average number of component calls per request:

Applications Activities View

Source file : C:\Documents and Settings\Owner.YOUR-B280B1E83B\My Documents\Portal\04 Portal Performance\070211-170654.zip
Time interval : 17:06:55 (11.Feb.2007) - 18:07:15 (11.Feb.2007)

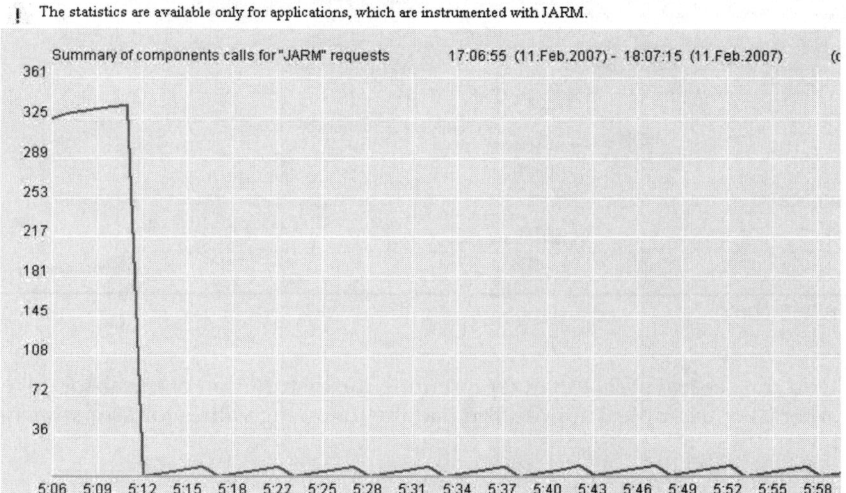

color	scale	unit	counter name	sum	count	avg	10%	50%	90%
	10	#	(ID19021350)Number of Component Calls for all Requests	23199	61	380.0	19	59	101
	1	#	(ID19021350)Average Number of Component Calls per Request	61	61	1.0	1	1	1

The table reports are Components by Groups, Components Performance View, Requests Performance View, and Users Activities View. Refer to Figures 27-5, 27-6, 27-7, and 27-8 to view the types of information that can be obtained from these table reports.

Using the Charts

In the line chart seen in Figure 27-9, the *count* column displays the number of times the counter has been measured in the reporting interval. The *sum* column displays the total amount of the measured value. For example, if the counter is the number of HTTP requests, then it would show the total number of HTTP requests received by the J2EE engine. The *avg.* column refers to the average value of the counter.

Components distribution in groups (ID19021350)

Source file : C:\Documents and Settings\Owner.YOUR-B280B1E83B\My Documents\Portal\04 Portal Performance\070211-170654.zip
Time interval : 17:11:57 (11.Feb.2007) - 18:07:15 (11.Feb.2007)

Distribution of components in groups			
Group	Number of used components	Group	Number of used components
AppServer:Security	12	UME:searchUsers	1
init(IServiceContext serviceCo	1	ADS:TrustManager	1
CleanJobTask()	1	SLD:OM	2
EP:PCD_Role.getRole pcd	8	EP:KM	12
EP:PRT_service	406	EP:PCD_Role.searchRoleNamesInternal (&(com.sap.portal.pcd.gl.AtomicName	1
ADS:Licensing	2	afterInit()	1
init(IServiceContext)	1	SLD:JDBC	3
getPermission(String)	1	ADS:ConfigurationService	2
com.sap.mw.jco.JCO.Client	1	UME:AbstractPrincipal	1

FIGURE 27-5 Components by groups

To the right, you can see *statistical values* representing the distribution of the absolute values of the counters. For example, suppose you had the following values for *used memory consumption:*

10%	50%	90%
50	350	700

What this means is that 10 percent of the time, the used memory consumption has been below 50MB, and 40 percent of the time (that is, between 10 and 40 percent), it has been

Reports

Capacity Planning View
Resource Consumption View
Error Statistics View
Applications Activities View
(ID19021350)Components by groups (JARM)
(ID19021350)Components Performance View (JARM)
(ID19021350)Requests Performance View (JARM)
(ID19021350)Users Activities View (JARM)

Components Performance View (ID19021350)

Source file : C:\Documents and Settings\Owner.YOUR-B280B1E83B\My Documents\Portal\04 Portal Performance\070211-170654.zip
Time interval : 17:11:57 (11.Feb.2007) - 18:07:15 (11.Feb.2007)

#	component name	number of calls			net time (ms)			gross time (ms)			outbound data (bytes)		
		min	accum	max	min	accum	max	min	accum	max	min	accum	max
1	EP:PRT_service:init:com.sap.ip.bi.base.application|mainservice	1	1	1	217	217	217	734	734	734	0	0	0
2	EP:PRT_service:init:com.sap.portal.appintegrator.sap.bwc|urlgenerator_bwc	1	1	1	28	28	28	28	28	28	0	0	0
3	EP:PRT_service:init:com.sap.portal.runtime.system.notification|SAPJ2EEHttpService	1	1	1	0	0	0	0	0	0	0	0	0

FIGURE 27-6 Components Performance View

Reports

Capacity Planning View

Resource Consumption View

Error Statistics View

Applications Activities View

(ID19021350)Components by groups (JARM)

(ID19021350)Components Performance View (JARM)

(ID19021350)Requests Performance View (JARM)

(ID19021350)Users Activities View (JARM)

Requests Performance View (ID19021350)

Source file : C:\Documents and Settings\Owner.YOUR-B280B1E83B\My Documents\Portal\04 Portal Performance\070211-170654.zip
Time interval : 17:11:57 (11.Feb.2007) - 18:07:15 (11.Feb.2007)

#	Request name	Number of executions	Number of components	Duration (ms)				Data volume (bytes)			
				min	avg	comp max	max	min	avg	comp max	max
1	EP:PCD_Role	12	1	0	2499	2499	24884	-1	-1	-1	0
2	UME:searchUsers	1	1	17	17	17	17	-1	-1	-1	0
3	ADS:ConfigurationService:ReadXML	1	1	1164	1164	1164	1164	-1	-1	-1	0

Figure 27-7 Requests Performance View

between 50 and 350MB. For the remaining 40 percent of the time between 50 and 90 percent, the used memory consumption has been between 350 and 700MB.

What this means is that there has been a wide variation in the memory consumption. So, to get a better understanding of the behavior, you may look at the Capacity Planning View, and find that the cause of increased memory consumption is increased user sessions.

While using the Performance Viewer tool, it could be helpful to use the following tips. Using the 10 percent, 50 percent, and 90 percent values, identify those counters that have wider variations. Using this list, you may be able to identify those counters that are impacted by each other. Compare the data for different servers in the system or between the server and dispatcher to identify any wide variations and hence discrepancies in the configuration.

Reports

Capacity Planning View

Resource Consumption View

Error Statistics View

Applications Activities View

(ID19021350)Components by groups (JARM)

(ID19021350)Components Performance View (JARM)

(ID19021350)Requests Performance View (JARM)

(ID19021350)Users Activities View (JARM)

Users Activities View (ID19021350)

Source file : C:\Documents and Settings\Owner.YOUR-B280B1E83B\My Documents\Portal\04 Portal Performance\070211-170654.zip
Time interval : 17:11:57 (11.Feb.2007) - 18:07:15 (11.Feb.2007)

Requests per user				
#	user name	number of requests	duration for all requests(ms)	average duration of request(ms)
1	NWDI.Developers	1	0	0.0
2	Administrator	4	520	130.0
3	RABIJAY01	1	578	578.0
4	NWDI.Administrators	2	0	0.0
5	Guest	11	275120	25010.0
6	Anonymous Users	6	0	0.0
7	ume_service	21	29989	1428.0
8	Everyone	11	18	1.0
9	Guests	6	0	0.0
10	admin	7	478	68.0
11		3964	5749	1.0

Figure 27-8 Users Activities View

PART VI

Resource Consumption View

Source file : C:\Documents and Settings\Owner.YOUR-B280B1E83B\My Documents\Portal\04 Portal Performance\070211-170654.zip
Time interval : 17:06:55 (11.Feb.2007) - 18:07:15 (11.Feb.2007)

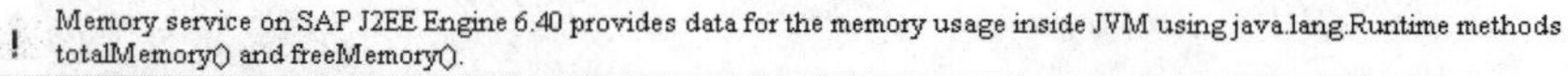

! Memory service on SAP J2EE Engine 6.40 provides data for the memory usage inside JVM using java.lang.Runtime methods totalMemory() and freeMemory().

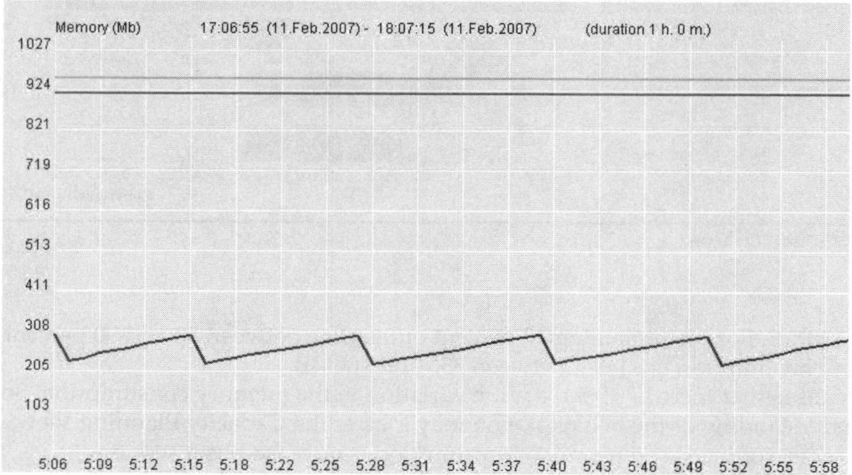

color	scale	unit	counter name	sum	count	avg	10%	50%	90%
	1	#	(ID19021350)/Services/Memory/AllocatedMemory	56059	61	919.0	919	919	919
	1	#	(ID19021350)/Services/Memory/AvailableMemory	58499	61	959.0	959	959	959
	1	#	(ID19021350)/Services/Memory/UsedMemory	16096	61	263.0	233	261	296

FIGURE 27-9 Resource Consumption View

For example, a problem may exist if one of the servers is accepting more requests than the other servers in the configuration. Another example is when the dispatcher threads are active, but the server threads are idle. Identify those counters that have similar trends in the variation of their measured values. This may help to identify resource bottlenecks such as if the memory consumption increases when the number of user sessions increases, or when the application threads queue increases in size and the response time increases.

Windows-Based System Performance Analysis

If the portal is installed on a Windows-based operating system, you can activate performance monitoring.

NOTE *Some of the performance metrics that can be measured at the operating system level are network throughput, disk throughput, memory utilization (OS and JDK), and CPU utilization.*

Windows has a number of objects that can be monitored, such as processes, memory, process, TCP, network interface, physical disk, and system. Each of these has a number of attributes based on which measurements can be made. These attributes are referred to by the name counters and examples of these counters are processor time, page outputs per second for memory, and so on.

1. Open the Control Panel.
2. Double-click Administrative Tools.
3. Then double-click Performance, and in the Performance window, click Performance Logs and Alerts in the right pane.
4. Right click Counter Logs and choose New Log Settings. Enter a name, and then click OK.

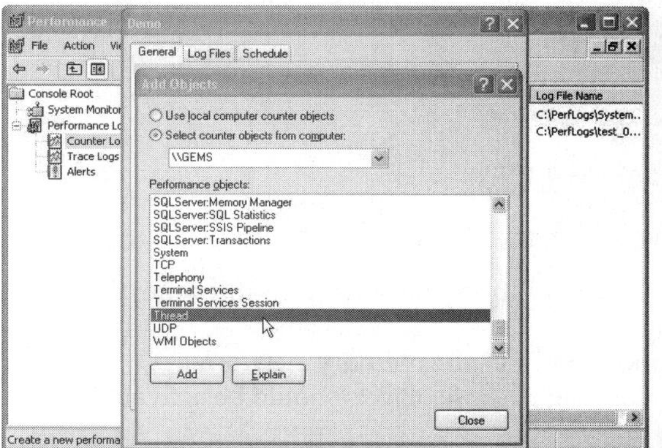

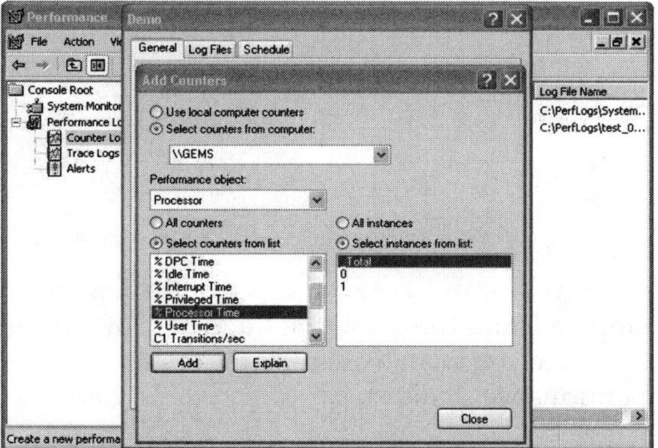

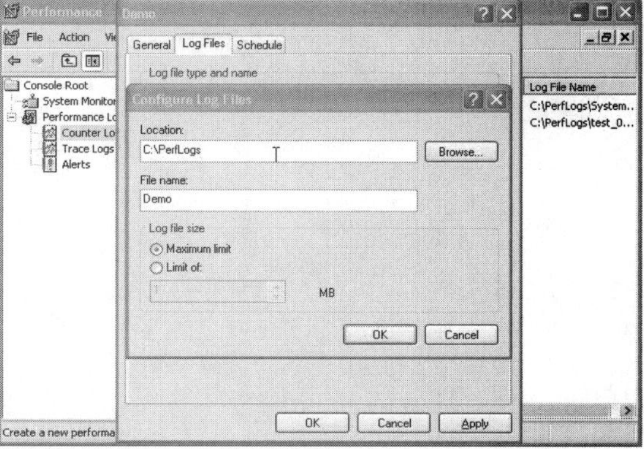

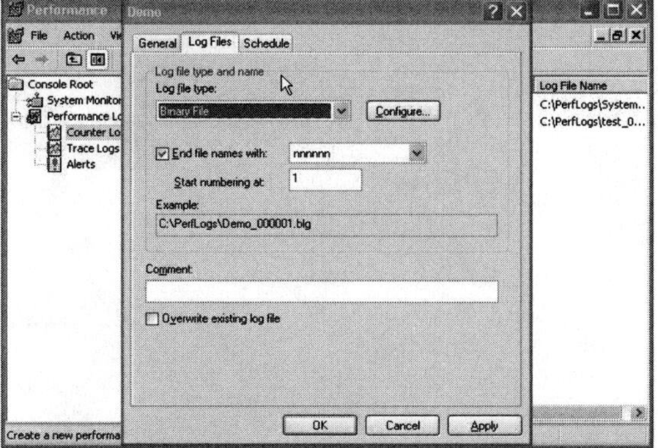

5. You can add either objects or counters by selecting either Add Counters or Add Objects. For additional details, click Explain.

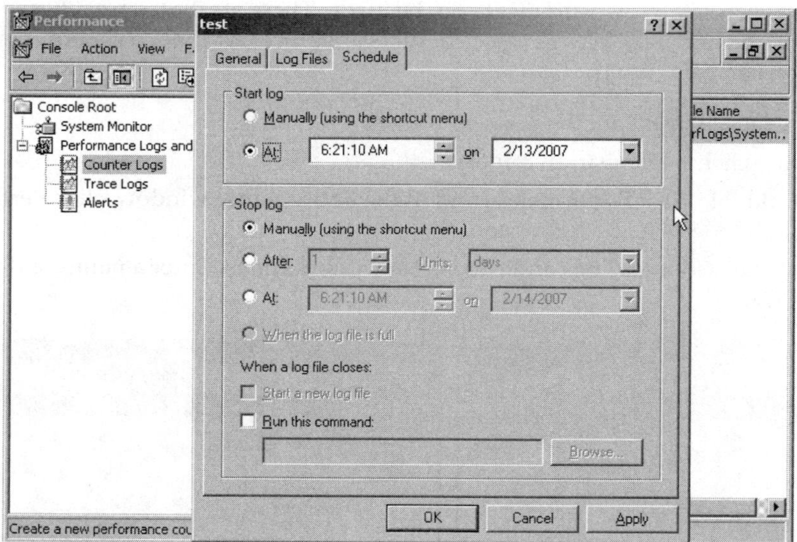

You can configure the name of the log files, the size, location, the start date and time, the stop date and time, and the frequency of sampling data.

Since you want to monitor the system performance, the CPU, the memory, network performance, and disk performance, the counters belonging to those objects should be activated.

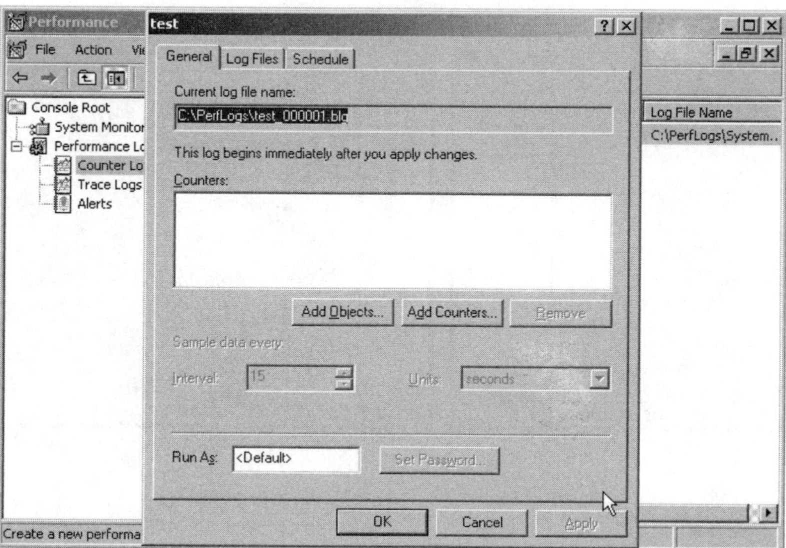

CPU-Based Monitors

Following are some of the CPU-based monitors that could be activated to analyze CPU performance.

Context Switches/Sec

For the system object, you would activate the context *switches/sec* counter that measures the rate at which all the processors in the system are switched from one thread to another. The switch between threads may occur due to the thread relinquishing the processor or when the thread is taken over by a higher priority thread. These activities could result in the CPU load and system latency as well.

The number of context switches should be 1500 times the number of CPUs. Thus, for a dual CPU, the number should be around 3000. If the number of context switches is very high, this could indicate that there are more application threads, which may result in garbage gollection, synchronization issues, I/O waits, and so on. In such situations, reducing the number of threads could be helpful.

% Privileged Time, % Processor Time, and % User Time

% privilege time is the time spent by the process threads in a privileged mode, which is the case when a system service is called that needs access to private system data. *% processor time* is the time spent by the processor to run a non-idle thread and is the primary measure of processor activity. *% user time* is the time spent by the processor in the user mode that is designed for applications.

TIP *Ideally, most of the CPU processor time should be spent in the user mode.*

CPU Time vs. System Time

Now let's see the preferred values for the CPU performance. Ideally, the total CPU time should be around 85 percent and the system time should be around 10 percent of the user time. To achieve this, you may have to change the client threads and the system threads accordingly.

The CPU should be busy for around 10 percent of the time due to I/O operations. High I/O operations may also result in high system activity. If threads are waiting to access a resource due to locks, this can also result in high system activity.

If the CPU is more than 85 percent loaded and if portal behavior is erratic, you should check the users logged in, request response times, and view the HTTP sessions. Check the log of the HTTP service and identify any unusual URLs that could potentially be the cause of such intensive usage.

Try to check a particular CPU load when the system performance is affected and check whether the ratio between user and system CPU time changes drastically. Try to match it with HTTP service info logs for more clues. Check whether threads are waiting for database connections and, if so, increase the number of connections till equilibrium is reached.

Memory-Based Monitors

Following are some of the counters that can be activated to analyze memory performance.

Pages Output/Sec

To identify whether any shortage of memory occurs, you should activate the pages output/sec counter. If this value is high, it could mean that a lot of pages are written to the hard disk to free up more physical memory.

Mbytes Content

The available Mbytes content should also be activated for memory. The higher this value, the better it is. It is the sum of zeroed, free, and standby memory.

Zeroed memory is pages in memory that are filled with zeroes so that the processes do not see the data that were used by a previous process. Free memory is the ready-to-use memory. Standby memory is the memory that is in the process of being removed to the disk from physical memory but can be recalled for use.

Regarding the memory, ideally there should not be any paging activity, and if there are more than 200 memory pages per hour, you should analyze further using other memory counters.

JVM Heap Size

When calculating the JVM heap size, the PermSize for all the JAVA processes in the portal, make sure that the heap size fits within the physical RAM to avoid any paging activity. The recommended solution when more RAM is needed, after allowing for all these Java processes, operating system, and other processes, is to add more RAM.

TIP *When calculating the PermSize, also allow some memory for the operating system and other processes in the system.*

If, on the other hand, free RAM is available and the server process consumes all of its memory allocated in the JAVA heap, accompanied by GC processes, then configuring an additional server node could be helpful.

Sometimes the dispatcher may consume more memory, and if it is also accompanied by full GCs and minor GCs longer than 10 ms, then more memory may be required for the dispatcher.

Process-Based Monitors

You should activate the thread count, percentage processor time, percentage privileged time, and working set counters for the process object.

% privileged time is the time spent by the process threads in privileged mode while executing system services. *% processor time* is the time spent by all the threads to execute instructions, which is the basic unit of execution in the system. There is at least one thread running in a given process.

NOTE *Every process has a number of threads running and the threads are responsible for executing an instruction.*

Working set is the set of memory pages that have been recently used by the threads in the process.

Network-Based Monitors

To analyze network performance, you can activate the counters for the TCP object and the network interface object.

TCP Counters

The TCP object contains monitors that measure the rate of transfer of segments using TCP. A number of counters monitor the connections such as connection failures, connections active, connections established, connections passive, and connections reset.

HINT *A high value for connections failure, or connections created and destroyed, could be reasons for poor performance.*

Network Interface Counters

The network interface object provides counters for measuring the bytes and packets sent and received over a TCP/IP connection. The counters that are helpful in identifying the data throughput through the network interface are bytes sent/sec, bytes received/sec, packets sent/sec, and packets received/sec.

The counter Output Queue length is the number of packets in the output queue. If it is greater than 2, it indicates a performance bottleneck. Packets Outbound Errors is the number of outbound packets that could not be transmitted due to error and is an indication of functionality error in the portal.

While checking the network connections, ensure the following:

- Connections are closed quickly
- Expired connections are not kept in keep-alive mode
- Connections at the OS level are not refused

HINT *Poor network connections could result in poor scalability, high response times, and poor CPU usage.*

If the dispatcher has low memory, it may be able to support fewer connections. The other issue could be that the OS itself is configured only for limited connections. The expired connections may still be in keep-alive mode due to the OS settings that prevent destroying connections in short time intervals.

Sometimes poor response times can be accompanied by poor CPU usage in dispatcher and server nodes. This could be due to delays in proxy servers and the network in general. NIPING values should be used to make further analysis. Sometimes the network could be slow due to the smaller size of TCP/IP packets and larger number of packets. Increasing the size of the TCP/IP packets could help.

Disk-Based Monitors

A physical disk stores file, program, and paging data. To measure the time spent by the disk on reading and writing, you can set up counters such as % disk time, % disk read time, % disk write time, and % disk idle time.

TIP *To measure the load on the disk, counters such as disk read bytes/sec, disk write bytes/sec, disk reads/sec, and disk writes/sec can be used.*

A busy disk can also be a performance bottleneck, and you can use the current queue disk length to measure it. For good performance, this should be less than 2.

The percentage of the active disk time should not be higher than 10 percent. If it is higher, check for log file activity and disable unnecessary log files, and use a high-speed drive and sufficient I/O buffer for storing logs.

As far as disk performance is concerned, the disk queue length is important especially if it is a database machine.

TIP *If logging is found to be creating the issue, reducing the log levels and decreasing the number of system and client threads could be helpful.*

Check for processes as well as real-time virus programs that consume a lot of I/O operations. To do this, go to the Task Manager and select the I/O Read Column and sort it.

Using the Task Manager

Use the Task Manager to conduct a snapshot analysis of the performance such as memory usage, I/O read/writes, CPU, VM size, threads, and so on. Under the Process tab, click Select Columns to add more columns. Check the checkboxes for Memory Usage, I/O Reads, I/O Writes, CPU Time, Virtual Memory Size, Thread Count, Page Faults, and Virtual Memory Size.

As shown in Figure 27-10, select View | Show Kernel Times. On the Performance tab, the red lines show the Kernel CPU times.

TIP *A high value for the kernel times could mean there is a lot of lock contention in the Java VM.*

Next, go to the Processes tab and sort by the CPU column to identify the process that consumes the highest CPU processing power. You will notice that a number of Java processes consume very high CPU power. If this machine is a 2 CPU machine and if one of the Java processes is consuming almost 50 percent of the CPU, it could either mean that there is a garbage collection process taking place or one thread is consuming all the CPU power, thus preventing other threads from running.

TIP *Check if the value for PF delta is high for the process, which, if true, means that there is a lot of paging activity for the process.*

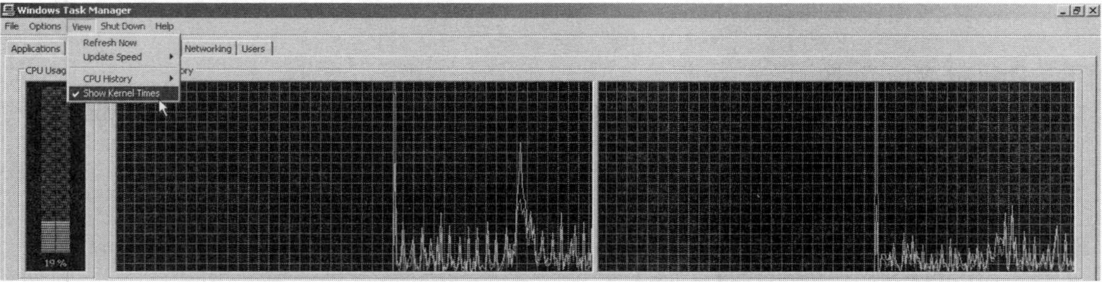

FIGURE 27-10 Performance tab of the Task Manager

Distributed Statistics Records (DSRs)

The J2EE engine contains the DSR service that generates the required statistics and trace information to the central monitoring system using the SAPCCMSR agent.

NOTE *For more about how to set up the central monitoring, see Chapter 32.*

For the DSR to be functional, the following must be true:

- The Central Monitoring System should be set up.
- The DSR service should be active in the J2EE engine.
- The DSR collector should be active and collecting the statistics for the component. The required configuration should have been done in using transaction ST03G.

The DSR records contain the performance data regarding the J2EE engine, which can be used to assess the system performance. The DSRs can be displayed using the ST03G transaction.

Another tool that can be used to assess performance is the JARM (Java Application Response Time Measurement), which is discussed in more detail in Chapter 28.

Relevant OSS Notes

Following is a list of relevant OSS notes:

- **764417** Information for troubleshooting of the SAP J2EE Engine 6.40
- **742395** Analyzing High CPU usage by the J2EE Engine
- **743207** Analyzing High CPU usage by the J2EE Engine: Windows
- **766598** Persist and Analyze Java Monitoring Data with J2EEEngine 640
- **780177** Setup of Solution Manager Diagnostics
- **975136** Initial Troubleshooting Steps for J2EE UME 640/700
- **984006** Remote Support for an Enterprise Portal
- **952795** Central Note for Debugging J2EE Engine
- **480213** Problem Processing in the Component EP-PIN
- **484894** Info Required by Dev Supp. for Messages Processing. Portal
- **981533** Performance Problem Related to the Support Platform
- **812688** Central Note - Support Platform for NW04

NOTE *For more details, refer to the* How to analyze performance problems *guide mentioned earlier and other performance related resources listed in Appendix B.*

Summary

In this chapter, you learned about the factors that affect portal performance and walked through few steps that can be taken when troubleshooting an issue. You took a look at the perfviewer web application and the Performance Reporter application for gathering monitoring data and to analyze the performance results. You then learned how you could use the Windows-based performance monitors to analyze performance.

28

CHAPTER

Portal Monitoring

In this chapter, you will learn how to use the Portal Monitoring tool and conduct user activity tracing. The Portal Monitoring tool can be used to measure the response times and the data volume of requests; by doing this, you can assess the portal workload and identify any expensive iViews.

Portal Monitoring Tool

The Portal Monitoring tool lets you drill down quickly to identify problems with relatively little effort. The tool is based on Java Application Response Time Measurement (JARM), which helps you to identify problems in the portal infrastructure as well as portal content such as iViews.

Workload Monitoring iViews

For portal monitoring, a number of workload monitoring iViews are available under the System Administrator role. Go to System Administration | Monitoring | Portal.

The Request Summary iView shown in Figure 28-1 contains summary information such as the average response time per request and the total number of requests since startup. This is the aggregated view of all the monitoring data since the portal was started. As you can see from Figure 28-1, it displays information on the following:

- Number of requests processed since the portal was started
- Average time taken to process a request
- Time of the first portal request
- Number of requests processed per second

Choosing Server Nodes for Analysis

To choose different nodes and check the values, click the arrow next to the Select Server field. These comparative values will help you identify whether any particular server node is overloaded or not.

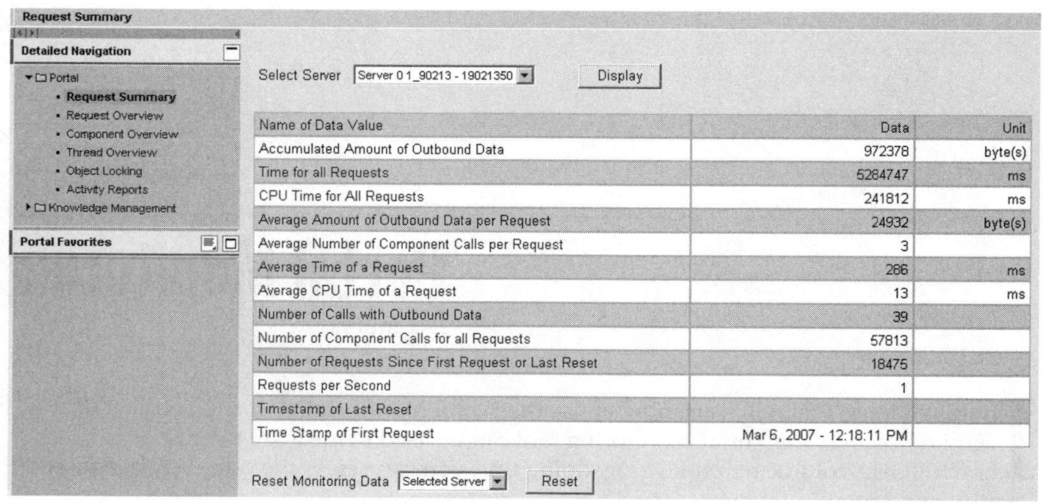

Name of Data Value	Data	Unit
Accumulated Amount of Outbound Data	972378	byte(s)
Time for all Requests	5284747	ms
CPU Time for All Requests	241812	ms
Average Amount of Outbound Data per Request	24932	byte(s)
Average Number of Component Calls per Request	3	
Average Time of a Request	286	ms
Average CPU Time of a Request	13	ms
Number of Calls with Outbound Data	39	
Number of Component Calls for all Requests	57813	
Number of Requests Since First Request or Last Reset	18475	
Requests per Second	1	
Timestamp of Last Reset		
Time Stamp of First Request	Mar 6, 2007 - 12:18:11 PM	

FIGURE 28-1 Request Summary iView

TIP *The values across different server nodes should be comparable if the load-balancing device is working properly.*

You can view information based on the following portal views by selecting them from the navigation pane on the left:

- **Request Overview** Contains an overview of the most expensive requests along with their IDs and response times. You can drill down into the individual requests for further analysis.
- **Component Overview** Contains the overall response time and the number of times the component has been executed.
- **Thread Overview** Contains information on threads that are currently being processed.
- **Activity Report** Contains information on the logged on users and their logon times.

Personalizing the iViews

To make the iViews more user friendly, you can personalize them so that at least 100 lines of information are displayed instead of the default of 15. To increase this number, choose Options | Personalize, and in the Personalization dialog box, enter a value of **50** for Number Of Displayed Requests as shown in the illustration on the right. If you select yes for Display Instrumentation Columns, this will add additional columns to the request overview that provide information on whether the request was successfully completed.

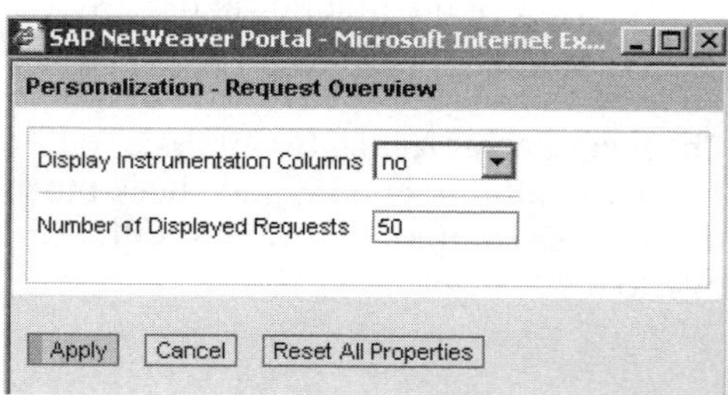

NOTE *The same personalization can be applied for the Component Overview iView.*

Request and Component Analysis

The JARM data consist of information on requests and components. A maximum of three top-level components are followed by any number of nested components at any level.

In Figure 28-2, you can see a process flow showing that the incoming HTTP request is processed by a thread named *Client_Thread_1.*

EP:PRT:*context* is the name of the incoming request, where *context* is the name of the page or iView. The incoming request is served by the portal components, namely, *EP:PRT_init, EP: PRT_action,* and *EP:PRT_render*. These are the top-level components that are displayed in the Request and Components overviews.

Naming Prefixes

The prefix *EP:PRT* stands for the portal runtime, and depending upon the subsystem to which the request and components belong, a number of prefixes can be used:

- **EP:PCD** Portal Content directory
- **EP:UME** User management engine
- **EP:KM:COLL** Knowledge management and collaboration
- **EP:KM:CM** Knowledge management content management

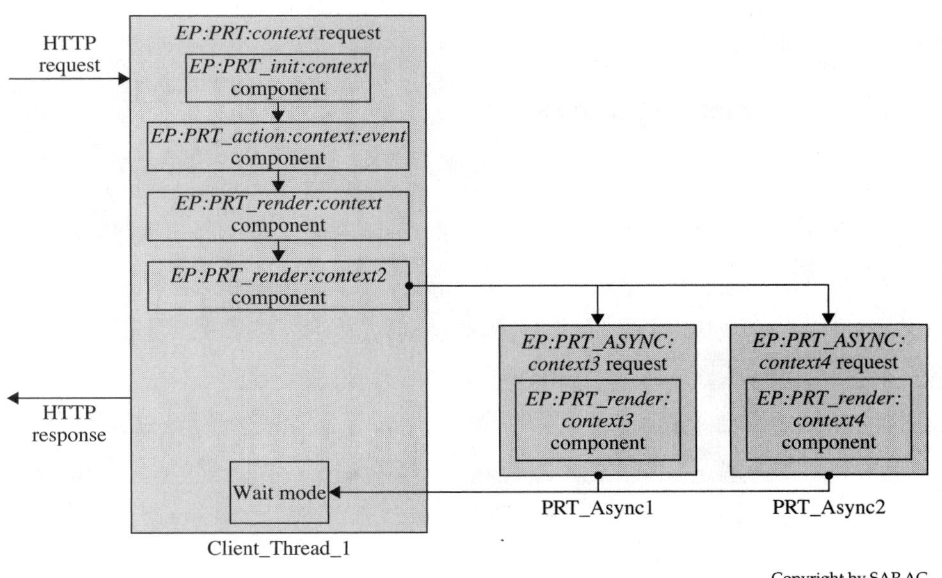

FIGURE 28-2 Process flow of an incoming HTTP request

PRT Components

The EP:PRT_action component exists only when a user action is triggered from the user interface. The EP:PRT_init is the least time-consuming and EP:PRT_render consumes the most time while serving the request.

The EP:PRT_init component is responsible for initializing the portal objects such as the Portal Object Model (POM), and the EP:PRT_render component is responsible for generating the HTML response and rendering the iView.

TIP *From an analysis standpoint, you usually need to focus only on the* EP:PRT_render *components.*

Delegation of Work

In Figure 28-2, you can see more than one EP:PRT_render portal component—one for the page and the others for the embedded iViews. The PRT_render components are delegated to other worker threads in the portal, namely, with the prefix *PRT_ASYNC*. These delegated requests are processed by asynchronous threads PRT_ASYNC1, PRT_ASYNC2, and so on.

Request Overview

Now let's go back to the Monitoring iViews on the portal and click Request Overview. A screen similar to Figure 28-3 will appear, displaying all the most expensive requests that were processed. If the same request were processed very quickly, it may not be displayed in the list.

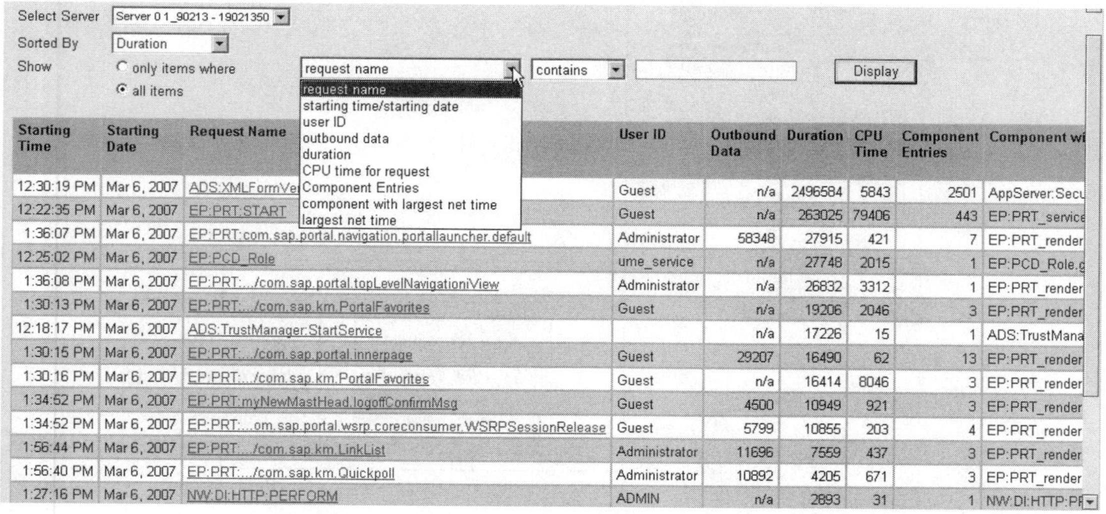

Select Server: Server 0 1_90213 - 19021350
Sorted By: Duration
Show: only items where / all items — request name — contains — Display

request name
starting time/starting date
user ID
outbound data
duration
CPU time for request
Component Entries
component with largest net time
largest net time

Starting Time	Starting Date	Request Name	User ID	Outbound Data	Duration	CPU Time	Component Entries	Component wi
12:30:19 PM	Mar 6, 2007	ADS:XMLFormVe	Guest	n/a	2496584	5843	2501	AppServer:Secu
12:22:35 PM	Mar 6, 2007	EP:PRT:START	Guest	n/a	263025	79406	443	EP:PRT_service
1:36:07 PM	Mar 6, 2007	EP:PRT:com.sap.portal.navigation.portallauncher.default	Administrator	58348	27915	421	7	EP:PRT_render
12:25:02 PM	Mar 6, 2007	EP:PCD_Role	ume_service	n/a	27748	2015	1	EP:PCD_Role.g
1:36:08 PM	Mar 6, 2007	EP:PRT:.../com.sap.portal.topLevelNavigationiView	Administrator	n/a	26832	3312	1	EP:PRT_render
1:30:13 PM	Mar 6, 2007	EP:PRT:.../com.sap.km.PortalFavorites	Guest	n/a	19206	2046	3	EP:PRT_render
12:18:17 PM	Mar 6, 2007	ADS:TrustManager:StartService		n/a	17226	15	1	ADS:TrustMana
1:30:15 PM	Mar 6, 2007	EP:PRT:.../com.sap.portal.innerpage	Guest	29207	16490	62	13	EP:PRT_render
1:30:16 PM	Mar 6, 2007	EP:PRT:.../com.sap.km.PortalFavorites	Guest	n/a	16414	8046	3	EP:PRT_render
1:34:52 PM	Mar 6, 2007	EP:PRT:myNewMastHead.logoffConfirmMsg	Guest	4500	10949	921	3	EP:PRT_render
1:34:52 PM	Mar 6, 2007	EP:PRT:...om.sap.portal.wsrp.coreconsumer.WSRPSessionRelease	Guest	5799	10855	203	4	EP:PRT_render
1:56:44 PM	Mar 6, 2007	EP:PRT:.../com.sap.km.LinkList	Administrator	11696	7559	437	3	EP:PRT_render
1:56:40 PM	Mar 6, 2007	EP:PRT:.../com.sap.km.Quickpoll	Administrator	10892	4205	671	3	EP:PRT_render
1:27:16 PM	Mar 6, 2007	NW:DI:HTTP:PERFORM	ADMIN	n/a	2893	31	1	NW:DI:HTTP:PF

FIGURE 28-3 Request Overview iView

NOTE *Only the most expensive execution of that request will be displayed.*

Restricting the Search Results

You can see that a lot of information is displayed on the horizontal layer and scrolling is required to see it all. Moreover, you can display a fewer number of records by restricting the search criteria based on request name, date, user ID, largest net time, and so on. One way to deal with these data is to restrict the search to today's date and a specific time.

After entering the required selection parameters, click the Display button. Using filters based on user ID and date is very helpful when you want to research performance issues lodged by a certain user at a certain point in time.

Analyzing the Results Using Excel Sheet

You can copy the results and paste them into an Excel spreadsheet to work with the data. To select the results, press the SHIFT button and use the mouse to select the top left area, scrolling down to the bottom right of the selection.

TIP *Using an Excel spreadsheet is very helpful because you can slice and dice the data to arrive at conclusions. Excel is also useful for reading the large PCD names of the requests and components.*

In the results page, shown in Figure 23-3, you can see a lot of useful information, such as the following:

- **Duration** Time taken overall to process the request. For example, in Figure 23-3, you can see that the EP:PRT:.../com.sap.km.Quickpoll request took about 4.2 seconds to be processed.
- **CPU Time** Time taken by the CPU to process the request. For EP:PRT:.../com.sap.km.Quickpoll, the CPU time is .67 second.
- **Components Entries** Number of components that processed the request, which for the EP:PRT:.../com.sap.km.Quickpoll is 3.

When you click the request name, you will be able to see all three components that were executed to serve the request.

Use the information shown in Figure 28-4 to identify the component that took the largest amount of time to process the request. The second component displayed in the list (EP:KM:CM:UI) shows a nesting depth of 1, which means that the first component delegated its work to the second component. This can be concluded based on the fact that the sum of the net CPU time for the first and the second components add up to the gross time for the first component in the list.

NOTE *The data presented here have been collected from a test system and are included for illustrative purposes only.*

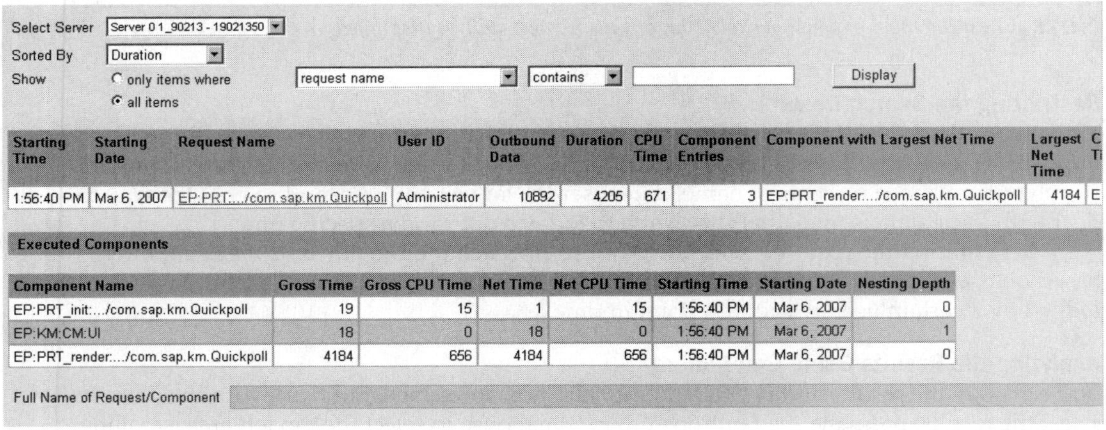

Select Server: Server 0 1_90213 - 19021350
Sorted By: Duration
Show: ○ only items where [request name] [contains] [ ] Display
● all items

Starting Time	Starting Date	Request Name	User ID	Outbound Data	Duration	CPU Time	Component Entries	Component with Largest Net Time	Largest Net Time	C Ti
1:56:40 PM	Mar 6, 2007	EP:PRT:.../com.sap.km.Quickpoll	Administrator	10892	4205	671	3	EP:PRT_render:.../com.sap.km.Quickpoll	4184	E

Executed Components

Component Name	Gross Time	Gross CPU Time	Net Time	Net CPU Time	Starting Time	Starting Date	Nesting Depth
EP:PRT_init:.../com.sap.km.Quickpoll	19	15	1	15	1:56:40 PM	Mar 6, 2007	0
EP:KM:CM:UI	18	0	18	0	1:56:40 PM	Mar 6, 2007	1
EP:PRT_render:.../com.sap.km.Quickpoll	4184	656	4184	656	1:56:40 PM	Mar 6, 2007	0

Full Name of Request/Component

FIGURE 28-4 Details of components serving the incoming request

Comparing Two Requests

If you want to check whether two requests are related to each other, you can check the starting times and dates for those requests; if they are spaced closely, it could indicate that they are related to each other. This is especially helpful if you want to check whether a request delegated its work to another ASYNC request.

HINT *You will be able to check that the delegating request has a slightly larger response time than the delegated request.*

Using the Components Overview

You can proceed with portal workload analysis using the Components and Requests overview information. To display the Components overview, click the Components Overview link on the navigation panel. Figure 28-5 displays all the components on the portal for all requests *(all executions* of the request and not just the expensive ones) since the portal was started.

TIP *The Components Overview is more reflective of the actual workload on the portal when compared to the Requests Overview.*

Analyzing the Components Overview Results

To begin with, try filtering the EP:PRT_render for analysis, and then copy it into an Excel spreadsheet and sort it by the average gross time. Figure 28-6 shows a sample Excel spreadsheet with the calculations for Gross % Time and % Calls included.

Select Server: Server 0 1_90213 - 19021350
Sorted By: Average Gross Time
Show: only items where | component name | contains | ep:prt_render | Display
all items

Component Name	No. of Calls	Gross Time	Gross CPU Time	Net Time	Net CPU Time	Average Gross Time	Average Gross CPU Time	Average Net Time	Average Net CPU Time
EP:PRT_render:com.sap.portal.navigation.portallauncher.default	1	27185	140	0	0	27185	140	0	0
EP:PRT_render:.../frameworkpage	1	26984	46	26841	0	26984	46	26841	0
EP:PRT_render:.../com.sap.portal.topLevelNavigationiView	1	26829	3312	26829	3312	26829	3312	26829	3312
EP:PRT_render:.../com.sap.km.NewsBrowser_0	1	14001	4203	13524	4000	14001	4203	13524	4000
EP:PRT_render:myNewMastHead.logoffConfirmMsg	1	10651	890	10651	890	10651	890	10651	890
EP:PRT_render:.../com.sap.km.LinkList	1	7553	421	7553	421	7553	421	7553	421
EP:PRT_render:.../com.sap.km.Quickpoll	1	4184	656	4184	656	4184	656	4184	656
EP:PRT_render:.../com.sap.km.docs	1	2108	1265	2	0	2108	1265	2	0
EP:PRT_render:.../com.sap.km.PortalFavorites	23	39404	11867	39287	11867	1713	515	1708	515
EP:PRT_render:com.sap.portal.runtime.logon.certlogon	8	10729	215	4	0	1341	26	0	0
EP:PRT_render:com.sap.portal.runtime.logon.default	8	10725	215	10725	215	1340	26	1340	26
EP:PRT_render:com.sap.portal.layouts.framework.dynNavArea	2	2536	390	2536	390	1268	195	1268	195
EP:PRT_render:.../com.sap.coll.Communities	2	2118	1249	2	0	1059	624	1	0
EP:PRT_render:.../com.sap.portal.innerpage	22	22126	445	21624	124	1005	20	982	5

FIGURE 28-5 Details of Components Overview

You can choose the values for Time For All Requests and the Number Of Requests since first request from the Request Summary view. These values are 5284747 ms and 18475, respectively (refer to Figure 28-1).

From the Components Overview, you can pick up the values for the total time taken for the component and the number of times it was called for execution. Add two new additional

	A	B	C	D	E	F	G	H	I	J	K	L
1	Component Name	No. of Calls	Gross Time	Gross CPU Time	Net Time	Net CPU Time	Average Gross Time	Average Gross CPU Time	Average Net Time	Average Net CPU Time	Gross % Time	% Calls
2	EP:PRT_render:.../com.sap.km.PortalFavorites	23	39404	11867	39287	11867	1713	515	1708	515	0.75%	0.12%
3	EP:PRT_render:com.sap.portal.navigation.portallauncher.defau	1	27185	140	0	0	27185	140	0	0	0.51%	0.01%
4	EP:PRT_render:.../frameworkpage	1	26984	46	26841	0	26984	46	26841	0	0.51%	0.01%
5	EP:PRT_render:.../com.sap.portal.topLevelNavigationiView	1	26829	3312	26829	3312	26829	3312	26829	3312	0.51%	0.01%
6	EP:PRT_render:.../com.sap.portal.innerpage	22	22126	445	21624	124	1005	20	982	5	0.42%	0.12%
7	EP:PRT_render:.../com.sap.km.NewsBrowser_0	1	14001	4203	13524	4000	14001	4203	13524	4000	0.26%	0.01%
8	EP:PRT_render:com.sap.portal.runtime.logon.certlogon	8	10729	215	4	0	1341	26	0	0	0.20%	0.04%
9	EP:PRT_render:com.sap.portal.runtime.logon.default	8	10725	215	10725	215	1340	26	1340	26	0.20%	0.04%
10	EP:PRT_render:myNewMastHead.logoffConfirmMsg	1	10651	890	10651	890	10651	890	10651	890	0.20%	0.01%
11	EP:PRT_render:.../com.sap.km.LinkList	1	7553	421	7553	421	7553	421	7553	421	0.14%	0.01%
12	EP:PRT_render:.../com.sap.km.Quickpoll	1	4184	656	4184	656	4184	656	4184	656	0.08%	0.01%
13	EP:PRT_render:.../com.sap.portal.dynamicNavigationArea	3	2914	467	13	0	971	155	4	0	0.06%	0.02%
14	EP:PRT_render:com.sap.portal.layouts.framework.dynNavAre	2	2536	390	2536	390	1268	195	1268	195	0.05%	0.01%
15	EP:PRT_render:.../com.sap.coll.Communities	2	2118	1249	2	0	1059	624	1	0	0.04%	0.01%
16	EP:PRT_render:.../com.sap.km.docs	1	2108	1265	2	0	2108	1265	2	0	0.04%	0.01%

FIGURE 28-6 Spreadsheet analysis of portal components

fields for Gross % Time and the % Calls in the Excel spreadsheet. Enter the formula for the two fields based on the following information.

Calculate the average gross percentage time for a request:

Gross % time = Gross time of the component / time for all requests (in %)

This value indicates the gross percentage time spent by the component in serving the request.

To calculate the % calls, do this:

% calls = No. of calls to the component / No. of requests since first request (in %)

This value indicates the percentage number of calls that were made to the component on an average for a given request.

In the Excel sheet, enter **=C2/5284747** in the Gross Percentage Time column. In the % Calls column, enter **=B2/18475**. (Here it is assumed that the second row in the Excel spreadsheet corresponds to the first row in the list of displayed components.) Copy the formula into the other rows. To convert the calculated values into a percentage, right click a cell and select Format Cells, and then select Percentage in the Number tab.

Testing the Most Expensive Portal Component

Now, by sorting by the gross % time, you can identify the portal component that takes the longest time to execute. You can either preview it in the PCD based on its PCD URL or directly access it in the URL using the component name: http://<*server*>:<*port*>/irj/servlet/prt/portal/prtroot/*component_name*.

As a next step, you can check whether it is an SAP or custom iView, check the cache property, and explore the possibility of caching. You can also explore whether it is possible to do some coding optimization. If none helps, you should conduct a deeper analysis using host analysis or create full thread dumps.

Importance of Test Data Quality

You should also ensure that there is a minimum value of 100 for calls for these values to be of significance in arriving at conclusions regarding the performance.

You must be cautious enough to eliminate the expensive requests that are generated during the portal startup due to loading of classes, filling up of caches, and so on. You can eliminate such expenses by setting up filters based on "time of first request".

To identify the most expensive request, you can sort the list by duration. Once you have identified the most expensive request, you can identify the most expensive component for that request based on the Component with Largest Net Time. Clicking the request name will take you to the Components Overview screen.

You can conduct the same analysis as before and identify the most expensive component. You may find that the request has poor response times either because of one large component or due to the large number of components, though individually they may be consuming very little time. Also take a look at the nesting levels, gross time, and net time for the components. The gross time and net time will be the same if the component does not call any other component that can be concluded based on the nesting level for that component. The gross time is the sum of the net times of all the components with nesting level that is below by one (meaning those components that are called by the calling component).

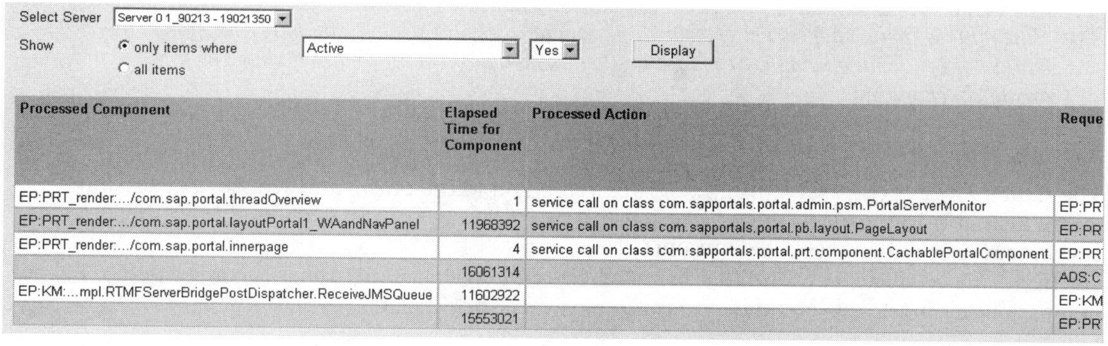

Select Server: Server 0 1_90213 - 19021350

Show: (•) only items where [Active] [Yes] [Display]
( ) all items

Processed Component	Elapsed Time for Component	Processed Action	Reque
EP:PRT_render:.../com.sap.portal.threadOverview	1	service call on class com.sapportals.portal.admin.psm.PortalServerMonitor	EP:PR
EP:PRT_render:.../com.sap.portal.layoutPortal1_WAandNavPanel	11968392	service call on class com.sapportals.portal.pb.layout.PageLayout	EP:PR
EP:PRT_render:.../com.sap.portal.innerpage	4	service call on class com.sapportals.portal.prt.component.CachablePortalComponent	EP:PR
	16061314		ADS:C
EP:KM:...mpl.RTMFServerBridgePostDispatcher.ReceiveJMSQueue	11602922		EP:KM
	15553021		EP:PR

FIGURE 28-7 Left half of thread overview screen

Also watch out for the parent requests that call the PRT_ASYNC request. A delay in the parent request could be because it has been waiting for the ASYNC request to complete and hence you would rather focus on the ASYNC request for further analysis.

Thread Overview

To make a proper analysis using thread overview data, restrict the display to *active threads* only. Try to copy the data onto an Excel spreadsheet and look for any threads that are hanging or identify a particular user and compare with other groups of users for whom the response times may be faster.

Try to identify any components that also have poor response times and for which the Elapsed Time for Component is very high or is constantly increasing. This could indicate a thread that is hanging. The most important view is the active threads view. And as always, try to copy the information into a spreadsheet for further analysis.

Figures 28-7 and 28-8 display the left and the right halves of the thread view information. The thread overview information can be used to link an expensive iView to the thread dump analysis using the thread name.

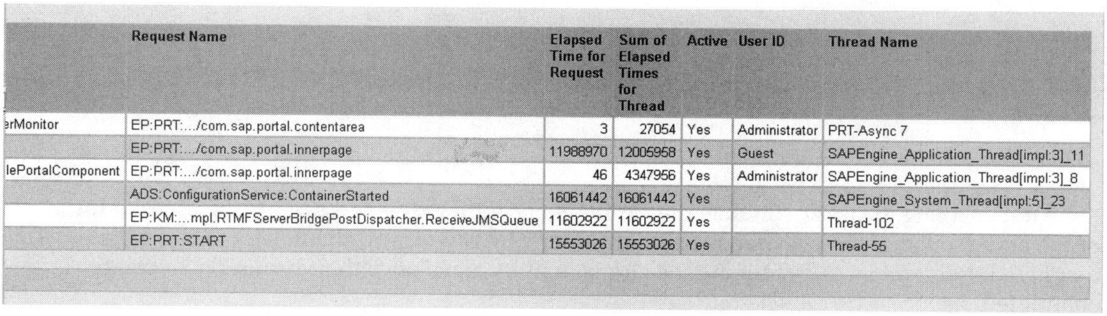

	Request Name	Elapsed Time for Request	Sum of Elapsed Times for Thread	Active	User ID	Thread Name
erMonitor	EP:PRT:.../com.sap.portal.contentarea	3	27054	Yes	Administrator	PRT-Async 7
	EP:PRT:.../com.sap.portal.innerpage	11988970	12005958	Yes	Guest	SAPEngine_Application_Thread[impl:3]_11
lePortalComponent	EP:PRT:.../com.sap.portal.innerpage	46	4347956	Yes	Administrator	SAPEngine_Application_Thread[impl:3]_8
	ADS:ConfigurationService:ContainerStarted	16061442	16061442	Yes		SAPEngine_System_Thread[impl:5]_23
	EP:KM:...mpl.RTMFServerBridgePostDispatcher.ReceiveJMSQueue	11602922	11602922	Yes		Thread-102
	EP:PRT:START	15553026	15553026	Yes		Thread-55

FIGURE 28-8 Right half of thread overview screen

TIP *Since this is just a snapshot overview of the components and requests that are still active, there should not be too much emphasis placed on the thread overview information alone, as it is constantly changing.*

Activity Report

The *Activity Report* consists of users who are logged on to the portal and whose user session is still available in the cache. If the user logs off or if the user session is deleted from the cache, that user will not appear in the list.

If, during analysis, you find that lots of users are logged on and this is accompanied by insufficient memory, this could be the cause of poor performance.

HINT *Sometimes users fail to log off the portal, and this can consume resources and cause poor performance.*

Single Activity Trace

A Single Activity Trace can be enabled for a particular user and can occur without a significant performance impact, even in production systems. The SAT trace uses the same monitoring data and the JARM instrumentation as that of the Requests and Components overview functionality.

NOTE *The SAT trace can be activated in the Visual Administrator for a single user or for all users.*

Activating the SAT Trace

After logging into the Visual Administrator, go to Server | Services | Performance Tracing and open the Runtime tab and then the Trace Config tab, as shown next. Enter the user name and click the Activate checkbox next to the Static SAT Trigger module. Click the Save button. To change the user, enter the new user, click Refresh, and click Save again. If the user is not entered, the trace is activated for all users.

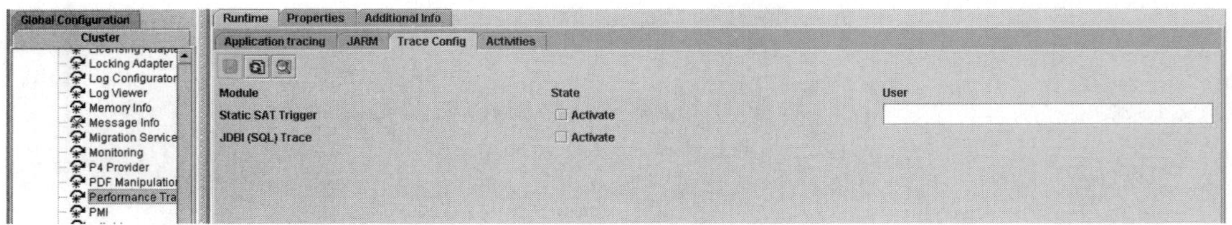

After enabling the trace, simulate the various steps for the user and capture the timestamps of the actual events, their response times, the steps involved, and the details of the pages displayed. Remember to deactivate the single activity trace once the simulation steps are completed.

Do *Remember to deactivate the single activity trace once the simulation steps are completed.*

The single activity trace log sat.trc.log is found at <*drive*>/usr/sap\J2E\JC01\J2EE\cluster\server0\log folder.

Tip *If you encounter any problem in creating a single activity trace, follow the steps covered in SAP OSS Note 655823.*

Interpreting the Log

To view the log file, you should use the Log Viewer. To open the Log Viewer, go to C:\usr\sap\J2E\JC01\j2ee\admin\logviewer-standalone and click logviewer.bat.

The log file is formatted with different colors and indentations, as shown in Figure 28-9. The entries in red with the prefix *EP:PRT* denote the requests, which can be classified as external requests and internal child requests.

The external requests are prefixed with *EP:PRT* and the internal child requests are prefixed with *EP:PRT:ASYNC.* The external requests and the components called from these external requests are processed by client_threads. The internal child requests are processed by the thread pool PRT-Async.

If the thread details are not available in the results output, place your cursor on the header columns and right click. Then select the required fields, which in this case will be Thread, to get the data for the threads.

The blue lines represent the JARM components and an indentation represents the nesting levels of these components. The gray lines represent the JARM actions and events and display information on an event or an implementation class that is behind the iView. To check the JARM actions, scroll down to the right and check under the Description column.

In Figures 28-10 and 28-11, you can view the class on which a service call was initiated.

Analyzing the SAT Trace

While analyzing the SAT trace, check whether the gross time of the component matches with the duration for any action the user takes, such as a click. If they don't match, perhaps more than one component has been called and you should therefore analyze all of them and identify the most expensive one.

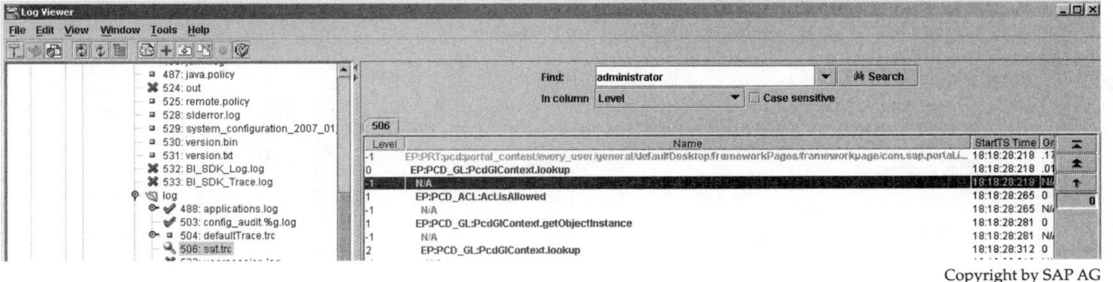

Figure 28-9 SAT.trc trace file viewed in Log Viewer

506

	StartTS Time	Gross CPU ...	Net CPU Time	Gross Time	Net Time	Out Data	Description	Username	Th
s/frameworkpage/com.sap.portal.i...	18:18:28:218	.171	N/A	.566	N/A	107484		Administrator	SAPEngine_Appl
	18:18:28:218	.015	.015	.096	.047	N/A		N/A	SAPEngine_Appl
	18:18:28:218	N/A	N/A	N/A	N/A	N/A	EP:PCD_GL:PcdGlContext.lookupat	N/A	SAPEngine_Appl
	18:18:28:265	0	0	.020	.020	N/A		N/A	SAPEngine_Appl
	18:18:28:265	N/A	N/A	N/A	N/A	N/A	EP:PCD_ACL:Acl.isAllowed	N/A	SAPEngine_Appl
	18:18:28:281	0	0	.029	.027	N/A		N/A	SAPEngine_Appl
	18:18:28:281	N/A	N/A	N/A	N/A	N/A	EP:PCD_GL:PcdGlContext.getObjectInstanceat	N/A	SAPEngine_Appl
	18:18:28:312	0	0			N/A		N/A	SAPEngine_Appl
	18:18:28:312	N/A	N/A	N/A	N/A	N/A	EP:PCD_GL:PcdGlContext.lookupat	N/A	SAPEngine_Appl
	18:18:28:312	0	0	.002		N/A		N/A	SAPEngine_Appl
	18:18:28:312	N/A	N/A	N/A	N/A	N/A	EP:PCD_GL:PcdGlContext.lookupat	N/A	SAPEngine_Appl
	18:18:28:312	0	0	.002	.002	N/A		N/A	SAPEngine_Appl
	18:18:28:312	N/A	N/A	N/A	N/A	N/A	EP:PCD_ACL:Acl.isAllowed	N/A	SAPEngine_Appl
	18:18:28:312	0	0			N/A		N/A	SAPEngine_Appl
	18:18:28:312	N/A	N/A	N/A	N/A	N/A	EP:PCD_GL:PcdGlContext.listBindingsat portal_c...	N/A	SAPEngine_Appl
	18:18:28:312	0	0			N/A		N/A	SAPEngine_Appl
	18:18:28:312	N/A	N/A	N/A	N/A	N/A	EP:PCD_GL:PcdGlContext.lookupat portal_conte...	N/A	SAPEngine_Appl
	18:18:28:312	0	0			N/A		N/A	SAPEngine_Appl
	18:18:28:312	N/A	N/A	N/A	N/A	N/A	EP:PCD_GL:PcdGlContext.getObjectInstanceat p...	N/A	SAPEngine_Appl

Figure 28-10 Log Viewer results

Also try to limit the scope of the trace so that you have a better handle on the traces and you have more limited content to conduct the analysis. Make sure that the screenshots of the activities conducted by the user are captured along with the time and duration taken for any action the user takes, such as a click.

When analyzing the logs, use the timestamp and the nature of user activity to identify the *first click* in the log file. Then look for the red lines that have the highest gross time. Then look for the blue lines under that red line that have the highest gross time. If you succeed in finding any red lines, scroll to the right to find the class used for that component from the gray lines.

After identifying the slowest component, check to see which subsystem (for example, EP: UME, EP: PCD) it belongs to. Once you have identified the subsystem, it is a matter of optimizing performance using techniques such as caching, reorganizing the roles, redesigning the iView, redeveloping the portal component code, and so on. Try to troubleshoot by removing

e	Out Data	Description	Username	Thread
	N/A		N/A	Thread[PRT-Async 7,5,
	N/A		Administrator	Thread[PRT-Async 0,5,
	N/A		N/A	Thread[PRT-Async 0,5,
	N/A		N/A	Thread[PRT-Async 0,5,
	N/A	service call on class com.sapportals.portal.navigation.workAreaiView	N/A	Thread[PRT-Async 0,5,
	N/A		N/A	Thread[PRT-Async 0,5,
	N/A		N/A	Thread[PRT-Async 0,5,
	N/A		N/A	Thread[PRT-Async 0,5,
	N/A		N/A	Thread[PRT-Async 0,5,
	N/A	service call on class com.sapportals.portal.prt.component.CachablePortalComponent	N/A	Thread[PRT-Async 0,5,
	N/A		N/A	Thread[PRT-Async 0,5,
	N/A		N/A	Thread[PRT-Async 0,5,
	N/A		N/A	Thread[PRT-Async 0,5,
	N/A		N/A	Thread[PRT-Async 0,5,
	N/A	service call on class com.sapportals.portal.pb.layout.PageLayout	N/A	Thread[PRT-Async 0,5,
	N/A		N/A	Thread[PRT-Async 0,5,
	N/A		N/A	Thread[PRT-Async 0,5,
	N/A		N/A	Thread[PRT-Async 0,5,

Figure 28-11 Rightmost section of the Log Viewer results

iViews, roles, and so on. As an alternative, try to enable server-side caching for the page or iView using this link: http://*<host>*:*<port>*/irj/servlet/prt/portal/prteventname/HtmlbEvent/prtroot/com.sap.portal.pcd.admintools.softcachebrowser.default.

Analyzing the Client, File System, LDAP, and Backend Systems Access

To analyze the client-side performance, you can check the CPU usage of the browser using the Task Manager or the PSList. Use this URL to download the PSList tool for analyzing Windows operating system processes: www.microsoft.com/technet/sysinternals/utilities/pslist.mspx.

File system access performance data can be analyzed using filemon, perfmon, iostat data, or the HTTP trace for remote connections. LDAP performance can be analyzed using the LDAP browser, activating the HTTP trace on the LDAP server, as well as the proprietary tools provided by the LDAP provider.

If the portal is connected to a backend system such as R/3, Oracle, or SQL, you should try to use the performance analysis tools provided by the respective backend systems. For example, in the case of an R/3 system, you can use ST04 trace; for SQL, you can use the SQL Server profiler; and so on. ST05 can be used for tracing RFC and ST03 for response time measurement.

To test the backend connectivity to an R/3 system that uses an RFC destination, you can use SM59.

Summary

In this chapter, you explored the workload monitoring iViews such as the Request Summary, Component Overview, and Thread Overview. You then learned how to use the iViews to analyze the workload and identify any component that contributes to a performance bottleneck. You then learned how to enable the SAT trace to conduct analysis for an individual user for a more detailed and specific analysis.

29 CHAPTER

JVM Garbage Collection Analysis

Java performance analysis focuses on monitoring the garbage collection, virtual machine performance, response time analysis, and bandwidth, and analyzing the thread behavior using thread dumps. JVM analysis could be viewed as a next step in performance analysis after conducting operating system and portal workload analyses.

This chapter discusses the importance of garbage collection, how to activate garbage collection, calculating the JVM parameters, and fine-tuning the J2EE JVM settings.

Garbage Collection Basics

Garbage collection (GC) analysis focuses on measuring the time spent by the JVM on garbage collection versus the time spent productively for the application. Performance issues arising out of poor application code or deadlocks while accessing network resources or database resources can be analyzed by creating thread dumps in the J2EE engine.

The garbage collection *trace* provides information on how much time was spent on full and minor garbage collection as well as the available memory before and after the garbage collection process. The verbose:gc logs contain information regarding the GC times, GC frequency, application runtimes, number of objects that were created and destroyed, rate at which objects are created, and so on.

Importance of GC Analysis

The intent of GC analysis is to do the following:

- Reduce the GC collection times
- Try to reduce the frequency of young and old GCs
- Identify memory leaks
- Size the old and young generation heaps

It is important to analyze the garbage collection process because it helps identify *memory leaks* and allows you to check whether the *memory consumption* is too high. Garbage collection analysis may turn out to be critical, because when garbage collection occurs, it can bring the system almost to a frozen state. It is important that the time taken for garbage collection is minimal compared to the total elapsed time.

Activating the GC Trace

To activate the garbage collection trace, you must include the option `-verbose:gc` in the JVM. Garbage collection has no performance impact on the system when it is activated.

Limitations of Garbage Collection

The garbage collection technique does not provide any information on the CPU time taken by the application when running function modules and similar performance data. For that kind of analysis, you should resort to application profiling techniques, which do have some performance impact. Also, garbage collection does not provide information on which application or system process is consuming the memory.

Java Heap Structure

The Java heap is divided into three generations: young generation, old generation, and permanent generation. Figure 29-1 displays the memory heap layout.

Young Generation Heap

The young generation consists of Eden and semi-spaces. The Eden space is calculated based on the *NewSize* and the *SurvivorRatio*. *NewSize* is the size of the young generation:

Eden = *NewSize* – ((*NewSize* / (*SurvivorRatio* + 2)) × 2

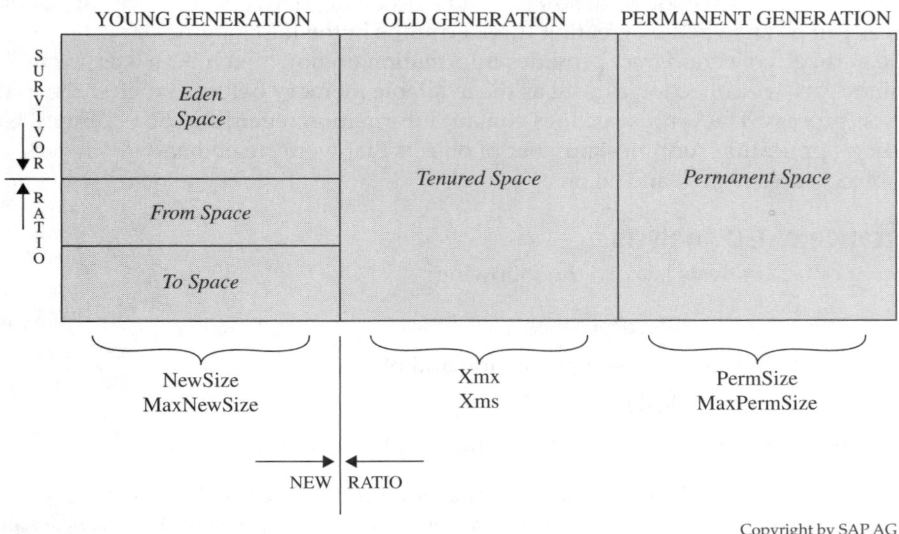

FIGURE 29-1 Memory heap layout

SurvivorRatio is an integer that can vary from 1 to a high value. *SurvivorRatio* controls the size of the Eden and survivor spaces. *MaxNewSize* is the maximum size of the young generation.

The *semi-spaces* are *From space* and *To space* and are calculated like so:

From space = (*NewSize* – Eden) / 2
To space = (*NewSize* – Eden) / 2

So, for example, for a 128MB young generation with an Eden size of 64MB, a semi-space size of 32MB will result in a *SurvivorRatio* of 2.

Old Generation Heap

The *old generation*, or the *tenured generation*, area is used to store the objects released from the young generation. The `-Xmx` parameter controls the maximum size of the older generation. The `-Xms` parameter decides the initial size of the older generation area, also known as the *heap*.

Permanent Generation Heap

This area is used to store the class objects and their related metadata. The parameters `PermSize` and `MaxPermSize` control the initial and maximum sizes of the permanent generation. The parameter `NewRatio` is the ratio of the young generation/old generation. You can also disable permanent generation collection by using the option `-Xnoclassgc`.

Garbage Collection Process

Let's discuss how the minor and major garbage collection works.

Minor Garbage Collection

To begin with, a Java object, when created, is located in the Eden area. When the Eden area is filled up, a minor GC process begins, during which time the JVM checks for those objects that are no longer referenced in the application. The JVM deletes those objects and moves all the referenced objects into one of the survivor spaces, namely, the To space.

The JVM also analyzes the survivor spaces for garbage collection and removes the unreferenced Java objects from the survivor spaces. This is known as *copy GC*. At the same time, it moves some of the Java objects that have survived a certain number of GC cycles into the old generation area. This is *promotion GC*. The promotion GC is a little costly compared to the copy GC as the garbage collector has to deal with the old generation heap collector. Also note that after every minor GC cycle, the Eden area is empty and one of the survivor spaces is also empty.

The minor GC is directly proportional to the size of the live data in the Eden space and the From semi-space. Decreasing the young generation size may result in increased frequency of minor GC and decreased GC duration because a lesser number of live objects would have been created. The reverse happens when the young generation size is increased. Increased duration between successive minor GCs provides time for objects with short-term data to die naturally.

TIP *Part of the tuning process's intent is to arrive at a right combination of values for the frequency, collection duration, and heap size.*

Based on the lifetime of objects, we can classify them as *temporary*, *intermediate*, and *long-term* objects. Long-term objects live long enough to survive many minor GCs and hence get promoted to the older generation area. Intermediate objects survive one minor GC, but get collected before promotion to the older generation area. Temporary objects die even before facing one minor GC.

Increasing the size of the young generation may help to convert the long-term objects into intermediate objects and the intermediate objects into short-term objects. This may result in lesser objects being promoted and hence reduce the overhead involved. However, it increases the time for minor GC and it should be explored if you can implement a parallel GC.

Developers should also identify objects that are alive longer than necessary, and simply assigning them to a null can help. Not creating some unnecessary objects should also be considered as an option. Other solutions are combining two objects into one and reducing the object size by converting non-static variables into static variables. As far as possible, you should try to keep the application stateless. You should avoid using complex structures and instead adopt flatter structures. Reducing the number of threads used may result in a reduced number of objects and hence increased performance.

TIP *Immutable objects such as String are not good candidates for GC and hence you should convert them into StringBuffers.*

Major Garbage Collection

Finally, a stage is reached when the old generation area is also filled and a major GC process is started. During the major GC process, the whole heap is subject to GC analysis and this takes a substantially longer time. The duration could be as much as 60 seconds, during which time the whole portal may look as though it is frozen.

TIP *Memory leaks can be identified when the frequency of major GCs and the duration of the GCs increase.*

Calculating the JVM Parameters

The JVM parameters required for the new generation are *NewSize, MaxNewSize, SurvivorRatio,* and *TargetSurvivorRatio.* The *NewSize* and the *MaxNewSize* are set to 1/6 the size of the 1GB heap size.

–*XX:NewSize* = 160m	–*XX:MaxNewSize* = 160m for 1GB heap size
–*XX:NewSize* = 320m	–*XX:MaxNewSize* = 320m for 2GB heap size

The *SurvivorRatio* decides how large the Eden space is compared to the survivor space. It is set to a value of *–XX:SurvivorRatio* = 2. The *TargetSurvivorRatio* decides when the objects are sent to the old generation after a certain percentage of the survivor space heap is used. It is recommended to keep the value to 90 as specified in *–XX:TargetSurvivorRatio* = 90.

The permanent space parameters required for the JVM are *XX:MaxPermSize* and *–XX:PermSize.* For J2EE 6.40, you can set these to 192m, and for 7.0, they can be set to 256m. If more applications are likely to be deployed, or if the application grows in complexity, you may need to increase these values subject to the virtual address space limitations.

GC Analysis

These sections discuss how to go about analyzing the GC process.

Total Memory Available for the Java Application

The total memory available for the Java application is calculated by subtracting the memory currently used from the size of the old generation area. Note that the Eden area and the survivor area are not considered in this calculation because they are not available for all practical purposes. For the same reason, the old generation area can be treated as synonymous to the heap size.

Time Spent on Garbage Collection

The other important value to be calculated is the time spent on garbage collection, because that is unproductive time not used by the application. It is calculated by subtracting the GC time from the elapsed time. These values can be obtained from the `-verbose:GC` parameter of the JVM as well as in the monitoring service of the J2EE engine.

Memory Leak

In Figure 29-2, the thickest line is the garbage collection process, the thin line is the available memory, the black dots are the durations, and the medium weight line is the total size used by the newly created objects in the Eden space. On the left Y-axis is the memory in bytes and on the right Y-axis is the time elapsed during GC. The black dots around the 20-second range represent the full GC and those close to the X-axis represent the minor GCs.

As you can see in Figure 29-2, the GC process is initiated every time the available memory (thin line) goes below the size of the Eden space (medium thick line). You can see that the available memory (thickest line) is slowly decreasing with time; this could be due to increasing users, memory leaks, or oversized and filled caches.

Considering that the JVM is striving to create available memory that is equal to the Eden space, the number of GCs increases as it becomes increasingly difficult to make free space in the older generation area that is equal to at least the Eden space.

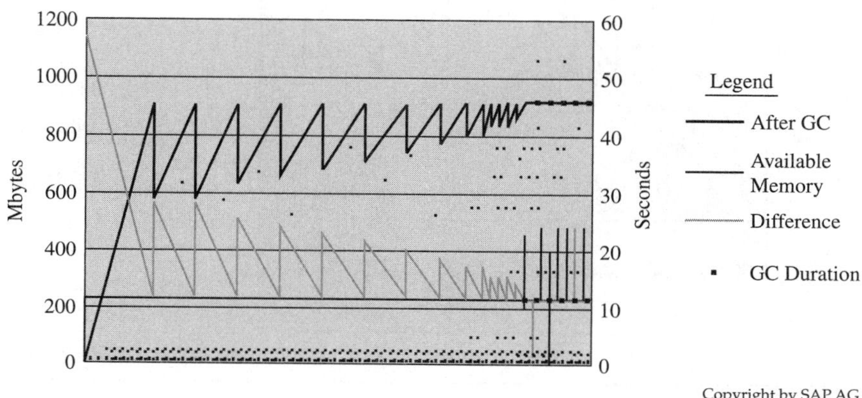

Figure 29-2 Memory leak

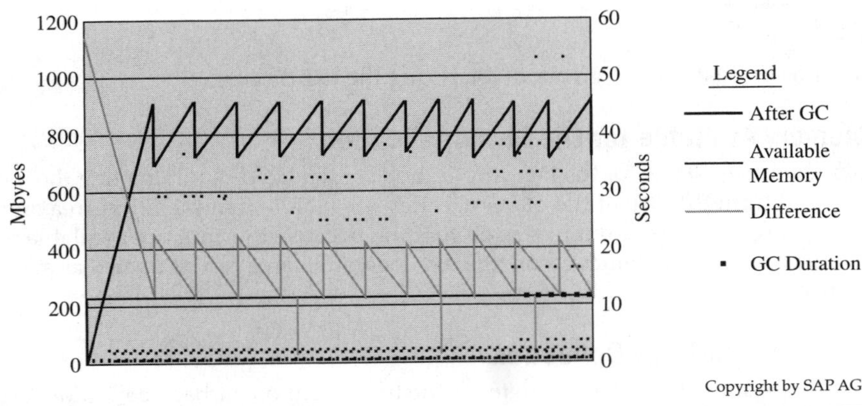

FIGURE 29-3 No memory leak

GC in a Well-Behaved System

Figure 29-3 reflects a well-behaved system, where the available memory comes back to its normal usage value after every garbage collection. There may be a small decrease in available memory over time due to increased user population, filling up of caches, and so on.

Memory Usage Under Load Test

Now take a look at Figure 29-4, which was probably taken during a load test. The available memory consistently goes down until it reaches a point where it is negative. With every GC, the JVM tries to restore the available memory at least to the size of the Eden space.

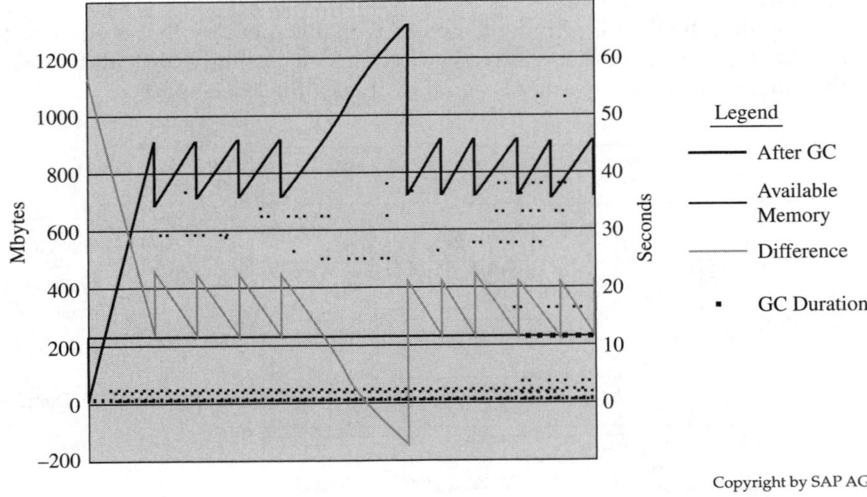

FIGURE 29-4 GC during load testing

With further load testing, a point has been reached where the garbage collection is unable to bring the available memory even to the level of the Eden space. At this point in time, the portal is probably frozen since the JVM is now fully focused on garbage collections till the available memory is restored to the level of Eden. Apart from heavy load on the system, another potential reason for this could be that the value for the *NewSize* parameter was set to a high value. The *NewSize* parameter controls the initial size of the young generation area.

Identifying Causes of Increased Memory Usage

Some of the main causes of increased memory usage and hence poor performance are increased size of caches, increased number of users, too many deployed and active applications, too many HTTP sessions, thread request queue size, and database pool waiting queue.

To identify the highest memory consumer, try techniques such as conducting a full garbage collection, then clearing the cache, and then conducting a GC again from the J2EE console. The additional available memory obtained will offer a good indication of the cache size.

In the same way, you can restart the services of an application and release expensive portal components in the Support Desk | Portal Runtime | Application Console. Then repeat the full GC again and check the change in the available memory.

Check whether the memory heap size is increasing with every GC; this could be a potential cause of *OutOfMemory* situation. Try to correlate this with the number of users on the portal, the number of HTTP sessions, and so on.

Identify the time when the system crashed using the console logs of the J2EE engine. Check the HTTP sessions, the waiting queues in the thread requests, database locks, network connections queue, and so on. Has there been a recent deployment of an application that is consuming memory to initialize variables? Check how much memory is available after the portal starts.

Check the threshold value for the number of users after the system crashes. Check the size of the portal cache. Try to identify whether the iView response time increases with increasing memory consumption. Some other tools available for memory analysis are SAP Address Space Viewer and profilers such as JProbe and OptimizeIT.

For setting up the GC parameters, a number of GC implementations are available in the JDK. It is recommended that you use *–XX:+UseParNewGC* because it parallelizes and therefore increases minor GCs. However, this does not work on Windows 2004/IA-64 Linux systems.

JDK Used for SAP J2EE Engine

Note that at the time of writing, the J2EE engine 6.40/7.0 is supported only by the JDK 1.4 family and not by JDK 1.3 or 1.5.

TIP *If you plan to change the JDK, follow the instructions in OSS Notes 718901, 731269, and 754699.*

GC-Related JVM Parameters

A number of parameters can be used for garbage collection in the JVM:

- **-XX:+PrintGCDetails** Prints the GC details
- **-XX:+PrintGCTimeStamps** Adds the timestamp information to the GC details

- **-XX:+PrintHeapAtGC** Prints GC heap information before and after GC
- **-Xloggc:filename** Prints the GC info to a log file
- **-XX:ParallelGCThreads** The default number of threads used for copy GC is equal to the number of CPUs; this parameter can be used to control that number of threads

Automatic vs. Manual Tuning of the JVM

To tune the JVM, you can use the configuration template as per OSS Note 739788. If not, you can manually set the JVM settings as per OSS Note 723909.

NOTE *The configuration template can be used only for installations beyond NW04 SP Stack 04 or J2EE engine 6.40 SP 7 and beyond.*

How to Configure JVM Settings for the J2EE Engine

Here's how to configure JVM settings for the J2Ee engine using the config tool:

1. Double-click the configtool.bat file under the <*drive*>:\usr\sap\J2E\JC01\j2ee\configtool folder. Ensure that the database is running, or you may face a DB-related error.
2. Click Yes, as shown next:

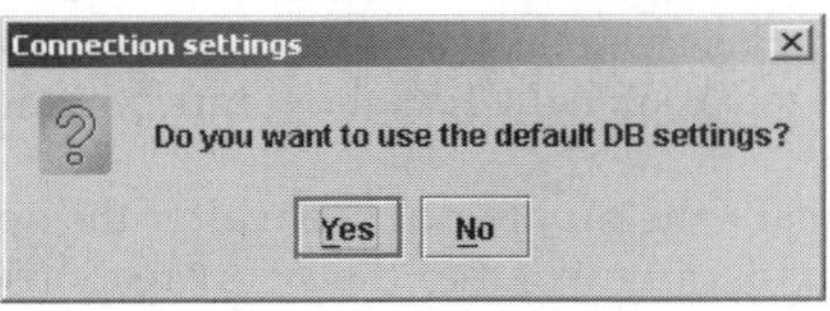

Copyright by SAP AG

3. Navigate to the dispatcher and the server nodes and double-click the nodes. The screen for the server will appear, as shown in Figure 29-5.
4. Enter the required parameter values and click the Save icon. Repeat these steps for the dispatcher and other server nodes, if required.

   The required parameters for activating the garbage collection for SUN JVM are

   ```
   -verbose:gc
   -XX:+PrintGCTimeStamps
   -XX:+PrintGCDetails
   -Xloggc :GC.log
   ```

5. GC.log is the name of the garbage collection file. Remember to restart the J2EE engine for the changes to take effect. If there are problems for the changes to take effect, refer to OSS Note 736557.

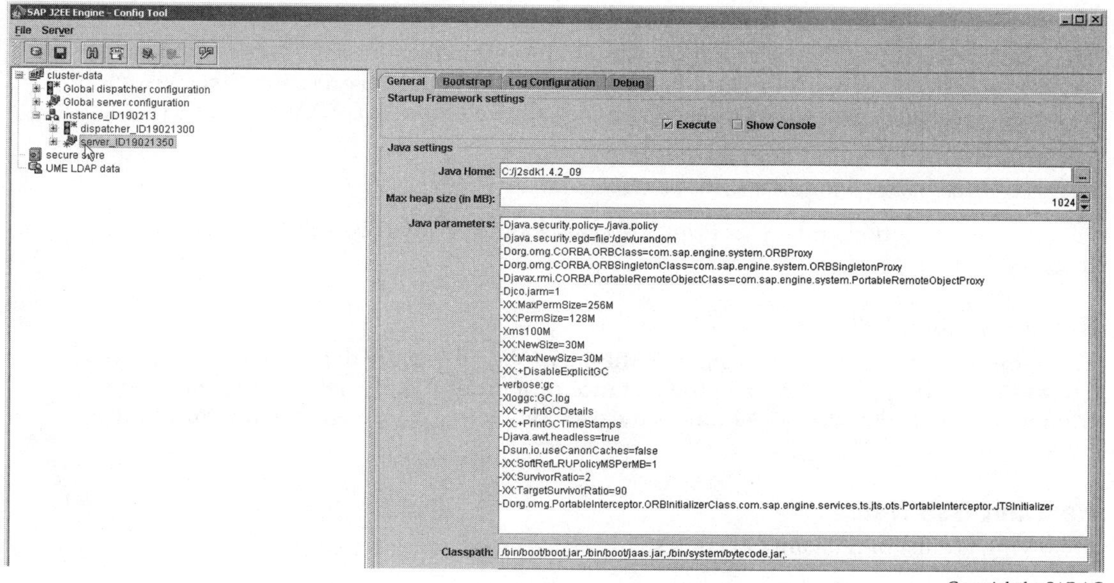

Copyright by SAP AG

FIGURE 29-5 Config Tool-JVM settings for server

Minimum and Maximum Heap Size for Server

For 32-bit machines and server nodes with 1GB RAM, the initial and maximum heap size can be set to *–Xmx1024m* and *Xms1024m*. However, sometimes it may not be possible to increase the heap size to the actual value of 1024M because of limitations with the *virtual address space* available for a given process.

Increasing the Heap Size vs. Adding a Server Node

Usually you can have up to 2GB for a Java process, but sometimes the loaded Windows DLLs will reduce that value for the JVM memory parameters. The *Xmx* and the *PermSize,* when added up, provide a value that should be available as a contiguous part in the virtual address space. Since that is sometimes not the case, you may have to reduce the value of the available virtual address space to about 1.7GB instead of 2GB. One workaround for this issue is to add another server node instead of increasing the heap size.

Dispatcher Heap Size

For dispatchers, it is enough to provide a heap size of 170m, and the young generation can be set to the default value, which is one-third of the size of the heap size. For instances that contain more than three server nodes, we may need to add 50MB to the dispatcher heap size for every additional server node.

Heap Size for All Server Nodes

The total heap size of all the server nodes should be within the physical RAM of the machine to avoid excessive paging. You should also allow for additional OS processes that consume memory. To calculate the number of server nodes allowed for a 1GB RAM machine, you can use this formula:

No of server nodes = Physical RAM available / 1.5

–verbose:GC option and *–XX:+PrintGCDetails* should always be used for getting GC data from the VM.

Server vs. Client VM

You should use the server VM instead of the client VM. To ensure this, you can add the line `jstartup/vm/type=server` in the instance.properties file. By default, the startup framework loads the server VM unless the `jstartup/vm/type` is set to a different type than the server.

Relevant OSS Notes

Following is a list of relevant OSS notes:

- **710146** How to Change J2EE Engine JVM Settings
- **723909** Java VM Settings for J2EE 6.40/7.0
- **1004255** How to Create a Full HPROF Heap Dump of J2EE Engine 6.40/7.0
- **709140** Recommended JDK and VM Settings for the WebAS630/640/7.0
- **718901** How to Change the JDK of the J2EE Engine
- **731269** Changing JDK Version with the Offline Config Tool
- **754699** Problem with User Mapping after Changing JDK
- **739788** SAP NetWeaver: Template-Based Configuration - Composite Note
- **736557** Changes Made with the Config Tool Are Disregarded

---

NOTE *For more details, refer to JVM related resources listed in Appendix B.*

Summary

This chapter discussed the importance of garbage collection analysis and how to activate it. It then analyzed the Java heap structure and discussed the garbage collection process. It explained how the JVM parameters can be calculated and compared the garbage collection behavior of a well-behaved system, memory leak system, and a system under load test. It discussed some of the potential causes of memory leak and how to configure the JVM of the J2EE engine.

CHAPTER 30

JVM Thread Dump Analysis

An important part of performance analysis is conducting JVM thread analysis. To conduct JVM thread analysis, you create a thread dump on the J2EE engine. The thread dump provides information on the thread name, the thread ID, and the call stack, and helps you to identify whether any Java deadlocks result in the system hanging.

NOTE *The thread dump can be triggered only if the JVM is still running and has not crashed.*

In this chapter, you learn about the importance of using thread dumps for analyzing CPU consumption, creating thread dumps, and using tools such as ThreadDumpScan and Thread Dump Viewer for analyzing thread dumps.

JVM Analysis Basics

JVM analysis can be especially useful when you see a lot of CPU consumption, even though there are no incoming HTTP requests or load on the system. A huge CPU consumption could be due to either genuine background jobs, garbage collection, or a bug in code.

To identify the cause of CPU consumption, you should supplement the information obtained from the thread dump with the information from the operating system on CPU consumption for threads. You can also use the information obtained from the portal monitoring for thread overview and requests and components overview, and combine it with the dump analysis and OS information on CPU consumption for threads.

The dump can be used to analyze the potential problem areas such as wait situations arising out of I/O operations when accessing file systems, database systems, and backend systems using Java Connector (JCO). It can also be used for identifying coding issues such as lock situations due to synchronized statements and poor performance due to deep nesting of loops.

NOTE *One of the benefits of using Java thread dumps is that no performance overhead is incurred in the J2EE engine when creating the dump.*

The dump, by itself, does not provide information on the CPU performance or the response time. It does provide limited help in analyzing memory issues and functional analysis. It needs to be supplemented with other information (such as CPU usage per thread) that can be obtained from operating system tools such as PsList.

Creating the Thread Dumps

Let's discuss the different ways you can generate thread dumps.

Using the SAP Management Console

To enable a full thread dump in J2EE 6.40, go to the SAP Management Console and click the J2EE Process Table under the instance. Then right click the server process on the right under the name column and choose Dump Stack Trace, as shown next:

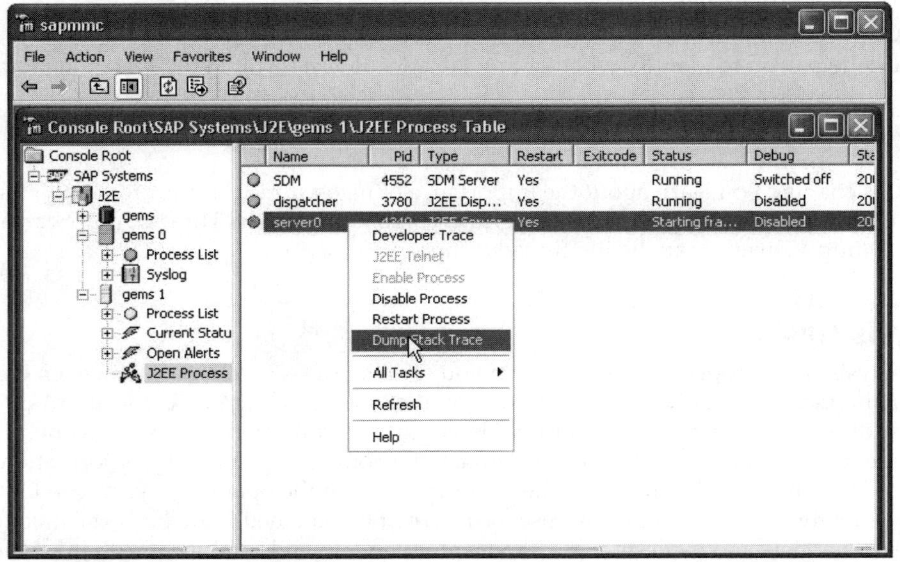

Copyright by SAP AG

A dump trace will be created in the following folders, depending on the version of the JDK:

- /usr/sap/<*SID*>/<*Instance*>/work/std_<*node name*>.out file (for JDKs from SUN and HP)
- /usr/sap/<*SID*>/<*Instance*>/J2EE/cluster/Javacore<*PID*>.<*timestamp*>.txt file (for JDKs from IBM)

Shown here is a section of the std_server0.out file where the thread dump output begins:

```
==============================================================================
getThreadDump : Wed May 30 05:31:39 2007

Timed out services:□
Service com.sap.portal.prt.sapj2ee > hard reference to interface tc~monitoring~api.□

==============================================================================
Full thread dump Java HotSpot(TM) Server VM (1.4.2_09-b05 mixed mode):

"SAPEngine_Application_Thread[impl:3]_8" prio=5 tid=0x040e5c20 nid=0xd0c in Object.wait() [5c1f000..5c1fd90]
        at java.lang.Object.wait(Native Method)
        - waiting on <0x14f91060> (a com.sap.engine.lib.util.WaitQueue)
        at java.lang.Object.wait(Object.java:429)
        at com.sap.engine.lib.util.WaitQueue.dequeue(WaitQueue.java:238)
        - locked <0x14f91060> (a com.sap.engine.lib.util.WaitQueue)
        at com.sap.engine.core.thread.impl3.SingleThread.run(SingleThread.java:147)

"CBS Request Orc" prio=10 tid=0x01124408 nid=0x824 in Object.wait() [5bdf000..5bdfd90]
        at java.lang.Object.wait(Native Method)
        - waiting on <0x14f90060> (a java.lang.Thread)
        at com.sap.tc.cbs.server.rt.impl.CourteousTimer.run(CourteousTimer.java:121)
        - locked <0x14f90060> (a java.lang.Thread)
        at java.lang.Thread.run(Thread.java:534)
```


Combining the PsList for Analysis

At the same time the dump trace is triggered, you should use an operating system tool such as PsList, one of the many tools that can be used to analyze the operating system. Note that the timing of the PsList and the full thread dump is important, because later on you will have to map the thread from the PsList with that in the full thread dump.

TIP *You can download the PsList tool from Microsoft's website at http://www.microsoft.com/technet/sysinternals/utilities/pslist.mspx. The tool is also available as an attachment to OSS Note 686254.*

Generating Java Thread Dumps Using Threaddump.class

OSS Note 686254 contains information on how to generate thread dumps using a Java class named *Threaddump.class.* In Figure 30-1, the column *Tid* stands for the *thread ID,* and this information can be used to identify the corresponding entry in the full thread dump for analysis.

While analyzing the PsList output, identify the threads that are consuming a lot of user time. Run PsList consecutively and check whether the user time increases to almost the same amount of time that occurs between the consecutive runs; this tells you that the thread is consuming a lot of CPU time.

Also check for the threads that are in running status. You can use that information, capture the native thread ID, and convert it into a hexadecimal value and use that to identify the corresponding record in the thread dump and identify the portal component for further analysis.

```
C:\WINDOWS\system32\cmd.exe

C:\PsTools>pslist -d | more

pslist v1.28 - Sysinternals PsList
Copyright ┌ 2000-2004 Mark Russinovich
Sysinternals

Thread detail for GEMS:


Idle 0:
 Tid Pri    Cswtch            State     User Time    Kernel Time    Elapsed Time
   0   0   6933858          Running  0:00:00.000   1:33:46.609     0:00:00.000
   0   0   8750848          Running  0:00:00.000   1:35:49.250     0:00:00.000

System 4:
 Tid Pri    Cswtch            State     User Time    Kernel Time    Elapsed Time
   8   0    428858    Wait:FreePage  0:00:00.000   0:00:26.812     0:00:00.000
  16  15     38254       Wait:Queue  0:00:00.000   0:00:01.015     3:04:04.812
  20  13     41390       Wait:Queue  0:00:00.000   0:00:01.156     3:04:04.812
  24  13     27533       Wait:Queue  0:00:00.000   0:00:00.515     3:04:04.812
  28  13     43374       Wait:Queue  0:00:00.000   0:00:01.281     3:04:04.812
  32  13     39545       Wait:Queue  0:00:00.000   0:00:01.171     3:04:04.812
  36  13    610854       Wait:Queue  0:00:00.000   0:00:16.578     3:04:04.812
  40  12     66821       Wait:Queue  0:00:00.000   0:00:01.750     3:04:04.812
  44  12    875552       Wait:Queue  0:00:00.000   0:00:23.562     3:04:04.812
  48  13     96290       Wait:Queue  0:00:00.000   0:00:03.265     3:04:04.812
  52  14     30940       Wait:Queue  0:00:00.000   0:00:01.187     3:04:04.812
  56  12     72985       Wait:Queue  0:00:00.000   0:00:04.078     3:04:04.812
  60  12   1026575   Wait:Executive  0:00:00.000   0:00:27.171     3:04:04.812
  64  15    126152       Wait:Queue  0:00:00.000   0:00:00.203     3:04:04.812
  68  14      8635   Wait:Executive  0:00:00.000   0:00:00.000     3:04:04.812
  72  18      5314  Wait:VirtualMem  0:00:00.000   0:00:00.359     3:04:04.750
  76  17      5582    Wait:FreePage  0:00:00.000   0:00:00.156     3:04:04.750
  80  16      8727   Wait:Executive  0:00:00.000   0:00:00.000     3:04:04.750
  84  17       528  Wait:VirtualMem  0:00:00.000   0:00:00.015     3:04:04.750
  88  23     26302   Wait:Executive  0:00:00.000   0:00:00.015     3:04:04.750
  92  16         1       Wait:Queue  0:00:00.000   0:00:00.000     3:04:04.718
  96  17         1       Wait:Queue  0:00:00.000   0:00:00.000     3:04:04.718
 100   8      5147   Wait:Executive  0:00:00.000   0:00:00.375     3:04:04.562
 104   8         1   Wait:Executive  0:00:00.000   0:00:00.000     3:04:04.046
 108   8    124510       Wait:Queue  0:00:00.000   0:00:02.015     3:04:03.625
 116   9        18   Wait:Executive  0:00:00.000   0:00:00.000     3:03:57.828
 120  16         3   Wait:Executive  0:00:00.000   0:00:00.000     3:03:57.796
 132   8         1       Wait:Queue  0:00:00.000   0:00:00.000     3:03:57.750
 136   8         1       Wait:Queue  0:00:00.000   0:00:00.000     3:03:57.750
 140   8         1       Wait:Queue  0:00:00.000   0:00:00.000     3:03:57.750
 144   8       149   Wait:Executive  0:00:00.000   0:00:00.000     3:03:57.750
 148   8      3661   Wait:Executive  0:00:00.000   0:00:00.015     3:03:57.734
 152   8      3522   Wait:Executive  0:00:00.000   0:00:00.015     3:03:57.718
 160   8        14   Wait:Executive  0:00:00.000   0:00:00.000     3:03:57.578
 164   8         2   Wait:Executive  0:00:00.000   0:00:00.000     3:03:57.578
 168   8         1   Wait:Executive  0:00:00.000   0:00:00.000     3:03:57.578
 252   8        20   Wait:Suspended  0:00:00.000   0:00:00.000     3:03:57.296
 256   9        20   Wait:Suspended  0:00:00.000   0:00:00.000     3:03:57.218
 260   8        20   Wait:Suspended  0:00:00.000   0:00:00.000     3:03:56.593
 268   8         3   Wait:Executive  0:00:00.000   0:00:00.000     3:03:50.203
 272  10      8979   Wait:Executive  0:00:00.000   0:00:04.406     3:03:50.187
 276   8        60       Wait:Queue  0:00:00.000   0:00:00.000     3:03:50.156
-- More  --
```

FIGURE 30-1 Using PsList for thread dump analysis

Tools for Analyzing Java Thread Dumps

Several tools are available for analyzing Java thread dumps.

Using the ThreadDumpScan Tool

To make the analysis of the thread dump easier, you can use a useful tool developed by SAP named the ThreadDumpScan tool. It can be downloaded from the SDN website under the Web AS download section. After downloading the file, extract it to a desired location. Then open the dumpscan.bat file and change the `classpath` and `JAVA_HOME` entries so that they point to the correct locations.

To create Excel files instead of CSV files, you need to download the poi-2.5-final-20040302 .zip file. Then extract the ZIP file and copy the JAR file into a desired location and update that location in the dumpscan.bat file again.

Open the Windows command prompt and then go the folder where the dumpscan.bat file is present and enter this command:

```
dumpscan <name of file>
```

The tool generates a number of XLS files containing useful information generated from the thread dump, such as garbage collection output, condensed view of dumps, and full thread dumps.

Shown next is a file generated by the ThreadDumpScan tool. This contains information on the threads, thread group, thread number, state of the thread, lines, priority, thread ID, native thread ID, and native stack trace location.

Name	Group	ThrNumber	State	Lines	Prio	tid	nid	native stack	
SAPEngine_Application_Thread[impl:3]_13	SAPEngine_Application_Thread[impl:3]_	13	in Object.wait()	9	5	06d72170	0x44c	null	at java.lang.Object.wait(N
SAPEngine_Application_Thread[impl:3]_12	SAPEngine_Application_Thread[impl:3]_	12	in Object.wait()	9	5	06d72008	0x1434	null	at java.lang.Object.wait(N
SAPEngine_Application_Thread[impl:3]_11	SAPEngine_Application_Thread[impl:3]_	11	in Object.wait()	9	5	6596058	0x10b4	null	at java.lang.Object.wait(N
SAPEngine_Application_Thread[impl:3]_10	SAPEngine_Application_Thread[impl:3]_	10	in Object.wait()	9	5	0748ce98	0xcf8	null	at java.lang.Object.wait(N
SAPEngine_Application_Thread[impl:3]_9	SAPEngine_Application_Thread[impl:3]_	9	in Object.wait()	9	5	6930490	0xf20	null	at java.lang.Object.wait(N
SAPEngine_Application_Thread[impl:3]_8	SAPEngine_Application_Thread[impl:3]_	8	in Object.wait()	7	5	03f11708	0x1338	null	at java.lang.Object.wait(N
SAPEngine_Application_Thread[impl:3]_7	SAPEngine_Application_Thread[impl:3]_	7	waiting on condition	7	5	06c4fe58	0x1334	null	at java.lang.Thread.sleep(
SAPEngine_Application_Thread[impl:3]_6	SAPEngine_Application_Thread[impl:3]_	6	waiting on condition	7	5	073f0e78	0x11b8	null	at java.lang.Thread.sleep(
SAPEngine_Application_Thread[impl:3]_5	SAPEngine_Application_Thread[impl:3]_	5	waiting on condition	7	5	066bed98	0xeb0	null	at java.lang.Thread.sleep(
Thread-26	Thread-	26	waiting on condition	2	5	03da4310	0x12fc	null	at java.lang.Thread.sleep(
CBS Request Orc	CBS Request Orc	0	in Object.wait()	3	10	066beab8	0x1298	null	at java.lang.Object.wait(N
CBS TCS-queue Reader	CBS TCS-queue Reader	0	waiting on condition	3	10	06c74c58	0x121c	null	at java.lang.Thread.sleep(
CBS AccessQueue Orchestrator	CBS AccessQueue Orchestrator	0	runnable	3	10	06c74af0	0xd58	null	at java.lang.Object.wait(N
CBS BSA Orc	CBS BSA Orc	0	in Object.wait()	3	10	03c8c038	0xf9c	null	at java.lang.Object.wait(N
CBS Resource Orc	CBS Resource Orc	0	in Object.wait()	3	10	03dc9ba8	0x3d4	null	at java.lang.Object.wait(N
JCoRequestDispatcher	JCoRequestDispatcher	0	runnable	7	5	03c7b408	0x94c	null	at com.sap.mw.rfc.driver.(
Thread-25	Thread-	25	waiting on condition	2	5	03c8ccf0	0x16cc	null	at java.lang.Thread.sleep(

Using the Thread Dump Viewer

For thread dumps in SAP J2EE Engine 6.40/7.0, you can use the Thread Dump Viewer provided by SAP. The Thread Dump Viewer is available from OSS Note 1020246 as an attachment.

Tip *To use the Thread Dump Viewer, the Java version should be at least 1.4.2.*

1. Download the attachment to a folder and open a command prompt in Windows. Enter the command **java –jar tdv640.jar**. The GUI will open, as shown in Figure 30-2.
2. Choose File | Open | Add To Current Dumps. Then select the thread dump file, std_server0.out, at C:\usr\sap\J2E\JC01\work.
3. Generate additional thread dumps spaced about 30 seconds apart and add the files to the Thread Dump Viewer using the technique described above. Then compare the threads to identify those that are locked or in waiting mode.
4. Generate the PsList so that you can identify the corresponding processes and their corresponding memory and CPU consumption from the Task Manager.

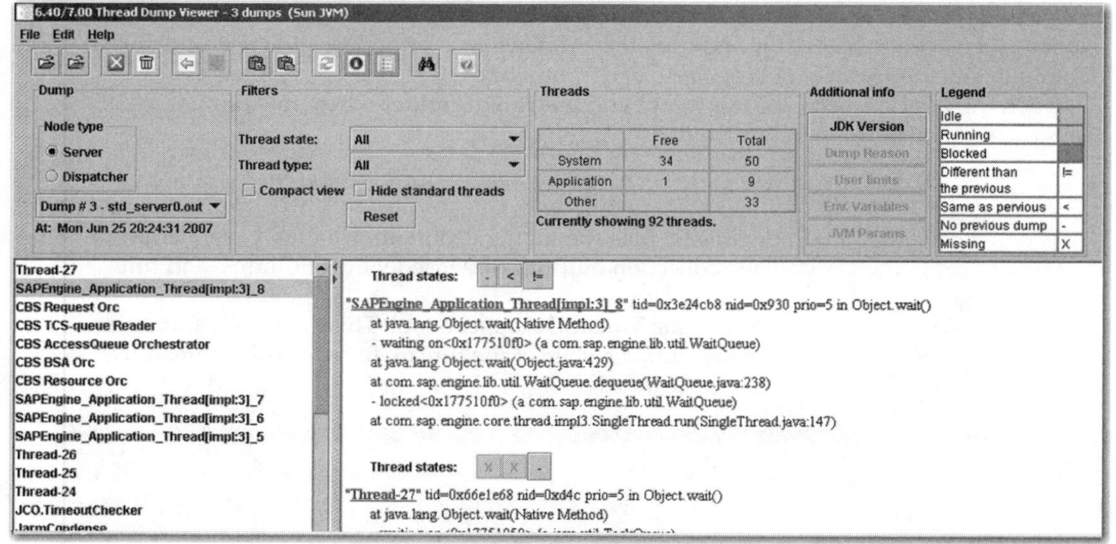

Copyright by SAP AG

FIGURE 30-2 Thread Dump Viewer application

Comparing Multiple Thread Dumps

When you need to add more than one thread dump to the viewer, you can compare the threads. You can filter the threads by either *thread states* or *thread types* using the filter shown here:

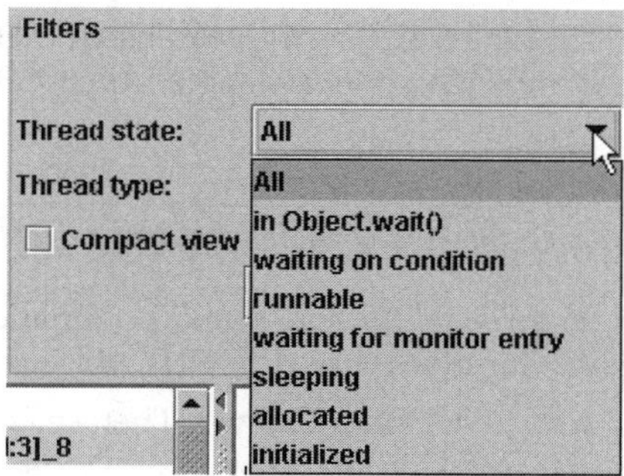

Copyright by SAP AG

You can also note the number of systems, applications, and other threads under the thread section. In this display, the lighter color of the thread states implies that the threads are idle.

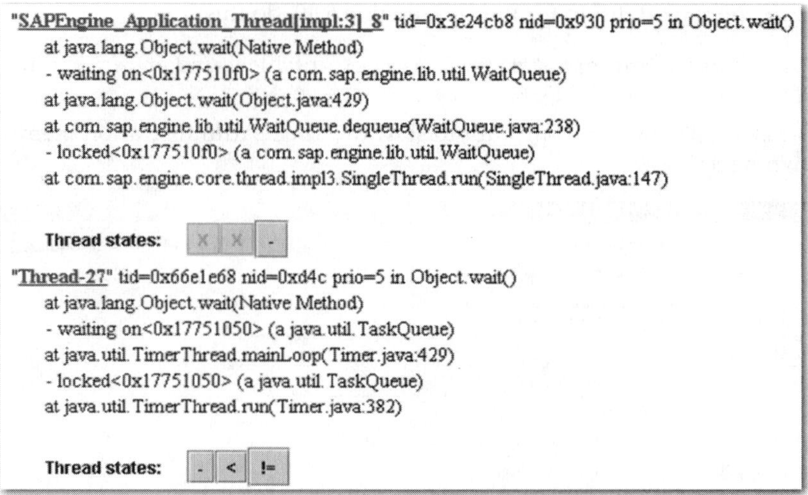

"SAPEngine_Application_Thread[impl:3]_8" tid=0x3e24cb8 nid=0x930 prio=5 in Object.wait()
at java.lang.Object.wait(Native Method)
- waiting on<0x177510f0> (a com.sap.engine.lib.util.WaitQueue)
at java.lang.Object.wait(Object.java:429)
at com.sap.engine.lib.util.WaitQueue.dequeue(WaitQueue.java:238)
- locked<0x177510f0> (a com.sap.engine.lib.util.WaitQueue)
at com.sap.engine.core.thread.impl3.SingleThread.run(SingleThread.java:147)
Thread states: X X -
"Thread-27" tid=0x66e1e68 nid=0xd4c prio=5 in Object.wait()
at java.lang.Object.wait(Native Method)
- waiting on<0x17751050> (a java.util.TaskQueue)
at java.util.TimerThread.mainLoop(Timer.java:429)
- locked<0x17751050> (a java.util.TaskQueue)
at java.util.TimerThread.run(Timer.java:382)
Thread states: - < !=

In this display, if you roll the cursor over the minus sign button, you'll see that this thread does not exist in the previous thread dump:

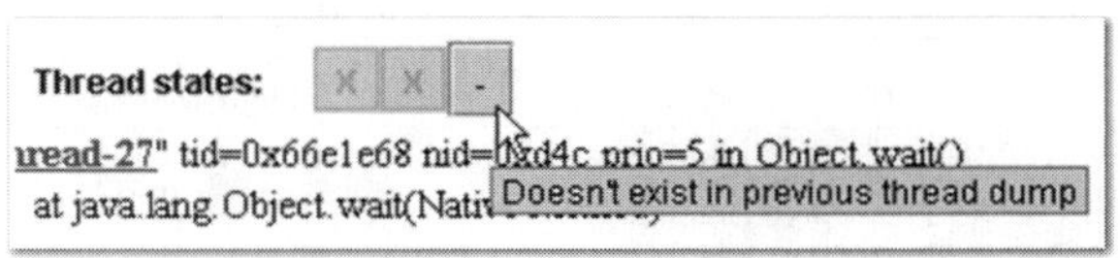

For additional information, refer to the legend shown on the right.

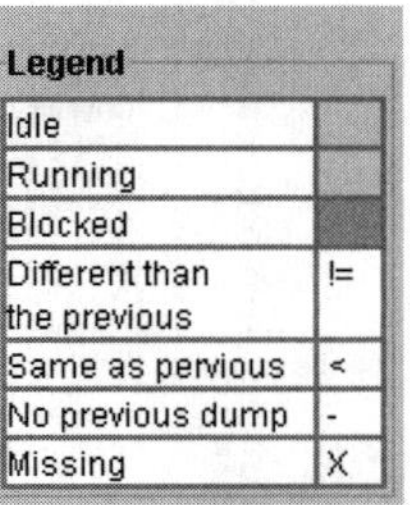

Legend
Idle
Running
Blocked
Different than the previous !=
Same as pervious <
No previous dump -
Missing X

The X implies the thread does not appear in this thread dump again. The green color next to Running implies that the thread is running. By using these legends, you can compare the threads in different dumps and identify threads that are available in both dumps and see how they behave with subsequent dumps. You can switch between different dumps by clicking the drop-down arrow:

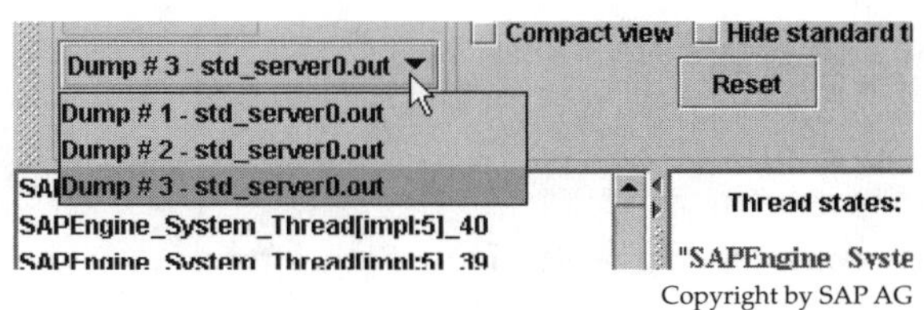

To generate the thread dump for the J2EE engine 6.40, do this:

1. At the command prompt, start the JCMon executable found at <*drive*>:\usr\sap\<*SID*>\SYS\exe\uc\NTI386.
2. Enter **20** at the command prompt to start the Local Administration menu, as shown next:

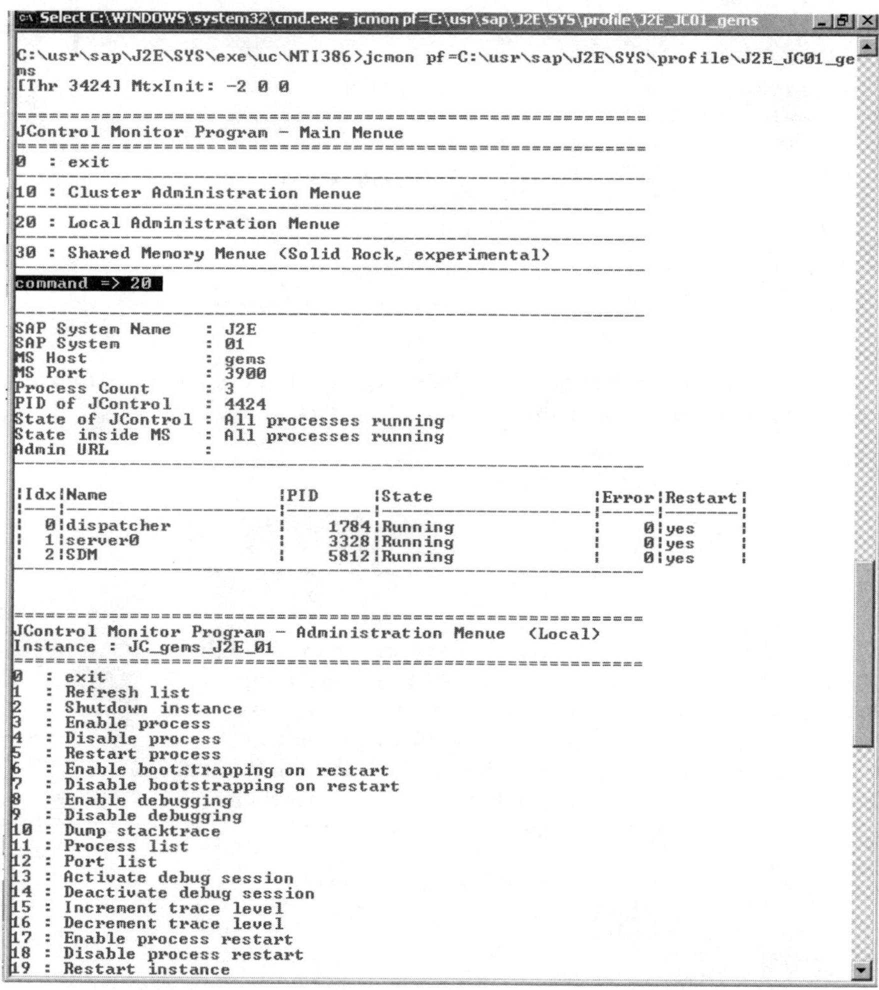

3. Enter **10** in the command prompt to trigger the Dump stack trace:

```
command => 10

Process Index : 1
```

4. Enter the process index from Idx column value for the server0 process as displayed next. For the dispatcher, the Idx is 0 and for SDM, it will be 2, as shown.

Idx	Name	PID	State	Error	Restart
0	dispatcher	1784	Running	0	yes
1	server0	3328	Running	0	yes
2	SDM	5812	Running	0	yes

5. Enter **y** to the question "Do you want to dump the stacktrace for process [1/server0]? <y/n>."

The dump will be successfully generated in the <*drive*>:\usr\sap\<*SID*>\JC<*instance_number*>\work\std_<*node_name*>.out file, if the JDK is from Sun or HP. If the JDK belongs to IBM, the thread dump can be found under the <*drive*>:\usr\sap\<*SID*>\JC<*instance_number*>\j2ee/cluster/javacore<*PID*>.<*timestamp*>.txt file.

Analyzing the Thread Dumps

Now let's discuss thread types, thread states, and how to use the thread dumps for analysis.

Example of a Stack Trace

Here's an example of a stack trace:

```
"SAPEngine_Application_Thread[impl:3]_13" prio=5 tid=0x06d72170 nid=0x44c in
Object.wait() [5e3f000..5e3fd90]
    at Java.lang.Object.wait(Native Method)
    - waiting on <0x14f90258> (a com.sap.mw.jco.RequestListenerGroup$RequestQueue)
    at Java.lang.Object.wait(Object.Java:429)
    at com.sap.mw.jco.RequestListenerGroup$RequestQueue.getRequest
(RequestListenerGroup.Java:698)
    - locked <0x14f90258> (a com.sap.mw.jco.RequestListenerGroup$RequestQueue)
    at com.sap.mw.jco.JCO$Server.loop(JCO.Java:8096)
    - locked <0x14f90258> (a com.sap.mw.jco.RequestListenerGroup$RequestQueue)
    at com.sap.mw.jco.JCO$Server.run(JCO.Java:8022)
    at com.sap.engine.core.thread.impl3.ActionObject.run(ActionObject.Java:37)
    at Java.security.AccessController.doPrivileged(Native Method)
    at com.sap.engine.core.thread.impl3.SingleThread.execute(SingleThread.Java:100)
    at com.sap.engine.core.thread.impl3.SingleThread.run(SingleThread.Java:124)
```

Let's take a look at the various parts inside the stack trace.

- `"SAPEngine_Application_Thread[impl:3]_13"` is the thread ID
- `tid` is the Java thread ID
- `nid` is the native thread ID that is used in the operating system
- `Object.wait()` is the state of the thread—that is, either `Object.wait()`, runable, or waiting on
- `[575f000..575fd90] - c` is the stack location

Thread Types

Now let's take a look at the common thread names in the full thread dump analysis.

- **Thread-49** Threads are not assigned any specific name and are usually created by third parties
- **Client Threads** These threads handle the incoming HTTP requests and are managed by the ThreadManager of the J2EE engine
- **SAPEngine_Application_Thread** A pool of system threads that are managed by the SystemThreadManager of the J2EE engine.

  Given below is a section of the thread dump.

  ```
  "PRT-AppBrkCleanRef-60000" prio=5 tid=0x03da2b18 nid=0x17ac waiting
  on condition [5f7f000..5f7fd90]
  at Java.lang.Thread.sleep(Native Method)
  at com.sapportals.portal.prt.core.broker
  .PortalAppBroker$ReferenceCleaner.run(PortalAppBroker.Java:1982)
  ```
- **PRT-AppBrkCleanRef-60000** These are threads that start with *PRT*. These threads are maintained by the portal runtime.

You may also have other threads with prefixes such as com.sapportals.portal.softcache .CacheCleaner, CBS Request Orc, and JCoRequestDispatcher.

Thread States

Threads can be in different states, such as runable, waiting on monitor, or suspended. Runable could mean that the thread is ready to run or that it is waiting for a CPU to be assigned. It could also mean that is already running using a CPU. Waiting on monitor state means that the thread is waiting for some event or notification to occur, which can be inferred based on the stack trace lists at `object.wait()`. If the PRT and the client threads are in the waiting mode, they are subject to closer analysis.

Analysis Using the Thread Dump

Following are some of the steps that can be adopted to conduct the analysis:

- **Group the thread dumps** To proceed with the analysis, it may be helpful to sort the dump by thread groups, then by status, and then by stack trace. While using the thread dump, check for the string full thread dump and if you see more than one dump, try to group them.
- **Identify deadlock situations** Search for string deadlock.
- **Check whether it is SAP or custom code** By analyzing the thread stacks, you can identify the location in the Java code where the thread is processing as well as whether it is SAP code or custom code.

- **Identify type of thread** You can also identify whether a given thread is a client thread, an application thread, a system thread, a third-party thread, a PRT thread, and so on.
- **Check the thread status** You can identify whether a given thread is idle, or waiting for network input or for database connection, and so on.
- **Waiting for monitor entry** Analyze the Client_Thread_, the PRT_Async_ and Thread- threads to see whether they have waiting for monitor entries. Check for the number of threads that are in this state. If you see many, that means they may have a performance issue while serving client requests as they are blocked.
- **Waiting on the socket** Then check whether the threads are trying to access database, network, and so on, and check for any methods such as `doContent()` or `service()`. This may help identify an iView.
- **Get OSS help** If you are not able to solve the problem using the thread dumps, send the problem to OSS for help. Check for threads that have a runnable state. Check the number of threads that have this state and check their stack trace.
- **Waiting for monitor** Check for threads that have waiting on monitor state. These threads are idle threads that are waiting in the thread pool for a task. This is normal behavior and hence can be ignored.
- **Compare with Task Manager** Identify the native thread IDs and use that information to check for those processes in the Task Manager. Check whether those threads have a high CPU consumption.
- **Identical stack traces** Check whether multiple threads have the same stack trace. If so, that could indicate a deadlock/starvation situation.
- **Longest stack traces** Take a closer look at threads that have the longest stack traces. Usually they have some problem.
- **Check for free threads** Check the stack trace for threads that have `Object.wait()` status. If they are missing, this could mean that no free threads are available, in which case you may need to increase the number of threads.

To check the number of threads for the server and dispatcher, go to the config tool and navigate to Cluster Data | Global Server Configuration | Managers | Thread Manager and Cluster Data | Global Dispatcher Configuration | Managers | Thread Manager, respectively.

Deadlock Issue: Portal Hangs

In some portal hanging situations, you can troubleshoot the problem by searching for the term *deadlock* in the trace. You can also try to access the J2EE engine directly by accessing the portal component through the following URL: http://*<server>*:*<port>*/irj/servlet/prt/portal/com.sap.portal.navigation.portallauncher.default

If it performs well, the problem may exist in one of the components in the web infrastructure such as a web server or load balancer. If the portal component is slow, you can try accessing the J2EE engine alone—http://<server>50100. If that works, the problem is in the portal runtime. If not, the J2EE engine itself is having an issue.

Relevant OSS Notes

Following is a list of relevant OSS notes:

- **1004255** How to Create a Full HPROF Heap Dump of J2EE Engine 6.40/7.0
- **686254** Thread Dump from J2EE Engine 6.20 Running as Windows Service
- **1020246** Thread Dump Viewer
- **710154** How to Create a Thread Dump for the J2EE Engine 6.40/7.0

NOTE *For more details, refer to the thread dump related resources listed in Appendix B.*

Summary

This chapter discussed the importance and limitations of using thread dumps for analysis and how to create thread dumps using the SAP management console and Threaddump. class. You then used the ThreadDumpScan tool and the Thread Dump Viewer to analyze the thread dumps. You learned how to use thread dumps for analysis.

CHAPTER 31

HTTP Performance Analysis

This chapter discusses HTTP tracing, which provides insight into the details of the HTTP communication between the client and the server and helps you identify potential bottlenecks from a network and client standpoint.

You will find the analyzing the HTTP trace can be useful when troubleshooting single sign on issues to identify what user ID and password is passed to the backend system assuming there is no encryption. You can use HTTP trace to analyze the following:

- Amount of data transferred between the client and the server, and vice versa
- The total end user response time, which is the sum of the server processing time, the network delay, and the client-side rendering time
- The status codes sent back by the server that indicate a server error, client error, or redirect
- The content type served by the server, such as HTML, images, JavaScript, CSS (Cascading Style Sheets).

HTTP Request and Response

When an HTTP request is submitted to the server and a response is generated, the HTTP stream follows a certain predefined format. The HTTP request consists of a start line, headers, and an optional message body. The first line of the HTTP request contains the method used to post the request, followed by the URL and version of the HTTP protocol—for example, `GET /home.html HTTP/1.1`. The first line is followed by zero or more message headers, with the format *<field-name>: [<field-value>]*—for example, `Content-Type: image/gif`.

The header is followed by an optional message body. The POST requests contain the parameters of the request, and the responses contain the content that was requested—for example, HTML, GIF, CSS, and so on. The GET request submits the required parameters to the server using name-value pairs through the URL. The POST request, on the other hand, does not have this limitation because the parameters are sent through the message body instead of the URL.

NOTE *One limitation with using the GET request is that the number of parameters is limited because only a maximum of 2083 characters (see Microsoft KB 208427) can be passed through the URL.*

The first line of the HTTP response contains the HTTP version followed by the return code. The HTTP version could be HTTP0.9, HTTP1.0, or HTTP1.1. The return codes are three digits.

Enabling the HTTP Trace

HTTP tracing can be done on the server, the proxy server, or the client browser. Each of these scenarios has some pros and cons.

Conducting HTTP tracing on the server comes with a few limitations. For example, when the tracing is done on the server, a small performance impact can result. Therefore, you may be limited to analyzing only the overall performance of the requests from all the users. You do not usually capture the request/response headers/bodies. In general, the server trace displays the request URIs, the response time, response length, and the return codes. In addition, you may experience a temporary disruption to service because of the requirement to restart the server.

NOTE *To enable the tracing on the J2EE engine, you need to configure the HTTP tracing service on the J2EE engine.*

Enabling the trace on the proxy server can be much more detailed, because there is very little performance impact and therefore analysis can be done at the user level. You can get detailed information regarding the request/response headers and bodies. Considering that the proxy can be located anywhere between the client and the server, measurements can be taken to evaluate the network delay as well.

Enabling the HTTP trace on the client can also include measurements of the performance impact due to the browser cache. However, an additional installation step of the HTTP trace will be necessary.

A browser plug-in called HttpWatch can be used to capture the HTTP requests. Because the plug-in is installed on the browser, it can be used to measure the HTTP requests that are not only submitted to the server, but also capture the requests that are handled by the browser cache.

When using a proxy to analyze the HTTPS trace, the proxy should have the ability to decrypt the incoming messages from the client/server and then re-encrypt the message before sending to the server/client.

HTTP Trace Analysis Tools

Some of the common proxy tools available in the market are HttpWatch (which must be licensed), the open-source Jakarta HTTP Client, HTTPLook, Grinder's TCPProxy, the open-source PortalSniffer (built from Grinder's TCPProxy), and SAP IEMon. All of these support SSL.

Setting up the HTTP Trace Tool

The HTTP trace tool can be set up on the client browser, the server, or in between the client and server. It can be installed on an Internet proxy for capturing HTTP traces for web applications on the portal that have links outside to the Internet. The location of the tool depends on what needs to be measured.

When the request is initiated by the client, the request reaches the trace tool, which then forwards the request to the server. The server then consumes some time to process the request and then sends an HTTP response back to the HTTP trace tool. The trace tool then forwards the response to the client. The client then parses the scripts and scriptlets in the response and executes them. This is also known as the *browser rendering time*. Figure 31-1 illustrates the time spent at the client, the server, and the network when the request is submitted to the server and a response is generated back to the client browser.

If the trace tool is installed on the server, it measures only the server processing time, because no network delay is involved between the server and the HTTP trace tool. On the other hand, if the HTTP trace tool is installed on the client, the tool measures not only the server processing time, but also the network delay between the server and the client. However, the HTTP trace tool would not measure the time delay involved due to the browser rendering time.

TCPProxy Tool

Here you'll install the TCPProxy from Grinder. You can download it from http://grinder.sourceforge.net/download.html:

1. Download Grinder 3 and install Java 2 standard Edition 1.4 or later. The actual zip file is located at http://sourceforge.net/projects/grinder.
2. Download The Grinder and then click the Download link next to the package The Grinder 3 (beta). You'll then see a page where you can find the link for grinder-3.0-beta33.zip file.

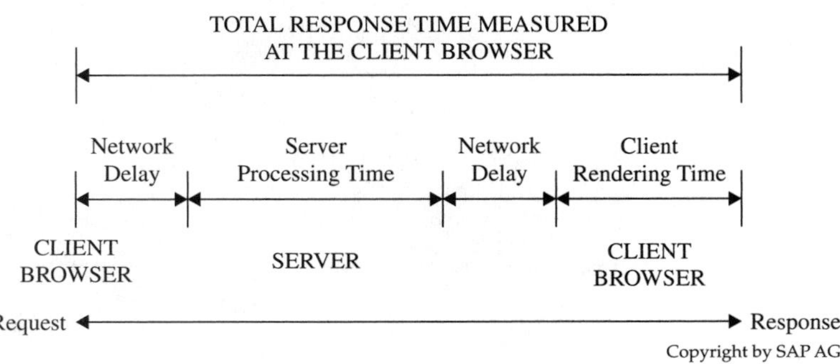

FIGURE 31-1 Time spent by an HTTP request

3. Save the ZIP file to your local machine and then extract it to the C: drive. After extracting the file, the contents of the extracted file should be visible in the folder, as shown here:

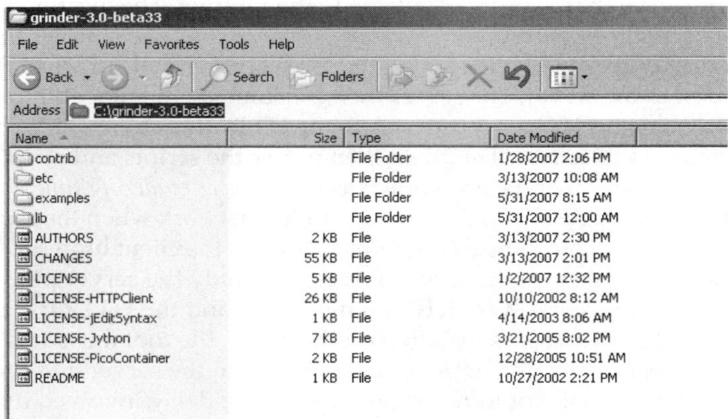

4. In the Internet Options applet on the Control Panel, change the browser LAN settings so that they now point to the proxy tool, without enabling automatic configuration and without checking the Bypass Proxy Server For Local Addresses. The illustration below shows port 8001 is where the TCPProxy is listening.

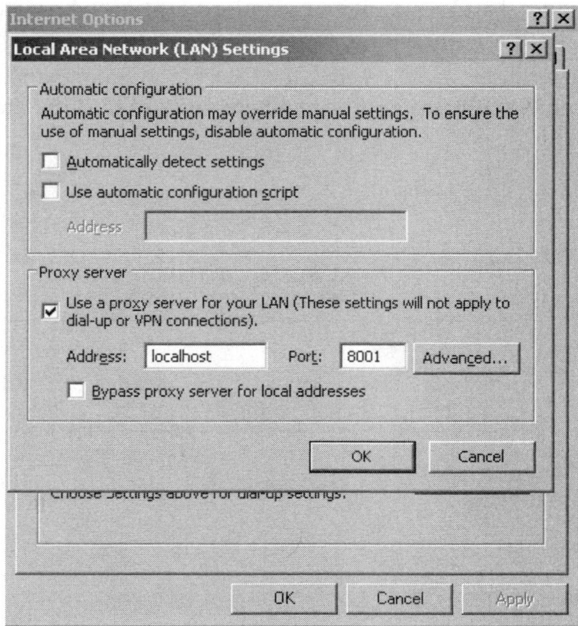

5. Clear the browser cache by selecting Tools | Internet Options in your Internet Explorer 6.0 browser. On the General tab, in the Temporary Internet Files section, click Delete Files button. When prompted, select the Delete All Offline content checkbox in the Delete Files dialog box and click OK twice. If you are using Internet Explorer 7.0, select Tools | Internet Options and then select the Delete button in the Browsing History section. Then select the Delete Files button in the Temporary Internet Files section of the Delete Browsing History dialog box. Click Yes, then Close, and finally click OK.
6. To activate the HTTP 1.1 Via Proxy option, navigate to Tools | Internet Options in your Internet Explorer browser. Then select the Advanced tab and then select the Use HTTP 1.1 Through Proxy Connections checkbox in the HTTP 1.1 settings section.
7. Remove the list of bypassing hosts. To do this, open Tools | Internet Options and select the Connections tab. Click the LAN Settings button and the click Advanced button in the Proxy Server section of the Local Area Network (LAN) Settings screen. Remove the entries, if any, in the Exceptions section of the Proxy Settings screen.

If any of the iViews on the portal is pointing to an external URL, the proxy should be configured to redirect such requests to the actual Internet proxy.

Conducting the Trace

To conduct the trace, open a Windows command prompt and then navigate to the folder where the file was extracted. Then set the `classpath` using the following command:

```
set classpath=C:\grinder-3.0-beta33\lib\grinder.jar
```

Follow this with the command `java.net.grinder.TCPProxy > trace`. The screen should appear similar to the following:

```
C:\grinder-3.0-beta33>set classpath=C:\grinder-3.0-beta33\lib\grinder.jar

C:\grinder-3.0-beta33>java net.grinder.TCPProxy > trace
5/31/07 12:11:01 PM (tcpproxy): Initialising as an HTTP/HTTPS proxy with the

parameters:

   Request filters:    EchoFilter

   Response filters:   EchoFilter

   Local address:      localhost:8001

5/31/07 12:11:01 PM (tcpproxy): Engine initialised, listening on port 8001

5/31/07 12:11:18 PM (tcpproxy):

5/31/07 12:11:18 PM (tcpproxy):
```

Capture the activities of the user on the portal, and repeat the user activities if you want to measure the performance of the cache. Then disable the trace of the HTTP tool by pressing CTRL-C.

PART VI

The captured trace file is now available at C:\grinder-3.0-beta33, or wherever you chose to store the results. The name of the trace file is *trace,* based on the value shown in the DOS prompt. Once the required traces have been captured, try to copy the HTTP trace onto an Excel spreadsheet.

Shown next is a sample of the entries in the trace file. Pay special attention to the request header and the other header tags such as `Host` and `Proxy-Connection`. The request is followed by a response section that starts with a first line that contains the version of the HTTP protocol followed by the return error code and a brief description.

```
--- localhost:1325|google.com:80 opened --
------ localhost:1325|google.com:80 ------
GET / HTTP/1.1
Accept: image/gif, image/x-xbitmap, image/jpeg, image/pjpeg, application/x-
shockwave-flash, application/vnd.ms-excel, application/vnd.ms-powerpoint,
application/msword, */*
Accept-Language: en-us,de;q=0.5
X-McProxyFilter: *************
User-Agent: Mozilla/4.0 (compatible; MSIE 6.0; Windows NT 5.1; SV1; .NET CLR
1.0.3705; .NET CLR 1.1.4322; Media Center PC 4.0; .NET CLR 2.0.50727)
Host: google.com
Proxy-Connection: Keep-Alive

--- google.com:80|localhost:1325 opened --
------ google.com:80|localhost:1325 ------
HTTP/1.1 301 Moved Permanently
Location: http://www.google.com/
Set-Cookie: PREF=ID=437ad3f44dc23708:TM=1180613834:LM=1180613834:S=dO6010N750Fh-
KXD; expires=Sun, 17-Jan-2038 19:14:07 GMT; path=/; domain=.google.com
Content-Type: text/html
Server: GWS/2.1
Content-Length: 219
Date: Thu, 31 May 2007 12:17:14 GMT
<HTML><HEAD><meta http-equiv="content-type" content="text/html;charset=utf-8">
<TITLE>301 Moved</TITLE></HEAD><BODY>
<H1>301 Moved</H1>
The document has moved
<A HREF="http://www.google.com/">here</A>.
</BODY></HTML>
```

NOTE *During the analysis, to get a better understanding of the contents of the HTTP header, refer to the RFC 2616 specification that deals with HTTP 1.1 - http://www.ietf.org/rfc/rfc2616.txt.*

Enabling the HTTP Trace on the Server

An HTTP trace can be activated on the server using one of three options:

- Internet Communication Manager (ICM) on the ABAP engine
- HTTP Provider Service on the J2EE engine
- SAP Web Dispatcher

Activating HTTP Tracing on the ICM

Go to the RZ10 transaction and maintain the parameter

```
icm/HTTP/logging_0 = PREFIX=/, LOGFILE=HTTP_ICM_%y%m%d.log,LOGFORMAT=%h %l
%u %t "%r" %s %b
```

- The `PREFIX` value defines the URL to be logged.
- `LOGFILE` defines the name of the log file and gets created in the work directory of the SAP R/3 Advanced Business Application Programming (ABAP) engine. The file gets created on a daily basis.
- `LOGFORMAT` defines the format of the content to be captured. The format defined by SAP is known as *CLF (Common Log Format).*

Activating HTTP Tracing on the J2EE Server

You can also enable the tracing on the J2EE server. To enable the trace on the J2EE engine, you should change the value of the properties of the HTTP provider service of the dispatcher after logging on to the Visual Administrator, as shown here:

- *HttpTrace*: enable
- *HttpTraceTime*: true

Tracing Requests/Responses or Headers Only

After logging on to the Visual Administrator, go to Cluster | Dispatcher | Services | HTTP Provider, as shown in Figure 31-2. The first value enables the J2EE engine to write all of requests/responses to the logs.

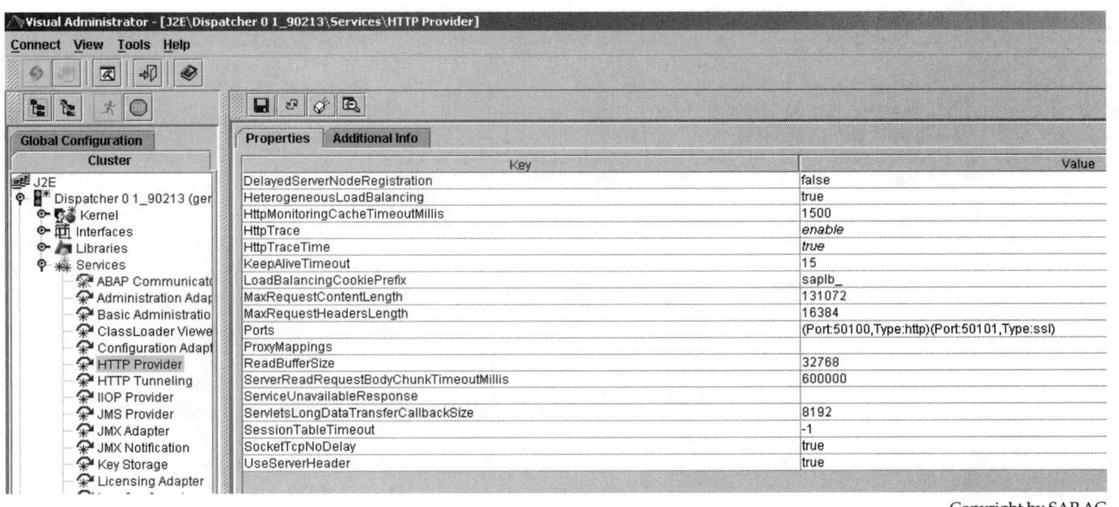

FIGURE 31-2 Enabling the HTTP trace

The other possible values for HttpTrace are *enableHeaders*, *enableHex*, and *enableHexHeaders*. The value *enableHeaders* will allow only the headers to be written to the log files. The other values, *enableHex* and *enableHexHeaders*, are similar to the *enable* and *enableHeaders* values, except that they are written in a 16-column hexadecimal format. Usually you capture the logs in hexadecimal format if the response is likely to contain binaries such as images or compressed gzip content.

NOTE *To disable the tracing, you need to enter* disable *for the* HttpTrace *property.*

Increasing the Level of Logging for HTTP Communication

By default, the log contains only messages with severity INFO. To add a more detailed level of logging, you should change the Log Severity of all log locations under com/sap/engine/services/httpserver. In the Severity drop-down list, select All, as shown in Figure 31-3. Click Copy Severity To Subtree. Save the changes.

Capturing the Dispatcher Response Time

Setting the *HttpTraceTime* property helps to capture the time taken to serve the request, which is the time taken from the moment the request is accepted by dispatcher to the moment the response reaches the client.

Locations of the Trace Files

So now the HTTP trace files will be written to either of the following log files depending upon the SP level. For SP12 and lower, it will be written to the /usr/sap/<*SID*>/<*instance*>/J2EE/cluster/dispatcher/log/defaultTrace.trc file and for SP13 and higher, it will be written to /usr/sap/<*SID*>/<*instance*>/J2EE/cluster/dispatcher/log/services/http/req_resp.trc.

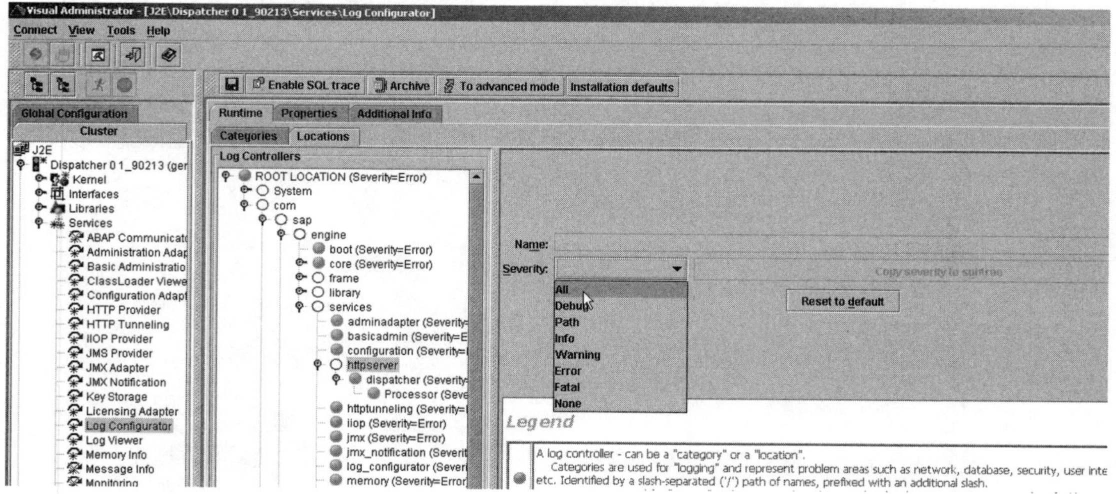

FIGURE 31-3 Increasing the logging level for HTTP communication in Visual Administrator

If you maintained the properties *HttpTraceRequestOutput* and *HttpTraceResponseOutput* in the dispatcher's HTTP service, the request and response traces will be created in the dispatcher folder.

For example, if you maintained these properties,

- *HttpTraceRequestOutput* = request.txt
- *HttpTraceResponseOutput* = response.txt

two files, request.txt and response.txt, will be created in the folder /usr/sap/<*SID*>/<*instance*>/J2EE/cluster/dispatcher.

Capturing the Server Response Time

To capture the server response time, enable the *LogResponseTime* property of the HTTP Provider service on the server by navigating to Cluster | Server | Services | HTTP Provider | Properties. The dispatcher and server response times can be found in the traces in j2ee\cluster\server0\log\system\httpaccess\responses.0.trc file.

Changing the Log Format

To use the common log format, you should change the setting *LogCLF* to true using the config tool, as shown in Figure 31-4.

Activating the Session Tracing

It is possible to trace all the requests pertaining to an HTTP request for troubleshooting purposes. To activate the session tracing, you need to configure the Performance Tracing service on the server in the Visual Administrator. In the Visual Administrator, go to Cluster | Server | Services | Performance Tracing | Runtime, Choose the Trace Config tab and choose the Settings icon.

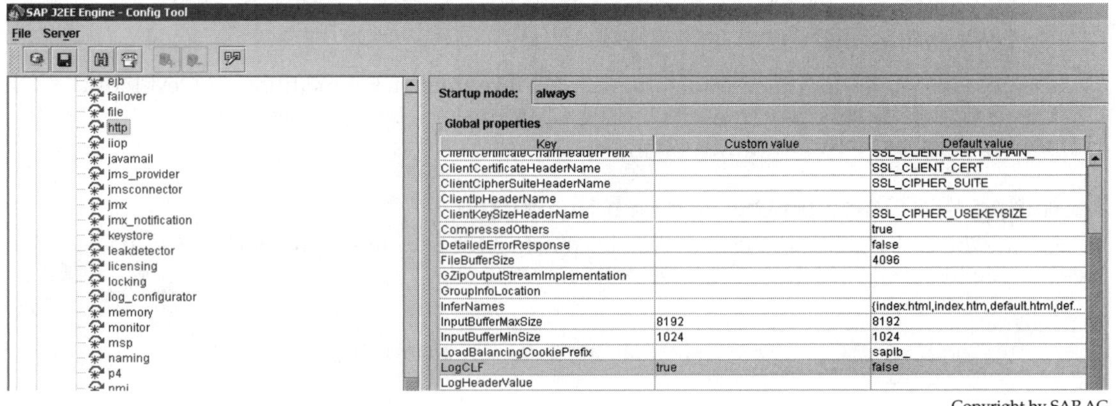

FIGURE 31-4 Config tool setting for *LogCLF*

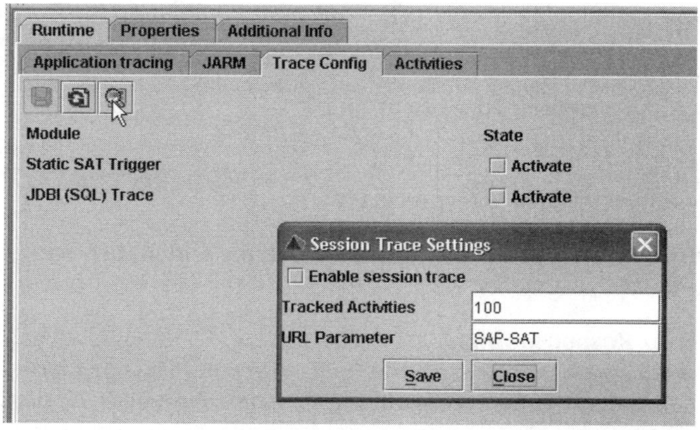

FIGURE 31-5 Session tracing in Visual Administrator

In the Session Trace Settings dialog box that appears, as shown in Figure 31-5, check the Enable Session Trace checkbox and click Save.

Tracked Activities represents the maximum number of activities to be traced. The URL Parameter with a default value of SAP-SAT represents the parameter that is used in the URL for passing in the values that define the scope of tracing and the level of tracing desired. Here is an example of the URL: http://*<host:port>*/irj/portal?SAP-SAT=scope-session,level-high.

The possible values for the first parameter are

- ***scope-request*** The current request is traced
- ***scope-session*** The session pertaining to which the current request is traced
- ***scope-none*** The session pertaining to the current request is not traced

The possible values for the second parameter are level-high, level-medium, and level-low.

The results of the session tracing can be found at Cluster | Server | Services | Performance Tracing | Runtime | Activities.

Activating HTTP Trace on the SAP Web Dispatcher

To activate the HTTP trace on the SAP Web Dispatcher, the setting should be changed in a local profile file used by the SAP Web Dispatcher:

```
# Logging
icm/HTTP/logging_0 =PREFIX=/,LOGFILE=HTTP_WD_%y-%m-%d.log,LOGFORMAT=%h %l
%u %t "%r" %s %b
```

Analysis Using the Trace

Let's now proceed with the analysis of the HTTP trace.

Analyzing the HTTP Error Codes

These HTTP responses also contain the status of the HTTP request. The HTTP status codes can be interpreted as follows:

- **1*xx*** These are informational
- **2*xx*** These are HTTP requests that are fully accepted by the server
- **3*xx*** These are HTTP requests that are redirected to a different URL
- **4*xx*** This status code is returned for client-related errors
- **5*xx*** These are generated for server-side errors

The error code in the status line is followed by a reason phrase that describes the nature of the error. The HTTP response contains a header that follows the status line. The header contains name-value pairs that provide information such as Server, Content-Type, Last Modified, Cache-control, Content-Length, and Date.

One of the things to look for is the number of redirects to a new URL as indicated by return code 302.

Tip *The number of redirect requests should be reduced to a minimum because they result in new connections.*

Check whether there is a response that also contains status *304 Not Modified*. If this occurs for the same resource—for example, an image or JavaScript file—it implies that the resource is obtained from the server and not the browser cache. This could indicate some problem with browser caching.

To detect the browser's caching behavior, first delete the Internet browser cache. Then check the user activity on the portal with the HTTP trace on. Close the browser, open a new one, and repeat the same activity again. Compare the two activities and check whether the number of requests during the second activity is less than the number of requests in the first activity because of caching.

You should also check for additional status codes such as 401 unauthorized, 404 NOT Found, 406 Not Acceptable, 409 Conflict.

Analyze the Header Fields

Content-Length defines the length of the message body. This is used only for HTTP 1.0, and problems may arise if the length defined in the header field is different from the size of the message body.

The field *Transfer-Encoding: chunked* is used if chunking of responses is activated. Chunking enables the HTTP response to be sent back to the client in separate parts known as *chunks* even before the length of the message body is known.

NOTE *In the case of HTTP 1.0, chunking is not active because the server needs to wait until the full message is created and the full length is known.*

The value *Accept-Encoding: gzip* in the request header indicates to the server that the client is capable of handling compression. The server response consists of the value *Content-Encoding: gzip* if the response is compressed.

The header fields *request (Cookie :)* and *response (Set-Cookie :)* provide information on cookies. The field *Accept-Language: de, en* provides information on the browser language.

You should check the Host header field to verify if the same HTML resource is requested either from different hosts or from different folders on the same host. For example, the same image could be retrieved from images/picture.gif or from image/picture.gif. To identify the host, check the Host header field.

Check whether the settings for the cache control and the Header fields have been properly set-for example, cache-control, expires, etag, and if-modified-since.

Analyzing the Response Time

The *response time* is the time elapsed between the first byte of the request and the last byte of the response that was received. You can repeat the activity on the portal and compare the response times. If all the requests take the same amount of time, that probably indicates a network problem. Otherwise, you may need to conduct traces such as a single activity trace or a session trace for deeper analysis.

Analyzing the URLs

Following are some of the commonly found URLs that demonstrate what was accessed by the client request. To verify the URL in the application, right click the iView/page and select Properties.

- **irj/portalapps** Corresponds to the C:\usr\sap\J2E\JC01\J2EE\cluster\server0\apps\sap.com\irj\servlet_jsp\irj\root\portalapps folder
- **irj/servlet/prt** PRT stands for the portal runtime servlet; if a value other than PRT appears, it points to a different servlet that probably belongs to a different J2EE application
- **/irj/servlet/prt/portal** Points to the portal iViews
- **/irj/servlet/prt/soap** Points to the Java-based web services
- **/irj/servlet/prt/portal/prtroot/myApplication.myComponent** Refers to the component myComponent belonging to the myApplication portal application

- **/irj/servlet/prt/portal/prtroot/pcdPCDlocation** Can be used to point any object in the PCD—for example, /irj/servlet/prt/portal/prtroot/pcd!3aportal_content!2fcom.sap.pct!2fevery_user!2fgeneral!2fcom.sap.portal.frameworkpage!2fcom.sap.portal.innerpage. After replacing *!2f* with *"/"* and *"!3a"* with *":"*, you can access the actual object using the PCD.
- **/irj/servlet/prt/portal/prttheme/theme/prteventname/submitEvent/prtroot** Refers to a user interaction on an iView

Analyze the Amount of Data Transferred

Check the amount of data in bytes transferred between the client and the server and look out for large images, CSS, or JavaScript resources. Explore the possibility of caching such extremely large content and optimizing the images and JavaScript files by using compression tools.

TIP *Remove unnecessary breaks, empty spaces, and tags, wherever possible, to reduce the CSS file size.*

Check whether compression is used by verifying the request header variable *Accept-Encoding: gzip, deflate* and the response header variable *Content-Encoding: gzip*.

Analyze the Number of Network Connections

Another factor that affects performance is the time taken to create new network connections. To reuse the same physical network connection for multiple HTTP requests, you should enable HTTP *Keep-Alive*.

NOTE *For HTTP 1.1, the default behavior is HTTP* Keep-Alive.

However, this must be activated explicitly in the header field *Connection: Keep-Alive* for HTTP 1.0. The value *Keep-Alive* can be used to keep connections open and the value *"closed"* can be used to close the connection. In HTTP 1.0, by default, the connections are closed after every response is sent to the client. This is also why SAP recommends that you use either HTTP 1.1 or *HTTP 1.0 with keep-alive* wherever possible.

If the trace contains the number of physical connections information, you can compare that information with the number of requests. If both these values are comparable, you can conclude that the HTTP 1.0 without the keep-alive feature has been used.

NOTE *For more details, refer to HTTP performance analysis related resource listed in Appendix B.*

Summary

This chapter discussed where to set up HTTP analysis and what can be analyzed using the HTTP trace. You learned some of the steps involved in setting up an HTTP trace on the server, ICM, J2EE engine, and SAP Web Dispatcher. You also learned about session tracing. You learned how to analyze the HTTP trace analysis using error codes, header fields, response time, URLs, amount of data transferred, and number of network connections.

32

CHAPTER

Configuring CCMS Monitoring and GRMG Availability Monitoring

As the SAP landscape becomes more and more complex with the implementation of additional SAP and non-SAP components with multiple interfaces and business processes spanning across multiple components, it becomes important that you have a monitoring infrastructure in place for centralized monitoring.

One of the activities that an administrator needs to be able to do as part of the job is to check the status of the process or component periodically. Administrators should be able to check the availability of the systems, monitor the performance of transactions, and check the functioning of interfaces.

NOTE *Monitoring the systems provide data that can be analyzed for resolving any issues.*

This chapter discusses the importance of setting up a central monitoring system and the steps involved in configuring the central monitoring system. You'll learn how to use RZ20 to display the monitors and alerts and how to analyze the monitoring data. The chapter also discusses the steps involved in setting Generic Request and Message Generator (GRMG) Availability for monitoring the availability of technical components and application processes.

Monitoring can be done from either a *business standpoint* or a *technical standpoint*. Monitoring from a business standpoint involves monitoring the business processes at runtime and, if required, alerting the business users for critical events in time. Some of the tools available for business process monitoring are SAP Business Workflow monitoring and alerts and Universal Worklist within the portal. To generate business key performance indicators (KPIs) for monitoring, SAP Business Intelligence (BI) can be used.

Monitoring from a technical standpoint involves monitoring the business processes as well as the underlying technical components at runtime. If required, you can generate alerts automatically so that administrators can be notified for resolution of issue.

Tools for Monitoring

Monitoring the business process from a technical standpoint can be done using Workflow monitoring and SAP Solution Manager. Pure technical monitoring of components for aspects such as status monitoring, activity monitoring, and performance monitoring can be done using tools such as Computing Center Management System (CCMS), SAP NetWeaver Administrator, and SAP Solution Manager.

Examples of components that can be monitored are BI, Enterprise Portal (EP), TREX, Internet Transaction Server (ITS), Business Connector (BC), and Exchange Infrastructure (XI). Reporting on technical KPIs can be done using CCMS, SAP BI, and SAP Solution Manager.

SAP NetWeaver Administrator

SAP NetWeaver Administrator is a Java application and is the central administration and monitoring tool for SAP NetWeaver systems available since mid-2005. It is meant to replace the Visual Administrator and the CCMS alert monitor (RZ20) functionality. It deals with both historic and current data. It can be used to monitor both Advanced Business Application Programming (ABAP) and Java systems centrally. Chapter 44 deals with SAP NetWeaver Administrator in greater detail.

CCMS Monitoring Infrastructure

NetWeaver Administrator, SAP Solution Manager, and the RZ20 display the same alert monitor data. The monitoring data are provided by CCMS monitoring infrastructure, which can be used to capture data based on predefined alert monitors. It is included in SAP NetWeaver as well as SAP Basis components as of 4.0 free of charge.

Central Monitoring Infrastructure

The central monitoring infrastructure resides on the ABAP stack, and monitored data such as performance history are stored and displayed centrally in the central monitoring infrastructure. One of the systems in the landscape should be identified as a central monitoring system and should be purely dedicated for system management. It should be at least SAP Web AS 6.20 or above. The monitored data are stored in local memory segments and can be displayed either centrally or in the Solution Manager, BI, or even third-party tools. The third-party tools also have the ability to send data back to the central monitoring infrastructure.

Configuring Alerts

Not much administrative activity is involved except when configuring alerts to be generated when a threshold value is exceeded and for setting up notifications through e-mail or Short Message Service (SMS). The alerts can be monitored proactively using the alert monitor, which is accessed through transaction RZ20. Another advantage is that you can drill down to a specific component that is being monitored so that you can remove the cause of the problem. If the necessary configuration is done, the corresponding auto-reaction methods such as issuing e-mail notifications are triggered.

Monitoring System Using Alerts

The administrator can use any central monitoring tool such as RZ20, NetWeaver Administrator, or SAP Solution Manager to view the monitoring views of the remote component that is being monitored. Administrators can then drill down into a remote component for troubleshooting and remove the alerts once the issue is resolved.

NOTE *System monitoring activities can be carried out with tools such as RZ20, NetWeaver Administrator, or SAP Solution Manager.*

Monitoring Objects

Basically, the monitoring infrastructure consists of a number of monitoring objects such as the CPU, the database system, and so on. Each of these monitoring objects in turn contains a number of attributes such as the CPU utilization, the disk storage percentage, and so on, that help you monitor the performance of the monitoring objects.

Predefined Data Suppliers

The monitoring architecture also contains a number of predefined data suppliers whose responsibility is to write the values of the monitored objects into a shared memory segment known as the *monitoring segment*. These stored data are then transferred to the Central Monitoring System using a predefined ABAP interface for SAP systems or using a CCMS agent. Figure 32-1 shows the central monitoring system architecture.

Monitoring Segment

The CCMS agent uses an RFC connection to the monitoring segment in the CMS and then updates the monitoring data. The CCMS agent is installed once per Java instance. The monitoring segment name is SAP_CCMS_*<host>*_*<System name>*_*<Instance number>*_x.

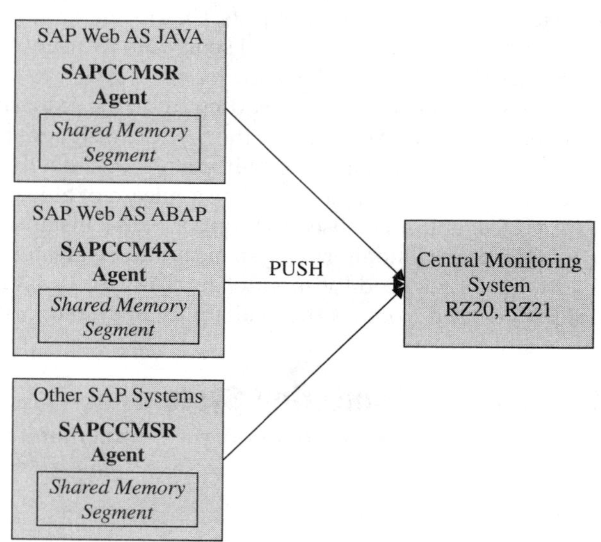

FIGURE 32-1 Central monitoring system architecture

PART VI

FIGURE 32-2 CCMS agents

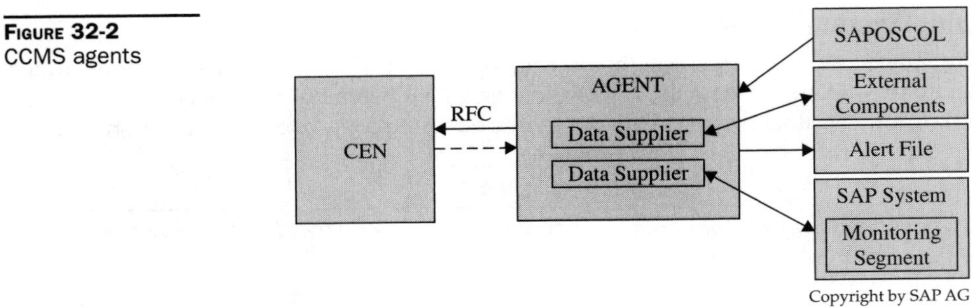

CCMS Agent

The CCMS technology is based upon *CCMS agents*, which run on all the servers that are being monitored. CCMS agents are independent processes that connect to a central monitoring system using RFC, and they have an interface to the shared memory segment in the server being monitored. The data that are being monitored are stored in the shared memory segment.

NOTE *Since the CCMS agents use the push technology to write/read data to/from the central monitoring system, the performance is not affected because the Central Monitoring System does not have to keep polling these agents.*

Operating System Collector

As shown in Figure 32-2, CCMS agents use the operating system collector SAPOSCOL to monitor processes at the operating system level. Using CCMS agents, you can monitor any log files, monitor operating system processes, create auto-reactions for alerts, and monitor network data. The CCMS agent uses exactly one monitoring segment to store the runtime information related to the monitoring objects. CCMS agents can be used to monitor portal, Content Management (CM), and TREX and send data to a central monitoring system such as SAP Web AS ABAP or Solution Manager.

A number of agents can be used, depending upon the scenario. For non-SAP and Java systems that do not have an SAP instance, the SAPCCMSR agent can be used for monitoring. Examples of such scenarios are log file monitoring, TREX, databases, and operating systems. The central monitoring system used should be a release of at least 4.6B.

The SAPCCM4X agent can be used to monitor ABAP instances with SAP BASIS releases greater than 4.X. The central monitoring system should be greater than or equal to BASIS 4.6C.

The SAPCM3X agent is used for monitoring SAP BASIS 3.X systems. Another agent called CCMSPING is used to check the availability of systems every minute.

Configuring the Central Monitoring System

The following steps are required to configure the central monitoring system:

Step 1: Create the CSMREG User

Create the CSMREG user in RZ21 in the central monitoring system. Go to Technical Infrastructure | Configure Central System | Create User CSMREG. Only the password needs to be assigned here. If the user already exists, the password remains the same as the original password.

NOTE *The CSMREG user is a communication user that the CCMS agent uses to connect to the CMS and to enter the monitored data in the central monitoring system.*

Step 2: Check That the SAP_BC_CSMREG Role Is Present

Ensure that the role SAP_BC_CSMREG has already been defined in the system. This role is automatically assigned to the user. If an error occurs in creating the user possibly due to a missing role, generate the profile for the role SAP_BC_CSMREG using transaction PFCG. This user should be created for every monitored system. Figure 32-3 displays the step for creating the CSMREG user.

Figures 32-4 and 32-5 display the roles and authorizations assigned to the CSMREG user.

Step 3: Activate Background Jobs

The data for the ABAP systems that are being monitored are collected using batch jobs that run periodically. To ensure that they run properly, the background dispatching should be activated using transaction RZ21.

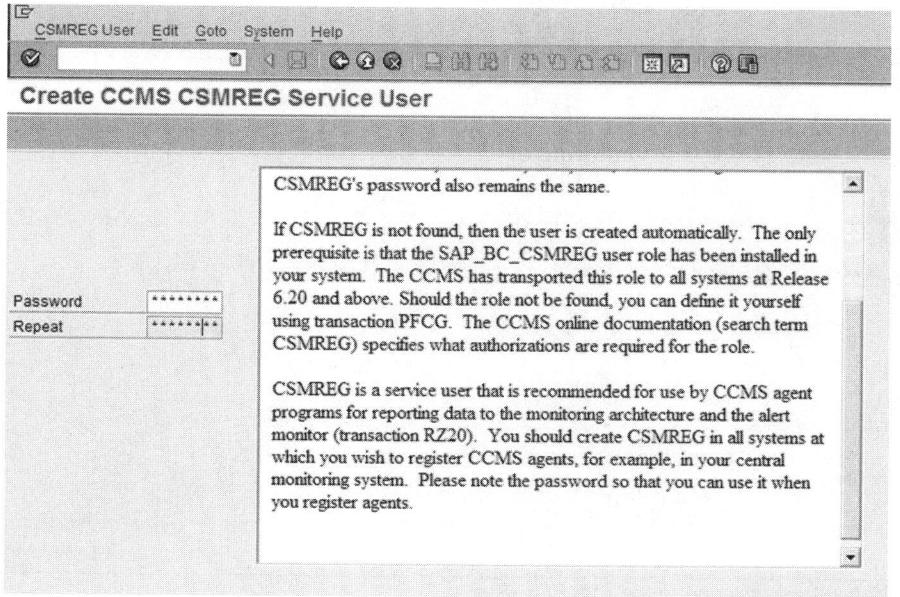

FIGURE 32-3 Create the CSMREG user

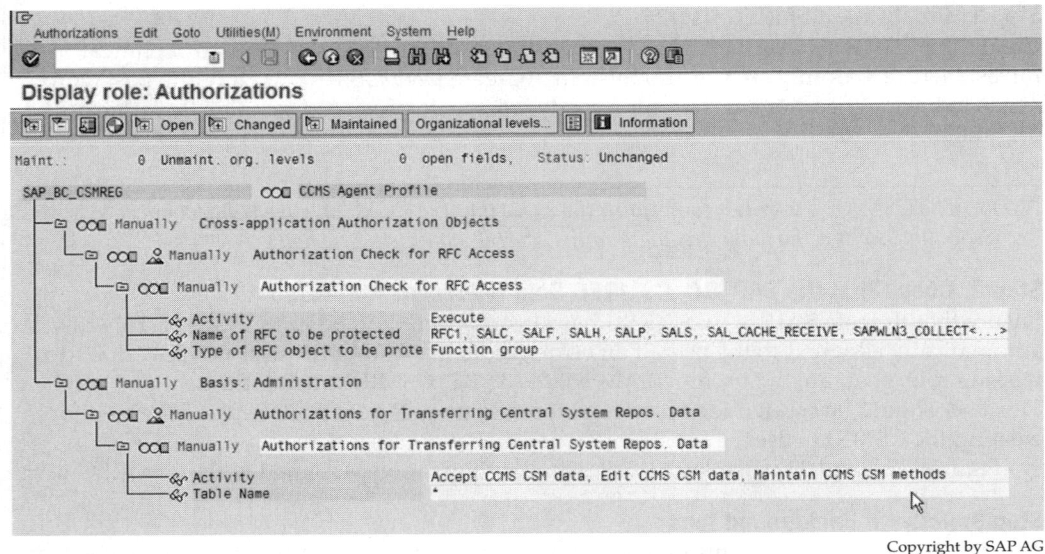

FIGURE 32-4 Authorizations assigned to the CSMREG user

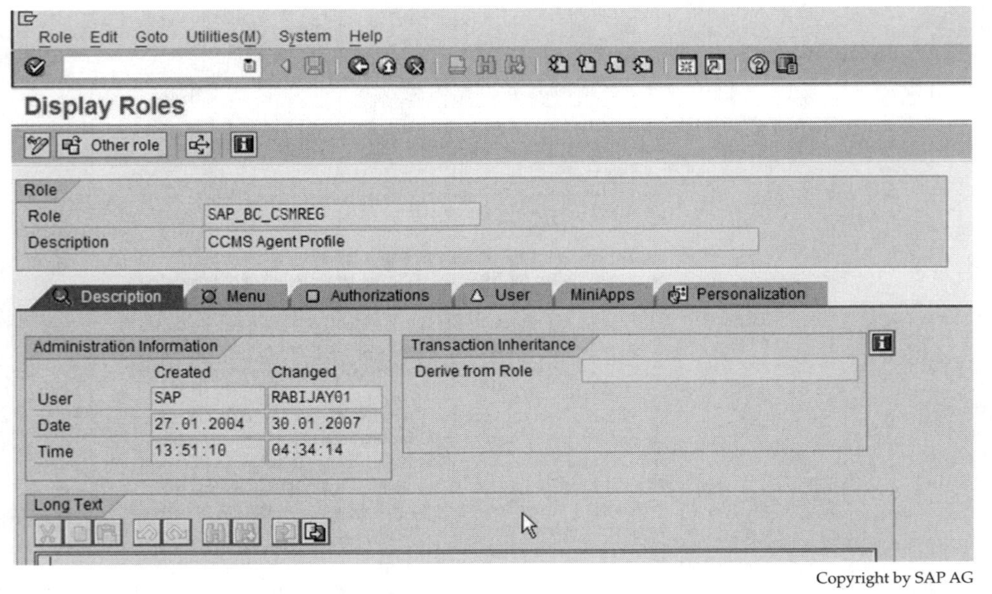

FIGURE 32-5 Role assigned to the CSMREG user

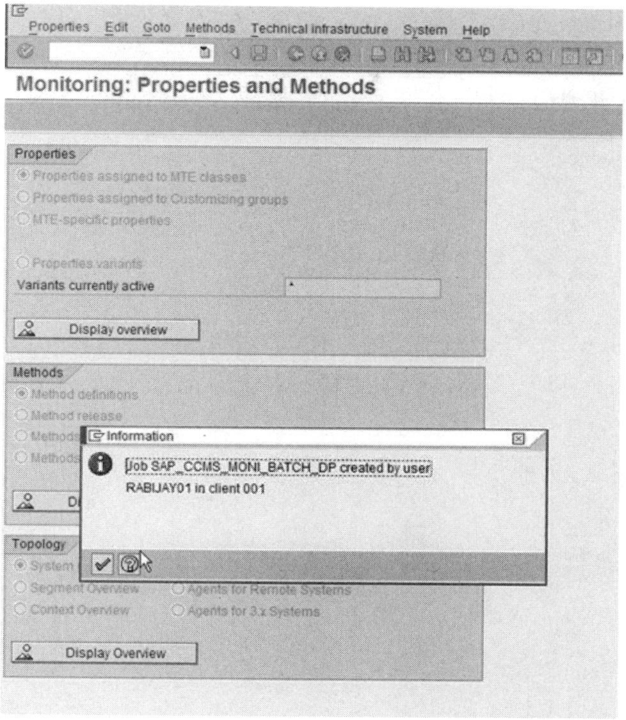

Copyright by SAP AG

FIGURE 32-6 Hourly job SAP_CCMS_MONI_BATCH_DP for background dispatching

Go to Technical Infrastructure | Local Execution Method | Activate Background Dispatching. An hourly job SAP_CCMS_MONI_BATCH_DP that runs background dispatching is created automatically, as shown in Figure 32-6.

NOTE *Since the SAP_CCMS_MONI_BATCH_DP job runs under your name, ensure that your user ID has the authorizations available in the role SAP_BC_BASIS_ADMIN.*

Step 4: Activate Central System Dispatching

By default, the auto-reaction methods are executed in the remote system that is being monitored.

If you want them to run in the central monitoring system, activate this by going to RZ21 | Technical Infrastructure | Configure Central System | Activate Central System Dispatching. The job that performs the central system dispatching is SAP_CCMS_CENSYS_DISPATCHER, as shown in Figure 32-7.

The steps involved in setting up monitors for remote systems are explained next.

Step 5: Create RFC Destinations

Create the required RFC connections using SM59 in the central monitoring system for connecting to the remote SAP system.

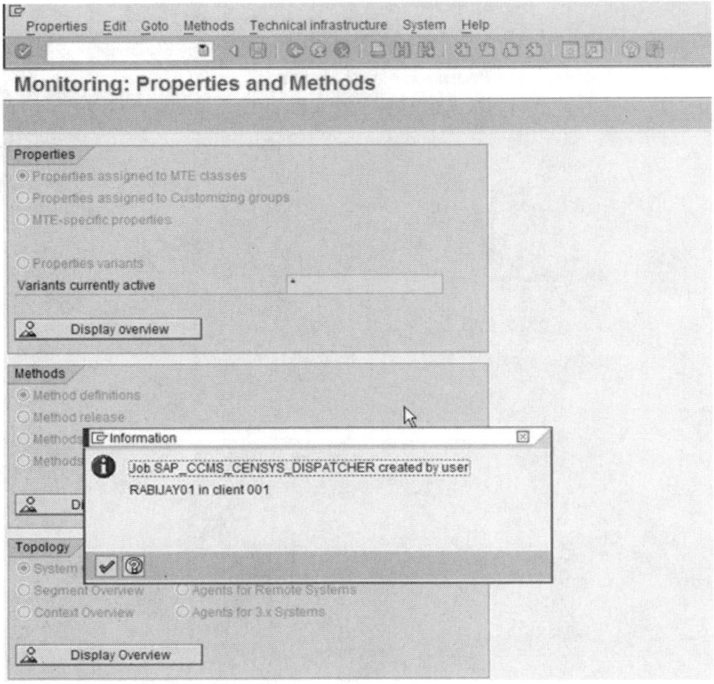

Copyright by SAP AG

Figure 32-7 SAP_CCMS_CENSYS_DISPATCHER job for central system dispatching

You need two RFC connections: one is used by the central monitoring system to connect to the remote system for transferring the monitored data in the remote system to the central monitoring system, and the other is used for conducting remote analysis of alerts in the alert monitor.

The first RFC destination uses the user CSMREG of type CPIC (for SAP BASIS 4.6D and below) or Communication. The second RFC destination uses the current user.

Step 5a: Create RFC Destinations for a Remote System

To create the first RFC destinations, go to Technical Infrastructure | Configure Central System | Create an Entry for a Remote System. Then choose Go to | RFC Connections. Click Create.

Enter the RFC destination ID, connection type as **3** for an ABAP system, and user name as **CSMREG**. Go to the Technical Settings tab and select Yes for Load Distribution. Enter the target system ID, message server host name in the Message Server field, and logon group in the Group field, and then choose IP address in the Save As field. Save the RFC destination and click Test Connection and Remote Login.

Step 5b: Create RFC Destinations for Remote Analysis

To create the second RFC destination, repeat the preceding steps, except that you select the Current User for the User field. This user must have authorizations for alert monitors and system management in the monitored system.

If you do not know the name of the message server, go to Transaction RZ03 and check for the instance with *M* in the services column. The first part of the name is the message server host name. To identify the group, go to SMLG transaction.

NOTE *When you save the RFC destinations, the system automatically checks whether the connectivity from the central monitoring system to the remote monitored system works.*

Finally, use RZ20 to change the monitors to include the monitoring tree elements from the remote monitored system. Go to RZ20 and load a monitor from a monitor set. Choose Extras | Activate Maintenance Functions and then choose Change Monitor and select the remote SAP system from the list of selectable Monitoring Tree Elements (MTEs). Log on if necessary to the remote system and add the MTEs from the remote system to your monitor.

Custom Monitors You can also create your own monitors, which would be necessary if you want to monitor a particular combination of monitors such as the CPU, the memory, and the threads. The monitors can span across multiple systems as well.

Static, Rule-Based, and Virtual Monitors Monitors can be static, rule-based, or virtual. *Static monitors* are manually selected, while *rule-based monitors* are selected by the system based on selection rules in the monitor. *Virtual monitors* can also be created; these are basically titles or labels that can be used mainly for visualization purposes by grouping together related MTEs.

Step 6: Register the SAPCCMSR Agent

Part of the installation process is the registration of the SAPCCMSR agent. For monitoring the Java systems, you should use the SAPCCMS agent. The monitored data are available in the monitor set SAP J2EE Monitor Templates in the alert monitor RZ20 of the central monitoring system.

The actual process for registering the agent would vary depending upon whether it is an SAP NetWeaver AS Java or SAP NetWeaver AS Add-in installation. In the case of SAP NetWeaver AS Java installation, the agent needs to be registered and started only once for each SAP NetWeaver AS Java instance.

Only one connection needs to be made to the remote central monitoring system. In the case of SAP NetWeaver AS Add-in installation, the agent should be registered once for the SAP NetWeaver AS Java to the local SAP NetWeaver AS ABAP system and then the agent should be registered to the central monitoring system for each Java instance.

Step 6a: Download the CCMS Agent

To download the CCMS agent, go to the service marketplace at http://service.sap.com/swdc. In the navigation bar, choose Download | Support Packages and Patches | Entry By Application Group | SAP NetWeaver | SAP NetWeaver | SAP NetWeaver 2004s | Entry By Component | Application Server ABAP | SAP Kernel 7.00 32/64 BIT | *<Operating System>* | Database Independent.

If the CCMAGENT.SAR file is not available for a given operating system, then go to the other links by choosing Download | Support Packages and Patches | Entry By Application Group | SAP NetWeaver | SAP NetWeaver components (*<SAP NW04>*) | SAP Web AS | SAP Web AS 6.20 | SAP Web AS ABAP | SAP Kernel 6.20 32/64-BIT | *<Operating System>* | Database Independent.

Look for the SAP R/3 version by choosing Download | Support Packages and Patches | Entry By Application Group | SAP Application Components | SAP R/3 | SAP R/3 4.6A | SAP Kernel 4.6D 32/64-BIT | *<Operating System>* | Database Independent. This file contains all three types of CCMS agents.

Step 6b: Download the SAPCAR Tool

Download the SAPCAR tool, if you do not have it already from the Additional Components section in the SWDC.

Step 6c: Decompress the CCMS Agent

Decompress the CCMS agent SAR file using the command

```
sapcar -xvf CCMAGENT_<VERSION>.SAR
```

Step 6d: Generate the CSMCONF File

Generate the CSMCONF file, which will contain the connection details for the agent to connect to the central monitoring system. Go to RZ21 | Technical Infrastructure | Configure Central System | Create CSMCONF Start File For Agents.

Save the file to the following path:

- **Windows** *<drive>*:\usr\sap\ccms*<SID>*_*<instance_number>*\sapccmsr
- **UNIX** /usr/sap/ccms/*<SID>*_*<instance_number>*/sapccmsr

This file should be copied to all the instances that need to be monitored. Figure 32-8 displays a section of the CSMCONF file.

FIGURE 32-8 CSMCONF configuration file for SAPCCMSR agent

```
# Configuration file for SAP CCMS agent program sapccmsr
# generated by D11 at 20070130 044123


CEN_CONFIG
  CEN_SYSID=D11
.


CEN_ADMIN_USER
  CEN_ADMIN_R3NAME=D11
  CEN_ADMIN_MSHOST=crmser
  CEN_ADMIN_LOADBALANCING=N
  CEN_ADMIN_ASHOST=crmser
  CEN_ADMIN_SYSNR=01
#  CEN_ADMIN_LOADBALANCING=Y
#  CEN_ADMIN_GROUP=PUBLIC
  CEN_ADMIN_CLIENT=001
  CEN_ADMIN_USERID=RABIJAY01
  CEN_ADMIN_PASSWORD=
  CEN_ADMIN_LANG=EN
  CEN_ADMIN_TRACE=0
.


CEN_GATEWAY
  CEN_GATEWAY_HOST=crmser
  CEN_GATEWAY_SYSNR=01
.


CEN_CSMREG_USER
  CEN_CSMREG_R3NAME=D11
  CEN_CSMREG_MSHOST=crmser
  CEN_CSMREG_LOADBALANCING=N
  CEN_CSMREG_ASHOST=crmser
  CEN_CSMREG_SYSNR=01
#  CEN_CSMREG_LOADBALANCING=Y
#  CEN_CSMREG_GROUP=PUBLIC
  CEN_CSMREG_CLIENT=001
  CEN_CSMREG_USERID=CSMREG
```

Step 6e: Ensure the CCMS Agent Is Running

In Windows, go to the directory *<drive>*:\usr\sap*<SID>**<instance_directory>*\, which contains the sapccmsr.exe file.

Depending on whether it is a Java standalone or a double stack, the *<instance_directory>* location will vary. For Java standalone, it is JC*<instance number>*. For the central instance of a double stack, it is DVEBMGS*<instance number>*, and for a dialog instance, it is D*<instance number>*.

If the EXE file cannot be found in any of these locations, it may be present in the Windows run folder at *<drive>*:\usr\sap*<SID>*\SYS\exe\runU (or ...\run).

Step 6f: Register the CCMS Agent in Visual Administrator

The agent is then registered with the monitoring service in Visual Admin as shown in Figure 32-9.

1. Navigate to Cluster | Dispatcher | Services | Monitoring | CCMS Agent Configuration.
2. Enter the following fields:
   - System ID
   - Enable CCMS Customizing should be checked. This automatically creates a JCO connection from the Java system to the CMS and an RFC connection from the CMS to the Java system.

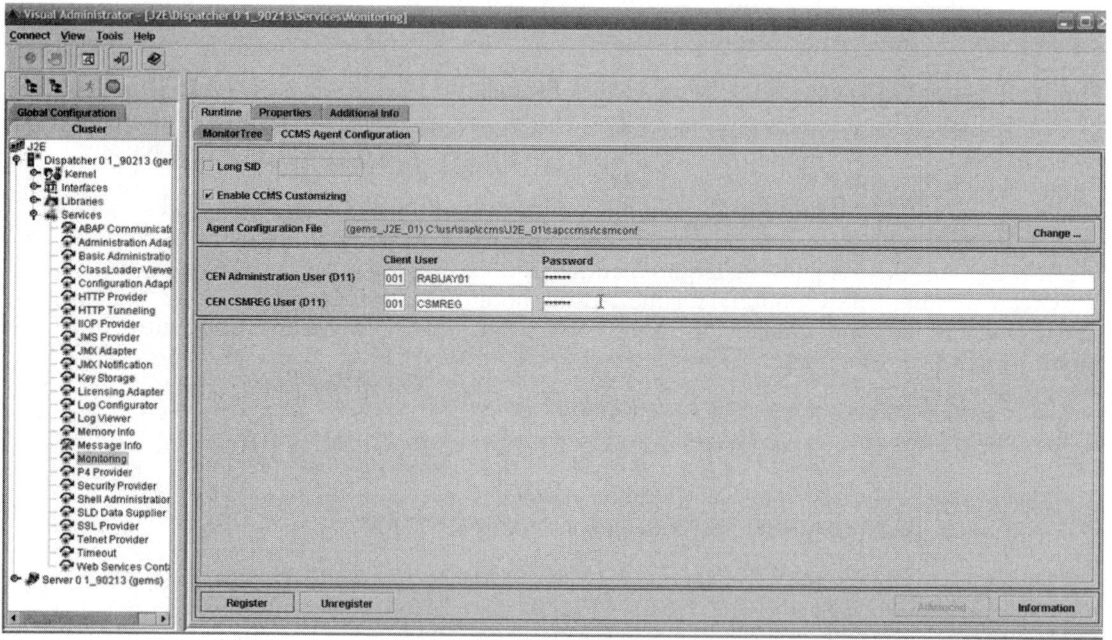

FIGURE 32-9 Registering CCMS agent in Visual Admin

- Agent Configuration File (/usr/sap/ccms/<*SID*>_<instancenumber>/sapccmsr/csmconf)
- Agent Executable (/usr/sap/<*SID*>/exe/sapccmsr.exe)
- Password for Administrator User (user used to create the CSMCONF start file)
- Password for CSMREG user

3. Click Register

NOTE *In Windows, the agent is registered as an automatic service. Sometimes you will have to configure it as automatic. In UNIX, it starts with startsap.*

Step 6g: Verify the Registration

To check whether the registration succeeded, go to System Overview | Display Topology | Agents for Remote SAP Systems in RZ21. If the preceding steps to register the agent in the Visual Administrator do not work, follow the manual steps as outlined here:

To start the agent, use this command

```
sapccmsr -j2ee -R pf=<path of the instance profile>
```

Note that you must be a local admin when running this command.

Confirm the connection data retrieved by the agent from the CMSCONF file by pressing ENTER. Enter the passwords for the CSMREG and the administration users, and confirm all the displayed values by pressing the ENTER key.

Step 7: Register the Agent for the Double Stack System

Now let's take a look at how to register the agent for double stack systems (both ABAP and Java). To begin with, you must first register the agent with the ABAP system and then register the agent with the central monitoring system.

Create a CSMCONF start file as mentioned in step 6d for the ABAP instance and save it as CSMCONF1 in the host with the Java instance that needs to be monitored. Ensure that the CSMREG user exists with the required authorizations.

Create another CSMCONF file for the central monitoring system and save it as CSMCONF2 in the same directory. Edit the CSMCONF2 file by changing CEN (central monitoring system) to CEN2:

- Change CEN_CONFIG to CEN2_CONFIG
- Change CEN_ADMIN_USER to CEN2_ADMIN_USER
- Change CEN_GATEWAY to CEN2_GATEWAY
- Change CEN_CSMREG_USER to CEN2_CSMREG_USER

Then you can merge the two files in the proper sequence and name them as CSMCONF file. The entries in the CSMCONF2 (for the CEN) file should follow the entries in the CSMCONF1 file. These steps should be repeated for all the ABAP instances so that you can have a final CSMCONF start file that can be used to register the CCMS agent in the Java instance host that needs to be monitored with that of the other ABAP systems and the CEN host.

The steps to register the agent are the same as the steps outlined in step 6f.

Step 8: Create Customizing Destination in Visual Administrator

If the manual process was followed to register the agent, you should create a customizing destination in the Java instance using the Visual Administrator as shown next.

NOTE *The customizing destination helps to change the monitor's threshold values from within the RZ20 in the central monitoring system instead of changing in the Visual Administrator.*

1. Create an RFC destination pointing to the central monitoring system by logging in to Visual Administrator in the monitored J2EE engine, then go to Server | services | JCO RFC provider | Runtime.
2. Select the Bundles tab and create a new RFC destination. In the Program ID field, enter **SAP.CCMS.J2EE.<*SID*>**, where <*SID*> points to the system ID of the JAVA instance that is being monitored. Refer to the connection parameters in the CSMCONF file and enter the connection data required for the central monitoring system.
3. Create an RFC destination in the ABAP system where the agent was registered before. Go to SM59, click Create, and enter the RFC destination name as **SAP .CCMS.J2EE.<*SID*>**, where <*SID*>is the system ID of the monitored Java instance.
4. Select T as the Connection Type. In the Technical Settings tab, select Registered Server Program in the Activation Type section and enter **SAP.CCMS.J2EE.<*SID*>** in the program ID input field, where <*SID*> is the SAP system ID.
5. In the Gateway option, enter the gateway information of the local ABAP system. Select Unicode in the Special Options or the MDMP and UNICODE tabs (depending on the version you are in).
6. Click Save.

Step 9: Update the System Topology

Now you need to update the system topology in the monitoring architecture using RZ21. For a double stack monitored instance, select Topology | Agents for Local System | Display Overview.

For a standalone monitored J2EE system, go to Topology | Agents for Remote Systems | Display Overview, as shown in Figure 32-10. Switch to change mode and enter **SAP.CCMS .J2EE.<*JSID*>** created in the previous steps in the column J2EE Customizing Destination. Click Save.

Troubleshooting

If problems occur, do the following:

- If the agent is not ONLINE in RZ21, check the sapccmsr service in the J2EE server.
- Check sapccmsr.log, install.log, and dev_rfc.trc files in the sapccmsr folder.
- Check the CSMCONF file.

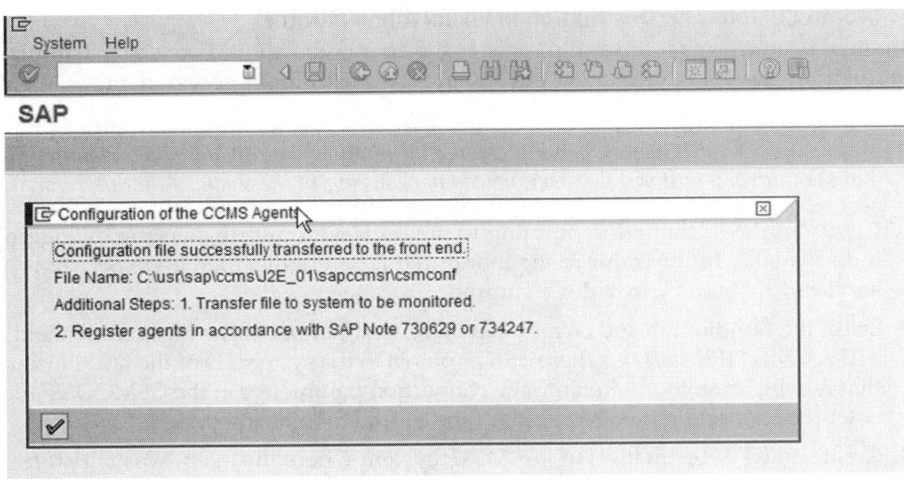

The following offers explanations for some of the fields shown in the Agents for Remote SAP Systems tab of the Monitoring Display Technical Topology (RZ21) screen, shown in Figure 32-10.

- **System** System ID of the monitored system
- **Destination** RFC destination of the monitored segment
- **Communication Status** *ONLINE* means the system is being monitored. *OFFLINE* means monitoring of the system was manually deactivated. *SHUTDOWN* means the system is not active. *COMM.FAIL* means the system RFC call failed.
- **Responsible Server** RFC destination used internally by the CCMS

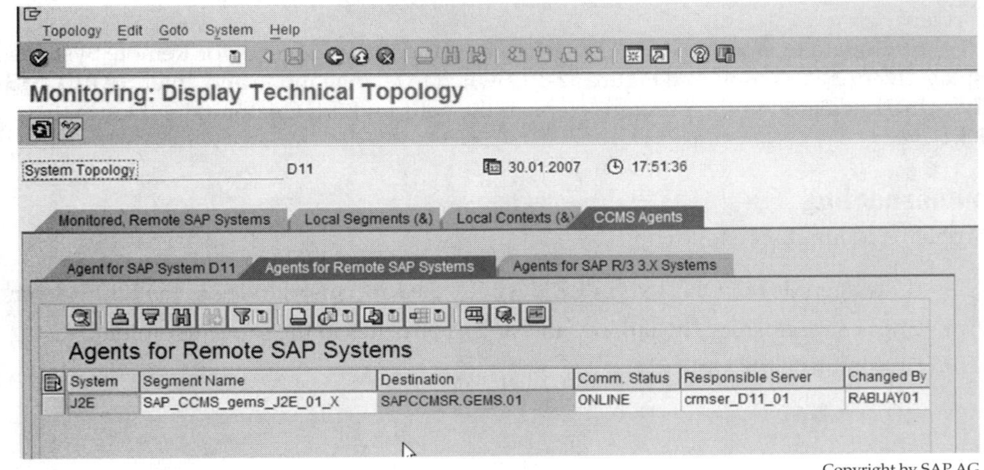

FIGURE 32-10 System topology for remote SAP systems

How to Use the CCMS Tool

Let's now discuss how to analyze the CCMS monitoring data using the RZ20 transaction.

Display the Monitors

To display the monitoring data, go to RZ20 and select SAP J2EE Monitor Templates. Then click the required monitors such as the engines monitor and applications monitor and choose Monitor | Start Monitor. The system will display all the objects and attributes under that monitor.

Choose Current System Status if that view is not already displayed. The MTEs will show different colors, conveying information regarding the status of the components. Green implies the component is okay, red implies there is a problem, yellow is a warning, and gray means no data are being supplied yet for the MTE. Choose Extras | Legend to obtain more info regarding the colors and icons.

Display the Alerts

Choose Open Alerts to display the alerts that have not been opened yet for analysis. The color coding now changes to show where the open alerts exist. Now click a yellow or red MTE and choose Display Alerts. The alert browser opens, listing all the alerts in the branch of the MTE tree that were selected.

Analyze the Alerts

Two options are available for analyzing an alert. Select an alert and choose either Start Analysis Method or Display Details. Choosing Start Analysis Method will open the problem analysis transaction or the method associated with the alert. Display Details will display the current status messages, current values, threshold values, and performance data for performance-related MTEs. For performance MTEs, select Display Performance Values Graphically to display the graphs. Finally, you can delete the alert from the Open Alerts view by choosing Complete Alert.

Standard Monitor Templates

SAP J2EE Monitor Templates contain the monitor sets for the J2EE Engine, Adobe Document Services (ADS), CCMS Self Monitoring, engine performance, engine services, engine systems, engines, and engines OS.

The engines monitor displays data regarding the status of the kernel, system, services, and performance. The applications monitor displays application data for SAP Portal, KM, and so on. The operating system monitor helps to monitor CPU performance attributes such as the CPU load in percentages, 5minLoadAverage, and Unused CPU; to monitor paging attributes such as PageIn for Windows systems, PageOut for UNIX systems; and to monitor process (server and dispatcher processes) attributes such as process count, CPU used, and VM consumption.

Autoreaction Methods

Alerts can be generated using auto-reaction methods to inform a problem. Alerts can then be set to Completed after the problem is addressed. They will also be set to Automatically Completed if the alerts were not set to complete manually.

After making all these changes, you should now be able to make the changes to the threshold values of the alert monitors using RZ20. You can also change the auto-reaction methods to configure what should happen when an alert is triggered and who should be notified when such an event happens.

Configuring the CCMS for E-Mail Alerts

To configure the CCMS for e-mail alerts, do the following:

1. Choose RZ21. Select Method Definitions | Display Overview | Select CCMS_OnAlert_E-mail | Edit Data.
2. Choose Display | Change, and open the Parameters tab. Enter the values for SENDER, RECIPIENT, and RECIPIENT-TYPE ID.
3. In the SENDER field, enter the name of the person in whose name the e-mail should be sent. The format is *C11:030:JOHN*, where *C11* is the system ID, *030* is the client, and *JOHN* is the name of the user in that system.
4. In the RECIPIENT field, enter the SAP username of the e-mail recipient or a distribution list that is maintained in client 000 with a list of recipients' names, fax numbers, e-mail addresses, or pagers.
5. In the RECIPIENT_TYPE ID, enter the value **R** for remote addresses.

Configuring the CCMS for a Specific Transaction

Here's how to configure the CCMS for a specific transaction:

1. Go to SE16 and enter **ATRAMONI** as the table name. Click Execute and choose Create.
2. Enter the name of the transaction and the client name. To monitor a client, simply enter * for the transaction and enter the client name. Enter the name for this monitoring object that will be displayed in RZ20. Enter the MTE class name as the same name as the monitor name. Enter the system ID as **<CURRENT>**. Click Save.
3. Go to RZ20, and select Extras | Activate Maintenance Functions.
4. Select the desired monitor set, and choose Create Nodes | Rule Node. Select Rule GET_MTE_BY_CLASS.
5. Click Continue and select the R/3 systems.
6. Enter **MTE class ContextR3DialogFocus**. Then click Continue and then Generate Monitor.

NOTE *Monitoring the transactions could come in handy when setting up SLAs and for ensuring that SLAs are strictly followed.*

GRMG Availability

The GRMG is part of the CCMS monitoring architecture of SAP Web AS ABAP and it consists of two main building blocks: the *GRMG infrastructure* and the *GRMG application*. GRMG availability can be set up to monitor the availability of both technical components and application processes. It can be used to monitor both Java and ABAP applications.

GRMG Application

Technically, the GRMG application is made up of Java Server Pages (JSP), servlets, or Business Server Pages (BSP). The GRMG application is the main component that is responsible for conducting the availability monitoring. To perform availability monitoring, the GRMG application is deployed in the component whose availability needs to be monitored.

The availability monitoring process is triggered when the GRMG infrastructure sends a GRMG request to the GRMG application. The GRMG infrastructure reads the required values from the customizing tables and uses these values to generate the GRMG request.

The GRMG request is then sent to the URL of the GRMG application. The GRMG application then responds to the GRMG request by sending back a GRMG response to the GRMG infrastructure.

The GRMG response is in an XML format. The GRMG infrastructure then receives the GRMG response from the GRMG application and displays the response in the CCMS Alert monitor.

GRMG Scenarios

In the scenario displayed in Figure 32-11, the web server receives the GRMG request from the GRMG infrastructure and forwards it to the GRMG application. The GRMG application then performs the availability monitoring on the monitored components and then compiles a GRMG response that is sent back to the GRMG infrastructure.

Consider a scenario where the request is sent to the SAP Web AS for monitoring an ABAP application. In this case, the GRMG request is sent to the service in the SAP Web AS, which can perform certain activities for availability monitoring and send back the response to the GRMG infrastructure.

FIGURE 32-11 GRMG architecture

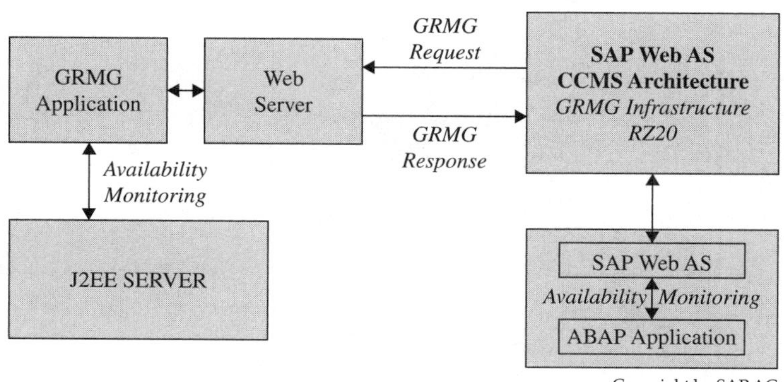

PART VI

Availability Monitoring Using Alerts

The availability of the monitored components is displayed as a percentage in the alert monitor and can be stored in the central performance history. This performance history data can then be used to monitor SLA performance. Alerts are also available in the monitoring architecture, which can then be used to generate auto-reactions for sending e-mails, faxes, and so on.

Availability Monitoring Configuration

GRMG availability monitoring configuration involves defining a GRMG scenario that consists of the applications, components, or processes that are required to be monitored.

NOTE *The GRMG availability monitoring requires a minimum of SAP Web AS 6.20 SP 12 or SAP Web AS 6.30.*

The information required for creating the GRMG request is available in a template file known as the GRMG customizing file. As shown in Figure 32-12, the GRMG customizing

```
 <?xml version="1.0" encoding="UTF-8" ?>
- <customizing>
  - <control>
      <grmgruns>X</grmgruns>
      <runlog />
      <errorlog />
    </control>
  - <scenarios>
    - <scenario>
        <scenname>J2EE_630</scenname>
        <scenversion />
        <sceninst>001</sceninst>
        <scentype>URL</scentype>
        <scenstarturl>http://gems:50100/GRMGHeartBeat/EntryPoint</scenstarturl>
        <scenstartmod>Unknown</scenstartmod>
      + <scentexts>
      - <components>
        - <component>
            <compname>HTTP</compname>
            <compversion>001</compversion>
            <comptype>Unknown</comptype>
          - <comptexts>
            - <comptext>
                <complangu>E</complangu>
                <compdesc>Test for HTTP servic</compdesc>
              </comptext>
            </comptexts>
          - <properties>
            - <property>
                <propname>Unknown</propname>
                <proptype>X</proptype>
                <propvalue>Unknown</propvalue>
              </property>
            </properties>
          </component>
        + <component>
        + <component>
        + <component>
        + <component>
        + <component>
        </components>
      </scenario>
    </scenarios>
  </customizing>
```


FIGURE 32-12 GRMG customizing file

file contains the information regarding the scenario, the components that are monitored, the URL details, and the RFC destinations for ABAP systems.

The CCMS agent should have been installed with the j2ee option in the SAP J2EE Engine and registered with the central monitoring system.

SAP J2EE Engine Availability Monitoring

SAP provides the availability monitoring template for SAP Web AS Java, which is at sap.com/com.sap.engine.heartbeat. This heartbeat is the availability monitor and is located in the monitor set SAP J2EE Monitor Templates in the central monitoring system. This heartbeat template needs to be configured for enabling availability monitoring of the EP. Here's how to install the GRMG availability monitoring for the SAP J2EE engine:

1. Log on to Visual Administrator, navigate to Cluster | Server | Services | Monitoring, and select the GRMG Customizing tab.
2. Under the customizing tree for the sap.com/com.sap.engine.heartbeat app, select scenario | scenariotexts | scendesc.
3. Enter ***<SID>_<host>*** for scendesc and save the changes.
4. Click the Upload icon. This transfers the customizing file to the CMS by the CCMS agent. The CCMS agent checks the /usr/sap/prfclog/grmg folder every 60 minutes.
5. Go to transaction GRMG in the CEN (central monitoring system) and choose Upload/Download | Query CCMS Agent for Scenarios. The scenario that was just uploaded will now be displayed under the URL (scenstarturl) and description (scendesc). This tells us whether the customizing file was indeed uploaded to the CMS.
6. Click the Start/Stop icon to start the GRMG scenario.
7. Go to RZ20. Choose the SAP J2EE Monitor Templates monitor set.
8. Start the Heartbeat monitor.
9. Expand the J2EE engine subtree. The J2EE engine for which the availability monitoring has been activated appears under scendesc.

SAP Portal Availability Monitoring

The template application available for portal availability monitoring is at sap.com/com .sap.portal.heartbeat.

Here's how to set up the GRMG scenario for monitoring the portal:

1. Start Visual Administrator and navigate to Server | Services | Monitoring | Runtime | GRMG Customizing.
2. Under the customizing tree for the sap.com/com.sap.engine.heartbeat application, select scenario | scenariotexts | scendesc.
3. Enter **Portal_*<SID>_<host>*** for scendesc and save the changes.
4. Click the Upload icon. This stores the XML template in the /usr/sap/prfclog/grmg folder and transfers the customizing file to the CMS by the CCMS agent. The CCMS agent checks the /usr/sap/prfclog/grmg folder every 60 minutes.

Additional steps are required for the portal. You need to create a user in the portal with Super Administration role and with no password change option.

NOTE *This step is necessary only when using usernames and passwords for authentication.*

1. Log in to Visual Administrator.
2. Go to Cluster | Server | Services | Security Provider.
3. Choose the User Management tab. Create a user, enter a user name, and enter a password twice. Then click OK.
4. In the User Management tab, enter the user name again and click Search. Select the user and add a checkmark to the No Password Change Required checkbox in the Authentication Group box.
5. Choose the Switch To Edit Mode icon on the top.
6. In the EP, choose User Administration | Roles
7. Enter **super_admin_role** and add the user.
8. Go to System Administration | Permissions | Portal Permissions | Security Zones | sap.com | NetWeaver Portal | high safety | com.sap.portal.heartbeats | components | PortalHeartbeat.
9. Go to Permissions Editor | add the user | assign authorization Administrator = Read | check the User checkbox | Save.

Verify the Uploaded Scenario in the Central Monitoring System

Now you need to verify the uploaded scenario in the central monitoring system:

1. Go to transaction GRMG in client 000 of the CMS.
2. Choose Upload/Download | Query CCMS Agent for Scenarios.
3. When prompted, click Yes.
4. Select the scenario with the description GRMG:J2EE.PI<SID>:<Host> and the URL http://<*Host*>:<*Port*>/irj/servlet/prt/portal/prtroot/com.sap.portal.heartbeats .PortalHeartbeat.
5. Choose Edit GRMG Customizing to adapt the template.
6. If you are using authentication based on username and password, do the following:
   - Set USE_BASIC_AUTHENTICATION to X
   - Set LOGON_USER and LOGON_PASSWORD
   - Enter the previously created username
7. If you are using a client certificate, add a row by clicking Insert Line, and enter the following:
   - Component: **GRMG_RT**
   - Version: **1**

- Property name: **SSL_CLIENT_ID**
- Property value: **ANONYM** (if only SSL and no certificate is used); **DEFAULT** (for standard SAP certificate); or the name of the SSL client PSE

8. Save the changes.

Start the GRMG Scenario and Heartbeat Monitor

1. Select the scenario and click the Start/Stop icon to start the GRMG scenario. If a scenario could not be started, click Start/Stop | Display Status Messages.
2. Go to RZ20 and choose SAP J2EE Monitor Templates monitor set.
3. Start the Heartbeat monitor.

Alternatively, go to SAP CCMS Monitor Templates and start the Availability and Performance Overview monitor. The scenarios will be shown under subtree GRMG-Tested Availability (Web Components).

Useful GRMG Transactions for Troubleshooting

Several problems may arise when dealing with the GRMG. The monitored components may not be available, or an agent may not be running or communications issues occur.

Several GRMG-related transactions can be used for monitoring. Before executing the ICM log transaction, go to transaction SMICM. Then go to Trace level | Set | 3. Then execute the scenario and display the ICM log by navigating to Utilities | ICM log. The ICM log displays any errors when creating the HTTP sessions. Then reset the scenario.

To perform a connection to the host specified in the URL, select Utilities. Then select Ping The Target Host. To trace the route taken by the GRMG request, click Utilities and choose Trace Route to Target Host.

NOTE *For more details, refer to the CCMS and GRMG related resources listed in Appendix B.*

Summary

This chapter discussed the various steps involved in setting up the central monitoring system and discussed how to use the RZ20 monitored data for analysis. It also discussed the steps involved to set up the GRMG availability for the J2EE and the portal scenarios.

33
CHAPTER

Tuning Portal Performance

This chapter discusses how to tune the J2EE engine, the portal server, the network, and the IE browser. When turning a system, you begin by creating a set of performance goals, and then you try to achieve those goals by fine-tuning the system. You need to understand how the application behaves under various conditions before you can finally arrive at a solution. The process involves both trial and error and constant tuning of performance-related configuration parameters to achieve your performance goals.

You should create realistic performance goals based on the available system hardware such as the number of CPUs, amount of available RAM, and other factors. Performance goals should be clearly defined so that they can be easily measured. Testing scenarios should be properly defined and well executed to ensure that the performance goals are achieved.

Tip *One example of a performance goal could be improving the login time in the portal.*

In this chapter, you will learn how to fine tune the J2EE engine by optimizing the JVM parameters, garbage collection settings, log file settings, and disabling the distributed statistics service. You will learn how to optimize network performance by optimizing HTTP compression settings, configuring HTTP service and IE settings. Finally, you will learn how to optimize the portal server by using isolation method property of iViews/pages, configuring server-side caching parameters, global caching parameters, page caching techniques, disabling monitoring and so on.

J2EE Engine Performance Tuning

The following steps are typically involved in tuning the J2EE engine.

Optimize the JVM Settings

The JVM settings can have a huge impact on the overall performance of a system, because right after the installation, these values may not be tuned properly. Performance tests can highlight any discrepancies and help you set the correct values. You can refer to OSS Notes 723909 and 724452 for setting memory settings. Compile a list of OSS notes to deal with memory management.

NOTE *Refer to Chapter 29 for more details on JVM performance improvement.*

Check the Garbage Collection

Check the garbage collection (GC) log to verify the time taken for minor GC and full GC.

You can minimize the number of full GCs and increase the heap size if possible to reduce the number of full GCs. To find the optimum value for the heap size and the ratio between the young generation and the older generation, make the necessary JVM changes and run the performance test for about 30 minutes and repeat it for different values. Check the number of full GCs that take place and choose the setting that contains the lowest value for full GC.

Configure the Log Files

In a productive system, logs should not be enabled during the initial installation as they are likely to consume resources unnecessarily. It is therefore recommended that the log settings be changed to a level that captures only errors.

Here's how to change the log settings:

1. Open the Visual Administrator.
2. Navigate to active Server | Services | Log Configurator.
3. Click Change To Advanced mode to switch to the advanced screen.
4. Open the Categories tab, and change the Severity field in all the logs to Error, as shown in Figure 33-1.
5. Repeat these activities on the Locations tab.
6. The same settings must be repeated for the active dispatcher by going to Dispatcher | Services | Log Configurator and repeating steps 4 and 5 above.
7. Finally, restart the server.

DO *These changes should also be made on other servers and dispatchers.*

If the CCMS is not being used, you should disable it by going to System Administration | System Configuration | Monitoring Configuration. Then, under the Java Application Response Time Measurement (JARM), uncheck Collect Monitoring Data.

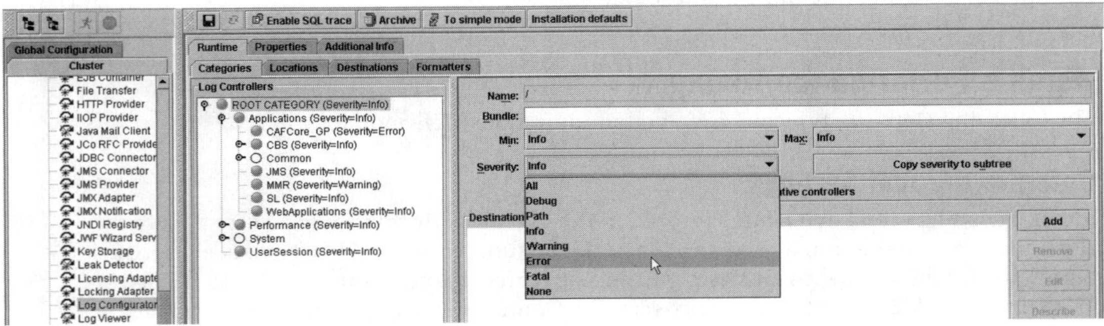

FIGURE 33-1 Changing the log settings in Visual Administrator

When troubleshooting the User Management Engine (UME) Portal Content Directory (PCD) issues, you may have increased the logging levels. However, after completing the troubleshooting activity, you must reduce the logging levels. Otherwise, the portal performance can be degraded to half or a third of its normal performance.

Disable the Distributed Statistics Service

When the number of concurrent users is high, a memory leak can occur when the distributed statistics service is active. Also, logging may result in large files with sizes greater than 40MB in the folders (usr/sap/ccms/dsr (UNIX) and \\\\<*hostname*>\prfclog\dsr (Windows).

Tip *It is helpful to disable the Distributed Statistics Service for NetWeaver 04, Support Package Stacks (SPS) 09, NW 04 SR1, and earlier.*

To disable the distributed statistics service, do the following:

1. Open the config tool and click Switch to configuration editor mode.
2. Choose Configurations | cluster_data | server | cfg | services and double click the Propertysheet dsr-runtime.
3. Click Switch between the view and edit mode icons in the toolbar.
4. Click Yes in the Switch To Edit Mode dialog box.
5. Double-click the property sheet dsr-runtime.

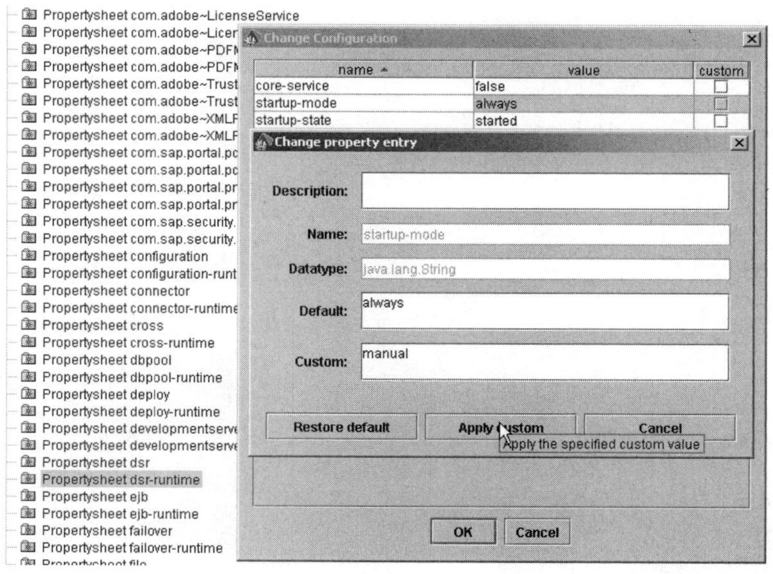

FIGURE 33-2 Disabling the distributed statistical records (DSR) in the config tool

6. Double-click Startup-Mode in the Change Configuration dialog box.
7. In the Change Property Entry screen, enter manual under the Custom field and click Apply Custom, as shown in Figure 33-2.
8. Restart the cluster.

Network Performance Tuning

Several steps are involved when tuning network performance.

J2EE Setting for HTTP Compression

You can improve response times by compressing HTTP responses. However, this may result in an OutOfMemoryError. In such cases, refer to OSS Note 746666 either to switch off compression or use a third-party product such as jazzlib library version 0.07 to implement compression.

Open the config tool, navigate to cluster_data | instance<*ID*> | server<*ID*> | services | http, and change the properties as shown in Figure 33-3.

NeverCompressed

Remove the content types that need to be compressed—*.PDF, *.css, *.js, image, text/JavaScript, application/PDF, and so on—under the NeverCompressed property. This property contains a list of file extensions and MIME types that should never be compressed with gzip encoding. File extensions should start with an asterisk. If the asterisk is missing, the entry is considered as a MIME type.

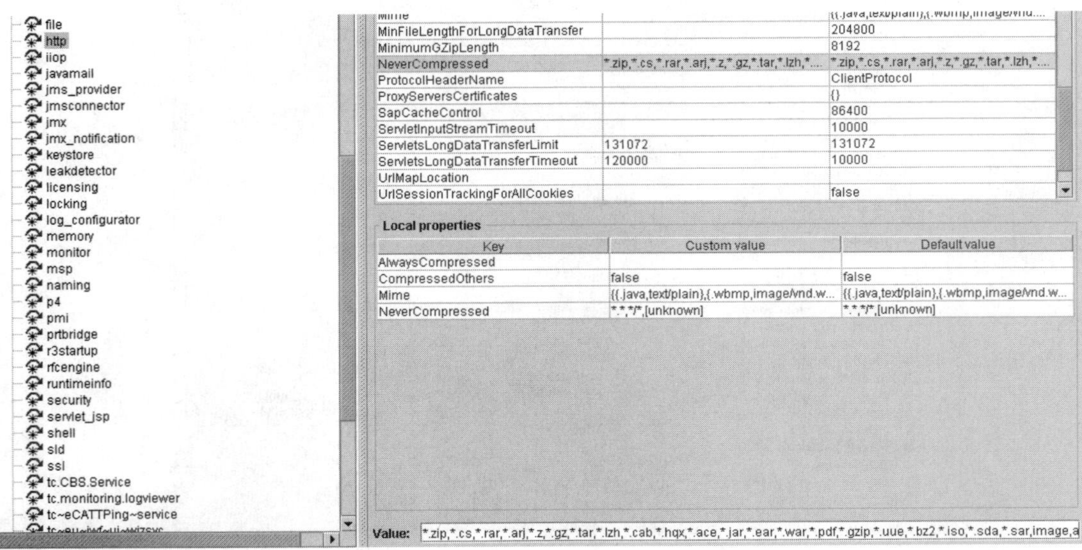

FIGURE 33-3 Changing J2EE settings for HTTP compression

AlwaysCompressed

The same rules apply for the property AlwaysCompressed, which defines the file extensions, and MIME types that are always compressed with gzip encoding. You can use the string *[unknown]* to include responses that do not have the header Content-Type set.

MinimumGZipLength

Both NeverCompressed and AlwaysCompressed work in conjunction with the MinimumGZipLength property. Only those responses that have lengths greater than the value in the MinimumGZipLength property are compressed. Change the MinimumGZipLength property to a lesser value (say, 1024) from its default value of 8192. Be aware that in the case of fast LANs, reducing this value may not help.

DON'T *Reducing the MinimumGZipLength value to less than 1024 is not recommended because of the increased processing power required by the clients while decompressing the content.*

CompressedOthers

The CompressedOthers property enables compression for content that is not defined in both the NeverCompressed and AlwaysCompressed properties.

MaximumCompressedURLLength

The MaximumCompressedURLLength property can be used to prevent compression for responses that are generated for long URLs whose size (in bytes) is greater than that specified in this property. This property will have no impact on compression if the value is –1.

CacheControl

Increase the CacheControl value to a higher value (say 604800 [seconds], which roughly equates to seven days). This controls the duration for which the response from the J2EE engine is maintained in the client cache. By increasing this value, you can reduce the network traffic because it eliminates a number of potential roundtrips to the server.

SapCacheControl

Increase the value of the SapCacheControl from its default value of 86400 (to, say, 604800 seconds). This controls the duration for which the response is stored in the ICM cache. So when a request for similar content is submitted, the request is served directly from the ICM rather than from the SAP NetWeaver AS.

You can also enable response chunking on the servlet_jsp service under cluster_data | instance<*ID*> | server<*ID*> | services. This is a feature of the web container service, which runs on the server nodes in a J2EE cluster. Response chunking can be used in HTTP 1.1 connections that use persistent connections.

Proxy Server Caching

You can also reduce the number of requests to the J2EE engine to almost 50 to 60 percent by implementing caching in the proxy server. Both software and hardware proxy/cache servers are available on the market. Examples of software proxy/cache servers are freeware such as Squid and Apache, and hardware proxy/cache server examples are NetCache and Cache Engine.

HINT *Hardware proxy/cache servers are more reliable than software proxy/cache servers, especially the commercial versions.*

Configure the HTTP Service

Another important service that can be configured is the HTTP service, a server socket that acts like a web server by listening to client connections, parses the incoming requests, forwards them to the correct module for processing, and generates the response back to the client. Shown next is a list of HTTP service properties that you could configure.

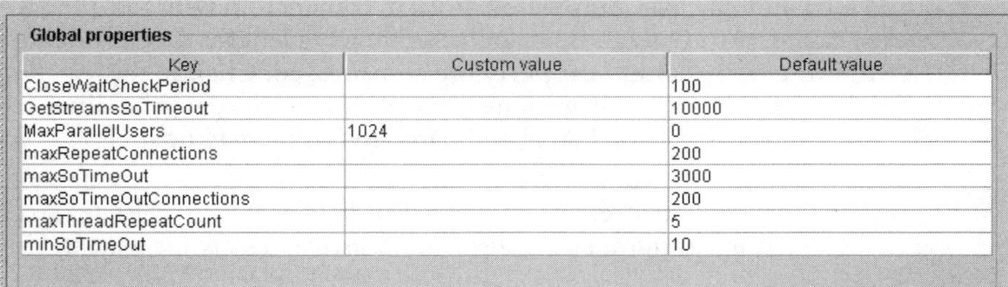

Global properties

Key	Custom value	Default value
CloseWaitCheckPeriod		100
GetStreamsSoTimeout		10000
MaxParallelUsers	1024	0
maxRepeatConnections		200
maxSoTimeOut		3000
maxSoTimeOutConnections		200
maxThreadRepeatCount		5
minSoTimeOut		10

IE Settings

In Internet Explorer, you can enable browser cache and HTTP compression. The browser cache helps to store resources such as images, Cascading Style Sheets (CSS), and JavaScript files and hence improves browser response time.

To enable the browser cache, open the Internet Options applet from the Control Panel. Then open the General tab and under Settings, check the Automatically radio button to check for newer versions of stored pages, as shown here:

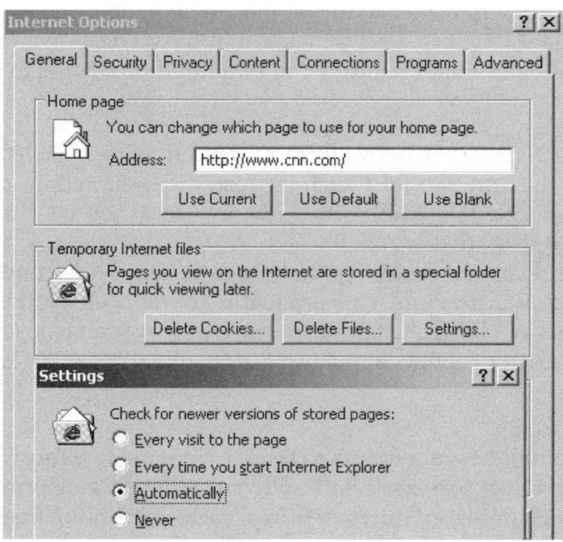

To enable HTTP compression, open the Advanced tab of the Internet Options applet. Scroll down to the HTTP 1.1 setting, and check the Use HTTP 1.1 checkbox, as shown next. If your company also uses a proxy, check the Use HTTP 1.1 Through Proxy Connections checkbox as well.

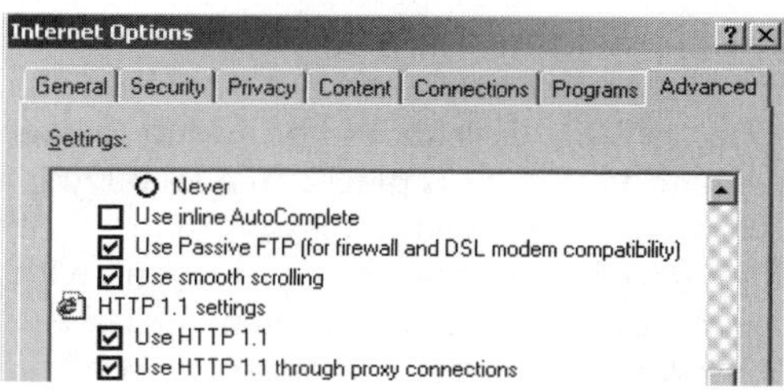

Tuning the Portal Server

Check individual hardware components of the portal platform for any potential performance bottleneck and address tuning possibilities on each one of them. Part of the process is to identify whether you need to add new servers for the J2EE engine either on the same host or on a different host. To make sure that the system is fully utilized, you should configure the memory parameters for the server and dispatcher of the J2EE engine after carefully reviewing the memory usage on these processes. The average CPU usage in the portal server should never be allowed to exceed 80 to 85 percent load for sustained periods of time. If multiple portal servers are installed to share the load, consider the potential increase in CPU utilization that is likely in the event of one or more of the portal servers failing. The load balancer can use SSL acceleration techniques to improve SSL encryption performance.

Do *Make sure that the operating system is properly tuned by referring to the installation guides.*

Isolation Method for iViews

Isolation properties can be defined for both pages and iViews. Isolation properties control how pages and iViews are rendered during runtime and can impact performance. Isolation methods for a page come into play when a page is defined as part of another page. During page design, you should consider whether you should have embedded iViews or isolated iViews.

Embedded iViews

When an embedded iView is used, the HTML source code of the iView is treated as part of the whole page in which it is embedded. The content is assembled at the server and rendered on the client without the involvement of the page builder. The page builder has no control over how the content is displayed. No scrollbars are added and the height of the iView cannot be controlled by the page. Embedded iViews are used when content is retrieved internally from the portal server. Embedded iViews should not be added to a Web Dynpro page. Both client-side (EPCF) and server-side (PRT) events are supported for embedded iViews.

The advantage of embedded iViews is that additional roundtrips to the server are avoided because only one request exists for both the page and the iViews inside the page. The disadvantage of embedded iViews is that whenever a user action is triggered on the iView, the whole page is reloaded along with other iViews on the page.

If one iView has some user information in its input field, it is likely to be lost when the iView is reloaded due to an action triggered on some other iView. For the same reason, embedded iViews and URL-isolated iViews should not be placed on the same page. Since EP 5.0, iViews are URL-isolated iViews, they should be added to pages that contain only URL-isolated iViews. If an embedded iView is placed in a Web Dynpro page, a warning message appears and the iView's isolation method is automatically changed to URL.

The page content area is a part of the desktop inner page along with the detailed navigation panel. So when a user action is triggered on the page content area, the whole desktop inner page is reloaded along with the other detailed navigational panel iViews. This could result in the user losing navigational capabilities because the whole navigational tree is reloaded.

Isolated iViews

In the case of isolated iViews, the client requests multiple requests depending on the number of iViews directly to the content source. So in the case of isolated iViews, the number of requests can be high, but the volume downloaded can be lower when compared to the embedded iViews. Isolated iViews are preferred in situations when content is retrieved externally to the portal server and when iViews will be assigned to the Web Dynpro page.

When the URL isolation method is used for an iView, the iView is placed in an iFrame, which in turn is inserted into the container on a page. Since the iView is placed in its own iFrame, any event triggered in that iView will not impact the other iViews in the page, except in cases where client-side eventing has been used. The page builder has full control over how the iViews are displayed, the height of the iView within the page, and the display of horizontal and vertical scrollbars for the iView within that page.

Note *Only client-side events are supported when using URL isolation methods.*

Since the iView request is treated as separate from the page request, the iView does not receive the input parameters automatically from the page request. You need to use the Parameters to Pass from Page Request property to define the set of URL-based parameters that should be passed from the page to the iFrame containing the iView.

Isolation Method for Pages

Pages that have URL isolation are contained within a separate iFrame within the Content Area. When navigating to the page for the first time, the desktop inner page loads first, followed by the loading of the page. Any subsequent user action that is triggered on the page does not load the desktop inner page. Only the page is reloaded. This results in improved performance, especially when you use iViews with embedded isolation on this page with URL isolation. Caching is also possible for pages that use URL isolation.

When a page with embedded isolation is used, the whole desktop inner page is also reloaded when a navigation action takes place to access the page. However, when a content action is triggered on the iView that has URL isolation, only the content in that iView is reloaded.

URL iViews: Client-Side vs. Server-Side Fetching

The isolation method of URL iViews is by default URL isolated and is therefore displayed within an iFrame in the page. The default value for the fetch mode is client-side, meaning the content is retrieved directly by the client's browser. When client-side fetching is used, the proxy setting on the client's browser is used, and when server-side fetching is used, the proxy setting on the server is effective.

When server-side fetching is used, the client request is submitted to the portal server, which then makes the request to retrieve the content from the content source. Server-side fetching can be slower due to the additional request between the portal server and the content source. When the server-side fetch mode is employed, you can use the portal server cache and the POST request.

TIP *Using a server-side cache can be useful when the actual content source is slow and remote.*

Note that for subsequent user actions, the request for content is made directly from the client to the content source and not through the portal server. Figure 33-4 displays the fetch mode property for iViews.

Server-Side Cache Settings: Cache Level

Server-side caching can be enabled, especially when dealing with static content, by setting the cache level of the iView or page to User, Shared, or Session. This is helpful because the number of requests to the server is reduced, which results in reduced network traffic as well as reduced load on the server. Figure 33-5 displays the settings for the Cache Level property:

- **None** The content is never cached and the iView retrieves content directly from the content source. This is useful for constantly changing information such as displaying news and stock information.
- **Session** The content is cached for a particular session and the cache is cleared for every new logon.
- **Shared** The content is shared across all users. This setting is useful for caching content that is common for all users.
- **User** The content that is specific to a user is cached. This is useful to display the user's daily tasks.

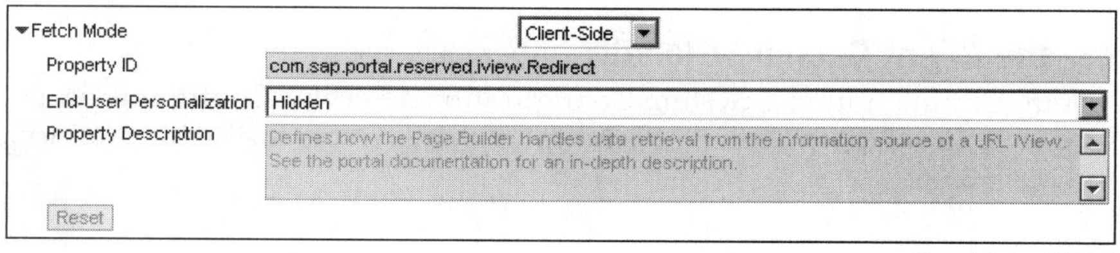

Copyright by SAP AG

FIGURE 33-4 Fetch mode property for iViews

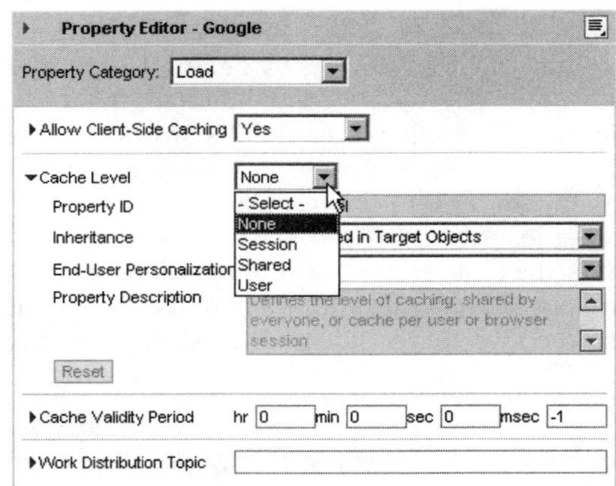

Copyright by SAP AG

FIGURE 33-5 Server-side caching levels

TIP *When trying to choose between Shared and User cache levels, choose the Shared level if the content allows such a choice. In the same way, when trying to choose between Session and User caches, choose User cache if possible.*

Allow Client-Side Caching

If this option is set to Yes, the iView's content is cached in the client browser and in the portal server cache. If the option is set to No, the content is not set in the client browser. If the setting for Browser Only is used, the content is not cached on the portal server, but is stored in the browser.

Cache Validity Period

Here you define the validity period, in milliseconds, for which the cache content is valid. When this period expires, the iView or page updates the content in the cache. Refreshing an iView or page from the Options menu forces the iView or page to retrieve content directly from the content source irrespective of the cache settings.

NOTE *If this value is set to –1, then caching is active at all times.*

Disabling the Client Caching Globally

Go to System Administration | System Configuration | Service Configuration | Applications | com.sap.portal.contentfetching | Services | contentFetchingService, as shown in Figure 33-6.

NOTE *The caching behavior is impacted by this setting only for dynamically generated content for iViews/pages and not for static content such as CSS, js, and images.*

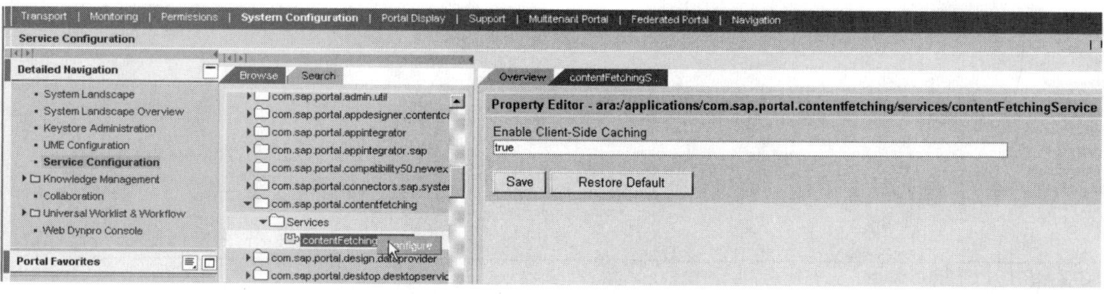

Copyright by SAP AG

FIGURE 33-6 Configuring the content fetching service globally

After making the necessary change, restart the service, as shown next:

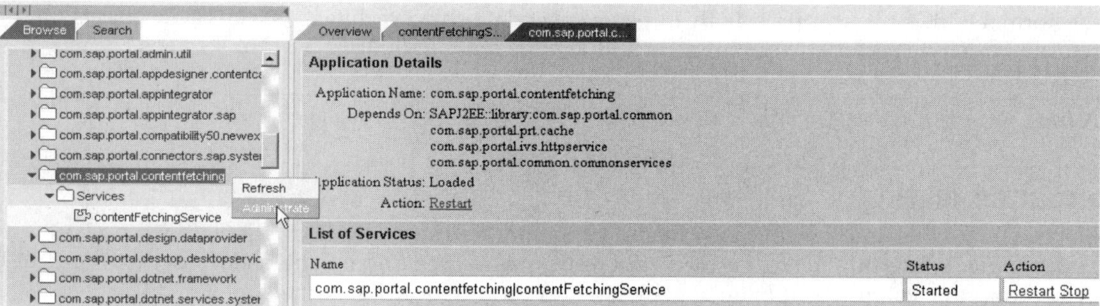

Copyright by SAP AG

Guidelines for Page Caching

Pages with an embedded isolation level should not be cached. If this page is embedded in another page, the `doContent()` method of the embedded page should be executed.

If the page contains iViews with embedded isolation, caching the page helps to cache the iViews as well. If the iViews do not have any caching, the caching parameters of the page will take over. The cache settings on the page should be more stringent than those on the iViews. For example, the cache validity period for the iView should be longer than the cache validity period for the page so that the page caching settings take over rather than the iView settings.

NOTE *If the page contains iViews with URL isolation, caching will not help, because the iView content is retrieved in an additional request.*

PRT Configuration: Turn Off Monitoring

Figure 33-7 displays the settings for PRT properties. In a productive environment, it is recommended that you keep the setting monitor.off set to true to disable the monitor.

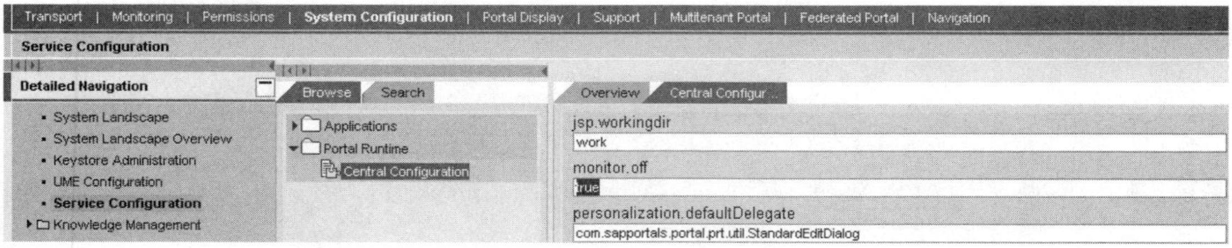

FIGURE 33-7 PRT configuration

Good Java Coding Techniques

To monitor the performance of the iViews, you can use the JARM API in the code to collect monitoring information of iViews. Adopting good Java development techniques such as connection pooling and data object caching can enhance the performance of iViews. To implement connection pooling, you should use the JDBC connector framework API instead of the normal JDBC or JCO approach. By implementing data object caching, you can cache objects returned from the backend systems and enable sharing among multiple users or sessions.

NOTE *Refer to Chapter 15 for more tips on how to develop content for good performance.*

Performance Testing

Before you go live, implement performance benchmarking so that you can track the performance after you go live. Performance testing should be implemented early in the project and the testing should aim at achieving certain performance targets.

GoingLive Check

Before actually going live, a GoingLive Check should be ordered from SAP to check that the system is ready to go live. As a part of the GoingLive Check, SAP will require information on the hardware, number of users, data volume expected, and the available interfaces within the system. The GoingLive Check consists of three phases:

- **Analysis** Around four weeks before going live, SAP checks the system availability and consistency. Proper configuration parameters and sufficient hardware configurations are checked. SAP looks into aspects such as hardware sizing, server configuration, CPU capacity, memory capacity, network connection, database configuration, and SAP configuration.
- **Optimization** Around two weeks before going live, SAP looks into the actual business processes and the transactions involved. Detailed analysis such as statistical records analysis, SQL trace analysis, and transaction optimization are performed. If performance is unsatisfactory, recommendations are provided to improve them.
- **Verification** Around four weeks after going live, SAP confirms the assumptions made during the analysis phase based on the historical data that are available after the Go Live. Additional recommendations, if required, are provided for improving performance.

NOTE *A GoingLive Check can be ordered from the service marketplace at http://service.sap.com/servicecat.*

After going live, you should always make sure that adequate performance testing is undergone and that any major functionality changes are implemented. Comparisons should be made with the pre–Go Live performance benchmark for major variances. The system performance should be periodically reviewed, especially during peak load conditions. Log settings should also be checked to see whether anything has changed that would adversely affect performance.

NOTE *For more details, refer to the documents* How to Fine Tune J2EE Engine Performance, *and* How to Fine Tune Performance of Enterprise Portal 6.0 *and other performance tuning related resources listed in Appendix B*

Summary

This chapter discussed the need for performance tuning and discussed some of the steps involved in tuning the system. In the J2EE engine, you learned about the need for tuning the JVM parameters, garbage collection, changing the default log levels, and disabling the distributed statistics service, if possible. To improve network performance, you learned about using HTTP compression on the J2EE server as well as using proxy server caching. The chapter also discussed portal server tuning aspects such as using the correct isolation property for iViews and pages, using server-side fetching for URL iViews, and choosing the correct server-side caching levels for the portal server.

PART VII

Portal Security

CHAPTER 34

Implementing Authorization Using Permissions, Security Zones, and UME Actions

This chapter takes a look at some of the options available for authorization of users to access content. You will learn about concepts such as permission models, security zones, safety levels, and User Management Engine (UME) actions. After reading this chapter, you will be able to assign appropriate permissions to portal contents, use security zones to secure URLs, and learn the importance of UME actions when assigning portal roles.

Authorization is different from *authentication*. Authorization helps to control whether a user can access a portal content object after login and the nature of actions that the user can take, such as create, change, and delete the object. Authentication is used to authenticate the credentials that a user submits before logging onto the portal. It is also used in the portal to authenticate a user who is trying to access portal content such as iViews and pages.

Authorization on the portal can be implemented using three techniques:

- Permissions model
- Security zone concept
- AuthRequirement property

Permission Model

Permissions are based on the access control list (ACL) concept; they help to define the user's rights regarding the objects in the Portal Content Directory (PCD). The portal content object can be assigned to an ACL, which is nothing but a combination of the level of access to that object and a list of roles, groups, or users who can carry out those actions.

Permission techniques based on the ACL methodology play an important role when setting initial permissions on the portal and also for implementing delegated administration of content.

NOTE *If permissions are not set properly after the implementation, some users may not be able to view the portal content objects in the PCD or the PAR files while creating iViews.*

Permissions can be set on all PCD objects—pages, iViews, worksets, roles, folders, systems, packages, and layouts. However, they cannot be set on the folders that exist within the role's content structure. Usually the ACLs are assigned to the various portal content objects by either the security administrator or the content administrator.

Levels of permission can be assigned to the portal content object and are broadly classified into the following:

- **Administrator-level permissions** Design-time permissions that control whether the administrator can create, change, or delete portal content objects during design.
- **End user–level permissions** Runtime permissions that control whether the end user can display the object during runtime.
- **Role assigner permissions** Applicable only to role objects; they control whether the user or the role or group to which the user belongs can assign roles to other users or groups, and vice versa. This permission is usually assigned to security administrators.

Administrator-Level Permissions

Following are the different levels of administrator permissions.

None This permission level is assigned mainly to roles when they have to be accessed purely in the runtime context. In such situations, end user access is assigned for that role. In the case of other portal content objects and folders, this permission level is not visible in the PCD.

Read This permission level allows the user, group, or role to view the object in the PCD using either browse or search. It allows the user to open the object in read-only mode, and allows users to create delta links and copies of the object. Once the object copy is created and then assigned to another object, the permissions on the object copy are determined based on the permissions on the target object. For example, if you created a copy of an iView and assigned it to a page, the new iView would assume the permissions of the target page.

Read permission allows the user to use the object as a template in the object creation wizards. It can also be assigned to PAR files, which will then appear in the iView creation wizards. The Edit Option will not be available for the objects in the PCD.

Write This permission level is applicable only to folders and not to objects within the folders. This permission level allows the user to create objects within the folder. It can also be assigned to the Everyone group if the end user is required to create and share content within the group.

Read/Write In addition to the access provided by the Read and Write permissions, additional permissions are possible. Read/write allows the user to add or remove child objects from a parent object and to edit the object properties. To copy an object, read permission on the object is sufficient, and adding that object to a destination folder using Paste or Paste as Delta Link requires read/write permission to that target folder. The Delete option will not be available for the objects.

Full Control Full Control provides the ability to delete, cut, and edit the object properties.

Owner Owner permission provides the ability to assign permissions for and delete an object.

Administrator-Level Permissions for Security Zones and Portal Components

The administrator permissions can be assigned to the portal components and the security zones, which can be accessed using the System Administration | Permissions in the top-level menu and Portal Permissions in the detailed navigation menu.

Following are some permission levels that can be assigned to the security zones and portal components:

- In the case of security zones, only Owner, Read, and None permissions are relevant, as shown here:

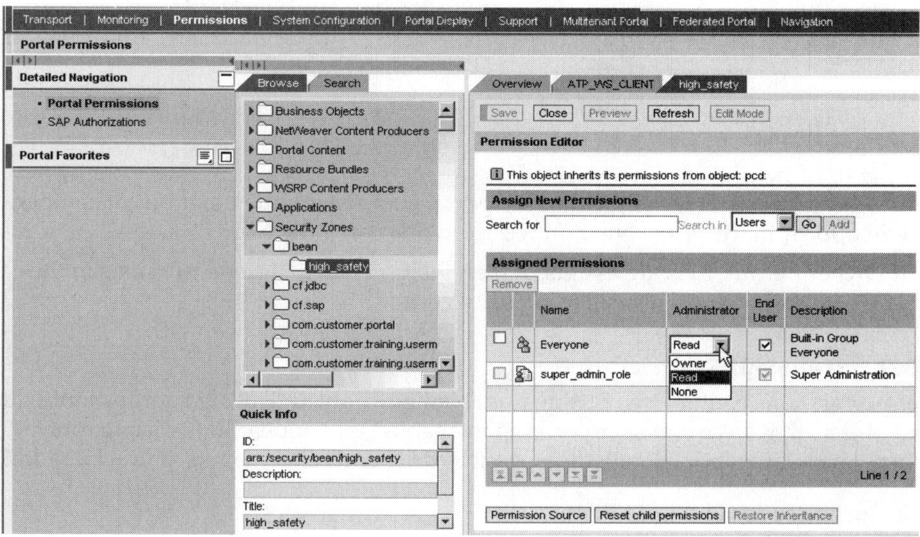

- If None is assigned to the security zones, then the security zones cannot be viewed by the user.
- If Read permission is assigned to the security zone, then it appears in the portal catalog for the user.

- Only Read and Owner permissions are allowed for the portal components, as shown next:

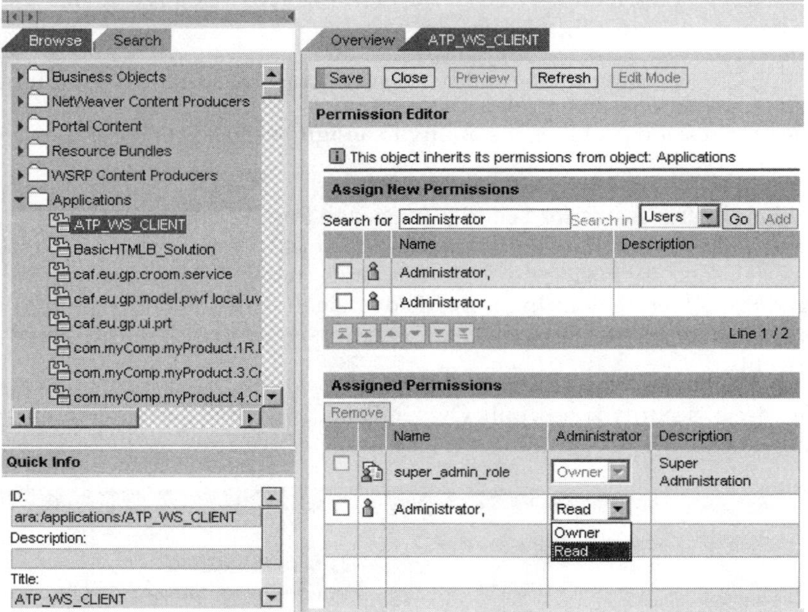

- If Read permission is assigned to the portal component, then that portal component will appear in the iView creation wizard while using the New From PAR option.
- If Owner permissions are assigned, then the user can assign permissions in the case of portal components as well as security zones.

End User Permissions

End user permissions contain two settings: enabled or disabled. During runtime, only those roles and objects that have end user permission enabled will appear in the navigation iViews (top-level navigation, detailed navigation, drag and relate targets, and related links).

Use Case Scenarios for End User Permissions

Some of the use case scenarios for end user permission are presented here:

- A content administrator can have administrator permissions assigned to a role that allows her to work with the role in the role editor, but if she does not have end user permission for that role, then she cannot view the iView or page contained within that role.
- End user permission allows access to a portal component directly through the URL, provided the portal component has been assigned to a security zone with end user permissions for the user. This provides an additional layer of security in addition to the access control provided by roles.

- If an iView is used to display data from a backend system, and if a system object has been created for that purpose, then that system object should have end user permission for that user.
- If a content administrator has full control on the iView but no end user permission for the iView, then that iView will not appear in the list of iViews for page personalization when the administrator is logged on to the portal as an end user.
- The end user permission is not available for portal components; it applies only to security zones.
- The end user permission does not apply to resource bundles, rule collection, portal desktop, or portal themes.
- Having end user permission for an iView does not determine which iView properties can be personalized during runtime. This would depend on the End-User Personalization settings for each property in the Property Editor. This was discussed in Chapter 14.

TIP *If end user permission is not assigned properly, the connectivity with the backend system will fail.*

Default Permissions for Super Administrator Role

The Super Administrator role has owner permission and end user permission on all objects within the portal. These permissions cannot be changed or deleted. This helps in situations when owner permissions have been deleted by mistake and you need to retrieve the user permissions again. In such a scenario, you should log in as the Super Administrator and set the permissions again.

The following illustration displays an example of permissions assigned to a content object:

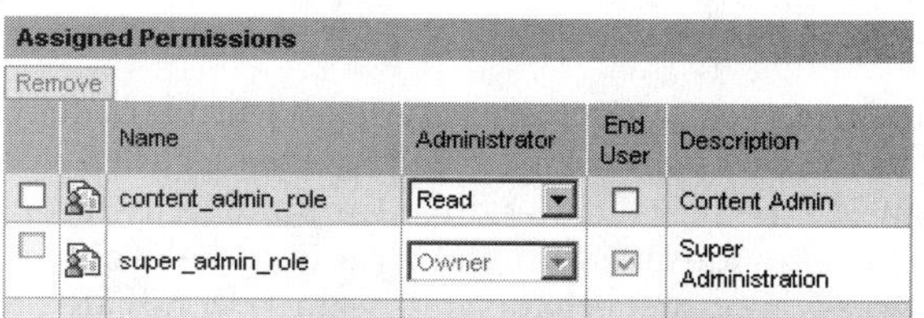

Copyright by SAP AG

Default Permissions for Portal Content and System Objects

The portal content directory and the system folder contain default permissions for the Super Administrator role and the Everybody group:

- The Super Administrator has full control and end user permissions.
- The Everybody group has read permissions and end user permissions.

Role Assigner Permissions to Folder

Role assigner permissions can be applied to roles directly or implicitly by assigning role assigner permission to a folder. The folder permission will then apply to the role objects contained within that folder. This controls which user, role, or group will be able to assign the role to a user or users belonging to group or role.

Multiple Permissions

If a user is assigned multiple permissions by virtue of being part of a role and a group, then the highest level permission will become effective. For example, if the role has full control permissions and if the group has read/write permissions, then the user will have full control permissions to that object.

Permission Inheritance Model

The permissions technique also follows the inheritance model, wherein an object can adopt the same levels of permission that have been set up for its immediate ancestor, if the object has not been assigned permissions explicitly. For example, the objects within a folder implicitly inherit the permissions set up for the folder.

However, when explicit permissions are set up in the content object, the inheritance relationship will be lost. The inheritance behavior can be restored by clicking the Restore Inheritance button in the object editor, as shown here:

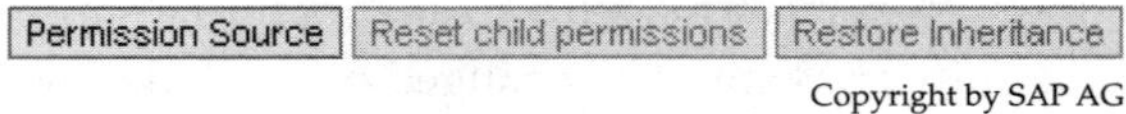

Copyright by SAP AG

Similarly, the child objects, such as the content objects within a role, the iViews within a page, and the contents within a workset, all inherit the permissions of the parent object. It is not possible to change the permissions of the child objects.

Security Zones

Now let's take a look at the concept of security zones and learn how they are used to secure portal components and services. The security zone provides security when an iView is accessed from a URL outside the portal either directly or indirectly through a portal component. Security zones provide an additional layer of code-level security in addition to the permissions-based access control mechanism. If security zones are not defined, the portal components can be accessed only through iViews after authentication and not through the URL.

TIP *Security zones are required if you need to access the portal component through the URL.*

Security zones can be accessed under System Administration | Permissions in the top-level menu and Portal Permissions in the detailed navigation menu. Navigate to Security Zones | *<application>*, right click application and select Open Permissions from the context menu. They are represented as a set of portal applications and services that can be attached to ACLs.

The security zone specifies the following for a component or service:

- Vendor ID
- Security area
- Safety level

Figure 34-1 shows the components of a security zone, in which sap.com is the vendor ID, NetWeaver.Portal is the security area, and high_safety is the safety level.

- **Vendor ID** Normally the ID of the content provider; in the case of SAP-provided content, it is usually sap.com.
- **Security area** A name assigned to the various categories that the developer has assigned to the security zone. This is freely definable. The portal components or services are attached to the security zones.
- **Safety level** Decides the level of authentication that may be required for accessing content that belongs to the security zone under consideration.

Assigning security zones is a two-step process:

1. The security zone is assigned by the content developer at the time of development in the deployment descriptor.
2. The content administrator or the system administrator assigns permissions to users, groups, or roles for the security zone.

NOTE *A portal component or service can belong to only one security zone.*

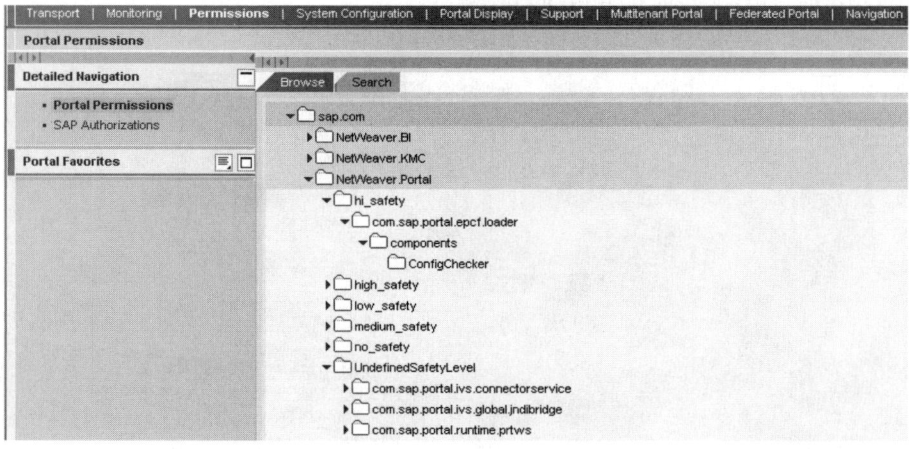

FIGURE 34-1 Components of a security zone

Requirements for Accessing a Portal Component or Service

Following are some of the basic requirements for accessing a portal component or service through the URL:

- The security zone should have been defined in the portalapp.xml file, as shown here:

```
<components>
  <component name="QuoteComponent">
    <component-config>
      <property name="ClassName" value="ws.quote.QuoteComponent"/>
      <property name="SecurityZone" value="ws.quote/high_safety"/>
    </component-config>
    <component-profile/>
  </component>
</components>
```


- The user, group, or role should have been assigned to the security zone with end user permissions.
- The security zones should be activated by setting the Dcom.sap.nw.sz to true.
- The security zone functionality should have been activated in the central configuration file of the portal, namely, the prtCentral.properties file, which can be found under \cluster\server0\apps\sap.com\irj\servlet_jsp\irj\root\WEB-INF\portal\system\properties.

In Figure 34-2, the value for portal.runtime.security.mode is *production*, which means the security zone is mandatory. If the value is *test*, then by default it is possible to access the portal component even if the security zone is missing. If the value is *development*, then there is complete access to the portal component.

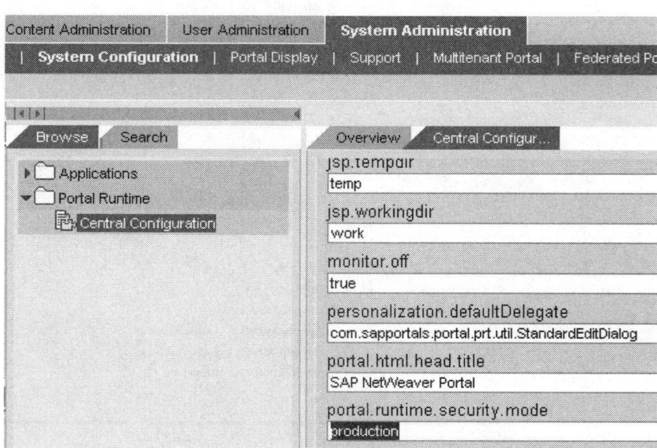

FIGURE 34-2 Portal runtime configuration for security zone

Defining the Security Zones

The security zones can be defined in two ways: via the *computed* method or the *fully specified* method. The computed method is the preferred method. The fully specified method is more prone to errors because of the need to specify the complete combination of vendor ID, security area, and safety levels. If any of the values for the vendor ID or the security area or the safety levels are not defined correctly, the component or service will get defined under the UndefinedVendor, UndefinedSecurityArea, or UndefinedSafetyLevel folder.

Computed Method

In the case of the computed method, the portal runtime computes the security zone based on the following:

- Vendor ID and SecurityArea, defined in the application-config section of the deployment descriptor, namely, portalapps.xml file
- SafetyLevel, defined in the component and service section of the deployment descriptor
- Based on the above values, the security zone is computed for components as *VendorID/SecurityArea/SafetyLevel/portal_application_name/components/component_name*
- For services, the security zone is computed as *VendorID/SecurityArea/SafetyLevel/portal_application_name/services/service_name*

Fully Specified Method

In the case of a fully specified method, a *SecurityZone* property is defined by the developer in the portal application deployment descriptor file known as portalapp.xml. The value of the security zone property is defined as shown here:

- *Vendor_ID/security_area/safety_level/portal_application_name/*
- *Components/component_name*
- *Vendor_ID/security_area/safety_level/portal_application_name/services/service_name*

TIP *If the security zone is fully specified in addition to the value obtained from the computed method, then the fully specified value will take precedence over the computed value.*

Shown next is the portalapps.xml file for the ATP_WS_CLIENT application. The portal component named *QuoteComponent* belongs to the security zone *ws.quote/high_safety*. The security zone is freely definable by the developer.

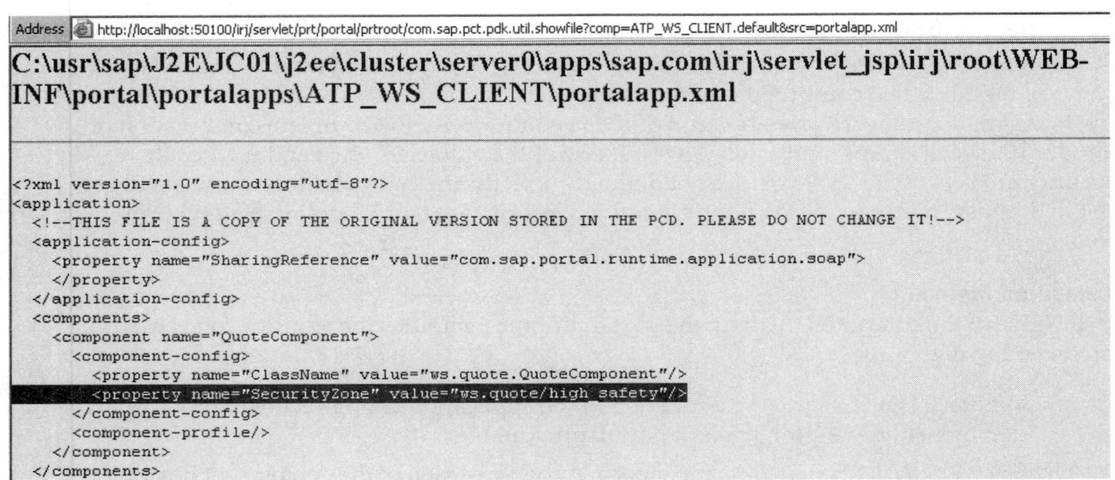

Shown next are the permission levels for the security zone defined by *ws.quote/high_safety*. The application ATP_WS_CLIENT belongs to this security zone and hence this permission level will be applied to that portal component.

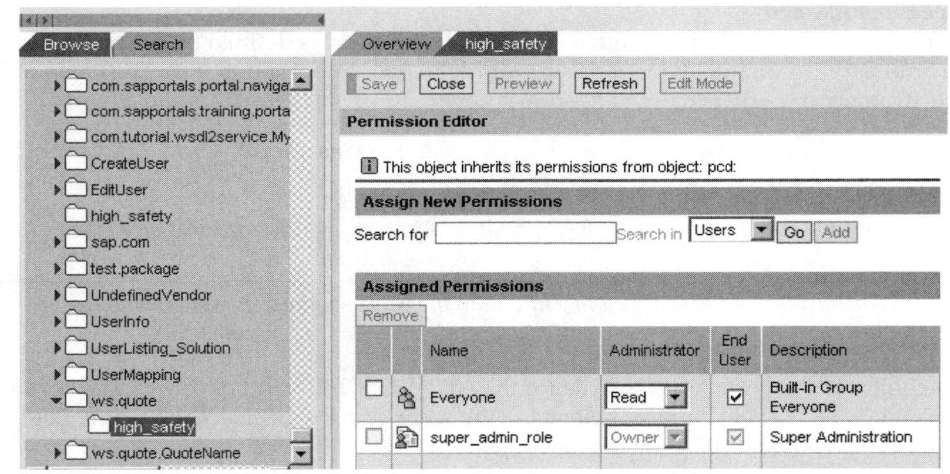

NOTE *Permission levels can be defined by the portal administrator after the developer has assigned the portal application to a security zone.*

Safety Levels

Safety levels are further classifications of the portal components and services into categories, which can in turn be assigned to different sets of ACLs. By doing this, you are able to maintain ACLs using safety levels instead of specifying ACLs at the level of portal components and services. This results in reduced maintenance effort.

Default Safety Levels

SAP comes with default safety levels and default permission levels, as shown in Figure 34-3. These permission levels will remain unaffected during a portal upgrade.

TIP *Permission levels need to be set for additional standard portal content that may have been created as a part of the upgrade.*

The NetWeaver.Portal Security Area contains various safety levels:

- **No_safety level** Contains the Everyone group, which has no administrator permissions but has end user permission enabled. This means that anonymous users can access this content.
- **Low_safety level** Contains end user permissions enabled for the Authenticated group. This implies that only authenticated users can access the portal components and services in this safety level. All the custom applications should be attached to either the low_or no_safety levels.
- **Medium_ and high_safety levels** Contain end user permissions enabled for the system administrator and the content administrator roles. This means that only users belonging to either system administrator or content administrator roles can access this content.

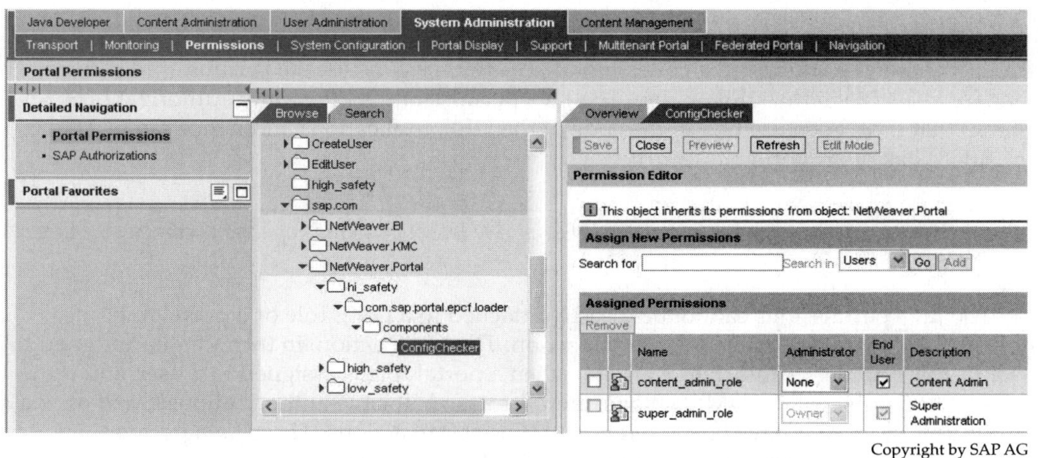

FIGURE 34-3 Default safety levels

Security Zones Example

Here's an example to help you understand the concept of security zones.

1. Access the Portal Administration console and try to upload an application with the security zone added to the application's deployment descriptor.
2. Go to the System Administration | Permissions in the top-level menu and navigate to Portal Permissions | Security Zones.
3. Right click the application and select Open Permissions. Now try to access the application using this URL:

   http://<host:port>/irj/servlet/prt/portal/prtroot/appName.portalComponent
4. You will find that you cannot access the application. Now go back to the permissions editor and add an end user with Read permissions to the security zone.
5. Now try to log on to the portal as an end user and, using the same browser, try to access the application again. You will see that you are now able to access the application.

AuthRequirement Property

The *AuthRequirement* property is available for the portal components and controls the minimum level of authentication needed to execute the portal component. This property can have the following values: User, Admin, None, or *<role list>*. None is used for anonymous content.

NOTE *The* AuthRequirement *property is mainly used for backward compatibility with EP 5.0.*

UME Actions

A UME action is nothing but a collection of Java permissions for the various applications that are available in the J2EE engine. The Java permissions are basically authorization checks that have been defined in the code of the J2EE applications and hence can be considered as programmable security.

NOTE *The Java permissions define at the J2EE engine level what kinds of actions can be taken by the user.*

The Java permissions cannot be directly attached to a UME role or a portal role; however, they can be attached to a UME action. The UME action, in turn, can be assigned to a UME role or a portal role. For example, when a portal role is assigned to a user, and if the portal role consists of the UME actions, then the user will have authorizations based on the Java permissions that have been assigned to those UME actions. These Java permissions will then allow the user to access any UME-based iViews or functions.

Standard UME Actions

A number of standard UME actions are available and are listed under the UMERole.xml file in the config tool under the com.sap.security.core.ume.service drop-down. The UME actions can be displayed either in the portal under the User Administration menu or in the J2EE engine's User Administration Tool section.

In the portal, go to User Administration | Identity Management and select Roles from the drop-down list. When you either create or change a role, you'll see a tab called Assigned Actions.

Default UME Actions

Following is a list of default UME actions available for a role.

UME.Manage_All for Super Admins and User Admins

This UME action is assigned to the Super Administrator and User Administrator portal roles. This action enables the user administrator to manage users belonging to any company, manage groups and roles, map users, export and import user data, and replicate users. The illustration below displays the list of UME actions assigned to the super admin role.

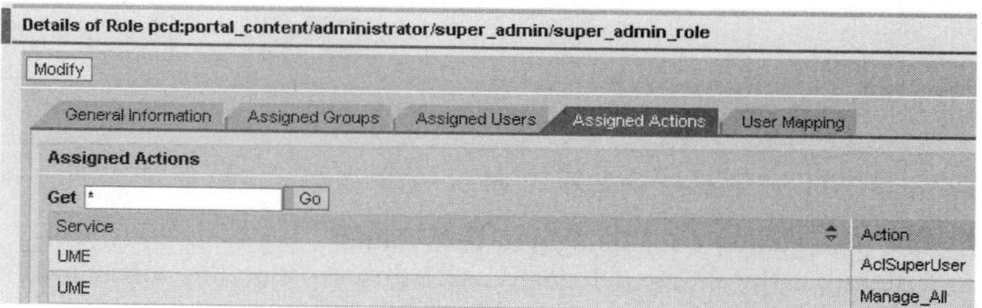

Any user that has a portal role that contains this UME action will automatically have role assigner permissions to all portal roles in the portal installation. This information will be helpful when creating custom portal roles.

The UME.Manage_All action is also assigned to the user administration role. The next illustration displays the list of UME actions assigned to this role.

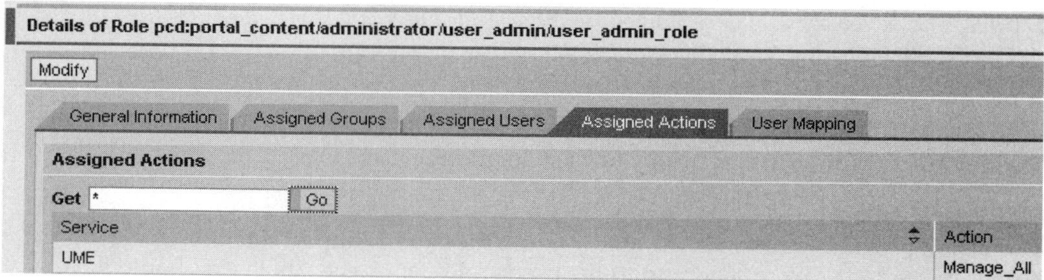

UME.AclSuperUser for Super Administrator

This UME action is assigned to the super administrator role on the portal and care should be taken not to assign this action to any other role. This enables owner permissions on all objects in the portal content catalog. This action is relevant only in the portal scenario.

UME.Manage_Users for Delegated User Admin

This action is used in delegated user administration and is assigned to the delegated user administrator role on the portal. This action provides the ability to delegated user administrators to administer users belonging to the same company as themselves. The illustration below displays the list of UME actions assigned to the delegated user admin role.

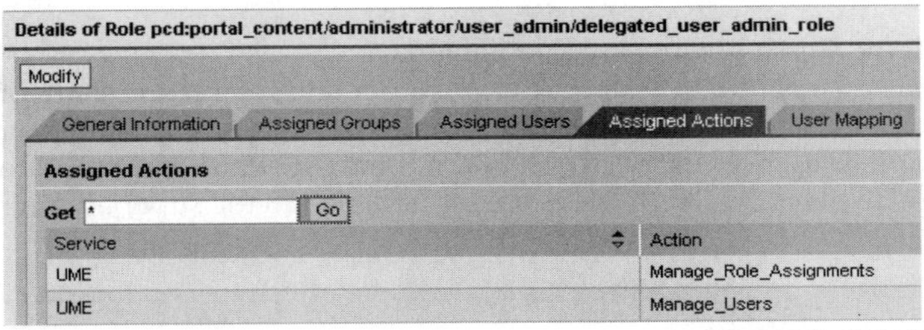

DON'T *Delegated user administrators should not have UME.Manage_All in their roles.*

UME.Manage_Role_Assignments for Delegated User Admin

This is used as a default action in the delegated user admin role on the portal. This allows delegated user admins to assign roles to other users in their company, provided the admins have the role assigner permissions for the roles they are trying to assign. However, this action does not allow the admins to assign roles to groups or change the actions in a role.

UME.Manage_Roles

This action is not relevant to the portal. This is UME-specific action and provides users with this action to add, delete, or modify UME roles.

DON'T *This action should not be assigned to the delegated user admins because this provides the users with the ability to assign administrator roles to themselves.*

UME.Manage_All_Companies

This UME action provides the ability to users to manage users in all companies.

UME.Batch_Admin

This action provides users with the ability to use the export/import functionality in the portal. To be able to export and import the users, roles, or objects, the users should have change access to those objects.

UME and Portal Roles

When you use the Identity Management menu in the portal or the UME console (http://<hostname>:<port>/useradmin) to assign roles, both portal and UME roles will be displayed. While the UME roles drive the actual authorizations in the J2EE engine, the portal roles are more for defining the content the user will view during runtime. Whenever a user is assigned a portal role, the user automatically acquires end user permission for that role, which allows the user to view the contents in that role. While the UME roles are stored in the UME tables of the J2EE database, the portal roles are stored in the PCD tables of the J2EE database.

Administering Portal Roles, UME Roles, and Groups

Let's now discuss the permissions and UME actions required for administering the portal roles and UME roles.

Changing Portal Roles

To create or change the portal roles in the portal content studio, the user should have either a content administrator role or the super admin role. No action is required to create a portal role. However, the user should have read/write permissions to the folder in which the role is created.

Changing UME Roles

To create or change the UME roles, the user should have either UME.Manage_All action or the UME.Manage_Roles action.

NOTE *Portal permissions are not required for UME roles.*

UME roles are created using the Identity Management functionality under the User Management menu on the portal.

Assigning UME Actions to Portal Roles

To assign UME actions to a portal role, either the Portal Content Studio or the Identity Management tool can be used; however, for assigning UME actions to a UME role, you can use only the Identity Management tool.

To assign the actions to a portal role, the following are required:

- Read/write permission on the role so that it can be edited by the user
- The UME actions UME.Manage_All or UME.Manage_Roles
- The user should belong to either a content admin role or a super admin role

Assigning UME Actions to UME Roles

To assign UME actions to a UME role, no portal permissions or roles are required. However, the user should have either UME.Manage_All or UME.Manage_Roles action. As already mentioned, you need to use the Identity Management tool to assign actions to UME roles.

Assigning Portal Role to Users and Groups

For assigning portal roles to users and groups, you should use the Identity Management functionality. The portal role should have the role assigner permissions on the role that is being assigned. However, if the user has UME.AclSuperUser action, then this check is not done when assigning the role. If the user has either a User Admin role or Super Admin role, then by default the user has the role assigner permission on all roles, so he or she can assign any role in the portal. However, this is not true for the Delegated User Admin role.

Assigning UME Role to Users and Groups

To assign UME roles, no portal permissions are required; however, the user should have either of the following combinations of actions: UME.Manage_Roles and UME Manage_Users or UME.Manage_All.

NOTE *For more details, refer to the content administration related resources listed in Appendix B.*

Summary

This chapter discussed the different methods available for implementing authorization. You learned about the different permission levels available including initial permissions and read about how they can be assigned to portal components and security zones. The chapter then discussed the concept of security zones and the need for them. You learned about the fully specified and computed methods for defining security zones, safety levels, and the various UME actions available.

35

CHAPTER

UME Architecture Components

The User Management Engine (UME) is an integral part of the J2EE engine and plays a major role in the user maintenance activities on the enterprise portal. This and subsequent chapters examine the UME architecture, the role played by the persistence stores, the UME principals, UME configuration, LDAP configuration, datasource configuration files, various UME scenarios, UME tools for user administration, and the user data replication functionality.

NOTE *The UME was delivered as part of the Enterprise Portal in Web AS 6.20, but from Web AS 6.40 onward, it has been delivered as part of the J2EE engine.*

Following are some of the salient features of the UME:

- The ability to store user management data in multiple repositories such as the portal database, the Advanced Business Application Programming (ABAP) R/3 systems, or the Lightweight Directory Access Protocol (LDAP) directory. Users who log in to the portal could be authenticated against any combination of these systems.
- The ability to leverage an existing LDAP directory in an organization for user credential information. The LDAP can be used to store user data for the portal as well as synchronize the user data of the LDAP with the central user administration, if this has already been set up for SAP R/3 systems.
- The ability to replicate user data to an external system such as SAP R/3 from the UME of the J2EE using XML.
- A set of UME administration tools are available for maintaining users and groups, changing passwords, unlocking users, and assigning users to groups.
- The ability to implement a self-registration functionality whereby external users can register on the portal and be subjected to approval by user administrators to become fully authenticated users on that portal.

UME Architecture

UME is responsible for managing user objects such as users, user accounts, roles, and groups. The components of the UME can be classified into the following broad categories:

- UME tools
- UME service
- UME API
- Persistence adapter
- Replication manager
- Persistence manager
- UME repository

The advantage of the UME is that all the different portal applications can share the same user objects, thus reducing the maintenance effort. The UME is also available as a web service so that it can be called by external applications.

NOTE *Unification uses the UME as a web service.*

Figure 35-1 displays the various building blocks of the UME. The UME architecture can be compartmentalized into the following layers:

- Portal component
- Portal service
- Portal runtime core

The UME-based tools in the portal component layer provide the user interface for creating, changing, or deleting user objects. Whenever a user administrator initiates a request in the User Management tool, the request is submitted to a portal component. The same thing happens when the portal applications make a call to the portal components. The iViews are based on the portal components and are triggered when the user makes a request to the iViews.

The portal component then calls the UME service, which is responsible for calling the appropriate UME API and for executing the necessary activity, such as creating, changing, or deleting user objects.

The UME API is part of the portal runtime core and is the actual source code that is responsible for creating the user objects. The UME API calls the persistence manager, which is responsible for coordinating with the different UME repositories available for storing the UME data.

The User API is useful for storing/retrieving user-related information such as first name, last name, and so on, while the User Account API provides the ability to create the actual user account and lock/unlock the account in the operating system.

The Group API helps to identify the group to which the user belongs, and the Role API can be similarly used for identifying the roles to which the user belongs.

Persistence Manager

The persistence manager knows which persistence adapter should be called for updating user data and which persistence adapter to call for retrieving the user data. This information

FIGURE 35-1 UME architecture

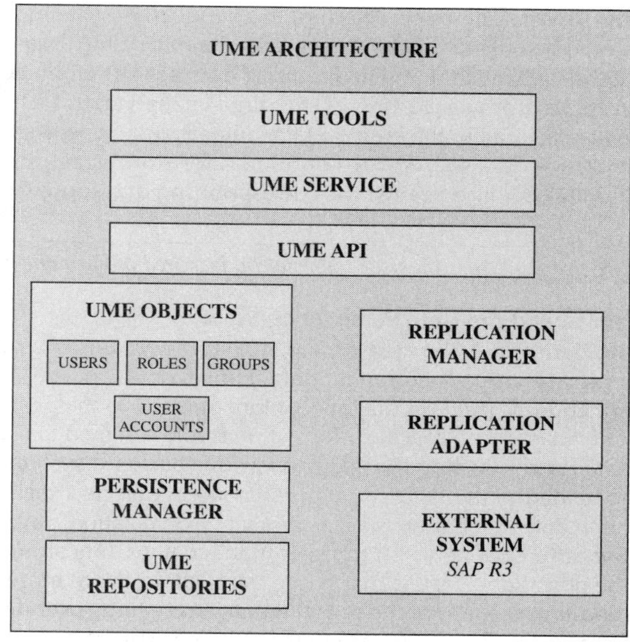

is stored in the UME configuration files, to which the persistence manager refers before calling the appropriate adapters.

NOTE *The persistence manager is discussed in greater detail in Chapter 37.*

Persistence Adapters

Every persistence repository or database has its own set of adapters, which is responsible for managing the connectivity to the corresponding databases. The persistence manager is responsible for choosing the appropriate persistence store for reading/writing user data and thus absolves the programmer or the calling application from having to know to which data source or persistence store to connect.

UME Repositories or Data Sources

The UME repositories (or persistence store) could be any of the following:

- LDAP system such as Sun ONE Directory Server, Microsoft Automated Deployment Services (ADS), or Novell eDirectory
- SAP R/3 system
- Web AS J2EE database in version 6.40

By default, the user management data are stored in the portal database in the case of Web AS 6.20 or the J2EE database in the case of Web AS 6.40.

TIP *By changing the UME configuration, you can store the data in an external R/3 system or an LDAP directory.*

When the LDAP system is configured in a productive system, you can configure it in a failover mode, where if one LDAP server fails, the other LDAP server takes over. It is possible to configure the UME such that when existing user's information needs to be retrieved, the information comes from an existing LDAP directory server, but when new users need to be created, they are created in the Web AS Java database.

When multiple data sources are configured for storing/retrieving user data, the authentication takes place against the corresponding datasource where the user is stored.

Do *Take care to ensure that the user information is stored only in one datasource.*

Portal Database and the UME Persistence Store

As shown in Figure 35-2, the user persistence store contains information on the basic user, group, and user-to-group assignment data. However, the portal database contains user management and information that are content-specific to the portal.

The user management–specific information is role assigned to users/groups and the user mapping data for connecting the users to various backend systems. The content-specific information related to the PCD is the portal content objects attached to the roles and other personalization data of the users such as iView personalization, page personalization, and so on.

Thus, the difference between the user management data stored in the UME persistence store and the portal database is that while the UME data are more focused on maintaining the user account information, the portal database contains user data that are required for displaying content to the users once they are logged into the portal.

Pool Manager

Before executing the appropriate user management activity, the UME service may call the pool manager to connect to the portal database. The UME service connects to the portal database to retrieve information on whether the user who initiated the request has the necessary role assignments or group assignments before connecting to the UME repository.

Types of Persistence Adapters

Examples of persistence adapters are *text adapters, database adapters, LDAP adapters,* and *SAP adapters:*

- **Text adapters** Used for storing user data in file systems; useful only for test systems and not used in productive systems.

Figure 35-2 Portal database and UME data store

PORTAL DATABASE

User Management Data
- User/group to roles
- User mapping

PCD Data
- Metadata about portal roles
- Content assigned to roles
- User personalization data

USER PERSISTENCE STORE (LDAP, R/3 or Database)
- User data
- Group data
- Users assigned to groups

- **Database adapters** Used for demo systems and can be used for storing user/role and role-to-group assignments. They also can contain the user mapping information, which contains the connectivity information for a given user for displaying information from various backend systems.
- **LDAP adapter** Most often used adapter for productive systems—even helpful in setting up a central user administration infrastructure that includes both SAP NetWeaver–based systems such as the Enterprise Portal as well as SAP R/3 systems.
- **SAP adapter** Used for creating group/user assignments on the portal based on SAP roles; uses the Java Connector (JCO) to connect to the SAP system.

Replication Manager

The replication manager comes into play when you configure the J2EE engine to use the replication adapter for creating users in an external system such as SAP R/3 every time a user is created on the portal. The replication manager replicates the user data by sending an XML file to an external system such as SAP R/3 or a legacy web application.

TIP *By setting up a replication mechanism, you can ensure that the SAP system and the EP system both use the same set of users.*

UME Data Partitioning

The UME can be configured to store user data in multiple repositories. This gives you a number of options for partitioning user data. While the different user data partitioning techniques and mentioned here, Chapter 37 explains how the UME can be configuring to implement these data partitioning options.

User-Based Data Partitioning

You can configure the UME to store certain sets of users in certain persistence stores, which is known as *user-based data partitioning*. For example when external users are created on the portal, the data can be stored in a portal database, but when internal users are created in the portal, the user information can be stored in the LDAP directory. This way, you can continue to maintain the different sets of users separately without polluting the integrity of the internal user information in the LDAP directory with external user data.

Attribute-Based Data Partitioning

You can also store different sets of user attributes for a particular user in different persistence stores. This is known as *attribute-based data partitioning*. For example, you can store certain SAP-specific attributes in the user master data in the SAP systems and other non-SAP–related data in the LDAP directories. Another example is when you store the user ID in the LDAP, but you store the role assignments or the user mapping information in the database.

Type-Based Data Partitioning

In this scenario, you can store users in the LDAP and groups in the database. This is known as *type-based data partitioning* because different types of principals are stored in different datasources. This scenario may be useful when groups are not maintained in the LDAP or when the groups that are maintained in the LDAP do not make sense.

Datasource Configuration Files

The details about which data source files should be connected to for reading data and which should be connected to for writing user data are available in the XML-based datasource configuration files. During the initial installation, if you are installing a pure NetWeaver AS Java system, then a NetWeaver AS Java database can be selected for storing the UME data. On the other hand, if a NetWeaver AS Java + ABAP system is installed, then the R/3 system user management can be used. If you selected the Java database as the UME datasource initially, then you can change the UME datasource to either NetWeaver AS ABAP or the LDAP system.

NOTE *If a Java database is not chosen as the initial datasource, it is not possible to change the UME data store.*

The details about which datasource is currently being used can be found in the *ume.persistence.data_source_configuration* property. If you want to change the datasource, some restrictions are applied, such as the new datasource should not have users with the same unique name or logon IDs as in the current datasource.

TIP *For more information, refer to OSS Note 718383.*

Tools to Administer Users

To administer the roles, actions, users, and groups, you can use either the Portal Content Studio or the Identity Management functionality in the portal. To manage UME roles, however, you cannot use the Portal Content Studio. Other web applications can be used to carry out the identity management activities: the NetWeaver Administrator, User Administration web application, Visual Administrator tool, and the portal user interface.

NetWeaver Administrator Available at http:// or https://*<J2EE_hostname>*:*<J2EE_port>*/nwa/identity. Figure 35-3 displays the NetWeaver Administrator functionality for identity management.

User Administration Web Application Available at http:// or https://*<J2EE_hostname>*:*<J2EE_port>*/useradmin. Figure 35-4 displays the User Management administration web application that can be used for administering users.

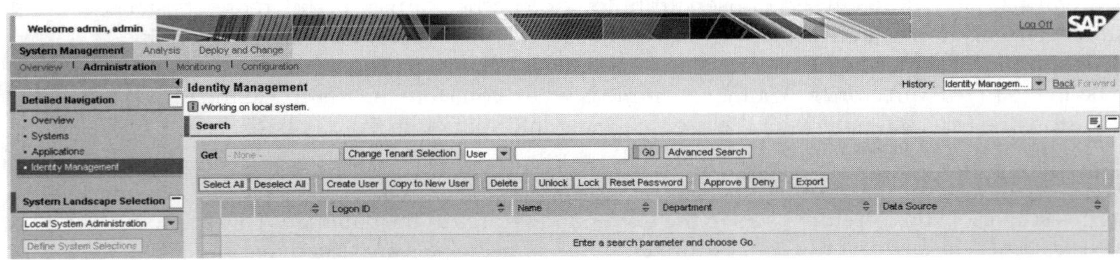

FIGURE 35-3 Identity management

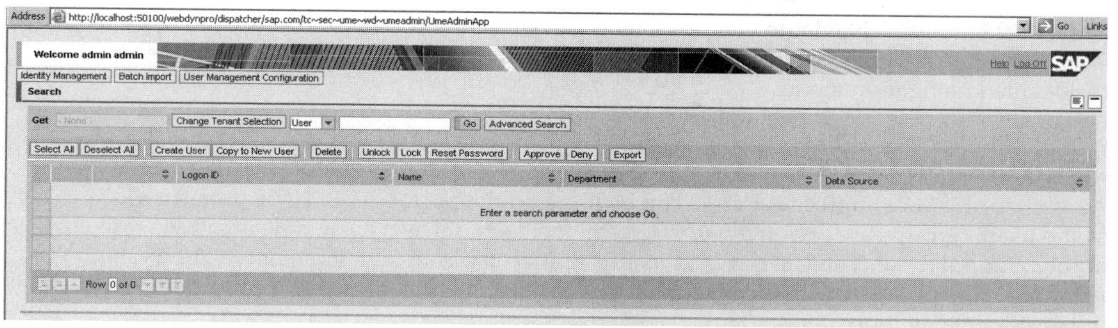

Copyright by SAP AG

Figure 35-4 User administration web application

Using the Visual Administrator Tool for User Administration You can also manage users and groups in the Visual Administrator tool of the J2EE engine by navigating to Cluster | Server | Services | Security Provider | Runtime | User Management tab, as shown in Figure 35-5.

Note *You cannot manage roles with the Visual Administrator tool.*

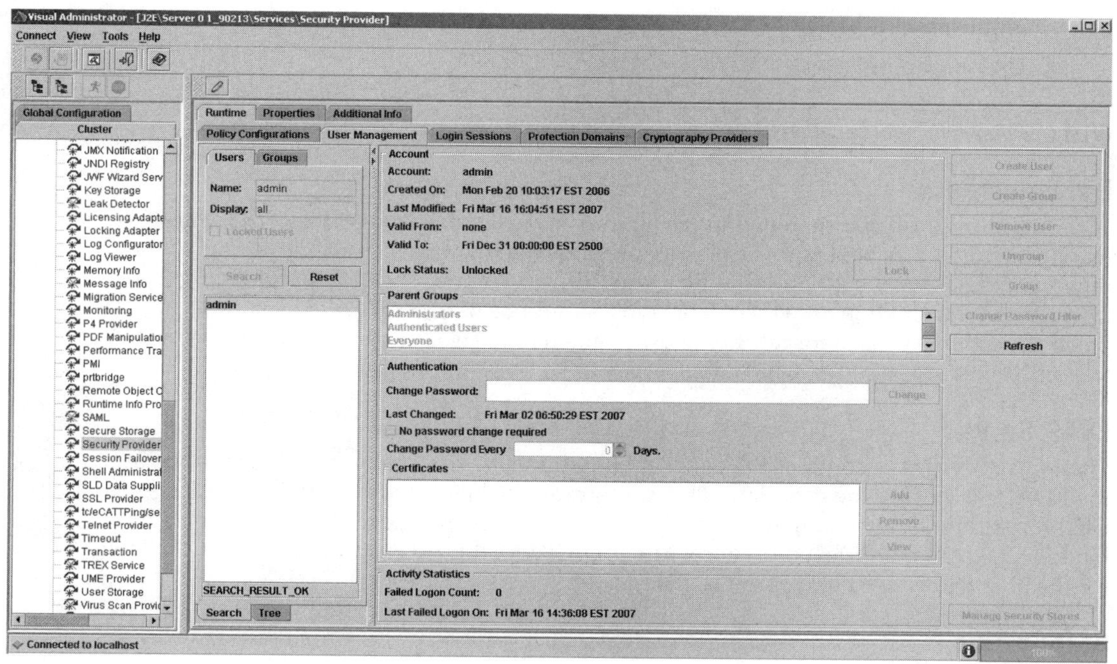

Copyright by SAP AG

Figure 35-5 Visual Administrator Tool User Management functionality

Portal User Interface Navigate to User Management on the portal by navigating to System Administration | System Configuration in the top-level menu and UME Configuration in the detailed navigation menu.

UM Configuration Tasks

A number of UM configuration tasks can be done on the portal. Also, UME data such as the users/groups are no longer stored in the portal database; these data are now stored in the J2EE database. The UME-related configuration tools are available under the System Administration | System Configuration in the top-level menu and UME Configuration in the detailed navigation menu.

NOTE *If you are using EP 6.0, functionality such as Direct Editing will not be available in EP 7.0.*

Several different configuration activities can be accomplished for the UME. The UME Configuration has the following tabs:

- Data Sources
- LDAP Server
- SAP System
- Security Settings
- Notification E-Mails
- User Mapping

NOTE *These tabs may be different depending upon the version of the portal you are using.*

Datasources

The Datasources tab is used for configuring the different datasources for storing user management data as well as for retrieving user management data. You can also upload and download datasource configuration files into the J2EE engine. The datasource configuration files contain information on which datasource should be used for storing user data and which datasource is used for retrieving user data. It may also contain information on which user attributes are stored in which database.

LDAP Server

The LDAP Server tab contains the connection parameters that are required for connecting to the LDAP for storing the user data. This configuration is required only if the LDAP server is used for storing or retrieving user data in the portal. Whether the user data can be stored in the LDAP or can be retrieved only from the LDAP depends on the authorizations available for the user that is used to connect to the LDAP.

SAP System

This tab contains settings for all the connection parameters that are required for connecting to an SAP R/3 system when the SAP system is used as the datasource for maintaining the portal users.

Security Settings

This tab contains provisions for setting up the security policy for maintaining the users' logon IDs and passwords. As you can see in Figure 35-6, you can set the following:

- The minimum/maximum length for the logon ID and the passwords
- The minimum number of lowercase letters, digits, or special characters required for logon IDs
- The minimum number of mixed-case letters, alphanumeric characters, or special characters required for passwords
- The maximum number of failed attempts after which the user is locked
- The time delay after which the user is unlocked automatically
- The password validity period, after which the user needs to change the password
- The period for which the logon ticket issued is valid
- Setting up the reference system for user mapping scenarios where the portal user ID is different from the SAP backend user ID, but the user IDs in all the SAP backend systems are all the same
- Other password policy requirements such as whether the logon ID can be part of the password, whether the old password can be part of the new password, and whether the users are allowed to change their passwords

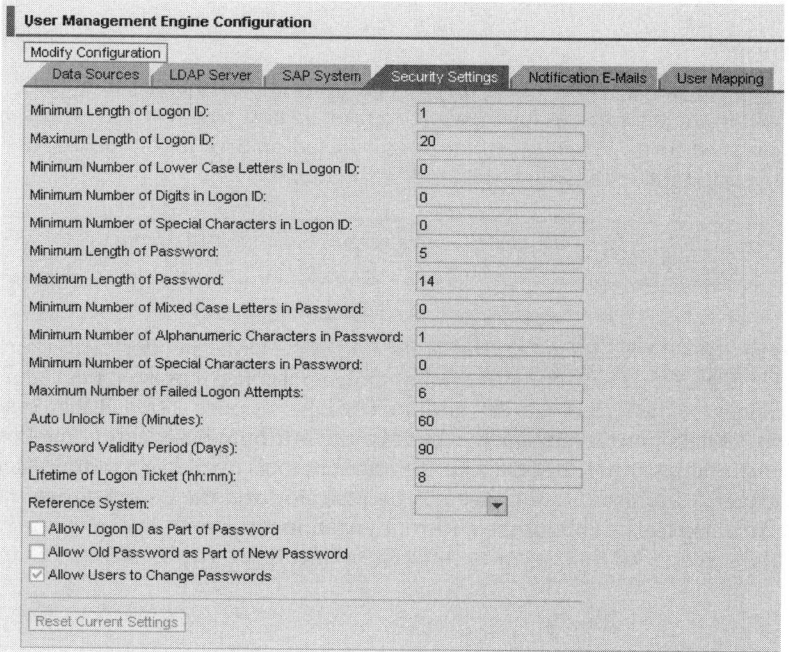

FIGURE 35-6 User Management Engine Configuration, Security Settings tab

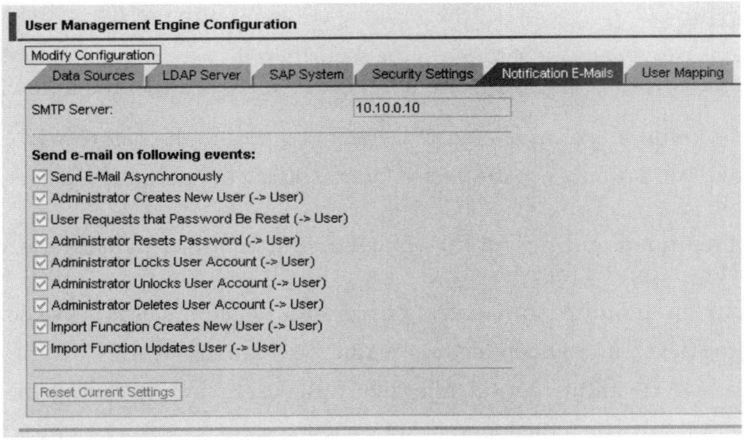

FIGURE 35-7 User Management Engine Configuration, Notification E-Mails tab

Notification E-Mails

Under the Notification E-Mails tab, shown in Figure 35-7, you can configure the SMTP server so that automated e-mails can be sent to the user for events such as when the user was created or when the user was locked/unlocked.

User Mapping

The User Mapping tab provides the ability to configure the user mapping data to be encrypted. When the user mapping is based on user ID and password, the password is stored in encrypted form. When user mapping is based on SAP logon tickets, the user ID is encrypted provided the user ID is not stored in the LDAP.

NOTE *For more details, refer to the UME related resources listed in Appendix B.*

Summary

This chapter discussed the salient features of the UME: the UME architectural components such as the UME service, the user management tool, persistence manager, persistence adapters, replication manager; UME data sources; and the UME persistence stores. It then discussed the different types of data partitioning such as user-based, attribute-based, and type-based data partitioning techniques. You learned about the different tools available to administer users such as the NetWeaver Administrator, the Visual Administrator, and the User Administrator web application. You also learned about the UM configuration tasks such as configuring the data sources, LDAP server, SAP R/3, security settings, notification e-mails, and user mapping.

36

CHAPTER

Administering Users with User Management Tool

An important aspect of user administration is the management of users, groups, and roles using the Identity Management iView. This chapter discusses a number of user administration tasks that can be performed. After reading this chapter, you will be able to administer users, import and export users from one portal system to another, enable users to maintain their own user profile, and test UME object and properties.

User Settings

To access the Identity Management iView in the portal, choose User Administration | Identity Management. When creating a user, the mandatory fields are Logon ID, Password, and Last Name. To modify information for a user, select a user name and click Modify, as shown next:

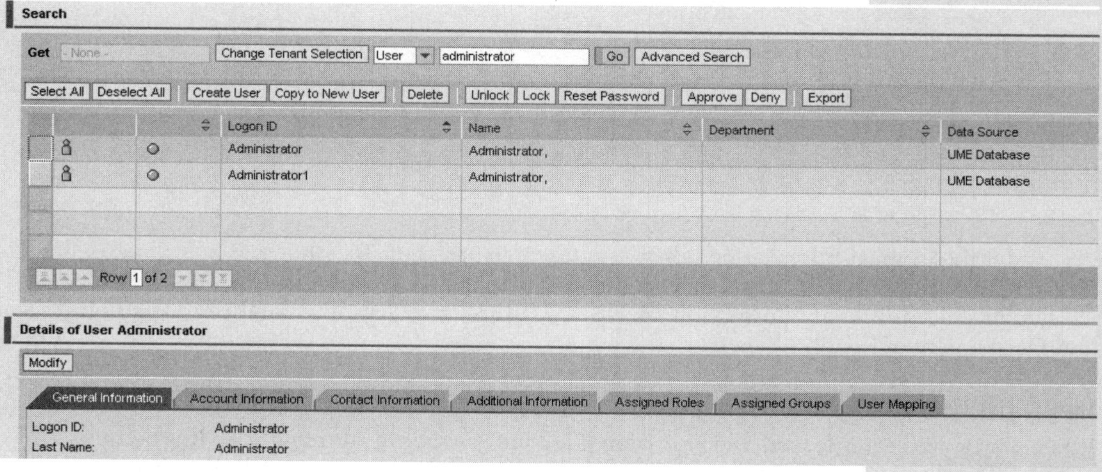

Search for Users

The portal provides some advanced features for searching user information. Under the Frequently-Used Information tab, you can search using Logon ID, Last Name, First Name, E-mail Address, Telephone, Fax, Mobile, Unapproved Users, and Security Policy.

You can also search for similar criteria under the General Information tab, as shown next.

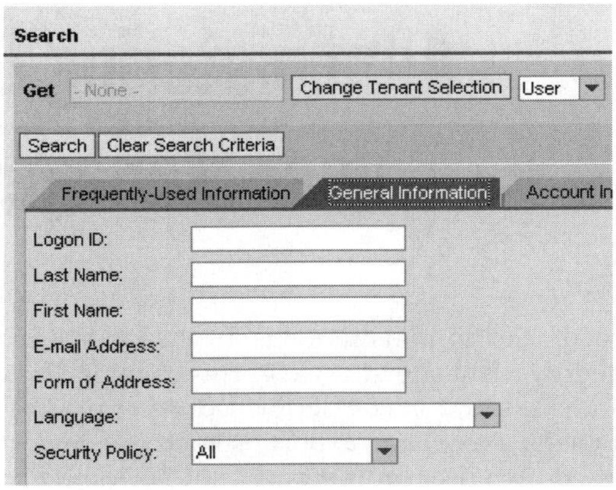

Copyright by SAP AG

Under the Account Information tab, you can search based on the locked status of the user account, the account creation date, the last password change date, and the start and end dates of account validity.

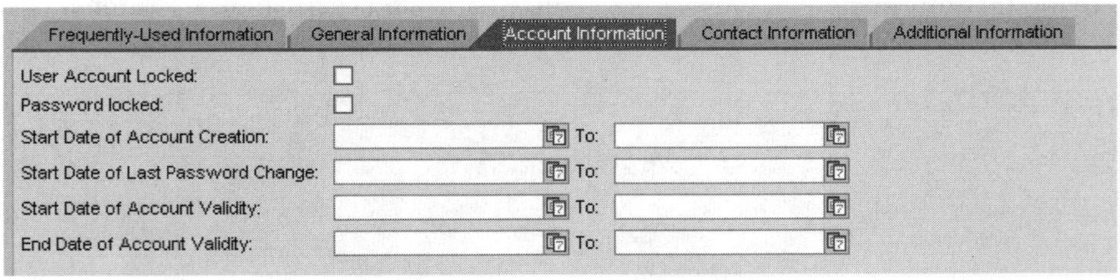

Copyright by SAP AG

Under the Contact Information tab, you can search based on Telephone, Fax, Mobile, Street, City, State/Province, Zip/Postal code, Country, and Time Zone.

Under the Additional Information tab, you can search for Organizational Unit, Position, and Department of Logon Alias.

Lock/Unlock Users

When a user account is locked, the user cannot log into the portal. You might do this because you do not want the user to have access to the portal temporarily. An optional reason for the lock can be entered and the reason will be displayed in the user's account history in the Account Information tab while displaying the user information.

Reset User Passwords

The administrator can reset a password for the user. When the user logs on the next time, he or she will still be required to remember the previous password. For this to work, the UME parameter *ume.logon.security_policy.password_change_allowed* must be set to TRUE. To change the UME parameter, you must use the J2EE Config tool.

TIP *To allow the user to change the parameter, the user should be assigned either a role that contains the UME action Manage_My_Password or a group that contains the role.*

You can set a new password or generate password automatically in the Identity Management iView, as shown next:

Details of User Administrator
Save Cancel
General Information | Account Information | Contact Information | Additional Information | Assigned Roles | Assigned Groups | User Mapping
Logon ID: * Administrator
Define Initial Password
Generate Password
Disable Password
Define Password: *
Confirm Password: *

Copyright by SAP AG

Export Users into a Batch File for Future Import

To export a user, simply search for the user, and then click the Export button:

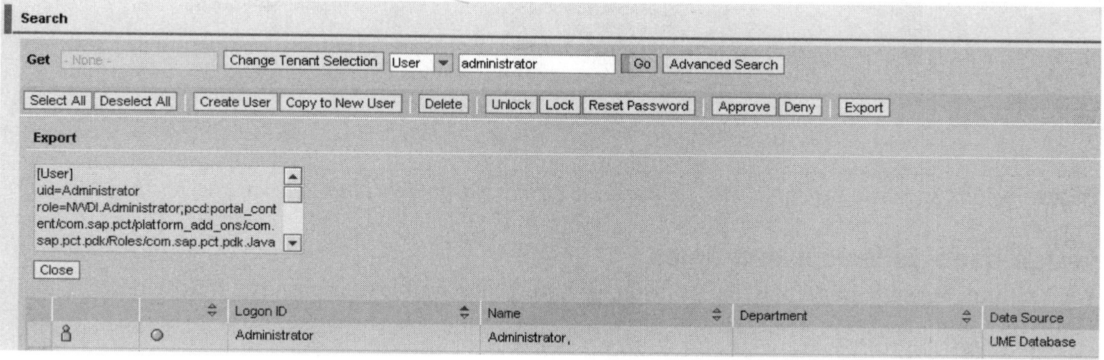

Copyright by SAP AG

Then put your mouse in the Export section, press CTRL-A and CTRL-C to copy the information, and paste it into a text document and save it. The saved file contents will look like this:

```
[User]
uid=Administrator
role=NWDI.Administrator;pcd:portal_content/com.sap.pct/platform_add_ons/com.sap.
pct.pdk/Roles/com.sap.pct.pdk.JavaDeveloper;JDI.Administrator;LcrAdministrator;
Administrator;pcd:portal_content/com.sap.gm.cnt/core/VCRole;
group=Administrators;NWDI.Administrators;GUEST_USERS_COMPANY;NWDI.Developers;
email_address=a@b.com
last_name=Administrator
```

As you can see, the user is identified by the `[User]` tag. The tags for groups will be `[Group]` and roles will be `[Role]`. A number of tags follow the `[User]` tag that defines the attributes for the user. `uid` is the logon ID, the tag `role` contains a list of roles attached to the user separated by `;`. The tag `group` contains a list of groups and a number of tags including `email_address` and `last_name`.

Import Users

To import the user, click Import under the User Administration tab, as shown next. You can either point to the file that contains the user batch file or simply paste the contents of the file in the field with space for content. Click upload button to create the users in the portal.

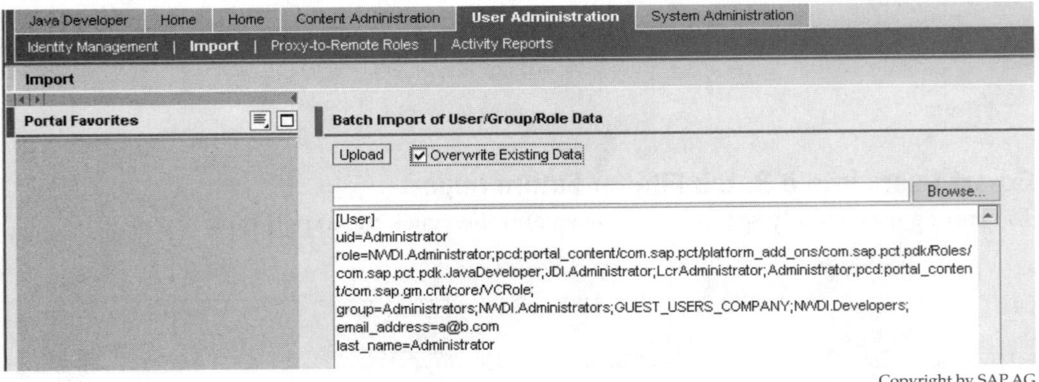

NOTE *Select Overwrite Existing Data if you want to replace any data that may already exist for the user.*

Assign Users to Groups and Roles

You facilitate user management by creating groups. It is possible to assign the following:

- Users to groups
- Groups to a group
- User to a role

- Group to role
- Roles to a user
- Roles to a group

By assigning roles to a group and then by assigning the user to the group, you can indirectly assign a number of roles to the user.

To assign groups and roles to a user, click Modify and then click Assigned Roles. Enter the required role in the Get field under Available Roles and then click Go. For example, to assign the end user role, enter ***eu*** in the Available Roles, and then click Go. Then select the role you want to assign in the results section. Then click Add. The newly assigned role will appear under the Assigned Roles section. Now Save the user data.

To add the group to the user, follow the same procedure described for assigning roles.

Display User History Information

To display history information regarding the user, click the Account Information tab. The account history contains information such as the following:

- When the user was created
- Status of the account
- Password change date
- Password reset date
- Locked/unlocked date

The following illustration shows the history information:

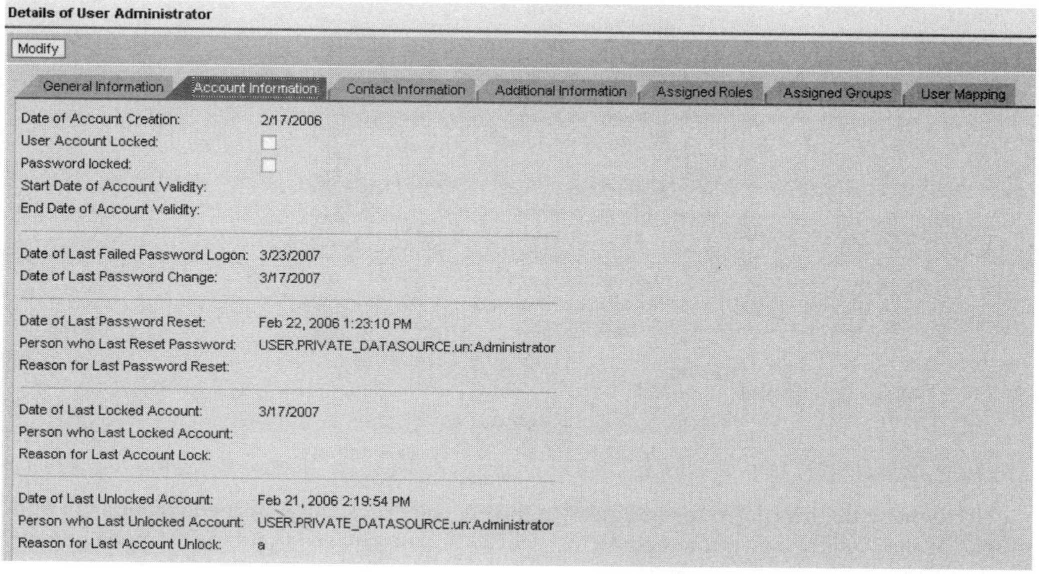

Details of User Administrator

Modify

General Information | Account Information | Contact Information | Additional Information | Assigned Roles | Assigned Groups | User Mapping

Date of Account Creation:	2/17/2006
User Account Locked:	☐
Password locked:	☐
Start Date of Account Validity:	
End Date of Account Validity:	
Date of Last Failed Password Logon:	3/23/2007
Date of Last Password Change:	3/17/2007
Date of Last Password Reset:	Feb 22, 2006 1:23:10 PM
Person who Last Reset Password:	USER.PRIVATE_DATASOURCE.un:Administrator
Reason for Last Password Reset:	
Date of Last Locked Account:	3/17/2007
Person who Last Locked Account:	
Reason for Last Account Lock:	
Date of Last Unlocked Account:	Feb 21, 2006 2:19:54 PM
Person who Last Unlocked Account:	USER.PRIVATE_DATASOURCE.un:Administrator
Reason for Last Account Unlock:	a

To create, change, modify, or delete a role, you must select Role from the drop-down in the Get field of the Search section in the Identity Management iView. For example, take a look at the end user role shown here:

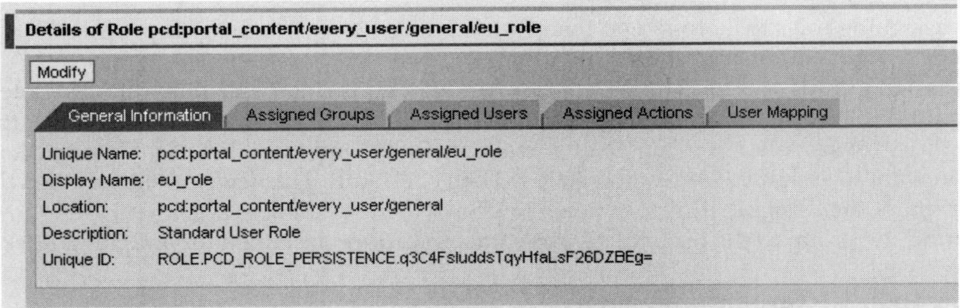

Copyright by SAP AG

You can see that the display name is *eu_role* and the location is *pcd:portal_content/every_user/general*. The unique name is the concatenation of the display name and the location. The actual location of the end user role can be located in the Portal Content catalog, as shown next, based on the location. In this illustration, the value in the Quick Info section under the ID provides the location of the end user role.

Copyright by SAP AG

To identify the list of groups assigned to the eu_role, click the Assigned Groups tab and enter * in the Assigned Groups section, then click Go. You can see that the Everyone group has been assigned to the eu_role.

In the same way, when you click on the Assigned Actions tab, you can see that the UME. Manage_My_Profile action has been assigned to the role. To export the role, click the Export button and the batch file for export will be automatically generated.

Shown next is an example of the batch file for the role:

```
[role]
rid=pcd:portal_content/every_user/general/eu_role
rdesc=Standard User Role
action=UME.Manage_My_Profile
user=collaboration_user;selfreg_user;enduser;bcuser;rabi;replica;cust_service1
group=Everyone
```

To create the role, you can then go to the Import menu and upload the file or the content as already discussed for the users.

Self-Management

Users can self-manage their profiles by doing the following:

- Changing their account details
- Changing their password
- Setting up user mapping

NOTE *If self-registration is activated, users can also register themselves as users in the portal.*

To allow the users to change their own profiles, you should assign the UME action Manage_My_Profile. This action can be assigned to the users via the end user role or the Everyone group. Once this action is assigned, users can update their user profile by clicking Personalize at the top-right corner of the portal desktop and then choosing User Profile.

The next illustration shows the screen that appears after the user clicks the Personalize link at the top-right corner of the portal desktop. The user can change his or her profile using this screen after clicking the Modify button.

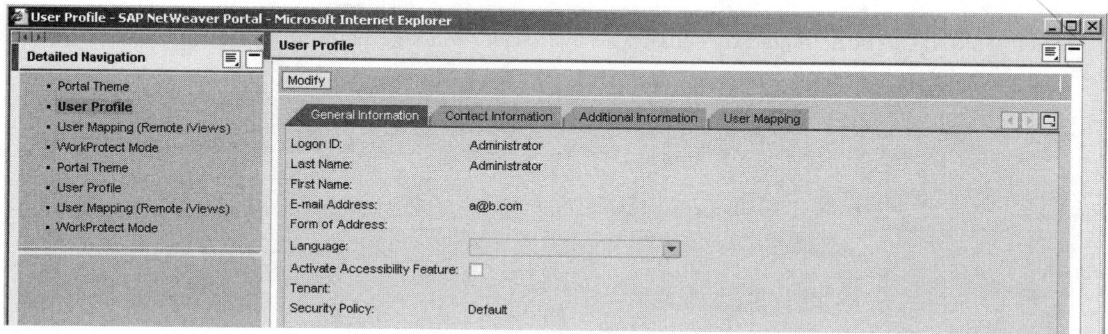

Test and Configuration Tools

Tool	Description
Status of UME properties	Shows the status of the properties currently used in the configuration
Cache monitor of UME objects	Shows the cache status of UME principal objects
Performance monitor of UME objects	Shows the performance status of UME data source adapters
Test component for UME objects	Use input fields to get information about principals

Back to Support Desk

FIGURE 36-1 UME Test and Configuration Tools

UME Test and Configuration Tools

To access the UME Test and Configuration Tools, choose System Administration | Support in the top-level menu and choose Support Desk in the detailed navigation menu, as shown in Figure 36-1.

The status of the UME properties can be analyzed by clicking the Status of UME Properties link. In Figure 36-2, the properties under the Active Property View display the settings in the database, whereas the properties under the File Property View display the properties in the disk.

You can also download the User Management Configuration by clicking the Download Files button and saving it to the file system. You can then send the configuration to the SAP OSS team for analysis.

By clicking Cache Monitor of UME Objects in the Test and Configuration Tools window, you can invalidate the caching related to the user or for the whole system, as shown in Figure 36-3.

You can analyze the performance of the UME adapters by clicking the link for Performance Monitor of UME Objects in the Test and Configuration Tools window. Figure 36-4 shows the results.

Figure 36-4 shows the average, minimum, and maximum time taken to carry out various tasks related to the UME adapters. It also displays the number of calls and the total time taken to execute the actions. Some typical tasks are search principals and populate principals. If you do not see any statistics, it could be because the User Management Performance Monitor has not been activated. It can be activated by clicking Activate User Management Performance Monitor.

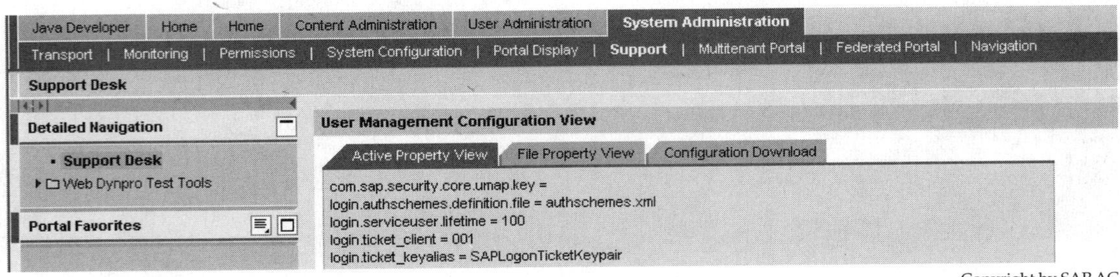

FIGURE 36-2 Status of UME properties

FIGURE 36-3 Cache Monitor of UME objects

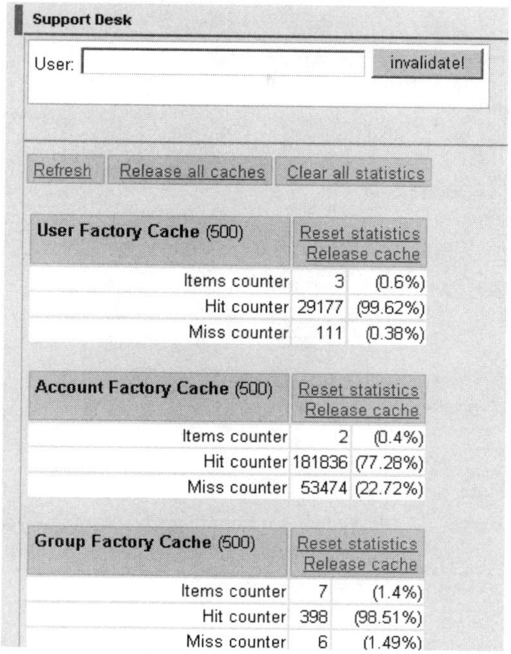

Support Desk

User: invalidate!

Refresh | Release all caches | Clear all statistics

User Factory Cache (500)	Reset statistics Release cache	
Items counter	3	(0.6%)
Hit counter	29177	(99.62%)
Miss counter	111	(0.38%)

Account Factory Cache (500)	Reset statistics Release cache	
Items counter	2	(0.4%)
Hit counter	181836	(77.28%)
Miss counter	53474	(22.72%)

Group Factory Cache (500)	Reset statistics Release cache	
Items counter	7	(1.4%)
Hit counter	398	(98.51%)
Miss counter	6	(1.49%)

FIGURE 36-4 Performance Monitor of UME objects

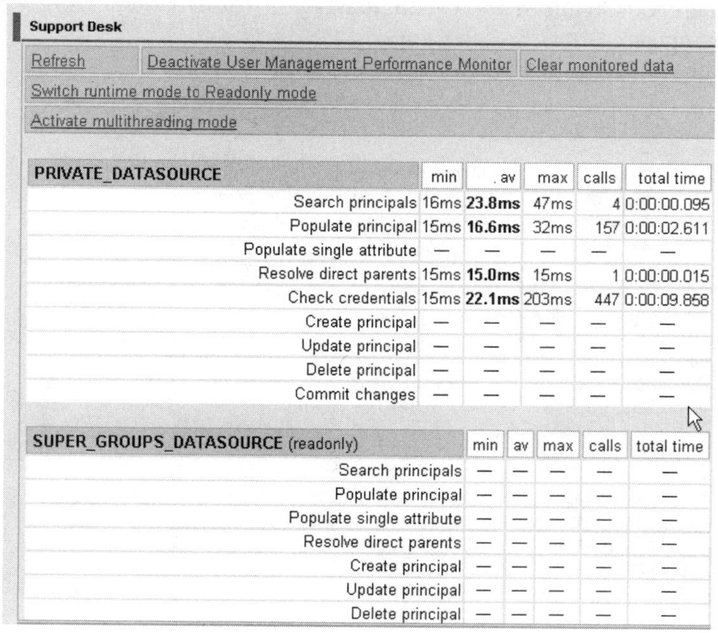

Support Desk

Refresh | Deactivate User Management Performance Monitor | Clear monitored data

Switch runtime mode to Readonly mode

Activate multithreading mode

PRIVATE_DATASOURCE	min	av	max	calls	total time
Search principals	16ms	**23.8ms**	47ms	4	0:00:00.095
Populate principal	15ms	**16.6ms**	32ms	157	0:00:02.611
Populate single attribute	—	—	—	—	—
Resolve direct parents	15ms	**15.0ms**	15ms	1	0:00:00.015
Check credentials	15ms	**22.1ms**	203ms	447	0:00:09.858
Create principal	—	—	—	—	—
Update principal	—	—	—	—	—
Delete principal	—	—	—	—	—
Commit changes	—	—	—	—	—

SUPER_GROUPS_DATASOURCE (readonly)	min	av	max	calls	total time
Search principals	—	—	—	—	—
Populate principal	—	—	—	—	—
Populate single attribute	—	—	—	—	—
Resolve direct parents	—	—	—	—	—
Create principal	—	—	—	—	—
Update principal	—	—	—	—	—
Delete principal	—	—	—	—	—

Support Desk

GET User

Get UME User	
Logonid of user	admin
Get	

Get EP5 User	
EP5 Id of user	
GetEP5User	

GET Group

Get UME Group	
UniqueName of group	
GetGroup	

Get EP5 Group	
EP5 Group Id	
GetEP5Group	

GET Role

Get Role	
UniqueName of role	
GetRole	

Get EP5 Role	
EP5 Role Id	
GetEP5Role	

EP5 Search

Search EP5 User	
Search user	
SearchUser	

Search EP5 Group	
Search group	
SearchGroup	

Search EP5 Role	
Search role	
SearchRole	

FIGURE 36-5 Test Component for UME objects

After clicking on the link for Test Component for UME Objects in the Test and Configuration Tools window, you'll get the screen shown in Figure 36-5. Here you can enter the required UME object and obtain information about that object. This is a low-level tool that can be used to check for memberships.

The result for the logon ID admin is as shown here:

Get user object by logonId took: 0ms

UME isMemberOf Group	
UniqueId	UniqueName
GRUP.PRIVATE_DATASOURCE.un:JDI.Administrators	JDI.Administrators
GRUP.SUPER_GROUPS_DATASOURCE.EVERYONE	Everyone
GRUP.PRIVATE_DATASOURCE.un:JDI.Developers	JDI.Developers
GRUP.PRIVATE_DATASOURCE.un:NWDI.Administrators	NWDI.Administrators
GRUP.PRIVATE_DATASOURCE.un:Administrators	Administrators
GRUP.COMPANY_GROUPS_DATASOURCE.GUEST_USERS_COMPANY	GUEST_USERS_COMPANY
GRUP.SUPER_GROUPS_DATASOURCE.AUTHENTICATED_USERS	Authenticated Users
GRUP.PRIVATE_DATASOURCE.un:NWDI.Developers	NWDI.Developers
UME Get groups took: 0ms	

UME assigned to Roles	
UniqueId	UniqueName
ROLE.PCD_ROLE_PERSISTENCE.VvlvkEGjiW9zPFaxR/4pd2/bX5Q=	pcd:portal_content/administrator/super_admin/super_admin_role
ROLE.UME_ROLE_PERSISTENCE.un:JDI.Administrator	JDI.Administrator
ROLE.PCD_ROLE_PERSISTENCE.q3C4FsluddsTqyHfaLsF26DZBEg=	pcd:portal_content/every_user/general/eu_role
ROLE.PCD_ROLE_PERSISTENCE.Tebd/Lyt41NnxNHxM5zp9TyR6j4=	pcd:portal_content/specialist/contentmanager/ContentManager
ROLE.PCD_ROLE_PERSISTENCE.vxLw9pkgokO0P5vLuimS6ZquOgM=	pcd:portal_content/every_user/general/eu_core_role

NOTE *For more details, refer to the UME related resources listed in Appendix B.*

Summary

This chapter discussed some typical user management activities such as creating, copying, and modifying users. It then discussed the different ways available to search users, lock/unlock users, reset passwords, assign users to groups and roles, and display history information. You learned how to use the import/export functionality on the portal and to enable self-management on the portal. You also read about some UME testing and configuration tools that can be used to test the UME properties, monitor the caching of UME objects, analyze the performance of UME adapters, and test the availability of UME objects.

CHAPTER 37

Configuring UME Datasource

The Lightweight Directory Access Protocol (LDAP) is useful when you want to maintain a metadirectory of users and groups in an organization. A number of different systems, such as e-mail, telephony, operating systems, application servers, web servers, and other applications, including central user administration systems, can be connected to the LDAP system as a central source for user management data.

This chapter looks at LDAP deep and flat hierarchies and configuring LDAP and SAP R/3 as User Management Engine (UME) persistence stores. It also discusses how to customize the datasource configuration for type-based, user-based, and attribute-based data partitioning techniques.

LDAP

LDAP is an industry-wide standard protocol that is supported by a number of application and hardware vendors. By configuring the UME to connect to an LDAP for storing user data, you can enable other applications to share their user information with SAP systems.

NOTE *To see a list of approved LDAP vendors, go to http://service.sap.com/securitypartners and look for Partners for Directory Services (Interface to LDAP enabled directories).*

The UME can be configured to write data, read data, or both to the LDAP. To share the data between SAP and other applications, the third-party applications should be authorized to modify the LDAP user data. Once the LDAP has been configured, it is then possible to synchronize the user information between SAP and the LDAP directory.

Two business scenarios are possible when using the LDAP. One is using the LDAP as a read/write datasource along with the portal database. The general user data can be stored in the LDAP and application-specific user data can be stored in the portal database using the attribute-based data partitioning technique. The other scenario is to use the LDAP as a read-only datasource for already existing users and store new users in the portal database.

Deep and Flat Hierarchies

Users and groups can be stored in the LDAP server either as: *deep hierarchy or flat hierarchy*. Inside the LDAP directory is a tree structure known as the *directory information tree,* which

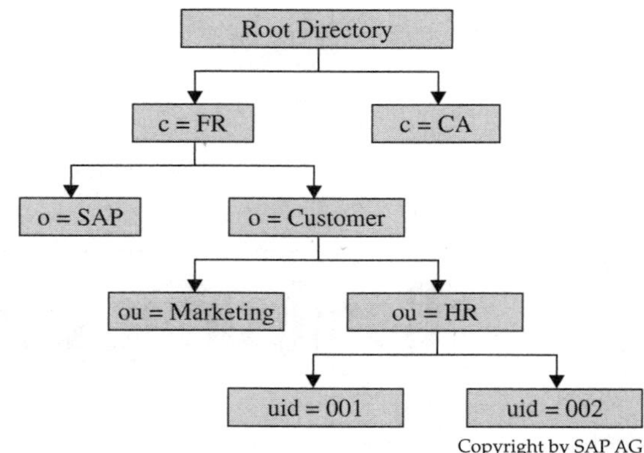

FIGURE 37-1 Directory information tree for deep hierarchy

contains a root node that serves as the entry point. The users appear at the bottom of the tree structure.

The difference between the two hierarchies is the way in which the users and groups are stored. For example, in the case of deep hierarchy, shown in Figure 37-1, the users are stored as separate entries below the group to which they belong. What this means is that the user can belong only to one group (and its parent groups) at any point in time.

NOTE *You cannot change this assignment of groups in the LDAP through the Identity Management tool or UME API.*

On the other hand, in the case of flat hierarchy structure, shown in Figure 37-2, the users are stored as an attribute list in the group to which they belong. In the same way, the groups are stored as an attribute of the user that lists the groups to which the user belongs. Thus, two separate branches are used for a flat hierarchy, one each for the user and the groups. The deep hierarchy uses the same branch for storing both users and groups. The advantage with this type of directory structure is that one user can belong to more than one group. The disadvantage is the amount of maintenance involved when a new user is added, and if that user belongs to multiple groups, you have to assign the user to all the groups explicitly.

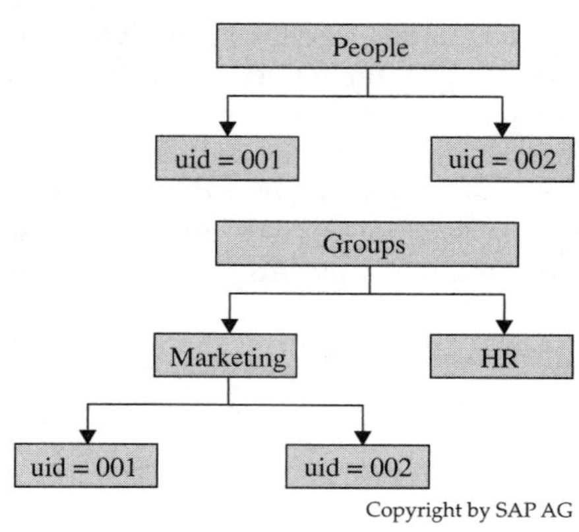

FIGURE 37-2 Directory information tree for flat hierarchy

TIP *A number of criteria, such as countries, organizations, companies, subsidiaries, departments, and organizational units, can be used to define the directory structure.*

Absolute and Relative Names

Every object in the tree structure could be a user, a group, country, department, or other unit and is identified by either *absolute* or *relative paths*. The absolute paths must be unique within the entire directory structure, but the relative paths have to be unique within their naming context. The absolute path names start from the bottom and go all the way up to the root node as shown here:

cn=John Smith, ou=HR, o=customer, c=FR

The path is relative to an entry point, as shown here:

cn=John Smith, ou=HR, and the entry point is *o=customer*

Thus the relative path just needs to be unique within the tree under the customer organization tree structure. The absolute name does not require the entry point to be defined because it goes all the way up to the root node.

SAP Schema Extensions

The directory information is structured using an object class hierarchy in which each object has a set of standard attributes that come with the LDAP server by default. However, if you want to configure it to use with SAP, you may need to add some new objects that contain additional SAP attributes such as roles. So you need to extend the standard LDAP structure, which is known as the *schema*, by using extensions known as *SAP schema extensions*. For example, you may extend the person object to include additional attributes such as *employeeID*, *title*, *department*, and *function*. The standard person object may include attributes such as *cn*, *givenName*, *sn*, *telephone*, *mail*, and so on.

Limitations When Using LDAP as a UME Data Store

Following are some limitations when using LDAP as a UME data store:

- The user used to connect the UME to the LDAP must have appropriate authorizations in the LDAP for read/write access.
- The distinguished names of the users and groups should not exceed 240 characters.
- The UME should not retrieve data from LDAP for Everyone, Authenticated Users, and Anonymous Users. This can be resolved during the UME configuration by configuring Unique Names of Blocked Groups.
- Similarly, you must configure the Unique Names of Blocked Users to prevent the UME from accessing duplicate users from the LDAP directory.
- You can assign users and groups to the LDAP groups only if those users and groups exist in the LDAP. However, you can assign LDAP users and groups to a group in the portal database.
- You cannot search for locked users.
- If the LDAP uses a deep hierarchy, you cannot assign users or members to a different group using the UME tool.

Multiple LDAP Directory Servers

When configuring the LDAP as a UME persistence store, the data can be stored in multiple physical LDAP directory servers or in multiple branches of the same LDAP directory server. Even though the users can be stored in multiple LDAP servers, the LDAP groups cannot span across multiple LDAP servers. Hence the LDAP groups can retrieve the users only from the LDAP server from which the groups are read.

NOTE *The maximum number of LDAP servers that can be configured is usually limited to five to avoid performance issues.*

LDAP Configuration

Given below are the steps involved in configuring the LDAP as the UME datasource.

1. Navigate to System Administration | System Configuration | UME Configuration.
2. Click Modify Configuration. To configure the LDAP for storing user data, the current UME configuration should be set up for storing data in the database.
3. In the Datasources tab, check whether the Datasource drop-down value is set either to *Database_only* or *..readonly* value for any database. If you had to change this value, restart the J2EE engine for the change to take effect.
4. If the value was changed and if the J2EE engine is now fully started, create a new user with the Super Administration role to verify whether you are able to log in as super administrator and access all the administrative tasks with the new configuration without connecting to an LDAP server.
5. Select the appropriate LDAP server from the Datasource drop-down under the Datasources tab, as shown next:

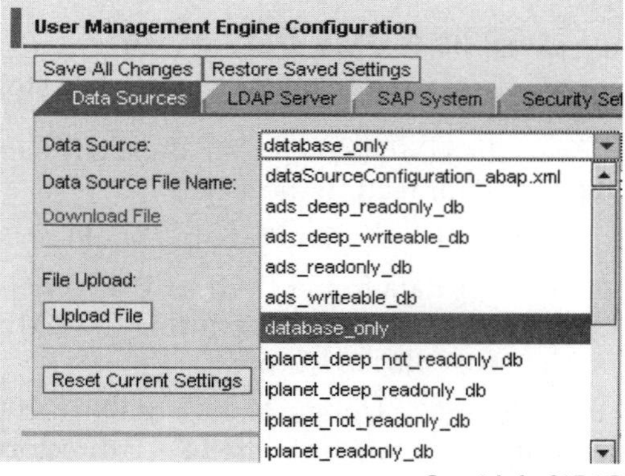

Copyright by SAP AG

Different combinations of datasources are possible based on which vendor it belongs to, the readonly/not readonly/writeable, and whether it is a flat or deep hierarchy.

If the datasource that is selected is readonly, then the LDAP server is a source for existing users, groups, or user accounts, but new users and groups are stored in the UME database and other principals are stored in the portal database. If it is not readonly and writeable, then the LDAP server is not only a source for existing users, groups, and user accounts, but it is also a store for new users and groups.

6. Now click the LDAP Server tab as shown in Figure 37-3 and enter the connectivity parameters to the LDAP such as the following

   Server name of the LDAP

   Port used by the LDAP directory

   Distinguished name of the user (for example, cn=LDAP Administrator)

   Password

   User path and the group path where the user data should be stored

   The user path is required only if a flat hierarchy is used, because it contains separate branches for the user and the groups. This gives the distinguished name of the branch under which the user is stored in the LDAP server. Example: *ou=Sales, o=company*. The group path (*ou=SalesNA, o=company*) is required for both the deep and the flat hierarchy structures.

7. Click Test Connection to ensure that the connectivity works, and then click Save All Changes. Then restart the J2EE engine for the changes to take effect.

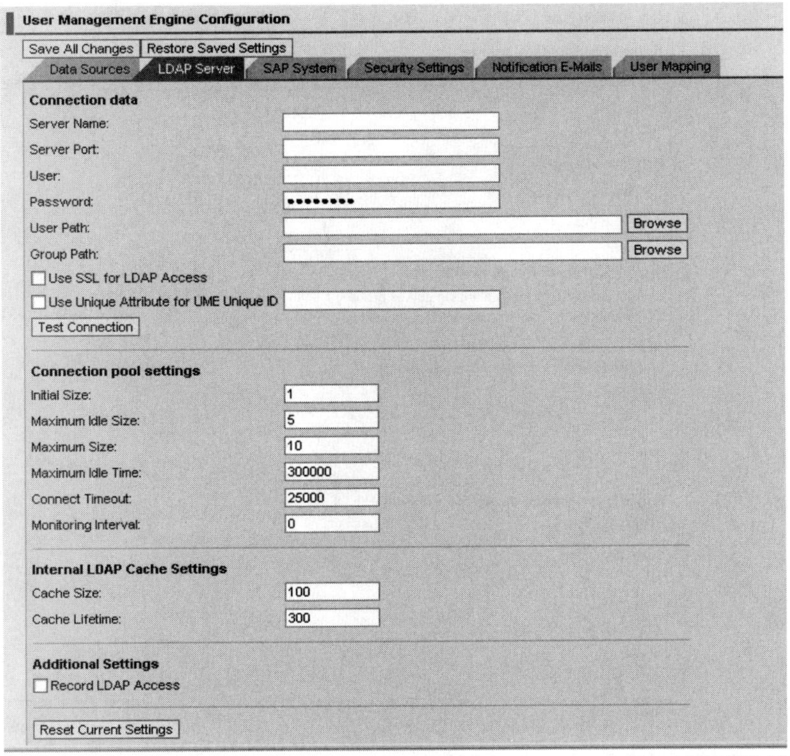

Figure 37-3 LDAP Configuration window

8. Log in to the portal using an LDAP user and verify whether you are able to log in successfully. Then log in as a database user and search for users and groups from the LDAP server as well as the database.

   If the user is not able to log in, check the log files, especially the portal startup files for clues regarding issues with LDAP connectivity. The possible reasons why the LDAP connection failed are incorrect user or password, the user does not have the required authorization levels to the nodes, the LDAP server is not running, or the DN (distinguished name) of the user is not valid.

Using the SAP System as a UME Database

If you plan to use the SAP system as the datasource, you will have to configure the connectivity parameters under the SAP System tab, as shown in Figure 37-4.

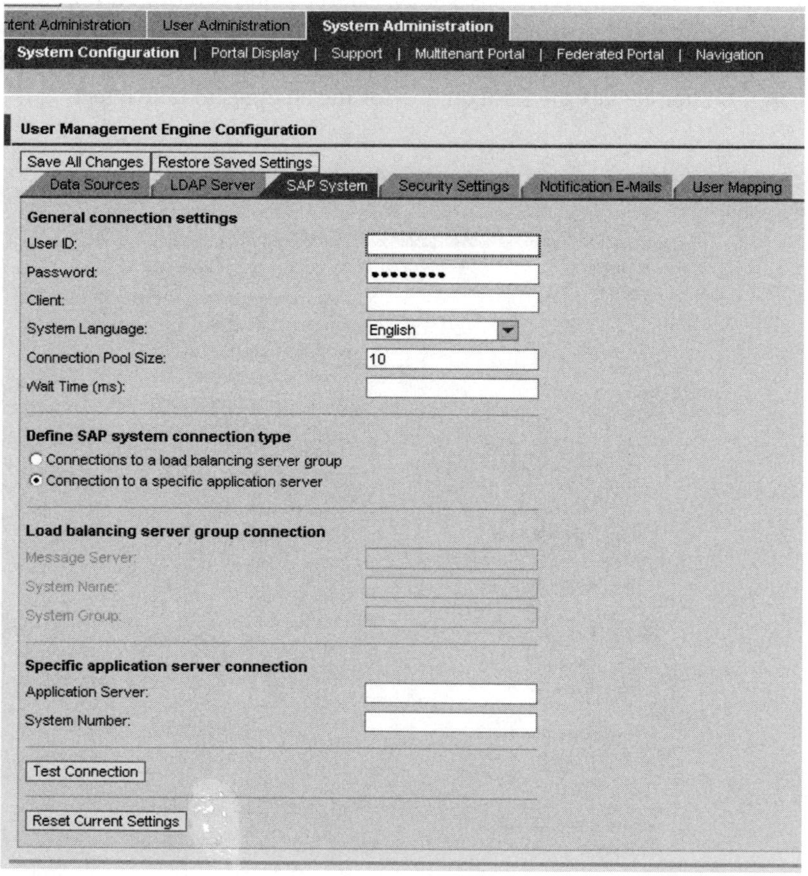

FIGURE 37-4 UME Configuration SAP System tab

The user used to connect to the SAP system should have the necessary authorizations to create and change the user profile. The error messages, if any, that are returned by the SAP system are displayed in the system default language selected here. The maximum size of the connection pool is limited by the memory size of the SAP system. The maximum wait time is the time for which the incoming request waits for a connection before throwing an exception. Sometimes this could be the case when the pool size of SAP connections is not sufficient.

The message server name is used to look up against the sapmessage.ini file located on the SAP server to identify the message server host address and the message server group. If the SAP system is a load-balanced system, and if the sapmessage.ini file is present in all the portal servers, then the message server name and message server group are used to identify the SAP system. If the SAP system is load balanced, but the sapmessage.ini file is not present in all the portal servers, then the combination of message server name, message server group, and message server host address is used to look up the SAP system. If, on the other hand, if the SAP system is not load balanced, then you can directly connect to the SAP system using the combination of the application server host address and the system number.

Customizing the Datasource Configuration File

The datasource configuration files may need to be customized if you want to implement user data partitioning methods such as type-based, attribute based, or user-based data partitioning. Whether you want to implement user-based, type-based, or attribute-based data partitioning would depend on your unique business requirements as discussed under section 'UME Data Partitioning' of Chapter 35. Configuring the configuration files should be done only if it is not possible to use the standard files.

NOTE *These changes are lost when the portal is upgraded.*

To change the datasource configuration file, you should not change the file that comes with the portal. Instead, you must rename the file and configure the UME property accordingly.

1. Start the config tool, and then go to Global Server configuration | services | com.sap.security.core.ume.service.

2. Change the value of the parameters *ume.persistence.data_source_configuration* to point to the newly created datasource configuration file, as shown next:

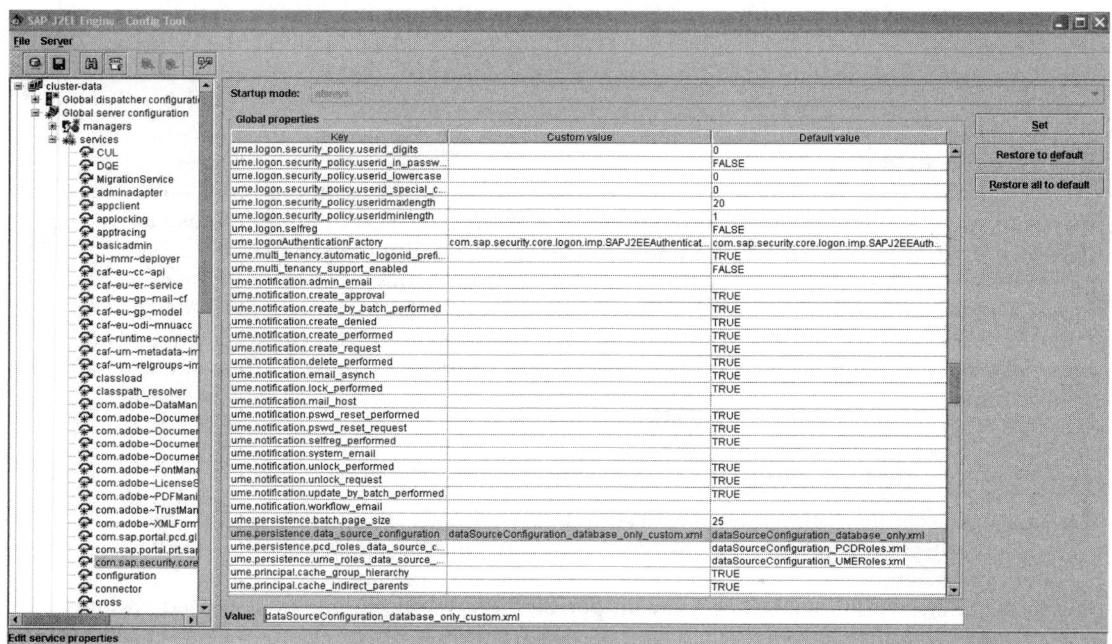

Copyright by SAP AG

3. To create the new configuration file, switch to the editor mode by clicking the Switch to Configuration Editor Mode icon in the config tool.
4. Navigate to Cluster_data | Server | persistent | com.sap.security.core.ume.service.

5. Double-click dataSourceConfiguration_database_only.xml, as shown next:

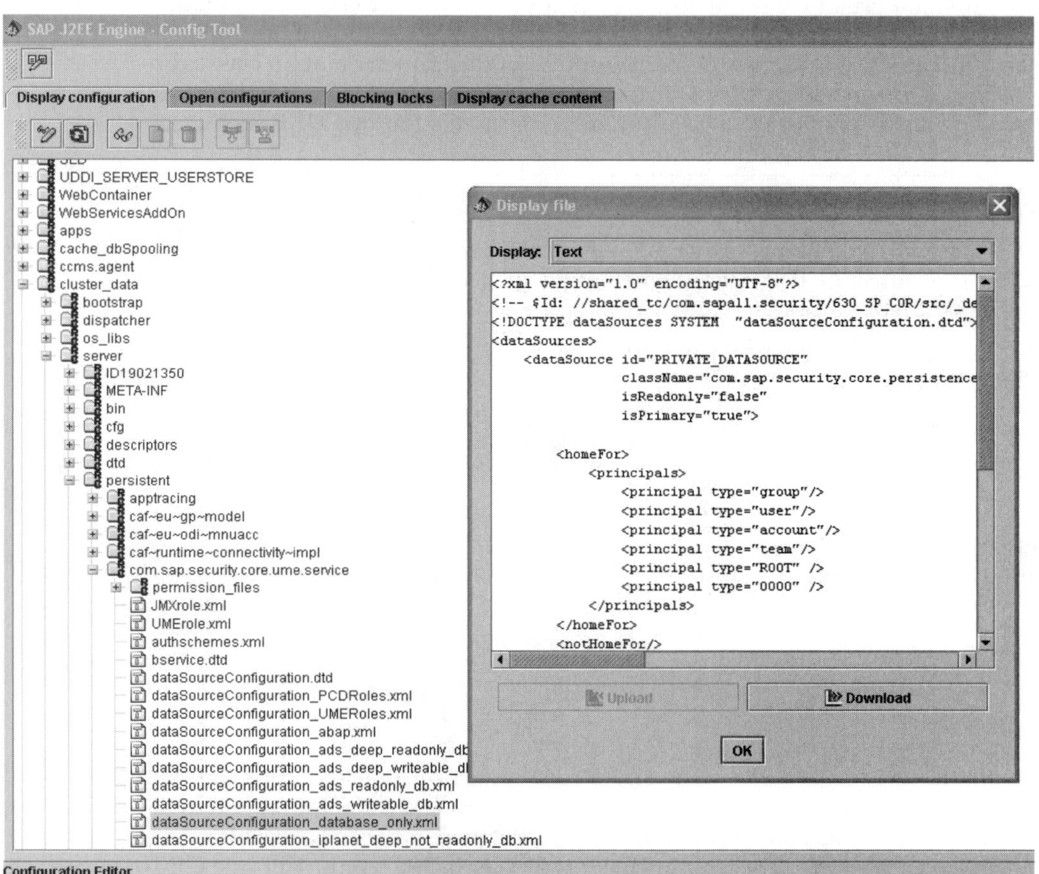

Copyright by SAP AG

6. Click Download to save the XML file to the file system, and then change it according to your needs to implement user data partitioning. Give it the same name you entered in the UME Parameters section for the *ume.persistence.data_source_configuration* property.

7. Return to the same location in the config tool and click Upload to upload the file into the J2EE system.

8. Restart the J2EE engine for the change to take effect. Two similar properties for Portal Content Directory (PCD) roles and UME roles are shown here:

   ume.persistence.pcd_roles_data_source_configuration
   ume.persistence.ume_roles_data_source_configuration

<dataSources> Tag

The first important tag is the <dataSources> tag, which defines the metadata about the datasource. It contains mandatory information such as the ID and the implementation class on which the datasource is based. Examples of the implementation classes are *com.sap.security.core.persistence.datasource.imp.DataBasePersistence* for the database, and *com.sap.security.core.persistence.datasource.imp.LDAPPersistence* for the LDAP server.

NOTE *The database ID must be unique and should not contain any decimals.*

The XML file also contains optional information such as the display name and the *isReadonly* attribute that defines whether the datasource is used for retrieving user information or for updating the user data.

TIP *At least one of the datasources should have a readonly value set to false so that you are able to write to at least one of the datasources for the portal.*

This example shows code dealing with an LDAP database that is used for retrieving user data:

```
<dataSource id="CORP_LDAP"
    className="com.sap.security.core.persistence.datasource.imp.LDAPPersistence"
        displayName="Customer Employees"
        isPrimary="true"
  isReadonly="true">

    ...
</dataSource>
```

In the above example, CORP_LDAP represents the LDAP database and the fact that the value of 'isReadonly' is true indicates that the user data cannot be stored in the LDAP database. For a datasource based on the J2EE database that can be used for storing user data, the file may look like this, where PRIVATE_DATASOURCE represents the J2EE database.

```
<dataSource id="PRIVATE_DATASOURCE"
    className="com.sap.security.core.persistence.datasource.imp.DataBasePersistence"
        displayName="Customer Employees"
        isPrimary="true"
        isReadonly="true">
    ...
</dataSource>
```

<homeFor> and <notHomeFor> Tags

The next important tags to look for are the <homeFor> and <notHomeFor> tags. The <homeFor> tag indicates that the datasource is the home database (primary) for the principal to be created.

NOTE *A principal can have only one database as its home database.*

The home datasource generates the unique ID for the principal that was created. The unique ID is composed of the following:

- Principal type
- ID of the datasource
- Unique name of the principal

Consider the example *USER.CORP_LDAP.jay,* where

- *USER* is the principal type
- *CORP_LDAP* is the datasource ID
- *jay* is the unique name of the user

The `<homeFor>` and the `<notHomeFor>` tags can be used for implementing type-based and user-based data partitioning.

Type-Based Data Partitioning Example

Following is an example of type-based data partitioning, where the principals of type *USER* are stored in the database and principals of type *GROUP* are stored in the LDAP directory:

```
<dataSource id="PRIVATE_DATASOURCE"
        className="com.sap.security.core.persistence.datasource.imp.DataBasePersistence"
        isPrimary="true"
  isReadonly="false">

    <homeFor>
        <principals>
            <principal type="USER">
            <!-- No substructure specified means home for all principals of type
                 "USER" except the ones in notHomeFor-Section -|
            </principal>
        </principals>
    </homeFor>
    <notHomeFor>
    </notHomeFor>
    ...
</dataSource>
```

It is clear from the italicized text in this example that principals of type *USER* are stored in the database.

It is clear from the following code example that the principals of type *GRUP* are stored in the LDAP datasource with ID *CORP_LDAP:*

```
<dataSource id="CORP_LDAP"
        className="com.sap.security.core.persistence.datasource.imp.DataBasePersistence"
        isPrimary="true"
        isReadonly="false">
    <homeFor>
        <principals>
            <principal type="GRUP">
```

```
            <!-- No substructure specified means home for all principals of type
                 "GRUP" except the ones in notHomeFor-Section -|
            </principal>
        </principals>
    </homeFor>
    <notHomeFor>
    </notHomeFor>
    ...
</dataSource>
```

User-Based Data Partitioning Example

In the case of user-based data partitioning, different users are stored in different datasources based on different user attributes. Consider this:

```
<dataSource id="PRIVATE_DATASOURCE"
        className="com.sap.security.core.persistence.datasource.imp.DataBasePersistence"
        isReadonly="false"
        isPrimary="true">
    <homeFor>
        <principals>
            <principal type="USER">
            <!-- Substructure specified means home for all
             principals of type "USER" if they have the
             namespace attribute value triple
             ($serviceUser$,SERVICEUSER_ATTRIBUTE,IS_SERVICEUSER)
             in their initial values -|
                <nameSpace name="$serviceUser$">
                    <attribute name="SERVICEUSER_ATTRIBUTE">
                        <values>
                            <value>IS_SERVICEUSER</value>
                        </values>
                    </attribute>
                </nameSpace>
            </principal>
        </principals>
    </homeFor>
    <notHomeFor>
    </notHomeFor>
    ...
</dataSource>

<dataSource id="CORP_LDAP"
        className="com.sap.security.core.persistence.datasource.imp.LDAPPersistence"
        isReadonly="false"
        isPrimary="true">
    <homeFor>
        <principals>
            <principal type="USER">
            <!-- No substructure specified means home
             for all principals of type "USER" except the
             ones in notHomeFor Section -|
            </principal>
```

```
        </principals>
    </homeFor>
    <notHomeFor>
        <principals>
            <principal type="USER">
            <!-- Substructure specified means home
             for all principals of type "USER", but not
             if they have the namespace attribute value triple
             ($serviceUser$,SERVICEUSER_ATTRIBUTE,IS_SERVICEUSER)
             in their initial values -|
                <nameSpace name="$serviceUser$">
                    <attribute name="SERVICEUSER_ATTRIBUTE">
                        <values>
                            <value>IS_SERVICEUSER</value>
                        </values>
                    </attribute>
                </nameSpace>
            </principal>
        </principals>
    </notHomeFor>
    ...
</dataSource>
```

In this example, all users are stored in the LDAP datasource except those that are of type *service*. The *service* type users will be stored in the J2EE database. This is evident from the fact that the <homeFor> tag for the database contains the entry shown next. The same entries are available under the <notHomeFor> tag for the LDAP, which means that the service users are not stored in the LDAP.

```
<nameSpace name="$serviceUser$">
    <attribute name="SERVICEUSER_ATTRIBUTE">
        <values>
            <value>IS_SERVICEUSER</value>
        </values>
    </attribute>
</nameSpace>
```

<responsibleFor> and <notResponsibleFor> Tags

The <responsibleFor> and the <notResponsibleFor> tags are used for defining which *attributes* of a principal can be stored in which datasource.

NOTE *The attributes of a principal can be stored in a datasource even if that datasource is not defined as the home datasource for that principal.*

If the attributes of a principal are not defined under the <responsibleFor> or <notResponsibleFor> sections, then the attributes are stored in the datasource that has been defined as the home datasource for the principal. The <responsibleFor> tag is useful for implementing *attribute-based data partitioning*, where different attributes of a principal are stored in different datasources.

Attribute-Based Data Partitioning Example

In the next example, the *firstname*, *lastname*, and *e-mail* attributes are read from the LDAP service. The tag 'populateInitially = true' indicates that the *firstname* and the *lastname* are populated initially with the values whenever the principal is read from the LDAP service, and they can be modified as they are not readonly. E-mail cannot be modified.

```
<dataSource id="CORP_LDAP"
      className="com.sap.security.core.persistence.datasource.imp.LDAPPersistence"
      isReadonly="false"
      isPrimary="true">
    ...
    <responsibleFor>
      <principals>
        <principal type="USER">
          <!-- Substructure specified means responsible
          for the specified namespace attribute tuples
          of principals of type "USER" -|
          <nameSpace name="com.sap.security.core.usermanagement">
            <attributes>
              <attribute name="firstname" populateInitially="true"/>
              <attribute name="lastname" populateInitially="true"/>
              <attribute name="e-mail" readonly="true"/>
            </attributes>
          </nameSpace>
        </principal>
      </principals>
    </responsibleFor>
    <notResponsibleFor>
    </notResponsibleFor>
    ...
</dataSource>

<dataSource id="PRIVATE_DATASOURCE"
      className="com.sap.security.core.persistence.datasource.imp.DataBasePersistence"
      isReadonly="false"
      isPrimary="true">
    ...
    <responsibleFor>
      <principals>
        <principal type="USER">
          <!-- No substructure specified means responsible
          for all namespace attribute tuples of principals
          of type "USER" except the ones in the
          notResponsibleFor subsection -|
        </principal>
      </principals>
    </responsibleFor>
    <notResponsibleFor>
    </notResponsibleFor>
    ...
</dataSource>
```

<attributeMapping> Tag

The `<attributeMapping>` tag can be used for mapping the logical attributes used by the UME API to the physical attributes used by the LDAP directory in the organization. For example, the *logical attribute e-mail* could be mapped to the *physical attribute mail* in the LDAP directory service.

In the next example, you can see that the *displayName* attribute is mapped to *uid* in the *com.mycompany.app1* namespace and to *sn* in the *com.mycompany.app2* namespace:

```
<dataSources>
...
...
<dataSource id="CORP_LDAP"
    className="com.sap.security.core.persistence.datasource.imp.LDAPPersistence"
    isReadonly="false"
    isPrimary="true">
  ...
  <responsibleFor>
    <principal type="account">
    ...
    </principal>
    <principal type="user">
      <nameSpace name="com.sap.security.core.usermanagement">
        <attributes>
      ...
        </attributes>
      </nameSpace>
      ...
  </responsibleFor>
<attributeMapping>
    <principals>
      <principal type="user">
        <nameSpace name="com.mycompany.app1">
          <attributes>
            <attribute name="displayname">
              <physicalAttribute name="uid"/>
            </attribute>
          </attributes>
        </nameSpace>
        <nameSpace name="com.mycompany.app2">
          <attributes>
            <attribute name="displayname">
              <physicalAttribute name="sn"/>
            </attribute>
          </attributes>
        </nameSpace>
        ...
      </principal>
    </principals>
  </attributeMapping>
```

Another scenario in which you can use this attribute mapping is when you want to substitute the logon ID of the user account for the e-mail address so that the user can log on to the application using his or her e-mail address as the logon ID. To enable this, you must map the *j_user* logical attribute to the *mail* physical attribute in the LDAP.

Adding New Attributes to User Account

Attribute mapping is also required when you add new attributes to the user account during customization. Suppose you wanted to get additional information from the LDAP user account. In this case, you have to include a logical attribute in the `<responsibleFor>` section and include the `<attributeMapping>` section under the `<responsibleFor>` tag for the logical attribute to map to the physical attribute in the LDAP.

If this attribute should be displayed in the user profile of the *Identity Management* application also, then you have to include the attributes in the *UME properties* as shown here:

```
ume.admin.addattrs=com.mycompany.app1:myCostCenter
ume.admin.self.addattrs=com.mycompany.app1:myCostCenter
```

<privateSection> Tag

Finally, the `<privateSection>` tag allows defining certain *configuration parameters* for the datasource such as the LDAP server—for example, LDAP-specific parameters for connectivity.

NOTE *These values have a higher priority as compared to the values maintained in the UME,* e.g., ume.ldap.access.properties.

Here's an example:

```
<dataSource id="CORP_LDAP"
    className="com.sap.security.core.persistence.datasource.imp.LDAPPersistence"
    isReadonly="false"
    isPrimary="true">
    ...
    <privateSection>
        ...
        <ume.ldap.access.server_type>MSADS</ume.ldap.access.server_type>
        <ume.ldap.access.authentication>simple</ume.ldap.access.authentication>
        <ume.ldap.access.user_as_account>true</ume.ldap.access.user_as_account>
        <ume.ldap.access.dynamic_groups>false</ume.ldap.access.dynamic_groups>
        ...
    </privateSection>
</dataSource>
```

The attribute mapping can also be used for implementing client certificates authentication. You can store the details of the client certificates as attributes in the user account in the LDAP. The logical attributes of the UME that need to be mapped are as follows:

- **certificatehash** Identifies the hash value of the certificate
- **javax.servlet.request.X509Certificate** Can be used for searching the LDAP certificate
- **certificate** Denotes the LDAP certificate itself

These attributes can be used to store the certificate in the LDAP directory and to search for the certificates.

These attributes must be stored in the <responsibleFor> section:

```
<principal type="account">
  <nameSpace name="com.sap.security.core.usermanagement">
    <attributes>
      …
      <attribute name="certificatehash">
        <physicalAttribute name="*null*"/>
      </attribute>
      <attribute name="javax.servlet.request.X509Certificate">
        <physicalAttribute name="usercertificate"/>
      </attribute>
      <attribute name="certificate">
        <physicalAttribute name="usercertificate"/>
      </attribute>
    </attributes>
  </nameSpace>
</principal>
```

NOTE *The actual values for the physical attributes will depend on the vendor specifications and hence the values may differ from what is shown here.*

NOTE *For more details, refer to the UME related resources listed in Appendix B.*

Summary

This chapter discussed how to set up the connectivity for configuring the LDAP as the datasource. It also discussed how the directory structure is maintained in the LDAP as flat and deep hierarchy. It discussed the limitations when using LDAP as a datasource. You learned how to use SAP as a datasource. You then learned how to customize the datasource configuration file for type-based, user-based, and attribute-based data partitioning techniques.

38

CHAPTER

Configuring Portal Authentication

This chapter examines the *authentication* mechanisms on the J2EE engine and the portal. The authentication on the portal takes place through the authentication on the J2EE engine. *Authentication* means checking the credentials of a user who is trying to log on to the portal. Once successfully authenticated, the user can access portal content based on his or her authorization levels. After reading this Chapter, you will learn how to configure the SAP provided login modules to change the authentication process for your applications based on your specific application requirements. You will also learn how you can modify the SAP provided authentication scheme.

Declarative and Programmatic Security

You can implement authentication based on *declarative* and *programmatic* authentication methods. Both declarative and programmatic authentication mechanisms are implemented using a technology that is based on login modules and login module stacks. Programmatic security uses authentication schemes in addition to login modules and login module stacks. The authentication scheme in turn refers to the login module stack for implementing authentication functionality.

NOTE *SAP provides a number of standard authentication mechanisms such as login modules and authentication schemes that you can use for your applications.*

Declarative Authentication

When you implement declarative authentication, the web container or the J2EE engine takes care of the authentication based on the entries in the deployment descriptor of the portal component in the case of portal applications and the web.xml deployment descriptor file for J2EE applications. You define the required authentication method in the deployment descriptor, which the J2EE engine refers to during runtime to trigger the required authentication.

NOTE *Since the web container handles the authentication, declarative authentication is also known as* container-based authentication.

Programmatic Security

When you implement in the case of programmatic security, the portal component itself, rather than the J2EE engine, triggers the authentication against the User Management Engine (UME). This kind of programmatic authentication is carried out by portal iViews and Web Dynpro. SAP provides standard authentication schemes that you can use for implementing programmatic security.

NOTE *Since the portal component authenticates itself against the UME, programmatic security is also known as* UME authentication.

How Programmatic Security Is Implemented

Portal iViews and Web Dynpro always use programmatic security and hence use authentication schemes. The portal iViews use the authentication scheme defined in the *AuthRequirement* property of the iView. In the case of Web Dynpro, the authentication schemes file contains a default login module stack that the application uses for authentication.

To change the authentication method for Web Dynpro applications, you must change the default authentication scheme in the authentication schemes file. This can affect the other portal iViews and J2EE web applications as well because they may be sharing the same authentication schemes file.

J2EE applications may or may not use programmatic security and consequently may or may not use authentication schemes. In order, to implement programmatic security, the J2EE applications need to specify authentication schemes directly in their call to the API.

How Authentication Works on the Portal

When the user tries to access the portal for the first time using the logon iView, the user is authenticated based on the credentials he or she submits. Assume that the user submitted the user ID and password for the first time. Once the user is authenticated, an SAP *logon ticket* is issued to the user and a new authentication scheme is added to the SAP logon ticket based on the type of authentication used by the user at the time of logon.

NOTE *Once the user is authenticated for the first time during logon, the user is logged in to the portal using the single sign-on (SSO) method, namely, using the* SAP logon ticket.

Authentication when Accessing Content

When the user tries to access another iView, the logon ticket is submitted to the iView for authentication. The information regarding the authentication scheme originally provided by the user at the time of logon is submitted to the iView for authentication. If the iView requires a stronger authentication scheme than what is provided in the SAP logon ticket, the user must re-authenticate based on the required authentication scheme. So the logon iView is displayed to the user again to re-authenticate.

For example, if the iView requires a client certificate for authentication, the user must either provide a client certificate for accessing that iView or submit some other authentication credential that has a priority higher than the client certificate mechanism. The logon iView continues to be displayed until the user gets locked out because the maximum number of invalid logons has been reached.

This kind of authentication based on content is possible only in the case of programmatic security. The authentication scheme is assigned to an iView using the iView property called *AuthRequirement*.

NOTE *To access the logon iView, anonymous access is sufficient.*

Standard Authentication Methods

SAP provides the following standard authentication methods:

- **Anonymous access/Guest access** You can also use anonymous logon to access content that does not require any authentication.
- **User ID/password**:
  - **Form based**
  - **Basic authentication** This is the default authentication mechanism used in the J2EE engine and uses the user ID and password.
- **X.509 digital certificates**
- **SAP logon tickets**
- **External methods** such as these:
  - Security Assertion Markup Language (SAML)
  - Header Variable authentication
  - Java Authentication and Authorization Service–Based Simple and Protected GSSAPI Negotiation Mechanism (SPNEGO) along with Kerberos authentication from Microsoft

---

TIP *You can configure higher levels of authentication by using client certificates, JSESSIONID for web applications, and SAP logon tickets for SSO in an SAP environment.*

Header-Variable–Based Authentication

In the case of header-variable login module authentication, SAP relies on trusted third-party systems to provide a username in the header variable that can be used for authentication. This may require that the network be configured to allow traffic only between the trusted system and the J2EE engine for a given port. You must also configure the IP verification service of the J2EE engine for IP filtering so that the J2EE engine accepts traffic only from certain URLs or IP addresses that belong to the external system such as Web Access Management used for authentication, or a proxy server or gateway server. This prevents the user from arbitrarily passing in the username in the header and logging on as an administrator or any other user.

External web access management software can also be used for authenticating. This software authenticates the user against a data store such as Lightweight Directory Access Protocol (LDAP), SAP, and so on, and then populates the request with a header variable that contains the user ID. This user ID is then submitted to the Web AS Java system, which tries to compare the user ID with the users in the UME data stores for authentication.

Form-Based and Basic Authentication

When you use form-based authentication, the user credentials are passed through the URL as a parameter value. In the case of basic authentication, the user credentials are passed to the server through an HTTP header variable, which is base-64 encoded.

SAP Logon Tickets

SAP logon tickets are stored as non-persistent cookies in the client's browser and they contain the *MYSAPSSO2* variable. They are issued by the portal server once the user is authenticated by any one of the other authentication mechanisms. They are digitally signed by the portal server and are verified using the portal server's public key by the accepting server during SSO. If the certificate is valid, the user is allowed access.

Integrated Windows Authentication

Integrated Windows Authentication is used in both NTLM and Kerberos authentication. It uses *HeaderVariableLoginModule* and requires the IIS Server. The user is allowed access to the portal without any authentication if he or she has already logged into a Windows Desktop session. Between the two, Kerberos is considered to be the more secure authentication mechanism.

Authentication Building Blocks

Let's now discuss some of the building blocks that are required for implementing authentication.

JAAS Specification

SAP's authentication functionality is based on the JAAS specification provided by SUN. The JAAS is part of the J2EE specification starting from JDK 1.4.2. Previously it was a standalone functionality that needed to be installed separately. The J2EE engine uses the JAAS specification to implement various authentication methods. So this provides you with the ability to choose the authentication methods required for your application using the JAAS specification.

Security Provider Service

The portal is basically a J2EE application that is running on the Web AS Java system, so this also means you can choose the required authentication method for the portal using JAAS. The authentication functionality is provided by the Security Provider service of the NetWeaver AS Java and the User Management functionality is provided by the UME service.

Login Modules and Stacks

The login modules are implementation Java classes that contain the actual logic required for the authentication. The login module stack, on the other hand, helps to define the sequence with which the login modules are called. This allows us to have different authentication mechanisms (different sequences of login modules) that can be used for different applications.

The login module stacks contain the list of login modules that are attached to JAAS control flags such as required, sufficient and so on. The authentication scheme contains the list of login module stacks that can be attached to the portal content.

Standard SAP Login Modules

A number of standard login modules are provided by SAP:

- **BasicPasswordLoginModule** Used for basic user ID and password-based authentication in a JSP and can be either Form type or Basic type
- **ClientCertificateLoginModule** Used for client certificate–based authentication
- **CreateTicketLoginModule** Used for creating SAP logon tickets after logging on
- **EvaluateTicketLoginModule** Used to evaluate SAP logon tickets
- **HeaderVariableLoginModule** Used for SSO using header variables
- **SAMLLoginModule** Used for SAML-based authentication
- **SPNegoLoginModule** Used for SSO using Kerberos authentication

Authentication Templates

SAP provides a number of predefined login module stacks that are also known as *authentication templates*. Some examples of SAP-provided authentication templates are listed here:

- **SAP-J2EE-Engine** Default stack for the J2EE engine
- **Basic** For basic authentication
- **Client** For client certificate authentication
- **Form** For form-based authentication
- **Ticket** For creating and verifying SAP logon tickets; especially useful for SSO
- **Evaluation assertion ticket** For verifying tickets issued between trusted systems

Login Module Flags

While the login module stack contains a number of login modules, the actual flow of control during the authentication process depends upon the login module flags. The four login module flags are as listed here:

Required For overall authentication to succeed, this login module should pass. Irrespective of the outcome, the control flows down the login module stack for further execution.

Sufficient The overall authentication can succeed, even if this login module fails. If this module passes, then the flow returns to the application. No more authentication logic needs to be applied. If the module fails, then the control flows down the list of modules.

Requisite This is required to pass for overall authentication to succeed. If this module passes, the control returns to the application. If the module fails, the control flows down the list of modules.

Optional The overall authentication can succeed, even if this login module fails. Irrespective of the outcome, the control flows down the login module stack for further execution.

Login Module Methods

A login module can be used in a variety of login stacks. For example, the *HeaderVariableLoginModule* can be used in both Web Authentication Management tools as well as for Windows-based Integrated Management.

The login module contains the following methods that get called during the authentication process:

- **initialize** () As is obvious from its name, this method is called first to initialize the relevant variables of the *LoginModule* with the required authentication and state information.
- **login** () This method is called during *phase 1* of the authentication process when the actual authentication process of the principal or the user takes place.
- **commit** () This method is called once the login method results in successful authentication of the user or principal. During this method, the authentication process is committed once the *LoginContext's* overall authentication succeeds. The LoginContext's overall authentication is deemed successful when the relevant SUFFICIENT, REQUIRED, REQUISITE, and OPTIONAL LoginModules have succeeded. This is considered *phase 2* of the authentication process.
- **abort** () On the other hand, if the login method did not result in successful authentication, the *abort()* method is called to abort the overall authentication process. This is *phase 2* of the authentication process and is called when phase 1 fails.
- **logout**() As the name implies, this method is called when the user explicitly logs out of the portal or when the system wants to log the user out because the authentication failed.

Authentication Login Module Process Flow

You can see from Figure 38-1 that once the sufficient login module succeeds, the control goes back to the application. The overall authentication is considered successful only if the required login module also succeeded. Even though the sufficient login module failed, the control went to the next login module in the list and the subsequent result depended on the outcome of the requisite login module (provided the required login module succeeded). Whether the optional login module fails or succeeds does not impact the overall authentication result.

Login Module 1 - required	pass	pass	pass	pass	fail	fail	fail	fail
Login Module 2 - sufficient	pass	fail	fail	fail	pass	fail	fail	fail
Login Module 3 - requisite	*	pass	pass	fail	*	pass	pass	fail
Login Module 4 - optional	*	pass	fail	*	*	pass	fail	*
Overall Authentication:	pass	pass	pass	fail	fail	fail	fail	fail

Figure 38-1 Authentication process flow based on login modules

NOTE *Usually the* CreateTicketLoginModule *is used as an optional login module for creating an SAP logon ticket.*

Even though the required login module passed, either the sufficient or the requisite login module is needed to be executed for success, because the flow passed down the login module list.

When the required function module fails, the overall authentication is deemed a failure even though the sufficient login module succeeded. The subsequent login modules become irrelevant to the outcome.

Policy Configurations

The various applications, services, and modules are registered in the Security Provider Service with the login module stack (or authentication template) that constitutes the authentication logic. This set of rules for various applications, services, and modules is known as *policy configurations.*

Managing Policy Configurations

To modify the Policy Configurations, navigate to the Security Provider Service in Visual Administrator by selecting Cluster | Server | Services | Security Provider Service. On the right-hand pane, select Runtime | Policy Configurations | Authentication | Components. Select the Switch To Edit Mode button as shown in Figure 38-2.

Under the Components tab, you see a list of applications, services, and modules for which you can set up the authentication rules using the login module stacks and

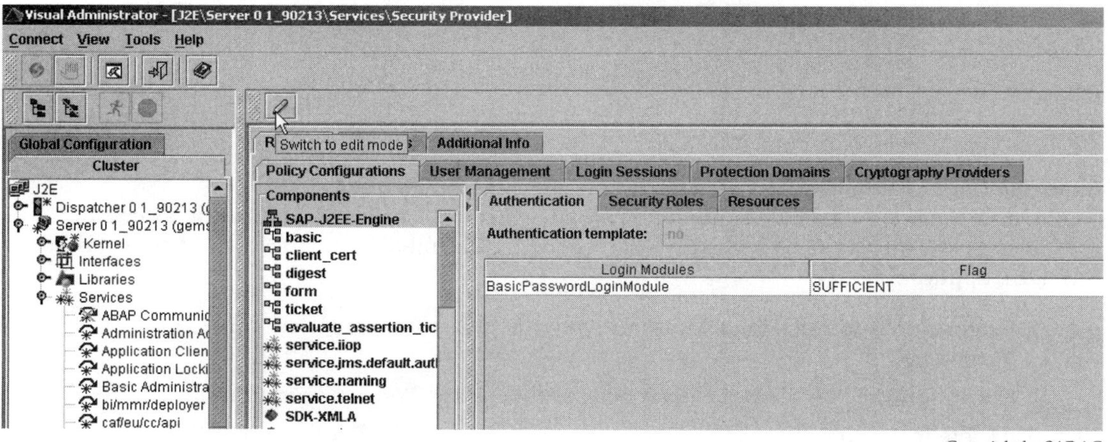

FIGURE 38-2 Login modules

login modules. To differentiate between the types of components, you should identify the icon that exists before the component's name, as shown here:

	Denotes the J2EE engine
	Denotes the login module stack
	Denotes the service
	Denotes the application

Under the Authentication tab, you can see the authentication template and the list of login modules belonging to that authentication template (or login module stack) for the component selected on the left. In Figure 38-2, the SAP-J2EE-Engine login module stack is selected, which is the default login module stack for the J2EE applications.

Tip *The SAP-J2EE-Engine login module stack contains the* BasicPasswordLoginModule *with the Control flag set as* SUFFICIENT, *which implies that user ID and password are sufficient for the authentication to succeed.*

To create a new policy configuration, click Add from the Components list and enter the name for the new policy configuration, as shown next:

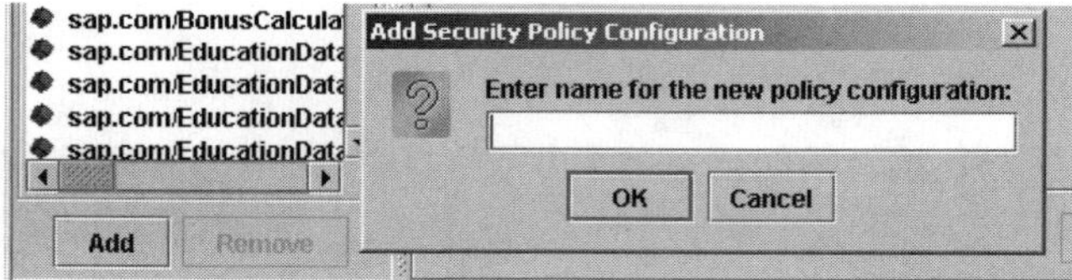

Copyright by SAP AG

Changing Initial Authentication Scheme for an SAP J2EE Application

To illustrate this example of login module templates further, consider the following example:

Given below are the steps involved when changing the initial authentication scheme of a SAP J2EE application.

1. Logon to Visual Administrator, and navigate to Server0 | Services | Security Provider.
2. Click Runtime on the right-hand pane and open the Policy Configurations tab.
3. Delete the current Login Module configuration for the SAP J2EE application under consideration by going to the components frame and selecting the SAP J2EE application.

4. Choose the Switch To Edit Mode button and set the Authentication Template to No by selecting "No" from the drop-down against the Authentication Template field.
5. Select the current login module and remove it by clicking Remove button, as shown next:

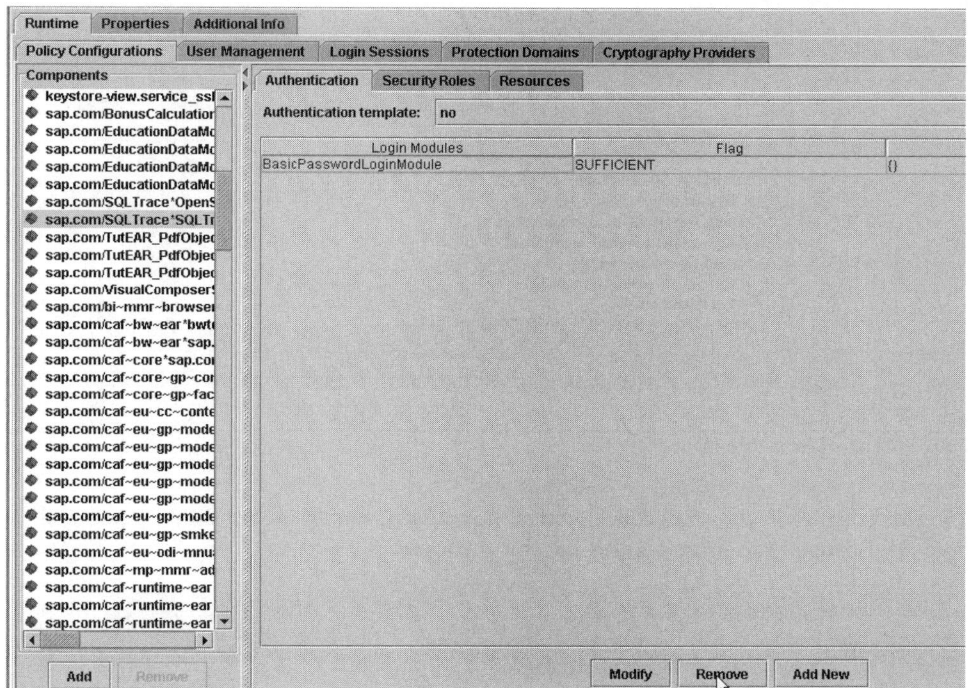

Copyright by SAP AG

6. Select the Add New button and select the EvaluateTicketLoginModule module from the Available Login Modules dialog box. Then click OK.
7. Log onto the portal and access the SAP J2EE application again. The application's logging behaviour will be different based on the new login module attached in the previous step.

Modifying the Authentication Template and the Login Modules

You can observe that the Authentication tab under the Policy Configurations tab in the Security Provider Service of the Visual Administrator provides the ability to change the authentication template or login module stack for the application; and remove, add, or change the login modules and their sequences as well as the control flags. Figure 38-3 displays a list of available login modules.

The next screen shows how to modifying an existing login module by modifying the Position and Flag fields. The Position field decides the position of the login module in the

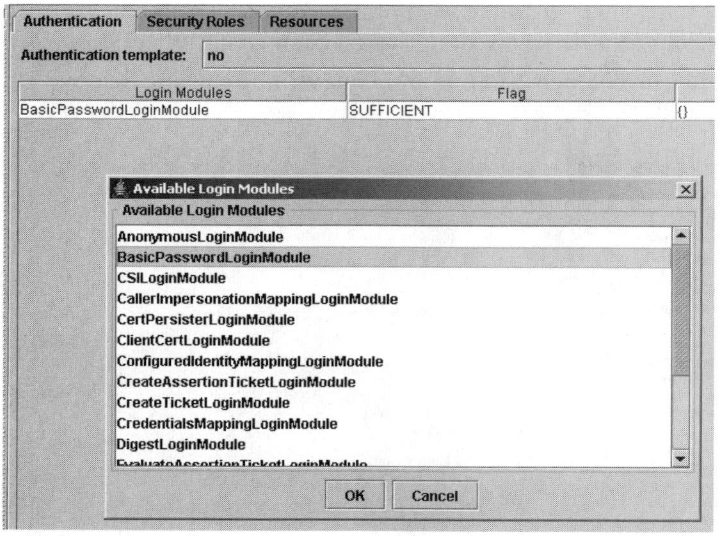

FIGURE 38-3 List of available login modules

list of login modules in the stack and decides the order in which the module is executed. The Flag field is used to set the control flag for the login module.

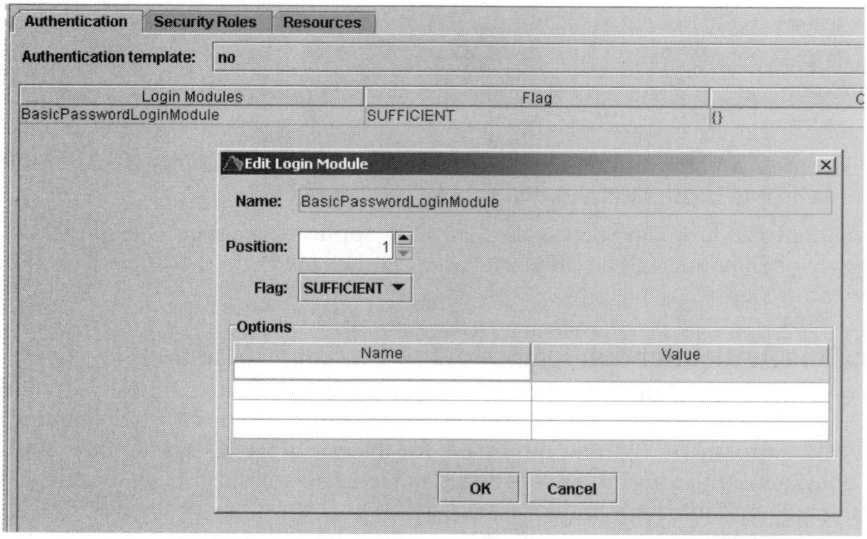

Authentication Scheme

The authentication scheme contains information on the following:

- Login module stack that is required for authentication
- User interface that is used to collect the information required to authenticate the user
- Priority that orders the various authentication schemes available in a desired sequence

Authscheme.xml File

The authscheme.xml file is a file under the J2EE/ume folder in the case of Enterprise Portal (EP) 6.0 SP2. Starting from NetWeaver 04, the authschemes.xml file is stored in the UME database and needs to be downloaded using the config tool.

The authschemes.xml file contains a number of authentication schemes defined using the `<authschemes>` tag. Individual authentication schemes are defined in the `<authscheme>` tag, and each authentication scheme refers to an authentication template, which is nothing but an SAP login module stack.

NOTE *Unlike EP 6.0 SP2, the authentication schemes are not defined in the authscheme.xml file but are defined in Visual Administrator.*

If you want to add a new login module, either standard or custom, you should log in to Visual Administrator and make the necessary changes to the template. Ideally, you can create your own login module stack and then add or remove the required login modules based on the required authentication mechanism.

Priority Number

You can have different levels of security for different iViews by assigning them to different authentication schemes. When accessing an iView, whether an authentication scheme is stronger than another authentication scheme is determined by the priority number that is assigned to that authentication scheme in the authscheme.xml file. Thus, if you assign a priority number of *20* for basic authentication and *50* for client certificate–based authentication, the client certificate–based authentication is considered stronger than the basic password–based authentication. Once the user is authenticated, the new authentication scheme is attached to the new logon ticket or the user session.

Sample Authschemes.xml File

In this section, let us take a look at the different authentication schemes files that are available for various authentication mechanisms.The following tags are contained in an authschemes.xml file:

```
<?xml version="1.0" encoding="UTF-8"?>
<!--  Configuration File for Authentication Schemes -|
<!--
<document>
<authschemes>
<authscheme name=" ">
```

```
<authentication-template></authentication-template>
      <priority></priority>
      <frontendtype></frontendtype>
      <frontendtarget></frontendtarget>
      </authscheme>
|</authschemes>
    <authscheme-refs>
        <authscheme-ref name=" ">
            <authscheme> </authscheme>
        </authscheme-ref>
    </authscheme-refs>
</document>
```

Following is a sample definition for the *uidpwdlogon* authentication scheme:

```
<authscheme name="uidpwdlogon">
<!-- multiple login modules can be defined -|
<authentication-template>
ticket
</authentication-template>
<priority>20</priority>
<!-- the frontendtype TARGET_FORWARD = 0, TARGET_REDIRECT = 1,
TARGET_JAVAIVIEW = 2 -|
            <frontendtype>2</frontendtype>
            <!-- target object -|
frontendtarget>com.sap.portal.runtime.logon.certlogon</frontendtarget>
        </authscheme>
```

You can see that the uidpwdlogon authentication scheme, which used in form-based authentication, contains the 'ticket' authentication template with a priority of 20. Following is a sample definition for the *certlogon* and *basicauthentication* scheme definition:

```
        <authscheme name="certlogon">
            <authentication-template>
                client_cert
            </authentication-template>
            <priority>21</priority>
            <frontendtype>2</frontendtype>
<frontendtarget>com.sap.portal.runtime.logon.certlogon</frontendtarget>
        </authscheme>
        <authscheme name="basicauthentication">
            <authentication-template>
ticket
                        </authentication-template>
                        <priority>20</priority>
                        <frontendtype>2</frontendtype>
<frontendtarget>com.sap.portal.runtime.logon.basicauthentication</frontendtarget>
        </authscheme>
```

From the above, you can notice that certlogonauthentication scheme as a priority of 21, which is higher than that of Basic Authentication and Form-based User ID/Password authentication schemes. So if the certlogonauthentication is attached to an iView using the AuthRequirement property and if the user has already accessed that iView successfully, then the user need not authenticate again to access another iView that has AuthRequirement property as either Basic authentication or Form-based authentication. Following is the authentication scheme definition for the *header* authentication type:

```
<authscheme name="header">
    <authentication-template>
    header
    </authentication-template>
    <priority>5</priority>
    <frontendtype>2</frontendtype>
    <frontendtarget>com.sap.portal.runtime.logon.header</frontendtarget>
</authscheme>
```

Following is the definition for *anonymous* authentication which has the lowest priority of –1:

```
        <authscheme name="anonymous">
            <priority>-1</priority>
        </authscheme>
    </authschemes>
```

Following is the authentication scheme reference, which should be included after the definitions for the authentication schemes:

```
    <authscheme-refs>
        <authscheme-ref name="default">
            <authscheme>uidpwdlogon</authscheme>
        </authscheme-ref>
        <authscheme-ref name="UserAdminScheme">
            <authscheme>uidpwdlogon</authscheme>
        </authscheme-ref>
    </authscheme-refs>
</document>
```

Notice that the default authentication scheme reference is based on uidpwdlogon authentication scheme, which implies that the User ID/Password authentication mechanism is the default authentication method. The `<frontendtype>` tag always has the value `2` for the portal. The `<frontendtarget>` tag contains the component name or the URL in the PCD for the iView that needs to be displayed when the authentication fails.

Changing the Authschemes.xml File

To change the authschemes.xml file, do the following:

1. Shut down the dispatcher and the server nodes in the cluster.
2. Start the config tool by clicking the configtool.bat file under the C:\usr\sap\J2E\JC01\J2EE\configtool folder.
3. Switch to the configuration editor mode.
4. Navigate to the cluster_data | server | persistent | com.sap.security.core.ume.service node.
5. Double-click the authschemes.xml file.
6. Click Download to save the authschemes.xml file in the local file system.

7. Switch to edit mode by clicking the icon shown here:

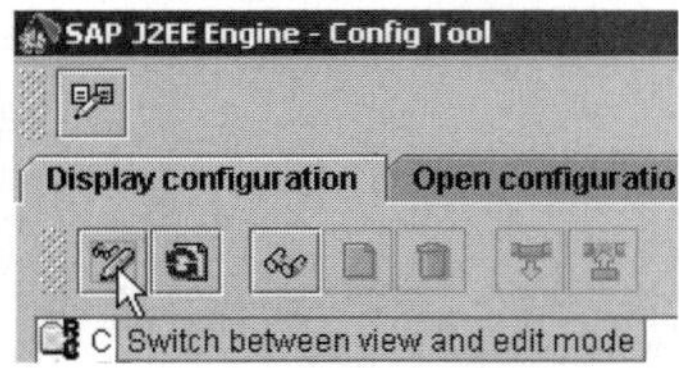

Copyright by SAP AG

8. Click Yes and then click the Create A Node Below The Selected Node button:

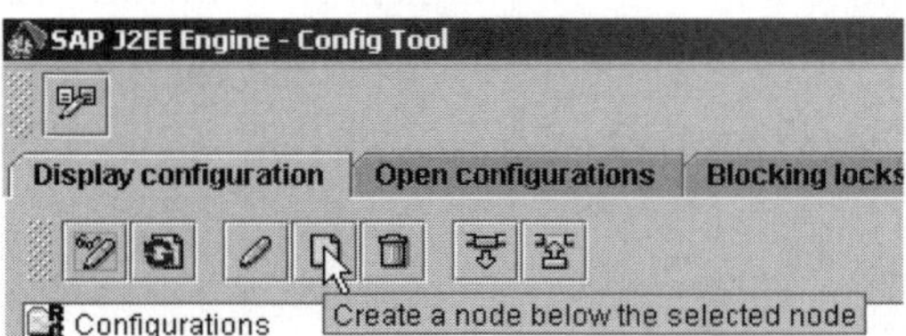

Copyright by SAP AG

9. Choose File-entry type:

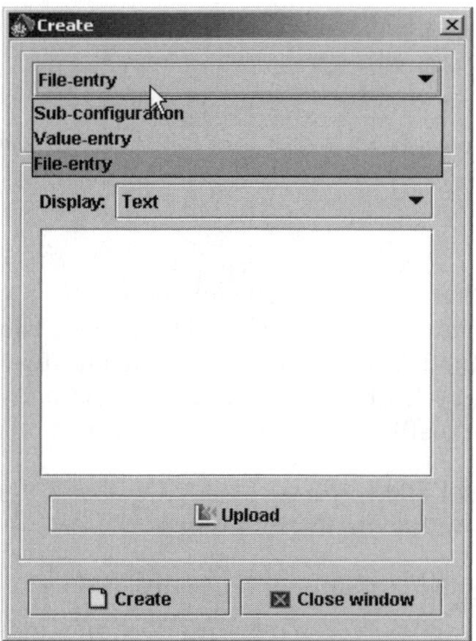

Copyright by SAP AG

10. Click Upload and select the file in the local file system where the changes were made.

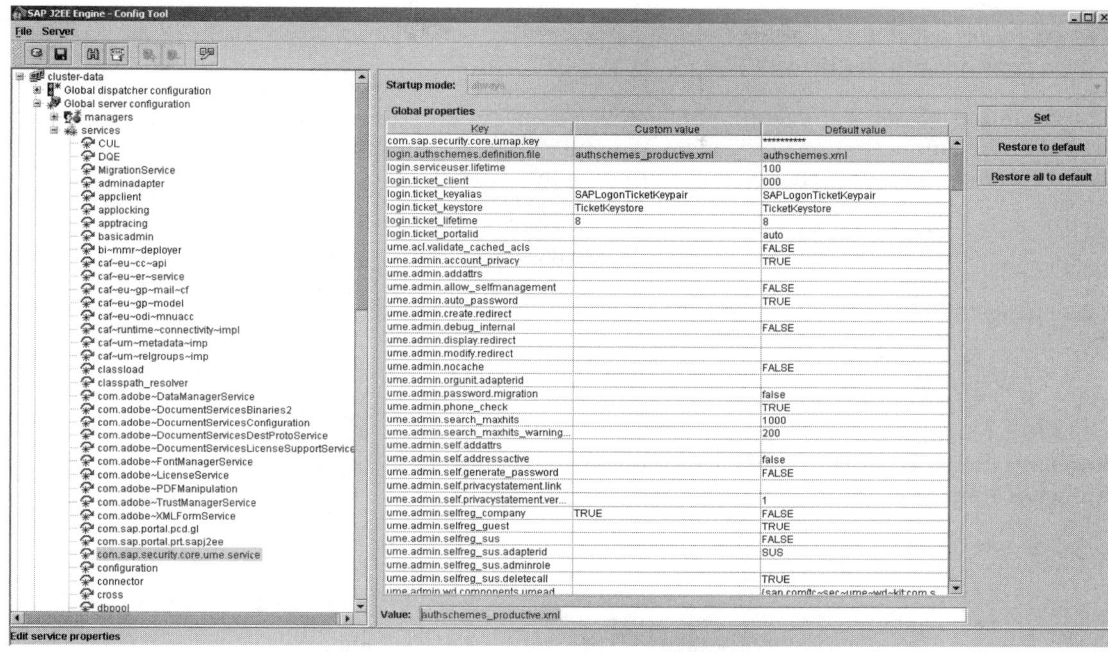

Copyright by SAP AG

FIGURE 38-4 Properties for com.sap.security.core.ume.service UME service

11. Change the default name in the Name field of file-entry type to **authschemes_productive.xml**.
12. Click Create and then click Close. The node will now be created in the tree structure.

Now, for the new changed file to take effect, you have to configure the UME property login.authschemes.definition.file, as shown in Figure 38-4. To do so, first change to the config tool mode.

1. Double-click the property sheet com.sap.security.core.ume.service after navigating to cluster_data | global service configuration | services.
2. Change the login.authschemes.definition.file property value as shown in Figure 38-4 and click Set. Click Apply Changes.
3. Click OK twice.
4. Restart the J2EE engine to activate the changes.

Changing the <authscheme-refs> Tag

On some occasions you'll have to change the authschemes.xml file. For example, the authscheme.xml file contains a tag called `<authscheme-refs>`. This tag is basically a pointer to the actual authentication schemes defined in the authschemes.xml file. The advantage here is that you can use the *authscheme* reference in the iView property.

NOTE *By default, all the iViews on the portal have a default authentication scheme in the iView property called* authscheme.

By simply changing the `<authscheme-refs>` tag in the authscheme.xml file to point to a different authentication mechanism, you can change the default behavior of all the iViews without having to change them individually:

```
<!--  References for Authentication Schemes, -|
    <!--  this section must be after authschemes -|
    <authscheme-refs>
        <authscheme-ref name="default">
            <authscheme>uidpwdlogon</authscheme>
        </authscheme-ref>
    </authscheme-refs>
```

After making the change, the file will look like the following. Here the default authentication mechanism is changed from user ID/password logon to the basic authentication mechanism.

```
  <!--  References for Authentication Schemes, -|
    <!--  this section must be after authschemes -|
    <authscheme-refs>
        <authscheme-ref name="default">
            <authscheme>basicauthentication</authscheme>
        </authscheme-ref>
    </authscheme-refs>
```

Once you make the change, the iViews will require basic authentication instead of form-based authentication.

Changing the Authentication Scheme Assigned to an IView

Go to Portal and choose Content Administration | Portal Content. Select the relevant iView, right click and select Open | Object. Choose an Authentication Scheme property under the Advanced Property Category, as shown next:

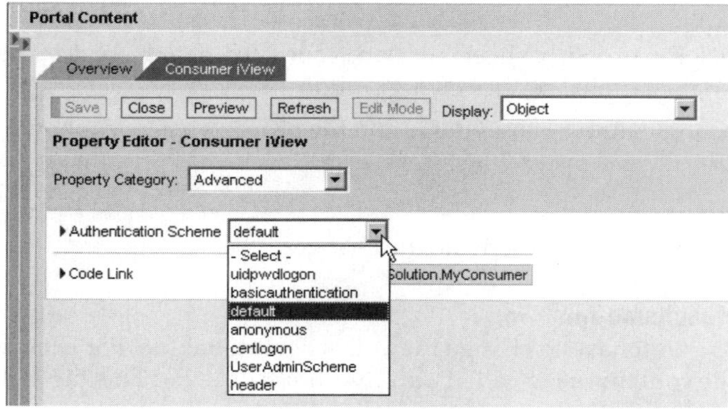

Another way to define the authentication scheme is to define the *AuthScheme* property for the component on which the iView has been based. Here's some sample source code:

```
<component-profile>
...
...
    <property name="AuthScheme" value="basicauthentication"/>
</component-profile>
```

NOTE *For more details, refer to the authentication related resources listed in Appendix B.*

Summary

This chapter discussed the declarative and programmatic security concepts and identified the differences between them. You looked at the various SAP standard authentication methods available and learned about the various building blocks of authentication such as JAAS specification, security provider service, login module stacks, login modules, authentication templates, and the login module flags. You learned about the login module process flow for authentication and learned how you can change the policy configuration to change the authentication method for applications. You then learned about the structure of the authentication scheme file and the tags used in the file.

39

CHAPTER

Transferring Role Between Portal and SAP

This chapter discusses the steps involved in transferring the roles between SAP and the portal. *Role upload* occurs when roles are transferred from SAP to the portal and *role download* occurs when roles are transferred from the portal to SAP. After reading this chapter, you will be able to transfer roles for SAP to portal and also distribute portal roles from portal to SAP.

Role Upload from SAP to Portal

Several steps are involved in transferring the roles from SAP to the portal. First, let's look at the initial upload.

Initial Upload

The roles, along with the transactions, can be uploaded from the R/3 Advanced Business Application Programming (ABAP) system using the upload tool within the SAP NetWeaver Portal. The role upload can be accomplished as an initial step to build content from the ABAP system. Note that the number of roles in the portal is limited (numbering in the tens rather than in the hundreds) as compared to the potential number of roles and objects available in the SAP system.

TIP *Take care to avoid the excessive proliferation of roles on the portal when using this automated method of transferring roles from SAP to the portal.*

Newly Created Content

The newly created content is created in the folder Portal Content | Migrated Content | SAPComponentSystems folder in the PCD catalog. The newly created content is automatically sorted based on the object type and the system to which it belongs. The MiniApps assigned to a role are created as pages, and for services such as transactions, MiniApps are created as iViews.

Subsequent maintenance of roles can then be done in the portal following the initial upload.

Do *Ensure that the required authorization profiles are generated in SAP every time a change occurs to a role on the portal.*

Maintaining the Authorization Profiles

Once the roles have been uploaded from the SAP system, you need to maintain the newly created content in the portal rather than from the ABAP system. However, the authorization profiles will still be maintained in the ABAP system. If the user assignments or the roles have been changed in the portal, the authorization profiles and the user assignments will have to be redone in the SAP ABAP system.

Note *Role upload from the SAP system is usually a one-time initial activity and further role uploads would be unnecessary.*

When uploading the roles from SAP into the portal, the authorization profiles that have been generated initially will continue to exist in the backend SAP system and are called into play when executing the transactions from within the portal.

Creating and Assembling New Content

After the roles have been uploaded into the portal, you may have to create some pages with iViews and attach them to the roles. If the newly created content has been created as worksets instead of roles, you may need to assign the worksets to the appropriate roles.

Single vs. Composite Roles

Either *single* or *composite* roles can be uploaded into the portal. Single roles always refer to a single SAP application and contain the authorizations available for the objects contained within that role. The authorizations could be *create*, *change*, or *display* and the objects could be transactions, Business Intelligence (BI) objects, business objects such as sales orders, and so on. The composite roles are combinations of single roles that help to create the overall menu structure. The composite roles differ from the single roles in that they do not have any authorization information.

Setting the Stage for the Upload

Let's now discuss in greater detail the prerequisites for the upload.

The objects that can be uploaded into the portal as part of the ABAP role are

- Transactions
- Business Intelligence objects
- Internet Application Components (IACs)
- MiniApps
- URLs

When uploading, you can decide whether to upload just the roles or to include the services (such as transactions, MiniApps, URLs, and so on) and attributes within the role as well.

You can also choose whether to overwrite the existing content in the portal. This is especially useful when you want to upload just the user assignments for the role without having to overwrite the role content.

Prerequisites for Uploading the Role

The prerequisites for uploading the role are dependent on the version of the SAP system.

- If the ABAP Basis release is earlier than version 6.20, the Enterprise Portal plug-in needs to be installed. This plug-in helps to connect the portal to the SAP R/3 backend system and to display data from the SAP system on the portal.

NOTE *The WP-PI plug-in is no longer available starting from ABAP Basis release 6.40 since it is now part of the PI_BASIS. For additional information, refer to OSS Note 723189.*

- The portal user who uploads the roles should be an administrator and the backend user should have the authorizations in the R/3 system S_RFC for the function group PWP2.
- A *system object* should be created in the portal for every backend system from which the role needs to be uploaded. The system alias name should be the same as the logical system name of the backend system.
- As far as possible, you should use identical users for both the portal and the backend system so that when the role assignments are also uploaded from the ABAP system, the newly created user in the portal is automatically assigned to the role.
- You should use the SAP logon ticket as the logon method for the system object. One way you can keep the users in sync between the portal and the SAP system is to configure the SAP system as the UME data source.
- If the users are not the same, you need to implement user mapping between the portal and the SAP users. Also, there should be one to one mapping between the portal and SAP users.

TIP *User role assignments will not work if more than one portal user is assigned to one SAP user.*

Configuring the Role Upload Service

You may be required to configure the role upload service as discussed here. For detailed troubleshooting, you can activate debugging by enabling the Activate Detailed Information For Debugging property in the Role Upload service. To do so, navigate to System Administration | System Configuration | Service Configuration. Then choose Application | com.sap.portal.pcd.rolemigration | Services, as shown in Figure 39-1.

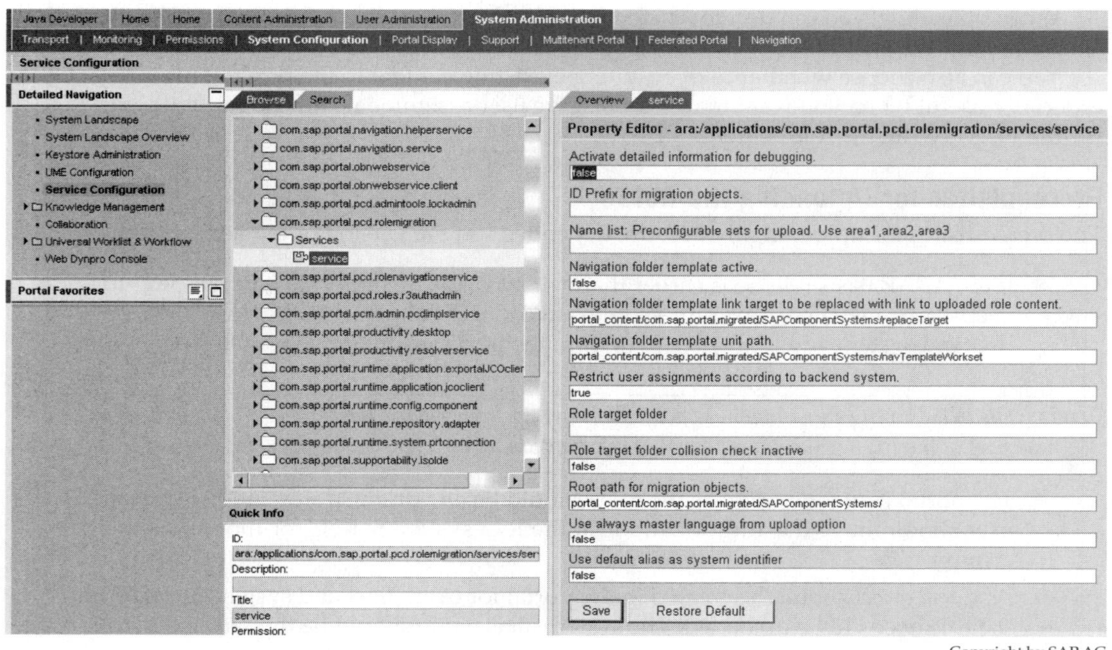

FIGURE 39-1 Configuring the Role Upload service

The ID Prefix Value For Migration objects is attached to every object created in the portal. Be aware that the newly created object will not be uploaded into the portal if the length of the object ID exceeds 100 characters after including the size of the ID prefix value.

The Restrict User Assignments According to Backend System default setting is *true*. If true, then the system removes user assignments in the portal, if they do not correspond to that in the SAP system. If false, then the user assignments in the portal are untouched and only the backend assignments are added.

As you can see in Figure 39-2, the newly created roles are created in the PCD folder as defined under the Root Path For Migration Objects property (see Figure 39-1). The default value is *portal_content/com.sap.portal.migrated/SAPComponentSystems/.*

For the Use Always Master Language from Upload Option property, the default is *false,* meaning the master language set in the upload options is not effective. If true, then the master language entered in the upload options is effective. This is discussed in detail in the next section.

NOTE *After changing any of these settings, the service must be restarted.*

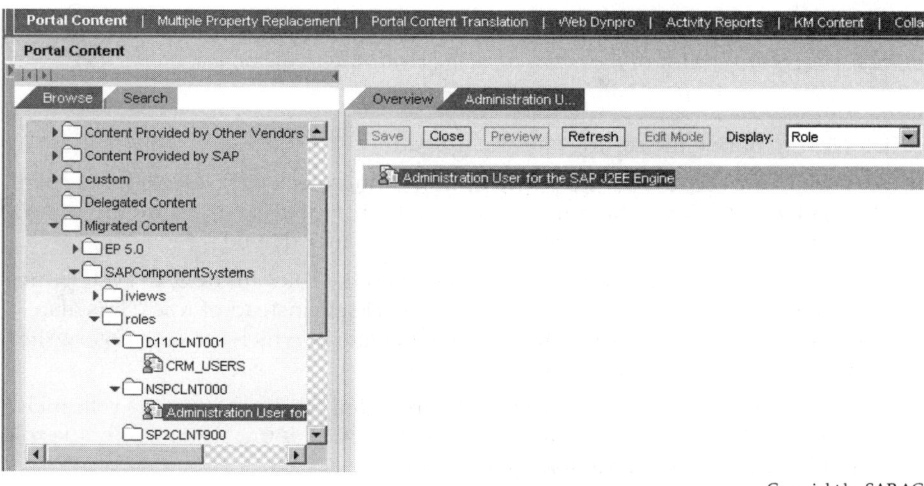

Figure 39-2 Newly uploaded roles

The Upload Process

To begin the upload process, first log on to the portal and navigate to System Administration | Transport | SAP Role Upload, as shown in Figure 39-3.

1. In the SAP System drop-down, select the required system from which the role needs to be uploaded. Then select the Object Type as either Roles or Transactions, and enter the required Search For ID value. Click Search.
2. Once the results are retrieved, select the objects so that they will appear under the List of Objects for Upload.

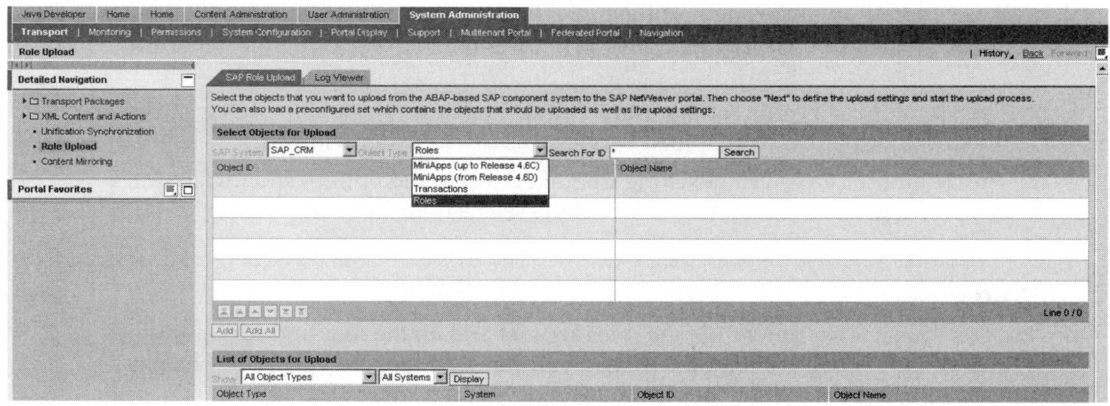

Figure 39-3 SAP Role Upload screen

NOTE *You can select objects for upload from multiple SAP systems, though it is not recommended. When these objects are created in the portal, they are created with the same value as that displayed in the Object ID field.*

3. Click Next to define the settings for the upload.
4. By default, the Upload User Mapping option is not selected. If selected, the users are uploaded along with the roles in the portal, provided the users are the same in both the portal and the SAP system or if the users are mapped.
5. The user assignments will not be uploaded when the roles in the SAP system are configured to be uploaded into the portal as worksets instead of roles. It is also possible to upload user assignments at a later stage, in which case the Overwrite Existing Content option should be left unselected.
6. If Upload Included Services is selected, the included objects within the role such as transactions are created as separate objects in the PCD. If unselected, only the role is uploaded without the transactions. The default is selected.
7. The top-level folders in the uploaded roles are by default defined as entry points. If this is not desired, Select First Folder Level as Entry Point should be unselected.
8. The default for Convert Roles to Worksets is unselected; if selected, the uploaded roles are created as worksets in the portal. As mentioned, the user assignments will not be uploaded into the portal.
9. The default value for Master Language is the portal's logon language. This is usually applicable to the objects that do not have language associated to them, which is the case for transactions. If this is set to a different language, the selected language setting will be applied to those objects that do not have a language (such as transactions).

NOTE *The language setting does not apply to roles since they have a language.*

10. The PCD Migration Folder setting is obtained from the role upload service and hence is read-only. This defines the target folder where the newly created roles are stored in the PCD. The default value is portal_content/com.sap.portal.migrated/SAPComponentSystems.
11. The use of the ID Prefix setting under the ID Prefix for Migration Objects setting in the Configuring the Role Upload Service was discussed previously.
12. The default for Overwrite Existing Content is a selected option, and this updates any existing content from the list of objects selected for upload.

Start Upload

Once the prerequisites for uploading the roles are met and all the required configurations for the role upload service are completed, then you can start the role upload by clicking Start Upload. If you want to interrupt the load, click Request Interrupt.

TIP *To check for errors, view the Details of the portal upload report. The LogViewer tab contains a list of the previously uploaded reports.*

Setting Up Detailed Navigation Menu

Another issue with using the role upload feature is that the top-level menu is populated with too many roles that make the portal navigation very unfriendly and cumbersome. There is a difference between the ABAP role and the portal roles in terms of their basic functionality. The ABAP role represents the menu of the SAP system for a given user and hence may have very deep navigation structures.

On the other hand, the portal role is designed more for portal navigation so as to meet the informational requirements of the portal user. So in such cases it is recommended that you display the newly created content in the detailed navigation menu rather than in the top-level menu. Newly created content, such as roles, will appear under Home | Work | Transactions.

NOTE *The steps for setting up the detailed navigation menu are defined in SAP OSS Note 762998.*

As outlined in OSS Note 762998, you need to activate the extended upload functionality by setting the Navigation folder template active property in the com.sap.portal.pcd .RoleMigration to *true*. This change enables the newly created content to appear in the detailed navigation menu instead of the top-level menu. Then follow these steps:

1. Download the navTemplateWorksetExample.zip attachment in the OSS Note and upload it into the portal.
2. Leave the current values for Navigation Folder Template Link Target To Be Replaced With Link To Uploaded Role Content and Navigation Folder Template Unit Path with their default values. These values are meant for the configuration related to the downloaded ZIP file.
3. The value for Navigation Folder Template Unit Path is portal_content/com.sap .portal.migrated/SAPComponentSystems/navTemplateWorkset, which points to the location of the uploaded content.
4. The value for Navigation Folder Template Link Target To Be Replaced With Link To Uploaded Role Content is portal_content/com.sap.portal.migrated/ SAPComponentSystems/replaceTarget. This points to the URL of the link target object. This link target object defines the position where the newly created content is inserted in the role or workset hierarchy.
5. Restart the service.
6. The workset template will create objects in the navigation path Home | Work | Transactions | backend role name. Since these folders are also available in the end user roles, the Merge IDs must be identical for these folders and the Can Be Merged property should be set to *true*. Now upload the roles as before.

   Keep the checkboxes selected for the following:

   - Upload User Mapping
   - Upload Included Services
   - Use Workset Template for …

Keep the checkboxes unselected for the following:

- Select First Folder as Entry Point
- Convert Roles to Worksets

7. Log on again as the end user and check the detailed navigation menu. You should now see the transactions available in the detailed navigation menu.

Role Distribution to SAP System

To transfer the portal roles to the SAP system and to generate the user assignments, the portal provides a role transfer tool. The transaction WP3R is used in the ABAP system to generate the role and the authorization profiles for the portal roles and then to assign them to the users.

Downloading Roles from SAP to Portal

When you have users in the portal with roles assigned to them, and if those roles contain iViews that contain transaction codes, then in order to run those transactions in the back end, you need to generate authorization profiles in the backend system and assign them to the backend user. If this is not done, the transaction iViews will throw an error.

It is not possible to transfer portal roles to the ABAP system on a one-to-one basis, because the two roles have different purposes and definitions. The roles created in the ABAP system are single roles and contain authorization data.

NOTE *Only those roles in the portal that contain objects in the SAP system such as transactions, MiniApps, and so on, are required to be created in the ABAP system.*

Prerequisites for Distributing Roles from Portal to SAP

The prerequisites required for distributing the roles to the SAP system are the same as the prerequisites for uploading the roles from the SAP system.

NOTE *The Enterprise Portal plug-in should be imported for the SAP Web AS 6.20. For more information, refer to OSS Note 723189.*

SAP Logon Ticket and User Mapping between Portal and SAP Users

If an SAP logon ticket logon method is used in the iView, the portal user is the same as the backend user. However, if the portal user is not the same as the user in the backend system, user mapping is required.

Creating the System Object

To transfer the portal role to the SAP backend system, you need to create a system object to identify that SAP backend system. The system object can be created under System Administration | System Configuration in the top-level menu and by choosing System | System Landscape Editor in the detailed navigation menu.

Distribution Process of Portal Roles to SAP

The distribution process of portal roles to the SAP system is a three-step process.

FIGURE 39-4 Portal roles corresponding to SAP roles in the backend system

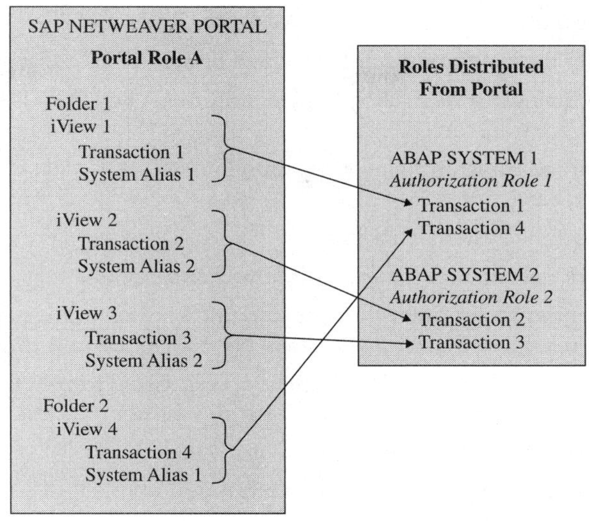

To begin with, the portal roles are transferred to the SAP system using the distribution function under System Administration | Permissions | SAP Authorizations. During this process, only those roles that have objects related to the ABAP system are transferred to the ABAP system. If required, as a second step you can follow it up by distributing the role user assignments from the portal to SAP using the Transfer User Assignment tool.

The third step is to follow up with the WP3R transaction in SAP to create an authorization role per portal role and per logical system. You can then assign these roles to the users in the SAP system.

Figure 39-4 illustrates how portal roles correspond to the roles in the SAP backend system. In the figure, iView 1 and iView 4 are part of role 1 in the backend SAP system. iView corresponds to transaction 1 and iView 4 corresponds to transaction 4. In the same way, iView 2 and iView 3 correspond to role 2 in the backend system. To start the role distribution from portal to SAP, do the following:

1. Log on to the portal as system administrator and navigate to System Administration | Permissions | SAP Authorizations. Then select Transfer Portal Roles.
2. Select the required SAP System, as displayed next:

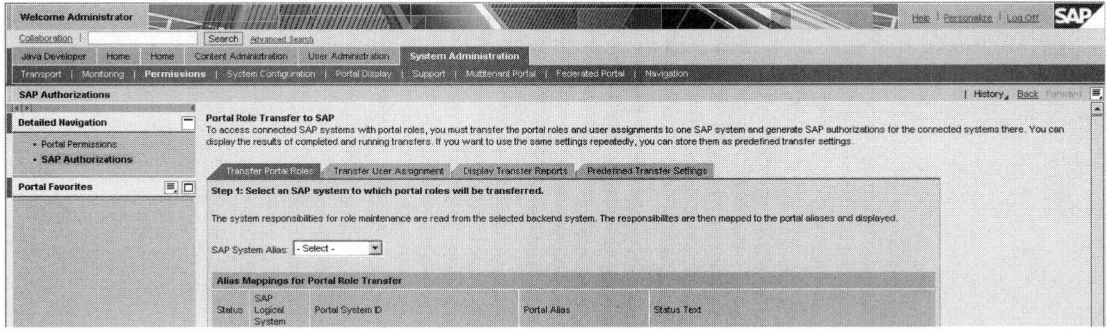

3. Select the checkbox Transfer All Portal Roles and click Next.
4. Only the system relevant roles will be selected for transport. Click Finish.
5. On the next screen, click Refresh and then click Details to see the log of the roles that are transferred.
6. Then, to transfer the user assignments, select the tab Transfer User Assignment and click Next.
7. Select the system, click Next.
8. Click Search. Select the required role and click Next.
9. The user assignment transfer starts now. Click Refresh and then click Details to see the results of the users that have been assigned and transferred to SAP.
10. Log on to SAP with the required access. Go to transaction WP3R and select the required portal role from the drop-down list.
11. Press F8 and select Create/Convert Role.
12. Enter a suitable name for the authorization role and create the required transport request.
13. On the Change Role: Authorizations screen, click the Generate icon. A pop-up Assign Profile Name for Generated Authorization profile will appear. Enter the required profile name and click Execute. The required SAP Roles and Authorization profiles are generated.

Relevant OSS Notes

Following is a list of relevant OSS notes:

- **723189** General information about Enterprise Portal Plug-In
- **762998** EP 6.0: Navigation structure for role upload

NOTE *For more details, refer to the role transfer related resources listed in Appendix B.*

Summary

This chapter discussed the importance of maintaining roles in the portal and the configuration steps required of the portal before uploading roles. It then walked you through the various steps involved when uploading roles to the portal from SAP. Finally, you learned the steps involved in downloading roles from SAP to the portal.

CHAPTER 40

Implementing Single Sign-On to SAP and Non-SAP Systems

This chapter discusses the benefits of using Single Sign-On (SSO) and the options available to implement SSO for both SAP and non-SAP applications. It walks through the details of different SSO scenarios available for implementing SSO to SAP backend systems and discusses the options available to integrate web content using the AppIntegrator and URL iViews. You will also learn how to connect a SAP transaction iView to the SAP backend system using SSO.

SSO to SAP Systems

SSO provides a number of benefits. It helps end users get authenticated once to the system so that they can access all the available applications, systems, and information in their organization. Examples of applications that can be enabled for SSO are intranet, extranet, workflow, Internet, Enterprise Resource Planning (ERP), Customer Relationship Management (CRM), Employee Self-Services (ESS), and Enterprise Buyer Professional (EBP) systems.

SSO is not only a matter of convenience for end users, but it also helps to improve the security of the systems. SSO helps overcome the hurdles that arise out of maintaining user IDs and passwords of different systems and password policies that mandate changing the passwords every few months. Users no longer need to maintain a cheat sheet of passwords or change passwords frequently.

SSO also helps administrators manage users (create users, lock and unlock users, delete users) from a central place. By enabling Lightweight Directory Access Protocol (LDAP) synchronization and maintaining a central repository of users, user maintenance can be simplified.

Implementing SSO for SAPGUI in Windows and the Web

SSO can be implemented for both SAPGUI in Windows and web environments. Following are some examples of implementing SSO in an SAP GUI on the Windows environment:

- SNC partner products
- Microsoft NTLM or Kerberos with Secure Network Communication (SNC)
- SAP logon tickets in SAP shortcuts

In the web environment, SSO can be enabled by using the following:

- Web access management tools
- X.509 certificates
- Integrated Windows Authentication using header-based authentication techniques such as Kerberos, Security Assertion Markup Language (SAML), Java Authentication and Authorization Service (JAAS), and SAP logon tickets

Authentication Mechanisms Using SSO

Let's now discuss the various authentication mechanisms that can be used for enabling SSO with both SAP and non-SAP applications.

User ID and Password

When the authentication mechanism is using user ID and password, you can use user mapping between the portal user IDs and the user accounts for the same user in the SAP and non-SAP backend systems to enable SSO. The user mapping is stored in the Enterprise Portal (EP) and can be managed either by the end users for their own user IDs or by the administrators as part of their administrative activities.

NOTE *Whether an end user or administrator maintains the user mapping information depends on the property* User Mapping Type *maintained for the system object that represents the backend system to which the SSO is being implemented.*

X.509 Certificates

You can use X.509 certificates for SSO to non-SAP applications. The SSO takes place using a direct connection between the client and the web server, and the EP redirects the request from the client to the web application on the web server to which the SSO is being implemented. The X.509 certificate is stored in the browser and is authenticated by the web server during the Secure Sockets Layer (SSL) handshake. For SAP applications, the certificate can be submitted either directly to the SAP application or through the EP from within an iView that makes a call to the backend SAP system through an RFC.

DO *The web application should be configured to accept client certificates.*

Integrated Windows Authentication

When using Integrated Windows Authentication for SSO, the SSO can be implemented for web applications that use Internet Information Services (IIS) using NTLM or Kerberos. Integrated Windows Authentication can also be used for SAP applications that are based on SAP EP 6.0 or Web AS Java 6.40 and above.

Third-Party EAM Software Agents

You can use third-party External Access Management (EAM) software agents for enabling SSO to non-SAP and SAP applications. You can use header-based authentication along with Web Access Management (WAM) agents for SSO with SAP applications deployed on EP 6.0 or Web AS Java 6.40 and above.

First you must log on to an EAM application such as Netegrity solution. This software will authenticate the user before accessing the portal. If you are using a URL iView, the client should be able to access the web application.

Security Assertion Markup Language

Security Assertion Markup Language (SAML) options are also available for non-SAP applications as well as for applications deployed on Web AS 6.40. The actual implementation of the SSO will depend on the specifics of the application.

Custom Log-In Modules

Finally, you can also develop custom logon modules for SSO using the JAAS specification in Web AS 6.40.

SSO to Non-SAP Applications

When using SAP logon tickets for SSO to non-SAP applications, web server filters and a ticket verification library are provided by SAP to implement SSO. For SAP applications, this is a relatively straightforward implementation because an SAP logon ticket is, after all, based on SAP's technology.

NOTE *For SAP applications, you need to configure the backend SAP application to accept SAP logon tickets.*

Implementation Options

When using SAP logon tickets for non-SAP applications, two different implementation options are available. The difference lies in where the ticket verification takes place.

In the first case, shown next, the SAP logon ticket is submitted to the web server filter located on the web server. The web server filter verifies the portal server's public key certificate using its local Personal Security Environment (PSE) and then populates the HTTP header field with the user ID for SSO to the non-sap web application.

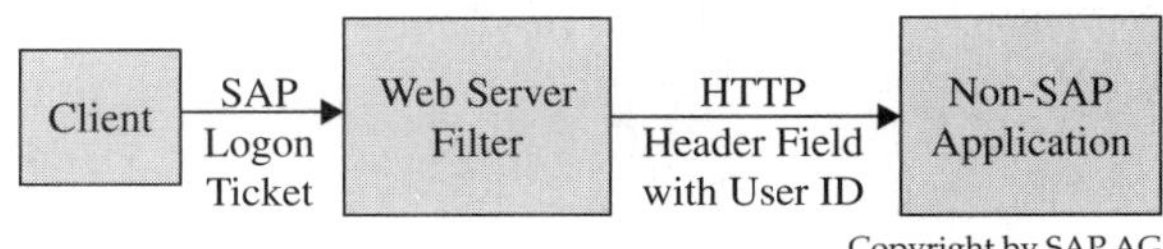

Web server filters are available for both IIS and Apache servers. They can extract the user ID as well as the authentication scheme from the SAP logon ticket.

TIP *Ensure that the portal server that issues the SAP logon ticket and the web application that needs SSO are in the same domain.*

In the second case, shown next, the SAP logon ticket is sent to the non-SAP application, which then verifies it using the ticket verification DLL and submits the user ID to the application for SSO.

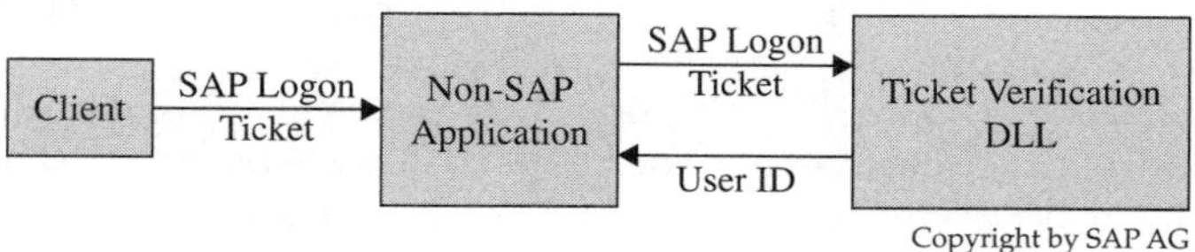

Ticket Verification Mechanisms

When the client accesses the third-party application, the application uses the ticket verification system to verify the logon ticket. The application may also check the access control list (ACL) to check whether the server name is included in it, and finally maps the user in the ticket with the user in the backend system before granting access.

A number of ticket verification mechanisms are available, as listed here.

Web Server Filter

The web server filter can be used for SSO to web applications that support HTTP header variable-based authentication. The filter verifies the digital signature of the ticket and then extracts the username from the ticket and populates the header variable named *remote_user_alias*. The *remote_user_alias* parameter is defined in the filter's configuration file.

TIP *The application should be able to read the header variable for authentication in order to succeed.*

Web Server Filter with Delegation to Windows Server 2003

No header variable is involved with this mechanism. The web server filter delegates the authentication mechanism to the Windows server that authenticates the user stored in the ticket. This filter makes use of the delegation functionality available in the Microsoft Windows Server 2003 and Microsoft ADS. The filter verifies the user stored in the SAP logon ticket and requests a Kerberos ticket for that user from the ADS. Then the ticket is used to access the Windows-based web application using SSO. This functionality can typically be used for accessing Outlook-based web access. The systems that support this are EP 6.0 SP2 and above, Windows Server 2003, and Active Directory Server 2003.

NOTE *Kerberos functionality is based on an ISAPI filter known as the* SSO2KerbMap module.

Java Ticket Verification Library

Some development is involved in this library and can be used for non-SAP Java-based applications. This library helps to extract the user ID from the SAP logon ticket for non-SAP applications. This is preferred over the C ticket library and DLL SAPSSOEXT methods for SSO.

C Ticket Verification Library

The C Ticket Verification Library can be used for C applications and is available in Windows 2000, Linux, and Solaris 8. It is also available in the wwpsso_v3.dll and helps to extract the user ID from the SAP logon ticket.

DLL SAPSSOEXT Library

The DLL SAPSSOEXT Library is used for both C and Java applications. This library is coded in C and contains Java Native Interfaces (JNIs). A number of C and Java sample examples are available.

NOTE *For more information, refer to the SAP help documentation and OSS Notes 442401 and 723896.*

Which SSO Option Is Best?

Your choice of SSO option depends on a number of factors, the chief among which is the existing security policy of the organization. If a public key infrastructure (PKI) is already in place, then a PKI X.509 certificate–based SSO would be the first choice. If a number of Windows-based applications are in use, then using Integrated Windows authentication may be a good choice. Of course, Kerberos-based authentication should be given the preference over NTLM-based authentication. If you have EAM software in use, you can leverage that for SSO for web applications. Finally, SSO using SAP logon tickets should be explored, especially for SAP applications. If none of these above options are feasible, your last resort is to use SSO using user mapping.

You can use three variants of SSO for SAP systems, as shown in Figure 40-1:

- **Scenario 1** SSO using logon tickets without user mapping
- **Scenario 2** SSO using logon tickets with user mapping
- **Scenario 3** SSO using user ID and password with user mapping

Which scenario you choose will depend on factors such as the following:

- The release of the SAP systems
- The customer's security policy, which may mandate the use of X.509 certificate–based authentication for self-service
- The user accounts in the portal server and the backend systems are the same
- The user accounts in the backend systems are the same but different from the portal server
- The user accounts in the backend systems are not the same for the same user

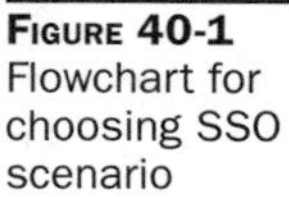

FIGURE 40-1 Flowchart for choosing SSO scenario

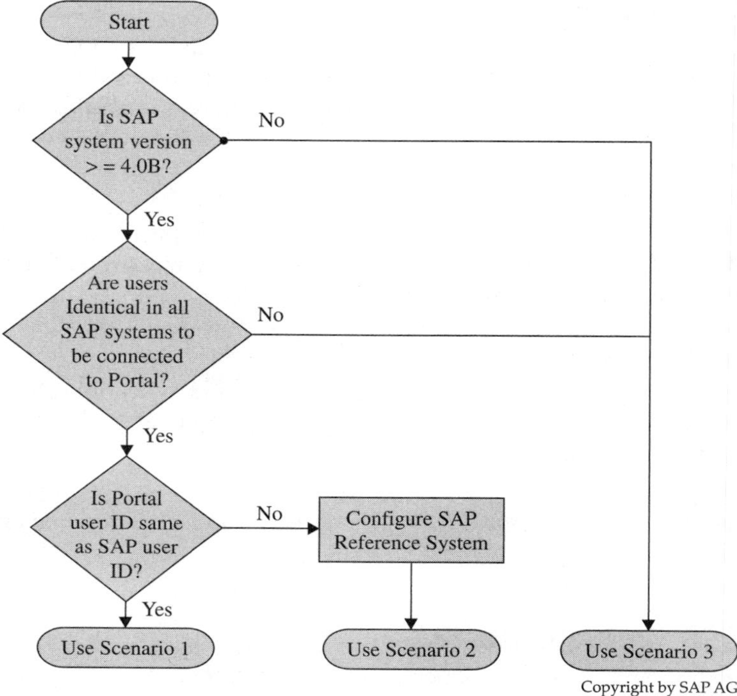

TIP *The SSO using logon tickets without user mapping is the most preferred way to achieve SSO and should be used whenever possible.*

Scenario 1

Scenario 1 is used when the users in the portal server as well as the backend SAP systems are the same and if the SAP systems that need to be connected are version 4.0B or later. To implement this scenario, you need to configure the portal server to issue SAP logon tickets and configure the SAP backend systems to accept and verify SAP logon tickets.

Scenario 2

Scenario 2 is used when the accounts for the user IDs in all the backend SAP systems are the same, but different from the user in the portal server. All the SAP systems should use a release later than 4.0 B. In this case, you should create an SAP reference system in the portal in addition to the steps mentioned for scenario 1. The user IDs in the portal should be mapped to the corresponding user IDs in the SAP reference system.

NOTE *Since the user IDs are the same in all the SAP systems, by mapping the portal user ID with the SAP reference system, you have indirectly mapped the portal user ID with that of all the other SAP systems.*

Scenario 3

Scenario 3 is used when either the systems are not later than version 4.0B or when the user IDs are different in the SAP systems. In this case, user mapping should be carried out between the portal user ID for that user to every individual SAP system to which SSO needs to be implemented. Moreover, the SAP systems should be at least version 3.1I or greater for the SSO to work. When user mapping is implemented, the user ID and password for the backend system are transmitted in plain text from the portal server to the backend SAP system.

TIP *You should enable encryption using HTTPS or SNC to prevent the user ID and password information from being compromised.*

SAP Logon Ticket Basics

An SAP logon ticket is a nonpersistent cookie that is stored in a client's browser and contains the following:

- Portal user ID and the mapped user ID in the backend system
- Authentication scheme used
- Validity period of the ticket
- Issuing system ID
- Digital signature of the portal server, assuming it has been configured to issue the SAP logon ticket

An SAP logon ticket is issued to the client once the initial authentication mechanism succeeds. The SAP logon ticket is then submitted by the client to the portal server for subsequent requests for accessing portal content. If the content lies with a backend SAP system, then the portal submits that logon ticket information again to the corresponding backend system for verification.

The backend system uses the public key information of the portal certificate stored in its certificate storage to match it with the private key information (digital signature) in the logon ticket. If the portal certificate is valid, the backend system extracts the mapped user ID and logs the user into the backend system without the need for a password.

Once the portal server issues an SAP logon ticket, it is then possible to access the SAP backend system directly or through the portal. In either case, the SAP logon ticket is used for authentication of the users—the only difference being that in the former case, the client is submitting the SAP logon ticket to the backend system and in the latter case, the portal submits the logon ticket to the backend system on behalf of the user.

Prerequisites for SSO

Before you proceed with configuring the portal and the SAP system for SSO, you need to be aware of the following prerequisites:

- For SAP systems earlier than 6.20, an Enterprise Portal plug-in must be installed.
- For systems earlier than 4.6C, the required kernel patches should have been installed including the relevant R/3 operating system patches.

- The SAP Security Library should be installed in all the application servers.
- The following profile parameters should have been set in all the instance profiles using transaction SSO2:

```
login/accept_sso2_ticket = 1
login/create_sso2_ticket = 0
```

- For releases 4.0 and 4.5, the profile parameter `SAPSECULIB` should point to the path of the SAP Security Library.

Configuring for Scenario 1

Several steps are involved in implementing SSO for scenario 1.

Configure the Portal Server to Issue SAP Logon Tickets To issue the SAP logon tickets, the portal server should be configured to be the ticket issuing authority. When the portal is started for the first time, the portal generates a cryptographic key pair, the private key of which is used to generate a digital signature. This digital signature is then stored in the SAP logon ticket that was issued by the portal to the client. The SAP backend system then uses this digital signature to verify with the public key information of the portal certificate that was installed in its key storage in a separate step.

To configure the portal as a ticket issuing authority, the two properties *login.ticket_issuer* and *login.ticket_client* should be maintained in the UME. To configure the UME, logon to the Config Tool by double clicking configtool.bat file in the portal server. Click Yes to the connection settings dialog box and Select File | Configuration Editor from the file menu. Switch to the edit mode by clicking the Switch Between View and Edit Mode button. Navigate to Configurations | Clusterdata | server | cfg | services and double click com .sap.security.core.ume.service property sheet. Select the entry login.ticket_issuer and enter the required value in the custom field and click Apply Custom button. Change the value for login.ticket_client also. You should restart the J2EE engine for the change to take effect.

NOTE *The value for the* login.ticket_issuer *is the portal server's SAP system ID and the* login .ticket_client *is usually maintained as* 000. *For additional portal servers that have the same system ID, the client can be* 001 *and so on.*

Configure the SAP Backend System to Accept SAP Logon Tickets The next step is configuring the SAP backend system to accept the SAP logon tickets only from the designated portal servers.

Export the Portal Server Certificate For this, you must first export the portal server certificate and then import it in the SAP backend system. To export the portal server certificate, go to System Administration | System Configuration in the top-level menu and choose KeyStore Administration | Content in the detailed navigation menu and click Download verify.der. Save the certificate information in the local file system.

Import the Portal Server Certificate and Add It to ACL To import the portal server certificate, go to transaction STRUSTSSO2 and navigate to certificate | Import. In the File Path field, browse to the verify.der file stored in the previous step and press Enter. Once the portal certificate has been imported into the SAP system, you must then try to add the portal server into the Public Storage Environment (PSE) using transaction STRUSTSSO2 (SAP Trust Manager) by clicking Add to certificate List button. After that, the certificate must be entered in the ACL. For this, click the Add to ACL button and enter the System ID (portal server's SAP system ID) and client values that were entered in the UME using the Config Tool in the previous step. Then save the STRUSTSSO2 transaction.

Check Whether the SAP System Can Accept SAP Logon Tickets Next, check whether the SAP system is set up to accept SAP logon tickets. Go to SA38 transaction and enter **RSPFPAR** as the program name. Then press F8 twice.

Search for the string *login/* and check whether *login/accept_sso2_ticket=1* and *login/create_sso2_ticket=0*, as shown next. These activities should have already been completed as part of the prerequisite check, but it is worth mentioning again.

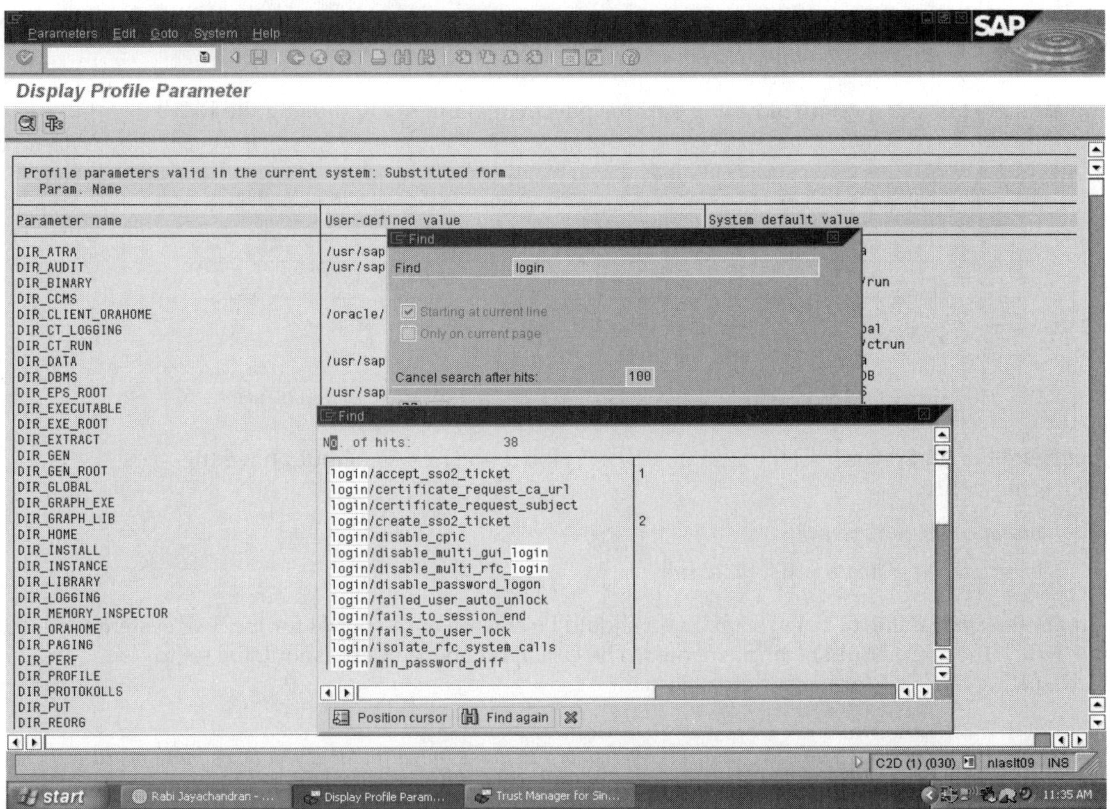

If the value is not set correctly, it should be changed using *RZ10,* as shown next. Click Change to make the necessary changes to the parameters and the system should be restarted for the change to take effect.

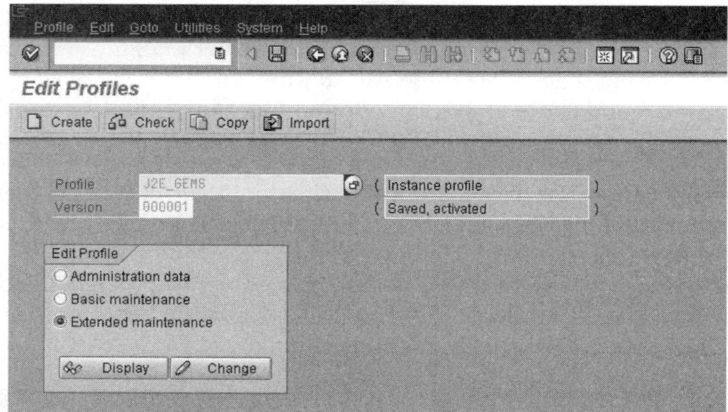

Copyright by SAP AG

The next illustration displays the various parameters maintained using the RZ10 transaction:

Parameter

24.09.2007 Active parameters 11:43:26

Parameter Name	Parameter value
rdisp/rfc_check	3
login/create_sso2_ticket	2
login/accept_sso2_ticket	1
login/ticket_expiration_time	48

Copyright by SAP AG

Configure the ITS System In the case of ITS, the global services file should have the following values:

~mysapcomusesso2cookie = 1

~login and *~password* must be blank

Create the System Object A system object should be created in the portal for the SAP system for which the SSO should be implemented. The *Logon* method property should be set to *SAPLOGONTICKET* for the system object.

NOTE *SAP logon tickets do not contain the password because the authentication takes place based on the digital signature mechanism. For issues with SAP logon tickets, refer to OSS Notes 701205 and 654982.*

Configure Multi-Domain SSO Note that the portal issues a logon ticket that is valid only for the Internet domain or the subdomain in which the portal is located. What this means is that the SSO will not work if the SAP backend system is located in a different domain when compared to the portal server.

It is recommended that either one DNS domain or subdomain be SSO-enabled for security purposes. This means that the cookie can be submitted only to the xyx.company .com or abc.company.com domain for authentication. SSO will not work if the domain is outside the company.com domain.

NOTE *The UME property* ume.logon.security.relax_domain_level *is set to 1 by default.*

Though not recommended, you can configure the SSO for multiple domains. For this, every domain should be configured as a ticket sending instance, and when the client tries to authenticate with the portal for the first time, the portal redirects the request to every one of those ticket sending instances. The ticket sending instances will send back the SAP logon ticket to the client and the client will get as many tickets as there are ticket sending instances.

NOTE *For more information, refer to the How to Guide on the SDN website.*

Configuring for Scenario 2

The following additional steps are required for scenario 2.

Logon Method Property for System Object in Scenario 2

The scenario 2 option is useful when the backend systems cannot be configured to accept and verify SAP logon tickets.

TIP *When user mapping is used, the backend system should not be configured for SAP logon tickets.*

While authenticating a user, the system checks for the user ID in the SAP logon ticket first. The system tries to authenticate the user based on the user ID and password only if the authentication based on the SAP logon ticket fails. So if the users are different for the SAP logon ticket and the user mapping scenarios, then depending on whether the logon ticket succeeded or the user mapping succeeded, the user allowed to log in to the SAP backend system could be different. This could mean the users may have different access, which may not be the desired end goal, thus leading to confusion.

Define the SAP Reference System

An SAP Reference system should be defined. Define a system alias for the required SAP reference system in the portal. Refer to Chapter 18 on how to create a system object for connecting to a SAP backend system. When defining the system, set the logon method property to *UIDPW* and not *SAPLOGONTICKET*. The property *UserMappingType* decides who can set up user mapping. The property *UserMappingFields* is additional credentials used for authentication. This can usually be left empty. Once the SAP system object is created, you can then update the SAP reference system as follows:

Navigate to System Administration | System Configuration | User Management Configuration | Security Settings. Enter the System Alias under the SAP Reference System field. Then carry out the same steps used for scenario 1.

User Mapping Between the Portal and SAP Users

You should next conduct user mapping for the portal users against the SAP Reference System. If no user mapping is found, the system will treat the SAP user ID as the same as the portal user ID. For this to work, the backend application should be able to accept the user ID and password combination for logon. Either the user or the administrator can do a manual mapping of the users. However, automatic uploading of users along with the user mapping information is possible starting from NetWeaver 04 using the batch import functionality on the portal. This is discussed in Chapter 36 under the Import User section.

NOTE *The user ID and password are sent in clear text; hence SSL should be used for increased security.*

Configure the User Mapping Type When creating system objects for user mapping, you can configure whether the end user, the administrator, or both can maintain the user mapping data. This is defined in the User Mapping Type property of the system object. You can also configure additional fields such as the server name, language, and so on, that can be added to the user mapping data for additional security along with the user ID and password. This is done using the User Mapping Fields and User Mapping Type properties in the system object.

UME Properties

The *UME* property defines whether the user mapping info is stored in an encrypted format for the following and should be maintained as such:

ume.usermapping.unsecure = T/F

NOTE *This setting is not possible in countries such as China and Russia because the cryptographic libraries cannot be exported to those countries for security reasons.*

The following defines whether the system checks the correctness of the password with the backend system when setting up the user mapping data for that system:

ume.usermapping.admin.pwdprotection = T/F

For ume.usermapping.refsys.mapping type parameter, you can use the *internal* setting when the reference system is an SAP R/3 system in which user mapping is done manually. However, it is also possible to use an LDAP as a reference system, in which case the value is *attribute*:

ume.usermapping.refsys.mapping.type = internal / attribute

The next setting is for the R/3 reference system and is used when the SAP logon ticket is used for SSO:

ume.r3.mastersystem

Verify the SAP Logon Ticket Contents

Once the SSO configuration has been completed, follow these steps to test the SAP logon ticket contents:

1. Upload the SSOSupport.par file (follow the steps in OSS Note 701205). Use the URL http://*<host>*:*<port>*/irj/servlet/prt/portal/prtroot/PortalAnywhere.default to deploy the PAR file.
2. Access the SAP Logon Ticket Analyzer. Use the URL http://*<host>*:*<port>*/irj/servlet/prt/portal/prtroot/PortalAnywhere.Go SSOSupport.
3. Click Send.
4. Notice the MYSAPSSO2 cookie used for authentication against the backend system.
5. Download the portal certificate, verify.der. Go to System Administration | System Configuration | Keystore Administration. Then download verify.der.zip and extract it.
6. Go to the SAP Logon Ticket Analyzer and click Send. Then click Browse and then choose verify.der. Upload certificate. You'll see the message "Ticket Check ***SUCCESSFUL***".
7. Change the *login.ticket_lifetime* to 24.
8. Go back to the SAP Logon Ticket Analyzer and verify the changes.

TIP *For troubleshooting, use OSS Note 495911 to activate the security log.*

To change the client ID, do the following:

1. Change the *ume.login.ticket_client* property to 001.
2. Restart the engine.
3. Check whether the client ID changed using the SAP Logon Ticket Analyzer.

Configuring for Scenario 3

There is no specific configuration required for scenario 3, however, the previous sections titled "User Mapping Between the Portal and SAP Users", "Configure the User Mapping Type", "UME Properties", and "Verify the SAP Logon Ticket Contents" are helpful when mapping portal users with the users in the SAP backend system.

SSO to an SAP Transaction Using an iView

Follow these steps to enable SSO to a backend SAP transaction:

1. Download the verify.der file. Go to System Administration | System Configuration | Keystore Administration. Download and unzip the verify.der file.
2. Launch the STRUSTSSO2 transaction. Import the verify.der file. Click Add to Certificate List and then click Save.

3. Create the ACL entry for the portal server. From the Cert. List area, double-click the entry for the portal server. Click Add to ACL and provide the system ID of the portal and the client ID of the portal server. Click Save and then Exit.
4. Create a system object with the saplogon logon method. To create a system object, navigate to System Administration | System Configuration | System Landscape.
5. Add the required permissions to the system object. The portal user trying to access the SAP transaction should have end user access to the system object.
6. Create a transaction iView and point it to the above system object. To create an iView, navigate to Content Administration | Portal Content. Right click Portal Content and select New | iView. Select iView Template option and click Next. Select Transaction iView from the template list and click Next. Enter iView name and ID and click Next. Select SAP GUI for HTML radiobutton and click Next. Select the system object created in step 4 before, enter the transaction code and click Next. Click Finish.
7. Create a role with Entry Point set to Yes.
8. Attach the iView to the role.
9. Add the role to the user.
10. Test the iView.

Integrating the Web Content

You can integrate the web content in two ways:

- URL iViews
- AppIntegrator

Using the URL iViews

It is easier to implement URL iViews for web applications. URL iViews allow user parameters to be passed through the URL, and those parameters can also be changed during personalization. It is not possible to use the POST protocol to submit the information to the server, and hence all the limitations of using a GET protocol such as limited length of the parameter value and poor security will also apply here. Both client-side and server-side fetching of content are possible. If links are available in the iView, the link should be accessible from the client.

Using the AppIntegrator

Using the AppIntegrator, you can integrate any remote web application, either SAP or non-SAP. The AppIntegrator allows you to use portal components that serve as templates for creating iViews that represent the remote application that needs to be integrated.

NOTE *The AppIntegrator provides a number of integration solutions for scenarios such as Business Server Pages (BSP), Internet Application Communications (IAC), Web Dynpro, Crystal Reports, drag-and-relate objects, and web-based solutions.*

In order for this to work, the client should be able to access the remote application directly, because once the content is loaded, the iView usually interacts directly with the remote application, bypassing the portal. Only client-side fetching of information is possible, but both GET and POST methods are possible.

Template Processor

When using the AppIntegrator to access content, you can pass parameters much more flexibly using the template processor. The templates allow passing static or dynamic information such as the following:

- Request information
- User information such as user ID
- User mapping information such as mapped user ID

Contexts The template processor contains a template with *tag expressions*, with the values that can be passed to the web application. The template processor uses a number of datasets called *contexts* to populate these tag expressions with runtime values before sending them to the remote application.

Following are some of the contexts that are available for populating the tag expressions:

- Request context
- Portal component profile context
- Portal context
- User context
- Look and feel context
- System landscape context

Custom providers are like user exits that can calculate the value for a specific parameter such as system.

Authentication Tag Of special interest is the Authentication tag, which can be used to pass credentials such as the user ID and password. To implement the AppIntegrator using this tag, you need to create a system object and configure the User Mapping Type and the logon method. If the logon method is set to *UIDPWD*, the `<Authentication>` tag is replaced with the *UserMappingTemplate* value. If the logon method is *SAPLOGONTICKET*, the `<Authentication>` tag is replaced with the *SSO2Template* value.

Since the user ID and password will be sent in clear text, the communication between the backend SAP and the portal should be encrypted. When user mapping is implemented using form-based logon, the source code of the logon page should be analyzed to get information regarding the method, the logon URL, and the inputs required for logging on. The type of method used can be found in the `<form ...method=` tag, and the logon URL can be obtained from the `<form ... action="...v` tag. The inputs can be obtained from the `<input name="..."`. You can also use any HTTP sniffer or similar tools to identify the same information.

TIP *Refer to OSS Note 796540 for more information.*

Relevant OSS Notes

Following are some relevant OSS notes:

- **442401** Web Server Filter for SSO to Third-Party Systems
- **701205** Single Sign-On Using SAP Logon Tickets
- **654982** URL Requirements due to Internet Standards
- **495911** Trace Analysis for Logon Problems
- **796540** EP 6.0: Problems with User Mapping
- **957666** Diagtool for Troubleshooting Security Configuration
- **320991** Error Codes During Logon (list)
- **912229** WEBAS Java: SSO Public Key Certificate Expires Every 2 Years
- **957707** Using Diagtool for Troubleshooting Single Sign-On
- **941423** UME: SSO Logon Fails Because of Password Lock
- **1050046** SSO Between Portal and Standard SAP JSP on J2EE Application

NOTE *For more details, refer to the SSO related resources listed in Appendix B.*

Summary

This chapter discussed the benefits of using SSO and the different authentication methods available for enabling SSO for both SAP and non-SAP applications. It then discussed the different variants available for enabling SSO for SAP systems and the factors that affect which SSO option is used. It walked you through the various steps involved in configuring the three different scenarios. It also discussed briefly how to integrate web content using URL iViews and the AppIntegrator.

41

CHAPTER

Implementing SSL on the J2EE Engine

The Secure Sockets Layer (SSL) needs to be implemented on the J2EE engine for enabling transport layer security when using Hypertext Transfer Protocol (HTTP), Peer-to-Peer Programming Platform (P4), or Lightweight Directory Access Protocol (LDAP). SSL encryption needs to be enabled in the J2EE engine when using it as a client, server, or intermediate proxy server. By enabling SSL, you can provide authentication of users, data integrity that provides immunity from tampering during data transfer, and data privacy that prevents eavesdropping.

This chapter discusses how to enable SSL on the J2EE engine and how to configure the client certificate authentication methods.

Configuring the SSL on the J2EE Engine

Configuring the SSL on the J2EE engine consists of two main steps: generating the key pair on each server of the J2EE engine and assigning the keys to a specific SSL port. Following are the detailed steps involved in enabling the SSL on the J2EE engine:

1. Download and deploy the SAP Java Cryptographic tool.
2. Download and install the Java Unlimited Strength Jurisdiction Policy Files.
3. Change the startup mode of the SSL provider and the key provider service.
4. Create the public and the private keys.
5. Create a certificate signing request.
6. Submit the certificate to the Certification Authority (CA).
7. Import the certificate request response into the KeyStore.
8. Assign the key pair to the SSL port.
9. Maintain the list of trusted certificates.
10. Test the SSL connection.

Download the Java Cryptography Extension Policy Files

Here's how to download the Cryptographic library:

1. Go to the J2SE download page at the java.sun.com website: http://java.sun.com/j2se/1.4.2/download.html. Navigate to the bottom of the page. Then click the link for downloading the library, as shown next:

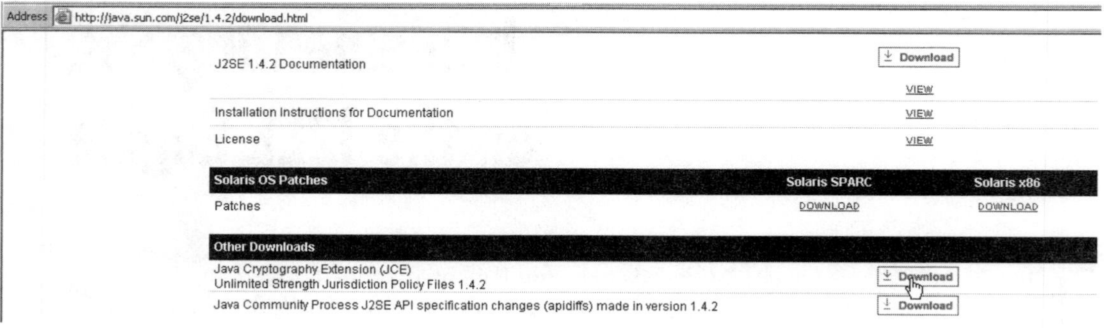

NOTE *The Java Cryptographic file should correspond to the version of the JDK that was installed as well as the JDK provider.*

2. Click Download and the File Download dialog appears:

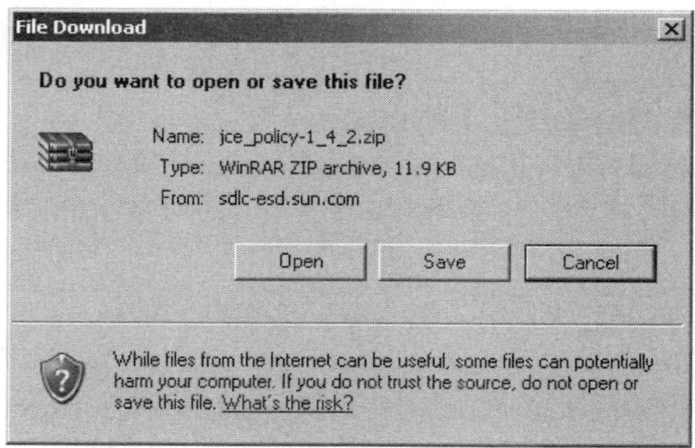

3. Save the jce_policy-1_4_2.zip file to a local folder.

Install the Java Cryptography Extension Policy Files

Extract the jce_policy-1_4_2.zip and you will see local_policy.jar and US_export_policy.jar files in the extracted folder. Copy these files and move them to the <*jdk_installation_directory*>\jre\lib\security and C:\Program Files\Java\j2re1.4.2_09\lib\security folder (required if you are using the JRE).

Download the SAP Java Cryptographic Tool

This step is required only if the SAP Java Cryptographic tool was not installed during the J2EE installation. The SAP Java Cryptographic library is already included in the default J2EE installation, but it does not have the necessary functions for implementing SSL.

NOTE *The SAP Java Cryptographic Library is subject to German export regulations as well as the local country regulations and hence may not be available for all customers.*

Here's how to download the SAP Java Cryptographic Library:

1. Go to http://service.sap.com/swdc and click Download.
2. Click SAP Cryptographic Software and a pop-up will appear as shown below. Select the checkbox for the Crypto Library relevant for the J2EE engine release 6.30, and click Add To Download Basket.

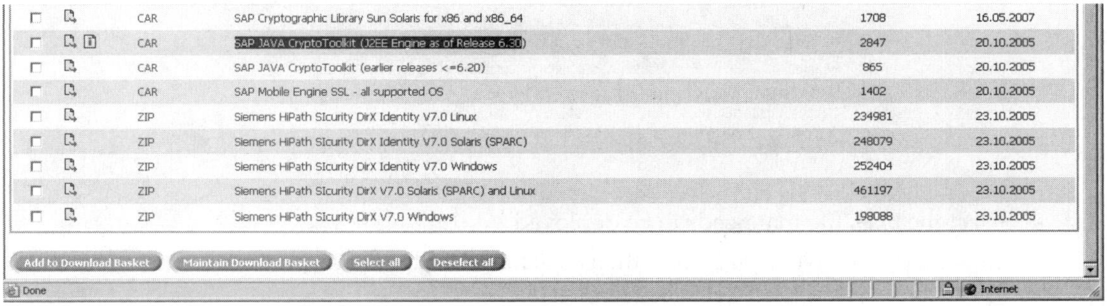

Type	Description	Size	Date
CAR	SAP Cryptographic Library Sun Solaris for x86 and x86_64	1708	16.05.2007
CAR	SAP JAVA CryptoToolkit (J2EE Engine as of Release 6.30)	2847	20.10.2005
CAR	SAP JAVA CryptoToolkit (earlier releases <=6.20)	865	20.10.2005
CAR	SAP Mobile Engine SSL - all supported OS	1402	20.10.2005
ZIP	Siemens HiPath SIcurity DirX Identity V7.0 Linux	234981	23.10.2005
ZIP	Siemens HiPath SIcurity DirX Identity V7.0 Solaris (SPARC)	248079	23.10.2005
ZIP	Siemens HiPath SIcurity DirX Identity V7.0 Windows	252404	23.10.2005
ZIP	Siemens HiPath SIcurity DirX V7.0 Solaris (SPARC) and Linux	461197	23.10.2005
ZIP	Siemens HiPath SIcurity DirX V7.0 Windows	198088	23.10.2005

Add to Download Basket | Maintain Download Basket | Select all | Deselect all

Done | Internet

3. Go to the SAP Download Manager by choosing Start | All Programs | SAP Download Manager | Download Manager.
4. Select the SAP JAVA CryptoToolkit (J2EE Engine as of Release 6.30) and click Download.

Uncar the Downloaded Cryptographic File

Once the download is complete, go to the download store and uncar the downloaded file. The location of the download store can be found in the SAP Download Manager Configuration | Download Store. To uncar the file, copy the CAR file into the directory where the sapcar EXE file is stored. Open the DOS prompt and navigate to the directory where the SAPCAR executable is available, as shown next. Enter **sapcar –xvf <*name_of_crypto_file*>** and press ENTER.

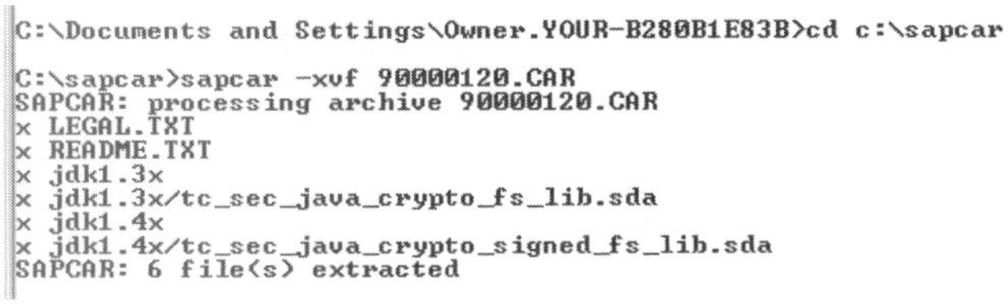

```
C:\Documents and Settings\Owner.YOUR-B280B1E83B>cd c:\sapcar

C:\sapcar>sapcar -xvf 90000120.CAR
SAPCAR: processing archive 90000120.CAR
x LEGAL.TXT
x README.TXT
x jdk1.3x
x jdk1.3x/tc_sec_java_crypto_fs_lib.sda
x jdk1.4x
x jdk1.4x/tc_sec_java_crypto_signed_fs_lib.sda
SAPCAR: 6 file(s) extracted
```

Deploy the SAP Java Cryptographic Tool

After extracting the crypto file, open the relevant JDK folder, which in this case is jdk1.4x, and deploy the tc_sec_java_crypto_signed_fs_lib.sda file. Here's how to deploy the SDA file:

1. Use the SDM tool by clicking the RemoteGui.bat file in the <*drive*>:\usr\sap\<*SID*>\JC<*instance_no*>\SDM\program folder.
2. Click Connect to SDM Server, and enter the SDM password.
3. Open the Deployment tab, and then click Add SCA/SDA to Deployment List (Local File Browser) – ALT+A icon, as shown here:

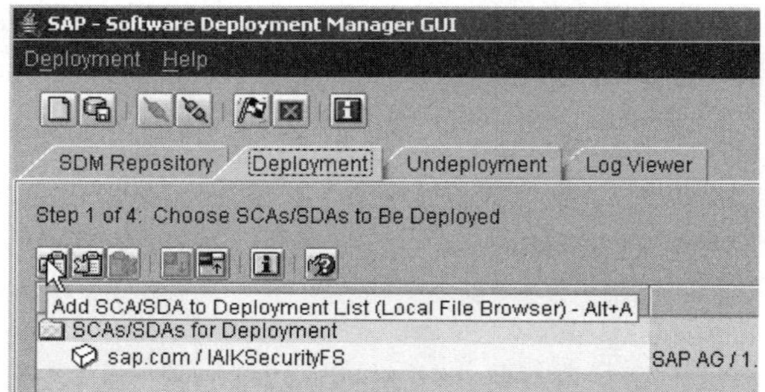

Copyright by SAP AG

4. Select the SDA file that needs to be deployed.
5. Click Next, click Next again, and then click Start Deployment.

TIP *Make sure that the library stored under Dispatcher | Libraries | core_lib is* iaik_jce.jar *and not* iaik_jce_export.jar.

Configure the SSL Provider and the Key Storage Service for Automatic Startup

The next step is to verify that the SSL Provider service and the Key Storage service for the dispatcher and the server have an automatic startup mode, so that they run every time the J2EE engine is started. Figure 41-1 shows the Startup Mode for the SSL Provider service, which is set to *ALWAYS*.

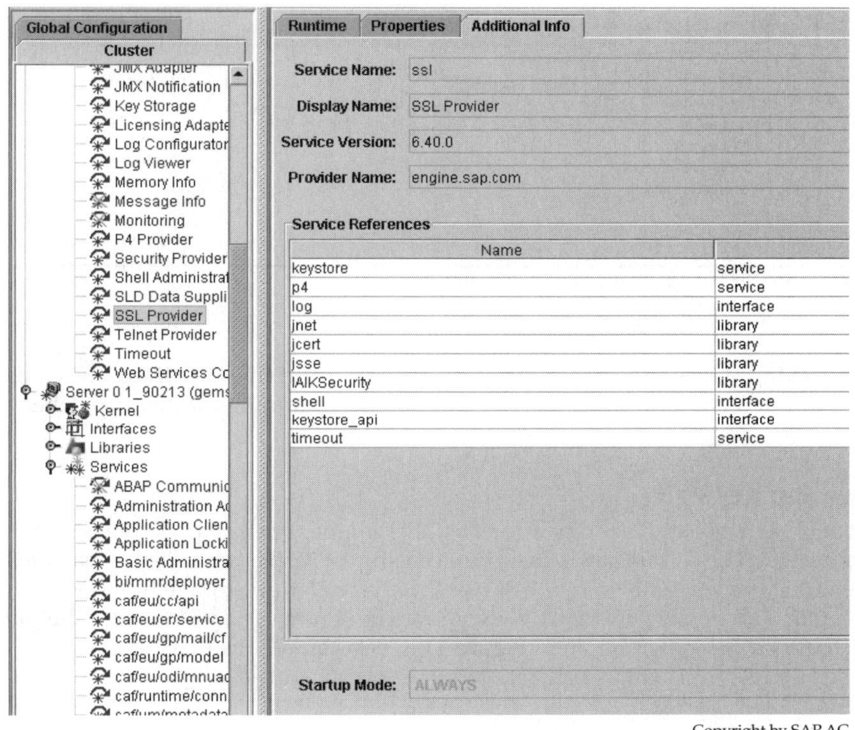

Copyright by SAP AG

FIGURE 41-1 Startup mode for the SSL Provider service

If any of the services is not running, go to the config tool, navigate to the SSL and KeyStore services for the dispatcher and server, and change the Startup Mode to *always*, as shown next:

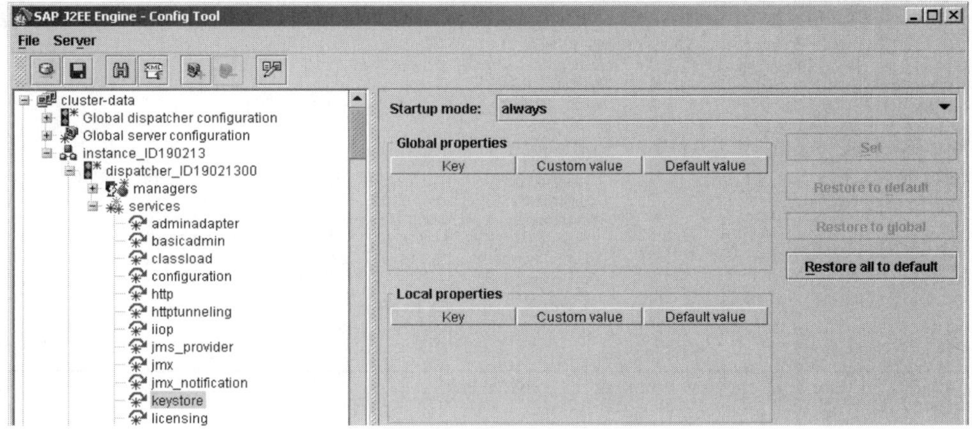

Copyright by SAP AG

FIGURE 41-2 The DEFAULT view displays the public key.

After making the changes, restart the J2EE engine and then log in to the Visual Administrator and check to see if these two services are running for the dispatcher and the server.

Generate the Key Pair

The next step is to create the key pair for the J2EE engine. The key pair consists of a *public* and a *private* key. The public key is distributed using an X.509 public key certificate.

To generate the key pair, go to the Server | Services | Key Storage in the Visual Administrator. Under the DEFAULT view, shown in Figure 41-2, you can see the public key; under the service_ssl view, shown in Figure 41-3, you can see the private key.

NOTE *The private and the public keys are provided during the default installation.*

When you click the ssl-credentials-cert entry in the Entries section, you can view the public key certificate that was signed by a test CA. You need to create a new certificate that is signed by an actual productive CA when running the J2EE engine in production mode.

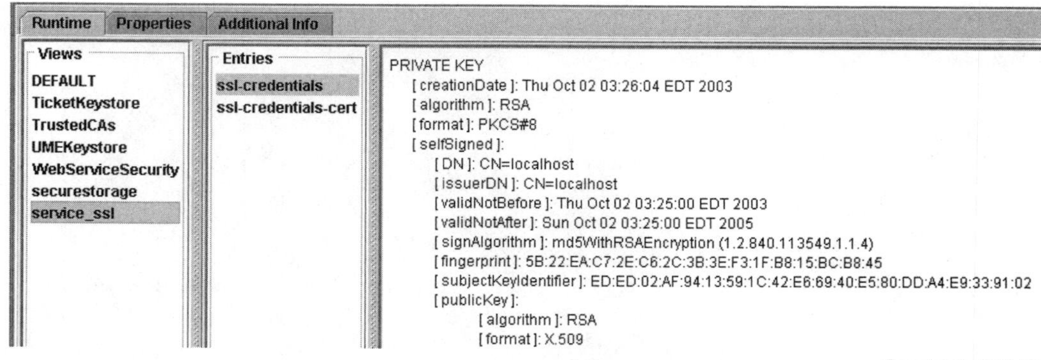

FIGURE 41-3 The service_ssl view displays the private key.

Here's how to create a new key:

1. In the Content tab of the Entries view, click Create.
2. Enter the values in the Key and Certificate Generation box. In the Common Name field, enter the fully qualified host name by which the portal server should be accessed.
3. If multiple servers need to be accessed using the same fully qualified host name, you should generate one key pair and use it for the other hosts as well. For example, when using a dual stack system, you would generate the key in the ABAP system and then upload it into the J2EE engine. Enter **Portal** as the Entry Name. This name will appear under the Entries section.
4. Select the Store Certificate checkbox so that you can save the certificate and export it later for future use.
5. Select RSA as the Algorithm, as shown next:

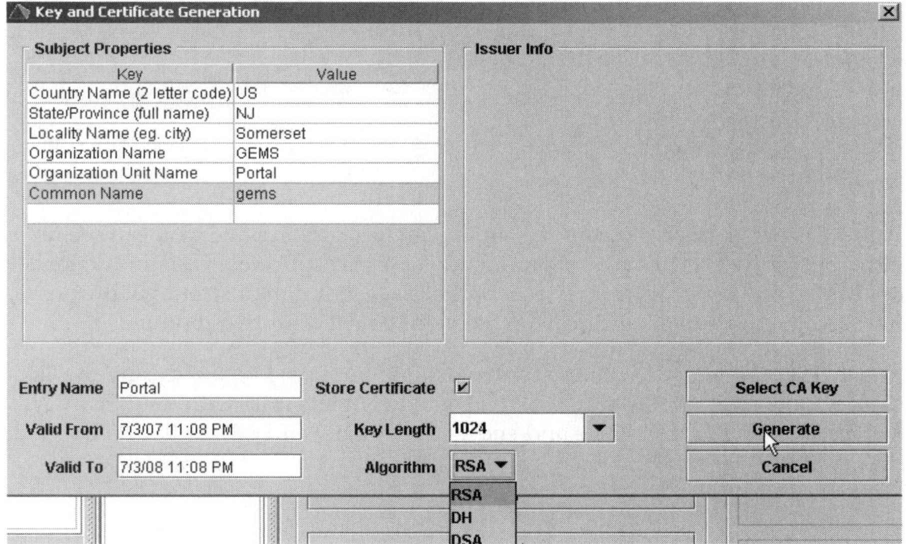

Copyright by SAP AG

6. Click Generate to generate the public key and the certificate.

You will see two new entries with the names *Portal* and *Portal-cert*. Portal is the private key and Portal-cert is the certificate. The key pair is not signed by a CA, so you now need to generate the Certificate Signing Request (CSR) and submit it to a CA for signing.

Generate the CSR and Import It into the J2EE Engine

You can use the SAP Trust Center or other CAs such as VeriSign to sign the key. To generate the CSR, click the private key entry and then choose Generate CSR Request. In the dialog box that appears, shown next, enter the file name and save it locally.

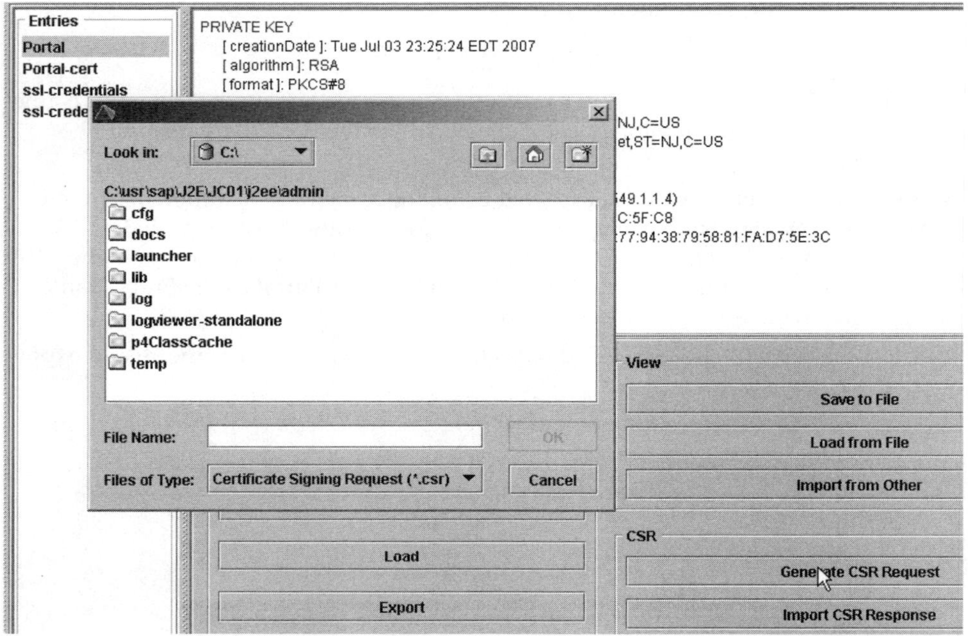

Then go to http://service.sap.com/tcs. In the left navigation pane, you can see links for getting either test server certificates or production server certificates. The production server certificates can be ordered from the service marketplace. For demonstrational purposes, we'll download the test server certificate, which will be valid for two months.

1. Click Test it Now and paste the contents of the file saved before during the Generate CSR Request step. Make sure that the pasted contents start with -----*BEGIN NEW CERTIFICATE REQUEST*----- and end with -----*END NEW CERTIFICATE REQUEST*----- as shown next:

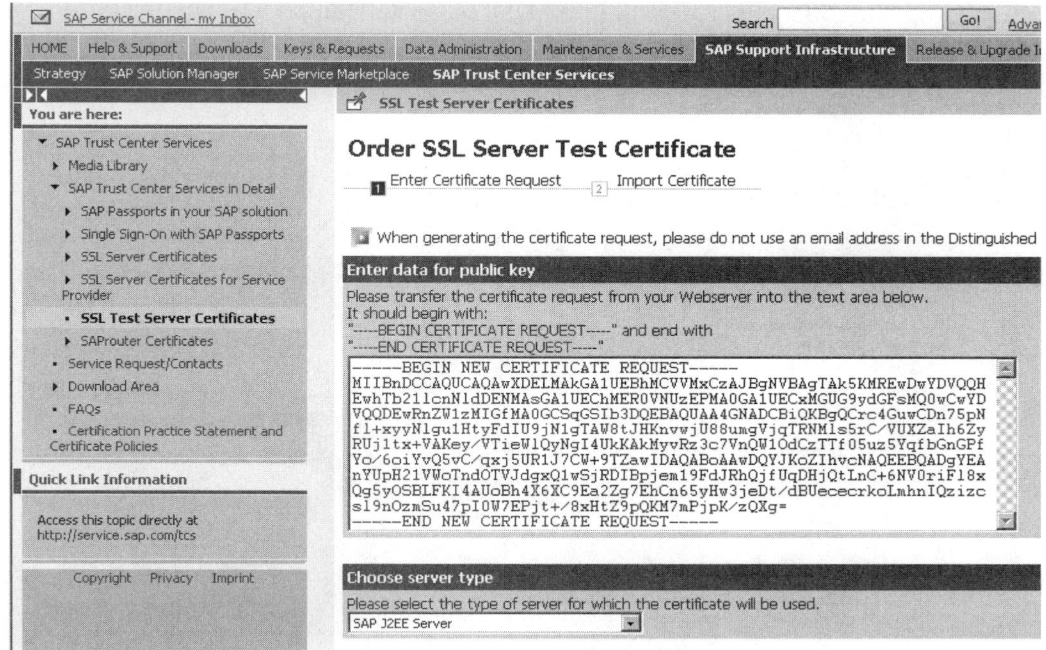

Copyright by SAP AG

2. Choose the SAP J2EE Server as the Server Type.
3. Click Continue. In the next screen, you will be able to view the CSR response:

Copyright by SAP AG

4. Copy this information as a file in the J2EE server and import it by clicking on Import CSR Response:

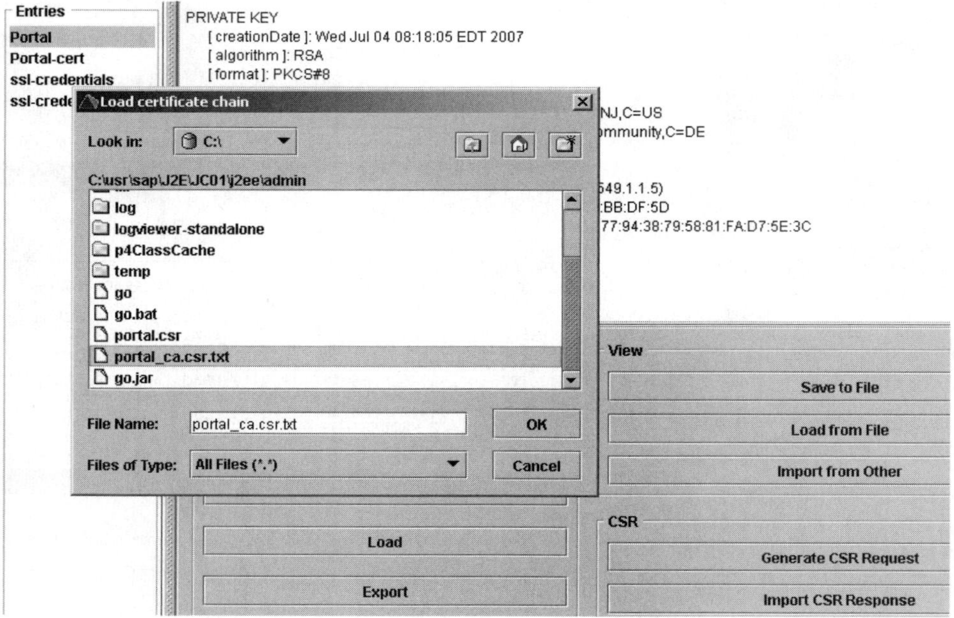

5. The imported private key is as shown here:

[validNotBefore]: Wed Jul 04 07:02:47 EDT 2007
[validNotAfter]: Sun Sep 02 07:02:47 EDT 2007

You can see that the private key has now been signed by the SAP Trust Community (as shown next) and also the validity period of the certificate is for two months based on the values found here.

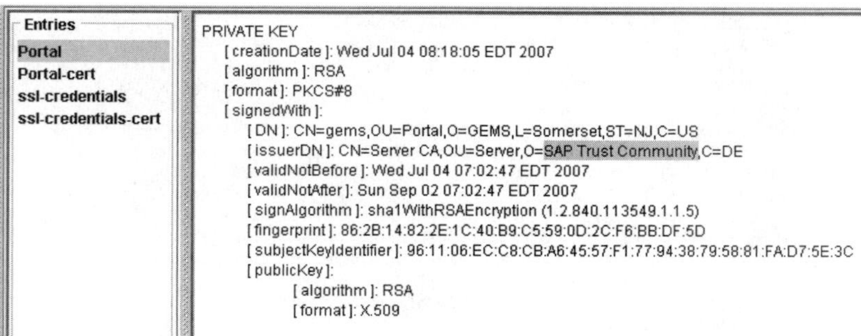

Bind the Key Pair to a Specific SSL Port

Your next step is to load this key pair entry into the Dispatcher's SSL Provider service under the Server Identity tab. The port to be used for SSL is based on the Ports property of the dispatcher's HTTP Provider service, as shown here:

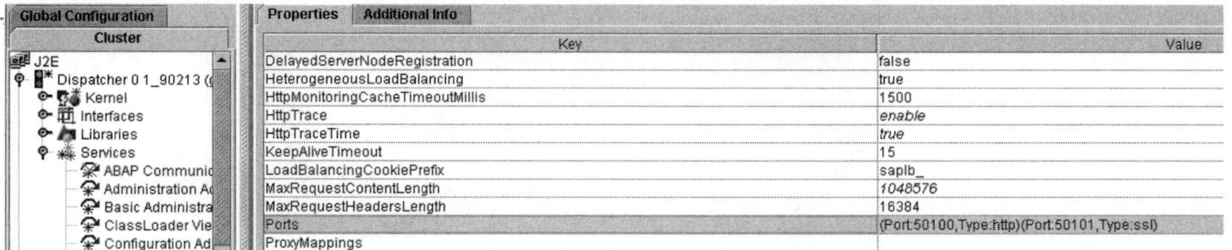

Under the Runtime | Configuration | Active Sockets, select the port relevant to HTTP protocol, which in this case is 50101. Three active sockets are available: 5<xx>01 for HTTPS, 5<xx>03 for IIOP with SSL, and 5<xx>06 for P4 with SSL. Click Add and select the newly added key pair named Portal in the Available Credentials dialog, shown next. Then click OK.

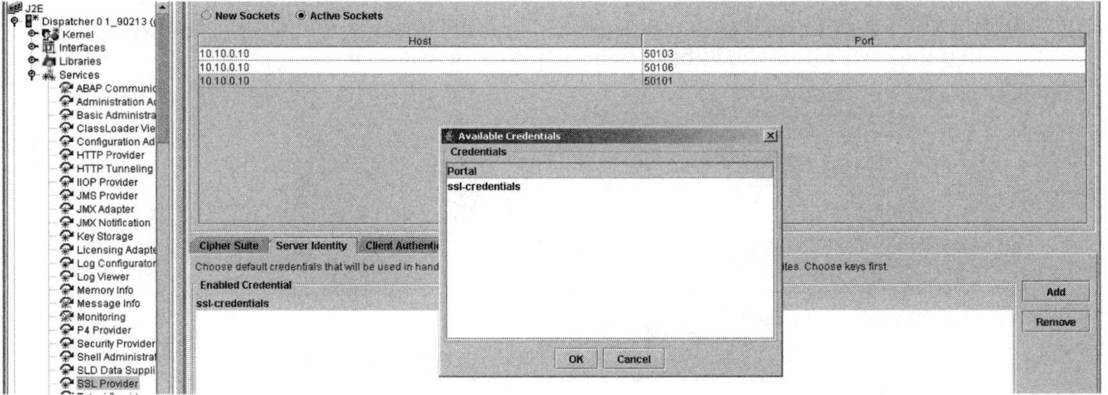

Test the SSL Functionality

Your final step is to verify that the SSL is working. Access the J2EE server using the URL https://*<your_common_name>*:50101. A Security Alert dialog may display, as shown in Figure 41-4, for the following reasons:

- The server certificate used by the J2EE engine is expired or invalid.

  The CA (which in this case is the SAP Trust Center) is not trusted by the client browser.

- The host name used in the URL to access the portal server (or the J2EE server) is not the same as the name found in the Distinguished Name in the server certificate.

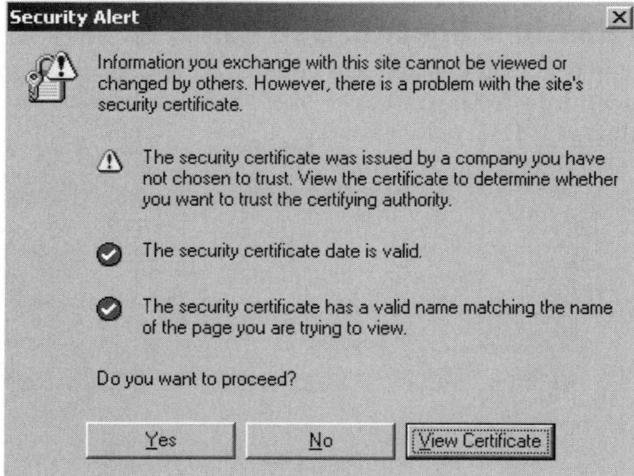

FIGURE 41-4 Security pop-up

1. Click View Certificate.
2. In the Details tab, shown next, you can display information on the Issuer, Valid from, Valid to, Subject, Public key, and so on. In the Issuer field, you can see who issued the certificate. The Subject field displays the user details.

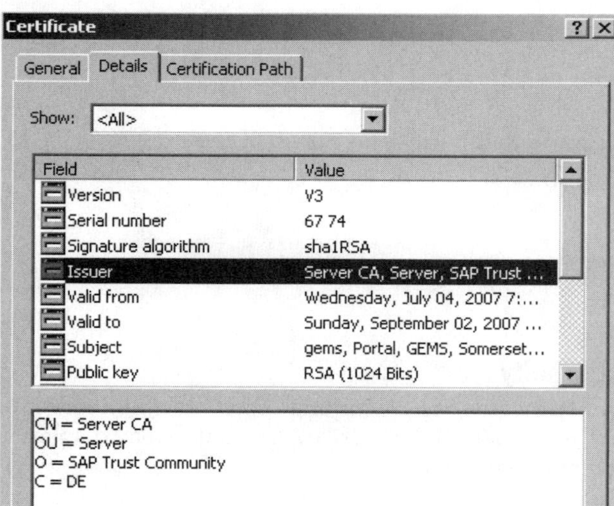

To trust the CA, you need to import the CA root certificate into the browser, as shown in the illustration on the next page. To access the import screen, go to Tools | Internet Options | Content | Certificates | Trusted Root Certification Authorities:

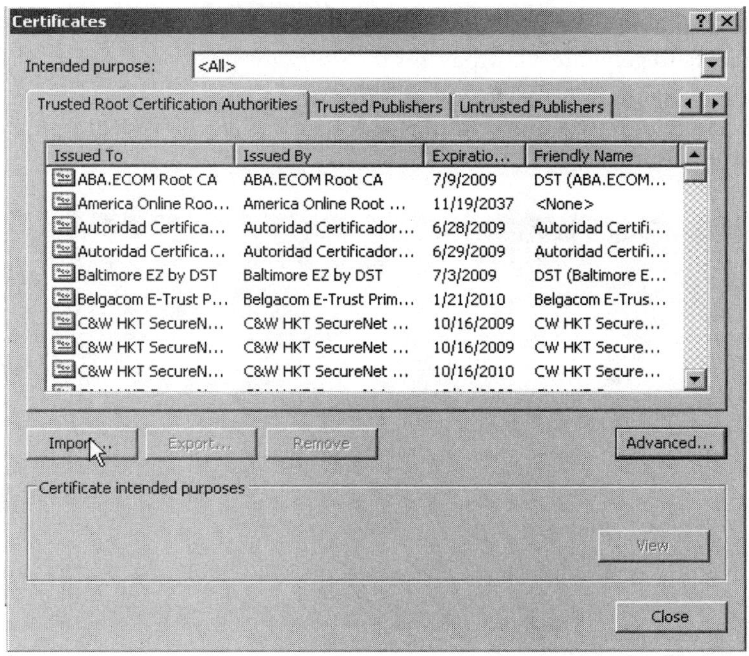

If, while testing, an HTTP 403 error code appears, check the Cipher Suite in the SSL Provider service of the Dispatcher. The Cipher Suite is used during the handshaking process, and you can change the priority of the Cipher Suite that is used if a particular cryptography is not supported.

HINT *If SSL works fine, click the lock icon at the bottom of the browser to view the server certificate.*

Configuring the Client Certificate Authentication Methods

Client certificates can be used to authenticate the user without entering the user name and password. This can be very helpful when implementing SSO. The J2EE engine uses the information available in the client certificate to authenticate the user. The J2EE engine can be configured to identify the user based on certain fields in the client certificate.

To configure the client certificate authentication, you need to do the following:

1. Set the *ume.logon.allow_cert UME* property to *TRUE.*
2. Log on to the config tool, open the com.sap.security.core.ume.service on the server side, and change *ume.logon.allow_cert* to *TRUE* as shown next. Restart the server.

com.sap.portal.pcd.gl
com.sap.portal.prt.sapj2ee
com.sap.security.core.ume.service
configuration

ume.logoff.redirect.silent		FALSE
ume.logoff.redirect.url		
ume.logon.allow_cert	TRUE	FALSE
ume.logon.branding_image		layout/branding-image.jpg

Copyright by SAP AG

3. Go to Server | Services | Key Storage and click the TrustedCAs entry.
4. Click Create to generate a key pair for the user.
5. Enter the credentials for the user in the Key And Certificate Generation dialog box. Enter a name under the Entry Name field, which is used for identifying the entry under the Entries section.

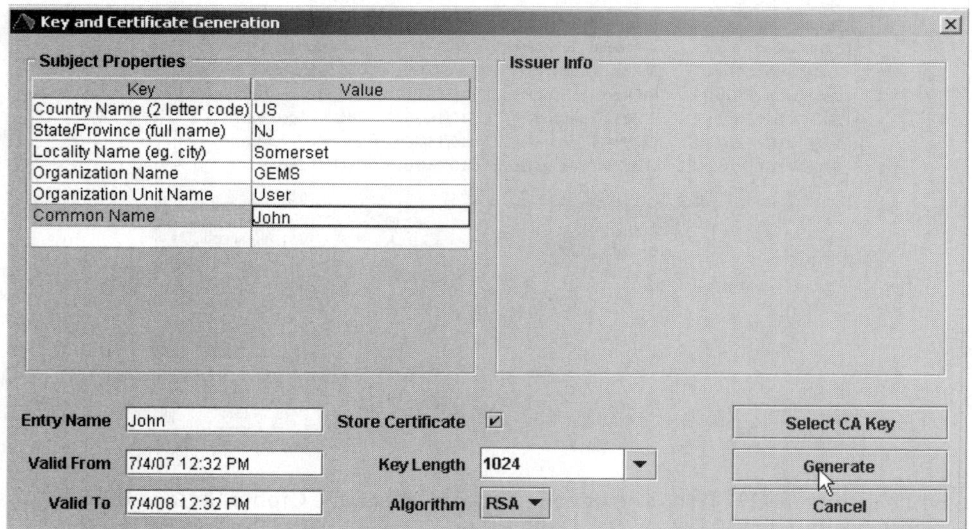

Copyright by SAP AG

6. Click to select the Store Certificate checkbox and click Generate.
7. To sign the client key pair, select the private key and choose Generate CSR Request.
8. Save the file in the local folder.
9. Then send that file to the CA and import the response from the CA into the User Entry by choosing Import CSR Response.
10. Now you'll enable the Client Authentication Requirement on the server. Go to the SSL Provider service on the Dispatcher and click the socket on which the client certificate should be enabled.

NOTE *The root server certificate should already be installed under the Server Identity tab.*

11. Click Add and select the client certificate, as shown here:

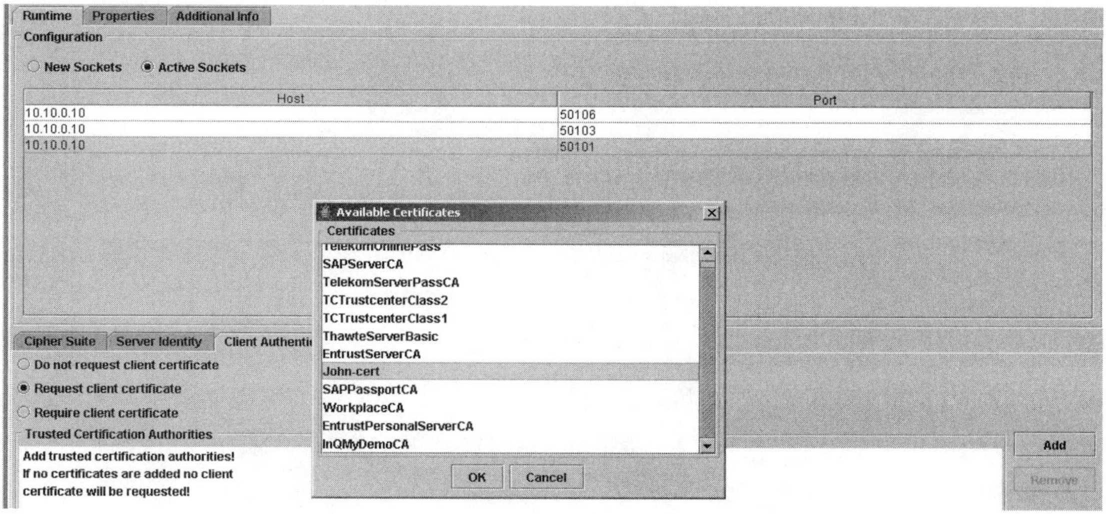

You have three options:

- Do Not Request Client Certificate
- Request Client Certificate
- Require Client Certificate

The difference between the second and third options is that in the case of Request Client Certificate, the client is prompted to submit a client certificate, but if the certificate is not submitted, then the authentication reverts back to Basic Authentication. In the third option, the client is required to submit the client certificate, and if not submitted, the authentication fails and does not proceed further. In both cases, the certificate should be issued by a CA that is trusted by the server.

Assign the Client Certificate to the User in User Management

Now on to the next steps:

1. In the Visual Administrator, go to the Security Provider service under Server. Click Switch To Edit Mode.
2. Open the User Management tab, and click the Tree tab below.
3. Click Administrators in the User Tree view, and then choose Create User.
4. Enter the user name and password in the Create New User dialog box and click OK.
5. Switch back to the Search tab, click the Users tab, and enter the user name (previously created user). Then click Search.

6. Choose the user and click Add under the Certificates view, to see the Add Certificates dialog shown next.

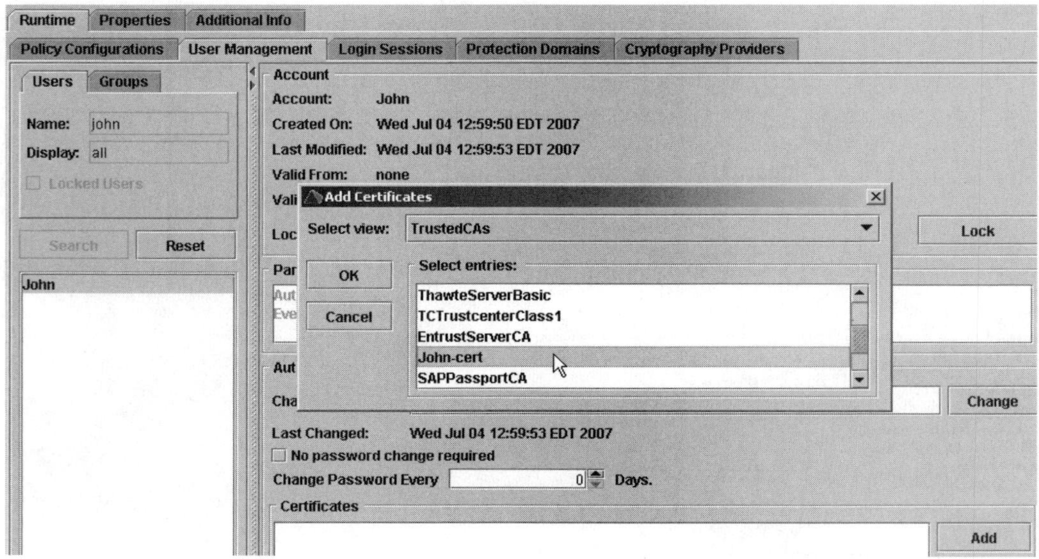

Copyright by SAP AG

7. Then choose TrustedCAs as the Select View, and select the required client certificate that was previously generated for the user.

Change the Application's Login Module Stacks

1. Go to Security Provider service | User Management | Policy Configurations.
2. Go to the application for which you want to enable client certificate–based authentication. Click Add New and select ClientCertLoginModule. Then click OK.

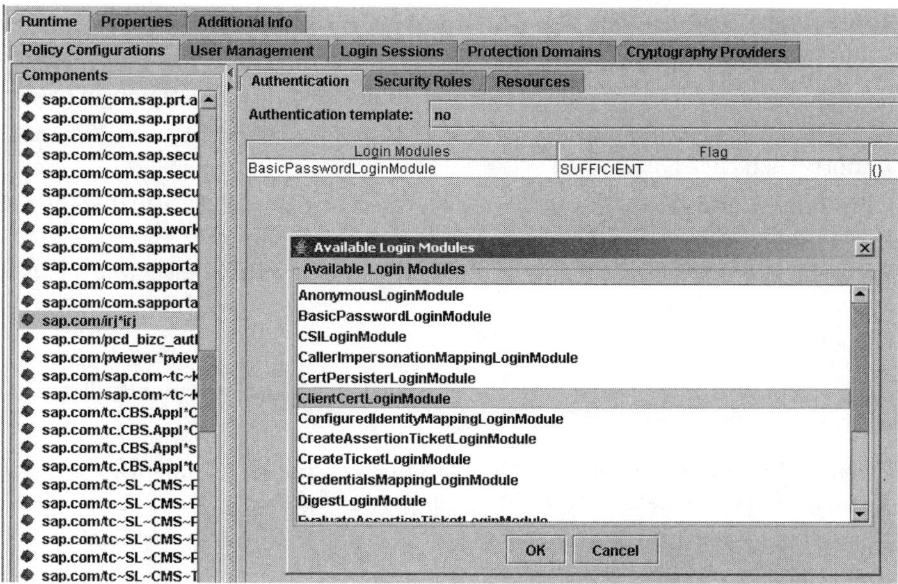

Copyright by SAP AG

3. Click Modify and change Position to 1.
4. Open the Security Roles tab and add the user to the required roles, as shown next:

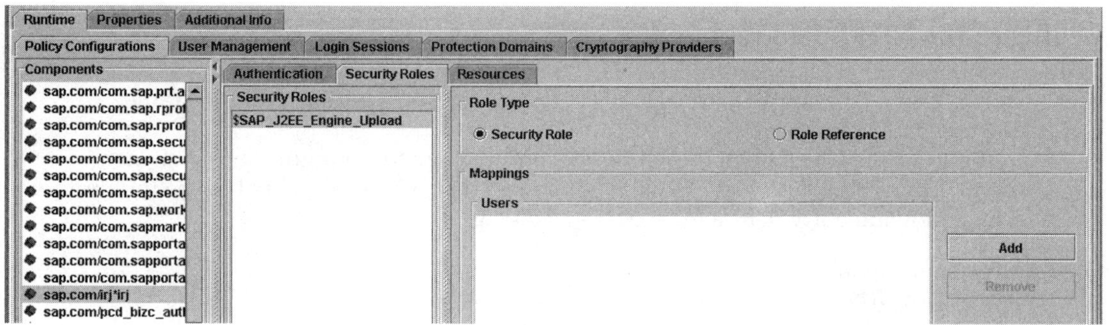

Copyright by SAP AG

HINT *You need not add the user to the roles under the Security roles tab, if the user belongs to the Administrator group.*

Export the Private Key, Import the Certificates, and Test

1. Go to Key Storage Service of the server, click TrustedCAs, and then click Export.
2. Save the certificate as a .p12 file in the local folder. Protect it by assigning a password.
3. Open the browser and go to Tools | Internet Options | Content | Certificates | Import. Then click Next.
4. Click Browse and select the previously exported private key. Ensure that the file type is .p12. Then click Next.
5. Enter the password used for exporting in the preceding step. Select Mark This Key As Exportable. Click Next.
6. Click Next, then Finish, and then Close.

If the CA has provided the root certificate, go ahead and install it under the Trusted Root Certification Authorities:

1. Open the browser and navigate to Tools | Internet Options | Content | Certificates | Trusted Root Certification Authorities | Import. Click Next.
2. Proceed per the instructions in the wizard to install the CA root certificate.
3. If the client certificate is not signed by a CA and is self-signed, then simply install the client certificate in the Trusted Root Certification Authorities store.
4. To test the functionality, go to the application for which the login module stack was modified and try to access it using the client certificate instead of using the user ID and password.

Configure the HTTPS Redirect on the J2EE Engine

You can configure the J2EE engine for the HTTPS redirect functionality so that every time a user tries to access a J2EE application using HTTP, the browser is redirected to the same URL using the HTTPS protocol.

To configure the redirect, open the config tool and then go to Configurations | cluster_data | server | persistent | servlet_jsp, which is shown next. Open the global_web.xml file and add the following entry before the </web-app> tag:

```
<security-constraint>
  <display-name>HTTPS-redirect</display-name>
  <web-resource-collection>
    <web-resource-name>allResources</web-resource-name>
    <url-pattern>*</url-pattern>
  </web-resource-collection>
  <user-data-constraint>
    <transport-guarantee>CONFIDENTIAL</transport-guarantee>
  </user-data-constraint>
</security-constraint>
```

As always, restart the J2EE engine for the changes to take effect.

Troubleshoot J2EE SSL Issues

The diagtool is a helpful tool that can be used when troubleshooting logon problems, single sign-on (SSO), User Management Engine (UME), and other authentication-related issues. You can use the diagtool to troubleshoot SSL-related issues on the J2EE engine, too. To do that, you must download the diagtool attached to OSS Note 957666 and follow the instructions in the note to generate a file that is named as diagtool_yymmdd_hhmmss.zip in the output folder of the diagtool.

Sometimes you may be required to generate SSL log output on the dispatcher for analyzing the SSL traffic for debugging purposes. Here's how to do that:

1. Start the Visual Administrator, and navigate to Dispatcher | Services | Log Configurator | Location.
2. Expand the com.sap.engine.services.ssl node and select ALL in the Severity drop-down.
3. Save the changes and then reproduce the error. Retrieve the latest dispatcher log files as in *<j2ee_engine_home>*/j2ee/cluster/dispatcher/log/defaultTrace.N.trc for further analysis.

DO *Remember to reverse the changes made to their original values to avoid impact to system performance.*

Relevant OSS Notes

Following is a list of relevant OSS notes:

- **1019634** Troubleshooting SSL Problems
- **957666** Diagtool for Troubleshooting Security Configuration

---

NOTE *For more details, refer to the J2EE SSL related resources listed in Appendix B.*

Summary

This chapter discussed the need for using SSL in the J2EE engine and walked through steps involved in implementing SSL on the J2EE engine and configuring the client certificate on the J2EE for authenticating the user.

42

CHAPTER

Implementing Portal Network Security

Security is becoming increasingly important as companies use portals to open up internal systems such as Customer Relationship Management (CRM) and Enterprise Resource Planning (ERP) to external business partners such as customers and suppliers using Internet and distributed systems. Some typical examples of Internet-based scenarios that can be set up with the mySAP Business Suite are mySAP ERP-based Employee Self-Service (ESS) and Manager Self-Service (MSS) applications, mySAP Supplier Relationship Management (SRM)–based SAP Enterprise Buyer, Supplier Self Service, Live Auction, and CRM-based business-to-consumer (B2C) and business-to-business (B2B) applications. This chapter discusses how to implement network security on the portal.

Organization-Wide Security

It is important that a company have an *organization-wide security policy* that includes the portal. Portal security is important to protect confidential and proprietary information such as intellectual property, to comply with the regulatory requirements such as the Sarbanes-Oxley Act, to comply with service-level agreements (SLAs) and contractual requirements, to maintain trust of business partners, to ensure continuity of business operations, and to maintain a good image.

Proper security can be achieved in the portal by implementing measures such as authentication, authorization, confidentiality, integrity, and non-repudiation. Security safeguards can also be implemented using organizational-wide measures such as these:

- Drafting a security policy for the portal
- Training and educating personnel
- Creating disaster recovery plans for portal infrastructure
- Protecting physical assets such as server facilities and computers

Security Threats and Safeguards

Security threats can affect the OS layer, the application layer, or the network layer of the portal infrastructure. To counter such threats, you must implement the necessary safeguards in those affected layers. Some of the common security threats for which you need to implement the safeguards are attempts to penetrate the portal systems, attempts to get more portal authorizations than what is allowed, denial of service attacks, eavesdropping of network traffic, spoofing, and masquerading.

To protect against these threats, safeguards can be implemented, including implementing adequate access control mechanisms, using digital certificate–based authentication, using firewalls, using encryption, using public key infrastructure (PKI), using portal system monitors, implementing the latest patches, using application gateways, using application security mechanisms, using virus-detection software, and using OS-hardening.

Security Policies

The organization's security policy should clearly specify the requirements for data and application security. In addition, it should highlight the importance of keeping the backend systems in their own security zones, far away from the relatively vulnerable Internet-facing security zones. If a security policy already exists, it is paramount that the policy is clearly understood so that it can be adhered to during the project implementation. A balanced security policy should take into consideration the security for application, data, infrastructure, collaboration, user access, infrastructure, and software lifecycle.

NOTE *An organization-wide security policy should address aspects such as authentication, authorization, privacy, data integrity, security auditing, and logging.*

Infrastructure Security

Infrastructure security mainly deals with protecting assets such as the network, the operating system and database platforms, system security, and frontend security.

Encrypting the communications can increase network and communications security, and using security devices such as firewalls, proxies, SAProuter, SAP Web Dispatcher, and network-based intrusion detection systems (IDSs) can do the same.

The operating system used for the SAP portal should be configured for increased security, and elements that make the operating system vulnerable should be eliminated. Use the database-specific security features to improve security. The operating system should be protected from viruses by integrating third-party virus checking products with the SAP systems. You can also install host-based IDSs as a step toward increasing operating system security.

In scenarios involving Exchange Infrastructure (XI), Internet Transaction Server (ITS), or SAP Business Connector (BC), system-to-system communication should be authenticated using Secure Sockets Layer (SSL) or Secure Network Communication (SNC). In some cases, you may need to encrypt database-to-application server communication using SSL or a virtual private network (VPN) solution.

Finally, adopting SSL for data replication, storage, and retrieval should increase frontend security for devices such as PCs, laptops, and PDAs. Secure session handling can be implemented for the SAP NetWeaver Application Server or SAP ITS by limiting the time period for which the cookies or SAP logon tickets are issued.

Data and Application Security

Encryption and authorization controls are the two main techniques used to protect data. Encryption is required to prevent access to data by users outside the portal. Authorization controls are required to prevent access to data by users that are not authorized to see such data.

Application security is required to implement authentication so that only authorized users can access the portal application. Application security protects data from being provided to unauthorized users—such as data about the portal system itself, such as server information, operating system information, and patches. When providing security for the portal, you should consider the ability to meet regulatory requirements for a country or industry.

NOTE *Data security is concerned with protecting data that are related to an application. Application security addresses the need for regulatory compliance, roles, and authorization for access control, data privacy, and security auditing.*

The portal system should comply with the data protection and privacy requirements such as ensuring that only minimal data are collected and retained for a limited period of time. It should also protect the rights of the customers to change incorrect data and also to know what data are being collected.

Auditing should be in place to help track any changes made to the portal systems and when.

NOTE *You should be able to audit processes, document flows, configuration changes, master data changes, and transactions.*

Network Security

It is important to protect the portal from various threats and implement the viable safeguards against those threats. The alternatives available to safeguard against attacks are personnel training, authentication, firewalls, encryption, OS-hardening, virus detection, patches, and application gateways.

The network topology should be designed well to avoid vulnerabilities at both the software layer and the network layer. Operating system and application security should be strong to avoid illegal access to the application servers, the database servers, and the LAN servers.

Using SNC and SSL

Security devices such as firewalls, SAP Web Dispatcher, and SAProuter should be used along with SNC and SSL to protect the network. Using SNC and SSL helps to provide additional protection such as authentication of communication partners, data integrity, and privacy of data transferred between client and server.

NOTE *SSL can be used for HTTP, Peer-to-Peer Programming Platform (P4), and Lightweight Directory Access Protocol (LDAP) and SNC can be used for dialog and RFC SAP protocols for secure communication between SAP systems.*

Cryptography can be used to encrypt the data that flow through the network. While this adds to the security of the data, it also limits the ability for the security devices such as firewalls to analyze the traffic. In such cases, you can use application gateways to terminate the SSL and resend the traffic for the remaining network.

Cryptography can be used for preventing eavesdropping, masquerading, and repudiation. By encrypting the data, you can protect against eavesdropping. To prevent masquerading, you can implement authentication using public and private keys. By signing the documents that are exchanged with a private key, the user who sent the documents cannot refuse that he or she did not send it.

NOTE *SNC communication cannot be used between the database and the application server. So it is important that the database and the application servers are located within a secure LAN protected from the Internet by a firewall and SAProuter.*

As far as possible, the database server and the application servers must be placed in a separate subnet instead of in an existing subnet. For more complex systems, it may be desirable to have multiple IP subnets for different groups of related systems. This allows you to provide varying levels of security.

Network Area Protected by SNC

Figure 42-1 displays how SNC can be used for the following communications:

- SAP GUI and the SAP system application server
- External RFC or CPIC Program and the SAP application server, and vice versa
- SAProuter and SAP application server
- SAProuter and SAProuter

Disabling Services

To increase server security, you should try to disable a number of services that are running in the servers. The list of the network services with their protocols and port information can be found at \winnt\system32\drivers\etc\services.

FIGURE 42-1
SNC communication

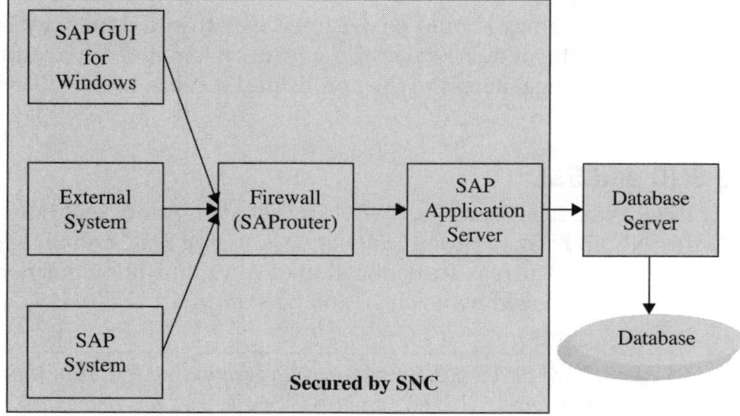

TIP *To get a list of the active services, run* **`netstat -a`**.

Intrusion Detection Systems

Intrusion detection systems are security devices that provide notification of any attempts to breach security. They can be installed in the networks or in the OS. Network IDS devices can identify attempts at the network level, but they cannot decode encrypted traffic, which limits their use. In such cases, OS IDS devices can be helpful. Both the network and the OS IDS systems gather their data and send them to the IDS server, which aggregates the information and sends a message.

Hardware and Software Infrastructure Elements

An important part of infrastructure security design is identifying the various hardware and software elements required to implement network- and application-level security. Some of the common hardware infrastructure elements are firewalls, web appliances, load balancers, and application gateways. During design, you can choose different combinations of these elements to provide additional security, increased performance, network bandwidth, and high availability.

The hardware elements can be combined with software infrastructure elements for access management and identity management. Access management is concerned with controlling access to URLs and provides SSO capabilities as well. Identity management deals with providing the user and role management functionality for enterprise applications.

Layered Network Design

You can establish multiple security zones that can be configured to provide security by using application gateways between the client and the portal infrastructure. You can increase the level of security by introducing firewalls between the zone layers. This helps you keep the sensitive components in the innermost zone. Figure 42-2 displays a typical network layered design possible in the portal scenario.

FIGURE 42-2 Network layered design

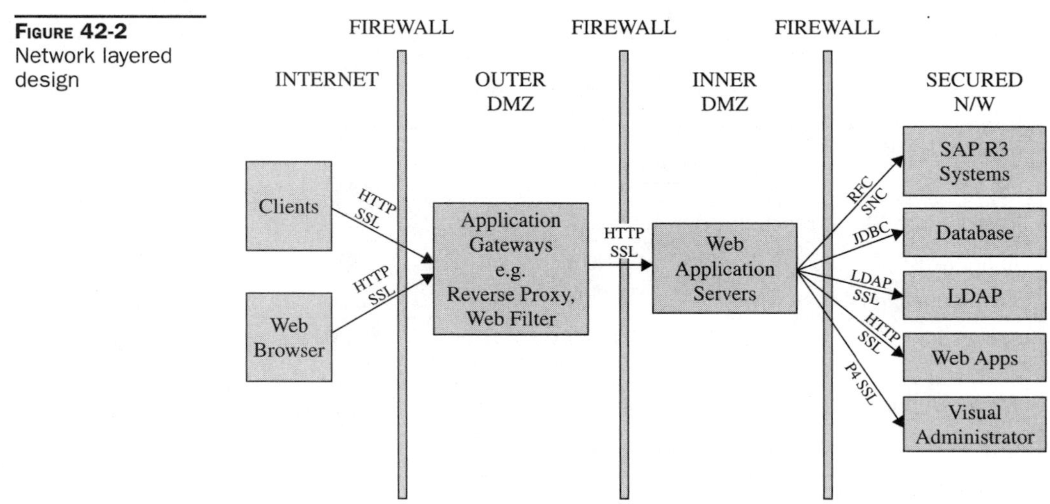

Source	Destination	Protocols	Ports
Client	J2EE Dispatcher	HTTPS	80/443
J2EE Dispatcher	J2EE Dispatcher	P4	50XX10/50XX11
J2EE(Portal) server	J2EE(Portal) server	P4	50XX20/50XX21
J2EE Dispatcher	J2EE(Portal) server	P4	50XX20/50XX21
J2EE(Portal) server	J2EE Dispatcher	P4	50XX10/50XX11
J2EE(Portal) server	Oracle DB	JDBC	1527
J2EE(Portal) server	LDAP	LDAP	389/636
J2EE(Portal) server	SAP	RFC	36XX/32XX
J2EE(Portal) server	Web application	HTTPS	80/443

TABLE 42-1 Protocols and Ports Used for Communication Between Portal Components

Protocols and Ports Used

Table 42-1 shows the protocol and port information that are required for communicating between the client, J2EE Dispatcher, J2EE server, web server, LDAP, database, and SAP systems.

Table 42-2 shows the default port and the range of ports that can be used for different services. NN represents the J2EE instance number.

Table 42-3 shows the protocols that are recommended between various components in the portal network.

Service	Port Number	Default	Range
HTTP	5NN00	50000	50000–59900
HTTPS	5NN01	50001	50001–59901
IIOP Initial context	5NN02	50002	50002–59902
IIOP over SSL	5NN03	50003	50003–59903
P4	5NN04	50004	50004–59904
P4 over HTTP tunneling	5NN05	50005	50005–59905
P4 over SSL	5NN06	50006	50006–59906
Internet Inter-Orb Protocol (IIOP)	5NN07	50007	50007–59907
Telnet	5NN08	50008	50008–59908
Java Message Service (JMS)	5NN10	50010	50010–59910
Server Join Port	5NN20 + x × 5 x = no. of servers	50020	50020–59995
Server Debug Port	5NN21 + x × 5 x = no. of servers	50021	50021–59996

TABLE 42-2 Ports Allowed for Services

Components	Secure Protocols
Between Web browser and Web server	SSL
Between Web server and SAP J2EE engine	SSL
Between Web browser and SAP J2EE engine	SSL
Between Portal Server and Database	SSL
Between Portal Server and LDAP	SSL
Between Portal Server and SAP Systems	SNC

TABLE 42-3 Recommended Secure Protocols Between Portal Components

Firewalls and Application Gateways

Firewalls can be used to allow only certain services such as mail or HTTP and to prevent services such as telnet between different networks. The firewall system can be composed of packet filters as well as application-level gateways.

Packet Filters

Packet filters are used with routers that help to route traffic based on IP addresses, ports, or protocols used. For example, mail requests can be routed to mail servers and FTP requests can be routed to FTP servers. Some advanced packet filters not only use the IP addresses and ports, but also track the TCP sessions and can add dynamic rules to configuration for protocols such as NFS and FTP.

NOTE *The packet filters provide only network-level security and cannot be used for detecting application-based attacks. In such cases, application-level gateways can be used.*

Application-Level Gateways

Application-level gateways differ from packet filters in the sense that they reject or allow network traffic based on the application content in the request. Apache is one example of an application gateway. Application gateways can be configured to allow requests only from certain URLs and to avoid known exploits. Access can be allowed based on information in the content, such as a user in the request, known threats, source network, sender address, and so on. Instead of directly allowing the clients to access the backend systems, you expose them through an application gateway, which checks the credentials of the user for authentication and redirects the user to a logon page, if authentication failed.

Unlike the packet filter–based firewalls, the application-level gateways can decode the encrypted traffic from the client and rebuild the TCP packets and send them to the server. Thus they can serve as the endpoints for SSL traffic.

NOTE *By having application gateways, you can avoid the possibility of hackers using brute force to access the backend systems simply by using their knowledge of SAP systems.*

Disadvantages of Application Gateways

One of the disadvantages of the application gateways is that they are slow because of their need to analyze the traffic content. The application gateways are known to have a number of bugs. It is therefore recommended that you store the application gateway separately on a dedicated host apart from the host on which the packet filter is located.

SAP Application Gateways

SAP provides application-level gateways such as SAProuter for dialog and RFC connections and SAP Web Dispatcher for HTTPS connections. The default port on the SAProuter is 3299 and should be allowed in the firewall for SAP protocols. The SAP Web Dispatcher can be used to enable load balancing and as a URL filter to filter HTTPS requests.

As shown next, client machines can access the SAProuter only on port 3299, which is enabled by the configuration of the router/packet filter. The SAProuter permits connections to the application servers only on port 3201, based on its configuration.

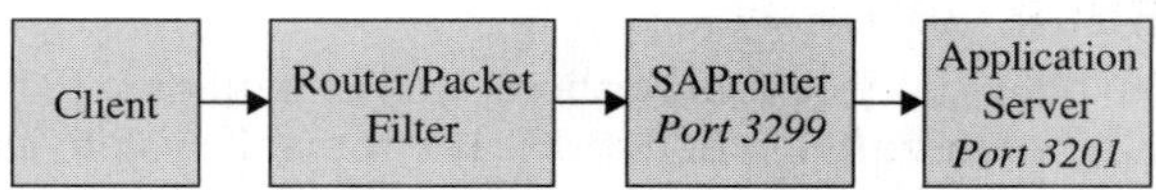

Router/Packet filter allows connections on port 3299 only
SAProuter allows connections on port 3201 only

This scenario is a more secure configuration than a simple configuration in which the client tries to access the backend systems directly through the URL, which resolves to the IP address of the backend system. Exposing the IP address to the users is not considered safe. In reality, you may have much more complex scenarios with multiple entry points, applications, and protocols.

Implementing Security Measures

Proper allowance should be provided during project planning for lead times related to security implementation. Development should not commence unless the security requirements have been gathered so that they can be incorporated into the design. Make sure that provision is made for testing programs and processes, with security elements, such as firewalls, SSO, web access management tools, SSL, and so on, in place.

Tip *Watch for any potential performance degradation after implementing security.*

Make sure that performance baselines are created with security implemented, and manage user expectations with the security infrastructure in place. Early assessment and implementation of security helps you understand the limitations and plan ahead for activities such as requesting exceptions ahead of time, procuring firewalls, setting up firewall rules, and so on. Encourage security team involvement by conducting audits and maintain openness so that proper security can be implemented.

Always use SSL/SNC communications even if not required as a matter of policy. Good password rules must be defined in the security policy and a decision should be made as to which application (whether it is the LDAP, the SAP application, or the portal) is responsible to drive the password policy. Provide the minimum possible access to all the technical users of the system. Issue administrator access to users for a limited period of time. Patches should be installed regularly as they could contain solutions for security-related issues. Unnecessary software or services should not be installed in the production system.

NOTE *For more details, refer to the portal security related resources listed in Appendix B.*

Summary

This chapter covered the need for portal security and how to ensure its compliance using an organization-wide security policy. It then addressed briefly the need for infrastructure security, data and application security, and network security. Finally you learned how firewalls can be implemented using packet filters and application gateways.

VIII

PART

Configuring System Landscape Directory

43

CHAPTER

System Landscape Directory

With a constant increase in the number of systems in an organization, it becomes difficult to manage systems in a controlled manner. The System Landscape Directory (SLD) provides help in this area by maintaining a central repository of information about systems that can be used by other systems such as Solution Manager, Exchange Infrastructure (XI), and so on. The systems in the landscape should be able to register themselves with the SLD automatically, which ensures that the information provided to the SLD clients (data consumer) is up to date.

In this chapter, you will learn more about the SLD, the SLD content types, system landscapes, SLD installation options, and how to configure and access SLD.

Since SLD is a Java-based application and considering that the data can be collected from both the Java and Advanced Business Application Programming (ABAP)–based systems, the SLD provides a Java and ABAP API to connect to these systems, respectively. The ABAP API is wrapped on top of the Java API using the Java Connector (JCO) RFC Provider service. It allows third-party systems to read and write data to the SLD in the role of data consumers and data providers, respectively.

NOTE *As of Web AS 6.40, the SLD runs as a* service *in the SAP J2EE engine.*

SLD is used in the NetWeaver Development Infrastructure (NWDI) for name reservation for development components and in XI to store information about business systems. SLD is used in Software Lifecycle Management for system landscape design, system landscape implementation, change management, software logistics, upgrade, and installation. SLD is also used in system monitoring solutions such as Solution Manager and Computing Center Management System (CCMS). It is also used in Web Dynpro for retrieving RFC destinations.

The SLD is based on the Distributed Management Task Force (DMTF) standards, namely, the Common Information Model (CIM) and the Web Based Enterprise Management. The CIM is an object-oriented model for modeling software and hardware elements in an implementation-independent way and has been extended by SAP to include SAP components.

SLD Content Types

CIM contains three schemas or SLD content types:

- **General component data** Used for installable software
- **Landscape data** Used for installed software and hardware elements
- **Namespace reservation data** Used for software development

General Component Data

The general component data include information on the software products and solutions such as SAP Customer Relationship Management (CRM); software components such as SAP_BASIS, SAP_APPL, releases, and support packages; as well as information on non-SAP products and components such as Siebel. The CIM also provides information on the dependencies between the various software and hardware components as found in the product availability matrix, the supported platforms and releases for the operating systems, databases, and so on.

The component information consists of software unit, products, and software component.

The *software unit* is a collection of software components such as SAP BASIS 7.0 and the CRM server. Several collected software units form a product.

Product components are delivered to a customer either for installation or upgrade. Examples are SAP CRM, SAP Supply Chain Management (SCM), and so on. Products are associated with releases—for example, CRM 4.0 and CRM 3.0.

Information on third-party *software components* should be maintained manually. When creating third-party components, you can create a product and then add the software unit and software components later on. You can also export and import third-party content to multiple SLD servers to keep the information consistent.

PPMS Repository and Master Component Repository

SAP has a PPMS repository (Product and Production Management system) from which the data for the Master Component Repository are downloaded. The Master Component Repository contains all the information about products delivered by SAP, such as information on products, software components, patches, versions, support packages, and so on.

Downloading the Software Catalog from SMP

This information is made available by SAP in the SMP (service marketplace) that can be downloaded and imported into the SLD (refer to OSS Note 669669). The software catalog contains a list of all installable products and software components along with the in support packages and dependencies between them.

To keep the software catalog up-to-date, go to service.sap.com/swdc | SAP Software Distribution Center | Download | Support Packages and Patches | Entry by Application Group | SAP Technology Components | SAP Master Data for SLD, as shown in Figure 43-1.

NOTE *You do not need to download the entire catalog every time you want to update the software catalog. Instead, you can download the updates to the software catalog, which are available as ZIP files.*

You can see in Figure 43-1 that cimsap1408_0.10000\3379.zip is the CIM model definition, where *14* represents the CIM model release number, *08* represents the Support Package level, *0* is the patch level, and *10003379* represents the model content compilation number.

In Figure 43-1, CRContent14_0.10003379.zip represents the initial CR content, where *14* represents the CIM model release number, *0* represents the patch level, and *1000379* represents the model content compilation number.

In Figure 43-1, CRDelta1416_0.10003379.zip represents the delta CR content, where *14* is the CIM model release number, *16* represents the SP level, *0* is the patch level, and *10003379* represents the model content compilation number.

To import the software catalog, click Content | Import and point to the downloaded ZIP file. The downloaded ZIP file should be located in the \usr\sap\<*SID*>/SYS/global\sld\model directory.

TIP *You do not need to import the initial content all the time. Importing the delta content is sufficient unless, of course, the CIM model changes, in which case you need to import the full initial CR content.*

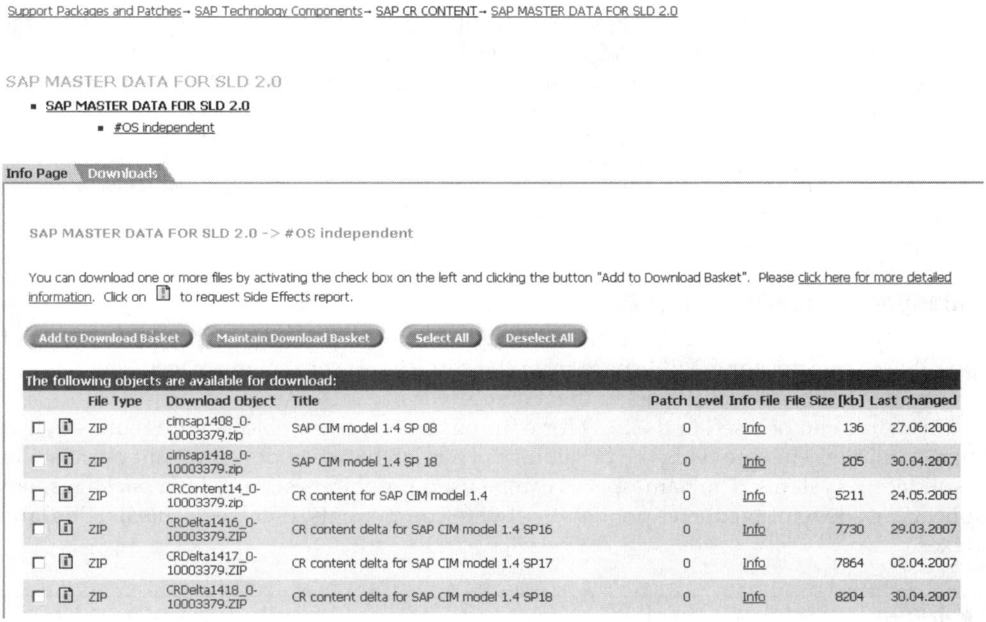

Support Packages and Patches→ SAP Technology Components→ SAP CR CONTENT→ SAP MASTER DATA FOR SLD 2.0

SAP MASTER DATA FOR SLD 2.0

- SAP MASTER DATA FOR SLD 2.0
  - #OS independent

Info Page | Downloads

SAP MASTER DATA FOR SLD 2.0 -> #OS independent

You can download one or more files by activating the check box on the left and clicking the button "Add to Download Basket". Please click here for more detailed information. Click on to request Side Effects report.

Add to Download Basket | Maintain Download Basket | Select All | Deselect All

The following objects are available for download:

File Type	Download Object	Title	Patch Level	Info File	File Size [kb]	Last Changed
ZIP	cimsap1408_0-10003379.zip	SAP CIM model 1.4 SP 08	0	Info	136	27.06.2006
ZIP	cimsap1418_0-10003379.zip	SAP CIM model 1.4 SP 18	0	Info	205	30.04.2007
ZIP	CRContent14_0-10003379.zip	CR content for SAP CIM model 1.4	0	Info	5211	24.05.2005
ZIP	CRDelta1416_0-10003379.ZIP	CR content delta for SAP CIM model 1.4 SP16	0	Info	7730	29.03.2007
ZIP	CRDelta1417_0-10003379.ZIP	CR content delta for SAP CIM model 1.4 SP17	0	Info	7864	02.04.2007
ZIP	CRDelta1418_0-10003379.ZIP	CR content delta for SAP CIM model 1.4 SP18	0	Info	8204	30.04.2007

FIGURE 43-1 SAP Master Data for SLD 2.0 downloads page

System Landscape Data

Using the SLD, a customer can create his own system landscapes by including SAP as well as third-party customer component types. The customer manually creates a system landscape. The system landscape is linked to the corresponding element in the component data.

System Landscape Types

Typically, a system landscape consists of technical systems, landscapes, business systems, software catalog, and reserved names. Landscapes can be of different types: administration (for monitoring), NetWeaver Development Infrastructure (NWDI), general (application systems such as SAP R/3, SAP CRM, SAP SCM), scenario (Software Lifecycle Manager), transport, and web service.

Technical Systems Technical systems are application systems such as CRM installed in the landscape. They are actual physical systems that provide data to the SLD. Technical systems can be directly linked to the component information available in the SLD. It is therefore important to keep the component information up to date. Whenever a change occurs in the technical system, such as a support package being installed, this information is updated in the SLD server by a batch job running on the technical system.

Different types of technical systems are available, such as NetWeaver AS ABAP, NetWeaver AS Java, standalone Java, third-party, and XI systems such as integration servers and adapter engines.

Business Systems Business systems are logical systems that are associated with technical systems. They are created to address a specific business purpose. Business systems are more commonly used in XI installations. Only one technical system can be associated with a business system, but more than one business system can be defined for a given technical system.

NOTE *Not all technical systems can register automatically, in which case manual registration of the technical systems is required.*

Namespace Reservation Data

The third type of SLD content is namespace reservation data, which is specific to NWDI. It is possible to register for a namespace from the service.sap.com/namespaces. The namespace can be maintained using the name server in the SLD.

This name can be used in the SLD for naming development objects with names that are globally unique. This prevents the possibility of a clash between development objects when consolidating systems. The namespaces can be used for objects such as Java packages, Java applications, development components, software components, database tables, fields, and indexes.

TIP *It is enough to have one namespace for a given landscape, but you can also have multiple namespaces for various landscapes such as for system landscape planning and design.*

Accessing the SLD

To access the SLD, go to http://*<hostname_of_j2ee_engine>*:*<port>*/sld. The port varies depending upon the type of NetWeaver AS installation.

For the Java stack, the default value is *5abcd*, where *ab* represents the system number of the NetWeaver AS system and *cd* represents the SAP J2EE engine port. This value can be changed in the J2EE config tool.

If the NetWeaver AS is a full installation consisting of both the ABAP and the Java stacks, the port is *8080*, which is defined in the SMICM transaction and can be changed, if required, for security purposes.

SLD User Interface

The SLD user interface mainly consists of two main pages: the Home page and the Administration page. The Home page consists of three categories that correspond to the three main types of SLD content: Landscapes, Software Catalog, and Development, as shown in Figure 43-2.

The Administration page consists of two sections: Server and Content, as shown in Figure 43-3. The Server page contains links for administering the server and the Content page contains functions for maintaining the component repository such as importing and exporting content.

SLD User Roles

A number of user roles are provided with the SLD. In NetWeaver 2004s, they are LcrUser(SAP_SLD_GUEST), LcrClassWriter, LcrSupport (SAP_SLD_SUPPORT), LcrInstanceWriterCR(SAP_SLD_ORGANIZER), LcrInstanceWriterNR(SAP_SLD_DEVELOPER), LcrInstanceWriterLD (SAP_SLD_CONFIGURATOR), DataSupplierLD (SAP_SLD_DATA_SUPPLIER), LcrInstanceWriterAll (SAP_SLD_ORGANIZER), and LcrAdministrator (SAP_SLD_ADMINISTRATOR).

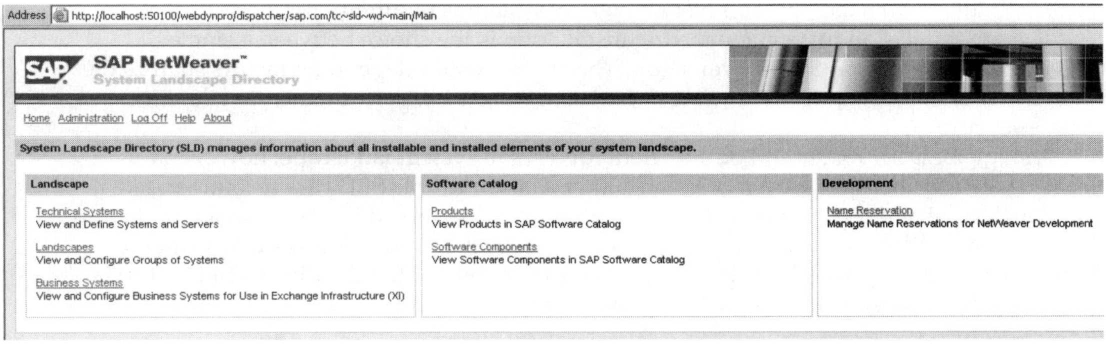

FIGURE 43-2 The System Landscape Directory Home page

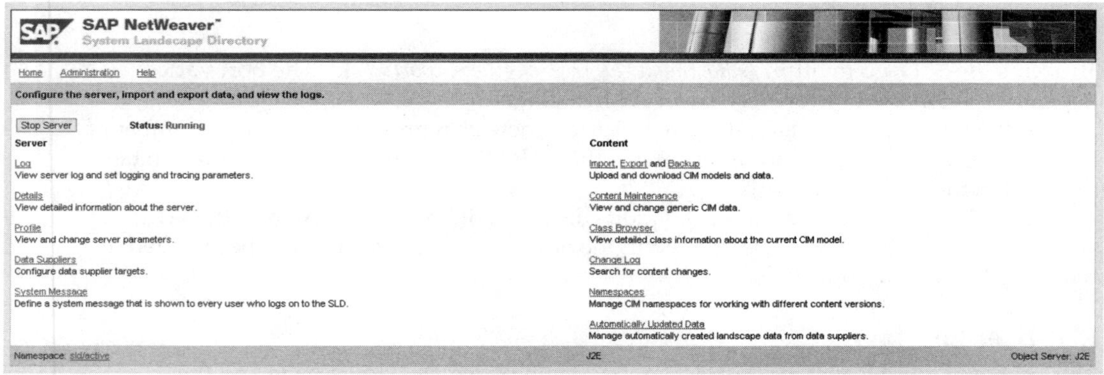

FIGURE 43-3 The System Landscape Directory Administration page

The J2EE engine administrator already has the SLD administrator role. If a full NetWeaver AS system has been installed, the SLD role can be mapped to the ABAP roles shown in parentheses.

NOTE *As a part of post installation, you may need to map the SLD roles to the corresponding ABAP roles.*

SLD Installation

Various installation options are available for the SLD.

The SLD server can be installed either as a standalone system (with only the Java stack) or as a full NetWeaver AS system with both ABAP and JAVA stacks. When installing SAP XI or SAP Solution Manager, the full NetWeaver AS system is required.

The other decision to be made during installation is the choice between a single SLD server and a distributed SLD server setup. The choice would depend on factors such as the cost, the ease of setup and subsequent maintenance, security, performance, availability, and data integrity.

A single SLD server should be sufficient for a small system landscape; however, for larger system landscapes with more than 100 systems, multiple SLDs are recommended. Obviously, cost and the effort involved in setting up a distributed SLD system are higher. However, in a distributed setup, it is possible to secure the production systems from the non-production systems. The performance and availability of the distributed SLD setup is also higher compared to the single SLD server setup.

NOTE *For more information on this topic, refer to OSS Notes 936318, 954820, and 764393.*

SLD Data Supplier Bridge and Suppliers

The SLD bridge is responsible for transferring the information provided by the data suppliers to the SLD server in a form that is CIM compliant. The SLD data supplier bridge also acts as a central receiving point for data from all data suppliers and then sends them to the local and remote SLD servers.

NOTE *The systems in the landscape can automatically register with the SLD during system startup and can report data periodically to the SLD through an SLD bridge.*

SLD Data Suppliers

SAP provides two data suppliers: one for ABAP and the other for JAVA. The data suppliers provide the required data back to the SLD periodically by virtue of a batch job that is set up to run periodically. Examples of data suppliers are SAP R/3, SAP NetWeaver AS, and SAP BI systems. The system data collected from these data suppliers are provided to the SLD clients such as SAP XI and Solution Manager.

ABAP Data Supplier The ABAP data supplier uses an RFC to connect to the SAP gateway service in the J2EE engine for sending data to the SLD Bridge, as shown next:

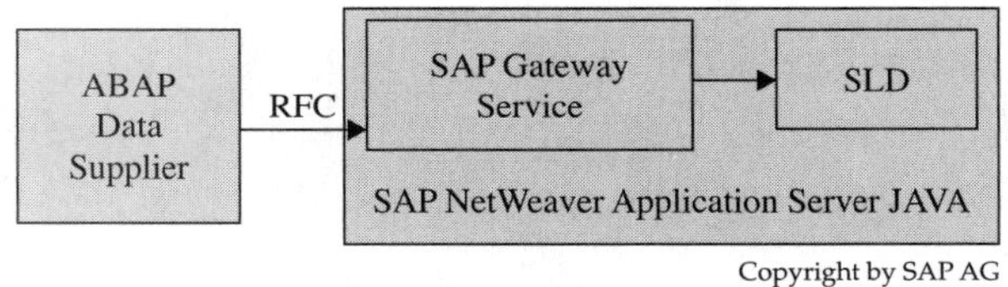

NOTE *In the case of a standalone J2EE engine, the RFC gateway service should be installed manually.*

Java Data Suppliers In the case of Java data suppliers, you can either use an RFC or HTTP to connect to the SLD bridge. If RFC is used, an SAP gateway service is required and hence the HTTP-based communication is preferred.

If multiple SLDs are installed, the SLD bridge should be configured to transfer data to multiple SLD servers. Systems other than ABAP and Java systems should use the sldreg executable to send data to the SLD.

Configuring SLD Data Supplier for ABAP

To configure the SLD data supplier for an ABAP system, use transaction RZ70:

1. In the SLD Bridge: Gateway Information group box, enter the gateway host name and the gateway service.
2. Choose Proposal under the Data Collection Programs group box.
3. Choose Import.
4. Click Yes to use the installation default settings.
5. Choose Activate Current Configuration.
6. Then start the background job for data collection by clicking Start Data Collection and Job Scheduling.

Set the SLD Server Settings Part of setting up the SLD is to set the server settings by navigating to Administration | Server | Profile. Select Server Settings under the Section drop-down. It is recommended that you keep the default settings as shown next:

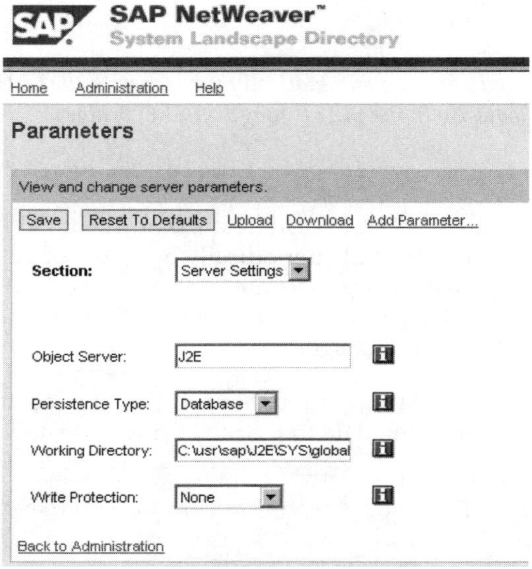

SAP NetWeaver™
System Landscape Directory

Home Administration Help

Parameters

View and change server parameters.

Save | Reset To Defaults | Upload | Download | Add Parameter...

Section: Server Settings

Object Server: J2E

Persistence Type: Database

Working Directory: C:\usr\sap\J2E\SYS\global

Write Protection: None

Back to Administration

NOTE *For more details, refer to the SLD related resources listed in Appendix B.*

Summary

This chapter discussed why you need SLD and how to implement it. It discussed the CIM model and the various SLD content types such as component, landscape, and name reservation data. It discussed the various SLD installation options available and the various SLD user roles required.

CHAPTER

Configuring and Using NetWeaver Administrator

In this chapter, you will learn about the architecture and functionality of SAP NetWeaver Administrator (NWA) and address some of the steps involved in configuring it. SAP NetWeaver Administrator (NWA) is a handy tool that lets you centrally monitor, administer, and configure Advanced Business Application Programming (ABAP) as well as Java systems. You don't need to log in to any of the individual systems to administer them. Moreover, NWA runs inside a Java system and a web-based client can be used for administration. NWA provides all the required monitoring and administration capabilities under one roof.

NOTE *NWA is available as of SAP NetWeaver 04 SP 12.*

NWA provides a "central cockpit" from which you can monitor all the systems belonging to the landscape. You can display the RZ20 monitor tree elements in a web format and display performance reports. Use a central log viewer to display and filter log files. Start and stop Java applications and configure systems centrally, and seamlessly navigate to other administration capabilities and programs, such as job scheduling, the User Management Engine (UME), and the System Landscape Directory (SLD).

NOTE *NWA is not intended to replace the Solution Manager. The Solution Manager is used for managing end to end from an application standpoint, whereas the NWA is a NetWeaver lifecycle management tool that can be used to administer and monitor from a systems standpoint.*

NWA Architecture

As shown in Figure 44-1, the SAP NWA uses the SLD to obtain information regarding technical systems that need to be administered or monitored. NWA resides in the Java stack of the central monitoring system (CEN). Use of the Solution Manager is not mandatory, but the NWA can use any information that the Solution Manager feeds to the CEN. The NWA uses the Computing Center Management System (CCMS) agents, Java Management

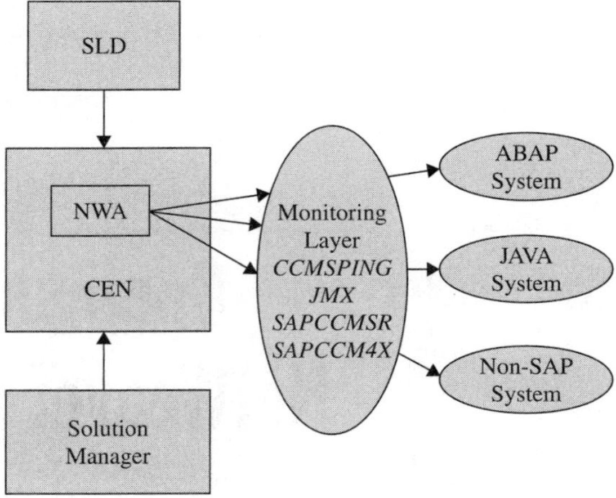

FIGURE 44-1 NWA architecture

Extensions (JMX), and so on, in the Monitoring and Management connectivity layer to communicate with the ABAP and Java systems that need to be monitored.

NWA Functionality

The home page of the NWA contains the System Management Overview tab, as shown next:

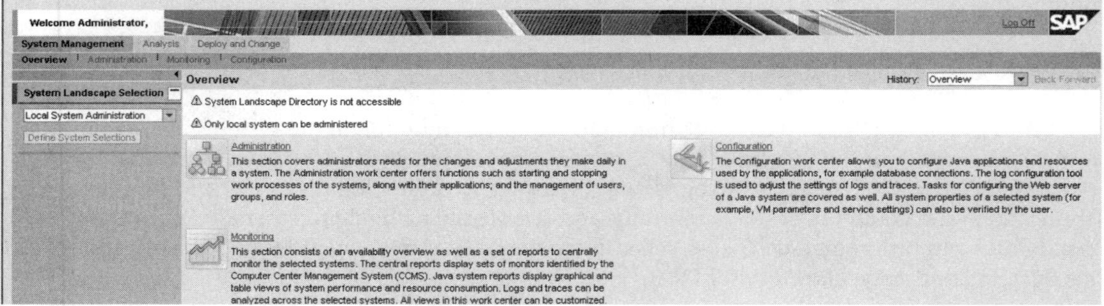

Under System Management are three work centers: Administration, Monitoring, and Configuration. On the left side of the page are options for choosing a system to work with. You can not only administer the entire system landscape centrally, but you can also manage local systems.

To work with the various systems in the landscape, you should have defined the systems in the SLD either manually or automatically. You can then log in to the NWA and select Define System Selection, where you do the following: choose All Technical Systems and choose the required system to work with, or enter the name of the Landscape type, enter the name of the system in the filter input, and click Go. You must define the system landscapes in the SLD and then create systems within that landscape. They will appear in the NWA under Define System Selections.

System Administration Capabilities

When you open the Administration work center, a detailed navigation panel appears on the left, where you can select the overview, systems, applications, or user and access links. When you click a system, the list of instances available for that system will appear on the right in a tree structure. You can then select any of the instances and start, stop, or restart the instance. A Details screen appears on the bottom when you select a system, displaying tabs containing System Details, Instance Details, J2EE Processes, and Services. You can manage the J2EE processes and services from these tabs.

Administering J2EE Processes

From the J2EE processes tab, shown next, you can start, stop, or restart any of the three processes: the J2EE server, the J2EE dispatcher, and the SDM process.

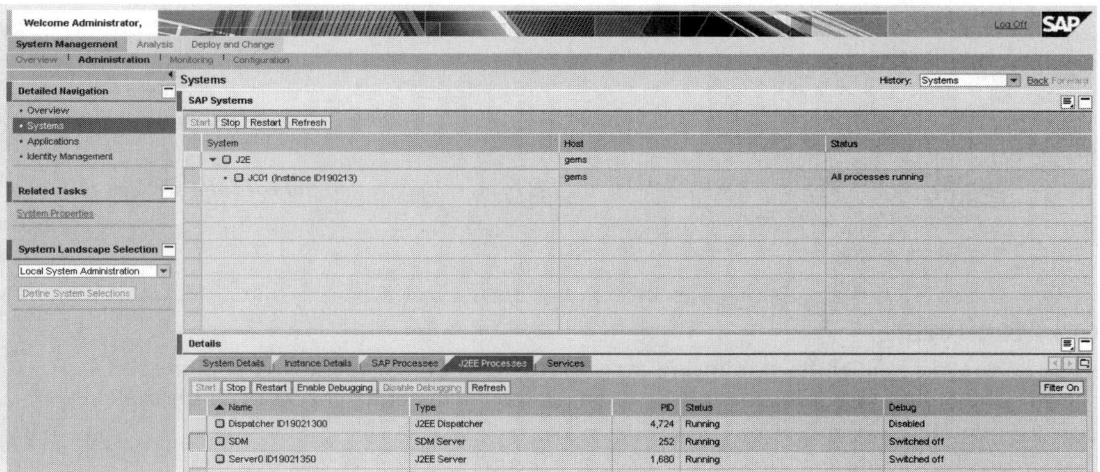

You can then click the System Properties link under the Related Tasks section in the left navigation pane to display the system properties. Clicking the server, dispatcher, or cluster on the Configurations tab will display the corresponding tabs: JVM properties, Kernel, and Services under the Details section.

Administering the J2EE Applications

As shown next, you can also manage the applications that belong to various systems by clicking the application's link in the detailed navigation menu and then selecting the system. You can start and stop applications as well as display their status, modules, resource, reference, deployment date, and other information. The system also provides the ability to search for applications based on the name, status, modules, resources, references, failover, and deployment date.

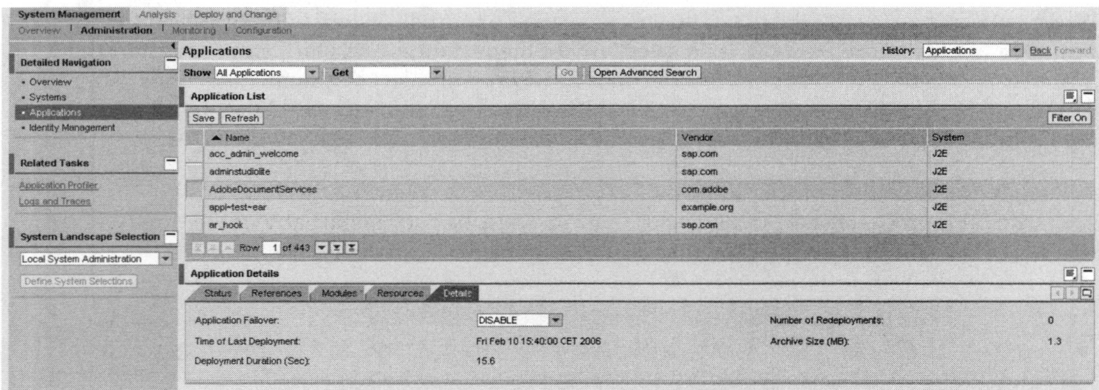

Copyright by SAP AG

Note *The references for an application refer to the list of other application libraries and services to which this application is referring.*

System Monitoring

Now let's take a look at the monitoring capabilities in the NWA, as shown in Figure 44-2. As a part of the monitoring functionality, you can conduct availability checks of all the systems in the landscape.

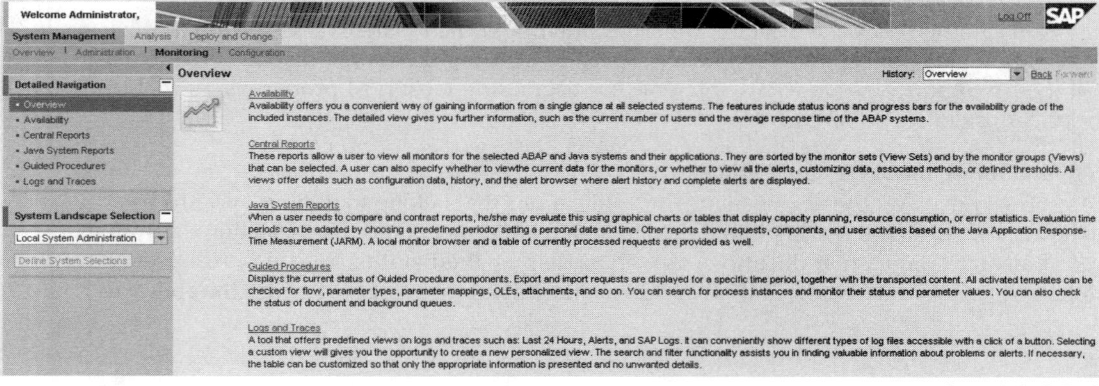

Copyright by SAP AG

Figure 44-2 System management monitoring interface

CCMSPING for System Availability Check

The availability check is performed using the CCMSPING agent in the CEN monitoring system. The CCMSPING agent pings the message servers of the monitored systems and returns the availability data to the CEN every minute.

System Availability

The System Availability overview screen in the NWA displays the availability of the systems as well as the number of instances that are running for both Java and ABAP instances. The detailed screen displays the number of users logged on, the average dialog response time, and the standard response time.

NOTE *The system instance information includes information on instance name, instance type, status, and availability in percentage.*

Central Reports: RZ20

The Central Report is simply the transaction RZ20 displayed in web format. You can display Central Reports in the NWA provided the necessary configuration has been completed in the CEN. All the multiple systems that need to be monitored should have been configured in the CEN and must be entered in the SLD. The SLD should be connected to the NWA and finally the connection to the CEN should be entered in the Visual Administrator of the J2EE engine host where the NWA is going to be used. You can do almost everything you need to do in the RZ20 in the NWA. To display the central reports, go to System Management | Monitoring | Central Reports.

Under the View Set drop-down list, you can select any of the monitor sets that are displayed in the RZ20 transaction. For each monitor set, you can display the current data, alerts, customizing data, the auto-reaction methods, and the thresholds for the monitor elements to generate the alerts.

First, select the systems that you want to monitor in the System Landscape Selection section. After selecting the systems, you must select the list of monitor sets and monitors that you want to analyze.

To view just a particular combination of monitors from different monitor sets, you can mark the individual monitor elements in different view sets and then click Show Marked.

When you click the individual monitor element, a detailed screen appears with tabs for Current Values, Configuration, Alert Browser, and History.

To display the alerts for a particular monitor element or node, click the Alert Browser tab. This view contains a list of all alerts that were generated because a threshold was exceeded. You can remove an alert from this list by selecting the alert and clicking Complete Alerts.

To analyze an alert, you need to click the Analyze link, which starts a transaction in the corresponding system so that you can process the alert. The Current Values tab displays the newest numerical values, maximum and minimum values, and any messages that may have been generated for that monitoring element.

Java System Reports

The Java System Reports can be used as a problem detection and analysis tool. It can be used for both monitoring and tracking the performance of the whole cluster or the instances in the J2EE engine.

A number of predefined reports are available: Capacity Planning, Resource Consumption, Error Statistics, Application Activities, Slowest Components, User Activities, and Current Activities. To access the reports, go to System Management | Monitoring | Java System Reports. When selecting the systems, remember to select the Java systems only.

NOTE *Performance reports are based on data collected by the Java Management Extensions (JMX) and Java Application Response Time Measurement (JARM) API.*

When displaying the reports or charts, as shown in Figure 44-3, you can select the time period with which you want to work. You can also export the history data. To create your own reports or charts, click the Open Customization button and then select the relevant performance monitors, JARM requests, application components, and users.

Two tabs are available: Charts and Reports. The Chart tab can be used to analyze performance based on performance data from a number of performance monitors and/or JARM monitors. Under the Reports tab, shown next, are a number of predefined reports such as the Resource Consumption report, which is a collection of Memory Consumption and Threads charts.

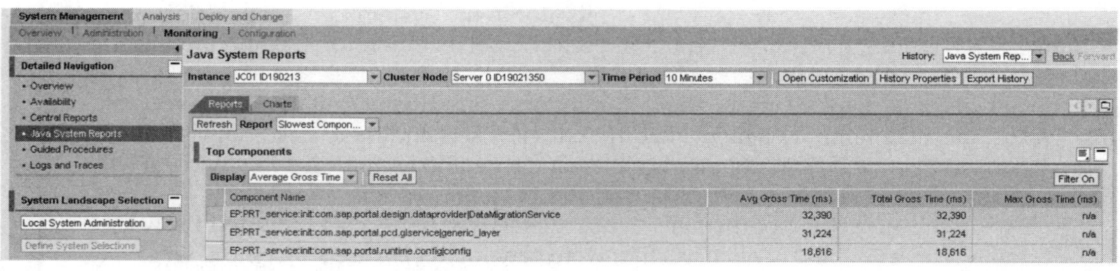

FIGURE 44-3 Java System Reports

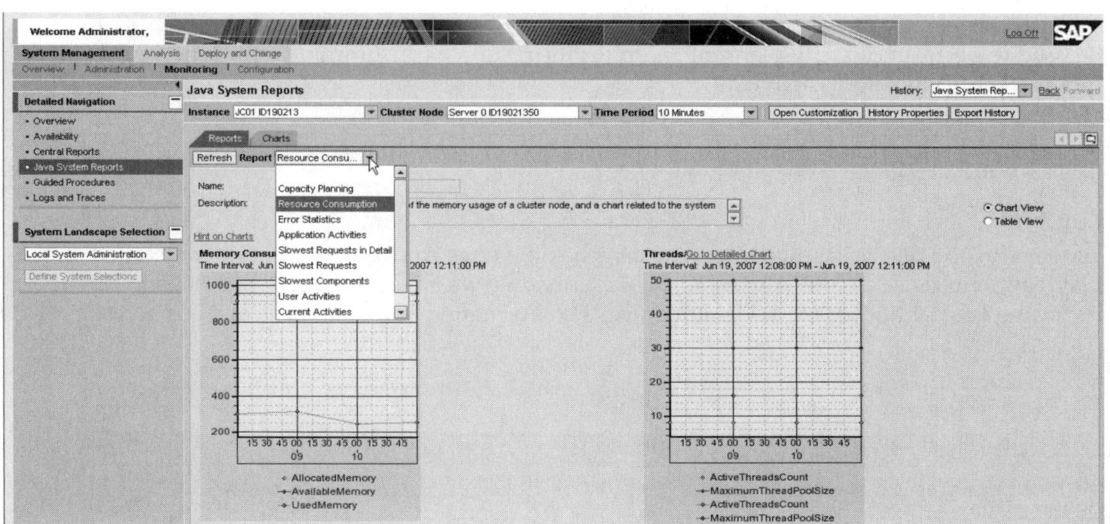

Copyright by SAP AG

As shown next, you create a Capacity Planning report that contains charts for displaying the incoming Requests, Average Response Time for these requests, Number of Sessions Available, and Communications. You can create charts for various parameters that are related to each other and then build reports from them.

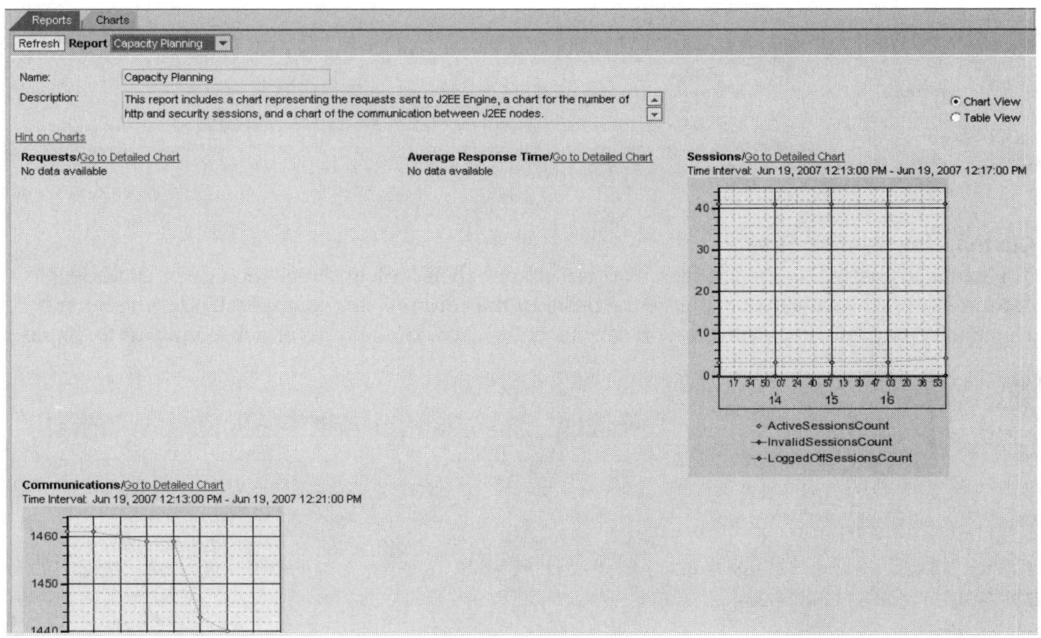

Copyright by SAP AG

You can also modify the standard reports to suit your requirements. Built-in reports can be used to perform capacity planning, monitor the resource consumption over time, and monitor the application's activity.

NOTE *In both Reports and Charts, you can toggle between chart and table view.*

Log Files

To view the log files, as shown next, you can click the Logs And Traces link under Detailed Navigation in the left pane. A number of predefined views are available for SAP logs, including Last 24 hours, Alert, Default Trace, Text Formatted Traces, Expert, and Archives.

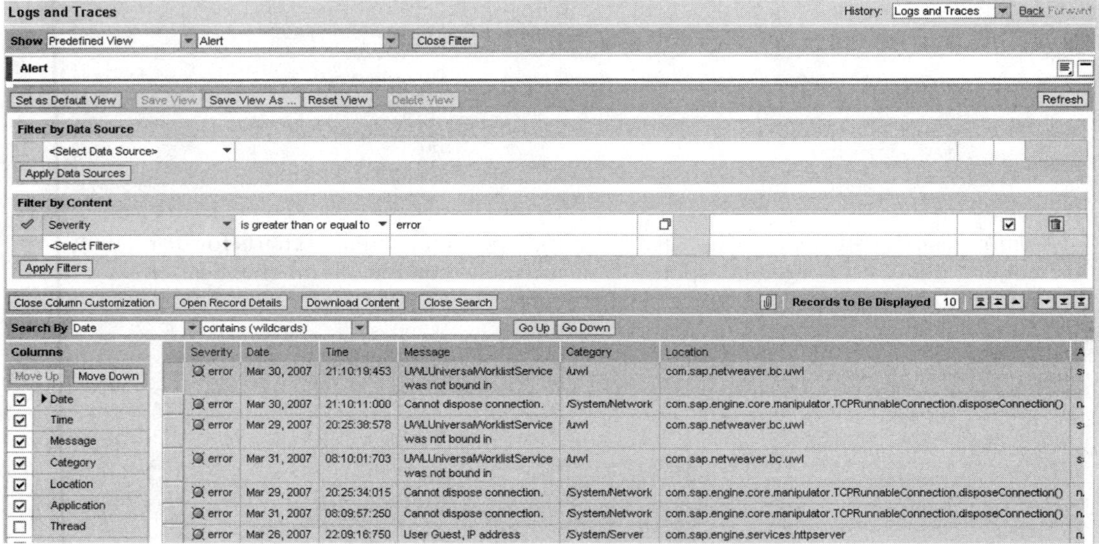

Customizing the Log Files

You can also customize the log files: You can change their look and feel, include or exclude columns from the display, or change the order of the columns, for example. Under the Filter by Data Source section, shown next, you can select the data source from which you want to display:

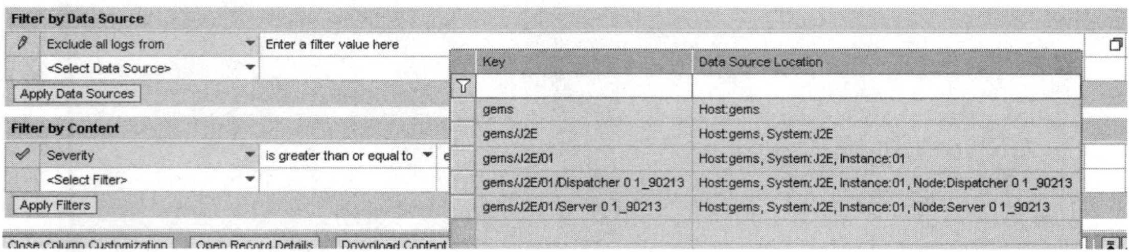

You can also filter log files by content by setting filters on columns such as Severity, Category, Data and Time, and so on, as shown here:

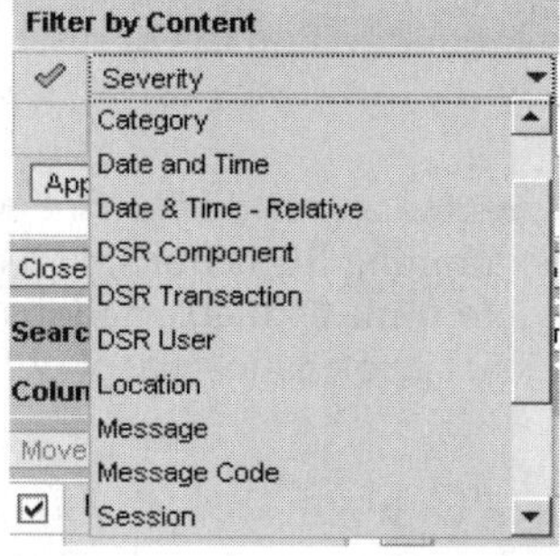

Copyright by SAP AG

You can save the customized view and re-import the view for later use from this toolbar:

Copyright by SAP AG

You can also display the log for a particular application by choosing System Management | Administration | Applications and then selecting the relevant application. You can then select the Logs and Traces under the Related Tasks to display the logs for just that application:

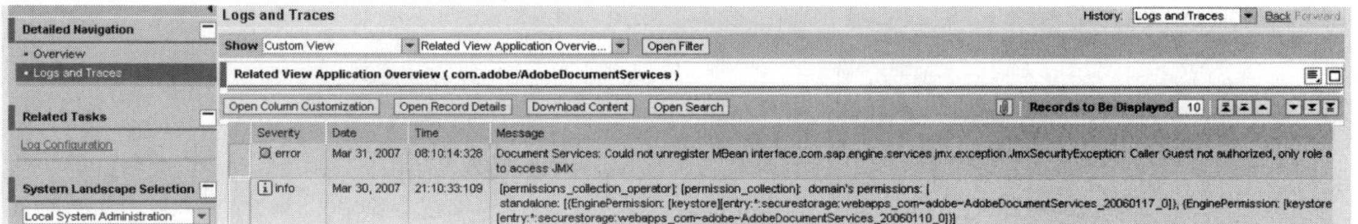

Copyright by SAP AG

Roles

Four roles are associated with using the NWA:

- SAPJAVA_NWADMIN_CENTRAL
- SAPJAVA_NWADMIN_CENTRAL_READONLY
- SAPJAVA_NWADMIN_LOCAL
- SAPJAVA_NWADMIN_LOCAL_READONLY

The SAPJAVA_NWADMIN_CENTRAL role provides pretty much complete access to all the NWA functionality. The SAPJAVA_NWADMIN_CENTRAL_READONLY role allows read-only access to all the central monitoring capabilities.

You can combine these roles to provide custom versions so that you can delegate specific administration tasks to a specific group of users. For example, you can create roles that allow only systems to be managed, or roles that allow only applications to be managed, and so on. You can create custom roles and assign the necessary actions to them.

NWA-Related Actions

To view a list of actions that are assigned to a role, display the role in the User Admin tool and select the Assigned Actions tab. By examining the actions, you can know which permissions are possible—for example, you can determine available actions for Applications_Display, Applications_Configure, Logs_Display, Performance_Display, Systems_Start_Stop, and so on.

Setting up the NWA

To connect to the remote systems from within the NWA, you need to perform certain configuration steps such as SLD configuration, central monitoring, and connectivity between the remote systems and the NWA as well as between the remote systems and the CEN.

Setting up the NWA consists of a number of steps:

1. Set up the SLD.
2. Set up the CEN.
3. Configure the NWA.

As shown next, the ABAP and J2EE systems are the satellite systems that can be monitored centrally. The ABAP systems can register with the CEN using RZ70 in the monitored ABAP systems where you can provide the gateway details for the CEN system. The ABAP systems communicate with the CEN using RFC, while the Java systems communicate with the CEN using HTTP.

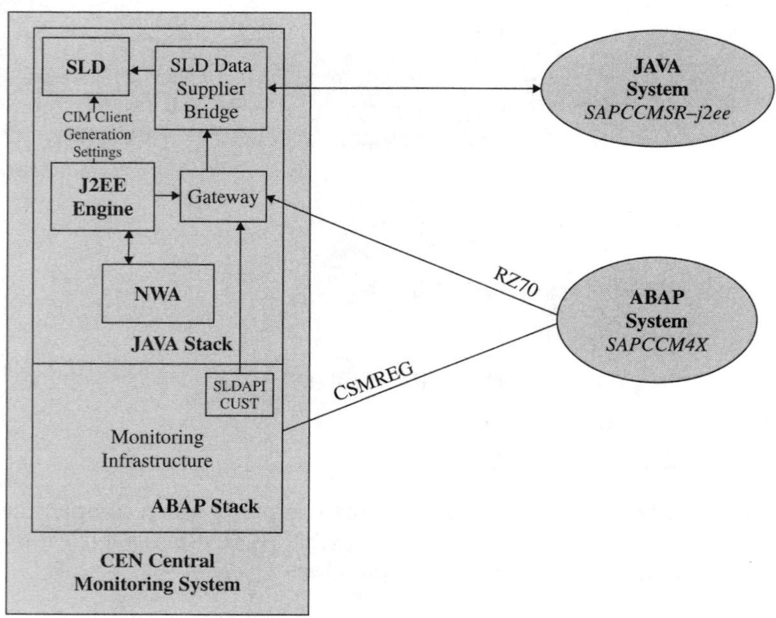

NOTE *You can register the Java systems directly with the Data Supplier Bridge of the SLD in the Visual Administrator of the monitored J2EE engine.*

The CEN system itself directly communicates with the SLD through a gateway and is configured using the transaction SLDAPICUST in the CEN system. An RFC destination named SAPSLDAPI is maintained in this transaction. The details regarding the monitoring systems and monitored systems are maintained in the SLD by the CEN system using this RFC destination.

Configuring and Activating the SLD

The SLD should be activated and running for the object server that should be activated by going to SLD, as shown next (http://<host> <port>/sld), and clicking Administration, and then Start Server if the server is not running.

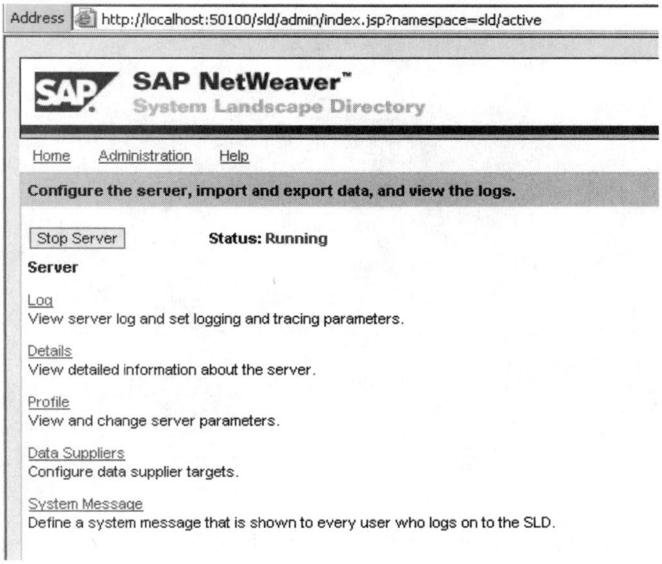

Address http://localhost:50100/sld/admin/index.jsp?namespace=sld/active

SAP NetWeaver™
System Landscape Directory

Home Administration Help

Configure the server, import and export data, and view the logs.

Stop Server Status: Running

Server

Log
View server log and set logging and tracing parameters.

Details
View detailed information about the server.

Profile
View and change server parameters.

Data Suppliers
Configure data supplier targets.

System Message
Define a system message that is shown to every user who logs on to the SLD.

The next step is to import the CIM model by clicking the Import link under the Content section and opening the file .../<*SID*>/SYS/GLOBAL/SLD/Model/CR_Content.zip.

NOTE *The CIM model contains details about the SAP products, the software components, and information on the schema relationships between the technical systems, landscapes, and business systems.*

To have the monitored systems automatically self-register with the SLD, you must enter the gateway information in the Data Supplier Bridge. This gateway information should then be entered in the monitored systems so that they can report data to the SLD using this bridge. Make sure that the bridge is started.

You then create an RFC destination in the CEN system using the SLDAPICUST transaction so that it points to the RFC server program in the J2EE engine where the SLD is installed. The CEN can then use this RFC connection named SAPSLDAPI to update the SLD with the information about the relationships between the monitored and monitoring systems.

The next step is to enter the data supplier bridge information in the monitored systems. For ABAP you should use the RZ70 transaction and for Java systems you should go to Visual Administrator and navigate to Server Node | Services | SLD Data Supplier | HTTP Settings, as shown here:

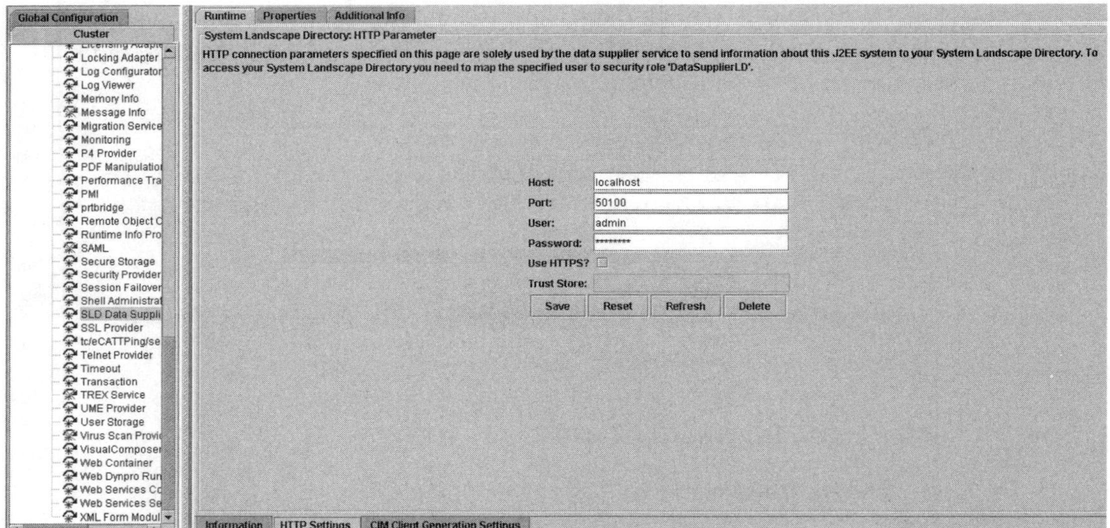

Activities in the CEN

The second major set of activities concerns setting up the CEN. The monitored ABAP systems should have been configured in the CEN using RZ21. The monitored Java systems should be registered with the CEN using the CCMS agent SAPCCMSR. The monitored ABAP systems should be registered with the CEN using the agent SAPCCM4X for 4.X systems and SAPCCM3X for 3.X systems.

Maintain JCO RFC between J2EE Engine and ABAP Stack

A JCO RFC connection should be created in the J2EE engine of the CEN pointing to the ABAP stack of the CEN. If this is not done, when you access System Management | Monitoring | Availability, you get an error saying "Not available in local mode; switch to central mode." First, create the destination SAP.CCMS.CEN.<*SID*>. To do this, open Visual Administrator and select Cluster | Server | Services | JCO RFC Provider and create the RFC destination SAP.CCMS.CEN.<*SID*> pointing to the CEN gateway host, as shown next:

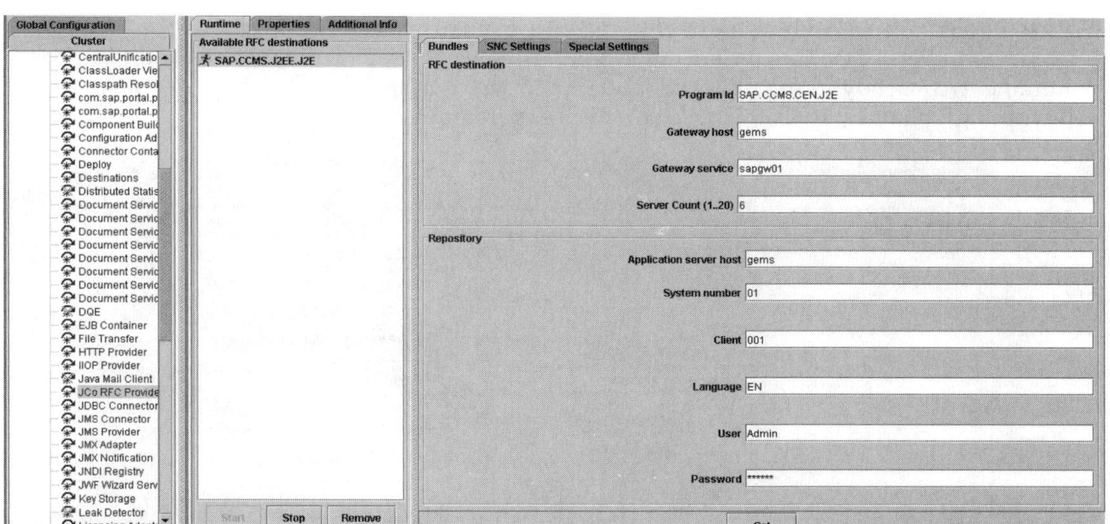

Copyright by SAP AG

NOTE *The JCO RFC connection is required so that the NWA, which is installed in the Java stack of the CEN, can collect the RZ20 monitored data as well as availability data from the CEN.*

Activate the Availability Monitoring in J2EE Engine

The availability monitoring should have been activated in the J2EE engine using the CCMSPING agent. It is also possible to have multiple CCMS agents that are dedicated to a particular set of systems. This is usually the case when the system landscape is large. If the CCMSPING agent is configured but is not running in the NWA, you can activate it by going to System Management | Monitoring | Availability. Then select the relevant instance and click Enable Availability Monitoring under the Configuration section.

Configure the NWA

The final step is to configure the NWA itself. To enable the NWA to get data regarding the systems available in the landscape, the NWA should be configured to connect to the SLD. This is done in the Visual Administrator of the NWA under the CIM Client Generation settings.

NOTE *If the CIM Client Generation settings are not configured, you will see a message that mentions that the System Landscape Directory server is not started and the Local System can only be administered. This is because the CIM client is required by the NWA to connect to the SLD.*

Log in to the Visual Administrator of the NWA and go to Cluster | Server | Services | SLD Data Supplier | CIM Client Generation Settings. Select the sap.com/tc~lm~webadmin~mainframe~wd/webdynpro/public/lib/app.jar and sap.com/tc~lm~webadmin~sld~wd/webdynpro/public/lib/app.jar. Then enter the SLD parameters:

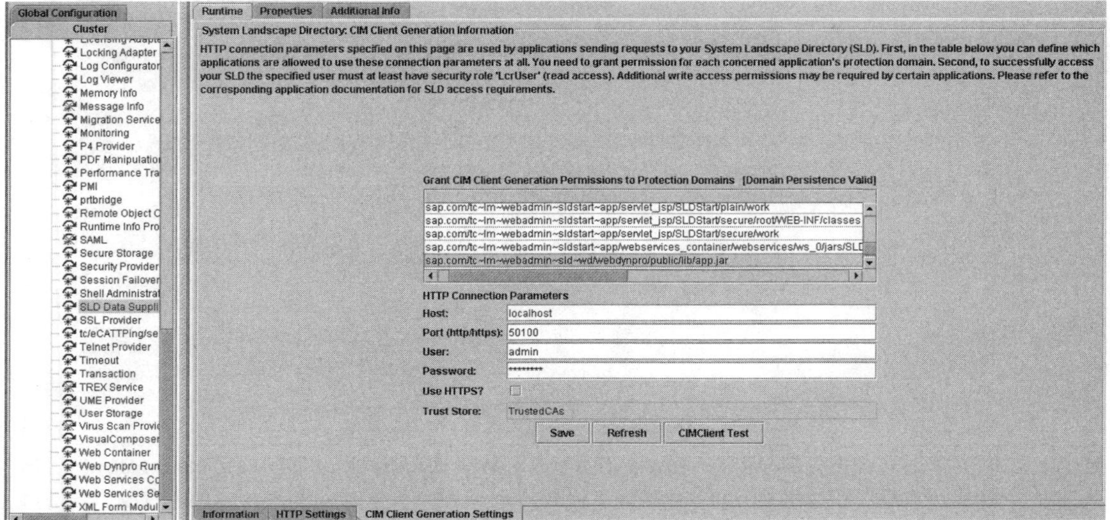

Copyright by SAP AG

Preconfigure Connections to Monitored Java Systems from NWA

Finally, when accessing the monitored Java systems from the NWA, you can pre-configure the connection parameters to the monitored Java systems so that you do not have to reenter the credentials for logging onto the Java systems before displaying their monitored data in the NWA. If this is not configured, you will see a JMX Connection Error pop-up.

To configure this, you should go to the Destinations under the Visual Administrator and enter the details of the HTTP destination. The HTTP destination name is sap.com/tc~je~jmx~wsconnector~sp/*<SID>*/*<host>* and the URL is http://*<host>*:*<port>*/WSConnector/Config1?style=document.

NOTE *For more details, refer to the NWA related resources listed in Appendix B.*

Summary

This chapter discussed the importance of using the SAP NWA as a central cockpit for monitoring systems. It discussed the essential components of the NWA architecture, the functionality, and some of the system administration capabilities of NWA. It discussed how to use the NWA for administering J2EE processes, J2EE applications, system availability, RZ20 reports, alerts, and Java System reports. You learned about the standard charts and reports available such as the resource consumption reports, capacity planning reports, and log file views. You then looked at how to set up the NWA, set up the SLD and SLD Data Supplier Bridge, set up connections between the CEN and the SLD, register the systems with SLD, and configure monitored systems.

PART

Appendixes

APPENDIX A

Installing the SAP NetWeaver 7.0 (2004s) - Java Trial Version

This appendix deals with the steps involved in installing an evaluation version of SAP NetWeaver 7.0 (2004s) - Java Trial Version. To install the evaluation software, do the following:

1. Go to the URL http://sdn.sap.com and click Downloads.
2. In the Downloads page, under the Free Download Catalog, click SAP NetWeaver Main Releases under the Software section.
3. In the SAP NetWeaver Main Release Downloads page, click SAP NetWeaver 7.0 (2004s) - Java Trial Version.
4. In the SAP NetWeaver 7.0 Java Trial Version page, click Click Here For Download.
5. In the SAP Download - License Agreement page, select the Java Edition File 1 radio button and click I Agree - Download Selected File button. Save the file to a local folder.
6. Repeat step 5 for downloading the Java Edition File 2 and Developer Studio files. Save the files in the same folder where the Java Edition File 1 is stored.
7. Navigate to the folder where the Java Edition File 1 was stored and extract it using WinZip or WinRAR. Note that this step will also unzip the contents in the Java Edition File 2 and Developer Studio files. You may face problems if the whole file was not downloaded completely, in which case you must re-download the files. The best way to check whether the files have been fully downloaded is to cross-check the file sizes mentioned in the SAP Download - License Agreement page and compare them with the sizes of files downloaded in your local folder.
8. After extracting the files, double-click start.bat or start.htm. This will open a Welcome to Sneak Preview SAP NetWeaver 2004s SR1 page.

9. Before proceeding with the installation, do the following:
   a. Install the Sun Microsystems J2SE SDK version 1.4.2_08 or 1.4.2_09. Avoid 1.4.2_10 or JDK 1.5 as they can cause issues.
   b. Ensure that you do not have a J2E system already installed in the computer.
   c. Check the services file in C:\WINNT\system32\drivers\etc\services for Windows 2000 or C:\Windows\system32\drivers\etc\services for Windows XP to be sure that it does not have the entries for ports 3601, 3201, and 50000 to 50030. To remove the entry, enter the hash symbol before the entry.
   d. Install the Microsoft loopback adapter if your computer is not connected to a network or if no DHCP server is available on your network.
10. Click the Installation link on the right and follow the instructions to install SAP Web Application Server Java 7.00 and portal, SAP NetWeaver Developer Studio, MaxDB Database Manager, and MaxDB SQL Studio.

APPENDIX B

References

The following list of resources from http://sdn.sap.com, http://help.sap.com, and http://service.sap.com have been cited in the course of writing this book and can be consulted for further information to master a given topic. To access any resource mentioned below, go to http://sdn.com and enter the resource name in the Search field and press Enter.

- Accelerate Your Deployment of Portal Content with SAP Business Packages
- Application Gateway with Apache - Multi-Backend
- Architecture of the SAP Web Application Server
- Authentication and Single Sign-On
- Authentication in SAP NetWeaver - Users, Groups, Roles, etc.
- Authentication Using the User Management Engine
- Availability Monitoring of HTML Pages with GRMG Lite
- Backup and Recovery of EP 6.0 SP2
- Backup and Restore SAP Enterprise Portal 6.0 and KMC on Web AS 6.40
- Best Practice for Transporting SAP NetWeaver Portal Content
- CCMS Agents: Features, Installation, and Operation
- CCMS Monitoring and Management of New Features in 6.20–6.40
- Central and Assigning Auto-Reactions in CCMS
- Central Monitoring SAP NetWeaver
- Change Management and Transport in the Enterprise Portal
- Client-Side Performance Optimization
- Configure Remote Role Assignment
- Configure UME for Multiple LDAP Data Sources
- Configuring the J2EE Engine
- Configuring the Monitoring Architecture
- Configuring the Portal for External-Facing Portal Usage

- Configuring the Sending of E-Mails as an Auto-Reaction
- Configuring WSRP Content Sharing
- Content Delegated Administration
- Creating a Rule-Based Monitor: SAP Web Application Server 6.10
- Customizing and Operating GRMG Scenarios
- Delegated Administration in EP6
- Enabling Generic Request and Message Generator Heartbeat Monitoring
- EP 6.0 Portal: Overview CCMS Solution Manager
- EP Scalability, Sizing, and High Availability
- EP6 Monitoring and Logging
- External Facing Portals
- Fine Tune the Performance of Your SAP Enterprise Portal
- Get Ready for Enterprise Portal 6.0
- HA Setups for NW04: Changes With SPS15/16
- High Availability for SAP Solutions
- High Availability of Portals on MS Windows Clusters
- How to Analyze Performance Problems
- How to Configure Permissions for Initial Content in SAP NetWeaver Portal
- How to Configure SSO in a Complex System Landscape
- How to Configure the SAP J2EE Engine for Using SSL
- How to Create New Portal Display Rules
- How to Perform Role and User Distribution in the SAP System
- How to Set Up the Landscape for a Federated Portal Network
- How to Transport SAP Enterprise Portal 6.0 Content (NW2004)
- How to Upload and Adapt ERP Roles to SAP Enterprise Portal (NW2004)
- How to Use Business Packages in SAP Enterprise Portal 6.0
- How to Use Security Zones in NetWeaver '04 SPS09
- How to Fine Tune J2EE Engine Performance
- How to Fine Tune Performance of Enterprise Portal 6.0
- How to Fine Tune Performance of Portal Platform
- Implementing a Federated Portal Network Overview
- Implementing an External Facing Portal
- Incident and Problem Management EP 6.0 SP2
- Increasing Infrastructure Security
- Initial Permissions Creator Demo
- Installation Guide - Enabling SSL for the SAP J2EE Engine

- Installation Guide - SAP NetWeaver 2004s SR1 Java on Windows: MS SQL Server
- Installation Tips for SAP NetWeaver 2004s
- Installing Additional Usage Types in SAP NetWeaver 7.0 AS Java
- Installing, Registering, and Operating CCMS Agents
- Introducing SAP NetWeaver Administrator - NWA
- Introduction to Iimplementing a Federated Portal Network
- Introduction to Java Support Package Manager
- Java Backup and Recovery Best Practice
- Java Support Package Manager - SAP NetWeaver 2004
- Java Support Package Manager SPS09 Demonstration
- Jumpstart Your Portal Implementation: Part 1
- Landscape Considerations in a Federated Portal Network
- Leveraging External Authentication Based on Industry Standards
- Maintain Portal Users More Effectively with Delegated Administration
- Master Guide - SAP NetWeaver 7.0
- Media List - SAP NetWeaver 2004s Support Release 1
- Monitoring Logging and Tracing the EP 6.0 SP2
- Monitoring OS Processes with CCMS
- Monitoring Setup Guide for NW 7.0 SP Stack 13
- New SAP NetWeaver Portal Functionality
- Performance Analysis and Tuning of SAP NetWeaver
- Performance Analysis in a nutshell
- Performance and Scalability
- Performance and Scalability of SAP Business Solutions
- Planning Guide - System Landscape Directory
- Portal Platform Architecture
- Portal Roles: Roles vs. Authorization
- Post Installation Guide - SAP System Landscape Directory on SAP Web AS Java 6.40
- Practical Guidelines to Build a High Availability SAP NetWeaver Infrastructure
- Remote Application Integration Demo
- Role and User Distribution in the SAP System
- Role Concept in SAP Enterprise Portal 5.0 and 6.0
- SAP Enterprise Portal 6 SP2 Performance Analysis
- SAP Enterprise Portal 6.0 - Decentralized Admin
- SAP Enterprise Portal 6.0 - Security

- SAP Enterprise Portal 6.0 - Security and User Management
- SAP High Availability - SAP NetWeaver 2004s Ramp Up
- SAP Infrastructure Security
- SAP NetWeaver 7.0 (2004s) PAM
- SAP NetWeaver Administrator: The Latest Tool for Monitoring and Administration
- SAP NetWeaver Rapid Installer
- SAP System Landscape directory: Intelligent System Landscape Handling
- SAP Web Application Server: An Overview
- Scalability Options of SAP NetWeaver
- Securing Internet Facing Portals
- Setting up and operating GRMG Monitoring Scenario
- Setting up portal roles in SAP Enterprise Portal 6.0
- Single Sign-on in Heterogeneous Environments
- Starting and Stopping the Application Server
- Step-by-step Setup of the SAP NetWeaver Administrator
- Strong Infrastructure and Network Security for Heterogeneous Applications
- System Landscape Administration with SAP NetWeaver Administrator
- Technical Infrastructure Guide - SAP NetWeaver 2004s
- Technical Infrastructures of SAP Enterprise Portal 6.0
- Technical Infrastructure of SAP Enterprise Portal 6.0 on SAP Web AS 6.40
- Transporting Portal Content
- Troubleshooting Enterprise Portal 60 SP2 Part 1 Master the Basics
- Troubleshooting for Administrators - Problem Detection and Analysis for SAP Web AS Java
- Troubleshooting on the SAP Web AS for Java Developers
- User Authentication in SAP Portal and Java Environments
- User Management and Authorizations - Overview
- User Management and Authorizations - The Details
- Using Logging and Tracing on the SAP Web AS Java
- Web AS 6.40 Performance Analysis
- Web Infrastructure concepts for Web application Server

The following websites offer more information:

- http://service.sap.com/asap
- http://service.sap.com/ha
- http://service.sap.com/instguides

- http://service.sap.com/maxattention
- http://service.sap.com/pam
- http://service.sap.com/quicksizer
- http://service.sap.com/releasestrategy
- http://service.sap.com/reviewprogram
- http://service.sap.com/scl
- http://service.sap.com/security
- http://service.sap.com/sizing
- http://service.sap.com/solutionmaps

Index

D

J

K